58515

DISCARD

D1565876

DATE			
DEC 0 2 1998			

BAKER & TAYLOR

U.S. Containment Policy and the Conflict in Indochina

U.S. Containment Policy and the Conflict in Indochina

William J. Duiker

Stanford University Press

Stanford, California

1994

Stanford University Press
Stanford, California
© 1994 by the Board of Trustees of the
Leland Stanford Junior University
Printed in the United States of America

CIP data appear at the end of the book

Stanford University Press publications are distributed
exclusively by Stanford University Press within the
United States, Canada, and Mexico; they are distributed
exclusively by Cambridge University Press throughout
the rest of the world.

Preface

This book began as a personal quest. I first became directly acquainted with the conflict in Vietnam in the mid-1960's, while serving as a foreign service officer with the U.S. Embassy in Saigon. At that time I was struck by the discipline and serious commitment shown by the communist-led insurgent forces in the country. I was also deeply troubled by the growing involvement of the United States in a war I increasingly felt it could not win.

After leaving government service, I embarked on a long-term project to study the rise of Vietnamese nationalism and the reasons for the success of the communists in their long struggle against France and the United States. But I retained my interest in how and why the United States became involved in the conflict in Indochina, and when it became clear that this question has continued to provoke debate among scholars, journalists, and other foreign policy observers, I determined to turn my attention to the issue.

Anyone who experienced direct involvement in the Vietnam War inevitably approaches the issue with strong emotional and intellectual attachments, not to say prejudices. In my case, the Vietnam experience presented me with a serious dilemma that was not entirely resolved by the end of the war. Having reached adulthood during the early years of the Cold War and entered government service on the eve of the heady era of the Kennedy presidency, I accepted the logic behind the U.S. policy of containment and supported its general application to Southeast Asia. I felt that the United States had both the right and the obligation to assist the peoples of the area in meeting the challenges of our day. But as the result of service in Vietnam I began to entertain serious doubts about the impact of U.S. intervention on the peoples of the region and became convinced that the survival of an independent South Vietnam could not be achieved at an acceptable cost. I also became persuaded that although the leaders of the insurgent movement in South Vietnam and their superiors in Hanoi were dedicated Marxist-Leninists, the driving force behind the Vietnamese struggle for national reunification was nationalism rather than ideology, a fact that had profound implications for the future of the region. The question in my mind, then, was how the United States could disentangle itself from an unwinnable and ultimately unnecessary conflict while at the same time preserving its security interests and those of its allies in Southeast Asia and elsewhere. In turn, this question related to the broader policy issue of whether and in what circumstances the United States should become engaged in civil disturbances where its security interests are not directly engaged. Events in Central America, the Middle East, and most recently in Somalia and the Balkans are a vivid demonstration of the continuing relevance of this question.

The result of that inquiry is this book. It was my original intention to pursue the question down to the fall of the Saigon regime in the spring of 1975, but as I discovered the complexity of the issues involved I realized that careful treatment would result in a book of unmanageable length. I therefore decided to conclude the analysis with the arrival of U.S. combat forces in the summer of 1965, leaving consideration of the actual conduct of the war to a possible later book.

There are, of course, other recent books on this topic, including George McT. Kahin's *Intervention* and William Conrad Gibbons's *The U.S. Government and the Vietnam War*. Gabriel Kolko has approached the topic from a neo-Marxist perspective in his *Anatomy of a War*. Specialized studies on the Vietnam policies of individual presidents have also appeared in increasing numbers. All of these books, in my judgment, have something important to offer, but each has its limitations, and in view of the importance of the topic I am convinced that additional consideration is justified. The approach adopted here will combine a detailed investigation of the early stages of U.S. involvement with a careful and dispassionate examination of the struggle for national independence and reunification as viewed from the other side. No study of the U.S. role in the war, in my opinion, can be complete without consideration of the view from Hanoi.

In the course of completing this book, I have incurred debts to a large number of people and institutions. I am grateful to the Harry S. Truman Library in Independence, Missouri, and to the Lyndon B. Johnson Library in Austin, Texas, for providing me with financial support to visit and consult materials dealing with the war. The staffs at both institutions, and especially David C. Humphrey, Archivist at the LBJ Library, were unfailingly helpful and cooperative. Ed Keefer, Charles Sampson, and Luke Smith of the Office of the Historian at the Department of State gave me valuable insights into policy issues during a visit to the office in 1989. Grants from the Social Sciences Research Council and from the Institute for the Arts and Humanistic Studies at The Pennsylvania State University in 1990 provided me with the opportunity to visit Hanoi, during which time I was able to locate crucial materials dealing with the communist side of the war. Mr. Tao Bingwei and Ms. Ye Xin of the Institute of International Studies in Beijing were very helpful during a visit to China in 1985, and the staffs at the Institute of International Relations, the Institute of History, and the University of Hanoi gave me considerable help in the course of several visits to Vietnam since 1985. Of particular help were Vu Huy Phuc and Tran Huu Dinh of the Institute of History and Professor Pham Xanh at the University of Hanoi. Gennadi Maslov of the Far Eastern Institute of the Soviet Academy of Sciences provided me with insight into Soviet and Vietnamese views of the war during a recent visit to Moscow.

I would like especially to thank William P. Bundy, Chuck Cross, Roger Hilsman, and Chalmers Roberts, all of whom kindly agreed to give me their comments and suggestions on various chapters of the manuscript. Others who have helped in various stages of this study include Paul Kattenburg, Fred Moritz, Al Patti, Forrest Pogue, and Stein Tonnesson, for their insightful comments on various aspects of the war over the years. Not least, I am indebted to a generation of students at The Pennsylvania State University, who have helped me to defend and shape my conclusions on the war. I would like to single out Jim Baer, whose comments on the war have always forced me to rethink my premises. For two years, Judy Shawley has gone beyond the call of duty to nurse the project along through an outmoded word processor and printer that should long since have been consigned to the dustbin. I alone, of course, am responsible for the contents and conclusions contained in this book.

Finally, I would like one more time to thank my wife, Yvonne, for her infinite patience and support in tolerating a housemate whose nose has all too often been buried in a book and whose attention always seemed to be on historical events in far-off Hanoi or Saigon, rather than on the more important problems of caring for home and family. To her, above all, this book is affectionately dedicated.

W.J.D.

Contents

Maps

U.S. Containment Policy and
the Conflict in Indochina

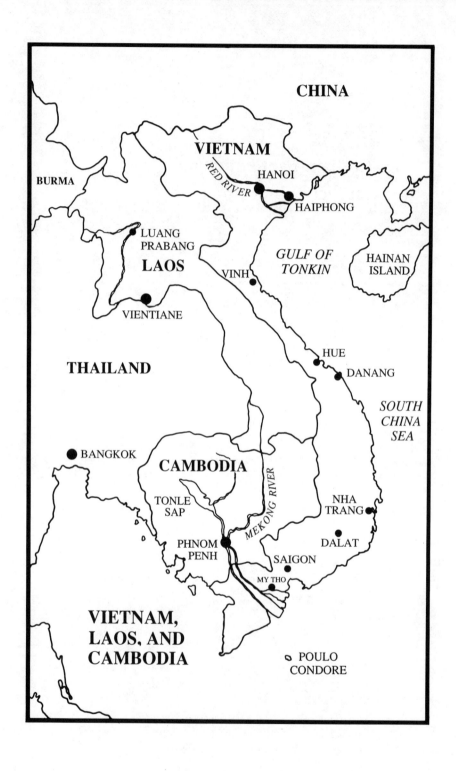

CHINA

VIETNAM

BURMA

RED RIVER

HANOI

HAIPHONG

LUANG
PRABANG

LAOS

*GULF OF
TONKIN*

*HAINAN
ISLAND*

VINH

VIENTIANE

THAILAND

HUE

DANANG

*SOUTH
CHINA
SEA*

BANGKOK

CAMBODIA

MEKONG RIVER

TONLE
SAP

NHA
TRANG

PHNOM
PENH

SAIGON

DALAT

MY THO

**VIETNAM,
LAOS, AND
CAMBODIA**

POULO
CONDORE

Introduction

From the end of World War II down to the dissolution of the Soviet Union, the primary objective of U.S. foreign policy has been to prevent the expansion of communism. Indeed, that objective was directly embodied in the so-called strategy of containment, a global approach to the pursuit of U.S. national security interests that was first adumbrated by George F. Kennan in 1947 and later became the guiding force in U.S. foreign policy.

At first, the concept of containment was applied primarily to Europe. It was there that the threat to U.S. interests from international communism directed from Moscow was first perceived, in the form of Soviet efforts to dominate the nations of Eastern Europe and extend Soviet influence into the eastern Mediterranean and the Middle East. Other areas of the world—Asia, Africa, and Latin America—were considered to be less threatened by forces hostile to the free world or more peripheral to U.S. foreign policy concerns. At least that was the view initially proclaimed by George Kennan himself, who identified five areas in the world as vital to the United States: North America, Great Britain, Central Europe, the USSR, and Japan. Only the latter was located in Asia.

By the end of the decade, however, the focus of U.S. containment strategy was extended to include East and Southeast Asia, primarily because of the increasing likelihood of a communist victory in the Chinese Civil War, which, in the minds of some U.S. policymakers, would be tantamount to giving the Soviet Union a dominant position on the Asian mainland. Added to the growing threat in China was the increasingly unstable situation in Southeast Asia, where the long arc of colonies that had been established by the imperialist powers during the last half of the nineteenth century was gradually but inexorably being replaced by independent states. The emergence of such colonial territories into independence was generally viewed as a welcome prospect by foreign policy observers in Washington, but when combined with the impending victory of communist forces in China it raised the unsettling possibility that the entire region might be brought within the reach of the Kremlin.

It was that menacing prospect that impelled President Harry S. Truman to assist the French in their struggle against communist-led insurgent forces in Indochina. As the decade of the 1950's dawned, Truman administration officials saw French Indochina, and specifically Vietnam, as the keystone of the U.S. policy of containment in Asia and an important link in the U.S. defensive perimeter throughout the region.

Later administrations appeared to agree. The Eisenhower administration went to the brink of war with China—and a possible nuclear exchange with Moscow—before drawing back at the Geneva Conference, when the United States accepted the temporary division of Vietnam into two separate zones, one communist and one noncommunist. Seven years later, President John F. Kennedy defined Vietnam as a "test case" of U.S. capacity to stem the advance of communism into vulnerable areas throughout the Third World. On becoming president in November 1963, Lyndon B. Johnson accepted his predecessor's view of the importance of the area and eventually committed half a million troops to its defense.

Given the official rhetoric regarding the importance of Indochina to U.S. national security, the reversal of that commitment was surprisingly rapid. In 1968, the Johnson administration agreed to begin negotiations under conditions that were bound to lead to a settlement that did not totally meet U.S. objectives. A year later, President Richard M. Nixon embarked on a program of withdrawal of U.S. combat forces that led to a final disengagement when the Paris Agreement was signed in January 1973. The U.S. effort to save Indochina formally came to an end in April 1975, when North Vietnamese forces marched into Saigon and placed the entire country under communist rule. By the end of the year, revolutionary governments had come to power in neighboring Laos and Cambodia.

The loss of South Vietnam did not bring an end to the U.S. strategy of containment in Asia. That policy, with some adjustments to meet changing conditions in China and the collapse of the USSR, continues today. But it did severely damage the national consensus on the validity of containment as the guiding principle of U.S. foreign policy and provoked a debate over the lessons of the Vietnam War and its implications for the United States. To some, U.S. involvement in Vietnam was a colossal mistake that not only led to the death of over 50,000 Americans but also placed the United States on the wrong side of history. To others, it was a noble cause that was sabotaged by a faulty strategy and a fractious press that undermined public support for the American effort.

In this cacaphony of voices there has been little effort on the part of either critics or defenders of U.S. policy in Vietnam to seek a reasoned debate over the key issues involved in the conflict. Many participants in the debate over the "lessons of Vietnam" have simply restated positions they had held during the war. To some degree, of course, these differences are fundamental and cannot be reconciled. They reflect divergent views over the role of the United States in the contemporary world and over the nature of the human spirit. In that sense, the debate over the war, like the ongoing disagreement in France over the meaning of the Revolution of 1789, will never be resolved.

Some of the questions raised by the war, however, are subject to resolution by factual analysis. Although sufficient evidence is not available to permit the writing of a definitive history of the war, documentary sources now being released in the United States provide the researcher with a much better understanding of the nature of the conflict, at least as it was seen in Washington. Material on the North Vietnamese side of the war has been slower to be made public, but official materials published in Hanoi have shed light on some of the key questions about communist strategy that were debated in the United States and in Saigon during the war. With the collapse of the USSR, Soviet sources on the conflict might soon become available to the historian. The time has now arrived for historians to seek to transcend the partisanship and polemics that have characterized the debate up to this point and put the conflict under the bright light of historical analysis.

The historian who seeks to contribute in some way to the resolution of issues raised during the debate over the war must answer several key questions. Some relate to the nature of U.S. objectives in the war. Why did the United States become involved in Vietnam? How did officials in Washington perceive the threat and what policy options were given serious consideration? Which voices within the government bureaucracy were strongest and why? What was the role of public opinion? To what extent did U.S. objectives change over time? Were U.S. objectives consonant with traditional U.S. interests in the region? If Vietnam was vital to U.S. security interests, why was the war not pursued to the point of success?

Another issue that deserves study is the quality of U.S. information about the situation. Did U.S. officials stumble blindly into a quagmire, or did they deliberately march in with their eyes open? How accurate were U.S. intelligence sources on the intentions and capabilities of the communists and of our allies in Saigon? How correct were U.S. policymakers' estimates of public support for the war? If U.S. officials had a distorted understanding of what was happening in Vietnam, was the fault with those who provided the intelligence or with those responsible for acting on it?

Further questions emerge from the strategy pursued by the United States in Vietnam. Why did the strategy fail? Was it a failure of conceptualization or of execution? Was it caused by problems that could be rectified in Washington, or was it a deeper question of forces operating in Vietnam that were not amenable to an "American solution"? In other words, would another strategy have succeeded, or was the result predetermined? Could actions have been taken to change the result, and if so, what and when?

Finally, questions emerge from the Vietnam experience that relate to broader issues of U.S. foreign policy. What does the U.S. failure in Vietnam tell us about the overall strategy of containment? Was the concept of containment faulty, at least as applied in the Third World countries such as Vietnam, or did the problem lie in execution? Are there lessons here that can be applied elsewhere, such as in Latin America, or is each case sui generis?

These issues are too complex to be given serious treatment in a single book. I have therefore focused my attention on how and why the United States became involved in the conflict, leaving the conduct of the war and its results for possible later consideration. The major questions to be considered here will be whether a U.S. effort to prevent or delay a communist victory in Indochina was justified and, if so, whether there were logical alternatives to the course that was actually followed.

In my search for answers, I decided to employ the chronological approach, not only because it is natural for someone with my training as a historian but also because it facilitates a better understanding of the assumptions and realistic options available to U.S. policymakers at a given point in time. Foreign policy, of course, is not composed in a vacuum but is a response to existing circumstances. This book will trace the steps that brought the United States into the Vietnam conflict and evaluate them in terms of conditions at the time and the information available to policymakers. Where relevant, it will present and examine the views of other participants in the conflict, including the government in Hanoi, and how such views related to policy decisions in Washington.

The final chapter will adopt a retrospective stance and attempt to answer some of the larger questions raised in the book. Was it a "noble cause" or a colossal error? Were there alternative strategies that might have fruitfully been pursued in Vietnam? Did the United States actually fail in Vietnam or, as some have contended, did it actually realize its overall objectives, albeit by inadvertence? What do events of the nearly two decades that have elapsed since the fall of Saigon tell us about the war and the U.S. role in it? Finally, are there any "lessons of Vietnam," or should the war be assessed as a unique experience that has little to say one way or the other about future U.S. foreign policy? With such intimidating questions before us, let us begin.

First Encounters

At first glance, it seems improbable that Southeast Asia would be the site of one of the most crucial showdowns in the Cold War. Up until World War II, the interests of the United States in the region were limited. Those of the Soviet Union were virtually nonexistent. Before the October Revolution in 1917, imperial Russia had no presence in Southeast Asia and in looking eastward had focused its attention on China and the Korean peninsula. After the Bolshevik rise to power, Soviet agents were sent into the area, and communist parties were formed in several colonial societies under Moscow's direction. But Soviet interest in the area was fitful, and by the late 1920's, Moscow concentrated its attention on the prospects for a revolution in China.

The importance of the area was hardly more firmly established in Washington. True, the United States had taken part in the land grab at the end of the nineteenth century that placed almost the entire region in the control of the Western colonial powers. After most of the region had been parceled off by the British, the French, and the Dutch, Washington had acquired its own possession in Southeast Asia in 1898, when it wrested the Philippines from Spain during the Spanish-American War. But the decision had been made on the spur of the moment and was viewed at the time more as a means of acquiring a stepping-stone into the China market than as an attempt to establish a permanent U.S. presence in the region. That attitude continued to prevail in later years, as the United States proved to be a reluctant sovereign and frequently appeared on the verge of restoring independence to its sole Asian possession.[1]

In fact, it was China that commanded the bulk of U.S. attention in the lands across the Pacific. Like most other imperialist powers, the United States took an active interest in exploiting economic opportunities in China, particularly in railroads, banking, and the sale of cotton, as well as in missionary activity. When those interests were threatened, Washington could occasionally be galvanized into a more active policy in the region. That happened at the end of the nineteenth century, when the seizure by several European states of new "spheres of influence" in mainland China provoked the administration of President William McKinley to propose a "gentleman's agreement" among the Great Powers to create an Open Door of equal economic opportunity in China while at the same time preserving the territorial integrity of the declining Manchu empire. Shortly after, when the Boxer Rebellion created political instability and theatened the lives of foreigners living in China, the United States provided troops for an international detachment to rescue the foreign legations in Beijing and punish the Manchu court for its role in encouraging the disturbances.

Yet there were some significant differences between U.S. policies in East Asia and those of its main rivals. As the Open Door notes (as the administration's two communications to other world powers are often labeled) demonstrated, U.S. policymakers were less interested in acquiring territory for its own sake than in keeping the area open to economic competition by all interested states. There were, of course, persuasive reasons for the United States to adopt such a position. As a continental power with substantial natural resources and a massive potential consumer market to exploit, the United States had a smaller economic stake in Asia than did the leading European commercial powers and was simply attempting to protect its limited interests with the least possible expense and effort. With such objectives in mind, the most practical strategy was a form of balance-of-power politics to prevent China and the region as a whole from falling under the domination of a single and possibly hostile power.[2]

America's Asian policy during this period also possessed a moralistic component that was somewhat less evident in the policies of its European rivals. That element was especially visible in the missionary enterprise that took thousands of Americans to China or provided them with financial assistance to convert the Chinese people to the Christian faith. As applied to Asia, American moralism was essentially a product of the nation's anticolonialist tradition, which viewed the United States as the champion of vulnerable peoples against the exploitative policies of the nations of the Old World. It could be pointed out, as indeed it was, that such a pose was somewhat hypocritical because the United States was rapidly becoming an imperialist power in its own right. The American pose of shouldering the "white man's burden" was qualitatively not so different from similar self-images of the "civilizing mission" adopted in Paris, the Hague, Brussels, or London. And of course it could be observed that the sanctimonious U.S. attitude toward colonialism was a consequence of its own fortunate economic circumstances, including a relative lack of dependence on foreign sources of raw materials and external markets for its manufactured goods.

Whatever the motives, however, Americans tended, at least in public, to be more sympathetic than citizens of other Western countries to the aspirations of Asian peoples for self-determination and economic development, and this national sense of moral fervor was occasionally reflected in U.S. foreign policy, notably after the Boxer Rebellion, when the McKinley administration attempted to reduce the punitive measures taken by other powers to punish the Chinese for the Manchu court's assistance to the Boxer rebels.

The Roots of Containment

Up until the end of the nineteenth century, then, U.S. foreign policy toward the nations along the Pacific rim was based on a combination of economic interest and anticolonial moralism. Increasing commercial activity and competition among the imperialist powers was beginning to focus U.S. attention on the Pacific, leading some observers to assert the need for a more active commitment to the area. In general, however, security concerns were viewed in Washington as limited, and policymakers preferred to rely on balance-of-power politics and the fragile framework of the Open Door to protect U.S. interests in East Asia.[3]

During the early years of the new century, the delicate ambiguity of the U.S. stance was given its first major test when Japan responded to the gradual decline of European interest in China after the Boxer Rebellion by adopting more aggressive tactics to expand its own influence in the region. Policymakers in Washington were clearly nervous at the prospect but were reluctant to undertake a solitary effort to restrain the Japanese. For two decades, the United States attempted to appease the Japanese by recognizing their interests in East Asia while luring them to undertake their activities within the framework of the Open Door policy. Where possible, as at the Washington Conference in 1922, U.S. policymakers attempted to mobilize the support of other powers with interests in Asia to contain the Japanese by limiting the number of capital ships the latter could maintain in the area.

At first, such efforts had some success. Tokyo was reluctant to risk a direct confrontation with the United States and during the 1920's gave at least lip service to the principles of the Open Door. But expansionist elements in Japan were restive under such restrictions, and when a combination of rising Chinese nationalism and the Great Depression threatened to undermine Japanese interests in North China, Tokyo decided to seek its objectives through military force and territorial expansion.

Washington reacted to this new threat to the balance of power in Asia with its habitual ambivalence. The Hoover administration condemned the Japanese seizure of Manchuria in 1931 on moral grounds, but President Herbert Hoover himself was adamantly opposed to sanctions, thus restricting Secretary of State Henry L. Stimson to an abortive effort to mobilize international support for a policy of nonrecognition of conquered territories. When that failed, Washington retreated to its earlier policy of countering Japanese expansion by a combination of moral opprobrium and appeasement. Even when tension between China and Japan broke out into open conflict after the Marco Polo Bridge incident in July 1937, President Franklin D. Roosevelt, restrained by the isolationist mentality of the American public, shied from a direct confrontation with Tokyo and turned a deaf ear to the pleas of Chinese leader Chiang Kai-shek to provide active support for China's struggle to protect its sovereignty and territorial integrity.

The threatened advance of Japanese military power into Southeast Asia finally galvanized the Roosevelt administration into action. When in 1940 the Japanese demanded military facilities and economic rights in French Indochina, the level of anxiety in Washington increased. Roosevelt imposed limited sanctions on economic relations with Tokyo, and in talks with the Japanese ambassador in Washington, Secretary of State Cordell Hull made it clear that U.S. patience was at an end.

Washington's reaction to Japanese moves in Southeast Asia reflected the new awareness by the Roosevelt administration of the importance of the area to U.S. security concerns. Although historically the United States had possessed few interests there, in the years following World War I Southeast Asia had become an area of increasing economic importance to the United States. In his study *The United States' Emergence as a Southeast Asian Power, 1940–1950*, historian Gary Hess points out that during the 1930's, U.S. trade with Southeast Asia increased steadily in size and significance. Although the total amount of trade compared to overall U.S. foreign trade remained relatively small (between 9 and 14 percent of total imports) the region was the source of some strategically vital raw materials, supplying 75 percent of the tin and 90 percent of the crude rubber in the 1930's. One U.S. oil company, Jersey Standard Oil, was refining 27 percent of the total oil output of the Dutch East Indies.[4]

There was, of course, a security dimension to these economic concerns. Japanese seizure of Southeast Asia would deprive the European colonial powers (or their governments in exile) of resources vital to their war effort against Germany. Although the United States traditionally had been critical of European colonialism, the loss of the area would represent a serious threat to the Allied cause in case the United States went to war with the Axis powers. Some administration officials viewed Japanese advances into French Indochina as a possible threat to the U.S. presence in the Philippines.

At first, the Roosevelt administration was reluctant to confront Japan directly over the area. When French governor-general Georges Catroux appealed to Washington for fighter planes to defend Indochina, the administration refused, claiming that all such aircraft would be needed for the possible defense of the Philippines. And the United States rejected British appeals for cooperation in protecting Thailand from falling under Japanese influence. But Washington's attitude was stiffening, and when Japanese troops occupied southern Indochina in July 1941, the Roosevelt administration froze all Japanese assets in the United States. During the fall, Washington continued to seek a negotiated settlement that would result in the neutralization of Southeast Asia and the removal of Japanese military forces from the area, but when it became clear that Tokyo and Washington were still far apart on their terms for an agreement, Roosevelt evidently concluded that war was virtually inevitable. In a meeting with British officials just before the Japanese attack on Pearl Harbor, he promised U.S. military assistance in case of a Japanese attack on British or Dutch possessions in Southeast Asia.

By the eve of World War II, then, the president, if not all the key members of his administration, had come to the conviction that Southeast Asia was important, if not vital, to the security of the United States. That importance, of course, was derivative in the sense that it stemmed from the belief that without the rich resources of the region, the Allies would be unable to secure victory against the Axis powers. But it nonetheless represented a substantial shift toward an activist policy of containment in Asia and reflected a growing view in Washington that, in a dangerous world, the United States must be prepared to use armed force to protect raw materials vital to its industrial might and military strength.

Southeast Asia in U.S. War Strategy

The strategic importance of Southeast Asia was thus a major factor in bringing the United States and Japan to the brink of war in December 1941. That assessment was initially reflected in U.S. war planning after the Japanese attack on Pearl Harbor in December. In planning operations in the Pacific theater, U.S. war strategists envisaged joint Allied operations against Japanese occupation forces in Burma. That plan was based partly on military considerations to make use of the military forces of Nationalist China, but it also corresponded with Roosevelt's belief that the key to the future peace of Asia was linked to the need to build a strong China friendly to the West and provide the basis for a stable peace in the region after the war.

By 1943, however, that policy had been superseded by a new strategy that focused on an attack on Japan directly across the Pacific. In part, that shift reflected a change in military concerns. But perhaps equally important was the growing feeling in Washington that Chiang Kai-shek's government, plagued with corruption and incompetence, would be unable to play the active role in war strategy that had previously been envisaged by Allied planners. One additional factor that may have influenced the decision was the tacit recognition that because adequate substitutes for natural rubber and tin had been discovered, the United States and its allies did not require the resources of Southeast Asia to wage a successful war effort. Those resources remained in Japanese hands until virtually the end of the war.

By 1943, then, mainland Southeast Asia had receded into the backwater of Allied war strategy in the Pacific conflict. Yet the area still commanded considerable importance in President Roosevelt's calculations about the postwar period. In Roosevelt's view, one of the prime causes of the war in the Pacific had been the weakness and division of the countries in the area, a condition that he ascribed in considerable measure to the legacy of colonialism and imperialism. In that sense the president shared the traditional anticolonialism that affected many Americans' view of the outside world. To Roosevelt, the essential prerequisite for a stable peace in postwar Asia was to bring the colonial era to an end and forge the emergence of stable and independent states in the area.

Roosevelt was particularly critical of what he considered the dismal record of the French in Indochina. This attitude was expressed forcefully on many occasions during the war years. In an oft-quoted memorandum to Secretary of State Hull in January 1944, he remarked that Indochina should not go back to France after the war but should be transformed into an international trusteeship with a view to future independence. "France has milked it for one hundred years," he remarked. "The people of Indochina are entitled to something better than that."[5]

Despite the vehemence of private comments, Roosevelt permitted a degree of ambivalence to creep into U.S. official statements about the status of the French colonies after the war. As early as August 2, 1941, Secretary Hull had implied that the United States might help the French to preserve their empire provided that they effectively resisted the Axis powers. On December 17, shortly after the Japanese attack on Pearl Harbor, Roosevelt had intimated his approval of that view in a letter to Marshal Henri Pétain in which he declared that the preservation by France of its overseas colonies was "essential . . . to the vital interests of the United States." A more formal statement of U.S. policy was made on April 13, 1942, when, in response to a formal request from Vichy's ambassador to Washington for a clarification of U.S. views on the subject, Acting Secretary of State Sumner Welles declared that the United States "recognizes the sovereign jurisdiction of the people of France over the territory of France and over French possessions overseas [and] fervently hopes that it may see the reestablishment of the independence of France and of the integrity of French territory."[6]

Despite such statements, FDR had no intention of permitting the return of Indochina to France after the war. Undoubtedly, Roosevelt's strong opinions on the issue were provoked in part by his critical view of French behavior in the struggle against Germany and Japan. In his eyes, France had shown little willingness to resist the Axis, either in Europe or in Asia. Moreover, by selling out in Indochina, Vichy France had given the Japanese a springboard for the conquest of the remainder of Southeast Asia. As he remarked to Soviet leader Joseph Stalin at the Tehran Conference in November 1943, Roosevelt felt that "many years of honest labor would be necessary before France would be re-established" as a strong nation after the war. To make matters worse, Roosevelt took a strong dislike to Free French leader Charles de Gaulle, whom he viewed as a man with dictatorial tendencies, delusions of grandeur, and obsessed by the desire to restore the French empire after the war.[7]

It is therefore not surprising that Roosevelt became convinced that at the close of the war Indochina should not be returned to French rule but should be transformed into an international trusteeship in preparation for future independence. Apparently the idea had first come up in discussions with British prime minister Winston Churchill at the Atlantic Conference in August 1941. But Churchill, an ardent imperialist, was reluctant to apply the concept of self-determination to colonial peoples and on his return to London made it clear that in the view of the British government the Atlantic Charter applied only to those areas under Nazi occupation and certainly not to India or Britain's other possessions in South and Southeast Asia.

Roosevelt was not daunted by such obstacles, and in the weeks after Pearl Harbor the issue of setting up trusteeships for dependent peoples after the end of the war came under serious study within the Department of State. The Intragovernmental Advisory Committee on Postwar Foreign Policy was set up with representatives from various agencies.

From the start, the administration's planning for postwar Southeast Asia was beset with difficulties. Few government officials had much experience in the area, and to provide expertise, scholars from the academic community were brought in to participate in the discussions. Once the deliberations got under way, it soon became clear that there was not only ignorance but considerable ambivalence about the future of the area. There was general agreement that the United States should promote the liberation of the peoples of Southeast Asia from colonial rule but much uncertainty about the speed of transition and the degree of U.S. involvement in the process. Some administration officials, such as Under Secretary of State Sumner Welles, wanted to force the European powers to accept a trusteeship system, but others, including the department's political adviser Stanley Hornbeck and former minister to China John MacMurray, wanted to limit U.S. involvement to moral suasion. There were also signs of potential discord over how to deal with French Indochina. Some agreed with the president and, because of the dismal French record, were inclined to separate Indochina from the rest of Southeast Asia and let the British and Dutch administer their own trusteeships under the supervision of a regional trusteeship council. Others were more cautious and questioned whether the United States was not already on record as supporting the restoration of French territory after the war. The first signs of official discord over U.S. Indochina policy had already appeared.[8]

From the outset, U.S. plans for postwar Southeast Asia ran into resistance from the leader of the Free French movement, General Charles de Gaulle. In the view of members of General de Gaulle's French Committee of National Liberation, based in Algiers, the most effective means of combating the multifarious threats to French authority in Indochina was for France to play a more significant role in the war effort in the Pacific, specifically in the Allied reconquest of Indochina. As de Gaulle noted in his memoirs, the French claim to Indochina would be strengthened if French blood were to be spilled in achieving its liberation from Japanese control.[9]

In this effort, the French hoped to receive considerable assistance from the British, who had promised to help France restore its overseas empire and who had an empire of their own to protect. In the spring of 1943, a Free French request to attach a French Military Mission under the command of General Roger C. Blaizot to Lord Philip Mountbatten's Southeast Asia Command (SEAC) was approved by the British War Office. According to the plan, the French hoped to use SEAC facilities to undertake military and intelligence operations in Indochina.

During the next few months, the Free French attempted to strengthen their position in preparation for a return to Indochina. With assistance from SEAC headquarters in Ceylon, they quietly began to undertake military and intelligence operations in Indochina (among other activities, the mission secretly parachuted a representative into Indochina with a message from de Gaulle to local French military authorities currently under Vichy command). A Free French Military Mission was set up in South China, and de Gaulle's representative in Washington, Henri Hoppenot, requested that a French representative be included on the Pacific War Council, a committee composed of delegates from nations actively involved in the war in the Pacific.

The Gaullistes also attempted to shore up their legal claim to Indochina. On December 8, 1943, the second anniversary of the Free French declaration of war on Japan (at which time the Vichy treaties and agreements with Japan had been solemnly repudiated), the Algiers committee formerly declared its determination to restore the French presence in Indochina at the close of the war. In an effort to deflect possible U.S. criticism, it added that "France intends to give a new political status to Indochina within the French community." Indochina would be extended economic reforms and broadened political rights, as well as participation in a new federally organized French Union. De Gaulle reiterated those views during a visit to the United States in July 1944. At that time he had promised Roosevelt that it was his intention to grant increased political participation to Indochina in a postwar French federal system.[10]

But such promises had little effect on Roosevelt, who continued his independent efforts to detach Indochina from French control at the close of the war. At a meeting of the Pacific War Council held on July 21, 1943, he had reaffirmed his determination to establish a trusteeship in the area in preparation for full independence at a suitable time after the war. Roosevelt's comments aroused heightened concern in London, where the British felt that his idea would weaken France in the postwar world and lead to Chinese domination over Indochina. Roosevelt was not deterred by British objections, however, and at the international conferences held in Cairo and Tehran he obtained the support of Generalissimo Chiang Kai-shek and Stalin for his trusteeship proposal.[11]

In early 1944 London instructed ambassador to Washington Lord Halifax to clarify the situation in talks with administrative officials. In conversations with Cordell Hull, Halifax found the secretary of state sympathetic to his view that the United States had already pledged itself to restore French sovereignty in its colonies. But when Halifax met with Roosevelt, the president reiterated his determination to pursue a trusteeship in Indochina and pointed out that he had the support of both Stalin and Chiang Kai-shek on the issue. He did promise Halifax that he had no intention of forcing a trusteeship on the British or the Dutch.[12]

On the issue of military operations in Southeast Asia, Halifax relayed a request from London that the French be permitted to take an active part in the planning of "political warfare" operations against the Japanese. The British proposals had already been taken up with the U.S. Joint Chiefs of Staff (JCS), who had tentatively approved them from a military point of view, with the restriction that the French should take part in political warfare only in the area of the SEAC. In the view of the Joint Chiefs, Indochina was in the Chinese theater and therefore was within the American sphere of responsibility. The British contended that there had been an understanding with Chiang Kai-shek that the SEAC was to be permitted to undertake operations in Indochina until firm boundaries were established, but they admitted that the understanding not been confirmed by the Joint Chiefs of Staff. The JCS suggested that the issue be discussed at the September 1944 conference between Roosevelt and Churchill in Quebec. Officials at the Department of State were also inclined to advocate the use of French troops in Indochina on the grounds that French support would be useful in operations against the Japanese. But in Quebec, FDR told Churchill flatly that he did not want U.S. forces involved in any military efforts toward the liberation of Indochina, in the conviction that any action on the matter would be premature.

This reply did not satisfy the British. On November 22, Halifax again raised the issue in Washington. Earlier that month, Roosevelt had replied to a memo by Edward Stettinius that the British were providing open support for French political operations in Southeast Asia by declaring that the United States should not become involved in French activities in Indochina. Now, pressed by Halifax, the president said with some asperity that he had discussed the issue with Churchill at Quebec in September:

I still do not want to get mixed up in any Indo-China decision. It is a matter for postwar . . . I do not want to get mixed up in any military effort toward the liberation of Indo-China from the Japanese. You can tell Halifax that I made this point very clear to Mr. Churchill. From both the military and the civil point of view, action at this time is premature.[13]

During the final months of the year, the ambiguity in the U.S. position led to increasing strains in relations with the British. In late November, U.S. ambassador to China Patrick Hurley informed Roosevelt that a so-called council of three empires (British, French, and Dutch) had been formed at SEAC headquarters with the goal of facilitating the restoration of the European colonies in Southeast Asia at the end of the war. The president replied that all Allied operations in Indochina should be coordinated with General Albert Wedemeyer, U.S. chief of staff to Chiang Kai-shek. In an effort to clear up misunderstandings, Wedemeyer met with Lord Mountbatten in Colombo in March, but the meeting did not alleviate the confusion. Wedemeyer thought that Mountbatten had agreed to undertake operations only with his prior approval. Mountbatten claimed that it had been agreed only that he would inform Wedemeyer of SEAC operations.[14]

The confusion at the upper echelons over Indochina policy affected U.S. units operating in the field, particularly officials of the Office of Strategic Services (OSS), some of whom were actively involved in attempting to promote intelligence operations in Indochina. Should OSS operatives cooperate with French intelligence units and provide assistance to them in Indochina and South China? Should they establish links with anti-French Vietnamese nationalist groups who were fighting against the Japanese and offered to provide information to the United States in return for weapons and political recognition? In October, William J. Donovan, chief of the OSS, had asked the Department of State to provide policy guidance for OSS units operating in the China theater. Stettinius had referred the matter to the White House, and on the sixteenth, Roosevelt had replied that U.S. units were to "do nothing in regard to resistance groups or in any other way in relations to Indochina—wait till things are a little clearer." Clearly, the president had not yet reached a final decision on U.S. activities in Indochina when the war in the Pacific came to a close.[15]

While statesmen and diplomats jousted over the Indochina issue in world capitals, Allied military and intelligence units in the Pacific attempted to interpret the policies of their governments and implement them to the best effect in the field. During the fall and winter of 1944–45, U.S. military and intelligence units in South China, lacking firm guidance from Washington, attempted to interpret Roosevelt's somewhat enigmatic rulings by cooperating informally with all resistance groups—French and Vietnamese—that were prepared to fight against the Japanese, without granting any open assistance that could be construed as overt political support. This was not always easy to achieve, for representatives of both the Free French and local nationalist groups did their best to obtain American military assistance and support for their cause.

To complicate matters, factional rivalry within both camps (in the French camp, between Gaullist, Giraudist, and Vichy elements; in the Vietnamese camp, between communist and noncommunist nationalist organizations) made it difficult for Americans to cooperate with such groups without being accused—however innocently—of political favoritism of one group over another. For OSS units in South China, charged with the responsibility of setting up intelligence networks in Indochina, the problem was particularly delicate. Such units had maintained contacts with both French and Vietnamese groups in exile, while attempting generally to avoid entanglement in political issues. But maintaining a nonpartisan stance was often difficult because all Vietnamese and French organizations viewed the United States as the primary source of military assistance and, in some cases, of political support. Under such conditions, when a firm policy from Washington was lacking, personal prejudices and political beliefs often predominated and gave rise to harsh charges of American favoritism.

For most U.S. units in the area, the two major protagonists were the French Military Mission under Jean Sainteny (and, after March, French units that had fled from Indochina after the Japanese coup d'etat of March 9, which abolished French administration in the territory) and the so-called Vietminh Front, led by the mysterious revolutionary later to be popularly known as Ho Chi Minh. Contacts between U.S. units and the French Military Mission had been in evidence since the latter's arrival in South China in 1943, but many members of the OSS were suspicious of French motives and—whether because of their knowledge of Roosevelt's views or their own political beliefs—were reluctant to cooperate with them. The French reciprocated and distrusted American intentions in Southeast Asia.

About Ho Chi Minh and his Vietminh Front (formally called the League for the Independence of Vietnam, or Viet Nam Doc Lap Dong Minh) U.S. officials knew almost nothing. Their first awareness of Ho Chi Minh (previously known by his earlier revolutionary alias Nguyen Ai Quoc, or Nguyen the Patriot) came in 1942 after he was arrested by local authorities in South China and placed in jail. By the time of Ho's release a year later, his anti-French and anti-Japanese Vietminh guerrilla movement was already becoming known locally for its political effectiveness and military prowess. Ho Chi Minh had approached U.S. officials in South China and offered to provide them with information on Japanese activities in Indochina in return for weapons and political support. Local OSS officials were aware of his revolutionary background but appeared to believe that he was above all a nationalist and, as the leader of the most effective anti-Japanese resistance group in the area, potentially useful in serving the Allied cause.

The Rise of the Vietminh

Whether Roosevelt's description of French Indochina as the most brutal and exploitative colonial regime in Southeast Asia is accurate is a matter of debate. Certainly exploitation of the colonial peoples was the rule rather than the exception throughout the region. None of the colonial powers had been especially successful in carrying out their self-declared "civilizing mission" of introducing Western technology and modern political institutions in the area. Virtually all had repressed efforts by indigenous patriotic groups to restore their national independence.

The French had been particularly thorough in their efforts to suppress anticolonial activities in Indochina, especially in Vietnam, which was politically and culturally more advanced than the neighboring French protectorates of Laos and Cambodia. Moreover, Vietnam had a well-developed tradition of national identity forged in the crucible of two thousand years of intermittent resistance to Chinese domination. That tradition, however, had not prepared the Vietnamese to face the challenge posed by European expansion in the mid-nineteenth century. The French completed their conquest of Vietnam in 1884 and divided the virtually defunct state into three separate segments, the protectorates of Tonkin and Annam in the north and the center and the colony of Cochin China in the south. By the end of the century, the three territories had been joined with the protectorates of Laos and Cambodia into the so-called Indochinese Union, governed by a governor-general appointed from Paris.

The division of Vietnam into three separate regions, each governed in a different manner, was probably undertaken for French administrative convenience, but it was destined to have momentous consequences for the future of French rule in Indochina and would eventually become a crucial factor in the Vietnam War. In Tonkin and Annam, French rule was relatively indirect, and French advisers at upper levels maintained contact with the local population through a Vietnamese administration. French policies there sometimes encountered strong resistance from the entrenched force of Confucian traditions, reflected both in the effete imperial bureaucracy and in the local leadership at the village level. Poor in resources and in some lowland areas densely populated, the two protectorates attracted relatively little direct French economic penetration and were affected only peripherally by French rule.

By contrast, in Cochin China French rule was direct, and the colony experienced intensive efforts at economic exploitation and cultural transformation. The process was facilitated by both historical circumstances and economic realities. The southern provinces had not been absorbed into the Vietnamese empire until the seventeenth century and remained a frontier region at the time of the French conquest three centuries later. In the wide-open spaces of the rich Mekong Delta, Vietnamese immigrants from the crowded northern provinces developed individualist values and entrepreneurial attitudes far removed from the tradition-bound provinces in the North.

After the arrival of the French, the marshlands of the lower delta were drained and the virgin lands opened up to cultivation. Along the Cambodian border, rubber plantations were established. In this hothouse atmosphere, an affluent Vietnamese bourgeoisie, its wealth based on commerce or absentee landlordism, began to flower. Centered in the growing metropolis of Saigon, this class had a curiously split personality reminiscent of urban attitudes in many of the great commercial centers of colonial Asia. Many were educated under French rule and studied in French schools. Often they developed an admiration for French culture, aped the living habits of the *colons*, and sought increased political influence and economic benefits within the confines of the French colonial system. Yet they were often scorned by French residents in Indochina, and many resented European domination over the local economy. The result was an amalgam of Francophile and xenophobic instincts that gave birth to a profound ambivalence about the alleged benefits of French rule.

These conditions made an indelible impact on the development of the Vietnamese nationalist movement, which began to emerge among educated Vietnamese in the first three decades of the twentieth century. Such groups ran the gamut from nonviolent reformism to advocacy of radical revolution. Many of the parties were split along regional lines. Much of the support for moderate reformist organizations came from Cochin China and was centered on the urban bourgeoisie in Saigon, where a small coterie of French-educated professionals formed the Constitutionalist Party to promote the broadening of political and economic freedoms for the local population in continued association with France in the Indochinese Union.[16]

In other circles, a different attitude prevailed. In the cities of Hanoi, Hué, and Saigon and in provincial and district capitals scattered throughout the country, anticolonial elements began to form clandestine political organizations dedicated to the eviction of the French and the restoration of national independence. Most prominent was the so-called Vietnamese Nationalist Party, or VNQDD, a radical nationalist group formed on the model of Sun Yat-sen's Nationalist Party in China. Such groups were formed mainly in Annam and

Tonkin, but some appeared in the South, where they received support from workers and petty bourgeois intellectuals in the Saigon area.

It was in this milieu that the Indochinese Communist Party (ICP) emerged. Some Vietnamese nationalists were introduced to Marxism through the radical ideas then fashionable in intellectual and working-class circles in Paris, where many had gone to work or study during and after World War I. Often they were first attracted to Marxist-Leninist doctrine less for its social millenarianism than for its anti-imperialist message, promising liberation for all colonial peoples from European rule. Such was certainly the case with the founder of the party, Ho Chi Minh. In 1920, then living in Paris under the revolutionary pseudonym Nguyen Ai Quoc (Nguyen the Patriot), Ho joined the French Communist Party (FCP) after reading Lenin's "Theses on the National and Colonial Questions," a document which, in his own words, attracted him as a means of liberating Vietnam and other oppressed countries from colonial rule. He had earlier been rebuffed in an attempt to present a demand for the independence of colonial territories to Allied leaders gathered at Versailles.[17]

In late 1924, after several months of training at the headquarters of the Communist International (Comintern) in Moscow, Ho Chi Minh returned to South China, where he was technically assigned as an interpreter for the Comintern's advisory mission to Sun Yat-sen's government in Canton. His real duties were to form the first Marxist revolutionary organization in Indochina. During the next several years he organized radical intellectuals throughout Vietnam into a transitional organization called the Revolutionary Youth League of Vietnam (Viet Nam Thanh Nien Cach Mang Dong Chi Hoi). Then, in February 1930, he presided over the creation of a Vietnamese Communist Party in Hong Kong. Eight months later, at the instructions of Moscow, it was re-named the Indochinese Communist Party, with responsibility for promoting revolution throughout French Indochina.[18]

Almost from the outset, the ICP became a leading force in the anticolonial movement. One indication of that fact was visible even before the creation of the party. Within two years, the Revolutionary Youth League's membership had shot up to about 1,000, and a significant number of that total had been recruited from rival nationalist organizations. But perhaps the most telling testimonial came from the French security services, who quickly assessed the league as the most serious threat to colonial authority and devoted a high percentage of their efforts to ferreting out its membership.

What was the secret behind the movement's early success? Part of the reason can be attributed to the shortcomings of its rivals. Despite the intensity of the Vietnamese sense of national identity, an intensity arguably stronger than in any other society in the region, the first anticolonialist parties in Vietnam were plagued almost from the beginning with chronic factional divisions and the lack of a mass base. Internal divisions, of course, were a common feature in many anticolonial movements throughout the Third World and were a product of various causes, including disagreements over strategy and tactics, regional or ethnic differences, personality conflicts, or even disputes arising from different visions of the final objective. In some instances, nationalist leaders were able to surmount such disagreements to form a broad alliance against the common adversary. Such had been the case in India, for example, with the Indian National Congress. Similar alliances were formed in Burma, Malaya, and the Dutch East Indies. In Vietnam, despite the relative homogeneity of Vietnamese society and the long tradition of national independence, nationalist parties were chronically unable to transcend regional differences, tactical differences, or personality disputes to achieve unity in face of the repressive efforts of the colonial regime.

Noncommunist political parties in Vietnam were equally unable to establish close links with the mass of the population. Because of their roots in the cities and their urban middle-class concerns, few patriotic intellectuals were particularly sensitive to issues vital to Vietnamese peasants such as land hunger, high taxes, and the prevalence of official corruption. The VNQDD recruited some of its followers from the working class and from native soldiers serving in the French colonial army. But the bulk of the membership came from the small but vocal bourgeoisie, and few came from rural villages. The party did issue a land reform program similar to Sun Yat-sen's "land to the tiller" in China, but it made no serious effort to build a base in the countryside and therefore was almost entirely wiped out after an abortive revolt in February 1930.

The Constitutionalist Party had even fewer ties with the overall population. Although the party's mouthpiece, Bui Quang Chieu's *La Tribune Indochinoise*, occasionally lamented the impoverished living conditions of the rural population, for the most part it spoke for the interests of the affluent bourgeoisie in Saigon and the landlord class in the southern provinces. Its primary concerns were to promote the interests of indigenous merchants and to achieve equal pay for equal work for Vietnamese employees with their European counterparts.[19]

The failure of noncommunist nationalism to take the lead in forming a broad-based anticolonial resistance movement in Vietnam left the door open for Ho Chi Minh's Indochinese Communist Party. Although in many respects Ho was a sincere Marxist-Leninist, he was convinced that the problem in Vietnam was at least partly a national one, involving the peasantry and patriotic members of the bourgeoisie and the patriotic land gentry, as well as the small indigenous proletariat. It was with that objective in mind that he had sought to create a broad front organization of patriotic and revolutionary elements under the aegis of the Revolutionary Youth League.[20]

At the time, a strategy emphasizing nationalism over class struggle coincided generally with the global approach pursued by the Soviet Union and its mouthpiece, the Comintern, and instructions to that effect were undoubtedly in Ho's baggage when he left Moscow for Canton in December 1924. But after 1928, Soviet strategy shifted radically to the left. Communist parties throughout the world were instructed to reduce their contacts with bourgeois nationalist organizations and seek to organize "united fronts from below" with workers and poor peasants in preparation for a wave of revolutionary violence in Asia.

It was in that context that the broad-based league was transformed into a formal Communist Party in February 1930 at the insistence of the Comintern. In the weeks and months that followed, revolutionary activists in Vietnam dutifully followed the shift in line ordered by Moscow and began to intensify their agitation in factories, rural villages, and rubber plantations for an anticipated insurrection against French rule. The shift would have disastrous consequences. During the spring and summer of 1930, provoked by a rapid downturn in the colonial economy, labor unrest and peasant demonstrations broke out in all three regions of divided Vietnam. Although caught somewhat by surprise by the violence and widespread nature of the popular protest, the party leadership attempted to take the lead of the movement to direct it into revolutionary channels. But the French reacted vigorously to the challenge, and the Nghe-Tinh revolt (so named because the largest uprisings took place in Ho Chi Minh's native province of Nghe An and neighboring Ha Tinh) was soon brought to an end. In the debacle, the party apparatus was virtually eliminated. The entire Central Committee was seized and an estimated 90 percent of party members were killed or sentenced to terms in prison. Ho Chi Minh, who was serving as Comintern representative for the Far East in Hong Kong, was arrested by British police as part of a general roundup of radical elements in the region. After his release in 1933, he spent most of the remainder of the decade in the Soviet Union. About all that could be said for the revolt was that it had demonstrated the importance of the peasantry to the revolutionary cause in Vietnam and the danger of a premature insurrection. As it would turn out, these were not insignificant lessons.[21]

It is a measure of the resilience of the party and its sturdy roots at the local level that it soon recovered from the debacle of the Nghe-Tinh revolt and reestablished its position as the most important force in the Vietnamese anti-colonialist movement. The ICP soon benefited from changes on the international scene. Amid growing signs that the Hitler regime in Germany was not, as Stalin had first believed, a temporary phenomenon, the Seventh Congress of the Comintern, held in August 1935, called for the formation of an alliance between the USSR and Western democracies against the common danger of global fascism. In response, the French government eased its efforts to suppress communist parties in the colonies. Now able to operate in a semilegal manner, the ICP began to revive, spreading its influence in the labor movement, among urban intellectuals, and in rural villages in the Mekong River Delta, where peasants were restive over high taxes, conscription, and the low price of grain.

But the emergence of the ICP from its clandestine existence during the early 1930's was short-lived. In 1938 the colonial authorities, frightened at rising social and political unrest, cracked down on the party's overt organization and closed a number of its newspapers. A year later, after Moscow signed a non-aggression pact with Nazi Germany, the party was formally outlawed. Party leaders were once again forced into hiding to escape the repressive efforts of the French Sûreté. Less than a year later, under severe pressure from Tokyo, French authorities were forced to grant military and economic rights to the Japanese in northern Indochina.

To Ho Chi Minh, still in Moscow, the rapidly changing world situation spelled opportunity, and in 1938 he received permission from the Comintern to return to China. After two years of service with the Chinese Communists, he resumed contact with members of the ICP. In May of 1941, at a meeting of the Central Committee held in the mountains near the Sino-Vietnamese frontier, the party created a new united front designed to appeal to all anticolonial elements within the country. It was known as the League for the Independence of Vietnam, or Vietminh.

The new front bore the marks of Ho Chi Minh's political genius. Making a firm break with the sectarian policies of the early 1930's, it focused not on the Bolshevik model of class struggle and urban insurrection based on the working class but on the two primordial issues in colonial Vietnam—national independence and the land revolution. The issue of national independence was designed to appeal, above all, to patriotic intellectuals and was directed against both French colonial rule and the growing Japanese military presence in the country. The emphasis on land reform reflected the ineluctable fact, demonstrated by the Nghe-Tinh revolt, that the peasantry—representing nearly 90 percent of the total population of the country—was potentially the most revolutionary force in Vietnam.

A key component of the new Vietminh Front was its allegedly bipartisan and nonsectarian character. Although the Vietminh was actually under firm party leadership, the guiding hand of the ICP was disguised so as to appeal to moderate elements in Vietnam and abroad who might be alienated by the social radicalism of Marxist-Leninist ideology. To avoid frightening patriotic landed gentry, the land reform program would be limited to rent reduction and the confiscation of land belonging to those who collaborated with the Japanese. There would be time enough for the party to carry through its dreams of social revolution. For the moment, the primary focus of the Vietminh Front would be national independence.[22]

After the formation of the new front, the ICP began to organize a network of mass organizations in cities and villages throughout the country while simultaneously building up guerrilla forces in a base area in the tangled mountains north of the heavily populated Red River Delta. Ho Chi Minh planned to prepare his forces for a combined political and military uprising to seize power from the Japanese and their French puppets at the moment of their anticipated defeat by Allied forces at the end of the war.

The U.S. and the Vietminh Front

For the most part, policymakers in Washington were ignorant of these developments in far-off Indochina. During the 1930's, reports from U.S. consular offices in Hanoi and Saigon made occasional references to political unrest in Indochina, but U.S. interests in the area were limited and conditions there were of little concern to U.S. diplomats. But the entrance of Japanese military forces into Indochina beginning in the fall of 1940, followed by the attack on Pearl Harbor the following year, radically changed the situation. During the early years of the war, the OSS established intelligence units in Indochina to gather information on Japanese troop movements and rescue U.S. fliers shot down while on missions over mainland Southeast Asia.

It was at that point that U.S. intelligence agents in Asia first became aware of Ho Chi Minh and his newly established Vietminh Front. According to Archimedes Patti, then a member of an OSS intelligence group operating in South China, the U.S. Embassy in Chungking reported Ho's arrest by Chinese authorities in December 1942. Several months later, the embassy received a request from a so-called Central Committee of the Indochinese Section of the International Anti-Invasion Association to seek Ho's release. At approximately the same time a similar request came from a Chinese Communist source, calling for his release from prison to aid the Allied cause. Ho had already earned a reputation in local circles for his ability to bring together disparate elements in a common front against the Japanese.[23]

Whether U.S. officials were instrumental in obtaining Ho's release from prison in August 1943 is not clear from available evidence. It is obvious that U.S. operatives in South China had some interest in using his services to promote anti-Japanese activities in occupied Indochina. Indeed, Ho Chi Minh cooperated by setting up or reorganizing antifascist organizations among Vietnamese living in exile in South China. One of these was the Dong Minh Hoi, an organization of Vietnamese nationalist groups formed by Chinese authorities to provide assistance to their own covert political and military activities in Indochina. U.S. officials in China and Washington were aware of Ho's revolutionary background and his ties to Moscow, and some were reluctant to see the United States become closely identified with him and his movement. Nevertheless, in early 1945 he was enlisted by the OSS to organize an intelligence network in Indochina.

For Ho Chi Minh an arrangement with the OSS could be useful in several ways. It would provide equipment and weapons for his movement at a time when the Vietminh was simply one of several nationalist and anti-Japanese organizations competing for support and visibility in South China. The amount of aid granted was minimal, but Ho Chi Minh used it to maximum advantage. Ho also hoped to solicit U.S. aid in preventing the return of the French after the end of the war. He was well aware that the United States was a leading capitalist nation with strong ties to the European powers. But he was also aware of President Roosevelt's determination to end French rule in Indochina and frequently expressed the hope that under Roosevelt's leadership the United States would support the struggle for democracy and national liberation in colonial areas after the war. Whether he believed such a contingency was likely cannot be said with certainty. In any case, he addressed several messages to President Roosevelt appealing for recognition of his movement as the legitimate representative of the national aspirations of the Vietnamese people. Given the apparent insignificance of his movement and FDR's reluctance to take action in Indochina before the end of the war, it is not surprising that none was answered.[24]

The Abandonment of Trusteeship

While Ho Chi Minh attempted to enlist U.S. support in his struggle for national independence, President Roosevelt's effort to prevent Indochina from reverting to French rule at the end of the war against Japan was becoming unraveled. At first, the primary resistance had come from the British and the French. But as the war neared a conclusion, FDR's plans for Southeast Asia came under fire from within his own administration. During the first half of 1944, discussions on the postwar status of the colonial areas in Southeast Asia continued in the Department of State. A clear difference of opinion began to surface between personnel from the Office of European Affairs and those from the newly created Division of Southwest Pacific Affairs (renamed in 1945 the Division of Southeast Asian Affairs).

The disagreement would bedevil U.S. policymakers for the next decade. Asianists were inclined to support Roosevelt's plans to remove Indochina from French rule by establishing an international trusteeship there at the close of the war, on the grounds that the United States must show its determination to stand at the side of colonial peoples in their demands for national independence and self-determination. Europeanists countered that such a decision would anger the French and impede postwar Franco-American cooperation. Some pointed out the importance of stabilizing Western Europe against the possible extension of Soviet power. In China, some U.S. diplomats added their voice to the debate, warning that Chiang Kai-shek's government in Chungking might attempt to use its influence over Vietnamese organizations in South China as a means of expanding its own activities in the region at the close of the war.[25]

In July 1944, Roosevelt met with Charles de Gaulle in Washington. At that time, de Gaulle indicated his intention to grant Indochina broadened political participation in a postwar federal system. Whether de Gaulle's promise affected FDR's attitude is uncertain. But Washington's recognition of de Gaulle's Committee of National Liberation as the provisional authority in France until elections could be held obviously complicated the president's plans to prevent the return of France to Indochina after the war. De Gaulle was not completely satisfied because he had wanted U.S. recognition of his government before elections were held.[26]

At the Dumbarton Oaks Conference, held in Washington, D.C., in August 1944, the United States submitted a new proposal for the postwar disposition of dependent areas. According to the proposal, trusteeships would be formed in only three cases: territories then under the mandate of the League of Nations, territories seized from the enemy because of the war, and territories voluntarily placed under the system by the states responsible for their administration.

The new proposal represented a qualified abandonment of Roosevelt's previous position, for under its provisions Indochina would become an international trusteeship only with French permission, something de Gaulle's government would patently be unwilling to do. The reasons for the shift have never been totally explained, but several factors may have been involved. In the first place, Roosevelt may have gradually given way (or at least feigned to have given way) under the persistent resistance of members of his administration as well as of the British and the French. Cordell Hull was quoted as observing that it might not be wise for the United States to insist on trusteeships—even on a national basis—if similar declarations could not be obtained from the British and the French. Second, as Hull pointed out in his memoirs, the War Department was opposed to a rigid insistence on trusteeships in the conviction that this would make it more difficult for the United States to obtain Japanese-mandated islands in the Pacific for defensive purposes after the war. Similar views were also apparently at work among working-level officials in the State Department. In discussions with representatives of the British Foreign Office, representatives from the Department of State had modified some of the administration's plans in an effort to allay British objections.[27]

Whatever the case, it is clear that Roosevelt had not yet totally abandoned his previous position. The U.S. proposal had not been raised for a formal decision at Dumbarton Oaks but was simply presented for discussion and later consideration. At the Yalta Conference, held the following February, the issue arose again, first in a conversation between Roosevelt and Stalin. At that time, Roosevelt indicated that he had not changed his mind on Indochina and in a somewhat rambling discussion remarked that he "had in mind a trusteeship" for the area. But when the issue was raised for formal discussion, the U.S. proposal earlier presented at the Dumbarton Oaks Conference and calling for voluntary trusteeships was approved. An indication of Roosevelt's willingness to accept the plan was forthcoming at a press conference held on the USS

Quincy returning from Yalta in which he remarked that although Stalin and Chiang Kai-shek had liked the trusteeship idea, the British had not because it might "bust up their empire."[28]

Further clarification of Roosevelt's position came in March, in a conversation with his adviser Charles Taussig. FDR observed that he was concerned about "the brown people in the East" who must be assisted in achieving their independence. Churchill, he said, did not understand that concept. When Taussig asked him if he had changed his mind on French Indochina, Roosevelt said no, that "French Indochina should be taken from France and put under a trusteeship." He hesitated and then said, "Well, if we can get the proper pledge from France to assume the obligations of a trustee, then I would agree to France obtaining these colonies with the proviso that independence was the ultimate goal." When asked if he would settle for self-government or a dominion status he said that "it must be independence. He said that is to be the policy and you can quote me in the State Department." On April 3, FDR reportedly approved a policy statement on Yalta plans that implied that Indochina would become a trusteeship only through the voluntary action of the French.[29]

Debate over the administration's Indochina policy continued into the spring, and the problem had not been resolved at the time of President Roosevelt's death in April. Shortly before his death, a memo written by G. H. Blakeslee of the Division of Far Eastern Affairs had attempted to craft a compromise between FDR's views and the concerns of Europeanists in the light of decisions taken at the Yalta Conference. Blakeslee recommended that no conditions be imposed on a French return to Indochina because conditions had not been imposed on other European colonial powers. Blakeslee also argued that although the Vietnamese were clearly capable of self-government, a preparatory period would be necessary to end factional strife and prepare the local population for assuming control of their own affairs. Nevertheless, Blakeslee sympathized strongly with the Vietnamese desire for national independence and hoped that an accommodation could be reached that would satisfy the concerns of the French and other colonial powers while at the same time placing the United States on the side of the dependent peoples of Asia in their struggle for national independence. Blakeslee and other State Department officials may have assumed that FDR still intended to press the French on the issue. In a cover document attached to the memorandum, the Far Eastern Division urged that the U.S. government should avoid any action that might prejudice a possible future initiative to move Indochina toward national independence.[30]

Blakeslee's effort to bridge the chasm between Asianists and Europeanists was not successful. After FDR's death the controversy flared up again when the department was instructed to prepare a position on Indochina in preparation for the upcoming San Francisco Conference, the primary objective of which was to set up a postwar international organization. The Offices of European

(EUR) and Far Eastern (FE) Affairs were directed to discuss various alternatives for the postwar disposition of Indochina. The report submitted by the Office of European Affairs supported the French position. Understandably sensitive to the potential problems a trusteeship in Indochina would pose for future U.S.-French relations, it recommended that the United States not oppose a restoration of Indochina to French rule. Stating that the Japanese coup d'etat of March 1945 (which had abolished French authority in Indochina and granted a spurious independence to local monarchist forces under Vietnamese emperor Bao Dai) and the increasing level of French military activities in the Pacific had created new conditions in the area, the report contended that the ambiguity of U.S. policy toward Indochina had "aroused French suspicions" and, furthermore, was not supported by our British and Dutch allies. Pointing out that there was "not the slightest possibility" that the de Gaulle government would consent to placing Indochina voluntarily under an international trusteeship, it recommended that the United States not oppose restoration of Indochina to French rule but instead exert its influence with the French "in the direction of having them effect a liberalization of their past policy of limited opportunities for native participation in government and administration."[31]

The Office of Far Eastern Affairs took a different view. While recognizing the complexity of the international situation and the dangers involved in antagonizing America's European allies over the colonial issue, its response declared that it would nonetheless be undesirable, in light of persistent French failures to develop representative institutions in Indochina, to restore the area to the French without imposing stringent conditions compelling them to extend democratic freedoms and self-government to the local population. Conceding that a period of preparation would be desirable before the granting of full independence, Abbot Low Moffat of FE asserted that the Vietnamese were a sophisticated people and as capable of self-government as the Thai. It would be desirable, he concluded, for the United States to "dissociate itself in every feasible way from the imperialism of the European powers in the Far East." Otherwise, "it might weaken the traditional confidence of eastern peoples in the United States." At the insistence of Under Secretary of State Joseph S. Grew, the two offices attempted to reconcile their differences, and eventually a compromise was reached whereby FE concurred with the assessment of the Europeanists, while urging that the United States "seek assurances from France that would extend a measure of self-government to Indochina."[32]

The French were aware of the direction of U.S. thinking and had attempted to anticipate U.S. objectives. On March 24, 1945, the provisional government declared that Indochina would enjoy "an autonomy proportionate to her progress and attainments" and promoted the idea of a French Union in preference to a trusteeship. At the opening of the San Francisco Conference in early May, French foreign minister Georges Bidault, in obvious reference to the Yalta agreement, declared publicly that the decision on the future of Indochina would rest with France alone, and he made it clear that the trusteeship concept would not be applied to Indochina. At the same time, he took the offensive in remarks to U.S. secretary of state Edward Stettinius, complaining that the American press had been implying that the United States would demand a special status for Indochina. In reply, Stettinius conceded that "some elements" in American public opinion (he did not mention that it had been the view of Roosevelt himself) were hostile to French policy and practice in Indochina but assured him that "the record was innocent of any official statement of this government questioning, even by implication, French sovereignty over Indochina."[33]

In the end, the conference resolved the issue by compromise. The U.S. delegation accepted the Yalta formula calling for the formation of trusteeships in colonial areas on a voluntary basis and did not press for the transformation of Indochina into an international trusteeship. But in deference to the views expressed in the State Department report, it "insisted on the necessity of providing a progressive measure of self-government for all dependent peoples looking toward their eventual independence or incorporation in some form of federation according to circumstances and the ability of the peoples to assume these responsibilities."[34]

This concept was incorporated into the United Nations Charter. Article 73 stated that the nations administering territories assumed the sacred trust or developing self-government and free political institutions.

After the close of the San Francisco Conference, the State Department issued a policy paper on Indochina policy which attempted to resolve the dilemma by admitting that the United States must harmonize the desire for security and freedom in Asia with the need to support the colonial powers in the global arena and U.S. security interests. It called for an "increasing measure of self-government" in Indochina. Otherwise, France would encounter "serious difficulty" in controlling the country.[35]

It has sometimes been asserted that the accession of Harry S. Truman to the presidency in April marked the transition of U.S. policy toward Indochina from insistence on a trusteeship to acceptance of a restoration of French sovereignty. As the above analysis demonstrates, this assertion is somewhat misleading, for it is clear that the evolution of U.S. Indochina policy away from the trusteeship idea was gradual and did not shift markedly in April, at the time of transition to a new president. The struggle between Europeanists and Asianists within the Department of State over the future course of U.S. policy toward the European colonies had already begun. Even Roosevelt had clearly begun to weaken in his view that Indochina should be taken away from the French and was prepared to accept a French return, although only under certain conditions.

President Harry Truman, who had not been kept abreast of foreign policy developments while he was vice-president and knew little about Southeast Asia, much less about Indochina, probably felt that he was following Roosevelt's intentions in good faith. In late May, he informed Under Secretary of State Joseph Grew that he would not insist on a trusteeship for Indochina without the consent of the French government but, according to Grew, said that it was his intention "at some appropriate time to ask of the French Government some positive indication of its intentions in regard to the establishment of civil liberties and an increasing measure of self-government in Indochina before formulating further declarations of policy in this respect."[36]

Still, some nuances distinguished Truman's position from that of his predecessor. Roosevelt had apparently insisted to the end that he would demand a commitment from the French that independence—not just autonomy or dominion status—would eventually be granted to the peoples of Indochina. Truman did not insist on such a commitment and appeared to be satisfied with the verbal declaration of the French government that the Indochinese people would receive political freedoms through the medium of the newly planned French Union. Whether Roosevelt would have insisted on French compliance with his own terms will never be known. What is known is that before his death, Roosevelt had been compelled, probably because of heavy pressure from his allies, to abandon his original position on Indochina. Whether he would have followed a different course of action than his successor had he lived will remain forever a matter of speculation.[37]

The French Return to Indochina

Under the influence of Roosevelt's instructions to avoid political entanglements in Indochina, U.S. officials in South China had treated Ho Chi Minh with caution and, though they forwarded his appeals for U.S. support to the U.S. Embassy in Chungking, carefully avoided any indication of overt support. In March of 1945, however, new directives from Washington granted more flexibility to U.S. units in the area, which were now permitted to provide assistance and cooperation to any and all resistance groups provided that such operations did not conflict with planned operations. American units, however, were still prohibited from aligning themselves with the French.[38]

Freed from earlier restrictions, some OSS officers began to cooperate more openly with the Vietminh against the advice of some U.S. diplomats and much to the irritation of Jean Sainteny and other French representatives in the area. Among those angry at U.S. policy were French military officials who had fled to China after the Japanese coup in March and wanted the United States to rearm them and provide them with supplies for a return to Indochina.

It is not surprising, though not always justified, that many French officials came to believe that the United States was systematically attempting to place obstacles in their way to assist Ho Chi Minh's Vietminh in seizing power in Indochina. The truth behind the controversy has been angrily debated and given rise to charges that cannot be resolved here. It is true that some U.S. officers involved in setting up operations in Indochina were anti-French and profoundly suspicious of French motives. But it is also true that many local French military or civilian officials were chronically suspicious of U.S. intentions and suspected that, under its claim of neutrality, the United States was conniving to replace the French in Indochina. It is no wonder that tensions between French and American officials in the area reached a high level as the war approached its close.[39]

Ho Chi Minh, already a master of the technique of dividing and isolating his adversaries, astutely played on these tensions and attempted to win the United States to his side by demonstrating the patriotic and democratic character of his movement. Some observers have asserted that, given his overall commitment to the Marxist-Leninist worldview, Ho Chi Minh was being hypocritical in making his bold bid for U.S. support. But Ho did not wear ideological blinders when he viewed the world scene, and furthermore he had little choice. The Vietminh movement was small and almost totally lacking in external support. The Chinese Communists and the Soviet Union, his closest ideological allies, were preoccupied with their own concerns and in no immediate position to provide assistance. Although Ho was not blind to the capitalist character of U.S. society, he may have sincerely believed that under the leadership of President Roosevelt, the progressive and democratic character of American foreign policy could be cultivated and put to good use in the struggle for Vietnamese national independence.

By the spring of 1945, the French in South China were becoming increasingly vociferous in demanding U.S. military assistance for projected French operations in Indochina. Ambassador to China Patrick Hurley, still confused over U.S. policy in the area, asked Washington for guidance. On June 10, he was informed by cable that as a result of the Yalta agreement, it was anticipated that the French would be permitted by the Allied command to restore their authority over Indochina. American assistance in this process was authorized so long as it was specifically directed at the overall objective of defeating the Japanese and did not interfere with planned operations. U.S. military forces, however, were to be used only against the Japanese.[40]

As a result of this directive, U.S. units were now permitted to provide assistance to the French, and the head of OSS operations in China, Colonel Richard P. Heppner, approved such aid on the condition that U.S. involvement maintained a low profile. In practice, however, the new policy had little impact on the local scene. Because of overall military requirements in the area, General Wedemeyer had instructed subordinates that U.S. weapons and other equipment could be provided to the French only for intelligence or rescue operations, and he informed General Gabriel Sabattier that all French operations against the Japanese had to be under OSS command.[41]

The new guidelines did not materially affect the nature of the growing U.S. relationship with the Vietminh. Ho Chi Minh continued his efforts to gain political recognition and military assistance from the United States through his contacts with the OSS and attempted to use such contacts to give the impression within Indochina that the Vietminh movement had official Allied support. When other methods of obtaining such official support proved unavailing, he resorted to subterfuge. Requesting and receiving a signed photograph of General Claire Chennault (with Ho Chi Minh standing beside him), Ho then displayed that photo in his travels throughout the area to prove that his movement had official recognition from the Allies.[42]

By the summer of 1945, it was evident that the war would come to a close without the necessity of undertaking Allied military operations in Indochina. Because of the rapidity of the American advance across the Pacific and the anticipated entry of the Soviet Union into the war against Japan in August, a planned offensive in South China was shelved, and the only remaining military problem relating to Indochina was to make arrangements for the entrance of Allied occupation forces to accept the surrender of Japanese troops at the close of the war. In retrospect, it is clear that the decisions made by Allied leaders at that time were destined to have momentous consequences for the future of Indochina. At the time, however, it appears that the decisions were made in good part because the United States did not wish to become involved in the political struggles that were bound to take place in Southeast Asia at the end of the war. It is ironic that U.S. unwillingness to participate actively in determining the postwar political process in Indochina would give rise to conditions that would lead to a return of U.S. political and military involvement under tragic circumstances less than a generation later.

The steady reduction in the level of U.S. involvement in the Indochina situation continued during the summer and fall of 1945. Reluctant to antagonize his European allies, President Truman did not act on Hurley's recommendation to take a strong stand against SEAC operations directed at restoring European colonial authority in Southeast Asia. Then, at the Potsdam Conference in late July and early August, he discarded the last U.S. trump card, accepting an earlier proposal that the occupation of Indochina be undertaken by British and Chinese but not by American forces. A British force would assume responsibility for all of Indochina south of the sixteenth parallel, while Chinese forces would occupy the area to the north. By default, the United States abandoned its capacity to exert effective influence over the future of Indochina.

If the significance of this decision eluded the attention of Harry Truman, it did not escape the sharp eye of Ho Chi Minh. Ho had been hoping that the

Allied advance into Indochina would be led by the United States, which he viewed as the most sympathetic of the Allies to the cause of Vietnamese independence and as a potentially powerful counterforce to the French. The British, however, were inveterate colonialists and would act as the stalking-horse for the restoration of French rule in Indochina. The Chinese, although viscerally anti-colonialist because of their recent humiliations at the hands of Western powers, had their own objectives in Indochina and, having already attempted to subsidize the formation of a pro-Chinese national resistance movement among Vietnamese exiles in South China, were not likely to favor the Vietminh, whose communist orientation was well-known to the Chinese leadership in Chungking. The decision at Potsdam complicated Ho Chi Minh's problems and added a new complexity to the already tangled situation in Indochina at the close of the war.

Conclusions

As the Pacific war drew to a close, U.S. policy toward Southeast Asia was in a process of transition from wartime concerns to a concentration on the effort to build a stable and enduring peace in the postwar era. Wartime strategy had focused on the need to control Japanese power throughout the Pacific; postwar strategy emphasized the importance of removing the underlying causes of the war and creating a new balance of power throughout the region.

As U.S. policymakers began to focus on the shape of the postwar world, they were still operating on assumptions based on what one historian has called the Yalta System. The foundation of the Yalta System was the creation of a policy of cooperation between the victorious Allied powers to defuse the roots of war and remove the threat of global domination by aggressive nations. A strong prerequisite for that effort, at least in the mind of Franklin Roosevelt, had been to bring the exploitative colonial system to an end and usher in a new era of independent nation-states in Asia and Africa.[43]

It was in that context that Southeast Asia took on considerable importance in U.S. postwar planning. In the Rooseveltian worldview, the war in the Pacific was the result of the political and military vacuum caused by the decline of China as a major actor in regional affairs and the imposition of colonial regimes in Southeast Asia. Roosevelt's primary postwar objective in Asia was to strengthen China as a major force in world affairs and bring the colonial system in Southeast Asia to an end.

Such a view was not simply based on the sentiment of global altruism. It also coincided with a hardheaded approach to traditional U.S. interests in the Pacific. Because U.S. concerns in the area were essentially limited to guaranteed access to major markets, the emergence of independent capitalist states in the region could only benefit the United States. Such an eventuality, in Roosevelt's eyes, was much more likely if the Allies played a conciliatory role in the restoration of independence.

From the outset, FDR ran into obstacles in bringing his vision into reality. The first major problem was China, which under Chiang Kai-shek proved unable to play its assigned role as a force for stability in East Asia. Washington's European allies had a different perspective on their own needs and did not share Roosevelt's vision of a postwar Southeast Asia composed of independent states. Even before the end of World War II, Washington was faced with the central dilemma that would constantly plague U.S. policy in Indochina for the next several years: the incompatibility between the objectives of the United States and its major European allies in Southeast Asia.

To complicate matters, the final building block of the Yalta System now appeared shaky because of the growing tension in U.S.-Soviet relations. In Europe, the transformation from alliance to hostility began over disagreements in Eastern Europe in the spring and summer of 1945. In Southeast Asia, the specter of the Cold War did not cast an immediate shadow. On the surface, Washington's decision to back the French at the expense of the aspirations of Vietnamese nationalists was based on the idea that French cooperation would be crucial for building a stable peace in postwar Europe. But the growing fear of Soviet intentions in the region may have played a role in the decision. As for the likelihood that frustrations in Southeast Asia could lead nationalist movements toward communism, Washington policymakers as yet showed little concern.

Chapter 2

The Restoration of French Sovereignty

After the close of the Potsdam Conference, hostilities in the Pacific ended with lightning speed, punctuated by the entry of the Soviet Union into the war and the dropping of atomic bombs on Hiroshima and Nagasaki. To Ho Chi Minh and other Vietminh leaders, the rapidly evolving situation presented both challenge and opportunity. Could the party mobilize its young and inexperienced forces to seize power before the anticipated return of the French? Would the victorious Allies accept the Vietminh Front as the legitimate representative of the national aspirations of the Vietnamese people?

Ho Chi Minh scrambled to keep up with rapidly changing developments. As soon as word of the Japanese surrender reached Indochina, a meeting of Vietminh leaders held at a jungle base north of Hanoi created a National Liberation Committee headed by Ho Chi Minh to serve as a provisional government of Vietnam and called for a general uprising to liberate the entire country from foreign rule. Ho's plan was to take advantage of the anarchic conditions at the moment of Japanese surrender and present the arriving Allied occupation forces with a fait accompli.

The August Revolution

In the northern part of the country, Ho's plan worked effectively. On August 19, urban militants combined with Vietminh units recruited in the neighboring villages and seized power in Hanoi in a bloodless coup. In towns and villages throughout Tonkin and Annam, Vietminh forces took over the local administration, often without encountering any resistance from demoralized Japanese occupation authorities. At the end of August, a Vietminh delegation was sent to Hué to persuade Emperor Bao Dai to abdicate. Bao Dai had formed a puppet Vietnamese government under Japanese tutelage in March. On learning of Japanese surrender, he had written a letter to the Allies on August 20 asking for recognition of his government but had received no answer. Under pressure from the Vietminh, to whom he had offered positions in his government, he abdicated the throne in return for appointment to the sinecure position of supreme adviser to the new Vietnamese republic, which was formally announced at a ceremony held in Hanoi in early September.[1]

The South presented a greater challenge. Whereas the Vietminh takeover in Hanoi had been virtually unopposed either by Japanese or by rival nationalist groups, rival political forces in Cochin China presented more competition. As a result, Vietminh activists were unable to establish the Front's total political dominance in the South as the war came to an end and were compelled to share power in the Committee of the South (Uy Ban Nam Bo) established in late August to represent Vietnamese national interests to the arriving British occupation forces. Although the chairman of the committee, Tran Van Giau, was a party veteran and a graduate of the famous "Stalin School" in Moscow, several members of the committee were members of noncommunist nationalist parties with a strong suspicion of the communist orientation of the Vietminh Front.

Allied occupation forces began arriving in late September. In the North, Chinese nationalist troops appeared to be more interested in plunder than in politics. The commander of Chinese forces was willing to permit Ho Chi Minh's government to remain in power on condition that he accept members of noncommunist parties, many of whom were politically linked to Chiang Kaishek's Nationalist Party, in his government, now formally called the Democratic Republic of Vietnam, or DRV. As a gesture to demonstrate his good intentions, Ho agreed to include noncommunists in his cabinet, and in November the ICP formally declared itself abolished, to be replaced by an innocuous Marxist Study Society. The party, as official sources later admitted, did not actually disband but went underground.[2]

Below the sixteenth parallel, the party was not so fortunate. General Douglas Gracey, commander of British occupation forces that began arriving in Saigon in early September, refused to recognize the legitimacy of the Committee of the South and dealt directly with the French. After a series of clashes between Vietnamese and foreign residents in Saigon led to heavy casualties on both sides, Gracey rearmed the Japanese as well as French troops released from detention camps and drove nationalist forces into the rural areas. According to the U.S. journalist Chalmers Roberts, who arrived in Saigon in late December, the French were so lacking in manpower and equipment that they used Japanese pilots flying Japanese planes as their transport service. By the end of October, French authority had been restored throughout most of Indochina.[3]

To later observers endowed with the benefit of hindsight, the results of the so-called August Revolution were an ominous forecast of things to come. Ten years later, the first phase of the Indochina War would come to an end at the Geneva Conference. The settlement at Geneva essentially recreated the situation in the fall of 1945, with two separate Vietnams, a communist one in the North and a noncommunist one in the South. The August Revolution appeared to have set a pattern that would not be erased until the final reunification of the country in 1975. What explains the ambiguous results of the August uprising? Why were the Vietminh so successful in the North and unable to achieve similar results in the South? Was the similarity with the situation after Geneva in 1954 simply a coincidence or a consequence of the iron laws of history?

We cannot entirely rule out the role of accident—what Marxist-Leninists describe as "subjective factors"—in the August Revolution. One reason for the Vietminh success in the North can be ascribed to the relatively tolerant treatment toward the DRV displayed by the Chinese occupation forces as compared with the attitude adopted by the British commander Gracey in Cochin China. Another explanation lies in the logistical problems faced by the Vietminh in extending their influence far beyond their power base in the mountainous regions surrounding the Red River Valley. Had the war lasted a few months longer, the Vietminh would probably have been in a stronger position to resist the restoration of French sovereignty in the South. Finally, the Vietminh benefited enormously from a famine that swept through the provinces of Tonkin and Annam during the winter and spring of 1944–45, causing widespread hunger and the estimated death by starvation of over a million Vietnamese.

In fact, however, the results of the August Revolution were by no means entirely an accident and probably represented the political realities in Vietnam at that time. The Vietminh power base at the end of the war was spread throughout the country, but it was not as strong in the South, at least comparatively, as it was elsewhere. The communist movement had been active in Cochin China since the mid-1920's, both in the urban labor movement in Saigon and among peasants in rural districts, but an abortive uprising launched by the ICP regional leadership in 1940 had resulted in the virtual destruction of the party apparatus in the South. The party had recovered somewhat as the war came to an end and had created its own front group—known as the Vanguard Youth (Thanh Nien Tien Phong) and led by the communist sympathizer Pham Ngoc Thach—but it encountered stiff competition from the moderate noncommunist political parties and factions that had emerged in the region during the interwar years. These organizations received the bulk of their support from an urban middle class based on commerce and absentee landownership tied to the rich rice lands in the Mekong River Delta, and they posed a serious obstacle to the activities of the Vietminh in urban areas in the South.

But resistance to the Vietminh in Cochin China did not come solely from the affluent middle class in Saigon and provincial capitals. It also came from two religious sects, called the Cao Dai and the Hoa Hao, which had recently won the support of a substantial part of the rural population, particularly in the provinces of the Mekong Delta. The popularity of these sects in the southern provinces was a consequence of the conditions relating to the original settlement of the area in the sixteenth and seventeenth centuries. Many of the Vietnamese who had settled in the area were adventurers or vagrants who had few ties to their original homes in the North and a reduced level of commitment to the traditional Confucian attitudes that pertained elsewhere in Vietnamese society.

French occupation in the nineteenth century further sharpened the distinctive southern personality of rural peoples in Cochin China. The opening of new rice lands in the Mekong Delta, which laid the foundations for the rise of a landowning middle class in Saigon, also led to widespread discontent among land-hungry peasants, many of whom became tenants on large landholdings owned by absentee landlords. This discontent was eventually siphoned off into the two religious sects, which combined religious millenarianism with social reform and a desire for political autonomy. By the end of World War II, the sects represented a major threat to communist plans to extend their base into rural areas of Cochin China.

The United States and the August Revolution

In late August 1945, French president Charles de Gaulle visited the United States for talks with President Truman at the White House. Truman attempted to make use of the occasion to persuade the French to liberalize their policies in Indochina and called on de Gaulle to make a direct pledge of independence, but the latter hedged. Although he gave private assurances that the French government was prepared to initiate steps leading to self-government in Indochina, he rejected U.S. pressure to make a public statement to that effect, which, in his characterization, would just be "fine words." France would first restore authority in Indochina and then seek agreement to establish appropriate policies there.[4]

Truman apparently did not press de Gaulle for a firmer commitment, and on August 30 Acting Secretary of State Dean Acheson transmitted a circular to all U.S. missions abroad reiterating U.S. acceptance of French sovereignty over Indochina. That decision was not transmitted to the U.S. Embassy in Chungking until early October, however, and in the interim the confusion in U.S. Indochina policy continued. General Wedemeyer ordered U.S. units to avoid involvement in the occupation of Indochina by British and Chinese expeditionary forces. A U.S. liaison team accompanied Chinese troops into Tonkin, but its role was limited to the supply and movement of troops. An OSS unit had been in Hanoi since the end of the war, but its members were instructed to avoid taking part in political disputes and to restrict their activities to aiding in the rehabilitation of Allied prisoners of war. Some U.S. personnel in Indochina, however, still operated under the assumption that the United States intended to oppose the restoration of French sovereignty in the area. In Hanoi, some U.S. officers sympathized with the Vietminh and agreed to send appeals from Ho Chi Minh to the Truman administration. Although most were aware of Ho's ties with the USSR and his attachment to Marxism, OSS officers such as Archimedes Patti were convinced that his primary goal was national independence and that he might respond to sympathetic treatment from the United States.[5]

Some Asianists in the Department of State were of similar persuasion and felt that the United States should assist the Vietnamese in their struggle to resist the return of the French. In late September, Abbot Low Moffat, chief of the new Division of Southeast Asian Affairs, suggested to his superior, John Carter Vincent, head of the Office of Far Eastern Affairs, that a joint U.S.-British commission investigate conditions in Indochina and hold discussions between U.S., British, French, and "Annamese elements."

At first Vincent agreed. He had talked with a British Embassy official who had expressed concern over General Gracey's actions in Indochina and had proposed talks to defuse this dispute. In a memo to Acheson, Vincent warned that the administration's hands-off policy could lead to a crisis in Indochina and recommended the establishment of a joint commission to study the situation. In the meantime, he advised that no additional French troops be dispatched to Indochina. Vincent conceded that France might oppose such a commission, but he felt that French pique was better than an explosion of Vietnamese nationalism.[6]

But the proposal was opposed by Europeanists on the grounds that it would delay France's recovery from the war. In a memo to H. Freeman Matthews, then head of the Office of European Affairs, James Bonbright of the Division of West European Affairs admitted that the situation in Indochina was serious but said that he was not convinced that it would take a major effort for the French to suppress the revolt. In the meantime, he proposed that the United States "go very slowly" in the matter. Setting up an international commission, he warned, "can only lead to one result—the eventual ejection of the French from Indochina." This would "be bad for the French and the West and generally bad for the Indo-Chinese themselves." In the end, Acheson agreed with Bonbright, and the proposal was shelved.[7]

On October 20, Vincent issued a statement reiterating existing policy and emphasizing that the United States did not question French and Dutch sovereignty but expected that the colonial powers would prepare their subject peoples for the duties and responsibilities of self-government. The declaration stated that the

US has no thought of opposing the re-establishment of French control in Indochina and no official statement by US government has questioned even by implication French sovereignty over Indochina. However, it is not the policy of this Govt to assist the French to reestablish their control over Indochina by force and the willingness of the US to see French control reestablished assumes that French claim to have the support of the population of Indochina is borne out by future events.[8]

Whether Ho Chi Minh was aware of the confusion in U.S. Indochina policy and the reasons for it is uncertain. But he was a master at seizing whatever opportunities circumstances offered, and during the fall he continued his attempt to make use of his amicable relationship with U.S. personnel in Hanoi to seek assistance from Washington. In late September he assured one U.S. listener that he did not expect full independence for ten years and that his government would operate through democratic processes and nationalize only natural resources. A few weeks later, he wrote a letter to President Truman in which he stated the legal case for recognizing the DRV as the legitimate government of an independent Vietnam. French rule had come to an end, he pointed out, on March 9, 1945, when Japan abolished the Treaty of Protectorate of 1884 and handed power to an independent government under Emperor Bao Dai. Bao Dai in turn had voluntarily abdicated the throne and transferred power to the DRV during the August Revolution. As for French claims of sovereignty, he asserted that France was not entitled to restore colonial rule because she had "ignominiously sold Indochina to Japan and betrayed the allies." The DRV was entitled to recognition on the basis of the Atlantic Charter.[9]

A few weeks later Ho Chi Minh followed up his letter with a request for cultural relations with the United States and a plea for U.N. intervention to achieve a political settlement based on the principle of self-determination. He enclosed an official pamphlet outlining the foreign policy aims of the DRV and reiterated his government's determination to seek friendly relations with the West. The letter and accompanying pamphlet were transmitted to Washington through the assistance of U.S. officials in Indochina. Within the Department of State, however, officials in the Office of European Affairs criticized the practice and were able to win approval for a policy of not responding to such messages.[10]

Ho Chi Minh had few options. Neither of his closest ideological allies, the USSR and the Chinese Communists in Yan'an, was in a position to provide assistance in his struggle to win international recognition for the DRV. Moscow was preoccupied with conditions in Europe and reluctant to offend the French by openly supporting the Vietminh. Chinese Communist leaders undoubtedly welcomed the rise of a viable revolutionary movement on their vulnerable southern flank, and Ho Chi Minh, while spending two years working with Chinese Communist Party (CCP) forces in various areas of China (during which time he presumably met briefly with Mao Zedong in Yenan), had undoubtedly cultivated their friendship and trust. But the CCP leadership was now locked in a bitter civil war with Chiang Kai-shek and in no position to provide assistance to Ho Chi Minh's forces far to the south.

Perhaps for that reason, despite Washington's coolness to his overtures, Ho Chi Minh did not despair of U.S. aid and continued to cultivate those Americans who remained in Vietnam. But he was apparently increasingly pessimistic about the attitude of the Truman administration and commented to one American observer that the United States did not seem to understand the Vietnamese determination to achieve independence.[11]

Officials in Washington were well aware of the situation in Indochina and of the popularity of the Vietminh movement among the local population. Concern within the administration over increasing Soviet influence in Asia was rising, and when U.S. civilian and military officials returned home in the late fall and early winter of 1945, many of them were asked to report their impressions. Perhaps most influential were the comments of General Philip Gallagher, chief of the OSS liaison team assigned to the Chinese occupation forces in northern Indochina. In a debriefing in Washington, Gallagher commented favorably on the strength and popularity of the Vietminh movement and said that he was impressed by the enthusiasm, dedication, and native ability of Vietnamese officials. But he added that they lacked executive experience, and in competition with other nations they would "lose their shirts." There was no doubt, he concluded, that Vietminh leaders were influenced by communism, but he stressed that they were primarily nationalists and "should not be labelled full-fledged doctrinaire communists." Asked whether the Vietminh had the capacity to defeat the French, Gallagher was dubious. They were too enthusiastic and too naive, he said, and "probably know that they will be licked." Still, they had a "deep-seated hatred for the French" and undoubtedly would resist their return to Indochina.[12]

Such reports must have made some impression in Washington, for in January 1946 the Department of State sent Kenneth Landon, a veteran Asian specialist and the assistant chief of the Division of Southeast Asian Affairs, on a fact-finding mission to Indochina. The visit took place at a delicate time in Vietnam. President Ho Chi Minh was negotiating with French representative Jean Sainteny on a peaceful settlement of the Franco-Vietminh dispute over the future of Vietnam. The French were also holding talks with the Republic of China (ROC) on the departure of Chinese occupation troops from northern Indochina. National elections held in early January had given the Vietminh a substantial majority in the new DRV National Assembly, but 70 seats and several key cabinet positions were assigned to the noncommunist parties as the result of a compromise between Ho's government and Chinese occupation officials. The presence of such noncommunist elements, many of whom were hostile to the Vietminh, complicated Ho Chi Minh's task because many nationalists were critical of his efforts to reach a compromise with Sainteny over a future French presence in Indochina.

Landon arrived in Indochina in late January, and after a short stay in Saigon he traveled to Hanoi, where he held discussions with Sainteny on the state of the Franco-Vietminh talks. The latter assured him that France was prepared to offer self-government to the Vietnamese. Landon was pleased with Sainteny's comments and in his report to Washington expressed cautious optimism about the prospects for a settlement.

Ho Chi Minh, however, was less sanguine. In several conversations with Landon, he stressed the depth of popular support for the Vietminh and the determination of the Hanoi government to oppose a restoration of French colonial authority. In a letter to President Truman relayed to Washington by Landon, he reflected an attitude of suspicion toward French motives and appealed to the United States to help the United Nations bring an end to the war. The White House did not respond to Ho's appeal. Similar letters to Great Britain and the USSR also apparently went unanswered.[13]

Ho's pessimism about French attitudes was amply justified by events. In discussions with U.S. diplomats in Paris, French officials were already beginning to qualify Sainteny's statements to Landon about French willingness to grant self-government to the Vietnamese. Ambassador Jefferson Caffery expressed the hope that the new government in Paris would adopt a more enlightened attitude on the issue because certain "old-line military leaders" in the de Gaulle government had exerted an "unfortunate influence" on colonial policy. But one official told Caffery that although France would adopt a progressive and enlightened attitude toward Indochina, independence was not under consideration.[14]

Franco-Vietnamese Negotiations

In Hanoi, Ho Chi Minh was under pressure, not only from ultranationalist elements in North Vietnam, who cited his willingness to compromise as a means of attacking his patriotic credentials, but also from militant members of his own party. According to former emperor Bao Dai, in late February Ho briefly lost his nerve and offered to resign his position as president in favor of Bao Dai in a desperate effort to placate the French and the ultranationalists. For unexplained reasons, however, he soon changed his mind and signed a last-minute agreement with Sainteny calling for the recognition of Vietnam as a "free state" in the French Union with its own army, parliament, and finances. The two could not resolve the issue of Cochin China (Sainteny pointed out that it was a French colony and thus not subject to the agreement) but reached a compromise calling for a plebiscite to put the issue before the local population.

In return, Ho Chi Minh agreed to accept a continued French cultural and economic presence in Vietnam and the token presence of 15,000 French troops to replace Chinese forces in the North, who were withdrawing as the result of a Sino-French agreement signed in February.

The agreement represented a major gamble by Ho Chi Minh, and he was severely criticized by militant elements in Hanoi. Yet there was a clear logic in his decision. For the Vietminh, the immediate priority was to remove the threat of continued Chinese occupation and postpone the likelihood of a military confrontation with the French. As Lenin had signed the Treaty of Brest-Litovsk with Germany in March 1918 to enable the Bolsheviks to concentrate on their internal enemies, so Ho was convinced that it was better to accept a temporary setback so as to avert a more certain disaster later.

The U.S. reaction to the Ho-Sainteny agreement was muted. The first reports from the field were optimistic, noting that domestic press reaction in Vietnam was favorable. But the mission in Saigon cautioned that opinion in Cochin China was divided, and many opposed unity with the North. In Washington, Secretary of State James Byrnes informed the French that the United States had no objection to the Sino-French treaty, which called for the end of Chinese occupation and the stationing of French troops in North Vietnam. Such arrangements, he said, "are a matter for determination by the Governments of France and China." The agreement, he added, "completes the reversion of all Indochina to French control." The department ignored a request from the DRV for diplomatic recognition of the new Vietnam as a "free state."[15]

It did not take long for the agreement to break down. By the end of March, Vietnamese sources were complaining that French elements aided by High Commissioner Georges Thierry d'Argenlieu (the new French title for the prewar governor-general) were delaying implementation of the agreement and trying to prevent the holding of a plebiscite in Cochin China. D'Argenlieu's uncompromising attitude was clear at the Dalat Conference, held in late April and early May and designed to allow French and Vietnamese negotiators to work out arrangements for formal negotiations at Fontainebleau. French sources were publicly pessimistic about the prospects for a successful conference and took a hard line on negotiations. On the key question of the referendum, d'Argenlieu asserted that a vote could not be held in Cochin China until law and order had been restored throughout the area.[16]

The Vietnamese were angry at what they considered French backsliding on the agreement and openly distrustful of their ultimate intentions. In Hanoi, Ho Chi Minh met with visiting U.S. consul to Saigon Charles Reed and expressed pessimism that the French would live up to their end of the bargain. Reed reported that the situation in Hanoi between the Vietnamese and arriving French troops was tense and that Ho had insisted that there would be no settlement unless Cochin China was permitted to join the new state of Vietnam.

But Ho had evidently still not despaired of a U.S. role in the dispute, emphasizing to his visitor that his government badly needed foreign assistance and technology.[17]

After Reed's departure, Ho continued his efforts to enlist Washington's support against the French. According to James O'Sullivan, the new U.S. consul in Hanoi, Ho gave the impression that he would "pay great attention to any suggestions made by the Department." O'Sullivan's reports also provided Washington officials with useful information on conditions in Vietnam. The Vietminh, he said, remained the dominant force in the government in Hanoi, and support for the government was widespread throughout the North. But their strength in Cochin China had declined because of French activities there. O'Sullivan also commented on French attitudes, reporting that French sources in Indochina expressed no objection to holding a referendum but were nervous that Vietminh agents would terrorize the local population in Cochin China, as they had during elections in the North. The outcome of a plebiscite, he predicted, would depend on conditions. Both French and Vietnamese observers felt that the vote would favor their own side, while neutral observers felt that an honest vote would be close.[18]

When the Fontainebleau Conference between French and Vietnamese representatives convened near Paris in late June, it quickly became apparent that agreement would be difficult. On the eve of the talks, High Commissioner d'Argenlieu announced the formation of a provisional government of the Republic of Cochinchina composed of pro-French elements in the South. In Paris, a new French government with reduced participation by the French Communist Party (FCP) came into office, and in early sessions at Fontainebleau it adopted an uncompromising attitude on negotiations with the Vietminh. Then, on August 1 d'Argenlieu dropped a bombshell, convening a second conference at Dalat composed of representatives from Laos, Cambodia, "southern Annam," and the new French-dominated Republic of Cochinchina. Back at Fontainebleau, the Vietnamese delegates broke off the talks and left Paris in anger, claiming that the French had broken the March agreement by convening the Dalat Conference.[19]

The Truman administration evidenced no immediate official reaction to these events, but the course of the talks was reported to Washington by U.S. missions in Paris, Hanoi, and Saigon. On August 9, Southeast Asian Affairs Division chief Abbot Low Moffat, whose irritation with the French attitude was growing more pronounced, wrote an internal memo to John Carter Vincent commenting on the situation. Moffat charged that Paris was attempting to regain control in Indochina in violation of the spirit of the March 6 Ho-Sainteny preliminary accords. He warned that a French decision to ignore the Vietminh could lead to a resumption of hostilities and urged that the department should be prepared to express to the French the U.S. expectation that they would abide by the spirit of the March 6 agreement.[20]

Ho Chi Minh had gone to France as an unofficial observer at the conference and spent much of his time behind the scenes in discussions with French acquaintances. After the adjournment of the conference in early August he remained in Paris to prevent a total rupture in Franco-Vietnamese relations. In mid-September he visited the U.S. Embassy at his own request and reported the breakdown of the negotiations to Ambassador Caffery. Ho denied that he was a communist and spoke of the desire of the Vietnamese people for a united Vietnam. He also reiterated his request for U.S. assistance. "I gathered," reported Caffery, "he would like to get us into the game and he would be very pleased if he could use us in some way or another in his future negotiations with French authorities." Caffery made no commitments.[21]

The following day Ho talked with George Abbott, first secretary at the embassy. Referring to his wartime association with the United States and the Vietnamese affection for Roosevelt, he reiterated his government's need for foreign capital, which, he claimed, the French could not provide. Finally, he said that Vietnam would approach several nations for assistance and hinted that he might seek military and naval cooperation and the possibility of an arrangement for a naval base at Cam Ranh Bay, along the central coast.[22]

The Truman administration, however, was in no mood to create problems with the new French government of Premier Georges Bidault, whose conservative complexion and independence from communist influence were welcome to U.S. policymakers nervous about the extension of Soviet power into Western Europe. Washington was also concerned at the threat of Soviet influence in Hanoi. A cable to the U.S. mission in Saigon in August asked for an evaluation of the relative strength of communist and noncommunist forces in Vietnam and the extent of contact between the DRV and communists in other countries. A few weeks later, Dean Acheson queried U.S. representatives in Vietnam on the significance of the DRV flag (a gold star in a red field) and asked for an assessment of noncommunist strength in the North.[23]

Some administration officials were clearly uncomfortable with the hardline position adopted by the French at Fontainebleau. From Saigon, Consul Reed expressed concern at the rapid buildup of French military forces in Indochina and noted that the Vietminh might well charge the United States with assisting the French because many jeeps and trucks purchased by the latter from U.S. surplus stocks still bore U.S. markings. But Washington said nothing. In September, lacking realistic alternatives and fearing the outbreak of war, Ho Chi Minh signed a modus vivendi with France calling for the resumption of talks early the following year. Then he returned to Vietnam by sea, arriving in Hanoi in October.[24]

The "Least Desirable Eventuality"

Ho Chi Minh arrived in a different Vietnam from the one he had left four months before. Before his departure for France, he had tried to secure an agreement with the VNQDD to avoid mutual provocations. But his fiery minister of defense, Vo Nguyen Giap, whom he had left in charge, lacked Ho's finesse in dealing with members of rival parties, and in Ho's absence the relationship between the Vietminh and noncommunist elements in the Vietnamese government had deteriorated. Attacks on the Vietminh leadership by nationalist newspapers led to government reprisals and in July to the arrest of key figures of the VNQDD. Many of the remaining noncommunist political leaders fled the country. On his return to Hanoi in October, Ho Chi Minh found many of his compatriots uneasy about the modus vivendi and whether it offered too much to the French. The government now moved decisively to the left. When the National Assembly convened to select a new cabinet, only two non-Vietminh members remained in the government.[25]

In the meantime, tensions were rising between the French and the Vietminh in the North. During the fall, clashes broke out between French troops and Vietminh militia on several occasions, culminating in mid-November, when French naval units seized a Chinese ship carrying contraband for the Vietminh. After clashes broke out in Haiphong, the French demanded that the Vietminh withdraw. When they refused, a French cruiser bombarded the native section of the city, killing several thousand civilians.

The incident at Haiphong stirred discomfort in Washington. Reports from U.S. officials in Indochina were critical of French actions, and in Paris Ambassador Caffery passed on such views to the Bidault government. But Washington's concern over French intransigence was counterbalanced by a rising anxiety over the communist complexion of the DRV and intelligence reports (many provided by the French) of Soviet influence over President Ho Chi Minh. The U.S. Embassy in Paris reported at the end of November that the French had "positive proof" that Ho Chi Minh was in contact with Moscow and had received Soviet instructions and advisers.[26]

In November, the department dispatched Abbot Low Moffat to Hanoi to assess the situation. Moffat was instructed to reassure Ho Chi Minh of U.S. support for the Ho-Sainteny agreement and the Fontainebleau discussions as a basis for settlement and to express U.S. sympathy for the efforts of the Vietnamese "to achieve greater autonomy within the framework of democratic institutions." But he was also told to advise Ho against the use of force to achieve such objectives and to point out that France had assured the United States that it would abide by the March 6 agreement and had no intention of reconquering Vietnam. Finally, Ho Chi Minh was to be advised to abandon his insistence on a referendum in Cochin China and to accept a compromise on its status. Washington hoped to use Moffat's visit as a means of assessing the possibility that Ho's government was dominated by communists and would be loyal to Moscow. In instructions sent after Moffat had already left for Saigon, Dean Acheson pointed out that the establishment of a communist-dominated, Moscow-oriented state in Indochina would be the "least desirable eventuality." To avert such a possibility, Moffat was instructed to make an assessment of the strength of noncommunist elements in Vietnam.[27]

Moffat arrived in Saigon on December 3. After three days of discussions with French officials, he left for Hanoi on the seventh, where he met with President Ho Chi Minh, who was seriously ill. Ho attempted to disarm U.S. suspicions, insisting that national independence, not communism, was his immediate aim. "Perhaps fifty years from now," he said, "the U.S. will be communist." In the meantime, he returned to his earlier efforts to lure Washington with offers of a greater U.S. presence, requesting U.S. economic aid and capital and offering the use of Cam Ranh Bay as a naval base. Lacking precise instructions from Washington, Moffat was noncommittal in his response. He expressed doubt that the United States had any interest in Cam Ranh Bay and pointed out that before the United States could establish direct relations with the DRV, its status would have to be settled through direct negotiations between the Vietnamese government and the French. In his report to the department, Moffat added his own analysis of the situation. The Vietnamese government, he concluded, was under strict communist control and in direct contact with both Moscow and the CCP leadership in Yenan. But he sensed a split in the government between moderate elements like Ho Chi Minh, who saw the need for settlement with the French, and militant elements represented by the military leader Vo Nguyen Giap, who feared collaboration but might be compelled to accept some degree of French presence and aid. Moffat concluded that for the present, a French presence would be essential, not only as an antidote to Soviet influence but also to protect Vietnam and Southeast Asia from a future Chinese invasion. He recommended a quick settlement; otherwise, French prospects would diminish.[28]

Because Moffat was a prominent Asianist in the Department of State with a reputation for sympathy for the cause of Asian nationalism, his report undoubtedly added weight to the growing concern over the danger of communist revolution in Southeast Asia. Although the bulk of Moffat's report expressed sympathy for the nationalist cause and some hope that the French could be brought to compromise, it is probable that the most influential part was the section that referred to the influence of communism in the Vietnamese government.

Why were U.S. officials suddenly so sensitive about the communist threat in Southeast Asia? Certainly the primary reason was the changing climate in

Washington, where concern over Soviet intentions in Europe had been rising since the beginning of the year, when George Kennan sent his famous "long telegram" on the problems of dealing with Moscow. But it is likely that an additional factor was the evidence of growing instability elsewhere in Asia, in China and in Southeast Asia itself, notably in the Dutch East Indies, where an attempted coup d'etat by militants led by the communist activist Tan Malaka almost unseated the moderate leadership of the Indonesian nationalist movement in July. Washington officials were also worried about strong leftist influence in Burma, where the Burmese Communist Party (BCP) played an active role in the nationalist movement led by Aung San's Anti-Fascist People's Freedom League (AFPFL), as well as in Malaya, where the local communist party threatened to become the dominant force in the struggle to bring an end to British colonial rule.

The Truman administration's preferred solution to such conditions was to pressure the colonial powers to hasten the transition to self-rule in order to favor pro-Western elements in the nationalist movements throughout the region. In November, the United States successfully pressured the Dutch to reach a temporary agreement with Sukarno's moderate wing of the Indonesian National Party. The British government on its own initiative agreed to discuss independence with Indian leaders and with the AFPFL in Burma. In Thailand, where rising leftist sentiment stirred concern in Washington, U.S. officials persuaded the British to abandon their demand for punitive peace terms stemming from Thailand's wartime alliance with Japan.[29]

In general, then, U.S. policy in Southeast Asia through 1946 continued to follow Roosevelt's line of attempting to support the aspirations of anticolonialist forces so as to guarantee the emergence of pro-Western regimes. For the most part, that effort succeeded. In Indochina, however, the strong communist orientation of the Vietnamese government in Hanoi led to a different emphasis. In a circular message to missions abroad on December 17, the department repeated Moffat's conclusions on the communist character of Ho Chi Minh's government and concluded that a continued French presence in Indochina was important, "not only as [an] antidote to Soviet influence, but to protect Vietnam and Southeast Asia from future Chinese imperialism." A delay in settling the issue, it predicted, would diminish French influence and it implied that neutral good offices or mediation might eventually be essential.[30]

War of National Resistance

If the Truman administration still believed that the problem of Indochina could be resolved without recourse to war, a more somber view prevailed in Hanoi. Ho Chi Minh had signed the modus vivendi in the hope of avoiding a direct confrontation with the French following the breakdown of negotiations at Fontainebleau, but he was clearly not optimistic. During the final weeks of the year, the DRV feverishly prepared for war. On November 5, Ho Chi Minh issued a decree calling for heightened efforts to increase production and mobilize guerrilla and self-defense forces in preparation for a protracted war of national resistance. Ho conceded that the struggle would be long and difficult and that the cities would have to be abandoned to build a base in the countryside. But he reassured his people that final victory would inevitably be theirs. In 1941, he said, the Vietminh Front had only a handful of comrades hidden in the mountains, and yet it was able to organize resistance against the Japanese and the French. Today the DRV has an army, and a people. Although the war may be long, the Vietnamese people will inevitably achieve the final triumph.[31]

By mid-December the situation in Hanoi was tense. O'Sullivan reported that the Vietnamese government appeared willing to await developments in Paris but that the situation was a powder keg, which "may explode at any time." He was correct. On December 19, Vietminh units attacked French installations in Hanoi and other cities in the North, while main force units withdrew to prepared positions near Tuyen Quang, in the mountains surrounding the Red River Delta. The first Indochina War had begun.[32]

Conclusions

Between the final months of World War II and the outbreak of the Franco-Vietminh conflict in December 1946, U.S. policy toward Indochina had undergone a significant shift in focus. The first step was the abandonment of Roosevelt's policy of favoring an international trusteeship in an effort to prevent the return of the French. Beginning in the summer of 1945, the Truman administration accepted the inevitability of a restoration of French sovereignty in Indochina but adopted an attitude of noninvolvement in the process and was often critical of the French for their reluctance to engage in serious negotiations with the Vietnamese government in Hanoi. By the end of the year, however, Washington had moved from an attitude of disinterested noninvolvement to a policy which, while still urging France to move more quickly toward granting self-determination to the Indochinese peoples, favored the continued presence of the French in Indochina in preference to an independent Vietnamese government under communist rule.

Some later observers have interpreted this shift as a transition from the Rooseveltian policy of anticolonialism to the Truman era's focus on anticommunism. That assumption is correct in the sense that fear of communism was becoming a salient feature in U.S. foreign policy toward Asia. But administration officials undoubtedly felt that the new approach was less a departure from tradition than a continuation of Rooseveltian policies under what were conceived to be new conditions. In Roosevelt's mind, U.S. attempts to bring the colonial era to an end in Southeast Asia were not simply based on altruistic motives but were primarily governed by the pragmatic calculation that only by removing the potential basis of war and instability in Asia could the United States hasten the emergence of pro-U.S. independent states in the region. For FDR, Great Power conflict and violent revolution were potential dangers that had to be avoided by preventive action.

Within months, even weeks, of Roosevelt's death, that vague sense of possible future danger was replaced by a palpable sense of threat, as Washington began to see itself faced with the growing menace of Soviet expansionism. At first, the danger was seen primarily directed at Europe and the Middle East. Indochina entered the picture only in terms of the effect of the conflict there on the French. But that attitude began to change in 1946, a reflection of the growing evidence of tension between communist and noncommunist forces within the nationalist movements in Southeast Asia. Washington now began to take a hard look at Ho Chi Minh and the allegedly communist character of his movement.

Washington's growing concern over communist influence in Southeast Asia did not bring an end to the traditional attitude of anticolonialism that had guided U.S. policy under Roosevelt. Indeed, in some respects the new situation made the transition to independent states a matter of even greater urgency. The Truman administration was convinced that the legacy of colonial rule was a major impediment to a solution of the problem and urged both the British and the Dutch to adopt conciliatory attitudes toward the indigenous nationalist movements in Burma and the Dutch East Indies to foster the emergence of moderate independent regimes in both areas. But in Indochina, the only effective anticolonialist movement was already under communist control, and there was no alternative in sight. But Washington hesitated to alienate the French at a time when the FCP was one of the most powerful parties in the political spectrum. French Embassy sources in Washington had made it clear that Paris would consider any implied U.S. support for the Vietminh an "unfriendly act." After an extended period of anguished indecision, marked by a bitter bureaucratic dispute between Asianists and Europeanists within the Department of State, the administration finally came down, however reluctantly, on the side of the French.[33]

In later years, observers searching for the roots of U.S. engagement in Vietnam would suggest that the failure to deal with Ho Chi Minh was a missed opportunity that might have prevented the later war in Indochina and met U.S. national security objectives in Southeast Asia. Among the most prominent spokesmen for such a view has been Archimedes Patti, the OSS officer whose book *Why Vietnam: Prelude to America's Albatross* is an autobiographical account of his contacts with Ho Chi Minh at the end of World War II.

In Patti's portrayal, Ho Chi Minh was a nationalist first and a communist second. He was "more concerned with Vietnam's independence and sovereign viability than with following the interests and dictates of Moscow and Peking." Had the Truman administration's vision not been distorted by its "communist blinders," argues Patti, Ho Chi Minh might have adopted an independent position in the Cold War and emerged as a buffer against Chinese expansion into Southeast Asia, thus serving a useful role in realizing American policy objectives in the region.[34]

The argument that Ho Chi Minh could have become an "Asian Tito" has become a centerpiece in the litany of "lost opportunities" that would later be voiced by critics of U.S. Vietnam policy. Such critics often do not deny that Ho Chi Minh was a sincere communist, but they cite evidence that Ho was a pragmatist who used Marxist-Leninist doctrine to achieve national goals, rather than the other way around. They also contend that Ho was well aware of Moscow's limited interest in Southeast Asia and wary of China's long-term goals in the region. A gesture of support from Washington might have induced Ho to revise substantially his domestic and foreign policy goals in the larger interests of Vietnamese nationalism.

The contention that more sympathetic treatment from Washington might have led Ho Chi Minh's government to adopt an independent foreign policy is not without merit. From the start of his revolutionary career, Ho had been an independent thinker who did not permit Marxist orthodoxy to undercut the Vietnamese struggle for national liberation. Ever the pragmatist, Ho avoided a direct clash with the Comintern during the 1930's, when his ideas were unpopular in Moscow, but quickly adopted an independent strategy in 1941, when it became clear that Soviet leaders were preoccupied with their own problems in Europe. In 1945, he was aware of Moscow's limited interest in Southeast Asia and probably would have gone to considerable lengths—such as the offer of Cam Ranh Bay as a naval base—to win support for his cause from the United States. So long as the United States did not oppose the overall foreign policy imperatives of the Vietnamese revolution, Ho Chi Minh would have tacked to the wind from Washington.

There are problems with this assumption, however. In the first place, it presupposes that Ho Chi Minh would have been able to persuade his colleagues in the party that a decisive shift in foreign policy alignment was in the long-term interests of the DRV. In view of the problems that he had already encountered in retaining the support of militant elements during his negotiations with the French, that assumption is open to serious question. Second, such an arrangement presupposes the existence of a relatively stable state system in the region such as prevailed in Eastern Europe during the era of Marshal Tito. Unfortunately, such conditions did not exist in postwar Southeast Asia, where the transition from colonialism to independence was marked by instability, both within each society and among the new states themselves. There is no strong evidence that Ho Chi Minh would have sought to play an active role in promoting communist-led revolutions in Burma, Indonesia, or Malaya. But the party had a strong interest in the fate of neighboring Laos and Cambodia that dated back to the precolonial era, when Vietnamese monarchs had competed with their counterparts in Thailand to dominate the lands in between. Could Hanoi and Washington, in the heat of the Cold War rivalries of the 1960's, have managed to avoid conflict over Vietnamese efforts to assist revolutionary movements in those two countries?

Even had the Truman administration been willing to take the risk that Ho Chi Minh and his colleagues could be weaned from their umbilical cord to Moscow, however, there was the equally serious risk that such a move might cause a severe strain in Franco-American relations. It is noteworthy that the opposition to dealing with the DRV within the administration came not from hard-line anticommunists but from the Europeanists in the State Department. Whether the latter exaggerated the risks of alienating Paris is beside the point. Given Washington's preoccupation with the Soviet threat to Western Europe, it seems highly unlikely that the administration would have sacrificed its delicate relationship with France for a hypothetical relationship with the Vietnamese nationalist movement.

In sum, the argument that the United States should have supported Ho Chi Minh in his struggle with the French, however tantalizing, is somewhat academic. It ran counter, not simply to the growing fear of communism in Washington, but to the traditional priority assigned to Europe in U.S. foreign policy. Many top officials in the Truman administration were Eurocentric in training and cultural predilection and undoubtedly saw the situation in Western Europe as more immediately threatening and ultimately more crucial to U.S. national security than the minor skirmish in far-off Indochina. France represented a keystone in the arch of U.S. security in Europe. Although a relatively pro-Western government had emerged in Paris during the summer of 1946, the danger of a communist presence in the French government remained in the shadows and, in the view of many Europeanists in the State Department, any gesture of support for Vietnamese independence from Washington could have had a disastrous effect on Franco-American relations.[35]

This is not to say that the Truman administration had no alternative to the policy that was eventually adopted. It is quite possible that the United States could have pressured the French to adopt a more conciliatory policy toward the Vietnamese without pushing French politics irrevocably to the left. There were, of course, internal dissensions over Indochina policy in Paris that the United States could have played on. During the height of the crisis in the fall of 1946, bitter debates erupted in French political circles over the wisdom of the hard-line policy in Indochina. Left-wing politicians accused d'Argenlieu of sabotaging the March 6 agreement and the modus vivendi, while the center and the right accused Socialist Party leader Marius Moutet, the minister of Overseas France and an old acquaintance of Ho Chi Minh, of seeking to give away a valuable colony. Yet it seems unlikely that Washington could have decisively reversed the drift toward war. In Paris, the balance ultimately shifted to the right, and when war broke out during the winter even FCP chief Jacques Duclos felt the pressure of maintaining colonial prestige, arguing in the National Assembly that France must protect its interests abroad.

No policy adopted in Washington could have satisfied all the objectives of U.S. foreign policy in the immediate postwar period. Yet given the conditions in the region and attitudes in Washington, the administration's decision seems virtually inevitable. Support for Ho Chi Minh would have been a risk and ran against the grain of the rising fear of communism. All told, the path of prudence seemed the wiser course.

Chapter 3

Years of Indecision

The Franco-Vietminh conflict began at a time when the global objectives of the United States were in transition. The breakdown of the wartime alliance with the Soviet Union ended Rooseveltian hopes for postwar cooperation between the Great Powers and led Washington to search for a new strategy to meet the changed contingencies. In Europe, these conditions resulted in the emergence of the new policy of containment. Sparked by the famous "long telegram" of George F. Kennan that portrayed Soviet expansionism as a product of Moscow's primordial insecurity and fear of the West, the Truman administration adopted a policy of patience and firmness to demonstrate to Soviet leaders U.S. determination to protect its vital interests in Europe and the Middle East. This led in March 1947 to the enunciation of the Truman Doctrine, often cited by revisionist historians as the opening shot of the Cold War. Although the specific purpose of the new doctrine was to provide economic and military aid to Greece and Turkey, the White House (influenced by the influential Republican senator Hoyt Vandenberg to believe that it was the only way to get the aid bill passed) had couched its appeal to Congress and the American public in terms of a worldwide struggle to protect the free world against the threat from the spreading tentacles of international communism.

But if the administration's response to the challenge of growing Soviet power in Europe was beginning to achieve a sense of programmatic coherence, its attitude and strategy toward Asia were less clear-cut. In part that lack of coherence was a consequence of the diverging views of Europeanists, who stressed the importance of maintaining close ties with the nations of Western Europe, and Asianists, who called for vigorous assertion of the traditional U.S.

commitment to anticolonialism to earn the gratitude and support of the peoples of Asia. In part, too, it reflected the prevailing view that U.S. interests in the region were nowhere near as crucial as in Europe. That attitude had been graphically portrayed by the architect of containment policy, George Kennan himself. When he identified five key areas that were crucial to U.S. national security interests, only one, Japan, was located in Asia.[1]

An additional factor that impeded the emergence of a coherent Asian policy in Washington was that many U.S. policymakers viewed the political and social instability in many areas of Asia less as a direct consequence of deliberate Soviet action than of the difficult conditions surrounding the collapse of colonial empires in the region. This, certainly, was a major factor in the administration's reluctance to become involved in the bitter civil war that erupted between the forces of Chiang Kai-shek and the communists in China.

The caution and uncertainty that afflicted the administration's policy in China was reflected in its reaction to the renewed fighting in Indochina. Washington officials were worried about the impact of the renewed conflict not only on the overall situation in Southeast Asia but also on the political situation in Paris, where French political circles continued to be badly divided over the government's response to the crisis. The news of the outbreak of war appeared almost simultaneously with an announcement that Marius Moutet, the minister of Overseas France, was to travel to Indochina to consult with Ho Chi Minh on a renewal of negotiations.

The contrasting incidents fueled the fires of political discord in France. Conservative forces were outraged at the implication that the government would adopt a conciliatory attitude toward the Vietnamese and called for a firm policy focused on suppressing the rebellion. In Saigon, High Commissioner Thierry d'Argenlieu, citing the murder of French citizens in Hanoi, declared that France would no longer negotiate with Ho Chi Minh and threatened to detach Cochin China from Vietnam and place it as a separate state in the projected Indochina Federation. Leftist parties were harshly critical of d'Argenlieu's actions, accusing him of sabotaging the Ho-Sainteny agreement and the modus vivendi that had been signed with Ho Chi Minh in September. In the heat of emotions inspired by the Vietminh attack in December, however, radical elements were placed on the defensive and unable to wage a frontal attack on the government's Indochina policy.[2]

At the outset, then, Washington adopted a cautious attitude toward the renewed conflict. On December 23, four days after the Vietminh attack, Under Secretary of State Dean Acheson met with French ambassador Henri Bonnet in Washington and informed him that the United States was "deeply concerned" about the situation and felt that it was essential to settle the conflict as soon as possible by conciliatory means. Acheson stated that the U.S. government did not wish to mediate the dispute but wanted to be helpful, and he advised the

French not to try to reconquer Vietnam by force. Bonnet was noncommittal, noting that he had little information on the situation, but he assured Acheson that the new French premier Léon Blum intended to be conciliatory if at all possible.[3]

Acheson's assurances that the United States had no immediate intention of intervening in the Indochina dispute were accurate, for the Truman administration had already rejected a suggestion by the Republic of China to mediate the conflict and informed the British that any outside intervention would be resented and rejected by the French. Washington preferred to await the results of the Moutet mission and a clarification of French policy.[4]

Not all U.S. officials were happy with the administration's position. Southeast Asian Affairs Division chief Abbot Low Moffat, making a tour of Southeast Asian capitals en route back to the United States from Indochina, wrote a report to the department which was bluntly critical of Washington's carefully neutral attitude toward the crisis. Writing from Singapore, Moffat recommended a vigorous effort to bring the war to an end. From an Asian perspective, he pointed out, Washington's hands-off posture appeared overly sensitive to European concerns and the political situation in France and implied U.S. approval of a French military reconquest of Vietnam. Even if the French were to be successful in quelling the insurrection, he warned, the resentment it would engender would prevent the French from restoring their authority in the country and could ultimately threaten Western interests throughout Southeast Asia. Moffat concluded that the United States should assert its moral leadership to mediate the conflict and bring about a political settlement, which, he believed, could be achieved only by French negotiations with the current Vietnamese government. He was still confident that French interests in Indochina could be preserved. The alternative would be to turn Indochina into a gigantic military camp.[5]

Similar views were expressed by the U.S. minister to Thailand, Edwin Stanton. Stanton pointed out that all Southeast Asians sympathized with the Vietminh and expressed his concern that the new governments set up within the French Union in Laos and Cambodia would attack the French and threaten the peace of Southeast Asia. But such suggestions provoked only a brief reply that the United States was doing all it could while awaiting the results of the Moutet mission.[6]

In early January a French Embassy official called on John Carter Vincent and conveyed the French government's rejection of the administration's offer of good offices. Paris appreciated Washington's "understanding attitude," he said, but preferred to restore order first and then open communications with the Vietminh. Vincent, who commented in his report on the conversation that the message was delivered "without much conviction," reiterated U.S. concern and sympathy but pointed out that as a Great Power, France had more responsibility than the Vietnamese to maintain peace in the region. He warned that it might be difficult to localize the conflict, which could spread elsewhere in Southeast Asia. The French diplomat responded sharply, pointing out that the United States shared responsibility for the problem because it had not provided material aid to the French in 1945.[7]

In early 1947, General George C. Marshall, just returned from an unsuccessful final effort to prevent the resurgence of civil war in China, replaced James Byrnes as secretary of state. In early February he sent a lengthy message to the U.S. Embassy in Paris on the unfolding situation in Indochina. Marshall's message was the first formal expression of the department's views on the subject and reflected the dilemmas that would characterize American policy in the area for the next several years. While expressing U.S. sympathy with the French predicament and a desire not to undermine the French position in Indochina, Marshall voiced his criticism of French methods: "We cannot shut our eyes to the fact that there are two sides [to] this problem and that our reports indicate both a lack [of] French understanding of [the] other side (more in Saigon than in Paris) and [the] continuing existence [of] dangerous, outmoded colonial outlook and methods in [the] area." But Marshall was not blind to the nature of the French dilemma: "On the other hand," he said, "we do not lose sight [of the] fact that Ho Chi Minh has direct communist connections and it should be obvious that we are not interested in seeing colonial empires and administrations supplanted by philosophy and political organizations emanating from and controlled by [the] Kremlin." Marshall conceded that the situation in Indochina was no longer a local problem but had taken on global connotations and could endanger vital U.S. economic and political interests in the area. But he had no solution to offer, except to suggest that the French should keep the negotiations open and "should be generous in seeking a solution."[8]

Presumably, administration policy was best reflected in the report of a special ad hoc interagency committee which stated that the objective of the United States in the area was a prompt and durable settlement providing for the "creation of a stable Vietnamese state that will remain in voluntary association with France and will meet the legitimate demands of the Vietnamese for self-government and be responsive to the fundamental interests." Such a state, concluded the committee, was "the best defense against disintegrative tendencies" in the area that could provide opportunities for the communists.[9]

The French Reject Talks

Ambassador Caffery passed Marshall's comments on to French foreign minister Georges Bidault, who replied noncommittally that France was well aware that nineteenth-century colonialism was dead and was seeking a solution. And there were indeed signs that France was reassessing the situation in

Indochina. Attitudes in France, however, were as divided as they were in Washington. The Moutet mission had achieved little because Moutet had been unable to meet with Ho Chi Minh, whom he dubbed a prisoner of the militant faction in the Vietminh leadership. Some were now determined to put an end to the Vietminh regime through the use of military force, while others proposed a negotiated settlement with presumably moderate elements around Ho Chi Minh.

In March, High Commissioner Thierry d'Argenlieu (whose increasingly obdurate attitude was becoming a political liability in Paris) was quietly replaced. His successor, Emile Bollaert, was a Radical Socialist parliamentarian whose appointment, new premier Paul Ramadier claimed, would inaugurate a new "constructive phase" in the Indochinese negotiations.[10]

But the first signs were not promising. On February 20, Ho Chi Minh appealed to the French for a reopening of peace talks on the basis of the restoration of the status quo ante bellum. But at a press conference held on March 7, Ramadier rejected talks with the DRV, claiming that the offer had not come through official channels and even questioning whether Ho Chi Minh was still alive (there had been persistent rumors of his death from illness). In a debate on Indochina policy in the National Assembly, Ramadier declared that France would wait for the emergence of a government with which it could talk. Ramadier's comments provoked a brief note of irritation from Washington; Dean Acheson wired the U.S. Embassy asking what the French expected if they refused to take advantage of Ho's offer of talks. But Ramadier's tough talk won wide support in the National Assembly, and even FCP delegates approved a directive calling for military action.[11]

In late March, Bollaert left for Indochina, arriving in Saigon on April 1. Before his departure he remarked that France would not recognize a government that would not follow democratic principles to represent the mass of the population. Ho Chi Minh, he warned, must eliminate the extremists from his government before Paris would agree to negotiate with him. In Vietnam there were rumors that the French had already begun to negotiate with Bao Dai, who was now living in Hong Kong, on forming a new government.[12]

Ho Chi Minh appeared to realize the need for moderation. In early 1947 he had reshuffled the DRV cabinet, and two prominent members of the ICP, Pham Van Dong and Vo Nguyen Giap, were replaced by independents. Ho turned over the Ministry of Foreign Affairs (which he had occupied concurrently with the presidency) to Hoang Minh Giam, a member of the small Socialist Party. In early April, Giam reiterated the DRV offer of negotiations and a cease-fire. In the meantime, the Vietnamese approached the United States, appealing for diplomatic recognition and mediation of the Franco-Vietminh conflict. In April and May, discreet contacts had been opened between Vietminh representatives and U.S. Embassy officials in Bangkok.[13]

On his arrival in Saigon on April 1, High Commissioner Bollaert at first appeared willing to adopt a conciliatory posture and sent his personal counselor, the French scholar Paul Mus, to hold private talks with Ho at his headquarters in the Viet Bac. But Bollaert's freedom of maneuver was severely restricted by the hard-line attitudes of key elements in Paris, and the conditions for talks transmitted to Ho Chi Minh were designed to be unacceptable. The latter flatly rejected the French demands, noting that "in the French Union there is no place for cowards. If I accepted these conditions, I should be one." [14]

The unyielding posture adopted by the French in negotiations with the DRV was probably a deliberate tactic to provide a pretext to break off talks and seek an arrangement with noncommunist elements in Vietnam. Bollaert had intimated as much when he stated in Saigon that "we do not admit that any group has a monopoly on representing the Vietnamese people." In fact, the French had been in contact with former emperor Bao Dai since March in the belief that he would be a more pliant instrument in the French Union. Bao Dai had briefly cooperated with the Vietminh after the August Revolution, when he served in the sinecure position of supreme political counselor, but he soon sensed that Ho Chi Minh had no particular use for him and used the opportunity for a suggested trip to China to change his residence to Hong Kong, where he was soon in contact with noncommunist nationalist elements living in exile. He soon assumed titular leadership of a mixture of nationalist groups under the umbrella of a National United Front. [15]

The French had set the stage for talks with Bao Dai by establishing constitutional monarchies within the French Union in Cambodia and Laos, two protectorates in which there was rising sentiment for national independence but little communist activity. Now the French began negotiations with Bao Dai. On January 21, 1947, Paris offered unity of the three regions of Vietnam and national independence within the French Union. Independence, however, would be limited, for according to the 1946 French constitution, Paris would retain control over national defense and foreign affairs. Bao Dai, sensing that he must demand more than the Vietminh to preserve his credibility as a nationalist leader, decided to "watch and wait." [16]

Washington Frets

The inflexibility of the French exasperated Secretary Marshall, who in mid-May renewed his pressure on Paris. In a message to Ambassador Caffery on the thirteenth, he pointed out that the uncompromising attitude adopted by the French was dangerous and could drive all of Southeast Asia into a posture of hostility to the West. Noting that the United States and France had common concerns in the region, which was at a critical phase of its history, Marshall instructed Caffery to warn Paris that a protraction of the present impasse could only lead to bitterness and destroy the basis for future voluntary cooperation. The best safeguard, he said, would be a close but voluntary association between the colonial powers and the newly independent peoples. Marshall also displayed his exasperation at the French flirtation with Bao Dai, noting with concern that the French attitude could lead to the creation of an "impotent puppet government" like the one in Cochin China.[17]

When Caffery passed on Marshall's views to Foreign Minister Georges Bidault, the latter assured him that the French had no intention of installing a puppet government under Bao Dai. But Caffery was skeptical and pointed out in a return cable to Washington that the French were caught in a dilemma. They did not wish to deal with Ho Chi Minh, but the noncommunist national movement was tainted with collaboration and lacked leadership and coherence. It was a symptom of the weakness of noncommunist nationalism, he said, that Paris had to turn to Bao Dai in the first place.

The lack of alternatives, of course, would eventually become an American dilemma as well. From Saigon, Consul Charles Reed (no admirer of Ho Chi Minh) reported that Ho's government was the only political force with a measurable degree of popularity and organization, and he voiced serious reservations that a government under Bao Dai would succeed in winning popular support from the Vietnamese people. At the same time he expressed doubt about the sincerity of Ho's claim that he was a moderate, but because the Vietnamese felt that he was the only legitimate leader and opposed any other candidates, he concluded that the French had no choice but to compromise. He predicted that French concessions (presumably to Bao Dai) could be disastrous if they gave the natives a free hand:

Many observers doubt whether they are capable of running an independent state and point to the fact that the Philippines after 40-odd years of benevolent tutelage, in which the advantages of education and instruction were available to all, are still not a model of good government. How much less would the Annamites have of making a success? The majority of these observers opine that without Occidental check or control the result would be chaos—and in that chaos either the Soviets or the Chinese would find their opportunity. The former would be able to establish their ideology in the very heart of teeming Southeast Asia, with millions of people to indoctrinate and to prepare for the ultimate struggle with the western democracies. The latter would be able to realize their age-old desire to dominate if not to take over this part of the Far East, a desire which is even now manifest. To many observers, the Chinese danger is the greater, even if not imminent because of China's preoccupation with her own political problems.[18]

Reed's message, combined with the seeming intractability of the situation, did not go unnoticed in Washington. In a message to U.S. missions in Saigon and Hanoi in July, Secretary Marshall ruminated over the implications of a Vietminh government in Vietnam. What were Ho Chi Minh's real views? How much of a role would alleged militants such as Dang Xuan Khu (commonly known under his alias Truong Chinh) and Ha Ba Cang (pseudonym Hoang Quoc Viet) have in an independent Vietnamese regime? What did noncommunist nationalists think of the Vietminh? Did they understand its communist orientation? Could they cope with the communists (presumably in a coalition government)? Could the DRV be induced to grant "reasonably free political expression"?[19]

Replies to Marshall's queries began to arrive in the department later in the month. Not surprisingly, they were ambivalent. In Hanoi, O'Sullivan was skeptical of the possibility of a split between Ho Chi Minh and the militants, but he said that the DRV would not necessarily be subservient to faraway Moscow, and he felt that the United States could possibly play a useful role in influencing policy in Hanoi. But he agreed with Reed's prediction of chaos and a police state without Western authority.

From Saigon, Reed's views were more pessimistic. A victory by the Vietminh, he felt, would seriously undermine any remaining Western influence and lead to the emergence of a political dictatorship in Vietnam. But Reed was not optimistic about finding an alternative to the DRV, which he had earlier described as the most popular political force in Vietnam. Dealing with Ho Chi Minh was a risk, he pointed out, but so was dealing with puppets. As for Washington's concern about Soviet influence, Reed felt that Vietminh leaders would not turn to Moscow until the time was ripe. Ho Chi Minh, he was convinced, was a "wily opportunist," and the assumption that he was opposed by militants might be a blind. According to Reed, few Vietnamese understood Marxism-Leninism, but they recognized strong leadership, thus increasing the possibility of a minority-led communist regime. So the removal of Western influence would lead to a police state and additional pressure on Laos and Cambodia. In sum, the danger of communism was a likely consequence if the Western presence were removed.[20]

In Washington, the possibility of a communist victory in Indochina had begun to stir concern in military circles. A staff report written by the director of the Intelligence Division of the Army Chief of Staff in July stated that Southeast Asia was an area of considerable importance because of its "strategic resources" and recommended that the United States consider the possibility of mediation to resolve the conflict in Vietnam. A few weeks later a study produced by the Plans and Operations Division warned that a communist victory in China would not only strengthen the Vietminh but also serve to bring it more directly under the influence of international communism.[21]

But U.S. irritation had little effect in Paris, where policy moved steadily throughout the summer toward a "Bao Dai solution" to the Indochina problem. With the FCP no longer a part of the French government, procolonial elements began to demand a tougher policy toward the DRV and negotiations with Bao Dai to bring him back as titular leader of a new Vietnamese state under French tutelage. On September 10, after consultations in Paris, Bollaert gave a policy speech at Hadong, near Hanoi, in which he envisaged an autonomous and united Vietnam within the French Union. He made no mention of national independence and emphasized that the French would maintain control over foreign affairs and national defense.[22]

Paris Fights and Negotiates

Having prepared the political ground, the French now turned to the military option. In early October French troops took the offensive in the mountains of the Viet Bac with the objective of sealing off the Chinese border and, if possible, destroying the Vietminh armed forces and capturing its leadership. Rumors of the coming offensive had circulated in September, arousing anxiety in Washington, where officials were concerned that it could have a serious effect on U.S. public opinion and in Congress, which was due shortly to vote on an aid package for Western Europe. Secretary Marshall asked Ambassador Caffery to inquire about the rumors and express U.S. concern. The French by now realized that the Truman administration was increasingly nervous about a communist victory in Indochina, however, and fobbed Caffery off with reassurances that they had no plans for a major offensive.[23]

The results of that offensive were meager. French units were able to cut a number of Vietminh supply routes into China, but traffic continued to move freely elsewhere along the border, and Ho Chi Minh and his colleagues eluded capture. After seizing some military supplies and destroying Vietminh defensive installations, French units withdrew back to the Red River Delta, leaving a limited number of troops in a string of border posts along the Chinese frontier.

In the meantime, negotiations with Bao Dai were moving forward, albeit at a glacial pace. Bao Dai, who was still in Hong Kong, had responded to Bollaert's speech of September 10 with a proposal to begin talks on Vietnamese national independence and unification, a stand that had been approved at a meeting of the National United Front held earlier that summer. In December, he met with Bollaert on a French cruiser at Along Bay, off the coast of Tonkin. The talks were apparently amicable but short on concrete results. Bollaert presented Bao Dai with a declaration that included the word "independence" but was vague on the actual powers to be awarded to the new state. Bao Dai countered that he was willing to return to Indochina, but only after France had agreed to Vietnamese demands for full independence and national unity. Bollaert proposed an immediate return, with negotiations to follow. In the end, Bao Dai agreed to sign the declaration, but by his own admission he was uneasy, and when the agreement was criticized by nationalist groups within the National United Front, he disowned it.[24]

As 1948 dawned, the talks were stalled. In January, Bao Dai refused a French proposal to resume negotiations and on March 26 he convened a meeting of nationalist groups in Hong Kong, where he agreed to form a provisional government headed by General Nguyen Van Xuan, a native of the South, to prepare for future talks with the French. At first Bollaert was angry at Bao Dai's patent effort to strengthen his base of support, but eventually he agreed to recognize the new government as a negotiating partner.

In June, the talks at Along Bay resumed and resulted in a new agreement based on the principle of Vietnamese national independence and unity within the French Union. Details were to be worked out later. In fact, very little had been settled. For whom did the new Vietnamese government speak? It had been created by nationalist parties living in exile and had no recognized base of support within the country. Its provisional president, Nguyen Van Xuan, was widely considered to be corrupt, and Chief of State Bao Dai had questionable credentials as a symbol of national identity. What about the DRV, whose Vietminh forces represented a concrete factor in the equation? Finally, what did the French mean by "independence" and national unity?

It did not take long for some answers to the latter question to emerge. Shortly after the signing of the agreement at Along Bay, Minister of Overseas France Paul La Coste Floret, no friend of the colonial peoples, declared that the agreement did not imply a French commitment to reunification of the three zones of Vietnam because the statute of the Republic of Cochinchina could be amended only by formal approval of the French parliament. Foreign Minister Bidault raised further suspicions when he opposed the use of the word "independence" in any form. On June 19, the Along Bay agreement was approved "in principle" by the National Assembly in Paris, but it was clear that hard bargaining lay ahead.

Defending the Asian Rimlands

While the French were moving slowly toward their "Bao Dai solution" to the Indochina problem, policymakers in Washington groped with the conceptual problem of how to protect U.S. interests in an increasingly dangerous world. Although Europe was the original focus of the administration's concern, the growing likelihood of a communist victory in the Chinese Civil War, combined with the unrest in Indochina, magnified alarms about a global communist victory directed from Moscow. The Truman Doctrine of March 1947, though specifically directed at shoring up the Western position in the eastern Mediterranean, had implied the need for a universalist response by the Western powers to the global threat of communism—a view that reflected the continuing legacy of the "One World" view popular during World War II that democracy cannot be protected anywhere unless it is defended everywhere. George Kennan's selective approach to the issue of containment was giving way to a more global approach to U.S. national security.[25]

But some administration officials and foreign policy observers were uncomfortable at such universalist objectives, whether because of concern over the lack of resources available to achieve them or because of doubt as to whether they reflected the true needs of U.S. national security. One of the skeptics was George Kennan himself. Although Kennan had been the intellectual founder of the containment strategy, he had become increasingly exasperated at the tendency of many policymakers and foreign affairs analysts to apply it indiscriminately throughout the world. Arguing that the United States was "greatly overextended" in what it was attempting to accomplish, he proposed that the administration should attempt to distinguish vital from peripheral areas and adopt a selective approach to defend strongpoints of considerable military and industrial importance such as Western Europe and the Middle East. In Asia, such areas of importance included the island nations of Japan and the Philippines.[26]

In this perspective, of course, not only most of Southeast Asia but all the continental rimlands from Korea to the Middle East were outside the defensive perimeter of the United States. Not only did Kennan consider these areas of limited strategic importance to the United States, but he argued that they would be difficult to defend both because of their location on the Asian mainland and of the power of resurgent nationalism. To an administration beset by a sense of growing threat and limited resources, such a view was reassuring and led to the formulation of a new White House strategy for Asia based on the defense of the offshore islands in the Western Pacific.[27]

Yet even as policymakers were attempting to reduce the role of the Asian mainland in U.S. global security interests, events in that area were increasingly forcing Washington's attention to the possibility of Soviet exploitation there. In China, the growing weakness of the government of Chiang Kai-shek prompted General Albert Wedemeyer, on a fact-finding trip for Secretary Marshall, to cable Washington on September 19, 1947, that he doubted it could be saved. In Southeast Asia, the transition to independence in Burma and the Dutch East Indies had led to political instability in both countries and continuing efforts by local communist parties to seize power on their own.

There was little firm evidence of direct Soviet involvement in these events. Despite public charges in the United States that Stalin had connived in the Chinese Communist occupation of Manchuria after the end of World War II, most knowledgeable officials were convinced that the CCP leadership was essentially independent of Moscow. But there were some signs of growing Soviet interest in the rising wave of revolution along the Pacific rim. One concrete indication that was often cited as evidence of this interest was the famous speech by Stalin's designated successor, Andrei Zhdanov, at the opening meeting of the Communist Information Bureau (Cominform) in September 1947. Zhdanov's speech, which was widely reported in the West, appeared to many to confirm signs of a shift from the wartime policy of cooperation with the West to a more aggressive effort to exploit Western weaknesses in emerging areas of Asia. Charging that the United States was now embarked on a course designed to realize world supremacy, Zhdanov said that Washington's dream of hegemony could only be opposed by the forces of socialism led by the USSR.

One area of Western weakness, Zhdanov declared, was the Third World, which was experiencing a "sharpening of the crisis of the colonial system" and "increased armed resistance" against the imperialist powers by the colonial peoples. Although he did not specifically threaten Soviet action in support of such anticolonial struggles, he did associate the USSR with the emerging nations of the Third World, pointing out that the world was now divided into two camps, the capitalist and the socialist. The latter, he said, included not only the Soviet Union but also Vietnam and Indonesia, and it had the sympathy of India, Egypt, and Syria.[28]

Skeptics could point out that Moscow's behavior did not entirely match its rhetoric. The Cominform, widely viewed at the time as a successor to the dreaded Comintern of the interwar period, did not include Asian communist parties in its membership. Nor apparently did it attempt to put into operation a new strategy to promote Soviet national interests in the Third World. In fact, Moscow, like Washington, was probably still groping to come to terms conceptually with the rapidly changing world situation. The rising tension between East and West was an irrefutable signal that the antifascist united front that had characterized relations with the United States and other Western nations during World War II was now at an end. Under those circumstances it was clearly in Moscow's interest to take advantage of the unstable conditions accompanying the decolonization process to promote Soviet influence in Asia.[29]

But it was one thing to decide on a more activist policy toward Asia and another to define a strategy to promote Soviet interests in the region. Any such decision presented Moscow with a strategic dilemma that had hounded Soviet foreign policy since the early 1920's: should the USSR support noncommunist nationalist parties and governments in a common front against the United States and its allies in the imperialist camp, or should it encourage communist revolutionary parties in emerging Asian countries to strike out to seize power on their own?[30]

During the early postwar period, Soviet policymakers had followed the first approach, giving verbal sympathy to noncommunist nationalist forces in Asia and apparently encouraging local communist parties to remain in united fronts with such groups against the common enemy of Western imperialism. But there is circumstantial evidence that Moscow shifted to a more confrontational approach in early 1948. Because the inauguration of the new policy coincided with a conference of youth organizations and radical parties held in Calcutta in February, some historians have surmised that the Soviet Union used the Calcutta Conference as a conduit to transmit instructions to Asian communist parties to break with their local united fronts and launch general uprisings to seize power on their own. In support of this hypothesis, they point out that in the months following the conference, communist parties throughout Southeast Asia became more aggressive and in several cases broke with their nationalist allies and launched independent insurrections. Others, however, argue that such uprisings were not launched on Soviet instructions but were a product of the local situation.[31]

Without full access to Soviet archives in Moscow, we are not likely to achieve a final resolution of this debate. In general, however, the evidence tends to support the hypothesis that although the conference may have served to promote the development of revolution in the region, it was unlikely that it had been used as a means of disseminating specific instructions from Moscow to communist parties in the region.[32] In the first place, several key leaders from the local communist parties did not attend the conference, which was also attended by representatives from a number of noncommunist organizations. Second, no declaration was issued at the conference. Although several speeches appeared to support the view that communist parties should strike out on their own—the Yugoslavian delegate, for example, was critical of the DRV for adopting a national united front strategy—there was no general attack on such a strategy or on the bourgeois democratic governments that were beginning to emerge in the region. Furthermore, an authoritative article by a leading Soviet commentator on Asian affairs, appearing in the Soviet journal *Bolshevik* in December, made no reference to the policy of armed struggle and specifically praised the united front model.[33]

Whatever role the Calcutta Conference played, the communist uprisings that followed the meeting undoubtedly convinced many policymakers in Western capitals that it marked the opening salvo in a new and more aggressive strategy in Asia. During the months following the conference, revolutionary uprisings led by local communist parties broke out in several areas in Southeast Asia. In Burma, the White Flag faction of the Burmese Communist Party, whose leaders had played a major role at the Calcutta Conference, launched an insurrection against the new moderate nationalist government of U Nu. Later in the year, armed insurrections also erupted in Malaya, the Philippines, and on the island of Java.[34]

All were abortive but, taken in conjunction with the Berlin Blockade and the Czech coup, as well as the deteriorating situation in China, they heightened sensitivities in Washington. Even Europeanists such as George Kennan, recently appointed chief of the Policy Planning Staff in the Department of State, were aroused. In February, Kennan requested a departmental study to determine which areas were vital to U.S. national security and to see to it that they remained in friendly hands. Shortly after, the newly created National Security Council (NSC) issued NSC-7, which described Moscow's drive for global domination as a threat to U.S. national security.[35]

This rising concern over the apparent growth of Soviet influence in Asia added urgency to the U.S. effort to find a solution to the conflict in Indochina and to the conviction that U.S. interests in the area demanded not necessarily a French truce with Ho Chi Minh but the emergence of a noncommunist government there. There is little evidence that the transition to a more aggressive posture by communist parties in the region had much effect on the Vietminh. Early in 1948, a report reached Washington that Ho had requested that U.S. observers visit his headquarters. But Washington officials were less interested than they had been the previous year. Asked to evaluate the proposal, officials in the Division of Southeast Asian Affairs considered two possibilities: that he was a puppet of Moscow, as some claimed, or that he was a true nationalist. If the latter were true, they concluded, a single report would not change anything so it would be a poor investment to send a U.S. official. Better, they suggested, to send a Chinese agent. This idea surfaced at a conference of U.S. diplomats held in Bangkok in June but was rejected on the grounds that if a "white face" would not be appropriate, a "brown face" could not be trusted.[36]

The Truman administration thus abandoned the relatively disinterested stance that it had adopted through the first year of the conflict and began to encourage the French to find a noncommunist alternative to Ho Chi Minh. In the summer of 1948, Secretary Marshall instructed that nothing should be left undone to strengthen truly nationalist groups in Indochina at the expense of the communists.[37] But Washington remained skeptical of the French effort to strike a deal with Bao Dai, and although it publicly welcomed the signing of the Along Bay agreement as a "forward step" toward the settlement of the troubled Indochina situation, it was disappointed at the slow pace of the negotiations and instructed the U.S. Embassy in Paris to inform the new government of Premier Robert Schuman privately that France faced a stark choice of granting the principle of Vietnamese unity and independence within the framework of the French Union or losing Indochina altogether. Washington promised that if France carried through with such commitments, the United States would publicly support it as a "forward looking step" toward the solution of the Indochina problem and fulfilling the aspirations of the Vietnamese and would reconsider its existing policy of withholding economic assistance to Indochina.[38]

The new consul general in Saigon, George Abbott, agreed. To Abbott, French reluctance to come to terms with reality held little promise for a long-term solution to the conflict. Abbott pointed out that the return of Bao Dai "with nothing to offer but vague hopes of future concessions" would have little effect on the situation inside Vietnam and simply add credibility to communist charges that Bao Dai was a "U.S. tool." He recommended that U.S. aid be held in abeyance until the French had made "irrevocable commitments" to give the fledgling Vietnamese government a better chance of success. State Department sources appeared to be thinking along the same lines, and the U.S. Embassy in Paris was instructed to inform the Schuman government that the only way to strengthen the noncommunists would be for the French to provide concrete evidence of a willingness to move promptly toward the creation of a unified Vietnam with all the attributes of a free state.[39]

For some, this was not enough. Charles Reed, now chief of the Division of Philippine and Southeast Asian Affairs, was concerned about rising Soviet influence in Indochina and called for a more active U.S. policy in the area, including propaganda to promote pro-Western attitudes and the creation of assistance programs in such areas as public health, medicine, and education. But Reed's superior W. Walton Butterworth, director of the Office of Far Eastern Affairs, held a more benign view of the situation and felt that Asian nationalism should be allowed to take its course.[40]

The shift in U.S. Indochina policy toward a more anticommunist stance was reflected in a major policy statement issued by the Department of State on September 27, 1948. The statement, which had been drafted by the Division of Philippine and Southeast Asian Affairs in July, listed four long-term U.S. objectives in the region: (1) to eliminate as far as possible communist influence and bring about the installation of a self-governing state friendly to the United States. This state, it emphasized, should be "commensurate with the capacities of the peoples involved" and patterned after the U.S. conception of a democratic state as opposed to a "communist totalitarian one"; (2) to foster the association of Indochina with the Western powers, particularly with France, so it would cooperate with the West in the political, economic, and cultural spheres; (3) to raise the standard of living so that the country would resist the communists; and (4) to prevent undue Chinese penetration so that the Indochinese people would not be pressured by "alien people and interests."[41]

The best means of achieving such goals, continued the statement, was to press France to grant the "basic aspirations" of the Vietnamese people for national unity, internal autonomy, and freely chosen membership in the French Union. To persuade the French to move toward such a solution, the administration had declined to sell them weapons and ammunition for use in Indochina. But Washington had chosen not to pressure the French to negotiate with Ho Chi Minh because of his record as a communist.

There was still hope, the author pointed out, that the nationalist movement could be removed from communist control because most Vietnamese nationalists were not communists, but this could be done only if the Vietnamese were accorded "the largest degree of political and economic independence consistent with legitimate French interests." The problem was, of course, that Ho Chi Minh was the strongest and perhaps the most able figure in Indochina, and any solution that excluded him was "an expedient of uncertain outcome." For that reason, the statement continued,

we are naturally hesitant to press the French too strongly or to become too deeply involved so long as we are not in a position to suggest a solution or until we are prepared to accept the onus of intervention. The above considerations are further complicated by the fact that we have an immediate interest in maintaining in power a friendly French government, to assist in the furtherance of our aims in Europe. This immediate and vital interest has in consequence taken precedence over active steps looking toward the realization of our objectives in Indochina.

What was the solution? "We are prepared," the statement declared, "to support the French in every way possible in the establishment of a truly nationalist government in Indochina which, by giving satisfaction to the aspirations of the peoples of Indochina, will serve as a rallying point for the nationalists and will weaken the communist elements." Such a solution would strike a balance between the aspirations of the peoples of Indochina and the interests of the French. A military conquest by France would not be desirable because the United States would inevitably share in the hatred produced by the denial of self-government. On the other hand, a French withdrawal would in all likelihood lead to communist domination or a political vacuum that would be filled by the Chinese.[42]

This statement neatly captured the dilemma of the Truman administration in Indochina. Whereas in 1945 Washington had been deflected from applying pressure on Paris to hasten the transition to an independent state in Indochina primarily because of the delicacy of the political situation in France, now a new factor was added in that a French withdrawal would enhance Soviet influence in an unstable region of Asia. But U.S. policymakers were still paralyzed by the apparent lack of political forces in Vietnam that could offer an alternative to the wily Ho Chi Minh. Beyond the suggestion that the United States increase its propaganda activities in Indochina to explain the nature of Western democracy to the Vietnamese people, the statement had little concrete to offer and based the realization of American objectives on the possibility that a conciliatory attitude in Paris could lead to the strengthening of the noncommunist nationalist movement.

The Elysée Accords

For the moment, suggestions from Washington had little effect on Paris, where hard-line attitudes were paramount. In September, with his own policy of compromise under increasing criticism, High Commissioner Emile Bollaert resigned and was replaced by Léon Pignon, a veteran colonial official who had earlier served as political counselor under d'Argenlieu. With assurances of support from former U.S. ambassador to France William Bullitt, who had met with him in Hong Kong, Bao Dai held talks with the new high commissioner to ascertain the views of the new government in Paris. Pignon was affable but noncommittal.[43]

But it was the Vietminh, not Bao Dai, who were the main problem for the French. During the early months of the war, Vietminh leaders had adopted a defensive strategy based on the first stage of the Maoist three-stage concept of people's war. Vietminh units were instructed to withdraw to secure areas while the leadership attempted to broaden the popular base of the movement and build up military forces for an eventual confrontation with enemy troops in populated areas of the country. Such tactics were not always easy to apply. Some Vietminh field commanders lacked experience in waging guerrilla war and imprudently squandered their resources by waging set-piece battles with the French. Other units lost discipline after encountering setbacks and fled in disorder from the battlefield. By the end of the year, however, such problems were beginning to be rectified, and Vietminh forces settled into a war of feint, deception, and rapid movement to keep the enemy off balance, while political cadres attempted to strengthen the base of the movement at the rice-roots level.[44]

In January 1948 the ICP Standing Committee formally decided to end the first stage of withdrawal and begin the second stage of equilibrium, involving selective attacks in areas of enemy weakness. Vietminh forces, some of which were now organized in battalion-sized units, began to attack French installations and convoys in selected areas of their own choosing. Lack of firepower was still a major problem, and with no means of importing equipment from abroad, the DRV was forced to manufacture its own weapons in primitive factories established in areas controlled by Vietminh forces. But prospects for the future were promising. Although there were as yet no clear signs of increased support from Moscow, a communist victory in China seemed probable, leading to the possibility of a fraternal ally established across the Sino-Vietnamese border.[45]

During 1948 the size of Vietminh forces increased rapidly, reaching nearly 250,000 at the end of the year. Much of the Viet Bac was under the control of revolutionary forces, as were rural districts along the central coast and in the Mekong Delta southwest of Saigon. According to an experienced French observer, more than half the population of the country was living in areas under Vietminh authority. Such successes were reported by the consulate in Saigon, which said that Vietminh prospects for forcing the withdrawal of the French were "excellent."[46]

In January 1949, the French finally met Bao Dai's demand that the former colony of Cochin China be included in the projected Associated State of Vietnam. That key concession resulted in the opening of formal negotiations led by Prince Buu Loc and to a formal exchange of letters between Bao Dai and French president Vincent Auriol in March. According to the agreement, signed at the Elysée Palace on March 9, France recognized Vietnamese independence and unity within the framework of the French Union. From Bao Dai's standpoint, the accords were a clear advance over the Along Bay agreement because they provided Vietnam with many of the attributes of an independent state. It was empowered to conduct its own diplomacy within the French Union, control its own finances, establish diplomatic missions abroad, and create a Vietnamese National Army (VNA). The only formal limitations stemmed from those imposed by membership in the French Union and the war situation in the country. Only time would tell whether those limitations imposed serious restrictions on national sovereignty.

The Elysée Accords, of course, would not come into force until they had been ratified by the French National Assembly. As it turned out, that was no inconsequential matter because a number of prominent French politicians, including Charles de Gaulle, were determined not to abandon national territory. In an attempt to pressure Paris, Bao Dai insisted that he would not return to Indochina until the matter was settled. In March, the French National Assembly created a temporary assembly in Cochin China to vote on the issue of unification. At first the assembly (many of whose members were closely tied to French interests in the South) was split on the issue, but after Léon Pignon applied pressure, it voted by a large majority for unity with the remainder of the country.[47]

The U.S. Reaction to the Elysée Accords

The French clearly hoped that the signing of the March 9 agreement would remove U.S. doubts about French policy in Indochina and open the door to economic and military assistance for the struggle against the Vietminh. Shortly after the signing of the accords, Paris appealed to Washington for financial aid to help create a Vietnamese National Army, warning that the Chinese People's Liberation Army (PLA) was nearing the Vietnamese frontier.

But the French had miscalculated, for the initial U.S. reaction to the Elysée Accords was lukewarm. In the weeks before the final signing of the treaty Dean Acheson, who had recently replaced George Marshall as secretary of state, informed the U.S. Embassy in Paris that it would be unwise for the United States to support any arrangement unless it was highly likely that it would succeed. He instructed the ambassador to inform the French that the administration would not approve the Bao Dai solution in its present form. Similar reservations were expressed by Under Secretary of State Robert Lovett, who cabled the embassy in January that there was no reason to commit U.S. support irrevocably to a new government that might lack popular support and become a mere puppet of the French.[48]

From Paris, however, came words of caution. In a cable to Washington shortly after the signing of the accords, Ambassador Caffery advised Washington to accept them as a "calculated risk" and to provide the new government with moral and economic support in the difficult days after Bao Dai's return, pointing out that such support would increase the possibility of success. The withholding of aid, he claimed, would constitute a negative rather than merely a neutral factor. Caffery conceded that if Bao Dai failed it would be damaging to the United States but contended that he was the only forseeable alternative to the communists.[49]

In Washington, Charles Reed took issue with such reasoning. In a memorandum to Walton Butterworth he expressed his skepticism of French intentions in Indochina. In April he had talked with the French Indochina expert Paul Mus during the latter's visit to Washington, and Mus had told him that Bao Dai had no support among the Vietnamese people. Mus also commented that Ho Chi Minh was a nationalist before he was a communist. Reed noted his skepticism of the latter contention but argued that even if Bao Dai was the only possible noncommunist alternative in Indochina, that was no reason, in view of his dubious chances of succeeding, to commit the United States to his support at this time. Should he turn out to be a puppet, Reed warned, we would be led blindly down a dead-end alley, expending our limited resources in money and prestige in a hopeless cause.[50]

Reed by now despaired of saving Indochina and felt that the United States should make its stand in Thailand. In a second memo to Butterworth in mid-May, he suggested an effort to sound out Ho Chi Minh to test his nationalist credentials. Rumors of a U.S. deal with Ho were circulating in the press. On April 25, *Newsweek* reported that the Truman administration viewed Ho Chi Minh as a nationalist and would attempt to persuade Bao Dai to form a coalition government with him. In an interview with *Newsweek* reporter Harold Isaacs, a veteran Asia-watcher, Ho had claimed that the contention that he was a communist was pure French propaganda. The DRV government, he insisted, was composed of many elements and was not a Soviet satellite.[51]

Secretary of State Dean Acheson was caught in the middle of these debates. A self-proclaimed realist and a partisan of the doctrine of containment, Acheson considered proposals for a deal with Ho Chi Minh chimerical. Responding to questions from U.S. representatives in Indochina that the United States might negotiate with Ho Chi Minh, Acheson aired his own views in a cable dispatched on May 20. The idea that Ho Chi Minh could be a "national communist" (by now the concept had been given renewed credence because of the ejection of Joseph Broz Tito from the Soviet bloc) was, he said, only a "theoretical possibility." The question of whether Ho was a nationalist or a communist was irrelevant because all Stalinists in colonial societies are nationalists. Once they had achieved independence their objective would be to subvert the state to communist purposes. Citing the example of Eastern Europe, he argued that including the Vietminh in a coalition government with Ho Chi Minh would only delay a communist takeover, not prevent it. So he saw no alternative to the present policy of supporting the French while encouraging them to make concessions to noncommunist nationalism.[52]

But Acheson had also been influenced by recent events in China, which, as he explained in the same cable, had shown that "no amount [of] U.S. military and economic aid can save [the] government, even if [it is] recognized by all other powers . . . unless it can rally support [of the] people against [the] commies by affording representations [to] all important nationalist groups and demonstrate real leadership." So he followed one part of Reed's advice. In a message to Saigon sent on May 2, he explained that the administration did not want to give a premature endorsement or de facto recognition to the Bao Dai regime in order to preserve its freedom of action on the matter. Acheson's attitude was apparently stimulated by the continued reluctance of the French government to ratify the Elysée Accords, raising suspicions in Washington that concessions from Paris were only a tactical maneuver to persuade Bao Dai to return to Indochina.[53]

In Saigon, Consul George Abbott shared such doubts. In a return cable to Acheson's message of May 2, he disputed Ambassador Caffery's view that lack of support could doom the Bao Dai experiment to failure and contended that French failure to act on Cochin China would be an even more grievous blow. He argued that the United States should insist that Cochin China be linked to Vietnam and that Bao Dai be induced to form a cabinet of sufficient stature to provide a reasonable chance of success. In the meantime he urged continued pressure on the French to implement the Elysée Accords rapidly and in a liberal manner. Under these countervailing pressures, Secretary Acheson held his ground. In a return message to Saigon on the tenth, he agreed with Reed that the administration could not afford to support a government likely to suffer the fate of a puppet regime and insisted that the Bao Dai government must through its own efforts demonstrate a capacity to organize and conduct affairs in such a way as to ensure popular support. Otherwise, he said, it would suffer the fate of Chiang Kai-shek's Kuomintang regime in China.[54]

But Acheson was not optimistic that pressure on the French would achieve salutary results. In a cable dated May 20 he noted that the French were unlikely to grant more concessions and predicted that U.S. efforts to press them would probably miscarry. It was his hope that the French would carry out the accords with generosity and in a "constructive atmosphere" and that the Vietnamese would appreciate the true character of the menace from China and the risk of losing all autonomy to the Chinese Communists. Acheson said such an outcome was not impossible if the French made it known that the Elysée Accords were not intended to define the permanent status of Indochina but would serve as the basis for a further evolution of Vietnamese independence. But if it should appear that the French offer was too little and too late, he promised that the department would not "rush into the breach" to support Bao Dai as a solution at the cost of its remaining prestige in Asia. For the moment, he said, the United States would avoid a commitment and seek to reach a common position with other governments.[55]

The issue of recognition provoked a new debate between Europeanists and Asianists in the State Department. In a meeting held on May 17 between representatives of the offices of Western European and Far Eastern Affairs, Charlton Ogburn of the Southeast Asian Division argued that the agreement would have little appeal for nationalist elements in Vietnam because it left the French in control of foreign affairs and the Vietnamese National Army. He suggested that since there appeared to be little the United States could do to alter the "discouraging prospects" there, the best policy would be to avoid a firm commitment while working toward a collective approach to the problem with other nations. But Europeanists countered that it would be useless to press the French to concede more. The meeting ended in an agreement that because the current prospects were "discouraging" no further action should be taken for the moment while efforts were made to seek a consensus approach with Great Britain, India, and the Philippines.[56]

A Pacific Pact?

The United States was under increasing criticism from its allies and other friendly states in the region, who saw the administration's policy in disarray and looked to Washington for leadership in Asia. Some of the concern was undoubtedly a reaction to the impending formation of the North Atlantic Treaty Organization (NATO), which committed the United States to the defense of Western Europe, while little was being done to stop the advance of communism in Asia. In March 1949, President Elpidio Quirino of the Philippines appealed to the United States not to forget Asia and suggested the formation of a Pacific pact among noncommunist states in the region. Similar expressions of concern came from Bangkok, where Ambassador Edwin Stanton reported that Thai leaders were uneasy at the growing power of the Chinese Communists and were interested in a U.S. defense commitment to guarantee their independence. Stanton expressed his concern that the Thai government might follow its historical pattern and bow to superior force, and he suggested that a carefully worded statement of support might alleviate the nervousness in Bangkok.

Washington's initial reaction to such appeals was cautious. At a press conference held on March 22, Secretary Acheson remarked that the United States was not yet ready to consider a Pacific pact. The situation in Asia, he said, was not like that in Europe, where all members of such an organization were capable and ready to make a full contribution to their mutual defense. Although he did not allude to the situation in China, Acheson and other top administration officials were undoubtedly influenced by recent events there. At a meeting of the National Security Council held on April 2, for example, Acheson argued that China was an area of "lower priority" in U.S. national security concerns and that "since the house appeared to be falling down there was not much to be done until it had come down." Too hasty action in the region, he said, would commit the administration to an "unpredictable course of action," and he suggested that no strategic planning be undertaken in the region until the situation in China had clarified.[57]

This "wait and see" attitude toward Asia came under increasing criticism in the United States, where the administration was under pressure from some members of Congress for its "do-nothing" policy in Asia. The administration had already begun to gear up in an effort to evaluate the situation in Asia in the wake of the debacle surrounding the collapse of the Nationalist government in China. In February, under George Kennan's direction, the Policy Planning Staff in the State Department initiated a study aimed at defining U.S. policy toward Southeast Asia. The paper began with a number of assumptions. First, the area was important to the United States because of its raw materials and its strategic position astride global trade routes. Second, if Southeast Asia were "swept by communism," the United States "shall have suffered a major political rout, the repercussions of which will be felt throughout the rest of the world, especially in the Middle East and in a then critically exposed Australia." With China falling to communism, Southeast Asia "represents a vital segment on the line of containment, stretching from Japan southward around the Indian peninsula." Finally, it concluded that Southeast Asia "has become the target of a coordinated offensive plainly directed by the Kremlin."[58]

But although staff members saw the problem in somewhat apocalyptic Cold War terms, their proposals were surprisingly modest. Noting that the major problems in the area were caused by cultural divisions, political immaturity, economic backwardness, and errors committed by the colonial powers, the report concluded that the United States should increase its own role in the area through a small aid program while at the same time working out a common position with friendly governments in the area. On Indochina, the report said only that the administration "should frankly tell the French what we think about Southeast Asia," while joining with Great Britain and India in an attempt to persuade the French to transfer sovereignty to a noncommunist regime. In the meantime, the United States should support resistance to communist encroachment in Thailand and cultivate it as a center of stability and U.S. influence while leaving Burma and Malaya as a British responsibility.

The draft of the staff paper was circulated in the State Department and presented at a meeting of high-level officials in early April. In the words of one historian, it "fell flat." Key department officials such as Soviet expert Charles

Bohlen were reluctant to encourage local governments in the region and recommended that the United States work with its Western allies on the matter. The paper was sent to Secretary Acheson who, after Kennan's urging, eventually approved it as PPS-51, but only for informational purposes, not for action. The administration still lacked a coherent policy for the region.

In the meantime, each office acted on its own. Some officials in the Division of Southeast Asian Affairs rejected a regional approach. Division Chief Charles Reed in particular wanted to abandon Indochina and concentrate on saving Thailand. Others, like Far Eastern Office director Walton Butterworth, shared his general pessimism but were not yet ready to write off Indochina entirely. In the end, Reed agreed to a policy of supporting Bao Dai so long as the French gave him a chance.[59]

Secretary Acheson discussed the problem of Southeast Asia with British foreign minister Ernest Bevin during the latter's visit to Washington in early April. Bevin was concerned over the situation in Malaya and Burma, where communist insurrections continued to fester, but he was not favorable to the idea of a military pact dominated by the Western powers to protect the area. The initiative, he said, must come from the Asian countries themselves. In any case, he felt that the threat to Southeast Asia was unlikely to be military in nature but was a matter of economic underdevelopment and the lack of self-confidence on the part of the governments in the area.

But Bevin was under pressure from within his own government. Malcolm MacDonald, British commissioner general in Malaya, had publicly warned that the West had to adopt an active regional approach in Southeast Asia to counter a similar strategy by the communists. In response, Bevin asked Acheson for U.S. support to persuade the Asian countries to help themselves while providing them with political and economic assistance. The British Commonwealth, he said, would be willing to provide such assistance but would not agree to become militarily involved in the area. On his departure he left a memo arguing his case.[60]

Secretary Acheson was in general agreement with Bevin's views on the defense of the region, and at a press conference held on May 18 he reiterated his position that the administration was not considering participation in any collective defense arrangement other than NATO, which he said was the product of specific circumstances in Europe. He also continued to hold a tough line on dealing with the French. In a conversation with the French ambassador in Washington on May 24, State Department counselor Douglas MacArthur II warned that the Elysée Accords had been "too little too late" and that the chances of success in Indochina were no better than even. The French government, he said, should not assume that U.S. military aid would be forthcoming under the Military Defense Assistance Program (MDAP). Washington's attitude would depend on the speed with which Paris ratified the agreement and the way it was implemented.[61]

The Indochina Debate Continues

Acheson's effort to push the French to grant further concessions drew a word of caution from the new U.S. ambassador in Paris, David Bruce. In a cable to the department dated May 30 Bruce said that French officials had assured him that they would be generous in interpreting the Elysée Accords. Noting that this was a major experiment for the French, Bruce echoed his predecessor in arguing that a positive statement from Washington was in order and that a degree of international recognition could provide the Bao Dai government with added credibility inside Vietnam.[62]

But Ambassador Bruce's appeal had no immediate effect in Washington, where Asianists continued to push for a firm position with the French. On June 6, a draft message to the French government was sent to the U.S. Embassy in Paris. The draft, which arrived while Secretary Acheson was in Paris for talks with French government officials, declared that the United States welcomed the signing of the Elysée Accords but felt that Vietnamese nationalists might resent those terms which implied a continuing status of inferiority to their erstwhile colonial rulers. If requisite French concessions were not forthcoming, the cable warned, the Vietminh would be the ultimate beneficiaries.

The draft drew a quick response from Ambassador Bruce, who called the proposal "poppycock" and, with Acheson's approval, replied that the message was unrealistic and would seem discouraging to the French. Bruce urged that he be permitted to convey the substance of the message in an oral presentation and simply urge the French to take a liberal interpretation of the accords. Faced with this concerted opposition from representatives on the spot, the department backed off. On June 16 Under Secretary of State James Webb, who had signed off on the original draft in Acheson's absence, agreed to an oral presentation but recommended that the French be warned against intransigence and that future U.S. actions would depend on implementation of the Elysée Accords.[63]

Actions in Paris helped to assuage U.S. irritation. On June 14 the French National Assembly passed a bill agreeing to uniting Cochin China with the other two regions of Vietnam. The French government announced that it would put the accords into effect even though the entire agreement had not yet been ratified by the National Assembly. Shortly after Bao Dai was named chief of state of the new Associated State of Vietnam.

The French action inspired appeals from some in Washington for a public statement of U.S. approval. Some Asianists were reluctant, but Secretary Acheson favored it, and the administration informed its allies that the United States was preparing to issue a statement welcoming the new state and considering how best to grant de facto diplomatic recognition and provide assistance to promote its chances for survival. The British expressed a general interest in coordinating their response with Washington but doubted the advisability of a statement welcoming the formation of the Bao Dai government at this time because they were convinced that success was unlikely and recognition would lead to failure and embarrassment. The Attlee government advised Washington that an approach to India might do more harm than good and could provoke Prime Minister Jawaharlal Nehru to launch another blast at colonialism in Asia. There was also reluctance in Bangkok, where Thai leaders considered the Elysée Accords inadequate because they provided no timetable for complete independence.[64]

Secretary Acheson, whose irritation with the French had apparently eased as a result of his recent trip to Paris, was not deterred by the lack of support from other quarters. On June 21, the department issued a statement calling the formation of a unified state of Vietnam a "welcome development" that should serve to hasten the reestablishment of peace in that country and could form the basis for the progressive realization of the legitimate aspirations of the Vietnamese people. The statement, which did not grant diplomatic recognition, was less than Ambassador Bruce had wanted, but it was equally displeasing to Asianists in the Office of Far Eastern Affairs, who feared that despite Léon Pignon's assurances to the contrary, Paris would interpret the March 9 agreement as an end in itself. Charlton Ogburn, one of the most vocal critics of French policy in the department, complained in a memo to Charles Reed that U.S. policy on Indochina had been "junked" and recommended that the administration limit itself to tepid support for the Bao Dai government and explain why it could not do more. Walton Butterworth sent the memo to the Division of Western European Affairs, which refused to countersign it.[65]

On August 31, 1949, Chief of State Bao Dai formally requested diplomatic recognition of the Associated State of Vietnam from the United States, but for the next several months the Truman administration held back from formal recognition, hoping that friendly and neutral governments in Asia would take the lead in giving a stamp of legitimacy and approval to the new state. In a joint meeting on September 13, Secretary Acheson and British foreign secretary Ernest Bevin agreed to pressure the French to ratify the accords and grant additional concessions, such as the transfer of Franco-Vietnamese relations from the minister of Overseas France to the Ministry of Foreign Affairs. But the British were reluctant to go further in granting approval to the new state and appeared sensitive to offending Asian members of the British Commonwealth, who were still suspicious of French intentions in Indochina. Bevin was especially concerned about the attitude of Indian prime minister Nehru and fearful that he might back Ho Chi Minh rather than Bao Dai.[66]

On September 17, Acheson, Bevin, and French foreign minister Robert Schuman held talks in Washington. Schuman promised that France would interpret the agreement liberally and would soon transfer French links with Vietnam to the Ministry of Foreign Affairs, but he pointed out that the new state was still very weak and could not stand alone without French military assistance. He noted that the French were fighting for the entire free world in Indochina. Schuman recognized that the United States could not give military assistance for political reasons but asked for economic aid to the new state and added that diplomatic recognition would help. Acheson was noncommittal on the issue of economic aid and said that Washington felt that Asians should be the first to recognize the new state, but he promised to try to persuade Thailand and the Philippines to take the step.[67]

Searching for an Asian Strategy

For U.S. policymakers in Washington, the problem of Indochina was only one facet of the larger issue of formulating a coherent Asian policy in the wake of the communist victory in China. The collapse of the Chiang Kai-shek government and its retreat to the island of Taiwan had a major effect on the thinking of top officials in the White House and the State Department, and in May 1949 President Truman instructed the latter to draft a "White Paper" to explain the fall of China to the American people. The thrust of the paper, drafted by China specialist John F. Melby, was that the communist victory was not the result of any action or inaction by the United States but of the failure of the Nationalist regime itself.

The fall of China provided an ominous backdrop for administration officials as they groped for a policy to stem the apparent retreat of American power before the forces of communism in East Asia. Although the White Paper presented a closely reasoned analysis of the underlying causes of the communist triumph on the mainland, the Truman administration was clearly on the defensive from congressional and public criticism as a result of the impression that it had a "do-nothing" strategy in Asia. That impression was at least partly justified in light of the opinion of such top-level State Department officials as Dean Acheson and Far Eastern Office director W. Walton Butterworth that the United States should take no hasty action to stem the tide of nationalism and revolution which was sweeping Asia but should, in Acheson's words, "let the dust settle."[68]

But even if the administration's policy of "wait and see" made sense from a long-term perspective, it was a public relations disaster at a time when the United States was suffering what the State Department's ambassador at large Philip Jessup called "an acute case of negativism" in its foreign policy in Asia. Noncommunist leaders in the Philippines and on Taiwan threatened to form a defense pact of Asian nations with or without the United States. Within the State Department, there was a rising consensus among middle-level officials of the need to begin the search for a coherent strategy to protect threatened U.S. interests throughout Asia. Several key figures offered suggestions to end the sense of drift and establish an affirmative policy in the region.

One source of action was George F. Kennan's Policy Planning Staff, whose earlier paper on Southeast Asia had received a mixed reception and had never been fully implemented. Although Kennan had earlier stated that the United States should not attempt to defend all of Asia, he and some members of his staff, including China specialist John Paton Davies, were reportedly impatient at the lack of action by Walton Butterworth and wanted a more dramatic policy to focus attention on U.S. interests and responsibilities in the region.

Consequently, in July Kennan agreed to forward a memorandum written by Davies to top officials for their consideration. The "Davies plan" was designed to provide dramatic evidence of U.S. determination to stake out and protect its interests and those of its allies in the general area of East and Southeast Asia. Based essentially on PPS-51 and the China White Paper, the Davies proposal called for a military defense pact built around the Philippines and Australia, two key U.S. allies in the area. Eventually he hoped to bring in New Zealand, Canada, and Japan and to consider possible participation by Indonesia and Thailand. The plan was not entirely military in scope but also included provisions for economic and educational programs to train Southeast Asian technicians to counter the dreaded Stalin School in Moscow. Indochina was conspicuous by its absence.[69]

An even more ambitious program was provided by Deputy Under Secretary of State Dean Rusk. Rusk, who had served as a staff officer with General Joseph Stilwell in Burma during World War II and was one of the few appointed officials in the administration with a strong interest in Asia, proposed the creation of a defense pact with noncommunist nations in the area, but he also wanted to provide full diplomatic recognition to the Republic of Korea and a technical aid program and diplomatic support for the Bao Dai government in Vietnam.[70]

Secretary Acheson was still resisting appeals from anticommunist nations in Asia for a Pacific pact, viewing them as a ploy to obtain U.S. financial assistance, but he agreed to discuss the Rusk plan with Rusk and several other top State Department officials, including Philip Jessup, Walton Butterworth, and Charles Bohlen, on July 16. He then took the issue up with President Truman, who authorized Jessup to appoint a study group to draw up plans for the defense of the noncommunist areas of Asia. Jessup was to assume that it was "a fundamental decision of American policy that the United States does not intend to permit any further communist domination on the continent of Asia or in Southeast Asia." Jessup then appointed Everett Case, president of Colgate University, and Raymond Fosdick, president of the Rockefeller Foundation, to the committee.[71]

The White House did not immediately implement the suggestions of either Rusk or Davies but decided to await the presentation of the Jessup committee report. But while top State Department officials were seeking to draft a new Asian policy, a second source of action came from the Department of Defense, headed by Louis Johnson. A West Virginia lawyer who had been one of the top fund-raisers for the Truman administration, Johnson had opposed the conclusions of the China White Paper and was increasingly impatient with the lack of direction from the State Department. In June he initiated his own policy review by sending a memo to Admiral Sidney W. Souers, secretary of the recently created National Security Council, recommending that its staff formulate a comprehensive plan to contain the advance of communism in Asia.[72]

The first draft of the NSC staff report, labeled NSC-48, appeared in October. It adopted an aggressive approach, calling for U.S. occupation of Taiwan and harassment of communist forces on the mainland. Such conclusions were anathema to top State Department officials such as Walton Butterworth as well as to the members of the Jessup committee, who had completed their own report in September. The committee report called for acceptance of the results of the civil war in China and an attempt to encourage Titoism on the part of the new leadership in Beijing. It also advised against any U.S. action to protect the island of Taiwan from a communist takeover. In considering U.S. policy outside of China, the committee advocated a major effort to side with the forces of Asian nationalism and provide economic assistance to newly independent nations in the area. The report was especially critical of European colonial influence over U.S. Asian policy and wanted an Asian-oriented approach to the region.

In late October, Ambassador Jessup met with Secretary Acheson and other top State Department officials to discuss the committee report. Their reaction was mixed. Acheson expressed his agreement with the need for the United States to side with Asian nationalism and pressure the French on Indochina, but he opposed adopting a regional approach to Southeast Asia, which, in his view, would give the erroneous impression that the United States was prepared to play a major role in the region. In particular, he rejected the adoption of a program calling for massive economic assistance, which would be impossible in the prevailing domestic climate. What was needed, he said, was "more brains and fewer dollars." The meeting touched briefly on Indochina but reached no consensus. Acheson, perhaps influenced by a recent conversation with Indian prime minister Nehru, commented that perhaps the United States should take a "closer look at Ho Chi Minh" because the Indian prime minister had contended that he was the only eminent political figure in the country.[73]

The Jessup committee report had thus not resolved some of the key issues in U.S. Asian policy, which still remained ambivalent on how to deal with China and the implications of the communists there on nations elsewhere in the region. During the remainder of the fall of 1949, the administration continued its policy review, which came to a climax in early December with an extended discussion of NSC-48. Asian specialists in the State Department had disagreed with Defense Secretary Louis Johnson's proposal to intervene actively in China and take steps to protect the island of Taiwan from communist occupation and had produced their own draft, which reiterated existing policy of avoiding involvement in the Chinese Civil War on the grounds that U.S. security in the area was based on the offshore islands and was not directly affected by the communist takeover on the mainland. It called for support to other nations in Southeast Asia to stem the tide of communism in the region but rejected the use of military force. It saw no solution to the problem of Indochina except to continue pressuring the French.

In late December, President Truman supported the State Department version, and NSC-48 was formally approved as the first comprehensive program of U.S. Asian policy since the end of World War II. Any effort to reverse the results of the Chinese Civil War was rejected, and future policy toward the mainland would be to encourage friction between the new regime in Beijing and the Soviet Union. In the meantime, however, the United States would continue to recognize the Republic of China until the situation had clarified.[74]

In other respects, the new program reflected the trend toward a more activist role in Southeast Asia that had begun several months earlier. It painted a grim picture of Soviet expansionism in Asia and declared that domination of the region by a single hostile power would seriously threaten U.S. national security interests. Pointing out that traditional U.S. policy had been to promote a system of independent states in the area, the paper said that the immediate U.S. objective must be "to contain and where feasible reduce the power of the USSR in Asia." To do so, the United States must assist, through diplomatic support and economic development programs, in the emergence of stable, friendly, and truly independent states in the area. Asian nations should be encouraged to develop regional associations to protect their own security, but the United States should not take the initiative in the process. It did state that the United States was willing to appraise the desirability of a collective security system in the area.

Perhaps the most noteworthy aspect of the NSC paper was its effort to draw a line of containment in Asia. Asia was important, it asserted, because "it is a source of important raw and semi-processed materials, many of strategic value." It defined as a minimum maintenance of the present U.S. military position in the offshore island chain. This island chain, which included Japan, the Ryukyu Islands, and the Philippines, was described as the first line of defense and, in addition, "our first line of offense from which we may seek to reduce the area of communist control, using whatever means we can develop without, however, using sizeable United States armed forces." Taiwan was to be protected if possible, but by diplomatic and economic means only. There was no reference to the strategic importance of Indochina, and the paper said only that "particular attention should be given to the problem of French Indochina and action should be taken to bring home to the French the urgency of remov-

ing the barriers to the obtaining by Bao Dai or other non-communist nationalist leaders of the support of a substantial proportion of the Vietnamese."[75]

The Issue of Recognition

While officials in Washington were huddled in debate over U.S. policy
options in Asia, the French position inside Indochina continued to deteriorate.
Conditions on the battlefield steadily worsened. An October estimate by the
Central Intelligence Agency (CIA) was somber, warning that with the forces
presently available, the French could do no more than maintain a stalemate. "If
present circumstances continue basically unchanged," the report predicted,
"the Vietnamese nationalists will probably be able to drive the French out of
Indochina within two years." Such a loss would represent "the critical breach in
the non-communist crescent around China, which now consists of India, the
Southeast Asian peninsula, Indochina, the Philippines, and Japan."[76]

To U.S. policymakers, the key to the situation was the continued reluctance
of the French to transfer authority to the new government in Vietnam. Chief of
State Bao Dai was also seen at fault for his failure to consolidate power and set
up the framework of the new government. He gave no indication of setting up
procedures to draft a constitutional statute but simply promulgated two "ordi-
nances" in July to create a provisional cabinet and a consultative national
council to rule in lieu of a legally constituted authority. Members of both bodies
were to be appointed by the chief of state.[77]

There were many in Washington who were still skeptical of the character of
the new Vietnamese leader, who had a reputation as a playboy, and were deeply
troubled over whether, in the best of circumstances, he was a realistic alternative to Ho Chi Minh. In a memo to Philip Jessup, Raymond Fosdick warned
that the "Bao Dai experiment" was doomed. He was equally critical of the
Elysée Accords, calling them a "shabby business" and a "cheap substitute" for
independence. To support the French was to attach the United States to the
"battered kite" of French colonial policy and ignore the forces that were sweeping Asia. To Fosdick, the only realistic policy was to accept reality and recognize
the DRV. Although he admitted that Ho Chi Minh was an unpleasant alternative, he said that Ho was an "unpredictable factor" because of the complex
relationship between China and Vietnam, which "in the end will be more
favorable to us than now seems probable."[78]

Fosdick's concerns about the character of Bao Dai and the likelihood of his
success were shared by others, but few went to the extreme of recommending
recognition of Ho Chi Minh's government. In two memos prepared for Jessup
in early November, Charles Yost, a Southeast Asian specialist in the State Department, conceded that Bao Dai was a risk but argued that Ho Chi Minh was
no angel either. If Ho really possessed broad popular support, argued Yost, that

fact should be accepted, but he was a stooge for the Kremlin and the communists dominated the nationalist movement only because of French stupidity. Yost had no easy solution to offer beyond urging continued pressure on the French to ratify the Elysée Accords. But he added that the United States should not commit itself to Bao Dai unless he showed a capability to win the support of his people. In the meantime, it should explore alternatives to either Bao Dai or Ho Chi Minh.[79]

Faced with evidence of foot-dragging in Paris and doubts about Bao Dai at home, the Truman administration held back from diplomatic recognition or the granting of economic and military assistance to the new state. During the spring, the State Department had agreed in principle on a modest program of technical and economic aid to the area, and officials in the Office of Far Eastern Affairs had discussed a small military aid program for Indonesia, Thailand, and perhaps Indochina, but no action had been taken.

In September, the passage of Section 303 of the Military Assistance Program forced the administration to make a decision on how to use the funds allocated under the program. The bill had originally been designed to provide funds for the Republic of China, but with the collapse of the Chiang Kai-shek regime on the mainland, State Department officials were informed that the funds could be used in neighboring areas such as Burma or Indochina. As the bill neared passage, French officials expressed interest in requesting aid under the program, and a few weeks later the Bao Dai government put in a bid as well.[80]

In October, Livingston Merchant, deputy chief of the Office of Far Eastern Affairs (the office was about to be renamed a bureau, and the divisions of Philippine and Southeast Asian Affairs were combined into a new Office of Philippine and Southeast Asian Affairs, PSA), made a tentative recommendation that $8 million from Section 303 funds be allocated to the French after ratification of the Elysée Accords. Additional funds were assigned to Burma, Thailand, and the Philippines. During the fall, however, no action was taken on the request, and Secretary Acheson fidgeted, complaining that by the time the French acted, it would be too late for Bao Dai to win the support of his people. In a cable to Paris in early December, he instructed Ambassador Bruce to tell the French that two further steps were needed—immediate ratification of the March 9 agreement and a declaration by Paris of a timetable for national independence within a relatively short period, along with a mechanism to prove its good intentions.

The courtly Bruce, a Europeanist if there ever was one, was as solicitous of French attitudes as his predecessor had been, and he warned Acheson that it was necessary to be practical. Realistically, he pointed out, the French could not withdraw because the 150,000 members of the French Expeditionary Forces alone could prevent a communist victory. French public opinion would not accept a timetable or an international commission to supervise steps toward Vietnamese national independence, nor would France agree to remain in Vietnam if it decided to withdraw from the French Union. Bruce urged that the administration simply urge ratification of the accords and the transferral of mutual relations to the French Foreign Office and hope that the limitations built into the accords would disappear with time. It was a risk, he conceded, but to assume Ho Chi Minh would win was "dangerous and defeatist."[81]

Support for Ambassador Bruce's position came from Saigon, where Consul General George Abbott warned that failure by the United States to support Bao Dai would be interpreted as evidence that the administration was indifferent and irresolute in opposing the advance of communism in Southeast Asia and would provide Ho Chi Minh with an opportunity to portray Bao Dai as a French puppet. Support for the new government, to the contrary, would provide it with international standing as a keystone in the free world defense of Southeast Asia.[82]

Conclusions

As we look back on U.S. foreign policy toward Indochina at the end of 1949, perhaps the foremost impression is one of uncertainty. The Truman administration had not yet formulated a clear policy on how to deal with the French and whether to support the Bao Dai government. There was not even a consensus on the nature of U.S. long-term interests in the area or the degree to which the United States should become involved in its defense.

One reason for this ambiguity was the continuing debate over the situation inside Vietnam. Although few doubted that Ho Chi Minh was a communist, or that his Vietminh forces were winning the war, there was some disagreement over whether he was a puppet of the Kremlin or a nationalist with potential Titoist leanings. There was similar controversy over whether the French would provide adequate autonomy to the new Associated State of Vietnam and whether Bao Dai had the strength of character to provide a realistic alternative to a Ho Chi Minh–dominated Vietnam.

Beyond such questions was a continuing struggle between Europeanists and Asianists within the State Department over foreign policy priorities. Many Asianists argued for a policy of backing Asian nationalism as the best means of preventing communist inroads in the region. Europeanists countered with the view that the support of France was crucial to the survival of the Western alliance. They pointed out that Paris could not be pressured to move faster because of French public opinion and added the irrefutable argument that without the presence of French military forces, there was no chance of saving Vietnam from communism.

A final factor that affected U.S. attitudes toward the conflict in Indochina was that at the end of 1949 U.S. policy toward Asia was itself in a state of flux. Until 1949 most leading figures in the Truman administration had opposed the application of containment strategy to Asia, believing that the forces of revolution and nationalism represented by the Chinese Civil War must be allowed to take their course. That policy had been formally expressed by Secretary of State Acheson in April, when he commented at a meeting of the National Security Council that the Chinese house was falling down and not much could be done about Asia until it was clear what was left after its final collapse. By late 1949, however, that hands-off view toward China was coming under question in Washington. Voices on Capitol Hill and even within the administration began to criticize the "let the dust settle" approach and wanted a tougher line to protect U.S. interests in the region.

As the decade came to an end, then, the Truman administration had not yet committed itself to the future direction of U.S. policy in Asia. But there were some suggestive indications that the thrust of events was beginning to move U.S. foreign policy toward a posture of more active support for the French in Indochina. The rising chorus of anticommunism in U.S. public opinion was certainly one factor, although there is no evidence that it had yet influenced administration policy. More concretely, the fall of mainland China undoubtedly triggered concerns in Washington that the shock waves might be felt throughout the region and the first signs of what later would be labeled the "domino theory" began to appear in official analyses of the situation in Southeast Asia. There seems little doubt that the communist triumph in China played a major factor in provoking U.S. foreign policy makers to begin thinking about the conflict in Indochina as an issue in the Cold War.

In this policy debate, Secretary of State Dean Acheson occupied a central position. Not only was he the senior administration official in charge of the shaping of U.S. foreign policy, he had the respect and the ear of the president. Although concerned about the expansion of communism in China, he was skeptical about the impact of a communist victory there on U.S. security interests in Asia. A practitioner of realpolitik rather than a moralist, he avoided the simplistic anticommunism of the day and actively considered the possibility of encouraging Titoist tendencies within the new government in Beijing. Finally, although like most top-level officials in the administration he felt instinctively that U.S. interests in Western Europe had priority over those in Asia, he was skeptical of French intentions in Indochina and reluctant to tie the U.S. ship of state to the "tattered kite" of French colonialism.

As the year ended, Acheson continued to resist the pressure to commit the administration to the struggle in Indochina. But the trend of events was evident, and despite his periodic comments to the contrary, it seems clear that the key issue was not whether the United States was going to support the French and the new Bao Dai government, but how much and how far it would do so. The administration's hesitation in granting formal recognition to Bao Dai and financial assistance to the French in fighting the war was a tactical ploy to extract greater concessions from the French rather than an indication that Washington officials were considering major alternatives.

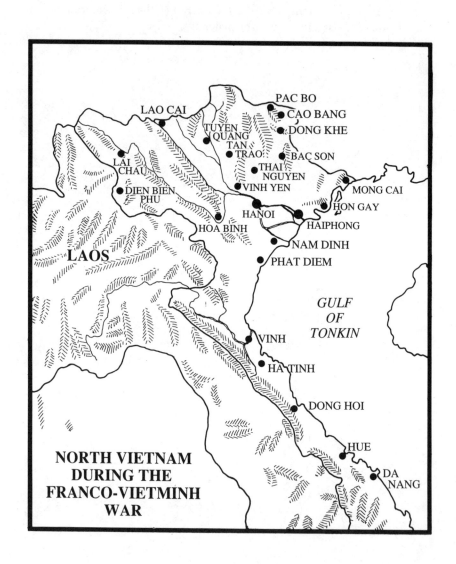

LAO CAI

PAC BO
CAO BANG
DONG KHE

TUYEN
QUANG
TAN
TRAO
BAC SON

LAI
CHAU

THAI
NGUYEN
VINH YEN

DIEN BIEN
PHU

MONG CAI

HANOI

HON GAY

HOA BINH

HAIPHONG

LAOS

NAM DINH

PHAT DIEM

GULF
OF
TONKIN

VINH

HA TINH

DONG HOI

NORTH VIETNAM
DURING THE
FRANCO-VIETMINH
WAR

HUE

DA
NANG

Chapter 4

Indochina Enters the Cold War

In retrospect, the year 1950 can be seen as a watershed in the history of modern Vietnam. It was in that year that the conflict in Indochina was transformed from an essentially local anticolonial struggle into a focal point of the Cold War. One factor in that transformation was the arrival of communist forces across the border in China. The other was the decision by the United States, spurred by the growing fear of the spreading red tide in Asia, to enter the struggle on the side of the French.

The reason for this development, however, was more than the fortuitous seizure of power by the communists in Beijing or the rising tide of Cold War sentiment in the United States. The situation in Indochina had taken on the character of a stalemate. In 1949, the French still possessed overall military superiority on the battlefield, but not sufficient to achieve a decisive victory against the growing political and military strength of the Vietminh. Led by the astute Ho Chi Minh, the revolutionary movement, widely viewed in Vietnam as a more legitimate representative of Vietnamese nationalism than the shaky government of former emperor Bao Dai, had begun to mobilize significant support from both urban nationalists and peasants.

But the DRV continued to have military weaknesses. Although the Vietminh forces were roughly equivalent to their adversaries in size, they lacked adequate firepower to wage conventional assaults on French-held areas in the lowlands. In the Maoist three stages of people's war, they had reached the second stage of equilibrium—placing them in a position to launch occasional surprise attacks by guerrillas or mobile forces on French outposts, Vietnamese district towns, and communications routes—but they still lacked the capacity to launch the final stage of general offensive to drive their opponents into the sea.[1]

To Vietminh leaders, the communist accession to power in China was a heaven-sent opportunity. For several years, they had struggled with minimal external assistance. The Soviet Union, despite statements of sympathy for struggles of national liberation in the official press, clearly viewed Indochina as an area of relatively low priority and in the early stages of the postwar era even viewed the Franco-Vietminh conflict as a potential obstacle to its goal of bringing the FCP to power in France.[2]

The arrival of communist power on the Sino-Vietnamese frontier thus offered the first serious prospect for external assistance to the Vietminh in their struggle against the French. The fear that China might benefit from instability in Indochina had been a factor in policy discussions in Washington almost since the end of the Pacific war. Now that power in China was in the hands of the vocally anti-Western Mao Zedong and his colleagues, the anxiety level in Washington, as in London and Paris, rose several notches and would provide an ominous backdrop to policy considerations in the region for the next several years.

Fears in Western capitals about the danger of a militant alliance between the new communist regime in China and the Vietminh were somewhat misplaced. During the two decades since the formation of the ICP in February 1930, relations between the two communist parties had been friendly but not close. The CCP had been intimately involved in the founding of the Vietnamese revolutionary movement in the 1920's, when radical activists under Ho Chi Minh sought refuge in South China and received their initial training in Marxist doctrine and revolutionary tactics at the famous Whampoa Academy in Canton, run by the CCP with Comintern support. That initial relationship, however, had been ruptured in 1927 when the Kuomintang-Communist alliance came to an end after Chiang Kai-shek's forces massacred communist demonstrators on the streets of Shanghai. After the CCP moved its headquarters to North China in the mid-1930's, ties between the two parties were almost nonexistent.

Relations between the two communist parties were gradually restored during and after World War II. Ho Chi Minh briefly visited Yan'an on his return to China from the USSR in 1938, and during the next several years he served with CCP units in various capacities in Central and South China. In 1940, he resumed contact with ICP leaders inside French Indochina, and during World War II his movement received some token assistance from Chinese groups sympathetic to the CCP. At the same time he borrowed selectively from Maoist revolutionary strategy and tactics and translated Chinese pamphlets on guerrilla warfare for the use of Vietminh units in Indochina.[3]

Until nearly the end of the decade, however, Chinese Communist assistance to the Vietminh was minimal. During the late 1940's, CCP leaders were preoccupied with the civil war in North and Central China, and there are few documented contacts between the two parties except for local units of the CCP operating near the Vietnamese border. There were unconfirmed intelligence reports, however, of Sino-Vietnamese agreements providing Chinese aid to the Vietminh. Still, Ho Chi Minh was careful to keep his options open and did not offer congratulations to the new government in Beijing until late November 1949, after Kuomintang units had been defeated by communist forces along the border.[4]

The situation began to change in mid-1949. According to a U.S. diplomatic source, Vietminh radio announced in April that units of the People's Liberation Army had arrived at the border and were providing "important support" to the Vietminh. That report may have been issued more to build up morale among revolutionary forces in Vietnam than to reflect reality, but it portended the possibility of increasing support in the future.[5]

The first public indication of the attitude of the new government in China to the conflict in Indochina came in November, when CCP leader Liu Shaoqi, in a widely reported speech at an international trade union congress held in Beijing, announced that the new People's Republic of China (PRC) would provide active assistance to national liberation movements in neighboring countries. He specifically mentioned the struggles in Indochina and Malaya. At a second speech later in the month, Liu called on the Chinese people to give support to the oppressed masses in the colonial countries of Asia and Australasia.[6]

In December Western intelligence sources reported the presence of a DRV military delegation in China, and in January Vo Nguyen Giap reportedly negotiated an aid agreement with the new government in Beijing. On January 18, 1950, the PRC recognized the Democratic Republic of Vietnam as the legal government of Vietnam (Moscow followed suit just two days later), and Ho Chi Minh traveled to the Chinese capital in March to sign the aid agreement.[7]

The precise scope of the agreement has never been divulged, although according to a recent Chinese publication it provided both for material assistance in the form of weapons, ammunition, and war material and for Chinese advisers and training for Vietminh troops. To facilitate the movement of men and matériel into Indochina, the Chinese began to build a series of roads, airfields, and supply dumps along the frontier. The effect of the new agreement was almost immediate. According to Western intelligence sources, in March alone the Vietminh received over 50,000 rifles and other weapons from the PRC.[8]

The new relationship with China soon exerted a visible influence on Vietminh policy and strategy. During the next few months, the DRV announced a number of institutional changes patterned on the Chinese model, and Western intelligence sources reported that "pro-Chinese" elements were occupying an increasingly dominant position within the front and the party. Vietminh sources also announced that the DRV had abandoned its policy of neutrality in the Cold War and had joined the democratic front led by the Soviet Union. New alignments in the government showed a stronger position for the communists.[9]

Washington Takes the Plunge

The communist victory in China and the prospects of increased Chinese aid to the Vietminh accelerated the sense of urgency in Paris regarding the need to complete the process of "perfecting" Vietnamese independence within the French Union and soliciting assistance and recognition for the Bao Dai government from the United States and other friendly nations. The Elysée Accords received final ratification by the French National Assembly on January 29 and were signed by President Auriol on February 2. The French government immediately appealed for diplomatic recognition for the new state and requested economic and military assistance from Washington.[10]

The Truman administration had delayed granting full diplomatic recognition to the Bao Dai government for several reasons. Washington officials hoped that postponement of the decision would apply pressure on the French to grant more meaningful concessions and interpret the agreement in a liberal manner. In particular, they hoped that Paris would issue a timetable for progress toward independence at the time of ratification. The delay may also have reflected continuing doubts about the viability of the Bao Dai government and its chances for survival in a hard-fought struggle with the Vietminh. Finally, administration officials were convinced that U.S. recognition would be more meaningful if it were preceded by a similar gesture from Asian nations such as India, Thailand, and the Philippines.

During the past several months, the administration had been lobbying governments in the region to grant recognition to the new associated state. Some, like Thailand and the Philippines, were reluctant to act, in the conviction that Bao Dai was a French puppet. India flatly refused because Nehru was convinced that Bao Dai lacked the character and the ability to counter the Vietminh, whom he viewed as the legitimate representatives of Vietnamese nationalism. The British had tried to help out by lobbying at a meeting of the Colombo nations but had no success because most Asian members were convinced that Bao Dai had no chance of survival.[11]

A CIA report dated February 10, 1950, confirmed such doubts, predicting that Bao Dai had little chance of winning the political support of an "appreciable fraction" of the resistance movement. The "great mass" of supporters, it said, would probably stay with the Vietminh. But Washington officials may have been more struck by another part of the report which noted that Soviet recognition made it clear that the Kremlin was prepared to exert greater pressure to install communist regimes in Indochina. Such fears may have been shared by Dean Acheson, who appeared exasperated by Asian reluctance to support Bao Dai, an attitude which, in his view, showed a lack of understanding of Ho's communist connections, with all the "sinister implications involved." William Lacy, who had replaced Charles Reed as director of the Office of Philippine and Southeast Asian Affairs, complained that the Southeast Asians were "on the fence" and should be brought to see "who is not with me is against me." Lacy suggested that the United States might make it known that aid would be withheld from unfriendly or neutral states.[12]

Faced with resistance from neighboring states in the region, Acheson decided to move ahead on recognition without them. He spelled out his reasons in a memo to President Truman on February 2. Recognition would encourage the nationalist aspirations of other noncommunist leaders in the region, establish stable noncommunist regimes near the Chinese border, support a friendly country in the NATO alliance, and demonstrate U.S. displeasure with communist tactics. In a cable to the U.S. Embassy in London, Acheson added that diplomatic recognition would give stature to Bao Dai in the eyes of noncommunist elements in Indochina. He rejected a British proposal to grant de facto recognition only as a bargaining ploy, arguing that the French had gone as far as they could for the moment.[13]

The proposal was unanimously supported by the cabinet and was formally approved by the president on February 2. Great Britain followed suit on the seventh, followed shortly by Australia and New Zealand. Most Asian governments, however, refused to follow Washington's lead. The first government in Southeast Asia to recognize the new Associated State was Thailand, but the decision, reached on February 28, split the cabinet and led to the resignation of Foreign Minister Pote Sarasin.[14]

In Paris, diplomatic recognition of the Bao Dai government was seen as only the first step in an effort to obtain economic and military assistance from the United States and other friendly nations for the struggle in Indochina. The French had broached the subject with U.S. officials early the previous year. In March, a French official had informally requested arms for the VNA, which, he said, would gradually replace the French Expeditionary Forces as the main force confronting the Vietminh on the battlefield. At that time, administration sources replied only that the issue was being studied. At the foreign ministerial talks in September, Foreign Minister Schuman raised the subject of economic aid, even if military assistance was politically impossible for the time being.

Washington had fended off all such appeals as premature. Then, on February 7, the French Foreign Office requested not only U.S. military assistance but also asked that the United States, the United Kingdom, and France undertake a joint review of the Indochina crisis in a global context, pointing out that Soviet and Chinese recognition of the DRV demonstrated that the French would be unable to resolve the problem on their own. A few days later Ambassador Bonnet followed up in Washington with a formal request to Acheson for military and economic aid, warning that without such assistance, France might have to withdraw from Indochina. He also mentioned French interest in holding joint staff talks to make a formal study of the military situation and asked for a tripartite declaration of solidarity against communist aggression. Acheson was noncommittal.[15]

The Truman administration was also under pressure from the British to achieve a measure of coherence in its Asian policy. Although the Labour government of Clement Attlee was opposed to a Pacific pact (which Nehru had publicly criticized as a "White Man's Pact"), some members of the Conservative Party, including Winston Churchill and Anthony Eden, had expressed themselves in favor of the idea, and similar sentiment for an anticommunist alliance also existed in other member countries of the Commonwealth such as Australia and New Zealand. Moreover, there was growing concern in British political and military circles over the Chinese threat to British possessions in East and Southeast Asia. At a conference of U.S. and British military leaders held in Singapore in November 1949, British representatives recommended that in the event of a Chinese attack the United States should fulfill its duty and assist the French in Vietnam.[16]

The French request for aid took place at a time when passions in Washington were inflamed by the issue of Formosa. Many Republican members of Congress, led by Senator William Knowland of California, were determined to force the administration to promise firm support to the Chiang Kai-shek regime. On another flank, Senator Joseph McCarthy of Wisconsin had just launched his attack on the loyalty of State Department China specialists such as John Carter Vincent and John Paton Davies. Acheson tried to hold his ground. In a widely reported speech before the National Press Club on January 12, he attempted to define administration policy in Asia. He pointed out that the United States was clearly committed to defend the Asian perimeter, by military force if necessary. But by implication he excluded Korea and Formosa. In Southeast Asia, he said, "the direct responsibility lies with the people concerned." Here the United States "could do no more than help."[17]

But conditions in Southeast Asia, not to speak of public attitudes in the United States, were beginning to call the offshore strategy into question. During his fact-finding trip to the area, Ambassador-at-Large Philip Jessup held talks with British commissioner to Malaya Malcolm MacDonald. The latter expressed his concern at the implications of Acheson's "island strategy," reporting that mainland Southeast Asia was in peril and an active role by the United States was needed to save it. MacDonald's somber message was reiterated at a conference of U.S. ambassadors held in Bangkok. Participants stressed to Ambassador Jessup that the mainland states were under heavy pressure and that the administration must do all in its power to save the region from communism.[18]

Jessup returned to the United States in mid-March more sensitive to the threat of communism in Southeast Asia and more inclined to take action to prevent it. He found that similar conclusions had been reached by many of his colleagues in Washington. In January, the Joint Chiefs, pointing out the crucial importance of Indochina to U.S. national security, had recommended the initiation of a modest aid program to help the new Bao Dai government. In response, Secretary Acheson had created a departmental study group composed of representatives from both PSA and the Office of Western European Affairs. The study group presented its report in early February, when it had become clear that the United States would recognize the Bao Dai government as soon as the French had ratified the Elysée Accords. Stressing the dangers of inaction in Indochina and pointing out that failure to help the French would severely damage U.S. security interests in Europe, the report recommended that military aid, not including U.S. troops, be made available to the French in Indochina out of MDAP funds.[19]

Two weeks later, the Bureau of Far Eastern Affairs produced its own report on the situation. The report emphasized that a purely military solution to the problem in Indochina was not appropriate because the key issues there were political and economic. But it conceded that without outside military assistance, the French, assisted by other indigenous noncommunist forces, would be unable to withstand the increasing threat presented by Vietminh units strengthened by aid from Communist China. It therefore recommended that both military and economic aid be provided to the new Associated States in Indochina as well as to the French. It proposed that as much aid as possible be provided directly to the local governments to avoid criticism that the United States was supporting French colonialism.[20]

On March 10, President Truman approved a grant of $15 million in military aid for Indochina and $10 million for Thailand. A discussion took place within the State Department over whether to continue to press the French to make an evolutionary statement before announcing the grant, and on March 29 Secretary Acheson tried again, pointing out in a message to the French that a large segment of public opinion throughout the world continued to regard the rulers of all three Associated States as French puppets and suggesting that the French government make a public declaration to convince the Asian countries that it intended to grant future concessions. But Paris refused, pointing out that such a statement would suggest that the existing accords did not constitute independence.[21]

While the administration continued to wrestle with the French, Washington officials also had to grapple with the problem of drawing up a coherent Asian policy. In late February, the NSC drafted a new policy statement labeled NSC-64 and sent it to the State Department for comments. The study painted a gloomy picture of the situation in Southeast Asia. Indochina, it pointed out, was under immediate threat from Communist Chinese forces across the border, and if it fell to communism, Thailand and Burma could be expected to fall in short order. The balance of Southeast Asia "would then be in grave hazard." To counter the danger, the NSC study recommended "all practicable measures" to prevent further communist expansion in the region and called on the administration to prepare "as a matter of priority a program of practicable measures to protect U.S. security interests in Indochina." In the new mood, the study was approved by the State Department with only minor changes.[22]

This was not enough for the Joint Chiefs, who wanted a stronger position. In their response, they concurred with the overall conclusions of the study and reiterated their conviction that mainland Southeast Asia was vital to U.S. national security. The area was of critical strategic importance because of its raw materials and its position as a crossroads between the Pacific and the Indian Ocean. The fall of Indochina would lead to the communist takeover of the remainder of mainland Southeast Asia. Japan, India, and Australia would be isolated, and the United States would be forced to use the Philippines and Indonesia as front-line bases for the defense of the Western Hemisphere.

Turning to policy considerations, the JCS took an even tougher line, arguing that the current situation, with small British and French contingents, supported by "small indigenous forces," was inadequate. The situation, they warned, was deteriorating, and without U.S. assistance, "this deterioration will be accelerated." They were thus led to adopt a more forceful position on the dangers inherent in the Indochina conflict than had been taken by the State Department. While conceding that in the long run, political and economic stability was the controlling factor, the JCS argued that the military situation in Indochina was of "pressing urgency" and required immediate action. They therefore proposed that programs to provide military assistance to Indochina and other nations in the area be approved and implemented as rapidly as possible and that funds that had been allocated for the region should be delivered by the earliest practicable date.[23]

But it was the State Department report, entitled "The Position of the United States with Respect to Indochina," that was adopted by the NSC on April 18 and signed by the president on the twenty-fourth, thus providing the first formal guidance for future policy on Indochina. The United States, for the first time, was committed to the defeat of communism in Indochina.

One of the problems for administration officials in providing aid was the question of how to balance the demands of the new government in Saigon with those of its patron in Paris. Bao Dai undoubtedly hoped to play off the United States against the French and in January had conveyed his own request for assistance to Philip Jessup, who was en route to the conference of U.S. ambassadors in Bangkok. A few days earlier he had named Nguyen Phan Long, a veteran journalist and longtime member of the noncommunist nationalist movement, as his prime minister. The appointment was undoubtedly made with the United

States in mind, for the new prime minister was known to be pro-American. Now Bao Dai's staff prepared a list of the new government's military and economic needs and presented it to Ambassador Jessup without the knowledge of the French. When the French became aware of Bao Dai's demarche, they responded with a memo demanding that all economic agreements between the United States and the Associated States be channeled through the French on the grounds that the latter would be actively involved in the management and distribution of the aid.[24]

That did not stop the Vietnamese. In late March, Defense Minister Phan Huy Quat outlined a plan for the United States to provide equipment, training, and advising to the VNA, an idea that Edmund Gullion, the U.S. chargé d'affaires in Saigon since the departure of Abbott, labeled "fantastic." To counter the Vietnamese, the French submitted their own requirements to Washington without consulting Saigon. Faced with two separate estimates, President Truman turned to the JCS, who declared that the French estimate was more realistic. The Joint Chiefs felt that aid to Indochina should have a high priority but that French requests should be carefully monitored by an interagency committee. They also suggested that a military assistance group be established in each Associated State to coordinate U.S. military aid with French operational plans.[25]

In the end, the three governments reached a compromise. The French agreed to provide the Vietnamese with an advisory role in submitting aid requirements to the United States, and a mixed Franco-Vietnamese Commission was established to receive and distribute equipment. French control over the entire process was implicit. In the process, Prime Minister Nguyen Phan Long had irritated both the French and militant Vietnamese nationalists and was forced to resign in late April. He was replaced by the veteran politician Tran Van Huu in early May.[26]

On one issue the French were disappointed. At a tripartite meeting of Western foreign ministers in May, Robert Schuman asked his British and American counterparts for a joint declaration to resist communism in Indochina, but British foreign secretary Bevin rejected the proposal on the grounds that it would have a negative impact among governments elsewhere in the region, and the idea was dropped. The final communique mentioned only support by the three Western powers for the independent nations of Southeast Asia.[27]

Implementing the Aid Program

While the Truman administration was debating how to respond to the French request for economic assistance, other officials were considering how to implement the program, should it be approved. In Bangkok, a conference of U.S. chiefs of mission recommended that primary emphasis be placed on Point

IV technical aid to increase the capacity of Asian states to help themselves. But a slightly different conclusion was reached by A. Robert Griffin, head of an economic survey mission sponsored by the State Department, which arrived in Saigon in March.

Griffin, a former official of the Economic Cooperation Administration (ECA) and currently publisher of the *Monterey Herald*, was optimistic about the Bao Dai government and felt that it was intensely nationalistic, but he also felt that it was fragile and was badly in need of prestige and a psychological shot of confidence if it were not to collapse. For that reason, he believed that the immediate purpose of U.S. aid should be to build up the local government through dramatic programs that could enhance its local and international prestige and bring immediate benefits to the local population. Long-range programs for rural rehabilitation and technical aid could follow later. Griffin recommended a total of $60 million for all of Southeast Asia, with $23.5 million earmarked for the three Indochinese countries.[28]

Griffin's recommendations were accepted by President Truman, and the aid program was approved by the White House on May 1. But as in the case of the military aid program, Washington, Paris, and Saigon differed over how to implement it. The ECA wanted to dispense aid directly to the Vietnamese, but the French insisted that they play an active role in distribution and management. A compromise was reached calling for the French and the Vietnamese to coordinate their efforts, but the United States agreed in a secret protocol that the French would be consulted at all times.[29]

The French were pleased with the aid agreement, and Foreign Minister Schuman promised to interpret the Elysée Accords in a liberal manner, but the reaction in Saigon was cynical, with many, including Bao Dai himself, expressing the view that the United States had given in to the French. Ambassador Bruce was exasperated with the Vietnamese attitude and lectured Bao Dai to stop being photographed hunting tigers and act like a commander in chief.[30]

By mid-spring, then, the United States was firmly committed to aiding the French in Indochina. The tentative quality of Acheson's famous press conference in January, when he had remarked that the Asian peoples must help themselves, had been replaced by a more activist approach whereby the Truman administration was categorically committed to defending the Indochinese countries from the threat of communism. In the process, the administration had apparently abandoned its effort to make U.S. aid conditional on concessions from the French. Testifying before the Senate Foreign Relations Committee in June, Dean Rusk, the newly appointed assistant secretary of state for Far Eastern affairs, explained that the United States must support the French in Indochina because without the French presence the communists would win. Asked to clarify U.S. objectives, he said that they were to support the Bao Dai government and the French until the former was a "going concern." In response to a further question,

Rusk added that he could not say how long the disorder would last, but he was not pessimistic about the prospects. Asia, he said, was waiting to see who won.[31]

Why had the Truman administration suddenly decided to extend its commitment to an area that had been considered to rest outside the U.S. defense perimeter as recently as January of the same year? One reason suggested by Dean Rusk's comments was a growing realization that the Bao Dai government was too weak to resist communist pressure without the presence of the French.

But perhaps a more important reason was to be found in the changing political climate in Washington, where attitudes toward the containment of communism had shifted dramatically since the beginning of the year. The "red scare" led by Senator Joseph McCarthy, along with the appearance of new faces such as Dean Rusk and Paul Nitze (who had just replaced George Kennan as head of the Policy Planning Staff) at the State Department signaled the emergence of a more aggressive approach to foreign policy symbolized by the approval of NSC-68 in April and the shift from an island strategy to a perimeter defense in Asia. Such attitudinal shifts undoubtedly provoked policymakers in Washington to take a new look at the situation in Indochina.[32]

Another factor that undoubtedly contributed to the hardening U.S. attitude on Indochina was the lengthening shadow cast by the new government of China. The communist ascent to power in Beijing, coupled with the recognition of the DRV by both China and the Soviet Union in January, put an increasingly global perspective on the events taking place in Southeast Asia and the ultimate implications for the United States. From Saigon, Edmund Gullion praised the decision to provide assistance to the anticommunist effort in Vietnam. Indochina, he said, was the focus of communist efforts in Asia as Greece was in Eastern Europe. If it were to fall, "most of [the] colored races of the world would in time fall to [the] Communists' sickle." Such fears were shared by voices in the U.S. media, and the decision to provide assistance was praised by none other than the *New York Times*.[33]

This shift in strategy indicated a reassessment of the nature of the threat posed by the forces of international communism in Asia. Previously, policymakers had seen the threat in somewhat selective terms. George Kennan had declared that the United States should defend only those areas vital to U.S. national security. Because American power was finite, other areas could be lost to the free world without a disastrous impact on U.S. national security. That view had governed the administration's approach to the Civil War in China.

By early 1950, however, a new factor had entered the calculations of policymakers in Washington. The position of the free world could be threatened, not only by a communist takeover of an area vital to the security of the United States, but also from the psychological impact of a communist victory anywhere in the region. That fear was especially evident in unstable areas such as Southeast Asia. Policymakers in Washington and other Western capitals expressed their concern that a Vietminh victory in Indochina could lead quickly to the fall of the entire region to the forces of international communism, thus weakening the position of the free world throughout Asia. Dean Rusk had alluded to that danger in his comments to the Senate Foreign Relations Committee in June that Asian opinion would be profoundly affected by the outcome of the war in Indochina. From here it was only a short step to the famous "domino theory" that would soon dominate U.S. foreign policy in Asia.

Drawing the Line

On June 25, 1950, North Korean forces crossed the thirty-eighth parallel in an invasion of the Republic of Korea (ROK) in the South. President Truman reacted quickly, ordering U.S. naval and air units to assist ROK forces in their hasty retreat down the peninsula. But the president and his advisers were concerned not only with the situation in Korea but also with its implications for communist moves elsewhere in Asia and even in Western Europe. At a meeting of key officials in the White House shortly after the attack, Dean Acheson suggested sending the Seventh Fleet to Formosa and stepped-up aid to Indochina. Truman agreed, declaring that the United States must "make a stand sometime or else let all of Asia go by the board." Much of this concern was a consequence of the panicked reactions from other world capitals, where government leaders voiced their concern that if the United States took no action in response to the invasion of South Korea, the rest of Asia could quickly collapse, with uncertain consequences for the Western position in Europe.[34]

Such concerns were probably on the president's mind when he declared that it was necessary to "draw the line at Indochina, the Philippines, and Formosa." On June 27 he ordered the U.S. Seventh Fleet to the Taiwan Straits to prevent a possible Chinese Communist invasion of the island, and on the same day he ordered an acceleration of U.S. military assistance to Indochina. During the next few days, U.S. aid through the Mutual Defense Assistance Program was increased by $16 million in accordance with recommendations by the Joint Chiefs, bringing the total amount of military aid to Indochina for the 1950 fiscal year to $31 million. On June 30, eight U.S. C-47 cargo planes with spare parts arrived in Saigon. More came later, when Congress passed a new general appropriations bill in September in which $13.5 million was scheduled for Indochina.[35]

The steady increase in military assistance during the last three-quarters of 1950 necessitated a serious look at the situation in Indochina. In July, a mission led by U.S. foreign service officer John F. Melby was sent to Indochina to study the overall military situation and make recommendations on how to maximize the effectiveness of the military assistance program. Melby, who had served in China during the crucial years immediately preceding the overthrow of the government of Chiang Kai-shek, was a cool and experienced diplomat who had shared Secretary of State Dean Acheson's view that the turmoil in Asia was a product of social and economic as well as Cold War causes.[36]

The Melby mission, including representatives from each of the military services, arrived in Saigon on July 15 and remained in Indochina for three weeks. The head of the military component was Marine Major General Graves B. Erskine. The mission report, submitted in August, echoed current administration views in asserting the importance of Southeast Asia to U.S. national security interests. And it accepted the new conventional wisdom in Washington and other Western capitals that the fall of Indochina would "inevitably precipitate the balance of mainland Southeast Asia into the communist orbit, including the possibility of the fall of Indonesia and the Philippines." But it broke with the official optimism that had marked much of the recent debate in Washington and painted a dark picture of the situation in Indochina. Vietminh strength was increasing and the French position, even in the vital Red River Delta, was precarious. French strategy under General Marcel Carpentier was essentially defensive and had allowed conditions in the area of the Chinese border to deteriorate. Carpentier appeared reluctant to use the new VNA units, probably out of fear (possibly justified) that its weapons would be turned against the French.

The Melby report also expressed concern over the political situation. The French appeared to believe that the problem could be solved by military force alone, ignoring the fact that the insurgency "was fueled as much by nationalist sentiment and hatred of the French as by stimulation from the outside." Bao Dai himself—who had returned to France in mid-June, allegedly to monitor the Pau Conference on the transfer of sovereignty—was "more confusedly irresolute" than ever and had totally failed to provide the new state with aggressive leadership. The report concluded by recommending greater use of Vietnamese forces, an effort to seal off the Chinese border, and more concessions on granting political autonomy to the Vietnamese government. It noted that the United States had only three alternatives—to cut its losses and disengage from the mainland, to engage in a holding operation until the situation changed, or to prevent a communist victory in Indochina at whatever cost on the grounds that the area was vital to U.S. national security. The Melby team clearly preferred the third alternative, on the grounds that Southeast Asia was vital to the United States because of its strategic location and natural resources.[37]

The Melby report reopened the debate within the administration over the proper tractics to use with the French and the wisdom of granting full-scale assistance to their operations in Indochina. It elicited a vigorous rebuttal from Donald Heath, a new U.S. minister in Saigon. Heath, a career diplomat who replaced Edmund Gullion in July, apparently viewed himself as a tough realist who, though occasionally critical of French failings, was convinced of the futility of pressuring Paris and felt that the primary need was to get on with the war.[38]

Heath was clearly put off by the implied pessimism reflected in the report submitted by the Melby mission, and in a series of cables to the department in August he took issue with some of its main conclusions. In his view, it was premature to write off the French effort and assume that the situation in Indochina had reached a stalemate. The French could be pushed to adopt a more aggressive attitude, but morale was still high and some progress was being achieved. French sources were confident that with U.S. aid and in the absence of overt Chinese intervention, the insurgency could be brought to an end within two years. Heath did agree that U.S. assistance should be used as a bargaining chip to force the French to accept Washington's advice and especially to move more rapidly to implement plans to create a Vietnamese National Army.[39]

Despite Heath's rebuttal, the Melby mission report was taken seriously in Washington. The issue was raised in a meeting of the Policy Planning Staff in mid-August and led to a discussion of the possibility of Chinese intervention. It was agreed that the United States would probably not send troops in the event of a Chinese invasion, nor (as the case of Korea had shown) would U.S. naval and air support be effective so the only solution was to persuade the French to adopt a new approach. If that did not work, the staff report concluded, the United States must reexamine its policy in Indochina.[40]

Others were even more pessimistic. In a memo to the assistant secretary of state on August 1, Charlton Ogburn returned to the attack, lamenting that Europeanists supporting the French position had left the United States with only two unattractive alternatives—abandoning the area to the communists or pouring dollars and lives into a losing cause. George Kennan agreed. In his own memo to Secretary Acheson on the twenty-first, he said that the French situation was hopeless and suggested that the only solution was to arrange a French withdrawal under some form of international auspices that could conveniently obscure the French defeat.[41]

The Melby report and the discussion it elicited prompted Secretary Acheson to send a cable to Saigon expressing U.S. concern at the deteriorating situation in Indochina and appealing for more action by the Bao Dai government and the French. Acheson suggested decisive action by both parties to create a dramatic effect on fence-sitters and prove the sincerity of the French commitment to the principles of the Elysée Accords. He concurred that the most essential step toward a psychological breakthrough would be to accelerate the development of the Vietnamese National Army, and he noted with approval the request of the new government of André Pleven to the National Assembly for additional funds to build up the VNA.[42]

Concern over the situation in Indochina was also increasing in the Department of Defense, where the Melby report had provoked an internal study by the

Joint Intelligence Committee. The committee's report, submitted on August 25, confirmed the conclusion of the Melby mission that Vietminh capabilities were increasing, and it predicted an enemy offensive during the fall. The JCS had already recommended a more active approach and urged that the United States provide tactical air and naval assistance to the French in the event of a Chinese invasion of Indochina. But civilian agencies rejected the proposal and brought about a compromise agreement that the United States should increase its aid to the French but not allow itself to be drawn into a general war with China.[43]

Such policy differences erupted in early September while Washington officials prepared for a meeting of the Big Three foreign ministers in the middle of the month. Responding to a State Department position paper calling on Secretary Acheson to press the French for political reform in Indochina, the Joint Chiefs declared that the recommendations included in the paper "[did] not reflect the urgency which, from the military point of view, should be attached to planning, preparing for, and providing adequate means to insure the security of Indochina." Pointing out the perilous nature of the situation, the JCS suggested that it "is to be viewed with alarm" and added that the French must take urgent and drastic action if they were to avoid a military defeat in the region. They recommended that the French be pressed to conclude the Pau talks immediately and to launch bolder measures. On the issue of joint staff talks, long proposed by the French, the Joint Chiefs asked that coordination not be limited to resources but also be extended to operations and recommended informing the French that additional aid would be provided compatible with U.S. capabilities and in accordance with plans acceptable to the United States. The mention of U.S. capabilities referred to military concern over the situation in Korea, and it was undoubtedly in this context that the Joint Chiefs suggested that Paris be informed that the United States "will not commit any of its armed forces under present circumstances."[44]

The meeting of the foreign ministers, held in New York City, took place in the shadow of the bitter battle of the Pusan perimeter on the Korean peninsula. Not surprisingly, the talks dealt with the situation in Asia but, despite prior indications, Secretary Acheson did not pressure the French on Indochina. The discussions on Indochina apparently centered on requests from the French. Pleven promised that they were determined to build up the VNA as a means of withdrawing their own troops, but he made it clear that they would need increased U.S. financial assistance in doing so. He also requested U.S. tactical air support in the event of a Chinese invasion and proposed tripartite staff talks for the coordination of military policy in the region. Acheson replied that the development of military forces in Indochina would receive high priority in Washington but that the administration required more information on French plans. He agreed to commence tripartite military talks as soon as feasible but rejected the French request for tactical air support.[45]

In the meantime, the running debate within the administration over Indochina policy was reflected in continued discussions over NSC-64, the document on U.S. Indochina policy that had been drawn up by the State Department early in the year. On October 11, a draft report by the NSC's Southeast Asia Aid Policy Committee was circulated to member agencies for consideration. The report reiterated the conclusions of NSC-64 that Indochina was of crucial strategic importance to U.S. security interests in Asia and that its loss would lead inexorably to the loss of all of Southeast Asia, but it rejected direct U.S. involvement under present circumstances. It recommended that U.S. forces not be committed to assist the French in case of overt foreign communist aggression, but that if such aggression occurred, the Department of Defense immediately be called upon to reassess the situation in light of new circumstances. It also called on the JCS to hold military talks with British and French military commanders in the Far East to work out a plan for the internal defense of Indochina and the coordination of any response to an outside invasion.

To at least some members of the JCS, such views did not reflect the urgency of the situation and the need for a clear U.S. policy. Army Chief of Staff J. Lawton Collins argued that a defeat in Indochina was "unacceptable, if we can possibly avoid it," and called for "all practicable measures" to deny the area to the communists, including "even the use of U.S. armed forces if the situation can be saved in no other way."[46]

The Vietminh Border Offensive

While officials at the State Department and the Pentagon were wrestling with policy alternatives, the anticipated Vietminh fall offensive erupted along the Sino-Vietnamese frontier. Rumors of a general offensive had been prevalent in intelligence circles since as early as May, in part because of the strengthening capabilities of the Vietminh, whose regular forces (now armed with Chinese weapons) were estimated at nearly 100,000 men, supplemented by an equal number of guerrillas. According to one estimate, nearly 10,000 had received training at recently established camps in China. During the late spring and summer, there were numerous intelligence reports of Chinese troop movements to the border area, as well as of the construction of transportation routes to the Vietnamese frontier. The Chinese apparently were careful, however, not to cross the border.[47]

From the Vietminh point of view, there was a strong logic for an attack on the Sino-Vietnamese border because it would facilitate the movement of supplies from China. The French had a string of base camps along the frontier, but they were poorly defended and there had been persistent rumors that General Carpentier intended to abandon them. If the border regions were to be taken over by the insurgent forces, some feared that the Vietminh could overrun the entire Red River Delta within weeks.

The border campaign began on September 17 and resulted in a heavy defeat for the French, who were badly mauled by Vietminh units attacking in regimental size for the first time. The French were forced to withdraw except for a lone redoubt at Mon Cay on the coast. Even at the time, the Vietminh fall offensive was seen as a significant event in the Franco-Vietminh War, and its impact on the political and military situation in Indochina was considerable. Not only did it serve to open up the entire region to Vietminh control and facilitate communications with China, it also opened a corridor to Laos and possible access to French positions in the Red River Delta and the urban centers of Hanoi and Haiphong. It was a serious psychological blow to the French, similar to the Tet Offensive during the American interlude nearly twenty years later. Like Tet, it revealed the unexpected strength of the Vietminh and the unlikelihood of a French victory unless Paris adopted a more offensive strategy. In short, it changed the entire strategic picture of the war.

The offensive shook the complacent mood in Paris. In mid-October, the Pleven government sent General Alphonse Juin, resident-general in Morocco, and Jean Letourneau, minister of state for the Associated States, to assess the situation in Indochina. The Juin-Letourneau visit led to the dismissal of General Carpentier (according to High Commissioner Léon Pignon, Carpentier's strategy was "so passive and defensive . . . that his qualifications for supreme military leadership must be questioned") and the decision to adopt a more aggressive effort to root out the Vietminh. The new commander in chief, General Jean de Lattre de Tassigny, also replaced Léon Pignon as high commissioner to provide him with increased authority and to eliminate the conflicts between civilian and political goals which had hitherto characterized French strategy. The French also promised to undertake a rapid augmentation of the size and role of the VNA and to offer political concessions to the Bao Dai government at the Pau Conference. The convention was finally signed in November.[48]

The new commander in chief, who had been in charge of French ground forces in Europe, arrived in mid-December with a mandate to reinvigorate the French effort in Indochina. De Lattre, whose dynamism and self-confidence were legendary, set the tone immediately by reversing a previous order to evacuate civilians from Hanoi and declared that the Tonkin Delta would be held and French units there would be reorganized for offensive operations. He also attempted to improve Franco-American relations. General Carpentier had complained publicly about the growing U.S. presence, placing severe restrictions on U.S. inspection trips and limiting U.S. contacts with the Vietnamese. De Lattre quickly relaxed such restrictions, and relations between the French and Americans in the area immediately improved.[49]

One final consequence of the Vietminh fall offensive was a French request for an additional increase in U.S. military aid. On October 12, Defense Minister Jules Moch appealed for the speedy delivery of U.S. equipment already budgeted and the immediate transfer of two squadrons of B-26 light bombers.

From Saigon, U.S. minister Donald Heath supported the request in a somewhat apocalyptic message pointing out that Washington had inadequately appreciated the danger of the present situation in Indochina and the importance of the area to "the eventual defense of the U.S." In a cable the previous day, he had painted the picture as "far graver" than the French had indicated and predicted that the loss of the entire frontier region was likely.[50]

The French request received a mixed reaction in Washington, where the intensification of the war in Korea raised anxiety over the capability of the United States to play an active role in Indochina. The Joint Chiefs questioned whether B-26s would materially aid the French, but they were overruled. Because of "political considerations," the White House ordered 21 B-26s to be sent immediately, with the remaining 9 to be provided the following year.

Under the surface, however, exasperation with the French and the Bao Dai government was mounting in Washington. On October 18, Secretary Acheson sent a message to Bao Dai, questioning the justification for his "pronounced holiday" in France and pointing out that his presence in Vietnam was vital. Two weeks later, he returned to the subject in a cable to Heath in Saigon, pointing out that it was not inconceivable that if Bao Dai's ineffectiveness continued, another "non-commie" Vietnamese nationalist leader might seek to replace him as chief of state and that the department might view such a development as "not obstructing the objectives we now seek."[51]

Acheson's anxiety about Bao Dai's effectiveness undoubtedly contributed to his growing unwillingness to pressure Paris. Despite de Lattre's efforts to placate the Americans, the U.S. mission in Saigon continued to complain about a lack of cooperation from the French. Acheson, apparently fearing the effect of criticism on French morale, said he would apply pressure only when the situation was favorable so as to encourage them to maintain their "primary responsibility" for the situation in Indochina. In an attempt to allay such criticism, Minister Letourneau made a statement in the National Assembly calling for independence "within the French Union" for the Associated States. At a press conference on November 27, Assistant Secretary of State Dean Rusk "welcomed" the announcement.[52]

The Vietminh fall offensive and the deteriorating situation in Indochina undoubtedly affected deliberations in Washington over policy in the region. The Joint Chiefs decided to delay their response to NSC-64 until hearing from General Francis Brink, chief of the new U.S. Military Assistance Advisory Group (MAAG) program in Saigon. But by the time they were ready to present their comments on the Southeast Asia Aid Policy Committee report, not only had the Vietminh launched their border offensive in Tonkin, but Chinese troops had intervened in Korea, adding to the Chiefs' reluctance to become more deeply involved in the conflict in Indochina. In their response in late November, the Chiefs now rejected General Collins's previous advice to consider the use of U.S. armed forces in Indochina, citing a report by the Joint Strategic Survey Committee that the introduction of such forces would be likely to lead to war with China and a possible global war in which the chief enemy would probably be the USSR and the principal theater of battle would be Western Europe. At the moment, the JCS argued, the strength of the Western alliance was insufficient to fight a war on both fronts.[53]

As a result, the Joint Chiefs now agreed with the draft report presented by the Southeast Asia Aid Committee in October that the United States should not at present become directly involved in the Indochina conflict. But the overall thrust of their argument was that the area was vital to U.S. national security interests and that the United States should take urgent action "by all means short of the actual employment of United States military forces" to prevent the fall of the area to communism. The key to solving the problem, they argued, was to give the people in the area something to fight for.[54]

The debate over U.S. Indochina policy in the fall of 1950 showed that mainland Southeast Asia was now increasingly seen, at least in the Pentagon, as vital to U.S. national security. The revolutionary movement in Indochina was viewed as a part of the worldwide conspiracy directed by the Kremlin, and the only reason to avoid the introduction of U.S. armed forces was to prevent war with China and to keep the French in the war.

A few voices were raised in protest against the expansion of U.S. involvement in the war. In November, John H. Ohly of the Office of International Security Affairs in the State Department called for a reappraisal of U.S. policy in Indochina. Pointing out that current policy would require expenditures of half a billion dollars in equipment and could have a substantial impact on U.S. military commitments in other theaters, he asked for a reassessment of U.S. goals in Indochina. Is the U.S. objective, he asked, to guarantee noncommunist control of the area, temporary noncommunist control, or just a continuation of the present situation? Does the United States have the manpower and the equipment to attain these objectives? Finally, do the French and the Vietnamese have the necessary will, morale, and leadership to continue the fight? Ohly's memo received short shrift from his superiors. The memo was answered by Deputy Assistant Secretary of State Livingston Merchant, who noted that the decision to aid the French had already been reached, and there was no point in reopening the issue.[55]

In Hanoi for Tet?

While officials in Washington debated over how best and how far to help the French in Indochina, Vietminh military strategists were making plans to drive the French out of Southeast Asia and bring the conflict to an end. An aid agreement had been signed with China calling for military assistance, the creation of a joint general staff, and possible coordinated activities. As a result of their successful border offensive the previous fall, the Vietminh now controlled virtually all the frontier region and had opened up communications with Communist Chinese forces. Much of North Vietnam was now in Vietminh hands. According to U.S. minister Donald Heath, all of the North except the Hanoi-Haiphong beachhead in the lower Red River Delta must now be written off, and even in Hanoi the situation was perilous. There were 185,000 Chinese troops on the border and rumors of a possible Chinese invasion. According to a National Intelligence Estimate (NIE) issued by the CIA in late December, there was "only a slight chance" that the French could maintain their military position long enough to build an independent Vietnamese government and a Vietnamese National Army.[56]

The political situation was equally unsatisfactory. French morale was deteriorating, and Bao Dai continued to display his customary lack of zeal. No amount of persuasion, lamented Heath, could spur him on to a sense of urgency and, as a result, no good men were willing to serve in his government, still under Prime Minister Tran Van Huu. Heath had appealed to him to create a provisional National Assembly, but Bao Dai had refused to hold elections. There were other potential sources for noncommunist leadership in Vietnam, including leaders of the VNQDD and the Dai Viet political parties, but in the view of most U.S. officials, they were not an impressive lot. Then there was Ngo Dinh Diem, a Catholic from Central Vietnam who had once served in Bao Dai's cabinet before World War II. He was a staunch nationalist and anticommunist and had political ambitions, but he was vague, obtuse, and wordy (the U.S. diplomat Edmund Gullion had described him as "monkist").[57]

In Vietminh headquarters north of the Tonkin Delta, such conditions were a promising augury of things to come. General Vo Nguyen Giap, chief architect of the 1950 border campaign, had designed it as a preparatory step to a large-scale general offensive to take place early the following year. Ho's military strategists, assisted by Chinese advisers, had been debating over the proper time to shift to the final stage of Maoist people's war since the spring of 1950. In his own account of the period, General Giap says that he and his colleagues had been speculating on the requirements for an offensive. Did the Vietminh need to have superiority throughout the entire battlefield? That could be a problem because insurgent activities had achieved relatively little success in the central and southern provinces, and an offensive launched by the southern Vietminh commander Nguyen Binh in early 1950 had been dealt a severe defeat by the French. Or, given the low state of enemy morale in the North, could the Vietminh succeed with local superiority in a given area? They eventually agreed on the latter and during the winter drew up plans for a series of attacks on the fringes of the Red River Delta designed to culminate in an attack on the city of Hanoi itself.[58]

The offensive opened in mid-January with an assault on the northwestern corner of the Red River Delta near the provincial capital of Vinh Yen. Fifteen Vietminh battalions, using Chinese human-wave tactics, descended from the surrounding mountains to attack French positions near the town, and the first press reports predicted that the defenders would be quickly overrun. But General de Lattre acted quickly, launching air raids that drove the Vietminh troops back with heavy losses. Later attacks on the fringes of the delta were similarly thrown back with heavy casualties. The failure of the campaign to achieve its objectives must have been a bitter disappointment to Vietminh strategists. Vietminh radio broadcasts had been openly boasting about the forthcoming attack for weeks, and some had proclaimed that Ho Chi Minh "would be in Hanoi for Tet" (the traditional Vietnamese New Year's holiday, based on the Chinese lunar calendar).[59]

In late February, while the 1951 general offensive was still under way, the party held its Second National Congress (the first had been convened at Macao in March 1935) at Tuyen Quang, in the heart of the Viet Bac. The timing of the congress suggests that party leaders had anticipated celebrating a major victory. As it was, the convening of the congress marked the beginning of a new stage in the history of the communist movement. It also signaled the growing influence of China on Vietminh policies.

Vietnamese sources have been consistently reticent about the Second Congress and what it meant for Sino-Vietnamese relations, but it seems clear that Chinese leaders had been implicitly critical of Ho Chi Minh's decision to place the issue of national independence over the antifeudal struggle in Vietnam and had probably advised him at the time of his 1949 and 1950 visits to Beijing that a stronger emphasis on class struggle was necessary to mobilize support from poor peasants and workers against the Bao Dai regime and its French sponsors.

The reappearance of the Communist Party in a new guise at the Second National Congress was almost certainly at least in part a result of Chinese advice. During the nearly six years since the dissolution of the ICP in November 1945, the party had continued to operate in secret, but its role as the vanguard element in the anti-French struggle had not been openly publicized. The public disappearance of the party undoubtedly helped to win support for the Vietminh cause from moderates, but it may also have aroused criticism from those who were convinced of the need for a stronger ideological focus within the movement. It is likely that Beijing added its weight to such concerns, and at the Second Congress the party was publicly reborn. In a keynote speech at the Congress, General Secretary Truong Chinh (often identified by Western intelligence analysts as a member of the "pro-Chinese" wing of the party) declared that after victory over the French had been achieved, the DRV would establish a "people's democratic dictatorship" on the Chinese model and advance toward the construction of a fully socialist society. Whereas a few months previously Ho Chi

Minh had sought to give an American reporter the impression that his government would adopt a neutral position in foreign affairs, now that the United States was openly helping the French there was no longer any reason to cultivate the image of neutrality in the Cold War. In deference to its new sponsor, the DRV would now openly lean in the direction of the socialist camp.

While responding to Chinese advice to move the course of the Vietnamese revolution decisively toward the left, party leaders sought to guarantee that the new orientation would not undermine the struggle for national independence. This determination was reflected in the name of the new organization—the Vietnam Workers' Party (Dang Lao Dong Viet Nam, or VWP). In the first place, the adoption of the term "workers' party," though reminiscent of parties that had recently been established in the people's democracies in Eastern Europe, represented a patent effort to allay concerns both in Vietnam and abroad as to the radical character of the party leadership and to convey the impression that the communist stage of the revolution would lie in the distant future. In the second place, the replacement of the geographical term "Indochina" for the more emotive "Vietnam" was designed to underline the importance of the national struggle in the current phase of the Vietnamese revolution.

Debate over the proper nomenclature for the Communist Party had a long history in the Vietnamese revolutionary movement. At the founding meeting of the party in February 1930, Ho Chi Minh had selected the title "Vietnamese Communist Party" for the new organization. The following October, however, the name had been changed to the Indochinese Communist Party at the instructions of the Comintern. This decision had aroused misgivings among some members of the revolutionary movement, who feared that the new name would reduce the party's appeal among patriotic elements in Vietnam, but the prevailing opinion in Moscow was that class struggle should take precedence over national independence as the guiding issue for revolutionary forces in colonial societies. Comintern strategists also believed that the liberation of colonial peoples from European rule could be realized only if they allied together in larger groupings against their more powerful adversaries.

In accordance with Moscow's guidelines, in 1935 the party had announced that after the eviction of the French, a closely knit Indochinese Federation (presumably under Vietnamese guidance) of the revolutionary governments in the three countries would be established. During the remainder of that decade, however, ICP activities in Laos and Cambodia had been minimal. The situation began to change after World War II, when nationalist sentiment appeared in both protectorates and Vietminh strategists began to see the importance of establishing a presence throughout Indochina to compel the French to disperse their forces. In 1950, national united fronts subordinated to the Vietminh Front were established in both countries. A Vietminh training document obtained by U.S. diplomatic sources that same year directed that revolutionary forces in

Vietnam, Laos, and Cambodia should cooperate in a common struggle to fight the invader, applying directives according to the situation in each country. Still operating under the guidelines established in 1935, that document declared that after victory over the French, an Indochinese Federation consisting of all three countries would be formed on a voluntary basis. During the next few months, guerrilla forces (popularly known as the Pathet Lao and the Khmer Issarak respectively) were formed and began to cooperate with Vietminh units operating in Laos and Cambodia.[60]

The next step came at the Second National Congress held in February 1951, when the old ICP was divided into three separate organizations—the Vietnam Workers' Party and "People's Revolutionary Parties" in Laos and Cambodia. Internal party documents make it clear that the decision to establish three separate parties had been made in response to growing nationalist sentiment among party members of Lao or Cambodian extraction. According to one internal party document written at the time, a failure to create three separate parties would

have prejudiced the support given by the Vietnamese revolution to the revolutions in Laos and Cambodia. The nationalist elements of Laos and Cambodia might have suspected Vietnam of wishing to control Laos and Cambodia. The band of imperialists and puppets would have been able to launch counter-propaganda destined to separate Vietnam from Cambodia and Laos, fomenting trouble among the Cambodian and Laotian peoples. Such an atmosphere of distrust could have harmed the unity of these nations in their fight against the French.[61]

There is no indication that China played a role in the decision to separate the old ICP into three separate parties. But there is little doubt that such a decision corresponded to Beijing's interests in the area. As later events would show, Chinese leaders were determined to prevent Vietnamese domination over the area and could not have been entirely pleased at the close relationship among the three Indochinese revolutionary parties. For their part, Ho Chi Minh and his colleagues made it clear that they intended to subordinate the new revolutionary organizations in Laos and Cambodia to the overall direction of the VWP. According to the document quoted above, the VWP reserved the right to supervise the activities of the other two parties and set up a special bureau under the Central Committee to handle Laotian and Cambodian affairs. Although China and the DRV were firmly linked by their common opposition to the forces of Western imperialism in Southeast Asia, the stage was set for a confrontation between the two in the future.[62]

Continued Uncertainty in Washington

In Washington, the failure of the Vietminh offensive brought a much needed burst of optimism in the midst of the generally dismal news from

Korea. But it was only a single ray of light in an otherwise gloomy picture. Although de Lattre's dynamic leadership was refreshing, he lacked political backing in France to take vigorous action to follow up the victory. Bao Dai continued to suffer from a narrow political base. After the dismissal of Nguyen Phan Long the previous spring, he had appointed Tran Van Huu, a wealthy Cochinchinese, as the new prime minister. Huu was a man of the people with antimonarchist leanings but was widely considered to be corrupt. In February, Huu attempted to form a broad-based government including a wide spectrum of political and social forces in the country, but most of the noncommunist political parties and the religious sects refused to participate, and when his cabinet was finally announced, the majority were pro-French elements from the South. The new government made little effort to deal with pressing issues of land reform and political democratization.[63]

The depressing conditions in Indochina forced the French government to swallow its pride and turn to its allies for aid. In talks with President Truman in late January, Premier André Pleven appealed for more U.S. assistance and coordination of military plans in the Far East. Truman was cautious, promising only that the aid program would continue as planned, barring unforeseen developments. He was not prepared to commit U.S. ground forces in the Indochina theater but would consider offering logistical support if the French decided to evacuate the delta. He rejected Pleven's appeal to create a tripartite Southeast Asian military command but agreed to U.S. participation in joint staff talks.

The Truman administration had been considering the possibility of staff talks since the previous September, when Foreign Minister Robert Schuman had raised the issue in New York. In December, Defense Secretary George C. Marshall had asked the Joint Chiefs for their views. With Korea still in the balance, they had advised against joint staff talks for the time being, but when Secretary Acheson argued that political considerations were overriding, they agreed to take part, so long as the talks did not deal with matters of strategy affecting U.S. global policy.[64]

It was a time of deep concern in Washington and other Western capitals over future prospects in East and Southeast Asia. Under the pressure of the Chinese offensive in Korea, the NSC briefly considered pulling United Nations troops out of the peninsula and reordering military priorities in Europe. The prospect of a French defeat in Indochina raised fears that the entire region might ultimately fall under some form of communist domination. One outspoken proponent of this view was Assistant Secretary of State Dean Rusk. In a memo to Deputy Under Secretary of State H. Freeman Matthews in late January, Rusk argued that it was generally acknowledged that the fall of Indochina would be followed in short order by the collapse of noncommunist governments in Burma and Thailand. It would then be difficult or impossible, he argued, for such newly independent countries as India and Indonesia to remain outside the Soviet camp.

A National Intelligence Estimate, issued on March 20, was more cautious, concluding that a victory by the Vietminh in Indochina would result in "increasing intimidation and subversive activity" in Thailand and Burma but not necessarily in the early establishment of communist governments in those two countries. If China intervened in Indochina, however, both governments would be susceptible to outside pressures and be obliged to seek accommodations with communist powers. Such an eventuality would greatly increase security problems for the British in Malaya.[65]

To the authors of the NIE, the key to the situation in Southeast Asia hinged on the possibility of Chinese intervention, a concern that had undoubtedly been heightened by the entry of Chinese forces into the Korean conflict. But top administration officials were not yet prepared to take action to dissuade Chinese leaders from intervening in Indochina. When U.S. minister Donald Heath supported a French request that the United States warn Beijing of the consequences of a Chinese attack, the State Department replied that such a statement could not be made at that time, although it was evaluating the situation and would keep him informed.[66]

Washington was not simply avoiding the issue. During the early spring of 1951, administration officials were engaged in a reappraisal of NSC-48, the existing statement of U.S. Asian policy that had been approved by President Truman in December 1949. An NSC staff study amending that document and approved by the president on May 17, 1951, had stressed the long-range importance of denying mainland Southeast Asia to the communists and called for a continuing program of U.S. assistance to keep the French from abandoning the struggle in Indochina. But it had also emphasized the limited nature of the U.S. role in the region. It was "not now in the over-all security interests of the United States to commit any United States armed forces to the defense of the mainland states of Southeast Asia. Therefore the United States cannot guarantee the denial of Southeast Asia to communism." According to the authors of the study, the main danger came from China. If Chinese forces attacked outside of Korea, the United States should consider a variety of responses, including a blockade of the Chinese coast and possible direct military action inside China. But the basic objective of U.S. policy must be to "continue its present support programs to strengthen the will and ability to resist communist encroachment, to render communist military operations as costly as possible, and to gain time for the United States and its allies to build up the defense of the off-shore chain."[67]

The Truman administration was thus not yet prepared to bear the primary responsibility for the defense of Southeast Asia against communist movements from within or outside the region. In Washington's view, that task was the responsibility of its allies—the French in Indochina and the British in Burma,

Malaya, and Singapore. If necessary, it was willing to accept the loss of much of the mainland to the communists. But Washington was willing to provide economic and military assistance to prevent such an eventuality and, if necessary, to stabilize a fallback position on the offshore islands.

One idea for strengthening Western defenses in Southeast Asia that had been under consideration in recent years was the proposal for a Pacific pact. The original idea had come from the anticommunist governments in South Korea and the Philippines, both of which were undoubtedly reacting to the formation of the North Atlantic Treaty Organization in Europe. The Truman administration had initially rejected the idea on the grounds that it would increase U.S. commitments in an unstable region of the world. But the issue had not died and was now revived in the unstable conditions surrounding the Vietminh offenses in Indochina. In December 1950 Secretary of State Dean Acheson wrote a letter to Defense Secretary George Marshall asking his opinion on a pact. The Joint Chiefs generally favored the idea but wanted the organization to be limited to island nations such as Australia, Japan, New Zealand, the Philippines, and possibly Indonesia. They specifically did not want Great Britain to be a member. On January 10, 1951, President Truman designated John Foster Dulles as his ambassador for defense arrangements in the Pacific region. Truman's letter to Dulles said that the United States was committed to the defense of Japan and was willing to consider a defense arrangement with Australia, New Zealand, the Philippines, and perhaps Indonesia.[68]

The British were irritated at being excluded from the proposed Pacific pact, not only because it implied U.S. unwillingness to assist in the defense of British possessions in the region but also because London was fearful that a "White Man's Pact" composed primarily of non-Asian nations would antagonize government leaders in the area and could have repercussions in Hong Kong and Malaya. But Washington was unmoved. Dulles rejected British proposals for a pact that would include states on the Asian mainland and said that the United States might consider the possibility of admitting the United Kingdom as a charter member of a consultation group to coordinate defense efforts in the region.[69]

In any event, the administration had little luck with Indonesia. The new government in Jakarta led by the nationalist leader President Sukarno was sensitive to the intentions of the Western colonial powers and preferred to maintain a position of neutrality in the Cold War. The government in Jakarta refused permission for a U.S. military mission under John F. Melby to visit Indonesia military installations. In the end, Washington abandoned the idea of a pact embracing both Asian and Western nations and signed a trilateral treaty with Australia and New Zealand (ANZUS) and reached separate bilateral security arrangements with Japan and the Philippines.

In the meantime, discussions on the coordination of mutual defense efforts between the United States, Great Britain, and France took place in talks held in

Singapore in May. The Joint Chiefs wanted to restrict the talks to matters dealing exclusively with Southeast Asia so as to keep their hands free in the event of global war. The chief U.S. representative at the conference, commander of the Seventh Fleet Admiral A. D. Struble, made it clear that he was not empowered to discuss "matters of strategy affecting United States policies and plans" and that the United States would make no commitments regarding areas currently under British and French administration. For the most part, the conference focused on the situation in Indochina. The conferees agreed that Tonkin was the key to Southeast Asia and that the French had sole responsibility for its security. But the potential Chinese threat to Burma and Thailand also came under discussion. The delegates agreed that although a Chinese invasion of Thailand was unlikely, if there were one, Thailand could not be defended. Struble asked for the views of his British and French counterparts on how to respond to such an attack, but they evaded the issue, describing it as a "political matter." In the end, the conferees reached no formal consensus but merely agreed to recommend periodic future meetings to discuss the regional situation and to exchange intelligence information on communist activity in the area.[70]

Resolving the Bao Dai Dilemma

By 1951, the Truman administration was firmly committed to the success of the Bao Dai experiment. With Cold War sentiment on the rise in the United States and Ho Chi Minh apparently settled in the socialist camp, Washington saw no alternative to supporting the Associated States of Indochina as a bulwark against communist expansion in the region.

It had been one of the fundamental goals of U.S. policy during the late 1940's to encourage the French to liberalize their policies in the area in order to mobilize the support of local nationalists for the government in Saigon, but the weakness of the Bao Dai government and U.S. preoccupation with the conflict in Korea limited the administration's options and made a continued French presence in Indochina vital to U.S. security interests in the area. Washington's growing dependence on the French obviously undermined its ability to pressure the Paris government to adjust its policies in the region.

It was a formula guaranteed to produce disharmony. By the summer of 1951 the military situation in Indochina had improved, and Washington began to focus on the role of the U.S. aid program. The agency responsible for administering U.S. economic assistance to the Associated States was the Economic Cooperation Administration in its new Saigon office headed by Robert Blum. Blum viewed the program as a means of building up the fragile confidence and enhancing the image of the Bao Dai government, and he hoped to strengthen the bilateral relations between the United States and the Bao Dai regime for that purpose even at the cost of friction with the French.

Blum, like many other U.S. officials stationed in Vietnam, believed in the importance of promoting U.S. democratic values. Some members of his staff were openly critical of French policies in the area and encouraged the Vietnamese to seek greater autonomy from Paris. High Commissioner de Lattre, a man of imperial pretensions and no little sensitivity to French prestige, took up the matter with U.S. minister Donald Heath, complaining that efforts by ECA officials to promote Vietnamese interest in U.S. culture were a gratuitous insult to the French "mission civilisatrice" in Southeast Asia. To emphasize his point, he refused permission for the governments of the Associated States to sign economic aid agreements with the United States until France had given its formal assent.

Donald Heath attempted to play a mediatory role in the dispute. In cables to Washington he noted that he shared some of his colleagues' criticism of French behavior and policies but that U.S. policy was to supplement, not to replace, the French. It was childish, he remarked, to think of the United States ousting the French and defeating the communists itself. Heath promised to discourage any member of his staff from encouraging the Vietnamese to seek to withdraw from the French Union.[71]

Blum had some supporters in Washington. In a memo to Dean Rusk, assistant director for non-European affairs in the Office of International Security Affairs Wade Bingham complained that Heath wanted to put U.S. officials stationed in Vietnam in a "hear no evil" situation that would weaken U.S. leverage with the French. It was hardly likely, he noted, that the French would either pull out of Indochina or refuse to accept U.S. assistance. Heath's cable also drew a response from Blum in Saigon, who said it was the Vietnamese, not the United States, who were undermining French rule. If strengthening the French was important, he added, strengthening the Vietnamese was even more crucial. It was important to be honest with the French, he concluded, and not apologize.[72]

The issue was eventually referred for decision to Livingston Merchant, deputy assistant secretary of state for Far Eastern affairs in the State Department. In a memo to Dean Rusk on July 27, Merchant temporized. Both sides in the debate had a point, he noted. Members of the U.S. mission should not publicly undercut the French, but de Lattre's imperious behavior had aroused the anxieties of many Vietnamese nationalists. He suggested that the department defer a decision until the visit of General de Lattre to the United States, scheduled to take place in September. Then it would be possible to assess the high commissioner's intentions.[73]

In the meantime, there were continuing strains in the field of military strategy. The appointment of General de Lattre as high commissioner and commander in chief of French forces in Indochina had been a tonic for French military fortunes and morale. The new commander had cleaned up the Red River Delta, reorganized French military forces, and markedly improved their future prospects. But the overall military situation was still weak, and the danger of Chinese intervention had not noticeably receded.

Washington had based its hopes on the French promise, incorporated in the Elysée Accords, to build a Vietnamese National Army. But progress had been slow. By May of 1951 there were still fewer than 40,000 men under arms, and of 34 battalions projected, only 24 were in existence. Only 7 had Vietnamese officers and, according to an American observer, few of these showed leadership capabilities. When recruitment efforts lagged, the Tran Van Huu government called for general mobilization, hoping to achieve the benefits of a shock effect, but U.S. officials were skeptical.[74]

General de Lattre arrived in Washington on September 13. If the aim of the Truman administration was to enhance coordination of the U.S. aid program and satisfy itself as to de Lattre's intentions, it was clearly the latter's objective to obtain increased U.S. assistance through talks with U.S. officials and public appearances before the American people. To that effort he devoted all of his ample charm and reputation. In talks at the White House and on television, he made a strong case for an increase in U.S. aid. While painting an optimistic picture of the situation in Indochina (he promised that if China did not intervene, the Vietminh could be eliminated in one or two years), in private talks with U.S. officials he complained about the slow delivery of items through MDAP and asked for additional equipment. He promised an increase in the size of the VNA but warned of the continuing possibility of Chinese intervention. The actions in Korea and Indochina, he pointed out, were all part of one war against communism and should be fought as such. Tonkin, he said, was the key. If the delta were to be lost, Indochina would "burn like a match." Then there would be no barrier to further communist expansion until the Suez Canal.[75]

Truman administration officials were not unprepared for de Lattre's request for additional U.S. aid because they had been warned by Donald Heath that he would be arriving with a shopping list. And there was some recognition in Washington that de Lattre had a point in complaining about the delay in deliveries of military equipment to Indochina. So Robert Lovett, who had replaced George Marshall as secretary of defense, promised to give sympathetic consideration to French requests for additional aid and to expedite the shipment of matériel already in the pipeline. But President Truman rejected de Lattre's request for a single logistical command in Asia, and the Joint Chiefs stated that although the United States recognized that Indochina and Korea were two parts of a single ideological struggle, "it would be wholly unacceptable . . . to attempt, under existing circumstances, to integrate the forces of the Western world engaged in the two wars."[76]

De Lattre's visit did serve to clarify some of the political issues that divided the two governments. In a meeting with the general on September 17, Dean Acheson attempted to reassure him about U.S. political objectives in Indochina, pointing out that the United States had no desire to replace the French or undermine the French Union. But he said that the administration needed reassurances as to the ultimate intentions of the French in the region and was convinced that it would be to the common benefit if the United States provided economic aid directly to the Associated States. De Lattre's reply was conciliatory. He had no objection to U.S. aid being funneled directly to the Associated States so long as it remained within the framework of the French Union. He did point out, however, that great harm could result if the "young missionaries" attempted to extend American influence in Indochina. In a reference to U.S. concern over the issue of greater autonomy for the Associated States, he pointed out that the French Union not only provided national independence but guaranteed it and was based on the idea of mutual assistance.[77]

The sense of optimism and confidence created in Washington by the dynamic presence of General de Lattre did not last out the year. During the fall, the long and bitter battle on the southern fringe of the Red River Delta at Hoa Binh, a battle labeled by the French scholar Bernard Fall as a "meat grinder," showed the continuing weakness of the French position in Indochina. De Lattre had ordered French forces to seize the city as a means of reducing the ability of the Vietminh to transport manpower and supplies from the southern provinces to insurgent units fighting in the North. The Vietminh counterattacked, and after an extended battle that was costly to both sides, the French finally withdrew in February 1952. In succeeding months, Ho Chi Minh's forces began to infest the Red River Delta, placing the metropolitan area of Hanoi under threat once again.

There were also disturbing signs of a lack of purpose in Saigon. On a tour through Southeast Asia in November, E. Allen Griffin, special regional representative of the ECA, stopped briefly in Saigon and reported that the real issue was not the French versus the Vietnamese but the lack of vitality, of public leadership, and of enthusiasm for improving the peasant welfare exhibited by the government of Prime Minister Tran Van Huu. The Huu government, he said, has no grass-roots appeal. It was not a servant of the people but represented the interests of landlords and government functionaries. So long as the Vietnamese government was composed of native mandarins, he warned, the revolution would continue.[78]

Griffin's comments provoked a testy reaction from Minister Heath in Saigon, who agreed on the inadequacy of the Huu government but questioned whether there were any alternatives. How could we press for the inclusion of popular leaders in the present government, he asked, when no leader with mass appeal would serve the present government on the basis of current Franco-Vietnamese relations? If such leaders existed, the French would not accept them, nor would they be proof against neutralism or Vietminh infiltration. Second, he pointed out that it was difficult to create a government based on popular suffrage during a civil emergency, and the United States could not accelerate the process without undermining the efficiency of the French. Heath recommended continuing efforts to provoke the Huu government into improving its own performance.[79]

Facing the Threat from China

Throughout the year 1951 the Truman administration had attempted to reinvigorate the French effort while avoiding an increased U.S. military commitment in Indochina. But both the British and the French continued to press Washington to commit itself, in accordance with the conclusions reached at the Singapore Conference in May, to tripartite talks on formulating joint strategy for the overall defense of Southeast Asia.

On October 30, the British Embassy in Washington, with the concurrence of the French, presented an aide-mémoire to the secretary of state proposing a tripartite meeting of the chiefs of staff during the upcoming NATO conference in Rome. The message noted that if China invaded Southeast Asia, outside forces would be needed and it would be desirable if the Western powers formulated a joint response. Acheson sent the British proposal to Defense Secretary Robert Lovett, who, after conferring with the Joint Chiefs, replied on November 19 that because it was U.S. policy to support anticommunist forces in Southeast Asia "by all means short of U.S. troops," there was no point in joint staff talks for the mutual defense of the area.[80]

But the British persisted, and after a meeting between Prime Minister Winston Churchill and Premier André Pleven in Paris in mid-December, the British ambassador returned to the subject, pointing out that while communism was being contained in Korea and Formosa and bilateral security treaties were being worked out between the United States, Japan, and the Philippines, no comparable arrangements were being established to the south. The British ambassador pointed out that neither France nor Great Britain, any more than the United States, was anxious to take on additional military responsibilities in Asia but that "no harm would come of exploratory talks" on issues of mutual concern related to the defense of Southeast Asia. Any discussions, he assured, would be purely exploratory and no participant would be committed to any course of action.[81]

The British appeal coincided with intelligence reports of Chinese preparations for a possible massive intervention in the Vietminh conflict. There were a reported 200,000 Chinese troops in Guangxi province, and Chinese aid to the Vietminh was on the rise. From Paris, Ambassador David Bruce reported that public support for the war in France was increasingly fragile and there were rumors of an impending pullout. On December 21, at a joint meeting representatives of the State Department and the Joint Chiefs of Staff held a wide-ranging discussion of current conditions in Southeast Asia and their implications for U.S. national security. The tone was set in introductory comments by Deputy Under Secretary H. Freeman Matthews, who portrayed a deteriorating situation in Indochina and the growing danger of a French withdrawal.

The focus of the meeting was on the danger of falling dominoes. Acting Assistant Secretary of State for Far Eastern Affairs John Allison declared that there was a real danger that all of Southeast Asia could be lost if Indochina went communist. Army Chief of Staff J. Lawton Collins was more skeptical. Though conceding that Burma and Thailand could probably not be held in the event of a Vietminh victory in Indochina, he insisted that because of its short defense line at the Isthmus of Kra, Malaya could probably be defended. But Collins painted a bleak picture of the political situation, warning that the defense of Indochina was a "one-man show." If de Lattre left, he warned, it could "go to pieces." That possibility incited Paul Nitze to remark that the adverse public consequences of a defeat in Indochina would be tremendous. That remark provoked a rejoinder from JCS chairman Omar Bradley, who said that he doubted that U.S. public opinion would "go along with the idea of going into Indochina in a military way." There was apparently no serious discussion of the possible introduction of U.S. combat troops because the issue was in the process of being investigated by an NSC study.[82]

Shortly after the joint State-JCS meeting, a message from French premier André Pleven arrived in Washington containing an appeal for a triparte conference on Indochina to be held at the earliest possible date. Convinced that U.S. officials were unaware of how serious the situation in Indochina really was, Pleven cited evidence of growing Chinese involvement in the conflict and pointed out that France did not possess the strategic resources to oppose a Chinese invasion. In a follow-up cable, Ambassador Bruce supported Pleven's views, noting that the French public had reached the point at which it might welcome a French abandonment of Indochina with "a sense of emotional relief." Although he did not feel that the French government would propose such a course of action in the near future, he warned that France could not bear its burden at the present tempo for more than another few months. Most French people agreed with their government that France was not just fighting for its own national interests but for the interests of all free nations. If the United States did not respond to French requests for additional aid, Bruce concluded, they might give up the struggle.[83]

Faced with political pressures from several directions, the Joint Chiefs abandoned their opposition to tripartite staff talks, and a conference attended by military representatives of all three countries convened in Washington in January 1952. The administration had intended to limit the talks to informal discussions dealing with measures to limit communist expansion throughout the region, but it soon became clear that the French were preoccupied with the possibility of Chinese intervention and wanted a U.S. commitment to provide air and naval support in that event. U.S. intelligence reports tended to discount the likelihood of direct Chinese involvement in the Indochina conflict, but the JCS felt that the Chinese threat was linked to the situation in Korea and were at least willing to discuss it.[84]

The administration was already discussing with other participants in the Korean conflict a statement that, in case of an armistice, Beijing would be warned that a renewal of Chinese Communist aggression in Korea would bring a U.N. reaction not necessarily confined to that area. Now the possibility of a similar warning on aggression in Southeast Asia was discussed. All agreed that this was an issue that should be considered by their governments, but the British and French representatives were apparently reluctant to discuss specific measures that should be taken in case China ignored such warnings. Among the measures raised were the use of atomic weapons, the imposition of a naval blockade of the Chinese coast, and the use of Nationalist Chinese troops. It was eventually agreed to turn the problem of retaliation over to an ad hoc committee composed of representatives of the three countries as well as Australia and New Zealand. It would be the responsibility of the committee to determine the capabilities of individual nations to participate in possible actions and to recommend military measures as a collective effort against China.

This decision was not sufficient for the French representative, General Juin, who was less interested in a warning to China than in a specific allied commitment of air and naval support in the event of a Chinese invasion. But General Bradley fended off Juin's request by pointing out that this was a matter that would have to be decided by civilian authorities.[85]

The conference thus adjourned without achieving any overall agreement on how to handle the possibility of Chinese intervention in the Indochina conflict. While awaiting a decision, the Truman administration decided for the moment to make a less dramatic warning. On January 28, 1952, John Sherman Cooper, the U.S. representative in the U.N. General Assembly, announced that any communist aggression in Southeast Asia would be a "matter of direct and grave concern which would require the most urgent and earnest consideration by the United Nations."[86]

A key problem that emerged from the joint discussions was that both the British and the French opposed U.S. proposals to respond to a Chinese attack with a blockade of the Chinese coast or any bombing campaign on the Chinese mainland except in direct support of operations close to the part of the border where the Chinese attack was launched. The French wanted to prevent their own forces from being diverted outside Indochina, while the British were anxious to avoid irritating Moscow and Beijing (the U.S. representative suspected that London was concerned that the Chinese would react to a military conflict by attacking Hong Kong or placing it under economic pressure). All rejected the use of Nationalist Chinese troops. In making his final report to the JCS, U.S. representative Vice-Admiral A. C. Davis noted that the committee had accomplished little. In fact, it highlighted a growing difference between the United States and its principal allies over how to handle the alleged Chinese threat to Southeast Asia. Reluctant to become directly involved in the military defense of the region, Washington wanted to avert the danger by attacking the source of the problem. London and Paris were fearful over the danger of an escalating war and wanted to limit it to the immediate area of Southeast Asia.[87]

The Pacific Pact Revives

In the meantime, the Western allies were no closer to an agreement over the advisability of forming a wide-ranging Pacific pact to protect noncommunist states in the region. Up through 1951 the administration had firmly resisted proposals to form such a pact involving mainland states in the region and had limited its offshore commitments to security arrangements such as the ANZUS treaty and bilateral agreements with the Philippines and Japan. But appeals from the British and the French for closer coordination of defense efforts in the region, combined with unhappiness in Bangkok that the United States had not agreed to consider security arrangements with Thailand, led to a reappraisal of the situation in Washington. In December, the State Department prepared a draft position paper on a possible Pacific security pact in preparation for an upcoming exchange of views with the British on the advisability of extending existing defensive arrangements in the area.

The paper was based on the prevailing assumption that while the maintenance of the offshore defense line—from Japan through the Ryukyu Islands and the Philippines to Australia—was vital to U.S. national security, the defense of the Southeast Asian mainland from communist domination, though highly desirable, was essentially the responsibility of the British and the French as well as of the Asian states in the area. Nevertheless, in deference to the feelings of U.S. allies, the paper expressed U.S. willingness "to consider the desirability of security arrangements either on a bilateral or multilateral basis, with countries of Asia other than those already aligned with the U.S., namely Japan, the Philippines, Australia, and New Zealand."[88]

The Joint Chiefs were not willing to be so forthcoming. In their comment on the paper written on December 28, they declared their firm opposition to any presently contemplated Pacific security pact along the lines of the NATO agreement. Current U.S. capabilities, they argued, "will not admit new arrangements or any extension of present arrangements in the Pacific area which would involve additional military commitments, particularly in view of the great extent and scope of present United States military commitments world-wide." Any extension of these commitments, they argued, must be preceded by an increase in U.S. military capabilities. Until the nations of the Pacific other than Japan, the Philippines, Australia, and New Zealand "have demonstrated the will and determination to develop the strength necessary to provide for their own internal security and to contribute at least to some extent to the security of the immediate area of which they are a part," the defense of the region should rest on collective measures under the aegis of the United Nations General Assembly. The result was a compromise. An amended paper written on January 2, 1952, replaced the phrase that the United States was willing to consider the desirability of new security arrangements in the area with a more general statement that it would "retain under active consideration" the problem of Pacific security in general and would give "eventual consideration" to proposals for security arrangements with Indonesia and the mainland states.[89]

The Debate over NSC-124

As 1952 began, the Vietminh were recovering from the debacle of the 1951 general offensive. During the last half of the previous year, they had begun to penetrate the southern portion of the Red River Delta and engaged the French in the grueling battle at Hoa Binh. The battle had resulted in heavy casualties on both sides, but its primary result was to undermine French morale in Indochina and provoke new reports of negotiations on a peace settlement. There was nervousness in Hanoi, and Donald Heath admitted that the battle at Hoa Binh had been a political and psychological reverse. The tonic that General de Lattre de Tassigny had provided to French spirits had dissipated.

The rapidly evolving situation in Indochina sparked demands from several quarters in Washington for a review of U.S. policy in Southeast Asia and the possible formulation of a new policy directive to supersede NSC-64, which had been approved in early 1950. The first step was an internal draft prepared by the NSC staff and submitted for consideration by the council on February 13. The study began with some familiar assumptions: the consequences of communist domination of Southeast Asia would be critical, both psychologically and politically, and would probably lead to "the relatively swift alignment of the rest of Asia and thereafter or [sic] the Middle East to communism, thereby endangering the stability and security of Europe." Tonkin was seen as the strategic key to the defense of Southeast Asia. If it were lost, the free world would be forced to adopt a policy of delaying action and perimeter defense of the coastal areas in preparation for evacuation. If Burma and Indochina were lost, Thailand would be exposed to infiltration and political pressure and Malaya placed under threat.[90]

The paper concluded that it was important to forestall communist aggression in Southeast Asia, but it appeared pessimistic about avoiding a disaster in Indochina. The military situation, at best, was a stalemate and there was no sign of political progress. Even worse, there was a real possibility that the French might opt for a diplomatic settlement that would probably lead to a withdrawal of their forces and a communist victory. But to the authors, the main danger was the possibility of Chinese intervention in the event of a peace settlement in Korea. The most effective means of deterring such intervention would be through a joint warning by the United States and its allies on the "grave consequences" of such action.

In exploring a variety of contingencies for U.S. action in Indochina, the authors declared that the United States should oppose negotiations leading to a French withdrawal. Should a withdrawal prove likely, the United States should seek maximum support from its allies for collective action to supplement the French, including the possibility of naval and air support, a naval blockade of China, or attacks on Chinese military targets. It would be desirable, however, to avoid the introduction of U.S. ground troops into Indochina. In the absence of an agreement for collective action, the authors concluded, the United States should probably not take unilateral action to prevent the fall of Indochina to the communists.

The NSC paper was circulated. In a response dated March 4, the Joint Chiefs pointed out that approval of the recommendations in NSC-124 would be dependent on political decisions as to whether the United States was willing to go to war with China to prevent Southeast Asia from falling into the communist orbit. They further noted that the British and the French opposed "even the concept of action against Communist China" except in the immediate area of aggression. Even if they should agree, they thought almost exclusively of defense of Western Europe and Southeast Asia, and their unwillingness to take measures in Southeast Asia indicated that "they may not recognize the actual long-term danger to themselves involved in the possible loss of Southeast Asia."[91]

To the Joint Chiefs, however, the situation in Indochina was different from that in Korea, in that any restrictions that would limit allied military actions to the immediate area would make it wholly defensive and consequently indecisive and prolonged. They thus recommended that any military measures taken to prevent China from controlling Southeast Asia by force of arms "should, from the outset, be planned so as to offer a reasonable chance of ultimate success." Military operations in Southeast Asia must therefore be accompanied by military action against the source of that aggression, namely Communist China itself. The JCS warned that such actions might be long in duration and expensive.[92]

In effect, the Joint Chiefs opposed acceptance of commitment under NSC-124 without a clear understanding that the United States must be accorded freedom of action, including operations against China. They repeated their warning that such action would risk global war and would be opposed by U.S. allies but stated that the United States should be willing to take such action unilaterally, if necessary. If not, they recommended that the United States should accept the possibility of the loss of Indochina, Thailand, and Burma to the communists.

Although these comments had focused on the issue of dealing with the possibility of Chinese intervention in the Indochina conflict, the Joint Chiefs felt that by far the greater likelihood was that the area would succumb to subversive tactics. They predicted that even without overt Chinese aggression it was still probable that before long the French would be unwilling or unable to carry on the war. They recommended increased U.S. military assistance as a means of forestalling such a likelihood but reiterated that the defense of the area was a French responsibility. U.S. ground forces, they said, should not be committed in Indochina, Thailand, and Burma, nor should the United States join in a combined military command for the defense of those countries.

A National Intelligence Estimate prepared by the CIA the day before tended to support the JCS arguments. It said that China had the capability to support 150,000 ground troops in Indochina but predicted that it would not intervene in force for the moment, although it could expand its assistance to the Vietminh and might introduce "volunteers" in small numbers. The NIE predicted a gradual deterioration in the military situation but no decisive victory for the Vietminh in the near future. The long-term outlook was for the increasing effectiveness of Vietminh forces leading to the growing possibility of a French withdrawal.[93]

The views of the Joint Chiefs were presented at a meeting of the NSC on March 5, but no final decisions were taken. Secretary Acheson complained that the military presented a chicken-and-egg problem. Possible courses of action could not be studied with a political decision, he noted, but it was hard to reach political decisions without a knowledge of the military capabilities to support certain courses of action. He predicted further deterioration of the situation in Indochina and said that the problem for the French was that they could not meet their commitments to NATO and Indochina at the same time. Acheson recommended a staff study to assign priorities and asked the Joint Chiefs to look further into possible military courses of action in Indochina.[94]

One of the few decisions taken at the meeting of March 5 was to call for further comments from appropriate branches of government. In late March the Policy Planning Staff offered its contribution to the debate in the form of a paper drafted by Charles Stelle. Stelle conceded that the area was one of significant political and economic importance to the United States and that the fall of Indochina would have "major political and psychological consequences for the West." He agreed that the current situation was unsatisfactory, with a stalemate on the battlefield and a visible decline in French will. He pointed out that the Associated States would face severe difficulties in achieving political stability even in the absence of communist military activity. Given the presence of a militarily powerful Vietminh, there was no guarantee that even increased U.S. involvement would necessarily stabilize the situation or prevent the United States from facing the stark choice between employing its own armed forces or accepting communist domination of the area. Even should the French with U.S. help manage to defeat the Vietminh and create conditions for the establishment of viable Western-oriented states in Indochina, there was a distinct possibility of Chinese armed intervention to prevent such a contingency.[95]

In considering U.S. options, Stelle found no magic panacea to solve the problem. The introduction of U.S. ground troops, he said, was not the answer because it risked provoking direct Chinese involvement. Beijing had demonstrated its sensitivity to the presence of U.S. forces near the Korean border, and it must be assumed that China was equally sensitive in the South. Moreover, it would relieve the French of their responsibility for the area. A truce along Korean lines was not a solution because the opposing forces did not face each other across a clear line of battle and it would be difficult to set up safeguards when there was no front to patrol. Stelle found little promise in inducing the French to grant additional political concessions to the Associated States because they already had more privileges than they could use. His conclusions were hardly startling: an increase in U.S. economic and military assistance to the Associated States to encourage them to broaden their political base of support but no introduction of U.S. forces to relieve French responsibility for the area.

To the Joint Chiefs, such recommendations were not particularly objectionable, but they did not offer a new approach, only the implementation of the present policy with variations. Moreover, the JCS took issue with Stelle's remark that the introduction of U.S. armed forces would be an undesirable course of action, contending that air and naval forces could be used effectively to offset the psychological presence of China in the vicinity as well as serve as a deterrent to the spread of communism elsewhere in the region. They also felt that Chinese intervention in the event of the introduction of U.S. armed forces was possible rather than probable and that more attention should be given to U.S. courses of action in the event of a French withdrawal. The Joint Secretaries were also unhappy with Stelle's paper, arguing that it was directed at preserving the status quo. They recommended their own program, calling for an expansion of the Military Assistance Advisory Group, the gradual phasing out of the French, and pressure on Paris to promise self-determination at a stated time.[96]

Faced with a multitude of objections from the Pentagon, the State Department sought a compromise. In a memo presented to Secretary Acheson on May 7, Assistant Secretary John Allison said that most of the differences between the two versions could be reconciled but that it was inadvisable to make contingency plans in the event of a French withdrawal because it was impossible to anticipate the surrounding circumstances. Allison had strong reservations about the proposal submitted by the Joint Secretaries. A set timetable for independence, he said, would be "dangerous in the extreme" because it would only encourage the French to retreat. There was no alternative to helping the French and persuading them to move gradually along the road to self-government for the Associated States.[97]

In an effort to reconcile remaining differences, the secretaries of state and defense met on May 12 and then held a final meeting a week later with General Bradley and President Truman at the White House. The final version of NSC-124, as approved by the president on June 25, stressed the dual approach that had characterized U.S. Indochina policy since early 1950—providing aid to the French while pressing Paris to move steadily toward granting greater autonomy to the new governments in Indochina. The paper recommended that if the French decided to withdraw, the United States should consult with its close allies on further action. If China intervened in the conflict, the United States should support a U.N. resolution condemning such action and seek British and French support for a joint warning of the consequences. If they did not agree, the United States should consider unilateral action.[98]

Selling the Allies

In late May, Secretary Acheson flew to Paris for a tripartite meeting of foreign ministers with Anthony Eden and Robert Schuman. Acheson's purpose was to persuade U.S. allies to approve its new program for victory in Indochina. But Schuman took the offensive from the start, pointing out that France hoped to build up the VNA to 174,000 men but lacked the resources to do so while simultaneously meeting its defense responsibilities in Europe. Expenses for Indochina, he asserted, made up one-third of the French defense budget, and they could no longer bear the burden alone.

Acheson was prepared for Schuman's appeal and responded that the French effort in Indochina was indeed in the general international interest, just like the U.S. role in Korea and that of the United Kingdom in Malaya and the Suez Canal. Indochina, he said, was of great strategic importance, not only for the security of Asia but also of the Middle East and Europe. For that reason, the Truman administration was prepared to consider increasing aid to the VNA and strengthening the effectiveness of the U.S. military assistance program. The United States would not provide ground forces in the conflict, but it was prepared to provide air and naval support for the defense of the region.

Agreement was harder to reach on how to deal with the danger of Chinese intervention. Acheson sought a consensus on the need to make a joint warning to China and on what action should be taken in the event it was disregarded. But both Eden and Schuman balked. Eden reserved his position on whether to issue a warning, suggesting that as in Korea it should be left to the United Nations to adopt further military measures in case of possible Chinese intervention. Schuman was equally cautious, pointing out that a warning itself could provoke an attack. Moreover, the French were skeptical that bombing the Chinese mainland was the answer to the problem of Indochina. It had not worked either in World War II or in Korea. But Schuman was no more enamored of Eden's suggestion to take the issue to the United Nations, which he said would be a lengthy process. The French undoubtedly also feared that the United Nations would raise the issue of French colonialism elsewhere in the world.

In the end, the meeting did not iron out the continuing differences between London, Paris, and Washington over war strategy in Indochina. At the close of the conference, the foreign ministers agreed to reexamine the conclusions of the ad hoc committee and return to the issue at a later date.[99]

At the foreign ministers conference, the French had appealed to their allies for quick action on an aid program to prevent a further deterioration of the situation in Indochina. The Vietminh had by now fully recovered from the setback suffered during their 1951 general offensive in the Red River Delta and had adopted a more cautious strategy designed to force the French to thin out their defense forces throughout the Indochina theater while awaiting the rise of antiwar sentiment in France. Vietminh forces were actively involved in Laos, where the Pathet Lao movement under their guidance was gaining strength in upland areas, and similar efforts were under way to mobilize the young Khmer Issarak forces in Cambodia.[100]

There were ample indications that the strategy might succeed. Apathy and war weariness were on the increase in both Paris and Saigon. General Raoul Salan, who replaced de Lattre as commander in chief after the latter's retirement for reasons of health (de Lattre died of cancer in December 1951), lacked his predecessor's flair for the dramatic and was described by one U.S. source as "conservative, overcautious, and defensive-minded."[101] In Saigon, Bao Dai continued to temporize, and the Tran Van Huu government failed to show any signs of gaining a grip on the situation. Even Minister Donald Heath, normally an optimist, was exasperated. In a cable to Washington in May, he complained of the Saigon government's failure to adopt crucial measures of political, social, and economic reform. Saigon's lack of drive was causing grave concern, he said, when contrasted with the unyielding will and drive of Ho Chi Minh's forces, who were more dedicated, more efficient, more disciplined, and more hardworking than their rivals. Part of the problem, he pointed out, was the French failure to persuade the Vietnamese that they intended to leave. What was needed were reforms, a buildup of the VNA, and an evolutionary statement emphasizing the principle of the independence of the Associated States. Acheson was sympathetic and promised to talk with Schuman, but in Paris Ambassador Bruce said that the French were sensitive to signs of U.S. interference. It would be best to raise the issue, he said, when Jean Letourneau, who took over as high commissioner (now renamed minister resident) in April, visited Washington in June.[102]

Letourneau arrived in Washington in mid-June on his return from an inspection trip to Indochina. He came with two major objectives—to obtain a commitment of increased U.S. aid to Indochina and to revive discussions over what actions to take if China intervened in the war. During meetings with Acheson and other officials held on the sixteenth and the seventeenth, he appealed for more financial assistance but rejected the introduction of U.S. ground troops because it could lead to Chinese intervention. Acheson responded that the United States was prepared to help, particularly with the buildup of the VNA, but was concerned at the lack of progress on the battlefield and Vietnamese complaints of continuing French dominance. Talks on the issue had little result, although Letourneau did promise that it would be possible to examine a new basis for French relations with the Associated States after the war was over.

Letourneau also attempted to reassure his hosts about persistent reports of secret peace talks with the Vietminh. Nothing was possible now, he said, because it would jeopardize the security of French fighting forces and undermine Vietnamese confidence. If Ho Chi Minh made an offer, he promised that France would consult its allies. In any case, Paris believed that there was no possibility of a settlement except through a general conference on East Asian problems in which Indochina would be a part. The final communique issued after the close of the meetings stressed the global nature of the war and included a U.S. promise to increase aid to the French Union.[103]

The talks with Letourneau had cleared the air over the aid issue but had not resolved the problem of China. While in London at the end of the month, Acheson raised the issue again with the British, stressing the U.S. view that it would be a mistake to issue a warning without allied agreement on possible actions to take. It would also be a mistake to attempt to defend Indochina *in* Indochina because the United States did not possess adequate ground forces so long as the Korean conflict continued. Air and naval action, combined with a blockade, would be preferable and need not go to the point of destroying China.

But once again, as in Paris, he was rebuffed and agreement was reached only to revive efforts by a working group of representatives of all three countries to resolve the issue. Eventually a five-power conference on the subject convened in Washington in October. But that meeting showed that consensus was as elusive as ever. The conferees agreed that actions against mainland China were the most promising means of forcing the Chinese to cease aggression, but the British and the French, supported by Australia and New Zealand, refused to commit themselves to such actions in advance. London and Paris continued to press Washington to take part in joint staff meetings to coordinate military planning in the region. The administration agreed, on condition that the meetings be informal and not be scheduled on a regular basis.[104]

During the remainder of the year, the situation in Indochina settled into an uneasy calm. The French, though continuing to possess superiority in numbers on the battlefield, settled behind their barbed wire and their strongpoints and, except for a brief sortie south of the Red River Delta in late summer, appeared content to wait for attacks in the hope of inflicting heavy casualties. The Vietminh had apparently decided to await further developments.

Saigon was briefly stirred to action by President Auriol's warning that France could not achieve a military solution by itself and needed help from the Associated States. Bao Dai appointed Nguyen Van Hinh as his chief of staff and promised to create six VNA divisions by the end of the year. But he lacked adequate funds and eventually delayed call-ups until the end of the year. In June he replaced Tran Van Huu as prime minister with Nguyen Van Tam. Tam, who had served effectively as a security chief, was vigorous and ambitious but was reputed to be too pro-French to appeal to Vietnamese nationalists. Tam promised land reform and political democratization but was viewed with suspicion by many Vietnamese nationalists, who refused to participate in his government. A National Intelligence Estimate published in August summed it up: the military situation was still at a stalemate, but the French Expeditionary Forces were gradually weakening.[105]

In December, after Dwight Eisenhower was elected as president of the United States, the Truman administration made a last effort to provoke the French to vigorous action at a meeting of the North Atlantic Council in Paris. At the meeting Jean Letourneau discussed the situation in Indochina and appealed for additional U.S. aid to counter a predicted Vietminh offensive in the Northwest. But Acheson was exasperated at the French attitude and made no commitments. After the formal meeting Letourneau and Foreign Minister Robert Schuman met privately with Acheson and Anthony Eden and raised the possibility of introducing "volunteers" from allied countries. Acheson dismissed the suggestion testily and returned to Washington.[106]

Conclusions

The Truman administration bequeathed to its successor an Indochina policy that was essentially without optimism and without ideas. In early 1950 the United States had granted diplomatic recognition and military and economic assistance to the new Associated State of Vietnam in the hope that the prospect of complete independence could inspire native resistance to the Vietminh. But reality soon set in. With the growing evidence of the weakness of Bao Dai and his government, it soon became clear that the United States needed the French presence to prevent a communist takeover as much as the French needed Washington's assistance to stay in Vietnam.

The disillusionment was equally striking in the military realm. At first, U.S. officials hoped to build up the VNA and frequently complained of the dilatory attitude of the French in carrying out their promise to create a vigorous and effective Vietnamese National Army. But the fragility of this hope soon became apparent to seasoned observers, and even Bao Dai in his more realistic moods admitted that it was a gamble because an armed VNA might desert en masse to the Vietminh.[107]

As a result, Washington was caught in a vicious circle. It wanted the French to withdraw to stimulate the local population to fight against the Vietminh, but it could not push the French out too fast because of the weakness of the Bao Dai government. Yet that weakness was in part a consequence of the French presence. Faced with the impossibility of squaring the circle, U.S. officials fell back on the hope that as the French gradually pulled out, Saigon would show greater initiative. By the end of 1952 it had become increasingly evident that that process was not taking place.

The issue was complicated by the prospect of Chinese intervention in the conflict. That fear, which began to intensify after the Chinese Communists consolidated their power on the mainland, was prevalent not only in Washington but in London and Paris as well. From the outset, U.S. intelligence estimates correctly predicted that direct Chinese involvement was unlikely, although they anticipated (also correctly) a significant level of Chinese aid to the Vietminh. To the credit of the Truman administration, relatively few top officials seemed to feel that Chinese intervention was probable, although it was not until mid-1952 that this became the accepted view in Washington.

Yet it seems indisputable that the communist takeover of mainland China, combined with the heightened fear of communist expansion elsewhere, exerted a major influence on the administration's view of the situation in Indochina. During the early years of the Franco-Vietminh conflict, Washington had cautioned Paris on attempting to seek a military solution to the dispute and expressed doubt that Bao Dai was an effective answer to the broad popular appeal of Ho Chi Minh. By 1950, it had committed U.S. prestige to that same Bao Dai and was encouraging the French to adopt a more aggressive posture on the battlefield.

What is extraordinary is that there was apparently little debate in Washington during this period over the wisdom of the administration's Indochina policy. Despite growing evidence that it was not working, there was no evident inclination to question first principles but simply to press on with wishful thinking. One lonely voice in the wilderness was that of Charlton Ogburn. In a memo to Dean Rusk in January 1951, Ogburn asked rhetorically why the United States must back a loser. The Soviets, he said, wait until the chances of an ally's survival are good to avoid losing prestige by backing a losing horse. According to Ogburn, U.S. policy in Indochina not only discredited it with Asians, who saw Bao Dai as a puppet, but also guaranteed his defeat because it undercut the need to strengthen Saigon's self-reliance. There is no indication that Rusk responded.[108]

The reason for this about-face, of course, was the almost unquestioned conviction that the loss of Indochina would lead inexorably to the fall of most of mainland Southeast Asia and perhaps have repercussions even further afield. The fear of falling dominoes is usually ascribed to the Eisenhower administration, but it began during the Truman presidency. Some have ascribed it to the Cold War mind-set that prevailed in the United States during the McCarthy era, but the evidence suggests that it was as prevalent in London and Paris as it was in Washington. In fact, there was an almost universal conviction in Western policy circles that the fall of Indochina would lead to the shift of Burma and Thailand toward communism, forcing the West to fall back on the Isthmus of Kra to protect Malaya.

By late 1949, of course, U.S. officials assumed that the fall of China could lead to the fall of mainland Southeast Asia and were prepared to accept that possibility. That had been the assumption behind the offshore island defense strategy and the basis for the security pacts that had been pursued in 1950. But in the more apocalyptic mood induced by the change in the domestic atmosphere in the spring of 1950, the administration became more concerned over the fate of the mainland. At first, Washington was reluctant to intervene directly in the area because of heavy U.S. commitments in Korea and the desire to avoid providing the French with an excuse to retreat from the area. As the Korean conflict began to wind down, administration officials were increasingly inclined to consider direct U.S. military involvement to forestall a communist victory in Indochina. In a debate over U.S. national security objectives at an NSC meeting in September 1952, Dean Acheson emphasized the growing U.S. responsibility in the Middle East and Southeast Asia because of the decline in British and French power and prestige. Truman agreed, noting that it was hard to get the American people "to realize the increased size of our responsibility in these areas."[109]

How realistic were the fears of U.S. officials that the fall of Indochina could lead to the falling of dominoes throughout the region? Obviously there is no easy answer to such a hypothetical situation. Today it seems ludicrous that governments in the region could be so affected by events in Vietnam, which most Asian leaders viewed as an exceptional case, that they would trim their sails to the prevailing wind coming from the North. But it is only fair to realize that in the conditions of the day, with inexperienced and unstable regimes facing internal rebellions by local communist parties and attempting to grapple with the serious problems accompanying the transition to independence, an uncertain policy on the part of the United States, combined with the image of a powerful and aggressive new government in China, must have been a powerful lure to a policy of neutralism or accommodation with the socialist camp. Thai officials reportedly admitted as much in private conversations with Western diplomatic sources.

Faced with the increasingly unacceptable possibility of an extension of communist power throughout Southeast Asia, the Truman administration overcame its doubts and committed the prestige of the United States in a conflict that, in clearheaded moments, most U.S. officials would have admitted it was unlikely to win. It was in 1950, not in 1954 or 1961 or 1965, that the United States first stepped into the quagmire of Indochina.

Chapter 5

The Road to Geneva

The Eisenhower administration came into office pledged to roll back the Iron Curtain, whose boundaries had expanded dramatically during the years immediately following the end of World War II. Although the new president and his immediate entourage did not sympathize with the tactics used by Senator Joseph McCarthy and other anticommunists to attack the judgment and sometimes the loyalty of key members of the previous administration, for the most part they did share the view that the Truman administration had been soft on communism, particularly in Asia, where Truman's policies, they believed, had contributed to the communist rise to power in China.

Yet there was a counterpoint to the anticommunist theme in the Eisenhower campaign platform. For although the Republican standard-bearer made a clarion call to take the offensive against international communism, he was also committed to a balanced budget and a reduction in government expenditures. This combination of Cold War rhetoric and fiscal parsimony would eventually lead to the adoption of the administration's "New Look" foreign policy based on the strategy of massive retaliation. The new policy called for a new approach that would take advantage of U.S. superiority in the field of nuclear weapons while lowering the costs of conventional arms. The administration hoped to preserve world peace by brandishing the atomic club to deter would-be aggressors. Simplified in the public mind by Defense Secretary Charles E. Wilson's catchphrase, "more bang for a buck," the new doctrine meant, in effect, that the United States would spend less on national security to achieve more.

President Eisenhower had some reservations about the new concept of massive retaliation. He liked the New Look for its promise of greater economizing in the area of national security but was nervous at its bellicose implications and hoped to make it clear that the policy was meant to deter war, not to start it. By nature a cautious man, Eisenhower was skeptical of any concept that promised total national security and was willing to accept the reality of a world characterized by diversity. Even the "rollback of communism" promised by the Republican Party platform, he said, should be peaceful. The new president was also skeptical of the universal relevance of the concept of massive retaliation and saw instinctively that it could not apply to all situations, particularly in dealing with political threats.[1]

But massive retaliation was more than just a pocketbook issue. Like his mentor George C. Marshall, Eisenhower was skeptical of the willingness of the American people to pay the long-term price for a policy of international activism. The police action in Korea showed how quickly the public grew tired of protracted and inconclusive wars. The doctrine of massive retaliation appeared to be an appealing way of using U.S. technological superiority to maintain a peaceful world in which "dirty wars" like Korea and Indochina could be avoided.

The inner contradictions in the new administration's foreign policy showed up quickly in its attitude toward Asia. The Republican Party had been vocal in its criticism of Truman's China policy and his failure to adopt an offensive posture to win the Korean War. Yet on close scrutiny it became clear that the concept of "rollback," if indeed it had any relevance, was directed primarily at Europe rather than Asia. During the campaign, Eisenhower pledged to bring the boys home from Korea, and Indochina did not figure prominently in his speeches. In his State of the Union Address given on February 2, the new chief executive simply noted that the Korean War was "part of the same calculated assault that the aggressor is simultaneously pressing in Indochina and Malaya, and of the strategic situation that manifestly embraces the island of Formosa and the Chinese Nationalist forces there." Any military solution to the Korean War, he said, would inevitably affect all those areas.[2]

Except for a prewar assignment in the Philippines, Eisenhower did not have much personal experience in Asia, but his new secretary of state, John Foster Dulles, had served the Truman administration as chief negotiator for the peace treaty with Japan and as roving ambassador in Asia. Dulles's views on foreign policy appeared to differ from those of the president in many respects. Eisenhower came into office with a reputation as a pragmatist and a conciliator, whereas Dulles was preoccupied with the menace of communism and appeared to approach the subject with an almost religious intensity. At the State Department he would be joined by another hard-liner on the subject, the new assistant secretary of state for Far Eastern affairs, Walter Robertson.

One of the first issues the new administration faced was the growing conflict in Indochina. In his briefing for the president-elect in November, Truman described the problem as one of lack of French aggressiveness and of fence-sitting on the part of the Vietnamese and said it was an "urgent matter" which the new administration would have to address. The news from Paris and Saigon in January added to the gloom. In France, the Pleven government fell, while in Vietnam Donald Heath was uncharacteristically pessimistic. The military situation, he reported, was still perilous; the Vietminh now controlled much of the Red River Delta and held the initiative throughout the North. If the Northwest were lost, the road to Laos and Thailand would be open. He was equally gloomy on political conditions in Saigon, where Prime Minister Nguyen Van Tam had had little success in mobilizing support for the war effort. Still, he was better than Bao Dai, in whom Heath no longer had any confidence.[3]

In early February Dulles was scheduled to go to Paris to consult with Prime Minister René Mayer, who had taken office on January 8. Before leaving Washington, he was briefed on the Indochina situation by civilian and military officials of the outgoing administration. In Paris, the new prime minister reminded Dulles of the promise of the NATO Council to provide additional support to the French and agreed to accept a working group from the United States later in the month.[4]

The working group arrived in France on March 8. In briefings, the French reported that the Mayer government intended to increase the size of the VNA by 40,000 men (in December 1952 it consisted of 53 battalions supplemented by national guard troops numbering about 28,000). France and the Associated States would bear the entire cost except for weapons. But the French implied that any future augmentation beginning in 1954 would have to be borne by the United States. There were tentative plans to add more troops, depending on the level of U.S. assistance. The overall plan was to create a VNA of eight divisions by 1955, permitting the French to turn the war gradually over to the Vietnamese.[5]

In Washington, the Department of Defense was undertaking its own analysis of the situation, based on a memo by the Joint Chiefs written on November 14, which recommended a speedup in the recruitment of indigenous forces and an improvement in logistical capabilities. On January 19, 1953, Deputy Defense Secretary William C. Foster requested a reexamination of the U.S. role in Indochina, with special consideration to the training of the VNA and maintenance of U.S.-supplied equipment. On March 13 the Joint Chiefs responded with suggestions that the French assign more responsibility to the Associated States and expand the VNA by 57 light battalions (40,000 men) to permit more offensive actions. They also recommended the addition of another squadron of support aircraft. But the JCS advised the administration to wait for France to submit these proposals for operations during the upcoming dry season. They recommended no training or combat role for the United States so as to keep the French in the war.[6]

The Mayer Visit

Later in March, the new French prime minister René Mayer visited the United States to meet President Eisenhower and consult with him on problems of mutual concern. Mayer brought with him a formal request for U.S. aid as promised by Secretary Acheson at the NATO meeting in December. Eisenhower's cabinet had met two days before Mayer's arrival and agreed that, as a top priority, Indochina should receive additional U.S. aid if the French presented a workable plan of action. In a comment at an NSC meeting on March 24, Dulles had noted that Indochina was more important than Korea because its loss could not be localized.

The two leaders met on the twenty-sixth, and Jean Letourneau explained French plans and future strategy in Indochina. According to Letourneau, Paris planned to add 80,000 men to the 40,000 already scheduled for 1953, leading to a total force of 250,000 by 1955. To a French request for assistance, Eisenhower adopted a cautious line and said that the United States could not help "without full knowledge" of French political and military plans so that the administration could see why its assistance was needed and how it would be used. Letourneau outlined French plans for a step-up in offensive operations leading to victory in two years. The new strategy called for pacification operations outside the Red River Delta followed by French attacks on Vietminh forces in Tonkin during the spring of 1955.[7]

Administration officials agreed to study the French plans, but they were disappointed at the long-term nature of the program and the lack of any plan to cut Vietminh links with China. Mayer informed Eisenhower that the plan could be accelerated to eighteen months, but to do so would require additional manpower and resources. Letourneau presented a hastily drawn-up plan on the thirty-first but said that the French would require a total aid package of $730 million for the period 1953–55. U.S. officials promised to consider the French aid request but remained unenthusiastic about French proposals, viewing them as too cautious and avoiding the heart of the problem—the Vietminh presence in the Red River Delta. Nor, in the opinion of the Joint Chiefs, did they assign sufficient responsibility to the VNA. But from Saigon, both Donald Heath and new MAAG chief General Thomas J. H. Trapnell defended the French plan as the best that could be expected under the circumstances. In the end, the JCS grudgingly pronounced it "workable" provided that French force levels were increased and the plan to regain the initiative was aggressively pursued.[8]

In late April representatives of the Departments of State and Defense met to seek a consensus on the French request. From the outset, officials representing the Joint Chiefs voiced their continued frustration at what they considered the lack of leadership in Indochina and the inadequacies of the French plan, and they argued that U.S. approval should not be extended until their reservations were satisfied. State Department representatives were not necessarily more optimistic, but they were more skeptical of the prospects of successfully pressing the French. Paul Nitze, director of the Policy Planning Staff, agreed that it was unlikely that the French plan would succeed but added that the alternatives were so "bleak" that "we probably should go along and give this plan a try even though it may not achieve what the French are saying it might." Army Chief of Staff General Collins assented but said that "we should first put the squeeze on the French to get them off their fannies." The meeting ended inconclusively with a decision to await Secretary Dulles's return from his talks with officials in Paris.[9]

Dulles had had little success. On April 22 he and other U.S. cabinet officials met with French foreign minister Georges Bidault and pressed him to instruct French military commanders to study the U.S. experience with large-scale operations in Korea. But the French were doubtful of the relevance of Korea to conditions in Indochina. Letourneau defended the French program and pointed out that it had seemed to be acceptable to listeners in Washington during Mayer's visit. Dulles remarked somewhat dubiously that he hoped Congress would approve the program and expressed the desire that the French would not reduce their overall military expenditures and leave the United States "holding the bag."[10]

The Vietminh Invasion of Laos

While these discussions were taking place, the situation in Indochina was rapidly evolving. In April, three Vietminh divisions crossed the border into Laos and, with the assistance of recently recruited local Pathet Lao forces, quickly overran two provinces in the northeast, reaching within ten miles of the royal capital of Luang Prabang. King Norodom Sihanouk of the Associated State of Cambodia was reportedly nervous and the Thai ambassador in Washington asked State Department officials about the administration's intentions. Eventually the Vietminh encountered logistical problems and withdrew from their advanced positions, but, as Ho Chi Minh and his colleagues undoubtedly had hoped, the shock effects were severe, both in Paris and in Washington.

In Paris, the deteriorating situation led to renewed demands for negotiations, not only from Radical Socialist deputy Pierre Mendès-France, who had been calling for talks for months, but also from the respected centrist journal *Le Monde*. Douglas Dillon, the new U.S. ambassador to France, noted that the political situation had not reached "dangerous proportions" but could evolve in that direction if there was no progress on the battlefield.[11] The situation in Laos also created a crisis of confidence in Washington. In late April the French had asked for the loan of C-119 "Flying Boxcars" to transport heavy equipment to

Laos. Prime Minister Mayer had suggested in Washington that U.S. pilots operate them during the period of the loan. Secretary Dulles discussed the request with President Eisenhower on April 27, and the latter agreed to send the planes but rejected the use of U.S. pilots because it would involve the United States in combat operations in Indochina. As a counterproposal, he suggested the use of civilian pilots. The French agreed, and after a meeting of the NSC on the following day, the administration agreed to send the planes.[12]

But perhaps the most important consequence of the Laos campaign was that it shattered the fragile confidence of the Eisenhower administration in the French capacity to resolve the conflict in Indochina. At the NSC meeting on the twenty-eighth, the president lamented that he was greatly disappointed over recent developments in Laos. Until then he had hoped that, however slowly, the French in due course would succeed. This hope was now shattered. If Laos should be lost, he said, the rest of Southeast Asia and Indonesia would soon follow, and the gateway to India, Burma, and Thailand would be open.

The problem, Eisenhower thought, was not only the lack of aggressiveness of French military commanders in the field but their failure to "instill a desire to hold" among the Vietnamese population. "What we had hitherto regarded as a civil war," he said, "had now come to look like nothing more than France engaged in fighting a traditional colonial war." The issue had been raised during a visit by King Norodom Sihanouk to the United States. Sihanouk had made a brief stopover in France and asked for a revision of the French Union, but President Auriol had refused on constitutional grounds. On arrival in the United States, Sihanouk complained of the lack of French responsiveness and warned that without true independence Cambodia would be forced to make common cause with the Vietminh.[13]

The new administration was thus now face to face with the central dilemmas that had frustrated its predecessor. Eisenhower returned to the problem at the next meeting of the NSC, held on May 6, remarking that only two things could save the situation in Indochina: an official French promise of national independence for the Associated States when the internal conflict was over and a dynamic leader for the French military forces on the battlefield. Those that had been sent out, he complained, were by and large "a poor lot." After the meeting the president sent a letter to Ambassador Dillon in Paris emphasizing the need for a "clear and unequivocal public announcement" on French intentions to grant national independence after victory against the Vietminh. He also referred to the need for a "forceful and inspirational leader" like de Lattre and specifically mentioned General Augustin Guillaume, commander of French forces in Morocco, or Lieutenant General Jean Valluy, now at Supreme Headquarters, Allied Powers Europe (SHAPE) headquarters in Europe.

The French, of course, had heard much of this before, but Prime Minister

Mayer badly needed U.S. backing to carry out his program in Indochina. In a meeting with Ambassador Dillon, he promised that France would insert a statement along the lines suggested by Eisenhower in a future speech. On the question of a new commander in Indochina, Mayer countered that Guillaume's health was bad and Valluy was ruled out because of his identification among ardent Vietnamese nationalists with the Haiphong incident of November 1946. As new commander of French forces in Indochina, he had targeted General Henri Navarre, chief of staff of French NATO forces in Central Europe, as the new commander in chief in Indochina. Two weeks later, the Mayer government resigned.[14]

The fall of the Mayer government, the Laos crisis, and the growing chorus of demands in Paris for a negotiated settlement of the war contributed to the rising level of anxiety in Washington over the possibility of a French withdrawal from Indochina and undoubtedly helped to spur active consideration of a higher level of U.S. involvement in the conflict. In late January 1953 the JCS, following the instructions of the outgoing administration, had ordered a study of possible U.S. military action to prevent a communist victory in Indochina if the French withdrew.[15] Then, in April, the five-power military conference requested by the French late the preceding year met in Honolulu and issued a report proposing the establishment of formal and continuous relations among representatives of the five countries to coordinate plans for the defense of Southeast Asia. In May, Admiral Arthur Radford, then commander in chief of U.S. forces in the Pacific (CINCPAC), was appointed U.S. representative to the group. Radford was just then in the process of completing a series of CINCPAC operational plans on Indochina called for by the JCS the previous December and was a vocal advocate of an active U.S. role to prevent a further advance of communism in Southeast Asia.[16]

The Vietminh invasion of Laos intensified the sense of urgency in Washington. On April 29, the National Security Council approved NSC-149/2, which suggested the possibility of direct U.S. intervention in Indochina in the event of Chinese aggression or other basic changes in the situation. On May 5, just before the NSC meeting the following day, Chief of Naval Operations Admiral W. M. Fechteler presented a paper discussing a variety of proposals for possible U.S. action in the region, including the option of armed intervention.[17]

At the NSC meeting on May 6, Special Assistant to the President Robert Cutler raised the issue for discussion. He pointed out that existing policy on Indochina contemplated intervention by the United States only in the event of overt or covert Chinese intervention to assist the rebels. Such a policy, he said, was irrelevant because Chinese intervention had not occurred and the deteriorating situation in Indochina had been brought about by the continuing civil war. NSC 149/2 contemplated intervention if a "basic change" occurred in the situation, and he asked whether the Vietminh invasion of Laos constituted such a basic change. In other words, was the United States now prepared to contemplate direct military intervention in the conflict?[18]

Faced with skepticism in the White House, the NSC took no decision on the issue, but three weeks later the JCS returned to the question of what action to adopt if the French decided to withdraw. In a report to the Joint Chiefs, the Joint Strategic Survey Committee noted that there were two conditions under which withdrawal would probably occur: in case of a Chinese invasion or of continued deterioration of support for the war in France. In the latter situation, the United States had several alternatives: (1) it could deploy U.S. and allied forces in Indochina to take over the French objective of "reducing Communist activity to the status of scattered guerrilla bands"; (2) it could provide just enough U.S. ground forces to hold critical strongpoints vacated by the French, while providing air and naval support for VNA operations; or (3) it could restrict itself to providing air and naval support for the VNA. In any case, the development of the VNA would continue. If the French withdrew slowly, the United States could forgo ground troops and use the VNA. But if China decided to invade, the report concluded, there was no feasible course the United States could take inside Indochina to prevent Chinese forces from overrunning the area. To succeed in thwarting such an invasion, the United States would have to contemplate applying all available coercive measures against the Chinese mainland, including a blockade and air strikes on military targets.[19]

The Navarre Plan

For the moment, such dire straits were only a possibility. The Eisenhower administration wanted to evaluate the situation and discuss plans with the new French commander in chief on the spot. It was not especially pleased with the choice of Henri Navarre to replace Raoul Salan. He had a reputation as unaggressive and even indecisive. Yet Washington was willing to give him a chance and received approval from the French to send a mission to evaluate the situation in Indochina and talk to Navarre about his plans. In late May, the Joint Chiefs selected Army Lieutenant General John W. "Iron Mike" O'Daniel, the new commander of U.S. forces in the Pacific, as the leader of the delegation. Known as a tough, no-nonsense officer, O'Daniel inspired a combination of fear and respect among his subordinates and could be expected to provide an honest and, if necessary, blunt report about the situation in Southeast Asia.[20]

O'Daniel arrived in Saigon on June 22. General Navarre, who had arrived only a few days earlier, consulted with his visitor on planned offensive operations. Although the two were almost extreme opposites in temperament, they evidently established a friendly relationship and, apparently with O'Daniel's assistance, Navarre quickly sketched out a new strategy which, according to a U.S. source, was an almost point-by-point response to U.S. suggestions. In contrast to the original plan presented earlier in the year by Jean Letourneau, it called for an almost immediate switch to the offensive against Vietminh main force units in the North and a reliance on big-unit rather than small-unit operations. Immediately following the current rainy season, French units would attempt to seize the initiative in small operations to disrupt local guerrillas; then, in the fall, they would launch aggressive operations to disrupt the antici- pated Vietminh fall offensive in the region of the Red River Delta.[21]

General O'Daniel was impressed with the new plan, and in his report after departing on July 10, he described it as "a new aggressive concept for the conduct of operations in Indochina." He was also pleased with Navarre's posi- tive attitude and willingness to cooperate with the United States and said that he had been invited back in a few months to "witness the progress we will have made." Back home, some of O'Daniel's colleagues were skeptical but were willing to give the plan a chance.

The real question, of course, was whether Paris would provide adequate backing for Navarre's new plan. At first the signs were promising. On June 26, after an interim of several weeks, Joseph Laniel, an Independent, was elected prime minister of a new French government. Although Laniel was viewed in some quarters as "uninspired and uninspiring," he came into office pledged to pursue the war to a successful conclusion. He adopted the Navarre Plan as his official strategy and backed up his promises with hints of new troops from France. Maurice de Jean was named the new high commissioner for Indochina, and in early July the new government issued a declaration vowing to "perfect" the independence of the Associated States "on the basis of equality."[22]

The O'Daniel report and the favorable news from Paris were a tonic for beleaguered officials in Washington, where the picture from Indochina had appeared so bleak in recent months. A National Intelligence Estimate prepared by the CIA in early June had predicted further deterioration in both the mili- tary and political arenas. Unless the French adopted a more aggressive policy, the authors predicted that the Vietminh would grow in strength and prestige and consolidate their position in the Red River Delta and Laos. The Nguyen Van Tam government was "more shadow than substance" and had suffered a notable decline in stability and popular support. Its promised land reform program was still in the planning stage, and Bao Dai as usual was unable to provide any semblance of leadership.[23]

The signs from Paris were not as promising as they appeared on the sur- face. The vote for Mendès-France, an outspoken advocate of French with- drawal, had been perilously high (he had failed by only thirteen votes to receive sufficient support in the National Assembly to form a new government), which prompted Ambassador Dillon to remark (prophetically as it turned out) that this might be the last chance to turn Indochina around. Former prime minister Rene Pleven warned Dillon that the prospect of an armistice in Korea made the longing in France for a similar settlement in Indochina almost uncontrollable. Navarre's hope to elicit a greater military effort was "out of the question." France, he said, could do no more.[24]

Back in Washington, representatives of the State Department and the Joint Chiefs of Staff met at the Pentagon on July 10 to discuss the situation in Indochina and the prospects for the Navarre Plan. The general reaction of the Joint Chiefs was favorable but conditional on the French capacity to carry it out. But representatives from State continued to probe U.S. military attitudes toward the situation. Robert Bowie, newly appointed director of the Policy Planning Staff, asked Army Chief of Staff General J. Lawton Collins why, if Southeast Asia was critically important to U.S. national security, he opposed the commitment of U.S. ground forces in Indochina. Collins replied that although the area was important, the JCS opposed the introduction of U.S. troops, particularly under present ceilings. When pressed for his advice on what should be done in the event the loss of Indochina was imminent, Collins hedged, recommending that the JCS would wish to talk it over with political leaders. "If we go into Indochina with American force," he warned, "we will be there for the long pull. Militarily and politically we would be in up to our necks." Moreover, he said, the United States would not be in as advantageous a position as it had been in Korea because it would have to defend the vulnerable port of Haiphong. It would, he said, be a "major and protracted war."[25]

French Blood, American Dollars

While civilian and military officials debated the problem in Washington, Secretary of State Dulles discussed Indochina with Foreign Minister Georges Bidault, who was in Washington for a meeting of the tripartite foreign ministers. Bidault mentioned the need for an increase in U.S. aid and stressed that the Navarre Plan would require either conscripts or a deactivation of French forces in Europe and Africa. But the crux of his message was that, despite evidence of new vigor in Paris, the Laniel government was determined to bring an early end to the war, by negotiations if necessary. Talk of peace in Korea had a contagious effect in France, he said, and he warned that the conflict in Indochina could not continue after a Korean settlement.[26]

To the Eisenhower administration, the idea of a negotiated settlement was anathema. Eisenhower had already expressed his negative opinion of the subject in talks with Canadian prime minister Louis St. Laurent in May, and studies undertaken in the State Department had stressed that the French needed to achieve a better military and political situation in Indochina before engaging in talks. A plebiscite under present conditions, said one observer, would certainly give a "thumping majority" to the Vietminh. So, in his conversation with Bidault, Dulles tried to pour cold water on alleged similarities between Korea and Indochina, pointing out the relevance of a negotiated settlement to the conflict in Indochina. In Korea, he said, the United States worked hard to get a settlement and let the enemy know it was willing to take certain measures to get it. The same tactic was necessary in Indochina—to use the Navarre Plan and the threat of action against China to make the enemy want to end the war. He also said that after the Korean conflict was over, Moscow and Beijing might want to keep the Indochina war going as a "colonial sore" in the side of the West. Dulles recognized that the war in Indochina could not be endless and suggested that if the situation had improved when the Korean conference took place, the United States would not oppose talks on Indochina. But negotiations from a position of weakness "would only end in complete disaster." Bidault conceded the logic of Dulles's arguments but countered that the French threat to add 20,000 additional troops in Indochina was not as credible as a U.S. threat to drop nuclear bombs in Manchuria.[27]

The outcome of the tripartite foreign ministers meeting in Washington could not have been reassuring to U.S. officials. Bidault's plea for negotiations made it crystal clear that French support for a continuation of the war effort, even within the Laniel government, was perilously fragile. The only hope lay in the Navarre Plan, and Bidault had already intimated that the chances for full funding of the plan in Paris were remote.

To Paris, the answer appeared to lie in a substantial increase—estimated at about 40 percent—in U.S. funding for the French effort in Indochina. Bidault had not been specific, but later in the month Paris asked for $400 million in new aid to cover increased costs of the Navarre Plan and help to reduce the French military budget. Previously, the United States had refused to provide aid to reduce the strains on the French budget, but now the Eisenhower administration approved the request, subject to a judgment by the JCS that the Navarre Plan had good prospects for success. The Joint Chiefs felt that the plan was still too cautious but finally on September 9 gave their qualified approval.[28]

Yet even as Washington shifted gears for an accelerated effort in Indochina, the mood in Paris was growing ever more pessimistic. Public support for the war was slipping rapidly. Vice-President Paul Reynaud reportedly felt that the United States had offered too little and wanted France to withdraw. Defense Minister Pleven warned that the Navarre Plan was too optimistic, and even Premier Laniel complained that Navarre was demanding resources that could not be provided. On July 22, Ambassador Dillon was informed by French officials that Navarre would not receive the twelve battalions he had requested from Europe. When the new U.S. aid agreement was signed in Paris on September 29, there were cries on the left of "French blood, American dollars." In the eyes of many Frenchmen and Frenchwomen, it had become Washington's war.[29]

Concern among U.S. officials that the French would not interpret the

Navarre Plan aggressively enough appeared confirmed when in early September Navarre submitted a new timetable that showed no indication that he intended to seize the initiative on the battlefield. If the enemy attacked, France would counterattack. Otherwise, Navarre planned only to launch diversionary operations. A general offensive against the major Vietminh battle corps was not scheduled until the fall of 1954. In the meantime, he would await reinforcements.[30]

In the realm of political reform, the French were beginning to move in a direction more in tune with U.S. desires. On July 3, the Laniel government announced its intention of perfecting the independence of the three Associated States. The first reaction in Saigon had been one of skepticism because many Vietnamese doubted the seriousness of the French offer, an attitude provoked in part by reports that some elements in the French cabinet around Foreign Minister Georges Bidault were opposed to granting increased autonomy to the Associated States of Indochina. Bao Dai had mixed feelings about the offer, fearing that it would encourage factionalism in Vietnamese society and bring the French closer to abandoning the fight. He told High Commissioner Maurice de Jean that since the French were still fighting to protect the Vietnamese from communism they were entitled to retain certain advantages and privileges in Indochina.[31]

Bao Dai's fear that the new situation would encourage factional struggles in Vietnam was justified. In part, it was a consequence of the French suggestion for the creation of a national assembly or other form of parliament to vote on the new relationship with France. Previously he had opposed national elections and the formation of a popularly elected assembly, citing the fractional character of Vietnamese society, and insisted that democracy could come about only after the end of the war. But his prime minister Nguyen Van Tam was in favor of the idea and in the fall announced his intention of holding elections for a national assembly. Bao Dai agreed to the plan but was clearly nervous about the consequences, remarking to former governor-general Georges Catroux that it would be a "magnifique faisceau de divergences. Nous verrons bien ce que en sortira." Now, in response to a French request, Bao Dai agreed to create a national congress to define the terms for negotiations on a new relationship with Paris. The first session, chaired by Prince Buu Loc, was held in Saigon on October 14. Two days later, the 200 delegates voted unanimously that Vietnam would join the French Union only on the basis of full equality. French anger was instantaneous, and the following day the issue was raised again, resulting in the addition of a qualifying phrase "in its present form" to the statement about Vietnamese membership in the French Union.[32]

But now the cat was out of the bag. Many delegates had wanted a full parliament in the first place and now demanded the creation of a formal national assembly. Bao Dai attempted to defuse the agitation by adjourning the congress, but Nguyen Van Tam countered by announcing plans to hold national elections for a legislature in December. An angry Bao Dai replaced him with Prince Buu Loc on December 17.[33]

The factionalism in Saigon was undoubtedly exasperating to U.S. officials at a time when they were desperately attempting to reinvigorate the war effort and keep France in the war. There were increasing signs of war weariness in Paris. The Laniel government had attempted to keep the pressure for peace under control, announcing that it was ready for negotiations on any basis that did not result in an abandonment of Vietnam. But on October 28, the French National Assembly endorsed a set of resolutions instructing the government to continue seeking an opportunity for talks and calling for the Associated States to take a greater military role in the war.[34]

The idea looked better on paper than on the battlefield. During the fall, French forces cleared an area near Bui Chu in the Red River Delta and then turned it over to newly created VNA light battalions to maintain local security. But nearby Vietminh units attacked immediately and, in the words of one U.S. historian, the VNA forces were "badly mauled." Vietnamese sources complained that they lacked artillery support and training to stand up to regular units of the Vietminh, but the incident tarnished the image of the VNA and appeared to substantiate French skepticism about the ability and will of the Vietnamese to defend themselves.[35]

There were also continuing signs of French nervousness about the possibility of Chinese intervention. Secretary Dulles had attempted to assuage such concerns in a speech before members of the American Legion on September 2. Noting that China had been training and equipping communist forces in Indochina, he warned Beijing that a Chinese invasion such as had taken place in Korea could have "grave consequences which might not be confined to Indochina." On the other hand, he intimated that a successful conference on Korea could lead to peace in the entire region. He amplified on those remarks at a press conference the following day, noting that if the atmosphere following an end of the Korean conflict seemed to be conducive to a settlement of the Indochina War, the United States would not be opposed.[36]

But Dulles's remarks did not relieve anxieties in Paris. On October 9, ambassador to the United States Henri Bonnet informed the State Department that French intelligence sources were reporting the possibility of Chinese air support for the Vietminh. Vietminh pilots were already being trained at Nanning and Chinese MIGs had flown sorties into Tonkin from South China. A few days later, Foreign Minister Georges Bidault returned to the issue in talks with Foreign Minister Eden and Secretary Dulles. Expressing his concern about possible Vietminh use of Chinese jets, Bidault asked what military help France's allies could provide in the event of a more active Chinese role in the war. Eden and Dulles promised to look into the matter.[37]

In early November, General O'Daniel arrived in Indochina for his second visit to evaluate French performance. As on the previous occasion, O'Daniel returned a few weeks later with an optimistic report that the French had regained the initiative and were making progress in the war. Other observers were not so sanguine. According to Brigadier General Paul W. Carraway, who had accompanied Vice-President Richard M. Nixon on a tour of Indochina shortly after O'Daniel returned, Navarre's optimism hid the fact that there was nothing stirring at the grass roots. Carraway reported that 60 percent of the Red River Delta was under Vietminh control and after nightfall the French had total security only in Hanoi and Haiphong. Similar reports from the U.S. army attaché in Saigon led General Mathew Ridgway, the army chief of staff, to criticize O'Daniel's report as "overly optimistic."[38]

Navarre had admitted to Donald Heath in November that though the French might launch some tactical operations, his policy would be mainly defensive in the North until the following summer. Ironically, one of those "tactical operations" was destined to affect the fate of the entire war. The French had been concerned about recent Vietminh moves into Laos. Not only did they divide French forces, but they also had political repercussions in the royal Lao capital of Luang Prabang. It was at least partly because Navarre was instructed by the Laniel government to provide greater security to the exposed royal capital in Laos that he decided to occupy the small border post of Dien Bien Phu in November. It had been seized by the Vietminh from the French during the former's 1952 offensive in the Northwest. Now it was retaken by the French on November 20 in an effort to interdict Vietminh supply lines into Laos and provide a base for guerrilla operations in the enemy's rear areas.[39]

Moment of Opportunity

The news of the French reoccupation of Dien Bien Phu reached Vietminh headquarters just as Vo Nguyen Giap was preparing to present the 1953–54 offensive campaign to his division commanders. Since the failure of the 1951 general offensive, Vietminh strategy had been generally to tie down French troops in fortified camps and then attack elsewhere, based on the idea of concentrating Vietminh strength against the enemy's weak points. At the Fourth Plenum of the Central Committee of the Party (now renamed the Vietnamese Workers' Party) held in January 1953, party strategists had decided to strike where the enemy was weak, even if in fortified camps, to force the French to disperse their troops.

The initial target was at Na San, in the Northwest, but that town was abandoned by the French during the spring. Then Giap's attention switched to Lai Chau, but that area was strategically unsuited for a large-scale offensive and would have minimal strategical impact. French forces were vulnerable in Central Vietnam and in upper Laos, but those areas were too far removed from the Vietminh zone of operations. So the news that Navarre had decided to reoccupy Dien Bien Phu was promising. From the Vietminh point of view, Dien Bien Phu had several favorable factors: it was located in mountainous terrain far from Hanoi, which would present serious logistical difficulties for the French; it was a strategic location on a key highway route into North Laos but also was located sufficiently close to Vietminh sources of supply in the Viet Bac and South China; and it provided an opportunity to achieve a maximum psychological advantage because the town had been chosen as a keystone of Navarre's military strategy in Indochina. After a wide-ranging discussion of possible alternatives, the final decision to attack the French fort was made by the high command on December 6. Three main force divisions were dispatched to the Northwest, while other Vietminh units were instructed to attack upper Laos during the winter months to compel the French to disperse their own forces in the area.[40]

The plan was an ambitious one, and it would require help from the Chinese. For three years the PRC had been providing increasing amounts of aid to the Vietminh cause—not enough to win, perhaps, but certainly enough to keep the struggle alive. It is impossible, given the lack of hard evidence, to know for certain what Chinese motives and objectives were in helping Ho Chi Minh's forces in Vietnam, but though some U.S. observers were seriously concerned at the possibility of direct Chinese intervention, it is highly unlikely that at that juncture China was prepared to take the risk of being drawn into the conflict. The war in Korea had already been costly in military, economic, and diplomatic terms, and there were subtle indications that Chinese leaders were anxious to improve relations with the West in order to facilitate plans for internal economic development. Moreover, the expansion of U.S. involvement in the war and the ominous warnings from Washington of the possibility of a direct U.S. attack on China must have caused anxiety in Beijing. But Chinese leaders must have equally welcomed the subtle hint in John Foster Dulles's American Legion speech that the United States was not averse to a negotiated settlement of the Indochina conflict. On August 24, Chinese foreign minister Zhou Enlai had stated that "other questions" could be discussed in connection with a resolution of the Korean conflict.[41]

Chinese interest in a peaceful settlement of the Indochina conflict coincided with an apparently growing desire in Moscow for a defusing of Cold War tensions. Since emerging as the dominant figure following the death of Joseph Stalin earlier in the year, Soviet prime minister Georgy Malenkov had made clear his own interest in improving relations with the West. On September 28 Moscow proposed the convening of a five-power conference to "examine measures for the relaxation of international tensions." On October 8 Beijing formally endorsed the Soviet proposal, although without mentioning Indochina as an appropriate subject for negotiations.[42]

The attitudes of Vietminh leaders toward a peaceful settlement of the Indochina conflict were undoubtedly more ambivalent. At the outset, Ho Chi Minh had actively pursued the diplomatic track, in clear recognition of the relative weakness of Vietminh forces on the battlefield. In a treatise on Vietminh revolutionary strategy written at the outset of the Franco-Vietminh war, VWP General Secretary Truong Chinh had indicated that party leaders might use diplomatic techniques to isolate the enemy and mobilize world support for the Vietminh cause. Chinh conceded the possibility of a negotiated settlement of the war once the French had lost the will to seek total victory, but the main thrust of his analysis was that the revolutionary forces could realize their objective of total independence only by force of arms. In a speech given in September 1951, he warned that the DRV should not be deluded into negotiations.

Although there is no firm evidence, it is likely that as Vietminh fortunes gradually improved in the fall of 1953, creating the possibility of a total victory, their interest in a diplomatic settlement declined, except in conditions of absolute revolutionary superiority on the battlefield. In September 1953, TASS reported a speech by Ho Chi Minh on the eighth anniversary of the formation of the DRV in which he said that peace could come about only through victory.[43]

In this context, Vietminh leaders may have viewed the groundswell of sentiment for a peace settlement in Indochina as a disturbing sign that their allies were prepared to betray Vietminh interests on the altar of an improvement in Great Power relations. Moscow had already made it clear that it viewed the struggle in Indochina as an issue of relatively low priority for Soviet foreign policy. China's support for the Vietminh had been more steadfast, but Vietminh leaders undoubtedly harbored lingering suspicions of China's long-term intentions in the region. According to one source, the issue was fiercely debated in Vietminh headquarters and then, on October 20, in an interview with a journalist for the Swedish newspaper *Expressen*, Ho Chi Minh broke a long silence and indicated the willingness of his government to attend a conference to seek peace in Indochina: "If the French Government wish to have an armistice and to resolve the question of Vietnam by means of negotiations, the people and government of the Democratic Republic of Vietnam are ready to examine the French proposals." A few days later China indicated its approval of Ho's demarche in an article in *People's Daily*.[44]

The flurry of comments in world capitals about the possibility of a negotiated settlement of the Indochina conflict aroused an acute case of anxiety in Washington, where the prospects of such a settlement were viewed by many as tantamount to total victory for the communists in Southeast Asia. In October, Prime Minister Laniel had reassured Secretary Dulles that France would not undertake negotiations without consulting the United States, but the momentum in Paris for a settlement had increased since then.

To prevent a serious split between Paris and Washington, Dulles had acceded to French pleas to keep the negotiations track open, but he was undoubtedly worried by a statement by Laniel in late October that France did not seek an all-out victory in Indochina. In a debate on the war in the National Assembly held on November 24, Laniel reiterated his government's interest in a peaceful settlement, alluding to the armistice in Korea as a possible model to follow. Once again, Laniel attempted to reassure Washington that no policy changes would be adopted before a meeting of the three allied heads of state scheduled to be convened in Bermuda before the end of the year. But Ambassador Dillon warned that Laniel was under heavy pressure from both the National Assembly and public opinion to bring an end to the war.[45]

At Bermuda, however, little was said about Indochina. Bidault, who replaced Joseph Laniel at most of the meetings because of the latter's illness, promised that the French effort in Indochina would continue and was still hopeful that the Navarre Plan might work, but he pressed the French interest in holding a five-power conference to include China and the Soviet Union. Eisenhower replied that the conference, with its implied recognition of the PRC, was a "bad word" for the United States. In the end, the communique laconically took note of the Soviet proposal to consider a five-power meeting and suggested that the idea could be discussed at a four-power foreign ministers conference scheduled for Berlin in January.[46]

Thinking the Unthinkable

The rapidly evolving situation in Indochina, notably the growing possibility of a French defeat or withdrawal from the area, had made the guidelines contained in NSC-124 increasingly obsolete as a basis for U.S. policy in the region. Approved in June 1952, at a time when a French defeat in Indochina was not an immediate possibility, NSC-124 had predicted that the loss of any country in Southeast Asia would have critical consequences for the United States and would probably lead in a relatively short time to communist domination of the entire subcontinent. But it did not suggest direct military involvement as a probable U.S. response to such a contingency. Now that the prospect of a French defeat appeared less remote, a reevaluation was considered advisable, and the NSC Planning Board began to look into the matter.

The Planning Board was assisted in its deliberations by a new NIE prepared in November by the CIA, which took issue with the dire predictions of some observers regarding the consequences of a fall of Indochina to the communists. According to the estimate, the primary impact of a Vietminh victory would be psychological. Thailand would be the key factor. So long as Thailand maintained its present orientation, other countries such as Indonesia and Burma would not be directly affected by a communist victory in Vietnam. But if Thailand became concerned at the lack of U.S. commitment to the region and began "to reorient toward the communist bloc," Burma and possibly Indonesia might abandon their neutrality and seek alignment with one of the power blocs. Other nations in the area would probably continue their present foreign policies. Japan would do so as well but might seek guarantees from the United States and expand its relations with communist countries in Asia.

The NIE also studied the possible reaction of Asian countries to the introduction of U.S. armed forces to prevent a communist victory in Indochina. It predicted that reactions would be divided. Those governments that currently leaned toward the West would quietly approve, whereas neutral states such as India, Indonesia, and Burma would disapprove and express their anxiety over an extension of the war. In the long run, the response would be largely determined by the degree of success of the U.S. intervention. If the Vietminh were to be quickly defeated, noncommunist Asian leaders would accept the new situation, but a protracted stalemate would "almost certainly reduce support for the U.S. throughout Asia." The deputy director for intelligence of the Joint Staff had dissented from these conclusions, arguing that the establishment of communist control over Indochina by military or other means would "almost certainly result in the communization of all of Southeast Asia" as well as exposing India, the Philippines, and Australia to increasing communist pressure. He recommended the addition into a new policy statement of a declaration of the benefits of U.S. armed intervention.[47]

During the next few weeks the Planning Board undertook its own analysis of the situation in preparation for a new policy statement that was eventually issued as NSC-177. In the process, urged on by the JCS representative on the board, Major General J. K. Gerhart, it reached similar conclusions that the loss of Indochina would have "the most serious repercussions on U.S. and free world interests and elsewhere." The loss of a single country, it said, might lead to the loss of the entire area, with grave economic consequences. It might seriously jeopardize U.S. security interests in the Far East and subject Japan to severe political and economic pressures. Based on these views, the Planning Board drew up concrete recommendations for consideration by the NSC. They were based on two possible contingencies. The United States should attempt to keep France in the war and warn China of the grave consequences of intervention. But if China should nonetheless intervene, the United States should seek international support for military operations while providing air and naval support to French combat troops in Indochina and considering direct military action against mainland China.[48]

These courses of action assumed that France would stay in Indochina. But General Gerhart pressed for consideration of alternatives in case the French decided to withdraw. To obtain military advice on such a contingency, the Planning Board turned to the Joint Chiefs, who referred the issue to the Joint Strategic and Logistical Plans committees for their views. The latter began work with certain assumptions: that there was no fighting in Korea, that China had not intervened in Indochina, and that a Vietminh victory there would have critical political, economic, and psychological consequences for the United States. They examined two possible alternatives (two others were rejected as offering no promise of avoiding a French defeat): (1) to deploy U.S. and allied forces in sufficient strength to assist the VNA to reduce the Vietminh to scattered bands, or (2) to assist the VNA to hold critical areas previously occupied by the French by providing air and naval support. They preferred the first alternative but viewed the second as a temporary measure while building up the VNA to handle the responsibility without outside assistance.

In considering the possibility of U.S. military intervention in Indochina, the Joint Strategic and Planning committees were not breaking entirely new ground. A National Security Council paper numbered NSC 162/2 and adopted in October 1953 had set out as the basic national security policy of the Eisenhower administration that certain countries, including Indochina, were of such strategic importance to the United States that, even though they were not allied to the United States by treaty, an attack on them "probably would compel the U.S. to react with military force either locally at the point of attack or against the military power of the aggressor."[49]

One question for Pentagon strategists facing the possibility of U.S. military intervention in Indochina was how to go about it. The administration's New Look policy, in seeking to reduce the need for large and expensive conventional forces, had called for the possible use of small nuclear weapons in limited wars. In October, NSC 126/2 had directed that in the event of hostilities brought about by Chinese or Russian aggression, "the United States will consider nuclear weapons to be as available for use as other munitions." Did that mean that nuclear weapons would be used in the defense of Indochina? If so, would they be most effective against enemy troops in the field or against lines of communications or industrial and military installations inside China? What would be the probable political and psychological effects at home and abroad of the use of nuclear weapons in Southeast Asia? Army Chief of Staff Mathew Ridgway pressed for systematic studies of these questions but with little success.

The use of nuclear weapons in the Indochina conflict thus raised some potential problems. But according to preliminary Defense Department estimates, the defense of Indochina without the use of such weapons raised equally serious questions. Studies undertaken by the Plans Division of the Army Staff in late 1953 concluded that should the French decide to withdraw, it would take seven U.S. army divisions plus a marine division to replace them. The effect on U.S. overall defense preparedness would be severe and would preclude further aid to NATO stockpiles and prevent the United States from fulfilling its NATO commitments in the event of a general war. Moreover, planners cautioned that successful military operations alone would not destroy the Vietminh political organization. That would take several years of intense political and psychologi-

cal warfare similar to what the British had undertaken in Malaya. In consequence, the Plans Division suggested that the United States undertake a "reevaluation of the importance of Indochina and Southeast Asia in relation to the
possible cost of saving it." Whether the Joint Strategic and Logistic Plans committees considered these views is not certain from the evidence. According to
the official history of the JCS, although the Joint Chiefs did not formally
endorse this report, they were in general agreement with its conclusions and
sent it to the NSC Planning Board to assist it in its own deliberations. The latter
then completed its study and sent it to the NSC as a Special Annex to NSC-177
for consideration and possible adoption.[50]

Before the National Security Council took up the proposed new policy
statement, it was sent to the Joint Chiefs for their evaluation. The JCS had just
received a gloomy estimate of the situation in Indochina from General Trapnell
in Saigon. The Vietminh had launched a new invasion of Laos, and French
intelligence sources reported that three Vietminh divisions, armed with antiaircraft artillery, were in the vicinity of the new French base at Dien Bien
Phu. The French had already requested 54 additional B-26s from the United
States and planned to ask for U.S. maintenance personnel to take care of their
upkeep.[51]

When the Joint Chiefs took up NSC-177 and its Special Annex at a meeting
held on January 6, 1954, they also had in hand a recommendation from the
Joint Strategic Survey Committee noting that because Indochina was critical
to U.S. security, the Joint Chiefs should press the administration to decide
whether to use military force if necessary to prevent the loss of the area to the
communists. The committee report recognized that political reasons might
compel the United States to accept the loss of Indochina, but it felt that the
United States should be prepared to do its utmost to prevent such a development and proposed that the Special Annex be revised to state that if the French
should decide to withdraw, the United States would provide all feasible aid to
the VNA, including the possibility of direct armed intervention (Alternative A
of the Special Annex).[52]

The Joint Chiefs discussed the proposal at their meeting on January 6 but
reached no decision. At a meeting of the Armed Forces Policy Council the
following day, the new JCS chairman Arthur Radford remarked that the JCS
had some comments on the Special Annex but needed time to study the paper.
But the proposal was attacked by civilian members of the council, and Secretary
of Defense Charles E. Wilson requested that the Special Annex be withdrawn
from further consideration.[53]

The issue was taken up again by the NSC at its meeting the following day.
In presenting the report, Admiral Radford said that the Joint Chiefs were not
yet prepared to make a judgment on NSC-177 or its Special Annex, but the
president set the mood, declaring (according to the note taker) "with great

force" that he "simply could not imagine the U.S. putting ground forces anywhere in Southeast Asia, except possibly in Malaya, which we would have to defend as a bulwark to our offshore island chain." To put U.S. troops anywhere else in the region was beyond his comprehension. The key, he said, was to get the Vietnamese to do the fighting themselves, and there was no sense even talking about U.S. forces replacing the French in Indochina. If that took place, Vietnam would absorb U.S. troops by divisions and the Vietnamese would transfer their hatred to the United States. He concluded that he was "bitterly opposed" to such an action and ordered that the Special Annex be withdrawn from consideration and destroyed.

But the president was more ambivalent about other forms of U.S. intervention. When Treasury Secretary George Humphrey opposed a suggestion by Admiral Radford to use U.S. combat aircraft to help save Dien Bien Phu, Eisenhower retorted that while he was determined to keep U.S. fighting men out of Asian jungles, it might be necessary to "put a finger in the dike" to protect our vital interests in the area. In the end, the NSC decided to approve the French request for B-26s and to defer final action on NSC-177 pending further consideration by the JCS.[54]

A week later, the NSC met again to consider minor amendments to NSC-177 offered by the Joint Chiefs and to vote on final approval. The final version called for continued U.S. aid to the French and assurances of U.S. support if they decided to negotiate. But it recommended that the United States insist that it be consulted if talks took place and then seek to influence the course of the negotiations. If China intervened overtly or covertly, the United States should seek U.N. and international support for military operations to support French ground forces in Indochina. If the French and the British did not support expanded military operations, the United States should consider taking such action unilaterally. In summing up, Secretary Dulles commented that the administration should not worry excessively over the possibility of the loss of Indochina because the United States could always promote guerrilla war there at low cost and teach the communists that we can "raise hell" too. NSC-177 was approved with minor changes as NSC 5405.[55]

In the end, the NSC had approved a new policy to keep the French in the war and prevent a further deterioration of the situation in Indochina. In the process it had reiterated the assumption of the previous policy statement that the loss of Indochina would "critically endanger" U.S. national security interests in Asia, but it had sidestepped the crucial issue of what action to take should the French decide to withdraw.[56]

Although the president had been instrumental in preventing a decision on how to deal with a French withdrawal, on January 16 he ordered the formation of a special committee composed of a number of his key advisers to undertake an analysis of the Southeast Asian situation and produce an action plan for the region. The committee was told to assume that a defeat in Indochina would be disastrous for U.S. national security and was asked to consider possible alternatives in case of a reverse in Indochina or elsewhere in the area.[57]

The first charge of the special committee was to evaluate a French request for additional B-26s and U.S. maintenance personnel. After some debate, the committee agreed to recommend the dispatch of 200 U.S. mechanics along with the B-26s, but reports of the decision reached Congress and caused a stir among those who feared that it could lead to a more direct U.S. role in the war. To placate critics, Eisenhower announced at a press conference on February 10 that the mechanics would be withdrawn by mid-June and would not take part in combat operations.

Eisenhower's assurances did not end public concern about U.S. involvement in Indochina. When one reporter asked whether U.S. actions could lead to direct U.S. involvement in combat operations, the president replied that "no one could be more bitterly opposed to ever getting the United States involved in a hot war in that region" than he was. "Consequently," he said, "every move that I authorize is calculated, as far as humans can do it, to make certain that that doesn't happen." Later he added that he "could not conceive of a greater tragedy for America" than to get heavily involved in an all-out war in any of those regions, particularly with large units. That is why, he said, we were supporting the French and the Vietnamese there.[58]

The Berlin Conference

While U.S. officials were wrestling with the French request for increased military assistance, the Laniel government continued its own efforts to find a negotiated settlement of the conflict. As the new year opened, attention in Paris focused on Berlin, where a conference of the foreign ministers of France, the United Kingdom, the United States, and the Soviet Union opened on January 25. The stated purpose of the conference was to discuss the situation in Germany and Austria, but the French hoped to use it as a forum to promote talks on Indochina. Moscow had its own hidden agenda but was apparently interested in easing international tensions. In Washington, there was an awareness of the possibility of a new attitude in Moscow, but key administration officials were wary that the Soviets might use the meeting not only to promote negotiations on Indochina but also diplomatic recognition of China.[59]

At the first plenary session held on January 25, Soviet Foreign Minister Vyacheslav Molotov, as expected, proposed a foreign ministerial conference, including China, to take place in May or June to consider "urgent measures for easing the tension in international relations." Dulles, ever fearful of opening the door to international recognition of Beijing, was reluctant, but he was under heavy French pressure and in late 1953 had already agreed to a conference if the

Korean talks went well. The French were encouraged in their attitude by the British, who had begun to undertake an agonizing reappraisal of the Indochina conflict. Officials at the Foreign Office in London had watched the situation with concern and feared that it could lead to a major Great Power confrontation. Previously, Prime Minister Churchill and Foreign Secretary Eden had felt no sense of urgency about the situation, but now Eden agreed to a suggestion by Georges Bidault to convene a five-power meeting to discuss problems in East Asia. Initially Secretary Dulles balked, but eventually he agreed to a conference if it were broadened by the addition of other interested countries. It was then agreed to hold a conference on Korea and Indochina at Geneva in May.[60]

On his return to Washington, Dulles attempted to justify his decision to attend a five-power conference on the grounds that the fall of the Laniel government in Paris could not only affect French staying power in Indochina but also imperil French membership in the European Defense Community (EDC), a vote on which was scheduled to take place later in the year. He added that the principle of no five-power conference had been upheld because the United States would negotiate with China only on a de facto basis.[61]

A few days after the Berlin Conference, the president's Special Committee on Indochina submitted its report to the White House. The report had been drafted by a working group under Marine Corps General Graves B. Erskine, the chairman of the committee, and it offered little that was new. It stated that the U.S. objective in Southeast Asia was twofold: to defeat the communists in Indochina and establish a Western-oriented complex of states including not only the three Associated States but also Thailand, Burma, Malaya, Indonesia, and the Philippines. It called for increased aid to the French for that purpose but warned that if that was insufficient, the United States "may wish to consider direct military action in Southeast Asia to ensure the maintenance of our vital interests in the area."[62]

Then the committee's report turned to the issue of negotiations. To obtain an evaluation of the military implications of a diplomatic settlement in Indochina, Secretary Dulles had asked the Joint Chiefs to undertake a study of how much the French could lose to the Vietminh without risking the loss of Indochina in its entirety. In their answering report dated March 12, the JCS found little potential benefit in negotiations without a "substantial improvement" in the military situation. A coalition government would lead to a communist takeover, while partition would represent a "partial victory" for the Vietminh and would be tantamount to recognition of territorial expansion based on armed force. If the country were divided at the sixteenth parallel, it would give Laos and Tonkin to the communists and open the Thai border to subversion. As for elections, a combination of factors, including widespread illiteracy and the lack of communications in rural areas, prevented the holding of a representative plebiscite, thus enabling the communists to pervert the elections and intimidate voters. The outcome of the election, the report said, would be hard to predict, but the current situation suggested that it would lead to an almost certain loss of the Associated States to communist control. Should Indochina be lost, the conquest of the remainder of Southeast Asia would inevitably follow. The report concluded that if France insisted on a negotiated settlement, the United States should decline to associate itself with such a settlement, thus preserving its freedom of action to pursue with the Associated States and its allies (notably Great Britain) the ways and means of continuing the struggle. The JCS further proposed that the NSC consider the extent to which the United States should commit its resources in Indochina with or without the French.[63]

These views were endorsed by the special committee working group, which added its own cover letter stating that from a strategic point of view, "no solution of the Indochina problem short of victory is acceptable." It pointed out that there were alternative courses of action to seek a favorable resolution at Geneva, including the possibility of U.S. involvement with air, naval, and ground forces in the event of failure at Geneva. The report was approved by Secretary of Defense Wilson and forwarded to the secretary of state on March 23.[64]

The Ely Visit

One reason for the growing sense of urgency in Washington was the increasingly ominous situation in Indochina. Until early March the situation appeared relatively stable. General O'Daniel, as always, was optimistic, and Harold Stassen, director of the Foreign Operations Administration, had just returned from Saigon with a report that the French appeared to welcome a Vietminh attack on Dien Bien Phu in the belief that it would lead to heavy enemy casualties. At a meeting of the NSC on March 4 he reported that the military situation in Indochina was "a great deal better than we had imagined."[65]

Within a few days, however, it became evident that such optimism was seriously misplaced. On the thirteenth, Vietminh infantry units attacked the French base at Dien Bien Phu in "human-wave" tactics and overran the French outposts on the northern perimeter of the base. Four days later, several neighboring strongpoints were lost, rendering two airstrips unusable.

A key factor in Vietminh success had been their ability to mobilize thousands of porters (many of them women) from rural villages throughout the country to transport heavy weapons, piece by piece, on their backs, over tortuous mountain trails from the Chinese border to Dien Bien Phu. Once arrived, the pieces were assembled and placed in tunnels dug into the hills surrounding the French base. From there they were able to pummel French defenses in the valley and gradually demolish the airfield.

By mid-March, then, it had become increasingly apparent in Paris that the

Vietminh threat to the French outpost at Dien Bien Phu was serious and that the collapse of French resistance there was a real possibility. Although General Navarre had earlier insisted to U.S. observers that the loss of Dien Bien Phu would not be a serious setback to the overall French military position, it had by now taken on major importance as a symbol of French determination to remain in Indochina, and a defeat there could have a disastrous effect on French public opinion.

Shaken by the prospect of imminent disaster, the Laniel government sent General Paul Ely, chairman of the French General Staff, to Washington to solicit an increase in U.S. military assistance to reduce the Vietminh threat to the beleaguered garrison. Ely arrived on March 20 and at a dinner with Vice-President Nixon, Admiral Radford, and other administration figures he painted a bleak picture of the situation at Dien Bien Phu, which he estimated had only a 50-50 chance of survival. A defeat there, he admitted, would be a serious blow to French morale. In meetings the following days with U.S. officials, Ely submitted specific requests, including additional B-26s and C-47 cargo planes, helicopters, and maintenance personnel. When he met briefly with Eisenhower on the twenty-second, the president was sympathetic and approved all of his requests except for helicopters (which would take too long to supply) and C-47s (which were not available).

On the twenty-third, Ely met with Secretary Dulles and asked if the United States would intervene in the event that Chinese aircraft became directly involved in the fighting in Indochina. Dulles hedged, saying that before such a decision could be reached, several factors would have to be examined because U.S. prestige would be involved. In any event, the United States would insist on playing a greater role in war planning and the training of the VNA than was currently the case. He also said that Washington would expect a firm French commitment to grant full independence to the Associated States.[66]

Ely went into further detail on the subject in private talks with Admiral Radford, who said Ely asked him for clarification on how the United States might be able to provide specific military assistance to the French garrison at Dien Bien Phu. Radford replied that 350 carrier-based planes could wage air strikes on Vietminh positions at Dien Bien Phu over a two-day period. He pointed out that CINCPAC had already worked out procedures for using carrier-based aircraft in Indochina but would require firm agreements with the French on command arrangements and base facilities. Such issues, he said, would have to be dealt with at a higher level.[67]

The meeting between Ely and Radford would inspire considerable acrimony between Paris and Washington during the complex period surrounding the end of the Franco-Vietminh conflict. General Ely apparently felt that he had obtained a commitment from Radford to seek unilateral intervention by U.S. forces. Admiral Radford has claimed that he made it clear to his visitor that higher authorities must decide whether to grant the French request, and a memorandum by a subordinate backs him up. And the record suggests that, whatever Radford might have said about the matter, Secretary Dulles and President Eisenhower had made it clear that a number of conditions needed to be fulfilled before direct U.S. military involvement in the Indochina conflict could be approved.

Still, in the days that followed, Radford pushed for U.S. air strikes at Dien Bien Phu (known as Operation Vulture), and Ely left Washington under the assumption that he had Radford's assurances that a French request for a U.S. air strike at Dien Bien Phu would be approved. Although a final judgment in the blame for the misunderstanding cannot yet be reached, it seems clear that, in the interpretation of historian George Herring, Radford had been indiscreet. By his own admission, Radford was an active advocate of intervention. But he felt that French measures to save Dien Bien Phu might be "too little and too late" and that only "prompt and forceful intervention" by the United States could avert the loss of Southeast Asia to the communists. He was convinced that the United States "must be prepared to take such action."[68]

To Intervene or Not to Intervene?

On March 24, Dulles reported to the president on the results of the Ely visit. Eisenhower agreed with Dulles that the United States should not get involved in the Indochina conflict unless there were political preconditions for a successful outcome. But he did not wholly exclude the idea of a single strike, if it appeared virtually certain to produce a decisive result. The main problem of the moment, however, was more political than military. In Paris, Pierre Mendès-France was calling for immediate talks with the Vietminh, and the Laniel government had been pressing the administration to recognize the PRC or lighten its trade embargo with the mainland to obtain a quid pro quo on Indochina. In a pessimistic phone conversation with Admiral Radford on the twenty-fourth, Dulles said that the United States must have a policy in case France decided to pull out of Indochina. "We could lose Europe, Asia and Africa all at once," he said, "if we don't watch out."[69]

On March 25 the NSC met to consider a memorandum from the Joint Chiefs asking for a decision on possible U.S. action in the event of a French withdrawal or defeat in Indochina. Dulles, with the support of Defense Secretary Charles E. Wilson, asked that the Planning Board prepare a report on the issue. Robert Cutler, special assistant to the president on national security affairs, consented but asked whether the report should deal with the possible intervention of U.S. armed forces, since the Special Annex on the subject, which had been submitted in January, had not met a favorable response from the president and had been withdrawn for destruction.

But now Eisenhower was apparently more willing to discuss the issue, replying that it was necessary to find out the extent to which we should go in employing ground forces to save Indochina from the communists. But the president said that he wanted to explore other possibilities such as an appeal by the Associated States to the United Nations or to specific individual states to join in a broadened effort to save Indochina. Such a grouping, he said, would have to be confined to nations in and around Southeast Asia because the inclusion of states such as Japan and Korea would be certain to incur hostility. Secretary Wilson suggested that the United States should forget Indochina for a while and concentrate on the effort to get the remaining Southeast Asian states to resist by themselves, but Eisenhower expressed his doubt that the idea was feasible because he believed that the collapse of Indochina would produce a chain reaction leading to the fall of the entire region to communism.

The meeting then turned to the problem of how to obtain congressional approval for any action the United States might take in Indochina. Dulles emphasized that the administration must consult with Congress on the issue but that no approach need to be taken immediately because there was no imminent danger of a French withdrawal. But, he added, this might be the time to explore with Capitol Hill what support could be anticipated in the event it seemed desirable to intervene in Indochina. The meeting concluded with instructions to the Planning Board to make recommendations before the Geneva Conference convened regarding the extent to which and the circumstances under which the United States should commit itself to support the Associated States, either with the French, in concert with other states, or on its own.[70]

The NSC meeting of March 25 had thus set forth two major objectives for the immediate future: to create a framework for possible united action to assist or possibly replace the French in Indochina and to consider possible courses of action in case the French decided to withdraw from the area.

The first duty fell primarily on the State Department. On March 27, Secretary Dulles informed British ambassador Roger Makins that the United States was considering an appeal to the United Nations or some form of regional grouping to undertake the defense of Southeast Asia in case the French decided to pull out of Indochina. Two days later, in a speech entitled "The Threat of Red Asia" before the Overseas Press Club of America in New York City, Dulles signaled the inauguration of a new policy. In a wide-ranging discussion of the situation in the area, he described the Vietminh as an integral part of the global communist movement headed by the Soviet Union and China and said that if the communists were to achieve uncontested control over Indochina or any substantial part thereof, they would surely resume the same pattern of aggression against other free peoples in the area. This, he said, would be a "grave threat" to the free community of nations, and the United States was convinced that it should be met by united action. Dulles conceded that such a policy might involve serious risks, but they would be far less than those that would arise a few years later if we dared not be resolute today.[71]

On the final day of March, the Vietminh opened a new offensive at Dien Bien Phu. In the interval since their earlier series of attacks, Vietminh leaders had reevaluated the "human-wave" strategy advocated by Chinese advisers (an approach that had been enormously costly in casualties without securing the final objective) and had now switched to a new policy of "slow but sure" advances characterized by a steady wearing down of French defenses and a heavy artillery bombardment of the French airstrip to prevent the French from reinforcing their position. The Vietminh 308th Division painstakingly dug a vast network of trenches within 50 meters of the French barbed wire, and the French outpost of Isabelle was surrounded on three sides. At a briefing of congressional leaders on March 29, Eisenhower announced that it might be necessary for the United States to take military action to save Dien Bien Phu from the communists. If so, he promised to inform Congress.[72]

The renewed threat at Dien Bien Phu and concern over the mood of defeatism in Paris pervaded the atmosphere in Washington as the month drew to a close. A few days before, the Special Annex that had been withdrawn from consideration in January was circulated among members of the NSC Planning Board for possible use in its future deliberations. At the Pentagon, JCS Chairman Arthur Radford had polled the remaining members of the Joint Chiefs of Staff on whether they would agree to recommend an immediate offer of U.S. air and naval assistance to the French. Radford's proposal was unanimously rejected.

On April 1, the NSC met to consider actions the United States might take to aid the French at Dien Bien Phu. After a briefing, during which Admiral Radford said that unless the garrison was reinforced there was no way to save it, Eisenhower raised the question of whether the United States should consider intervening to prevent the fall of the outpost to the communists. Referring to the Joint Chiefs' rejection of Admiral Radford's proposal for an immediate air strike, he said that though he realized the terrible risks involved, he saw no reason why the proposal for intervention should not be taken under consideration. But the president apparently wanted to keep his options open, and at his insistence, the meeting took no immediate action on the matter. Eisenhower met with key members of the council in his office after the meeting. There is no record of what went on at that meeting, but other evidence suggests that a decision was reached to consult immediately with key congressional leaders on possible air and naval action to restrain China. At a luncheon held shortly after the meeting in his office, Eisenhower mentioned that the United States might have to send in a squadron of planes from carriers off the coast to bomb Vietminh positions at Dien Bien Phu. If so, he said, "we'd have to deny it forever."[73]

The next morning, the president met with Dulles, Charles Wilson, and Admiral Radford at the White House. Dulles presented the draft of a possible congressional resolution on the Indochina situation, which pointed out that China and its agents in Indochina were attacking the legally constituted governments there. Because such action gravely endangered the peace and security of the region, the United States was prepared to retaliate, either with the United Nations, through united action or by the inherent right of individual self-defense. It asked for a congressional resolution authorizing the president "in the event he determines that such action is required to protect and defend the safety and security of the United States, to employ the Naval and Air Forces of the United States to assist the forces which are resisting aggression in Southeast Asia, to prevent the extension and expansion of that aggression, and to protect and defend the safety and security of the United States." In commenting on the draft, Secretary Dulles remarked that he and Admiral Radford might be in disagreement on its ultimate purpose. Radford might view it as authorization for a possible air strike regardless of whether allied unity was realized, whereas he himself viewed it as a deterrent to Beijing and a strong position through which to seek to realize united action with our allies and other states in the area. Radford, perhaps sobered by lack of support from the other Joint Chiefs, replied that the outcome at Dien Bien Phu would be determined in a matter of hours and thus the situation did not call for U.S. participation, although he did not exclude future events. In the end, the president approved the draft but instructed that it not be raised before sounding out the thinking of congressional leaders on the subject.[74]

The same day, Admiral Radford, apparently on the instructions of Defense Secretary Charles Wilson, convened a second meeting of the Joint Chiefs to seek their recommendation on how the United States should respond to a French request for U.S. air and naval assistance in Indochina. This time the answer was ambivalent, with Ridgway and Marine General Lemuel B. Shepherd opposed, Admiral Robert B. Carney ambivalent, and General Nathan Twining giving his qualified approval.[75]

On April 3, Secretary Dulles and Admiral Radford met with key congressional leaders from both political parties. Dulles explained the dangers facing the United States as a result of the deteriorating situation in Indochina and asked for congressional backing on the possible use of U.S. air and sea power to achieve U.S. objectives in the region. At first the response was positive, but after further discussion a consensus gradually emerged that there should be no congressional action until the secretary had obtained political and material commitments from U.S. allies. Dulles and Radford assured the lawmakers that the administration did not contemplate the introduction of U.S. ground forces, but one congressman expressed the view that once the flag was committed, the use of land forces would inevitably follow. At the close of the meeting, Dulles agreed to seek definite commitments from Great Britain and other U.S. allies and said that he had already begun to discuss the issue with foreign diplomatic representatives in Washington. It was the consensus of the meeting that if such commitments were obtained, a congressional resolution could be passed authorizing the president to commit U.S. armed forces in the area.

The following evening, President Eisenhower held a meeting of key officials at the White House to discuss Indochina. The president agreed with Secretary Dulles and Admiral Radford that U.S. forces could be sent to Indochina under strict conditions: that the intervention take place in the form of a united action including the United Kingdom and other key states interested in the area, that the French agree to maintain their own responsibilities in the area, and that the Laniel government make a specific commitment to grant full independence to the Associated States.[76]

Eisenhower's decision to consult with key members of Congress on the issue of using force has provoked considerable debate among scholars and other observers. His action has been lauded as a welcome contrast to the unilateralist behavior of his successors in the White House. Some have asserted that he deliberately used the meeting to isolate hawkish members of his own administration such as Radford and Richard Nixon, who advocated direct U.S. intervention in the war. Others have maintained that Eisenhower had no intention of permitting direct U.S. involvement in Indochina and used congressional doubts as an excuse for inaction.

Unfortunately, available evidence does not permit a definitive conclusion on Eisenhower's intentions. It does seem clear, however, that although the president was reluctant to intervene directly in the Indochina conflict, he was willing to consider it under certain circumstances and sought a blank check from Congress to free his hands to approach the allies for possible united action. Had he actually been scheming to use congressional reluctance as a pretext to avoid direct involvement, it seems improbable that he would have sought to remove such constraints on his future decision-making authority. More likely he had not yet decided on future courses of action and hoped to keep his options open for whatever contingencies might arise.[77]

After the meeting, a cable arrived from Paris. Ambassador Douglas Dillon had been called to see Premier Laniel and was handed an urgent request for intervention by U.S. carrier-based aircraft at Dien Bien Phu. In making the request, Laniel explained that General Ely had returned from Washington with Radford's personal assurance that he would do his best to obtain approval for U.S. naval and air action in Indochina if the situation required it, and he added that evidence of increased Chinese involvement made it necessary. The following morning, Dulles replied that the United States could not commit itself to belligerent action in Indochina without a full political understanding with the French and on a coalition basis with British Commonwealth participation. In addition, he said, congressional action would be required. Dillon saw Foreign Minister Bidault on the sixth and reported that the latter, though disappointed, had understood the reasons for rejection. But the French continued to hope for at least limited U.S. assistance to save the situation at Dien Bien Phu and requested ten to twenty B-29s, complete with the necessary maintenance personnel, to be put at the disposal of the French but based in the Philippines.[78]

The National Security Council met the same day to discuss the French request as well as the report by the Planning Board on possible U.S. intervention that had been requested at the meeting on March 25. The NSC refused the French request for the B-29s on the grounds that the planes could not be put in operation in time to have an effect on the battle at Dien Bien Phu. It was eventually decided that additional B-26s would be sent instead.[79]

Most of the meeting was devoted to the report by the Planning Board and its implications for U.S. policy in Southeast Asia. The report supported the request of the Joint Chiefs for an immediate decision on whether to intervene in Indochina. But Eisenhower, who a few days earlier had appeared receptive to U.S. armed intervention, now returned to the reluctance he had expressed in January. The president repeated his opposition to unilateral intervention, arguing against the assumption that the loss of Indochina would lead necessarily to the loss of all of Southeast Asia and citing the difficulties in getting Congress to agree. Secretary Dulles, in a manner that suggested it might have been prearranged, lent his support to the president, pointing out the reluctance of Congress and the British, and said the key issue was not intervention but the creation of a coalition to make it unnecessary. As a result, the NSC decided once again to postpone action on the proposal and to concentrate on creating a regional alliance for the defense of the area before the convening of the Geneva Conference.

The NSC then turned to a second report prepared by the special committee to recommend courses of action if Indochina were to be lost. Like the Planning Board report, it called for the creation of a regional organization to prevent the loss of Indochina to the communists or, failing that, "to oppose further communist progress in Southeast Asia." Eisenhower expressed himself in favor of the report, remarking that it was better to have a multinational political organization for mutual defense than emergency military action, but not all were reassured. Vice-President Nixon said that the proposed alliance might prove useful in preventing overt aggression, but he warned that the main problem in the area was not outside aggression but internal subversion. Would such an organization meet that threat, he asked, if local governments were unable to meet the danger themselves? Dulles answered in the affirmative.[80]

Harold Stassen, director of the Foreign Operations Administration, also had reservations. Stassen saw only three stark alternatives for U.S. policy in Indochina: to give up and perhaps lose all of Southeast Asia, to intervene at the risk of war with China, or, finally (which he preferred), to save the southern part of Indochina and form a regional organization to defend it and the remainder of Southeast Asia from further communist encroachment. Stassen's proposal provoked a hostile response. President Eisenhower interrupted to state that the United States could not be the colonial power that succeeded the French. Defense Secretary Wilson argued that the proposal was unsound because Tonkin was the key to Southeast Asia and that Stassen's idea to hold the South was, in Radford's words, a "temporary solution at best." Concern was also expressed by Treasury Secretary George Humphrey, who complained that if the United States formed a regional organization in Southeast Asia, it would end up "policing all the governments in the world." Where, he asked, would it end? Eisenhower testily asked Humphrey for his alternative. No free government ever went communist by its own choice, he commented, and we cannot say that internal communist subversion is none of our business. The meeting ended without a consensus on the proposal to reach a decision whether to intervene in Indochina with combat troops, but it did decide to proceed toward the formation of a regional grouping before the convening of the Geneva Conference, while simultaneously pressing the French to accelerate the program for national independence of the Associated States.[81]

Mission to London and Paris

Following the meeting of the NSC on April 6, Secretary Dulles initiated plans to round up support for united action on Indochina. He had already discussed the issue with the ambassador from New Zealand to try to help with the British, whose attitude, in Dulles's words, was "disappointing." In his view, Foreign Secretary Anthony Eden had shown little understanding of the seriousness of the situation during the Berlin Conference and had dealt with it as a private matter between the United States and France. So he suggested that President Eisenhower send a private letter to Prime Minister Winston Churchill to urge his support before the tripartite talks to be held at Paris in the middle of the month. Churchill's reply was noncommittal, but he did invite Dulles to London to discuss the matter.[82]

Dulles also raised the issue with French Ambassador Henri Bonnet, who visited the State Department to say that France wanted to study the U.S. proposal further. Dulles took advantage of the opportunity to discuss negotiations. He argued against a settlement that would be only a disguised surrender. Nor, he contended, would a demarcation line work because the Vietminh were everywhere. The only solution, he insisted, was to seek united action through a coalition of states to convince China of the dangers of intervention. If such an organization were to be formed in advance of the Geneva Conference, it would strengthen the allied position in the talks. But Bonnet was dubious, pointing out that French public opinion was now strongly in favor of a cease-fire and a peace settlement.

On April 10 Dulles left for London to consult with the British before proceeding on to the tripartite talks in Paris. He must have arrived in London with some trepidation. Eden's hesitation about Indochina had already exasperated him on several occasions, and the British ambassador in Washington had warned him that the British were increasingly pessimistic about the situation and felt that partition would be the "least undesirable solution."

Washington's impression that the British were balking was correct. In the weeks leading up to the meeting in London they had undergone their own agonizing reappraisal of the situation in Indochina and had come to the conclusion that the best solution was to await the results of the talks at Geneva. The fact was that Eden simply did not accept U.S. premises. He saw no will to act in Paris and no value to allied intervention, which could not be limited to air and sea power. A warning to China would be "dangerous and unnecessary." Nor did he take an apocalyptic view of the consequences of defeat in Indochina. Whereas Dulles and other Eisenhower administration officials expressed the view, at least in public, that the loss of Indochina could lead to the loss of all Southeast Asia, Eden felt that Malaya and perhaps other areas could be saved.[83]

In his talks with Dulles in London, Eden took a conciliatory but evasive position. To his guest's insistence on the need for united action he agreed that it was important to undertake a common effort to hold as much of Southeast Asia as possible but argued that there was no basis for collective action before the conference in Geneva, admitting frankly that "he did not know whether Indochina could be held." Rather than debating the contrasting premises, Eden and Dulles then sparred over the membership for the proposed regional organization. Eden, ever solicitous of Commonwealth concerns, argued that it was necessary to seek the support of Asian nations in the area. Burma, and perhaps India and Pakistan, would probably not wish to participate, but it was important to ask them. Dulles, whose impatience with the neutralist sentiments of many Asian leaders was legendary, countered that it would then be necessary to include the Republic of China, South Korea, and possibly Japan.[84]

In retrospect, this may have been the time for Eden and Dulles to clear the air over their fundamental differences. But neither was willing to risk a break over the issue and the British, in the words of one observer, were "too shamefaced in their new realism" to make clear to the United States and to their own people their reluctance to get involved. Eden, concerned at maintaining Anglo-American amity, hoped to move the United States imperceptibly toward the British position. Dulles, preoccupied with the Indochina crisis and still hoping to save the area from a Vietminh takeover, wanted to avoid a split and failed to understand the underlying message behind Eden's comments. In the end, they settled on an anodyne communique that declared that the two governments were ready to take part with others in an examination of the possibility of establishing a collective defense within the framework of the U.N. Charter "to assure the peace, security and freedom of Southeast Asia and the Western Pacific." On his departure for Paris, Dulles cabled President Eisenhower that he felt he had succeeded in dissuading the British from the idea of doing nothing before the convening of the Geneva Conference.[85]

After his arrival in Paris, Dulles met with Foreign Minister Georges Bidault and explained to him that the United States was prepared only to provide increased military assistance in Indochina as part of a program of united action to resist a communist takeover. He admitted that the British were balking but said that Thailand and the Philippines were receptive. But Bidault was cautious. If this opportunity had appeared three years ago, he remarked, France would have welcomed it, but now the French people wanted peace and the Laniel government was reluctant to do anything that might disturb plans for Geneva. After lunch the two resumed their discussions. Dulles pressed for a French commitment to give the Associated States legal permission to withdraw from the French Union, but Bidault demurred. The final communique said only that France and the United States, in concert with other nations, would examine the possibility of forming a collective defense organization to defend the area.[86]

The Collapse of United Action

Dulles returned to Washington on April 15 and reported the results of his trip to the president, who shared his disappointment at the evasive British response and expressed anger at the French attempt to obtain U.S. support as a "junior partner" while retaining full authority over war policy. He was also exasperated at the French refusal to grant full independence (using "weasel words") to the Associated States.

Dulles was not deterred from action and immediately initiated plans for a meeting of allied representatives to explore the concept of united action. But on the eighteenth the British unexpectedly indicated their refusal to attend. Eden said he had overlooked the meeting of Colombo Powers scheduled to be held in late April and added that any organization not including India, Pakistan, and Ceylon would produce criticism that would be "most unhelpful." Eden concluded that Great Britain could not attend such a meeting until after the meeting of the Colombo Powers, and even then he doubted that London would agree.[87]

Secretary Dulles took the news calmly and reorganized the proposed conference into an expanded meeting to explain the results of his recent trip to Europe. But privately he was angry with Eden, who he felt feared intervention would bring on World War III. A few days later he returned to Paris for a meeting of the Atlantic Council and met with Eden and Bidault to confer on the impending Geneva Conference. In Paris he discovered that morale was at a new low. The French outpost at Dien Bien Phu was still under siege and was now down to 3,000 men. The situation in the Red River Delta was shaky, with the Vietminh holding the entire area except for the Hanoi-Haiphong corridor. Georges Bidault, who appeared "close to the breaking point," informed Dulles that massive intervention was the only way to save Dien Bien Phu. Dulles reiterated that Washington would intervene only as part of a broad coalition, but Bidault replied that if Dien Bien Phu were to be lost, the French people would regard coalition as a trick to keep them fighting and would probably pull out of Indochina. The French might not win the war with U.S. assistance, he admitted, but they would feel honor bound to continue the battle. Dillon had warned Dulles that unless the United States agreed to help out at Dien Bien Phu the Laniel government might fall, but Dulles refused to budge, reiterating to Bidault that any U.S. action would require congressional approval and the formation of a coalition. The use of B-29s was "out of the question" under present circumstances because that would constitute a belligerent action and require congressional approval. He did promise to relay the request to Eisenhower, but in a message to Washington he said that the application of armed force by executive action was not warranted under the circumstances because U.S. national security was not under threat, nor was it clear that such action would be in its long-term interests.[88]

Dulles's meetings with Bidault would later cause additional misunderstanding and acrimony. In August, shortly after the conclusion of the Geneva Conference, Bidault claimed that in a private conversation with him during an intermission between formal talks, Dulles had offered atom bombs to the French for the defense of Dien Bien Phu, a charge he later repeated in his memoirs. When informed of this claim by the U.S. Embassy in Paris, Dulles said he had no recollection of making the offer and insisted there must have been some misunderstanding. In an effort to clear up the matter, a member of the U.S. Embassy talked to a French official, who agreed that Bidault had been almost incoherent that day, even to members of his own staff, and had probably misunderstood Dulles's meaning. Without further evidence to the contrary, this seems to be the most likely explanation because the use of atomic weapons in Indochina had already been considered and rejected as unsuitable, and Dulles was habitually careful not to overstep his authority.

Yet Bidault's contention that Washington might consider offering atom bombs to the French for possible use in Indochina was not far off the mark. At a meeting of the NSC Planning Board on April 29, the issue of using the "new weapons" in Indochina was raised for discussion. Some board members argued that use of U.S. atomic power in Indochina could deter the Chinese from retaliation, while failure to do so might suggest to Beijing that the United States was afraid to take advantage of its technological superiority. Robert Cutler discussed the issue with the president and vice-president the following morning, and they replied that it was unlikely that atomic weapons would be appropriate for use at Dien Bien Phu. But they agreed that the United States "might *consider* saying to the French that we had never yet given them any 'new weapons' and if they wanted some *now* for possible use, we might give them a few." Both Eisenhower and Nixon agreed, however, that the formation of the regional grouping was more important than the possible use of atomic power in Indochina and that our allies should not be informed in advance of the administration's attitude on the question.[89]

While in Paris, Dulles also met separately with Eden in an attempt to clear up the misunderstanding that had arisen as a result of his visit to London earlier in the month. Dulles stressed the importance of the appearance of united action to strengthen the French hand at Geneva as well as the need for plans to hold the remainder of the region if the French withdrew. But Eden remained skeptical. He was concerned at the effect of allied intervention on world opinion and the reaction of the Vietnamese to the possibility of a Chinese entry into the war. Admiral Radford, who had accompanied Dulles to Paris, tried to reassure Eden on the danger of a Great Power confrontation (the acceptance of risks was necessary, he said, to avoid being "nibbled to death"), but Eden was unconvinced. He conceded that Indochina was critical to the security of Southeast Asia and promised to take the issue to the cabinet, but he was apprehensive about the state of British public opinion.[90]

At the final meeting of the tripartite foreign ministers on the afternoon of April 24, Dulles asked Bidault point-blank what the French would do if Dien Bien Phu fell. Bidault replied that he and Laniel would wish to continue the fight, but the loss would be of "tremendous symbolic importance" and he could not guarantee what position the government would eventually adopt. Dulles then showed Bidault the draft of a letter of reply to a request from General Navarre for immediate U.S. air strikes on Dien Bien Phu. The letter noted that U.S. conditions on intervention in Indochina still stood. It stated that the United States was not convinced that an air strike would lift the siege at Dien Bien Phu, or that the fall of the outpost would significantly alter the French position in Indochina. It concluded that the best way to save Indochina was through united action.[91]

But Dulles's continuing effort to revive his proposal for united action ran into more difficulties. Eden met with members of the British cabinet and the Chiefs of Staff on April 25. They agreed with his position that although the situation in Indochina was grave, intervention would not be either politically or militarily effective. The cabinet decided to take no action before the Geneva Conference but to "study measures" to ensure the defense of the rest of Southeast Asia in the event that Indochina fell to the communists.[92]

The president instructed Admiral Radford to stop in London to talk to the

British on his return from Paris, but Radford had no success. Field Marshal Sir John Harding told him that military action would have little effect and that in any case the British were confident they could hold Malaya whatever happened in Indochina. Later, Radford talked with Churchill, who said that only the atom bomb ("that horrible thing") would save Indochina. In a philosophical mood, Churchill observed that sometimes it was necessary to accept defeat. Britain had its India, he said, and France would have its Dien Bien Phu. There was a danger of general war, he warned, and "it would be folly to squander our limited resources around the fringes."[93]

Dulles still did not give up and tried to sound out the Australians on the issue, but, following the lead of the British, they refused to take action before Geneva. Even in the United States, reports of possible U.S. intervention had inflamed public opinion. An extended debate had taken place in the Senate on April 6, and several lawmakers expressed their opposition to unilateral U.S. involvement in the Indochina conflict. Senator John F. Kennedy of Massachusetts argued that a satisfactory solution to the problem could not be achieved until France granted total independence to the Associated States.[94]

The following day, President Eisenhower raised the issue at a press conference. Alluding to the strategic and economic importance of the area to the free world, he warned of a possible domino effect if Indochina were to fall to the communists. Eisenhower expressed his doubts that a satisfactory settlement could be achieved at the Geneva Conference, but he refused to comment on whether the United States might decide to intervene as a last result to prevent a Vietminh victory. Two weeks later, however, in a speech to the American Society of Newspaper Editors, Vice-President Richard Nixon expressed the opinion that American troops should be sent to Indochina if the French decided to withdraw. In an effort to calm the ensuing public uproar, the administration claimed that Nixon had made an off-the-record reply to a hypothetical question and that his comment did not represent a departure from official policy. But concern continued, and on April 26 President Eisenhower assured Republican congressional leaders that U.S. combat troops would not be introduced into Indochina except as part of a coalition of interested nations to resist the spread of communism in Southeast Asia. He doubted that ground troops would be needed and said that it would be a tragic error for the United States to intervene alone. In any event, he promised, Congress would be consulted in advance.[95]

On April 29 Eisenhower held a news conference to calm public speculation on the war. He promised that the United States would not become involved in Indochina except "through the constitutional process which, of course, involved a declaration of war by Congress." A collapse of the anticommunist position there, he said, would be unacceptable, but he warned that a totally satisfactory solution could not be expected. The most that could be anticipated would be "a practical way of getting along."[96]

The issue came to a head at a meeting of the NSC held immediately following the presidential news conference on April 29. CIA director Allen Dulles reported that the fall of Dien Bien Phu would have very serious but not catastrophic consequences. Admiral Radford took immediate issue with that view, citing a warning from General Ely that if Dien Bien Phu fell, the VNA would "melt away." But the members were sobered by Acting Secretary of State Walter Bedell Smith, who passed on the view of Secretary Dulles (who was in Geneva preparing for the conference) that open U.S. intervention in Indochina could bring the Chinese Communists into the war. In a cable to the State Department, Dulles reported that the French were now inclined to accept a settlement that would assign them enclaves in all three regions of Vietnam, to be protected by U.S. air and sea power. If the United States supported the plan, he predicted, the ANZUS nations would eventually go along, although the British might initially resist.

The president was the first to comment on Dulles's cable. He said that British views "had nothing whatever to do" with U.S. decisions on whether to assist the French but that he did not see how the United States could intervene without the participation of other nations and a request from the Associated States. Harold Stassen revived his proposal for unilateral U.S. intervention in southern Vietnam, if necessary with ground forces, and expressed confidence that Congress and the American people would support such a decision if it were made clear that it was necessary to save the entire region from communism.

But Stassen's proposal elicited a quick rejoinder from Eisenhower, who pointed out the problems in such an approach. To the Asian peoples, he said, the United States would look like a colonial power because few in that part of the world understood the cause of the free world. Moreover, he added, where would we obtain the necessary armed forces? Finally, he pointed out that unilateral U.S. intervention in Indochina could mean a general war with China and perhaps the Soviet Union.

Stassen did not back down, expressing his doubts about Chinese intervention and asserting that if the United States showed a lack of courage it could lose support from nations throughout the free world. This was the time and place to make a stand, he said, and threaten the ultimate sanction of an all-out attack on China if it retaliated. But Eisenhower remained skeptical and reiterated that a policy of collective action was the only posture consistent with U.S. national security as a whole. To go in unilaterally in Indochina or elsewhere, he said, amounted to an attempt to police the entire world and opened up the charge that the United States was motivated by imperialist ambition. Without allies, he said, the leader is just an adventurer like Genghis Khan. The cause of the free world would never win, he said, if resources were frittered away in local engagements. When Stassen retorted that the United States could avoid that danger by making it clear that general war would result if the communists crossed national boundaries, the president replied that if he had to make that decision he would have to consider whether to launch a world war.

The confrontation between President Eisenhower and Harold Stassen did not conclude the deliberations of the NSC that afternoon. In an effort to reconcile opposing views that would later become a familiar tactic in the long-running Vietnam debate, Walter Bedell Smith sought a middle way between doing too much and doing nothing. Could Asian nations be induced to join in collective action—even without the British—thus meeting U.S. conditions for intervention and making possible an air strike at Dien Bien Phu? Even if the outpost should fall to the Vietminh, he said, the French might be willing to continue the struggle in Indochina. The president replied that this was what he had in mind until the Australians had indicated their refusal to join in united action under such conditions. But he expressed willingness to continue seeking to form a regional grouping even without the participation of the British so long as the French indicated a willingness to remain in Indochina. But he wanted no mention of the possibility of introducing U.S. ground troops. The American people were frightened, he said, and opposed to the idea.[97]

The NSC meeting of April 29 thus did not reach any positive decisions on possible actions to take in Indochina. But it brought an end to speculation over the possibility of unilateral U.S. intervention in the Indochina conflict and apparently crystallized President Eisenhower's opposition to the use of U.S. ground combat forces in the war. From that point on, administration strategy would focus on seeking to form a multinational grouping of states to defend the interests of the free world in Southeast Asia and influence the upcoming peace talks at Geneva. During the next few days, administration officials continued to discuss the possibility of united action with U.S. allies. In a conversation between Secretary Dulles and Anthony Eden in Geneva on April 30, Dulles complained at the lack of cohesion in the Western alliance and insisted that U.S. policy was not to seek war with China or large-scale intervention in Indochina but to avoid those eventualities through a show of common resolve. Eden, apparently anxious to mend the split that had developed after Dulles's visit to London three weeks earlier, said that he had prevented the Colombo Powers from taking an anti-Western position on the Indochina issue and handed Dulles a memorandum offering to begin bilateral talks on Southeast Asian regional security. On May 5, the British government indicated its willingness to take part in five-power staff talks on the situation but said it was still not prepared to undertake any commitments on military action in Indochina before the conclusion of the Geneva Conference. Dulles was placated but still felt that it was not enough.[98]

Conclusions

When the Geneva Conference convened in early May 1954, some of the key elements of the Eisenhower administration's Indochina policy were beginning to fall into place. After considerable hesitation, the president had made it clear that he had no intention of intervening on a unilateral basis to save the French from defeat in Indochina, either with air strikes or with ground troops. Eisenhower appeared to be dead set against the introduction of U.S. ground troops in Indochina under any circumstances, although he had vacillated on the subject earlier in the year. In the course of deliberations in the NSC, he had emphasized that although Indochina was important, it was not vital to U.S. national security and certainly not worth the risk of global war. Based on such considerations, Washington decided to sit back and await the results of the Geneva Conference.

Yet the administration was sufficiently concerned about the situation to consider united action to prevent the fall of the area to communism. At first, Eisenhower had insisted that no collective action could be undertaken without the active participation of Great Britain. But when Anthony Eden made it clear that London would not agree to participate in any military action in Indochina before the Geneva Conference, the president agreed to explore the possibility of forming a grouping without British participation.

Why was the administration willing to accept the risk of direct military involvement through united action when it had apparently decided that Indochina was not worth the risk of global war? To put the question another way, inasmuch as it had already recognized the difficulty of mobilizing the support of the Vietnamese people for the Bao Dai government, with or without the support of the French, how did they expect to achieve victory in the struggle against the Vietminh?

The conventional answer is that the Eisenhower administration was mesmerized by the threat of communism. It is certainly true that key figures within the administration such as John Foster Dulles and Admiral Arthur Radford were motivated by a strong hostility to communism. But the record presented here shows a more hardheaded and pragmatic approach to the question, at least on the part of Secretary Dulles and President Eisenhower, than usually emerges from historical interpretations of the period. It seems clear that both Eisenhower and Dulles were prepared to accept the loss of at least part of Indochina without necessarily bringing into play the concept of massive retaliation that had been advertised as the administration's answer to the threat of global communist expansion. If they were prepared to consider direct U.S. involvement, it was only (at least initially) on a limited basis and as part of an international alliance to seek a final resolution of the Indochina crisis. It is clear, however, that Eisenhower hoped that united action would not be necessary. Rather, it appears from the record that the administration attempted to use the *threat* of U.S. involvement as a weapon to assist the French in continuing the war, or at a minimum in achieving a more satisfactory peace settlement at Geneva. If Paris decided to negotiate, Washington would not attempt to undermine the effort but would shift its focus to building a collective defense organization to save the remainder of the area from communism.

There is, of course, the possibility that Eisenhower had no intention of permitting direct U.S. involvement in the Indochina conflict but imposed the condition of united action to deflect domestic criticism and create a weapon to assist the French in obtaining a more favorable peace settlement at Geneva. Although there is no way of reading Eisenhower's mind, this argument has plausibility. The president's familiar tactic of arguing on both sides of the issue, so frequently adopted in the debates on Indochina within the National Security Council, may have been a deliberate effort to solicit varying opinions and keep options open for possible future action. The establishment of several key conditions as a prerequisite for U.S. involvement in the conflict may have been the president's way of deflecting the demands of Admiral Radford and other advocates of immediate action and buying time for a less risky solution to the crisis.

Yet this interpretation should probably not be carried too far. Not only is it purely speculative in the absence of further evidence, but it also fails to explain Eisenhower's willingness to abandon British participation as a condition for united action in Indochina and the administration's continuing efforts to persuade the French to reject negotiations and continue the struggle. A more likely explanation is that the president was genuinely ambivalent about the issue and driven by two potentially irreconcilable objectives: to save Indochina from communism and avoid an escalating risk of global war.

If such is the case, it seems clear that Eisenhower had reached a decision by the pivotal NSC meeting of April 6 that Indochina was not worth the risk of global war, and it is quite possible that the April 6 meeting was orchestrated in such a way as to bring about that result. But the administration was as yet unwilling to abandon the effort to dissuade the French from a negotiated settlement and made an apparently sincere last-minute effort to create a coalition of states to assist the French in continuing the war. Only when that effort collapsed did Washington, however reluctantly, signal its willingness to give the peace process a chance.[99]

The End of the Beginning

The U.S. attitude toward the Geneva Conference could probably be best summed up in the concluding section of a speech that Secretary Dulles gave to the nation just as the talks convened on May 7. If the French could conclude a settlement on terms that did not endanger the freedom of the peoples of Vietnam, he said, this would be a real contribution to the peace of Southeast Asia. But the United States would be "gravely concerned if an armistice or cease-fire were reached at Geneva which would provide a road to a Communist takeover and further aggression. If this occurs, or if hostilities continue, then the need will be even more urgent to create the conditions for united action in defense of the area." Dulles elaborated on U.S. policy in brief instructions to the U.S. delegation at Geneva led by Under Secretary of State Walter Bedell Smith. The United States, he said,

is not prepared to give its express or implied approval to any cease-fire, armistice, or other settlement which would have the effect of subverting the existing lawful governments of the three aforementioned (*i.e.*, Vietnam, Laos, and Cambodia) states or of permanently impairing their territorial integrity or of placing in jeopardy the forces of the French Union in Indochina, or which otherwise contravened the principles stated . . . above.

If, in Undersecretary Smith's judgment, a peace settlement was likely to be concluded that was inconsistent with these principles, he was to inform Washington and recommend either withdrawal or a reduction of the U.S. role to that of observer.[1]

From the outset, the administration was nervous about the intentions of the French and feared that in its haste to achieve a settlement, the Laniel government might sell out the interests of the West. Specifically, it felt that the initial French proposal, which called for a regroupment of forces of both sides supervised by an international control commission (ICC) and guaranteed by the nations represented at the Geneva Conference, was sketchy and ambiguous and could be watered down by determined Vietminh negotiators. But administration officials also feared that if they did not back the French, the latter would attempt to shift blame for failure onto the United States. As a result, the United States decided to welcome the French proposal in public, while privately lobbying for tighter controls.

This anxiety about French intentions was clearly displayed in an additional set of principles that the administration sent to the U.S. delegation at Geneva on May 12. The following principles were basic to any acceptable settlement on Indochina: (1) international control machinery in place before a cease-fire, (2) representatives of the ICC guaranteed unrestricted movement, logistical support, and free access throughout Indochina, (3) some provision for U.N. supervision (or a satisfactory substitute) over the ICC, (4) adequate measures to guarantee the security of troops and population in Indochina, (5) an orderly liberation and evacuation of prisoners of war, (6) evacuation of Vietminh forces from Laos and Cambodia, (7) provisions for an examination of political and economic problems after the agreement, and (8) no provisions of a political nature such as early elections or troop withdrawals that would surely lead to a communist takeover.[2]

The Vietminh delegation, led by Acting Foreign Minister Pham Van Dong, must also have come to Geneva with some misgivings. Like the United States, it might have preferred that the conference not take place at all, or at least not in the prevailing circumstances. The dry season campaign of 1954 had been a brilliant success. Dien Bien Phu had fallen to a massive Vietminh assault on the very eve of the conference. Not only did this cause a disastrous drop in support for the war effort in France, it also opened up the entire Red River Delta to infiltration and possible attack by Vietminh troops. At a briefing given at the NSC meeting held on May 8, CIA director Allen Dulles estimated that with 500 trucks, the Vietminh should be able to transport their forces from the far Northwest to the Tonkin Delta within two or three weeks. Although French forces in the delta numbered nearly 200,000 as against only 76,000 Vietminh regulars, the French were plagued by low morale and enclosed in fixed strongpoints surrounded by a hostile or indifferent population. As for the VNA, General Navarre dismissed the Vietnamese forces under his command as "rabble."[3]

Vietminh delegates were thus not likely to be in a hurry at Geneva and could afford to take a hard line in the negotiations. They accepted the French demand for a cease-fire before the settlement of political questions, but thereafter their demands differed widely from those of the French. Their first proposal called for international recognition of the sovereignty and independence of all three countries, the withdrawal of foreign troops, and the holding of early free elections, supervised by local commissions. In addition, they demanded that representatives of the revolutionary movements in Laos and Cambodia, the Pathet Lao and the Khmer Issarak (the latter would eventually become better known as the Khmer Rouge), be seated at the conference. As a sop to the French, they expressed their readiness to examine membership in the French Union based on free will and a recognition of the economic and cultural interests of the French in the three Indochinese states.[4]

To the U.S. delegation, as to the French, the Vietminh proposal was totally unacceptable because it implied that the Democratic Republic of Vietnam would be the sole representative of all the Vietnamese people, as the Pathet Lao and the Khmer Issarak would speak for the peoples of Laos and Cambodia. The Vietminh proposal for the formation of local commissions to supervise elections was reminiscent of the procedures adopted in Eastern Europe after World War II which led to the formation of leftist regimes dominated by local communist parties.

In reality, neither of the two initial proposals reflected the actual conditions in Indochina or the relationship of those conditions to the Great Power balance on the basis of which a final settlement would eventually have to be achieved. Both were essentially propagandistic documents which presumed a degree of military and political imbalance that did not exist and could not form the basis for a compromise resolution of the issues involved. With the two proposals now on the table, the delegates at the conference could get down to the serious issues dividing the two sides: how to achieve a cease-fire, the nature, scope, and composition of a control commission to supervise an armistice, and how to deal with the problem of Laos and Cambodia.[5]

The Issue of Partition

The question of how to achieve a cease-fire, which eventually focused on the issue of partition, proved to be one of the more complex and tendentious points of contention at the conference. While all of the states with strong interests in the region—including the United States—appeared to oppose the division of Vietnam into two separate sovereign states, it was equally obvious that an essential element of any cease-fire would be the establishment of separate regroupment zones for the military forces of the two contending parties. But should this cease-fire be based on a flat partition of Vietnam into two separate regroupment zones or by the creation of enclaves controlled by each side throughout the country (popularly known as the "leopard spot" approach)? At first, the French preferred the enclave concept. The Laniel government clearly expected to retain control (for France or for the Bao Dai government) in the South. Yet the French also hoped to retain a base in the Red River Delta, including control over the major cities of Hanoi and Haiphong, and were willing to give some enclaves to the Vietminh in the Center and the South as a price. This would serve to protect French economic and political interests in major urban areas, while at the same time leaving their armed forces in a position to resume combat if necessary.[6]

For a time it was assumed that the Vietminh would prefer the same solution as a means of providing them with the opportunity to continue their activities throughout the country. But on May 26, the Vietminh delegation surprised observers with a proposal to partition Vietnam into two separate zones. Each side would receive total administrative and economic control over its own zone, and following the establishment of a demarcation line, the troops of each side would be withdrawn into its zone. A similar arrangement was proposed for Laos and Cambodia, with separate zones for the royal governments of the two Associated States and the revolutionary forces supported by the Vietminh. Pham Van Dong made it clear that this partition of the three states of Indochina should not be construed as interfering with the essential unity of each country, for the division would be temporary and lead eventually to national elections to achieve the reunification of all three states.

The decision by Vietminh leaders to seek partition rather than a "leopard spot" approach was apparently based on their belief that the latter solution would restrict the territory under Vietminh administration to small enclaves in rural areas, where communications would be difficult and the party would encounter problems in consolidating its authority. Under such conditions, the United States might be tempted to intervene. A single regroupment zone, of course, would provide a territorial base for beginning the march toward socialism and resuming the struggle for reunification at a later date. There was evidently an extensive debate among Vietminh strategists over the issue.[7]

The Vietminh proposal for partition presented the Eisenhower administration with a dilemma. The statement of principles sent to the U.S. delegation at Geneva on May 13 had clearly stated that the United States was opposed to partition as a means of settling the Indochina conflict. The French, as well as the Bao Dai government, had opposed the idea, and the Joint Chiefs, who in any case had always felt that Tonkin was the key to the defense of the Southeast Asian peninsula, felt additionally that partition would provide the Vietminh with contiguous territory within which they would be able to reorganize their forces.

Yet it was obvious in Washington that the French, for both political and military reasons, would have to concede some division of the country, as Walter Bedell Smith admitted in a press conference held on May 27, when he observed that one could not ignore Ho Chi Minh's well-organized, disciplined, and formidable military force, which controlled a considerable proportion of the country. That could not be wished out of existence. The United States, he explained, was groping for possible solutions that would not violate its principles but might produce the objective it was seeking, that is, the "termination of hostilities on an honorable basis."[8]

For a time General Smith attempted to follow Washington's instructions. At a press conference on June 2 he responded to a question by saying that "at the present time our position is we cannot associate ourselves with any formula which partitions or dismembers Vietnam." Later in the conference, he clarified the statement to mean permanent partition, while adding that once even a temporary line was drawn for the establishment of regroupment zones it could result in de facto partition. He conceded that it would be a complicated question to resolve.[9]

General Smith and other members of the U.S. delegation were apparently uncomfortable with the administration's opposition to partition as well as with the general policy of disassociating the United States from responsibility for an agreement. When on June 4 a high French official told Ambassador Donald Heath that it was his "personal opinion" that partition was the only practical solution, Smith wrote a private letter to Secretary Dulles asking him to consider that solution. He conceded that the United States could not associate itself with any settlement that bore the appearance or carried the name of partition but pointed out that the situation was deteriorating rapidly and might bring about its own solution. He recommended that the United States should play the role of helpful friend and not obstruct any reasonable military compromise the French would be able to achieve. In a brief reply Dulles was noncommittal, stating simply that he shared Smith's views but emphasizing that the administration would continue to seek to avoid identifying itself with partition or the creation of two separate states.[10]

A second issue related to the question of partition was the creation of a control mechanism to police the results of the conference. The administration wanted an international control commission, preferably based on the United Nations, while the Vietminh proposal for local supervision represented a procedure that, in U.S. eyes, had been discredited by the experience of postwar Eastern Europe.

On May 26, Smith asked Washington for guidance on the issue: should he stick to the official U.S. position and demand an ICC under U.N. auspices? Would it also be applied in Laos and Cambodia, as the Vietminh delegation had demanded? What was the optimal and minimal position on composition? He was told that the control mechanism should not be solely restricted to U.N. members because that would raise in "acute form" the issue of Chinese representation. The minimal position was that the communists should not possess a veto, while the optimal was an ICC composed of noncommunist Asian countries. British foreign secretary Anthony Eden had met the latter condition when he proposed a commission composed of the Colombo nations, but the DRV insisted that at least half the representatives should come from communist states.[11]

The Issue of Laos and Cambodia

A third problem concerned a settlement of the conflict in Laos and Cambodia. The two Associated States had been granted their independence by the
French in 1953 and were represented at the conference by their monarchical
regimes. The Western position was that the only issue in Laos and Cambodia
was the withdrawal of Vietminh forces from each country, a question that
should be treated separately from the problem of achieving a cease-fire in
Vietnam. But in his opening speech on May 8, Pham Van Dong, with the
support of China and the Soviet Union, had proposed that representatives from
the revolutionary movements in each country be invited to take part in the
conference. When Western delegates protested that the Pathet Lao and Khmer
Issarak movements had minimal local support and could not be classified as
governments, Pham Van Dong argued that Laos and Cambodia were all part of
a single Indochina theater and should be treated similarly with Vietnam at the
conference.[12]

The Vietminh demand that delegates from the Pathet Lao and the Khmer
Issarak be seated was not just a bargaining ploy. The creation of a militant
alliance of revolutionary states in all three Indochinese countries had been a
guiding principle in Vietnamese communist strategy since the formation of the
party in the early 1930's and had taken on concrete form in the early 1950's,
when revolutionary movements were formed in Laos and Cambodia to cooperate with the Vietminh in a broad regional campaign to drive the French out of
Indochina.

For several weeks, the Vietminh delegation refused to compromise on the
issue. At first, they were supported by Chinese foreign minister Zhou Enlai and
Vyacheslav Molotov, chief of the Soviet delegation, but neither China nor the
USSR considered the issue a matter of high priority, and Anthony Eden informed Zhou Enlai, who had displayed a conciliatory tone throughout the
conference, that the issue was dangerous and could undermine prospects for a
settlement. Walter Bedell Smith discussed the problem with Molotov, who
seemed detached and willing to compromise. Even the Indian government
warned Molotov that Vietminh insistence on the question of Laos and Cambodia would alienate other Asian states.[13]

United Action Revives

The failure to achieve any breakthroughs on key issues related to a settlement led to an increasing mood of pessimism among Western delegates at the
conference. On June 9 Eden told General Smith that because there was no sign
that these questions were being resolved he intended to leave Geneva, at least

for the time being. In a cable to Washington, Smith commented that the British might now be willing to move ahead on the stalled talks for a coalition to defend Southeast Asia from communist expansion. Although Eden still seemed pessimistic about Vietnam, he might be willing to adopt measures to save Laos and Cambodia.[14]

The prospects for a breakdown of the talks was probably good news to Secretary Dulles, who was ready for a final adjournment of the conference so long as the French did not attempt to blame the United States. He told Walter Bedell Smith to prepare to follow Eden's lead and leave Geneva. On June 17, Anthony Eden returned to London, leaving the Marquis of Reading in charge. Three days later, Smith departed for Washington, and the capable career foreign service officer U. Alexis Johnson became head of the U.S. delegation. John Foster Dulles now began to revive the U.S. proposal for united action.

Actually, the proposal had never entirely died. On May 8, the day after the conference opened, Secretary Dulles had told Ambassador Bonnet that the United States was still prepared to talk about internationalizing the war. The French had previously expressed little interest, but Bonnet now said that Paris would like to consider the issue in case the negotiations failed. The following day Laniel met with U.S. ambassador Douglas Dillon and told him that the degree his government could resist Chinese demands would depend on the amount of support it received from the West. The only way to impress China, he said, was to raise the threat of U.S. intervention.[15]

Dulles was well aware that the French viewed the talks on united action primarily as a means of strengthening their position at Geneva, and he was reluctant to move too quickly. Still, he felt that it would be useful for Laniel to know in at least general terms what conditions Washington would require to be met before considering intervention. They were (1) that U.S. aid be formally requested by both France and the Associated States, (2) that Thailand, the Philippines, Australia, and New Zealand agree to participate and that Great Britain agree to take part or at least to be acquiescent, (3) that some aspect of the problem be submitted to the United Nations, (4) that France promise not to withdraw its forces during united action, (5) that agreement be reached on training the VNA and a command structure, and (6) that France grant complete independence to the Associated States, including the unqualified option to leave the French Union at any time. If all these conditions were met (and endorsed by the National Assembly and the French cabinet), the president would be prepared to ask Congress for authorization to use U.S. armed forces in Indochina.[16]

Laniel was pleased that the United States no longer posed British participation as a prerequisite for action in Indochina. And he had no serious problems with the announcement of national independence (the treaty granting full independence to the Associated State of Vietnam was signed on June 4, but the signing of related conventions did not take place until July 21). But he did object to the condition that the Associated States should have the right to withdraw from the French Union at any time. Why was it necessary, he asked, since they had never requested it? Dulles suggested that the administration might be flexible on the issue, but "there cannot be any equivocation on the completeness of independence." The United States, he said, was not prepared to intervene purely as part of a Western coalition shunned by all Asian states. Another point of misunderstanding was the possible use of U.S. ground troops. The United States (at Eisenhower's insistence) had used the phrase "principally air and sea," but the French wanted at least token participation by U.S. ground forces. Dulles explained that the U.S. position did not exclude antiaircraft units and limited combat troops to protect U.S. bases. As for the suspicion that the French were using the negotiations as a means of strengthening their position at Geneva, Dulles informed Dillon that he had no objection to this tactic provided that French actions were consistent with U.S. principles.[17]

The administration now began to draw up a contingency plan for possible U.S. entry into the war. According to plans drawn up by the Joint Chiefs, the U.S. contribution would initially be based mainly on a carrier task force with a support element, as well as air force units based outside Indochina. There were no plans for introducing ground troops because the French already possessed a five-to-three numerical advantage over the Vietminh. If China intervened, JCS plans called for destroying Chinese forces inside Indochina and reducing Beijing's capacity to continue through a naval blockade of the China coast and the possible use of atomic weapons on the mainland.[18]

These plans did not satisfy the French. But despite French requests, Eisenhower refused to approve the use of U.S. air power without an agreement on united action. And the French were unable to obtain a U.S. commitment to introduce at least some ground troops. There were also signs of continuing discord on political issues. The French had attempted to meet Washington's conditions by announcing the signing of the treaty of independence on June 4, and Laniel told Dillon that he felt France had thus satisfied U.S. demands in the political arena so that military talks could begin in Washington immediately. But Dulles felt that this was a serious overstatement and cabled Paris that there must first be assurances of participation by other governments. Even after all conditions were met, he said, the United States still would not consider itself morally committed and must have an opportunity to make its own decision.[19]

During the next few days, the haggling between Paris and Washington continued unabated. The news from Indochina was somber. Intelligence sources reported that Vietminh losses at Dien Bien Phu were less than had been estimated, and an attack by Vietminh main force units on the Red River Delta was predicted for late June. General Valluy asked Admiral Radford if U.S. Marines could help evacuate French troops if necessary, but Dulles refused to make any commitments without an agreed plan of action. He also refused to be specific on how the United States would respond to Chinese intervention in the conflict although he did state in a speech on June 11 that the United States would consider overt Chinese aggression in Southeast Asia as a deliberate threat to its national security.[20]

It is doubtful, in any case, that Dulles entertained high hopes that united action might eventually be forthcoming. The Australian ambassador told the secretary that only an "absolute global emergency" would induce his government to commit itself before forthcoming national elections. On June 14, Ambassador Dillon reported his impression that the chances of the French agreeing to internationalize the war were virtually nil. Concerned that a serious military defeat in Indochina could lead the French to blame the United States for its failure to intervene, he recommended that Washington inform the French that it was not prepared to intervene under any circumstances and advise them to accept Vietminh peace terms. But Dulles was less concerned because to him it was clear that the French had no intention of formally requesting U.S. intervention. The threat of U.S. intervention was simply a card to play at the bargaining table.[21]

Breakthrough

The Laniel government failed to achieve a vote of confidence in the National Assembly on June 12 and resigned the following day. Shortly after taking office on the seventeenth, the new prime minister, Pierre Mendès-France, issued a statement announcing that he would resign if a cease-fire on reasonable terms had not been reached by July 20.

For the Eisenhower administration, the fall of the Laniel government and the emergence of Mendès-France as the new French leader represented a worst-case scenario that had been feared for several months. Mendès-France had spoken against "la sale guerre" since 1950, arguing that it required a political and not a military solution. At first he had been virtually alone, even within his Radical Socialist Party, but as the "dirty war" continued he gradually drew on new sources of support. In June 1953 he failed by only thirteen votes of being elected prime minister. Now he had his chance.

One of the first priorities of the new government in Paris was to reassure Washington. On June 20 Mendès-France met with Ambassador Douglas Dillon and assured him that France wanted peace but not surrender. But it was clear that united action was dead. Mendès-France would focus his attention on the bargaining table at Geneva.[22]

Mendès-France ascended to power at a fortuitous moment in the negotiations. On the fifteenth, Molotov had suggested a compromise on the composition of the ICC and proposed that India chair the commission. The Soviet

Union also agreed to treat military issues first so long as political concerns were not ignored. There were also signs of progress regarding Laos and Cambodia. In private talks with Zhou Enlai, Anthony Eden had emphasized that the allies would not back down on the issue. On the fourteenth, Zhou had said cryptically that his delegation was preparing to submit a new proposal for consideration. Two days later, he stated that the PRC was willing to recognize the kingdoms of Laos and Cambodia as neutral nations like India and Burma and to permit them to retain the right to request French advisers so long as no U.S. bases were established there. In the course of subsequent conversations, Zhou said that the Pathet Lao would need a regroupment zone in Laos but that no such arrangement would be necessary in Cambodia. When asked whether the Vietminh would agree to acknowledge the presence of their troops in Laos and Cambodia and remove them, Zhou replied that they could be withdrawn in conjunction with the removal of all foreign troops from both countries.[23]

On June 18, Zhou Enlai raised the proposal again at a formal negotiating session. Pham Van Dong followed, indicating the willingness of his government to remove its forces from both countries on condition that no foreign military bases be established anywhere in Indochina. The primary issue remaining was the question of the formal neutralization of the two countries and their right to request foreign military advisers. The Chinese and Vietminh delegations were willing to permit the Lao and Cambodian governments to hire foreign advisers so long as they were not from the United States. They also conceded their right to join alliances "in conformity with the UN Charter" so long as they did not join the defensive alliance proposed by the United States.[24]

It was apparent, even at the time, that the breakthrough on Laos and Cambodia had come about primarily at the behest of Zhou Enlai. Why had he decided to compromise on the issue? At the time, participants assumed that China was anxious to avoid a breakup of the Geneva Conference and feared the establishment of U.S. bases in Laos and Cambodia. This may well be true, but according to Vietnamese sources, China may also have had other objectives in mind. In a White Paper published at the height of the Sino-Vietnamese dispute in 1979, Vietnam charged that Zhou Enlai's behavior at the Geneva Conference was motivated by China's desire to incorporate Laos and Cambodia into its own sphere of influence. If this is the case, Zhou Enlai may have been willing to settle for the establishment of neutral states in the area in preference to an Indochina dominated by the Vietnamese.

There is little evidence to substantiate this claim, but based on fragmentary evidence at the time and the subsequent history of Sino-Vietnamese relations, it is plausible. During the later years of the Vietnam conflict, the PRC frequently indicated its determination to maintain Chinese influence in Laos and Cambodia and after the end of the war in 1975 openly intervened on the side of Pol Pot to prevent the formation of a "special relationship" among the three Indochinese states. Still, it is likely that China's primary concern at the time was to prevent the establishment of U.S. bases in Laos and Cambodia. In a conversation with Mendès-France on June 23, Zhou stressed this view and was plainly pleased when the French prime minister indicated that he shared the same opinion.[25]

Why did Pham Van Dong accept Zhou Enlai's compromise proposal at the conference? It is likely that the Vietminh, like the Chinese, were concerned that the United States might attempt to establish military bases on Indochinese soil and feared the possibility of a wider war in the event of a failure to achieve a settlement. But a more persuasive reason was the pressure imposed by both of its major allies—the Soviet Union and the PRC—to adopt a conciliatory position in order to reach agreement on a cease-fire. Vietminh leaders privately expressed anger at what they considered China's betrayal of the Vietnamese revolutionary cause in the interests of realpolitik and Chinese imperialist ambitions. In a meeting with Ho Chi Minh in early July, Zhou Enlai attempted to assuage Vietnamese bitterness by promising to continue supporting the Vietnamese struggle for national liberation, but the seeds of suspicion had been planted in the minds of Vietminh leaders and after a long period of dormancy those seeds would sprout in the bitter conflict that emerged after the fall of Saigon in 1975.[26]

There was also movement in the direction of agreement on a cease-fire line. In secret military talks with the French, Vietminh delegates had made it clear that they wanted a contiguous territory for a regroupment zone consisting, among other things, of the entire Red River Delta, including Hanoi and the port city of Haiphong. The French had not immediately agreed but had implied that if they did, they would want a free hand in the South and at least a temporary enclave in the North to complete the evacuation of their troops and civilians.[27]

When this was reported to Dulles in Washington, he lamented that the trend toward de facto partition was taking place under conditions such that the "communist takeover of all Vietnam looms ahead clearly," and he emphasized that the United States would not take part in any effort to "sell" such an idea to the Bao Dai government. On June 18, U. Alexis Johnson met with French delegate Jean Chauvel and informed him that the United States was not prepared to give its approval to any settlement that would subvert the Associated States or impair their territorial sovereignty and added that a French decision to surrender even a minimal enclave in the North would contravene U.S. principles and require it to dissociate itself from the agreement. Privately he assured Chauvel that the United States would continue to help. Chauvel expressed his understanding of the U.S. position but said that the French had decided that a "leopard spot" approach was "impracticable and unenforceable" and preferred to create a reasonably defensible line behind which to build up a noncommunist Vietnamese government. As for the enclave in the Red River Delta, it was better to abandon the idea rather than to concede one to the Vietminh in the South.[28]

In a last-minute effort before his departure for Washington on the eighteenth, Walter Bedell Smith met with Soviet foreign minister Molotov to discuss the issue of partition. Smith explained that the idea of partition was repugnant to the United States and complained that in demanding the entire Red River Delta the Vietminh were asking too much, but Molotov replied that in demanding territory throughout the South, Center, and North, the French were being unreasonable. If partition was repugnant to the United States, he concluded, nationwide elections should be held to decide one way or the other.[29]

Despite U.S. misgivings, the French decided to accept the Vietminh proposal for partition, although they did not immediately abandon hope for an enclave in the Red River Delta. On June 26, Chauvel saw Donald Heath (who was on his way to Washington) and told him that the new French government would pursue a division of the country and hoped that the United States would help to build a solid noncommunist state in the South and Center. He also hoped that the Associated State of Vietnam, under its new prime minister, Ngo Dinh Diem, would accept partition. If so, he said, agreement was possible in ten days. It soon became clear, however, that Chauvel's estimate was overly optimistic. The Vietminh delegation demanded a partition line at the thirteenth parallel, a proposal termed "totally unacceptable" by the French.[30]

In Washington, sentiment was divided and confused. Walter Bedell Smith, who had returned to Washington on June 20, was convinced that the United States should accept the settlement proposed by the French. In a memo to the president on the twenty-third, he argued in favor of accepting the inevitability of partition and the desirability of guaranteeing it, noting that in such a case the other side would not be tempted by the weakness and disunity of the opposition to violate the settlement. Others had a different view. Sentiment within the Defense Department was apparently strong that the Red River Delta was crucial to the defense of all of Southeast Asia. A North-South partition would thus be merely a prelude to a communist takeover of the entire region. This view had been supported at a five-power military conference held in early June, which recommended that any cease-fire agreement should provide for the retention of the Hanoi-Haiphong area by French forces, although there was some hope that a line could be held at Thakhek–Dong Hoi, just south of the eighteenth parallel.[31]

Some civilian officials in Washington were equally opposed to partition. With the approval of Robert Bowie and Edmund Gullion, Charles Stelle of the Policy Planning Staff drafted a memo to Secretary Dulles pointing out the dangers of partition and proposing that the United States indicate its willingness to send its own armed forces—if necessary without French approval—to defend a line at Dong Hoi. He admitted that neither the French nor the British were likely to accept such a proposal and offered a fallback position that the United States make it clear that it would not accept less than the Dong Hoi line and if necessary would send troops to protect it.

Ambassador Donald Heath thought this view was virtually unanimous in Washington. In a letter to Philip Bonsal in Geneva he said that "all the people below the Secretary and Under Secretary are unanimous that we should intervene or rather make up our mind to intervene now with or without the French." Bonsal replied that sentiment was different in Geneva, where U.S. delegates at the conference doubted that intervention would produce desirable results.[32]

Whatever the views of middle-level officials in Washington about partition, Dulles appeared willing, however reluctantly, to accept it. At a meeting with congressional leaders on June 28, he remarked that signs of a solution were developing. A partition line was taking shape that would place Thailand, Laos, Cambodia, and part of Vietnam under free world control. If such a line were drawn, he said, it must be one that the people in the area were willing to defend because the United States would not rush in single-handedly. It was a matter of making the best of a bad situation, as in Korea, he concluded.

Dulles was also reluctant to agree to Stelle's proposal to send U.S. troops to Indochina. At a meeting with other State Department officials on June 30, he cited the likely opposition of Asian and European public opinion, as well as the difficulty in persuading Congress and the American people. What he would prefer, he said, was to play a game of tit-for-tat with the communists (e.g., "when the Commies grab land we grab some from them"). If the Chinese crossed their national boundary, the United States might consider taking over Hainan Island in retaliation.[33]

Although the new French government had decided to reach an agreement on the best terms it could get, it was conscious of the need to maintain the appearance that it had the backing of its chief allies to strengthen its bargaining position at Geneva. On June 26, just two days before a head of state meeting between President Eisenhower and Prime Minister Winston Churchill, Paris asked the United States and Great Britain to include a statement in their final communique that a "serious aggravation" could result if there was no reasonable settlement of the Indochina conflict at Geneva. British and U.S. officials did agree on a compromise statement that listed their conditions for an acceptable settlement and included a warning that a failure at Geneva could seriously aggravate the situation. But Anglo-American differences remained. U.S. officials had hoped to persuade the British not to accept less than this, but the British were willing only to express the hope that the French would not settle for less. The breach between Washington and London had not been mended.[34]

According to the final communique, the two governments were willing to respect an agreement that contained the following: (1) preservation of the integrity and national independence and removal of Vietminh troops from Laos and Cambodia, (2) preservation of at least half of Vietnam and, if possible, an enclave in the Red River Delta (they were unwilling to accept a line south of Dong Hoi), (3) no restrictions on the maintenance of stable and secure non-communist regimes (including the right to import foreign advisers and weapons) in all three countries, (4) no political provisions that would risk the loss of the retained area to communist control, (5) no exclusion of the possibility of unity by peaceful means, (6) peaceful transfer of refugees from one zone to the other, and (7) an effective control mechanism.

Mendès-France was pleased with the joint U.S.-U.K. statement, which he felt generally paralleled the French position, but he was puzzled by the ambiguity of some of the provisions. In particular he felt that the conditions calling for national unity with no threat of communist takeover were potentially contradictory because if national elections went badly a communist domination of all Vietnam could result. He was also concerned at the meaning of the word "respect."

Dulles replied on July 7. He admitted that the conditions in the U.S.-U.K. communique were no guarantee that Indochina would not someday pass into communist hands but were intended to provide the best chance that it would not occur. Because national elections posed a risk, it was important that they be held as late as possible and without intimidation to give democratic elements the best possible chance to succeed. Dulles explained that the promise to "respect" the agreement meant the United States would not oppose such an agreement, although it might not guarantee it or support it publicly.[35]

The following day Secretary Dulles added a further condition that the Associated States, and particularly the government of Vietnam, must accept the agreement. This was likely to be a problem because the new prime minister, Ngo Dinh Diem, a Catholic from Central Vietnam, was determined to retain the Catholic bishoprics of Phat Diem and Bui Chu in the Red River Delta and was convinced that southerners were too easygoing to resist the communists by themselves. Mendès-France asked Washington to help persuade Diem to accept French proposals on partition, but it refused.[36]

Mendès-France had assured his allies that his government would try to stick to its bargaining position on partition, but during the next few days of negotiation the French were driven inexorably toward compromise. Pham Van Dong held fast on the Vietminh demand for the thirteenth parallel and refused the French request for an enclave in the Red River Delta. There were also continuing disagreements over the composition of the ICC and the date for holding national elections. On the latter issue, the Vietminh proposed a date six months after a cease-fire and the French held out for a two-year delay.

On July 8, French ambassador Henri Bonnet passed a note to Secretary Dulles strongly urging that either he or Walter Bedell Smith return to Geneva to take part in the ministerial meetings that were scheduled to resume on the twelfth. Anthony Eden had already decided to return, and he appealed to the United States to follow suit, arguing that partition was the best solution because the Vietminh would undoubtedly win national elections if they were held in the near future. From Paris, Ambassador Douglas Dillon agreed with the prognosis, recommending that the United States take an active part in the negotiations and guarantee the final agreement on the grounds that the French would otherwise settle for less and blame the United States for their failure.[37]

But Dulles was still reluctant. A few days earlier he had complained in a cable to Dillon that the French might agree to a settlement that superficially resembled the U.S.-U.K. seven points but would contain clauses that would lead to the communist takeover of all of Indochina within a few months. He also worried about the possibility that Paris was operating under the assumption that the United States would be a party to the settlement or that the communists would demand it. So he concluded that the continued absence of a high-level U.S. delegation would avoid a spectacular break with the French.

At first President Eisenhower had agreed, but Press Secretary Jim Hagerty argued in favor of fighting for U.S. views on the spot, pointing out that remaining aloof would make the Americans look like a "little boy sulking in his tent." Hagerty's plea evidently made the president rethink his position, and at a cabinet meeting on July 10 he said that he had not yet made a decision on the issue but that he hoped "we will see our way clear to send either Dulles or Smith back to Geneva."[38]

Dulles met with the president on the morning of July 10. Eisenhower wanted to send a message to Paris indicating U.S. willingness to send either Dulles or Smith back to Geneva but, in response to Dulles's pleas that it would place the administration in an awkward position, agreed to withhold a decision until the nature of a final settlement had been clarified. If it appeared likely that the French were about to obtain a settlement the administration could agree to, Dulles or Smith would return to Geneva.[39]

On July 12 Eisenhower instructed Dulles to go to Paris to confer with Eden and Mendès-France on the issue. When the three met the next evening, Dulles learned the latest information from Geneva. Apparently as a result of Zhou Enlai's mediation, Pham Van Dong had been induced to offer a partition line at the sixteenth parallel, and Zhou intimated to Mendès-France that the DRV might be persuaded to concede more. The Vietminh had also agreed to recognize the unity of Laos under the royal government but wanted a regroupment zone for the Pathet Lao. They would accept a French training mission in Laos but no U.S. military personnel or bases, and they indicated a willingness to compromise on the election issue and the composition of the control mechanism.[40]

Based on such signs of progress, Mendès-France pressed Dulles to return

to Geneva, but he demurred, explaining that the United States could not afford
to be associated with an agreement that would be portrayed to the U.S. public
as a second Yalta, and said only that he would think about it. Mendès-France
made a final plea for a U.S. declaration that it would "view with grave concern any action from any country which will endanger the maintenance of
peace in Indochina." Dulles said such a unilateral statement would present no
problem.[41]

The following day a second meeting was held at which Dulles reiterated
that the United States could not join in any guarantee to the communists of the
fruits of their aggression but would make a unilateral declaration to the effect
that it would not resort to force to upset such an agreement and would seek to
bring others to act in a similar fashion. After the meeting he called President
Eisenhower to request that Under Secretary Smith to return to Geneva. Eisenhower agreed.[42]

On the day after his return from Paris, Dulles presented a report of the
meeting to the National Security Council. The administration, he explained,
was on the horns of a dilemma. The "Yalta business" of guaranteeing Soviet
conquests must be avoided, but flatly to reject the French proposals would have
exposed the United States to the hostility of French public opinion as the
country responsible for blocking a settlement of the war. There would have
been more talk of "stiff-necked Presbyterians" and sanctimoniousness. But
there was also the danger that U.S. representation might stiffen the French to
reject a settlement and then ask the administration to take part unilaterally in
the war. Either of these possibilities, he warned, could lead to Franco-American
friction and an end to hopes for the European Defense Community. The administration had hoped to avoid the dilemma by withdrawing from Geneva
inconspicuously but was unable to because of French urging.[43]

Walter Bedell Smith, recovering from an illness, left for Geneva on July 16.
He was armed with two alternative declarations. If the armistice conformed
substantially to the seven points, he was authorized to declare that the United
States "took note" of the agreements, would refrain from the threat or use of
force to disturb them, and would view any renewal of the aggression in violation of the agreements "with grave concern." But if the terms differed materially
from the seven points, the United States would not be asked or expected by
France to accept the armistice and might decide to disassociate itself publicly
from the agreement.[44]

During the next few days the conferees at Geneva hammered out agreement on the remaining points of issue: the line of partition in Vietnam, national elections, the ICC, the issue of foreign bases and alliances in Laos and
Cambodia, and a regroupment zone in Laos. Mendès-France indicated to Eden
and Smith that the French were willing to accept a tripartite ICC composed of
India, Poland, and Canada with limited veto powers and to drop their demands

for the Dong Hoi line in favor of the sixteenth parallel in return for a two-year waiting period for national elections. A compromise was arranged on Laos and Cambodia when Eden promised Zhou Enlai that if the governments of the two countries were allowed to join alliances, they would agree not to join the projected anticommunist alliance proposed by the Eisenhower administration. At the last minute both governments got the right to join alliances if they conformed to the U.N. Charter.[45]

The final problem for the Eisenhower administration was whether to take note of the agreement or to disassociate itself totally from it. According to Herman Phleger, special legal adviser to the State Department, the final agreement and conference declaration did not conform to the seven points in several respects. Not all the Associated States had granted their approval because Vietnam had refused to voice its approval of the Political Declaration, which called for consultations on reunification elections between representatives of the two regroupment zones one year after the agreement was signed. There were some limitations on the ability of Cambodia and Laos to protect their national security, and the political provisions in the declaration threatened the loss of the South to communism. Finally, the ICC had no enforcement powers and could act only by unanimous agreement, thus giving the communists a de facto veto over its actions.[46]

Nevertheless, Prime Minister Mendès-France urged the United States to approve both the military agreement (signed only by the French and the Vietminh) and the Political Declaration. In forwarding his request to Washington, Smith asked for some latitude in making a final decision, pointing out that the French considered the declaration an integral part of the agreement and would be sorely disappointed if the United States did not at least "take note" of its existence. Washington ultimately decided that Smith could make a unilateral declaration on behalf of the United States, including a reference to Article 9 on the election issue. That unilateral declaration, presented by Under Secretary Smith at the final plenary session on July 21, stated that the government of the United States "took note" of the cease-fire agreements bringing the war to an end and declared that it would "refrain from the threat or the use of force to disturb them"; furthermore, it would "view any renewal of the aggression in violation of the aforesaid agreements with grave concern and as seriously threatening international peace and security." With respect to the statement in the declaration concerning elections, it said that "in the case of nations, now divided against their will, we shall continue to seek to achieve unity through free elections, supervised by the United Nations to insure that they are conducted fairly."[47]

That same day President Eisenhower held a press conference in Washington. While declaring his pleasure that agreement had been reached to stop the bloodshed in Indochina, he explained that the United States had not been a party to, nor was it bound by, the decisions taken by the conference because the agreement contained features it did not like. He further noted that the U.S. government was now actively pursuing discussions with other nations on the formation of a collective defense organization to prevent further direct or indirect aggression in Southeast Asia.[48]

Two days later, John Foster Dulles spoke to the press. From now on, he said, the important thing was to prevent the loss of North Vietnam from leading to an extension of communism elsewhere. One good aspect of the agreement was that "it advances the truly independent status of Cambodia, Laos and southern Viet-Nam" because Prime Minister Mendès-France had promised to complete the transfer of authority to the Associated States by the end of the month.[49]

Conclusions

The Eisenhower administration came into office pledged to stem the red tide in Asia as part of its overall program of rolling back communism throughout the world. From the start, its bark was worse than its bite. Not only did it accept a compromise settlement in Korea, but in Indochina it limited itself to a modest and generally ineffective effort to persuade the French to revive the war effort against the Vietminh, an approach that combined rhetorical toughness with strategical caution. It was neither the first nor the last time that a U.S. administration would make a sufficient commitment to achieve a stalemate but not enough to produce a victory.[50]

The moment of truth came in March 1954, when General Ely came to Washington to request direct U.S. assistance to save the besieged garrison at Dien Bien Phu. Before the abyss, Eisenhower hesitated. He did not refuse assistance, but he placed conditions on U.S. participation that, if accepted by the French, would have significantly transformed the nature of the war effort in Indochina. According to one of his biographers, in insisting that the United States would not enter the Indochina conflict except as part of an international effort, Eisenhower was setting forth conditions that he knew could not be fulfilled. In so doing he protected himself from criticism from the right wing of the Republican Party and the interventionist proposals of JCS Chief Arthur Radford.[51]

There is no doubt that the White House was under severe pressure from right-wing elements, especially the China lobby, to avoid any impression of conciliating the communists. Still, I do not find this argument convincing for several reasons. In the first place, Eisenhower probably had no reason at the time to know that the British would refuse to participate in a multilateral effort in Indochina because, according to one British official who was involved in the negotiations at the time, Anthony Eden had not disclosed his intention to seek a settlement of the war. Even after discovering that the British were not willing to follow Washington's lead, Eisenhower made an apparently sincere plea to Winston Churchill to reconsider.[52]

Moreover, after it became clear that Churchill and Eden could not be budged, Eisenhower abandoned the condition of active British participation and expressed his willingness to explore the possibility of united action with other states in the area. He discarded that effort only when it became clear that Australia would not cooperate. This is not the action of a man who is searching for a pretext to avoid intervention. In fact, the record of Eisenhower's comments in formal and informal situations at the time suggests a man who was genuinely tortured by uncertainty about the situation and the proper way to respond. It may have been a relief to the president when it became clear that united action was no longer a feasible option. But I suspect that his initial attempt to reinvigorate the war effort was sincerely motivated.

On another issue Eisenhower may have dissembled to get his way. Although the record suggests that Eisenhower vacillated on the issue of introducing U.S. ground forces into the Indochina conflict and did not make clear his rejection of the idea until an NSC meeting held in June, it is possible that he had no intention of putting U.S. combat troops into the war and simply played "devil's advocate" during NSC meetings as a means of orchestrating the discussion to get his way. Once the decision was made, there was apparently no further discussion of the issue.

During the course of the negotiations at Geneva, the administration continued to advocate united action. To some critics, this has been interpreted as an attempt to sabotage the conference and the prospects for a peace settlement in Indochina. The record suggests, however, that Washington was reconciled to an agreement and was not deliberately attempting to undermine it. The threat of united action was publicized primarily as a tactic to induce the communist nations to accept moderate terms at Geneva.

By all indications, this tactic succeeded. Washington's tough words (notably Dulles's speech in September that threatened massive retaliation if China became directly involved in the Indochina conflict) aroused anxiety and criticism at home and in Europe but may have been instrumental in bringing about the relatively moderate position adopted by Beijing and Moscow at Geneva. The threat of direct U.S. intervention may have been a factor in persuading the DRV to accept concessions in the final agreement. Although the New Look strategy proved to have little relevance to the conflict in Indochina, the Dulles concept of brinkmanship helped to reduce the cost of failure.

Whether the Eisenhower administration was wise in refusing to commit the United States to the final settlement is another question. Although Washington was anxious to provide whatever help it could to the French as they sought to bring the conflict to an honorable solution, John Foster Dulles firmly rejected all appeals that an active U.S. role in negotiating and guaranteeing a settlement would be the best way to limit the damage that a settlement would cause to U.S. national security. Dulles's reasons (and it appears from the record that the secretary of state, rather than the president, was instrumental in maintaining that position) are not well documented, but his comment that the United States could not afford to ratify a "Yalta-type" agreement that would validate an expansion of territory under communist rule suggests that the primary source of his concern was moral, with perhaps some overtones of domestic politics. Dulles was aware that his position exposed him to the criticism of sanctimoniousness, and he attempted to limit the damage to Franco-American relations by being helpful to the French in other ways, but he was adamant in defense of his position.

Whatever the reasons, the U.S. refusal to give its approval to the Geneva Accords freed Washington's hands to adopt an independent position on the issue in later years. But one can only speculate whether a decision by the Eisenhower administration to approve and guarantee a settlement might not have provided a means of strengthening the control mechanisms to keep the peace.

Evidence from recent scholarship suggests that one reason why the Eisenhower administration was unwilling to commit the U.S. government to the Geneva settlement was its fear of a hostile reaction from anticommunist elements connected with the China lobby. Administration leaders were well aware that there were differences between Moscow and Beijing over the Indochina issue, and an NIE published in June had predicted that in the event of a U.S. military attack on China, the USSR would continue to send military assistance to its ally but "would probably refuse Chinese Communist demand for full Soviet participation in the war." Such fissures in the Sino-Soviet alliance, of course, provided an opening for U.S. diplomatic efforts to widen the rift, and in the same month, President Eisenhower had reportedly asked Prime Minister Winston Churchill if under the appropriate circumstances he would agree to lend his good offices to seek an improvement in Sino-U.S. relations.[53]

These openings, however, were not followed up, and Dulles did not take up the olive branch that Zhou Enlai had proferred during the later stages of the conference. In part, that decision reflected Dulles's belief that it was U.S. toughness, not conciliatory gestures, that had induced Beijing to soften its stance on key issues connected with an Indochina settlement. But it also stemmed from administration sensitivity over congressional reaction to perceived White House "softness" on communism—a sensitivity undoubtedly sharpened by what had happened to the Truman administration four years previously. The result was a decision to proceed on that path with extreme caution. As it turned out, the failure of Washington and Beijing to mend, or at least reduce, their differences had tragic consequences for both sides.

It has been said that Vietminh leaders were as eager for a negotiated settlement as were the French. In his memoirs, Nikita Khrushchev claims that Ho Chi Minh was desperate and asked for Soviet help in bringing the war to an end. According to this version, the battle at Dien Bien Phu had exhausted the Vietminh and they were anxious for a period of peace to recoup their fortunes.

This argument is not convincing. Although Vietminh losses at Dien Bien Phu had undoubtedly been high, French intelligence sources reported the massive movement of Vietminh units toward the Red River Delta in late June and July, and French officials informed U.S. Embassy personnel that the situation was worse than Paris had been willing to admit. If a Vietminh offensive had been launched, one source stated, it was doubtful that the French could hold Hanoi.[54]

Why, then, did the Vietminh war planners not launch their general offensive anticipated in late June? One possible reason was suggested by VWP General Secretary Le Duan in a letter written in May 1965. The Vietminh did not achieve a complete victory at Dien Bien Phu, he remarked, because they lacked a strategic reserve to exploit the weakness of the French. If that is the case, French concerns that Vietminh units were preparing to seize the entire Red River Delta in June and July were exaggerated. But it is also likely that the fear of a U.S. reaction, combined with the pressure from Beijing and Moscow to await the initiatives taken by the new Mendès-France government in Paris, may have induced the Vietnamese to hold their hand and await the results of the negotiations.[55]

All in all, given the perilous situation that followed the fall of Dien Bien Phu in early May, the final settlement was undoubtedly more favorable to the United States than could have been anticipated at the start of the conference. It is not impossible that when the conference closed, the most disappointed delegation at the conference was the one represented by Pham Van Dong.

Chapter 7

Experiment in Nation Building

The comments by Secretary of State John Foster Dulles at his press conference on July 24 to the effect that the United States could now assist in building "truly independent states in Cambodia, Laos, and southern Vietnam" sent a clear signal to the international community that, whatever the fine statements in the Geneva Conference declaration about reunification elections in Vietnam, Washington interpreted the agreement as having created two separate Vietnams divided by the Cold War. It would now be the objective of the United States and its allies to strengthen the fragile government in the South and prevent a further erosion of the free world position in Southeast Asia.[1]

Dulles and other Eisenhower administration officials were perfectly aware that it would be a formidable task. For the previous several years, U.S. policymakers, at least in private, had conceded the strength, the discipline, and the rice-roots popularity of the Vietminh movement, as well as the charismatic appeal of its leader Ho Chi Minh. By contrast, the Associated State of Vietnam under Bao Dai had been weak and fractionalized and lacked any solid base of popular support among key groups in the Vietnamese population.

This pessimism was reflected clearly in U.S. intelligence estimates as the Geneva Conference came to an end during the summer of 1954. The CIA, whose analysis of the political and military situation throughout the Franco-Vietminh conflict had been generally accurate, pointed out the disparity of talent and commitment between the communists in the North and their non-communist rivals in the South. The chances for the development of a strong anticommunist regime in South Vietnam, it asserted, were "poor," and it predicted that the situation was likely to deteriorate progressively over the next year, increasing the possibility that the government in Saigon would be taken over by elements that would seek unification with the DRV in the North. The situation was only slightly better in Cambodia and Laos but depended to a certain extent on developments in Vietnam.[2]

One of the key problems was the personality and character of Bao Dai. During the early years of the Franco-Vietminh conflict, U.S. officials had tended to assign the primary blame for the situation to the dominant position of the French, but it became increasingly clear after the formation of the Associated State of Vietnam that Bao Dai lacked the capacity or the will to lead the struggle to prevent a Vietminh victory. During the spring of 1954, U.S. officials had vainly attempted to persuade Bao Dai to leave his refuge in Cannes to return to serve as commander in chief of Vietnamese forces in Indochina. Washington's exasperation with Bao Dai's behavior showed clearly in official cables to the U.S. Embassy in Saigon. Even Ambassador Donald Heath, originally one of his defenders, commented on "his cowardliness at this crucial moment in his country's history" and said that he had "no intention of going back" to lead his people. Under Secretary Walter Bedell Smith concluded that the only sensible solution was to find someone to take his place.[3]

Secretary of State Dulles shares such doubts, although for a time he was willing to reserve his judgment. In May he commented in a cable to the U.S. delegation in Geneva that Bao Dai was "an ally of uncertain value for the long push." If and when the United States decided to play a more active role in the Indochina conflict, he said, it must work toward the rapid establishment of an authentic national government. If Bao Dai did not soon show improvement, he could be "largely neutralized." In late May Dulles told the NSC that "drastic action" might be required if Bao Dai did not regain a measure of control over his government.[4]

A Man from Another Planet

Washington's increasing skepticism about the leadership qualities of Bao Dai was reflected in its treatment of him during the Geneva Conference. The administration carefully avoided making any formal commitments to him and delayed action on his request for an increase in U.S. aid to expand the VNA. When Walter Bedell Smith met with Bao Dai in early June, Dulles warned Smith against making any pledges of future assistance or cooperation "in view of his dubious future role" in Vietnam. The problem, as it had been for years, was that the noncommunist nationalist movement had consistently failed to produce a figure of widespread rice-roots popularity or administrative competence. Certainly none of Bao Dai's prime ministers had been impressive. This political vacuum in Saigon had been a matter of concern in Washington, although curiously there had been little discussion of its implications.[5]

Whether Bao Dai was aware of Washington's growing disenchantment with him is uncertain. Dac Khe, his minister of democratization, described him as "physically and mentally depressed." In his memoirs he described the United States as the only hope in avoiding a disastrous settlement at Geneva, but he noted that even U.S. support for the Vietnamese cause was limited. By his own account, it was with the expressed desire of strengthening Washington's commitment to Vietnam that in June he replaced Prince Buu Loc as prime minister with the ardent nationalist Ngo Dinh Diem. Bao Dai viewed Diem as "difficult" because of his fanaticism and his messianic tendencies, but he felt that the Eisenhower administration would appreciate his intransigence on the subject of communism. Many other observers already viewed Diem as being "in the American pocket." Whatever the truth of that assumption, he was truly, in Bao Dai's words, "the man of the moment."[6]

Diem, of course, was already well-known to many in Washington. He had come to the attention of consular officials in Hanoi in 1947 when he went to Hong Kong to talk politics with Bao Dai. In the early 1950's he went to the United States to stay at the Maryknoll Seminary in New Jersey. While there, he made frequent trips to Washington to meet middle-level officials of the State Department (apparently at his own request) as well as several influential congressmen, some of whom saw him as the charismatic leader needed to galvanize anticommunist sentiment in South Vietnam. Many appreciated his stubborn hostility to communism and his anti-French attitude. Others, notably in the State Department, apparently found him something of a nuisance. That he was a Catholic undoubtedly reassured some of his commitment to Western values. Certainly it provided him with a natural constituency in the Catholic community in Vietnam, many of whom were among the best educated and politically active in the entire country.[7]

The problem was that many U.S. officials shared Bao Dai's assessment of Diem's character limitations. Ambassador Douglas Dillon, who met him in mid-June just before his return to Saigon to take up his duties as prime minister, was skeptical. In Dillon's view, Diem was sincere but "may have little to offer other than to reiterate that the solution of the Vietnamese problem depends on increased responsibility by the U.S." From Saigon, Robert McClintock described him as a "messiah without a message." His only emotion other than a lively appreciation of himself, McClintock observed, was a "blind hatred of the French." McClintock prophetically described him as "a curious blend of heroism mixed with a narrowness of view and of egotism which will make him a difficult man to deal with."[8]

Understandably, Diem was not popular with the French. Although the son of a well-connected court official in Hué and a former minister in Bao Dai's cabinet in the 1930's, he had resigned his post in protest against French domination of his country. The French official Jean Chauvel complained that he was highly unfamiliar with the facts of life in Vietnam and was generally unrealistic. Some Vietnamese observers agreed. Dac Khe said that Diem was "an honest mystic of an age that passed," good in eliminating corruption but not very good at leading peasants because he did not believe in land reform or the creation of a popular assembly. Even one relative described him to a Westerner as not just from another culture and another hemisphere but from another planet.[9]

It has been widely believed that the Eisenhower administration was instrumental in pressing Bao Dai to appoint Diem as his prime minister. Some have pointed out that Diem had established good relations with the Catholic hierarchy in the United States, through whom he was introduced to John Foster Dulles. There is little evidence to support this contention. Bao Dai makes no reference to such a claim and says he did it on his own initiative to improve the prospects for U.S. support for his government. According to Paul Kattenburg, who was a young foreign service officer in Washington at the time, Diem had not been introduced to any high-level officials in Washington at least through mid-1954. As late as May 22, Dulles had said to the U.S. delegation that there was "no immediately available substitute" for Bao Dai. So it is unlikely that Washington played a direct role in his appointment.[10]

Diem's performance as prime minister during the final weeks of the Geneva Conference had not been reassuring. He had been adamantly opposed to partition, in particular to the French decision to abandon the Catholic provinces in the Red River Delta, and commented on one occasion that he would be willing to trade Hanoi in order to maintain control over the bishoprics, a statement that showed more religious zeal than tact or realism.[11]

As the conference came to an end, U.S. officials harbored serious doubts about the competence of the new prime minister and the prospects for survival of his government. They were also concerned about French intentions. It was still assumed that the French would continue to play a major role in South Vietnam, and the administration was reluctant to antagonize the Mendès-France government by pitting Saigon against Paris. On July 28, Dulles asked Ambassador Dillon to ascertain whether the French were likely to support Diem or to seek a replacement. According to Dulles, U.S. intelligence reports indicated that the French were attempting to undermine Diem in the hope of replacing him with a more pliant successor. The secretary remarked that since Diem had gone about as far as he could in accepting the decisions taken at Geneva without losing nationalist support, it would be in the best interests of both Paris and Washington to support Diem under the present circumstances. A week later, Dillon reported the results of a conversation with Guy La Chambre, the new French minister in charge of relations with the Associated States. La Chambre had said that the French had serious doubts about Diem. Not only was he too much of a mandarin to support land reform, but he lacked the popular appeal that would be needed if the noncommunists were to fare well in the upcoming national elections.[12]

Diem did have some supporters. Ambassador Heath expressed reservations about Diem's ability to surmount the obstacles facing him but took issue with French opinion of the new prime minister and remarked that so far he had shown good sense in avoiding a confrontation with the religious sects while not caving in to their demands. Heath said that there was a widespread sense in Vietnam that the United States was about to abandon the country, and he urged the administration to send a presidential letter of support and to establish an economic aid program. General O'Daniel, the new MAAG chief, supported Heath's views and added his own recommendation for a step-up in military assistance. This would be a good place, he pointed out, to test the U.S. ability to counter communist tactics.[13]

O'Daniel's views received strong support in the Pentagon. The Joint Chiefs agreed with his recommendation for a MAAG program in Saigon, providing that political stability could be achieved in the South. Secretary Dulles pointed out that the Geneva Accords set limits on what the United States could do, but he saw no problems with setting up a program to train the VNA since the French were pulling out. In mid-August the NSC adopted a policy paper calling for new efforts to strengthen Southeast Asia and promote democratic reforms in South Vietnam (while cooperating with France "only insofar as necessary"). Dulles then sent a letter to Mendès-France explaining the administration's decision to begin sending economic and military aid directly to the Vietnamese. He conceded Diem's lack of realism and experience but argued that his government "initially at least, has a better chance of rallying and holding nationalist sentiment than most of the Vietnamese who seem to be now on the scene, or in the wings."[14]

Signs of Washington's growing role caused problems with the French, who had been suspicious of U.S. intentions in Southeast Asia since early in the twentieth century. Mendès-France wanted to cooperate with Washington as much as possible, and in the weeks following the Geneva Conference Washington and Paris attempted to cooperate to put a stable government in Saigon, but long-term differences of approach plagued such efforts. Although both saw the weakness of the Diem regime, the French viewed it as a terminal problem and preferred to work with pro-French elements such as the former prime ministers Tran Van Huu and Nguyen Van Tam. Washington, on the other hand, saw Diem as the best of a bad lot and felt that he should be strengthened so as to maximize his chances of survival. Paris interpreted such attitudes as a U.S. attempt to replace the French and force South Vietnam out of the French Union.

France had reason for concern. Relations between Washington and Paris were increasingly strained because of the French decision not to join the EDC. The administration had apparently assumed that Paris would ratify the treaty and felt betrayed when it did not. Some U.S. observers were convinced that the French had made a deal with Moscow to obtain its support during the negotiations at Geneva.[15]

In October, the administration began to consider sending a letter to Prime Minister Ngo Dinh Diem offering a program to assist the government of Vietnam in "building a strong, viable state, capable of resisting attempted subversion or aggression through military means." The news that Washington intended to send a presidential letter to Diem aroused irritation in Paris, where officials expressed concern that increased U.S. involvement in the South could cause disquiet in communist capitals and undermine the Geneva settlement. Paris was undoubtedly also unhappy that such a letter could strengthen Diem's authority and prestige in his struggle for survival against his rivals in Saigon.[16]

In Saigon, the political intrigue was deepening. The leaders of the Cao Dai and the Hoa Hao, two religious sects whose political influence among the peoples in the vicinity of the Mekong River Delta had been growing significantly since before World War II, had been alienated by Diem's efforts to bring their territories under government authority and began to conspire with pro-French elements to engineer his overthrow. Ambassador Heath was caught in the middle. Although he continued to be convinced that criticism of Diem's mysticism and political ineptitude was all too valid, he reported to Washington that there was no alternative figure who could appeal to nationalist elements in the South. He appealed to General Paul Ely, the new French commissioner general, to help prevent a coup and received backing from Washington, which instructed the U.S. Embassy in Paris to caution the French that a coup would produce a "most unfortunate effect" in the United States and raise doubts about the prospects for a free Vietnam.[17]

Despite their misgivings, the French appeared determined to avoid a break with Washington on the issue, and in late September the two governments managed to cover their disagreement. In a joint communique, Paris agreed to acquiesce in direct U.S. aid to both South Vietnam and Cambodia and to pressure Bao Dai to stop conspiring against Diem. But the French had now decided to work with Ho Chi Minh. Jean Sainteny, the suave international lawyer who had negotiated the preliminary agreement with President Ho in March 1946, was sent to Hanoi and met with the Vietnamese president in mid-October amid press reports that Paris would offer economic aid to the DRV.[18]

But even Washington still had doubts about Diem. In a cable to the U.S. Embassy in Saigon on September 28, Under Secretary Walter Bedell Smith asked for the embassy's views on whether Diem was foredoomed to failure or whether the United States could make a "synthetic strong man" of him. Heath, who had seen Diem reject his advice to conciliate the sects, answered with a qualified affirmative. The United States should stick with Diem for a while, he said, but should also "look around urgently as so far we have been doing without success, for a relief pitcher and get him warming up in the bullpen. Diem's intrinsic faults may yet create a situation making his replacement necessary."[19]

During the next few weeks the U.S.-French accords on Vietnam began to unravel. Bao Dai, still in Cannes, reluctantly agreed to cooperate with Diem, but intrigues in his name continued in both Paris and Saigon. Some U.S. officials accused the French of bad faith, but Ambassador Heath attributed most of the problem to Diem's intransigence. Diem had already alienated the articulate sector of the population, he complained, and "everyone in the Embassy" was convinced that he could not organize or administer a strong government. Still, Heath remained ambivalent because there was no successor in sight. Time was needed, he said, to prepare what Prime Minister Mendès-France called "another structure of government."[20]

Back in Washington, the National Security Council met on October 22 to formulate a new policy for Indochina. State Department officials recommended a crash program to build up the VNA to meet immediate security needs in the South and enhance Ngo Dinh Diem's support among high military officers, to be followed by a long-term program to strengthen the ability of the regime to protect itself from external aggression or internal subversion. The Joint Chiefs were somewhat reluctant to embark on a long-term military commitment in the South because of the danger of political instability but recognized the "hen and egg" relationship between military security and political stability and indicated their willingness to approve a program if political considerations were considered paramount. On the following day, the president's letter was delivered to Prime Minister Diem in Saigon. It stated that the United States was prepared to examine a program of aid to the government of Vietnam providing that the latter was "prepared to give assurances as the standards of performance it would be able to maintain in the event such aid were supplied." The letter also noted that the administration expected that the Saigon government would undertake needed long-term reforms.[21]

Donald Heath passed on Eisenhower's letter to Prime Minister Diem, but he warned Washington that there was a possibility that "even with wholehearted complete backing Diem cannot succeed in forming a viable government" and recommended that the administration press on Diem the necessity of reorganizing the government and formulating a workable plan to win back the villages from the communists.[22]

The Southeast Asia Treaty Organization

To administration officials, of course, the defense of Indochina was only part of the broader problem of defending the entire region from communist expansion. At their summit meeting in late June, Eisenhower and Churchill had agreed to pursue discussions on a collective defense organization for Southeast Asia, and preparatory talks were held in Washington in mid-July. But the agreement to confer disguised the continuing differences between London and Washington on the geographical scope and powers of such an organization. The latter wanted a specific military pact with provisions for action to deter aggression. The British were willing to consider such a pact, but only if the Geneva Conference failed. If it succeeded, they preferred a more general approach focusing on developmental issues to provide the states in the area with a sense of commitment and regional identity. The two governments also differed on membership. The United States wanted to invite its key allies in the region such as Thailand, Korea, the Philippines, and Japan. The British preferred to include the members of the Colombo Pact, and they worried that if the Republic of China were to be invited, India would refuse. There was no question of membership by the Indochinese states. At the Geneva Conference, Zhou Enlai had stressed to Anthony Eden that membership by the Associated States in a collective defense pact led by the United States could wreck the peace talks, and Walter Bedell Smith had told Washington that membership by the Associated States should not be contemplated unless the Geneva Conference failed.[23]

Even within the United States there was disagreement over membership in the proposed organization, and some members of Congress expressed skepticism over the value of a "White Man's Pact." The Joint Chiefs questioned the desirability of a pact when few states in the area could provide for their own defense and current U.S. policy was to strike directly at China in case of external aggression. At a meeting of the NSC on July 22, Secretary Dulles suggested the possibility of a two-stage process, beginning with a military pact restricted to selected Asian states, and later, when conditions permitted, moving toward a broader regionwide organization focusing primarily on economic development. State Department officials explained that the purpose of such an approach was to build the confidence of Southeast Asian states to defend themselves against subversion as well as to serve as a deterrent to China. But the JCS remained skeptical and expressed their concern that such a pact would simply encourage Asian nations in the mistaken belief that the United States would protect them.[24]

Such doubts did not deter the administration. At an interagency meeting on July 24, Secretary Dulles argued that a regional organization would provide the president with discretionary authority to use against China if necessary. Defense Secretary Charles Wilson proposed beginning with an economic agreement, but Dulles argued that it would be an "unmitigated disaster" to abandon the idea of a military pact in prevailing conditions. A military pact, he said, would ensure that the United States would not have to act alone in case of Chinese aggression in the area.[25]

With the formal decision to proceed out of the way, the NSC Planning Board attempted to fill in the details. An initial draft, entitled NSC 5429, was circulated to appropriate agencies in early August. It called for a security treaty involving the United Kingdom, France, Australia, New Zealand, Thailand, the Philippines, and other interested Asian countries. The draft provided two alternatives on how to respond to a military attack on the signatory parties. Alternative A called for "immediate retaliation against Communist China if Communist China directly or indirectly (such as through the Viet Minh) commits armed aggression against any free nation of Southeast Asia, including Laos, Cambodia, and South Vietnam." Alternative B would "commit each member to treat an armed attack on the agreed area as dangerous to its own peace and safety and to act and to meet the common danger in accordance with its own constitutional process." In either case, the treaty was designed to provide the president with a legal basis, without further congressional action, to take military action against Communist China, including the possible use of atomic weapons, in the event it committed armed aggression.[26]

The draft also presented two alternative proposals for dealing with the problem of local subversion. Alternative A stated that since limited military and economic assistance would probably not prove adequate to cope wih communist subversion in Indochina, the United States should issue an immediate warning to the Chinese Communists that further communist expansion in mainland Southeast Asia "will not be tolerated" and would in all probability lead to a military attack "not necessarily restricted to conventional weapons against the source of the aggression (i.e., Communist China)." The United States would act alone if necessary. Alternative B simply stated that the United States should be prepared "either unilaterally or under the terms of the Southeast Asia Security Treaty, if requested by a legitimate local government, to assist it by military force, if necessary and feasible, to defeat local Communist subversion or rebellion which does not constitute external armed attack." Finally, the draft proposal presented four possible strategies, ranging from conciliation to seeking a casus belli, for dealing with the growing power of Communist China in Asia.[27]

The draft met heavy criticism. Asianists in the State Department criticized it for its simplistic treatment of complex issues (Kenneth T. Young described it as "the worst hodge-podge that has ever been submitted to the President and the Council in my span of five years' experience with NSC papers"). Army Chief of Staff General Mathew Ridgway registered his strong opposition to a strategy that appeared to offer no alternatives to appeasement or war with China. Ridgway proposed instead that the United States attempt to split China from the Soviet Union and show the former that its interests were with the United States.[28]

The paper was debated at an NSC meeting on August 12. Secretary Dulles expressed his personal preference for Plan A in dealing with armed attacks, but was doubtful that U.S. allies would be willing to accept it. President Eisenhower preferred Alternative B on the grounds that he would act without consulting Congress only in a dire emergency. He also wished to preserve his prerogative to decide what to do at the time aggression occurred rather than to be tied to "automatic counter action." The council also discussed means of dealing with internal subversion. John Foster Dulles preferred Alternative B but was concerned whether the United States could meet such commitments at current force levels. Eisenhower added that he was "frankly puzzled by the problem of helping to defeat local subversion without turning the U.S. into an armed camp." After further discussion, the issue was postponed until the following week.[29]

Debate resumed on the eighteenth. In the interval between the two meetings, Defense Secretary Wilson, never one to hide his opinions, had registered his strong disagreement with the decision to include Vietnam, Laos, and Cambodia within the purview of the treaty. In a note to John Foster Dulles he said he had a "minimum amount of optimism" about what could be accomplished at that stage. Dulles agreed but felt that the administration had no alternative. In a conversation with the president on August 17, the secretary had expressed his concern at committing U.S. prestige in an area "where we had little control and where the situation was by no means promising." But failure to go ahead, he felt, would represent "total abandonment of the area without a struggle." Including the Indochinese states in the pact was a risk but the "lesser of the two evils." Eisenhower agreed.[30]

At the NSC meeting on August 18, Secretary Dulles presented a revised draft of the section dealing with local subversion. In such conditions, it read, "the President should at once consider requesting Congressional authority to take appropriate action, which might if necessary and feasible include the use of U.S. military forces either locally or against the external source of such subversion or rebellion (including Communist China if determined to be the source)." On the issue of dealing with China, the council rejected General Ridgway's proposal to promote a split between Moscow and Beijing (there was a general consensus in favor of the president's view that "it was hopeless to imagine that we could break China away from the Soviets and from Communism short of some great cataclysm") but was equally disinclined to adopt a provocative policy toward the mainland on the grounds that such a posture would have no support from U.S. allies or from world public opinion. In the end, the administration's China policy was left unchanged.[31]

During the late summer, the administration worked out the question of membership in the new organization. At the request of Britain, Australia, and New Zealand, South Korea, Japan, and the Republic of China were not invited. Burma, India, and Indonesia were issued invitations but refused. At their own request, the United States agreed to argue for South Vietnam, Laos, and Cambodia to be included in the area covered by the treaty under an "umbrella clause" despite some concern within the administration over legal implications and political risks.[32]

Negotiations on the treaty began in Manila on September 1. Dulles attended with some misgivings over the attitudes of other participants, who were expressing reservations about inviting representatives from the Indochinese states to the conference and about including the word "communists" in the treaty. Our allies, he lamented to Livingston Merchant, "seem to have no desire or intention to hold the balance of Indochina." Is it good "to tie oneself up with people who are not willing to fight?" But at Manila, Dulles got most of what he wanted. Article IV, dealing with the response to armed attack, called for member states to act to meet the common danger in accordance with their "constitutional processes." In case of aggression other than armed attack, "the parties shall consult immediately in order to agree on the measures which should be taken for the common defense." South Vietnam, Laos, and Cambodia were included in the terms of a treaty by a separate protocol. There were no specific references to "Communist aggression," but the United States made it clear that it understood its commitments under the treaty to apply only to communist aggression.[33]

The Collins Mission

The letter sent by the Eisenhower administration to Prime Minister Ngo Dinh Diem in October further undermined U.S. relations with the government of Pierre Mendès-France. Paris felt that the letter had gone beyond the Franco-U.S. understandings achieved during the summer that the two governments would look elsewhere if it appeared that Diem would be unable to survive. The French were also angry that Washington had not consulted them on U.S. plans for a strengthened MAAG office in Saigon. In a letter to Prime Minister Mendès-France in October, Dulles tried to mend fences, but high administration officials were increasingly suspicious of French activities in Saigon and determined to replace them in Indochina.[34]

Nor did the presidential letter have much effect in stabilizing the situation in Saigon, where political intrigues against the Diem regime continued. At a meeting of the NSC on October 26, Defense Secretary Charles E. Wilson, who had earlier expressed doubts about the advisability of a U.S. commitment to Indochina, remarked in frustration that Washington should let the area "stew in its own juice." He saw nothing but grief for the United States there.[35]

Eisenhower replied that U.S. national security would be gravely affected by a retreat from the area, but administration officials realized the need to monitor the situation closely. At the end of October, the White House decided that the

United States needed a representative with more prestige and authority than Ambassador Donald Heath (and perhaps more confidence in President Diem), who had served ably in the post since recognition of the Associated State of Vietnam in 1950. In early November, General J. Lawton "Lightning Joe" Collins was appointed special U.S. representative to Vietnam with the rank of ambassador. Collins, who had earned his nickname for his aggressive tactics as a corps commander in World War II, was a close friend of the president. His written instructions were to direct and coordinate U.S. activities in Vietnam, and he was given broad authority to use all available local resources to reverse the "rapidly deteriorating situation" and help the government in Saigon to establish internal security and political stability. In private he was informed that the administration's inclination was to back Diem because there was no real alternative.[36]

After his arrival in Saigon, Collins told General Ely that it would be U.S. policy to take over the role of training the VNA and gradually phase out the French. On a visit to the United States in mid-November, Prime Minister Mendès-France warned his hosts that the decision could arouse suspicion in Hanoi, where the DRV had just reestablished its capital, and in Beijing as well. Dulles tried to reassure Mendès-France that the administration was not trying to replace the French but simply to guarantee the survival of South Vietnam. In fact, Dulles was concerned that if the United States took over the entire military role in Saigon, it would be faced with full responsibility in case of a defeat, which, he told Deputy Defense Secretary Robert B. Anderson, would be a "terrible blow to our prestige in that area." At the end of the meeting, the two governments reached a compromise calling for joint efforts to stabilize the situation in Saigon.[37]

On November 23, the CIA issued a new National Intelligence Estimate on the situation in Indochina. Even by the standards of the time, it was very pessimistic. The situation in South Vietnam had steadily deteriorated since the conclusion of the armistice, and on the basis of present trends it was unlikely that the government in Saigon would have the strength necessary to counter subversion. Almost certainly the Diem regime would be unable to defeat the communists in nationwide elections. Strong pressures could arise for the formation of a coalition with the Vietminh, whose strength in the South was increasing. If South Vietnam should fall, the pressure on Cambodia and Laos would increase.[38]

Reports from General Collins in Saigon were hardly more reassuring. Collins did his best to improve relations with the French on the spot, an attempt that was facilitated by his warm personal friendship with General Ely. On November 14 the two worked out an understanding, according to which the United States would run the training program for the VNA but would informally seek French advice. Collins also explored ways to strengthen Diem's popular appeal by setting up a land reform program and democratic institutions. Following the lead of his predecessor, Collins attempted to persuade Diem to broaden his political base by appointing such political figures as the Dai Viet party leader Phan Huy Quat to his cabinet. But Diem viewed Quat as a rival and refused. Frustrated at Diem's stubbornness, Collins grew more skeptical over his chances of survival, and in a cable dispatched on December 13 he asked Washington to give him until early January. If Diem had not shown improvement by then, it might be necessary to turn back to Bao Dai or withdraw entirely. The latter course, he warned, may be the "only sound solution." Collins's report caused a stir in Washington. It was passed to Donald Heath for comments, and he declared that Collins ignored the basic fact that U.S. withdrawal from South Vietnam would assist a communist takeover. The least that should be done, he suggested, was to buy time while attempting to strengthen Laos, Cambodia, and Thailand. Senator Mike Mansfield, a onetime history professor who was earning respect for his understanding of foreign policy issues, agreed, pointing out that if U.S. support for Diem was withdrawn, the French would appoint a candidate of their own and make an approach to Ho Chi Minh.[39]

Diem's failure to stabilize the government confirmed the French suspicion that he was not worthy of support. In talks with John Foster Dulles during a tripartite foreign ministers meeting in Paris in mid-December, Mendès-France said that he was willing to support Diem, but only if he was presented with stiff conditions and if active consideration were given to a possible replacement. Dulles agreed to apply greater pressure on Saigon but refused to give up on Diem until a promising substitute was located. "Even a slight chance of success," he said, was worth a considerable investment. In the end, Mendès-France agreed to support Diem while looking actively for an alternative. Dulles agreed but added that if there were no alternative to Diem it would be necessary to consider whether to make a further investment in Indochina.[40]

On his return to Washington, Dulles replied to General Collins in Saigon. A withdrawal from Vietnam, he said, would hasten a communist takeover and have adverse repercussions throughout Southeast Asia, so the current policy was justified even if only to buy time and build up strength elsewhere in the region. Unless the situation became hopeless, he felt, the United States had no choice but to aid Diem because there was no alternative. Bao Dai was no solution. On December 29 the administration decided to "take the plunge" and begin directing aid to Saigon while moving ahead with negotiations to set up a training program in Cambodia.[41]

In mid-January General Collins was recalled to Washington to report to the NSC on the situation in Saigon. In the interval since his pessimistic cable in December conditions had improved slightly, and in a meeting held on January 20 Collins reported that with U.S. and French support, Diem had a "reasonable chance of success." Collins set forth a program of action calling for political, economic, and military reforms and reported that the regime, with U.S. assistance, had drafted a decree establishing a provisional elective assembly with limited legislative powers. Diem had not yet decided what to do about Chief of State Bao Dai but was determined to carry through with a land reform program and was about to sign a contract with Michigan State University to set up a school of public administration. At a second meeting on January 27, the NSC approved Collins's program and he returned to Vietnam.[42]

On his arrival back in Saigon, he found the nation again at war. Diem had launched a pacification program to destroy the power of the religious sects, an action that led to widespread turbulence. Collins had little respect for the sect leaders, calling them "stupid and childish," but Diem's failure to use more conciliatory means to resolve the problem undermined Collins's fragile confidence in the regime, and in a cable to Washington in March, he said that Diem was virtually isolated. Once again he recommended that the administration seek alternative leadership, such as Foreign Minister Tran Van Do, Phan Huy Quat, or even Bao Dai.[43]

Collins's latest cable received immediate attention in Washington. When Dulles and Eisenhower discussed it over the telephone on April 1, the latter expressed surprise at the news and advised Dulles to tell Collins not to give up until it was certain Diem could not survive because the United States had "bet on him heavily." Dulles, who in any case felt that General Collins was inclined to be too hasty, agreed, and a cable was dispatched the same day advising Collins that "we do not think a switch would be desirable or practicable at present time." But Dulles left the door open. If the situation became critical, he said, Collins could tell Diem frankly that the United States might have to stop supporting him.[44]

During the next weeks, the debate between Saigon and Washington over Diem's fate continued while Diem continued his effort to extend his authority over the sects and the infamous Binh Xuyen, the river pirates who controlled gambling and opium dens in Saigon. As the situation neared the point of anarchy, Collins came under pressure from General Ely to persuade Washington to permit Bao Dai to dismiss Diem as prime minister. But Dulles, backed by Senator Mike Mansfield, wanted no more of Bao Dai, claiming that Congress would not agree to provide aid to a government that bore a clear French imprint. In a private letter to Collins he said that if Diem could not make it, the United States would call the whole business a failure. But Collins stood his ground, replying that Diem, who "lacked personal qualities of leadership and executive ability," was not indispensable. Tran Van Do and Phan Huy Quat, he argued, were nationalists too.[45]

By April 11, Dulles appeared ready to give in and with the apparent approval of the president drafted a cable to Collins authorizing him to acquiesce in plans to replace Diem so long as the replacement would not be represented as a French puppet. But after reading a memo from Kenneth T. Young, recently appointed director of the Office of Philippine and Southeast Asian Affairs, suggesting that there were interim solutions in which Diem might be retained in some capacity, the secretary had misgivings and later the same day drafted a second cable postponing a decision until the French provided further information on a possible replacement and the procedures that could be followed.[46]

Washington was receiving a different picture of the events in Saigon from another source. Colonel Edward G. Lansdale, a U.S. military officer with the MAAG mission in South Vietnam and well-known for his successful efforts to help President Ramon Magsaysay suppress the Huk rebellion in the Philippines, had become convinced that Diem was the best hope and sent cables to Washington appealing for a decision to stick with him. On April 16 Dulles recalled General Collins to Washington for consultations. Before his departure, Collins had another unsatisfactory meeting with Diem on appointing new members to his cabinet. In the meantime, the French voiced their unhappiness at Washington's reluctance to reach a decision on a change of leadership in Saigon. Dulles told the French ambassador that the United States would not act unless it was "absolutely certain that alternative would be preferable."[47]

On his return to Washington, Collins had lunch with the president on April 22. At the White House and in meetings with officials at the State Department he reiterated his view that it would be a major error to continue supporting Diem in view of his marked inability to govern and lack of constructive ideas. Asked for his alternatives, Collins suggested Phan Huy Quat but added that in his view the Vietnamese were not yet ready for a republican form of government, nor were elections feasible. Diem himself had little support outside of Central Vietnam.[48]

In his own words, Collins's report "caused a stir" in Washington. Some, like Senator Mike Mansfield and Kenneth T. Young, strongly disagreed with Collins's recommendations. But Dulles, just returned from talks with French officials in Paris, gradually gave way under Collins's relentless insistence on the need for a change and agreed to consider approaching Bao Dai to name a new prime minister. But he remained concerned about the French attitude and wanted their full support for a new government which, in his view, should result as much as possible from genuine nationalist sentiment in Vietnam. He also insisted that any new government in Saigon must be able to reduce the power of the sects and energetically carry out the reform program formulated by General Collins in December.

According to a memorandum written by Kenneth T. Young, the decision to replace Diem was reached at a lunch attended by General Collins and Secretary Dulles on April 25. The Department dispatched two telegrams to Paris two days later asking the ambassador to inform the French of U.S. plans to carry out a gradual shift of power to anti-Diem nationalist elements in Saigon.[49] But such plans were quickly overtaken by the course of events in South Vietnam. On April 23, a government radio broadcast offered talks with Binh Xuyen and Hoa Hao leaders and promised a national referendum on political questions to be followed by national elections for a national assembly four months later. There was no immediate reaction from the rebel leaders, and fighting broke out in the early afternoon of the twenty-eighth, Saigon time. Army units loyal to the government—referred to in contemporary documents as the Armed Forces of Vietnam (FAVN)—stormed Binh Xuyen strongpoints in the Saigon sister city of Cholon, and resistance quickly melted away. When the news of Diem's victory reached Washington, Dulles wired Paris to block further action on the tele-grams of April 27 until further notice and called for a meeting of the NSC the next day.[50]

Before the council General Collins reiterated his views that Diem was not indispensable and would have to be replaced if outright civil war were to be avoided. Dulles, however, remained reluctant, pointing out that the French had been unable to come up with a satisfactory replacement. Moreover, he said, the mechanics of a change would be difficult because it would require the coopera-tion of Bao Dai, who was known to be dependent on the Binh Xuyen for financial support. The recent events in Saigon could lead either to Diem's overthrow or to his emergence as a "major hero." In the end, the NSC approved Dulles's suggestion to postpone a decision by continuing to support the govern-ment in Saigon while recognizing that a change might have to be made and keeping the situation under constant review.[51]

After the meeting Collins returned to Saigon, where he found that the situation had changed radically since his departure a few days previously. Diem was now clearly in charge, and the situation in Saigon was quiet, although relations between the government and the French were tense. On April 30 a Revolutionary Committee was formed at the Saigon Town Hall and called for the abdication of Bao Dai, the formation of a new government under Ngo Dinh Diem, the withdrawal of French military forces, and the holding of elections for a national assembly. There were widespread rumors about who had founded the committee, but Collins believed that it had been orchestrated by Diem's younger brother Ngo Dinh Nhu.[52]

The situation was equally volatile in Washington, where Senator Mike Mansfield spoke out in favor of Diem and recommended a cessation of U.S. aid if he were replaced. Congressional opinion appeared to be strongly pro-Diem, with many prepared to believe that any replacement would be a French puppet. On May 1, Dulles cabled General Collins that because of congressional and public opinion it would be domestically impractical and detrimental to U.S. prestige abroad to participate in a scheme to remove Diem. The administration would therefore continue to support him while counseling him to improve his relations with his rivals and the French. Perhaps, Dulles concluded, a broad-based government with or without Diem would evolve out of the present crisis. Secretary Dulles may have been encouraged by a Special NIE dated May 2, which reported that Diem's recent triumph over his rivals had given him initiative and predicted that with U.S. support and French acquiescence the situation would stabilize under the current government. But the authors were still critical of Diem's lack of administrative ability and warned that success could make him even less amenable to policy guidance. It would be extremely difficult, at best, for any government in South Vietnam to build sufficient strength to meet the long-range challenge of the communists.[53]

In succeeding weeks General Collins continued to counsel Diem to reorganize his government and carry out the Franco-U.S. program presented the previous December. He remained dubious about Diem's future prospects, however, and argued that if after a reasonable period of time there were no signs of improvement the United States should either withdraw or join with the French in seeking a replacement.[54]

But Washington had decided to stick with Diem. On May 8, Secretary Dulles met with British foreign minister Harold Macmillan and the new French prime minister Edgar Faure in Paris. To the latter's complaint that Paris had gone as far as it could in backing the present regime in Saigon, Dulles replied that whatever its views in the past, the United States now felt that Diem represented the only way to save South Vietnam and counteract revolution. He pointed out that the administration had not picked Diem and was well aware of his weaknesses but saw no feasible alternative. It would still be willing to consider a replacement if one could be suggested, but in the meantime it would not allow Diem to become "another Kerensky." Prime Minister Faure said that the French could suggest no easy solution, but they were convinced that Diem was leading Vietnam to catastrophe and in the process causing a serious breakdown between Paris and Washington. Paris was prepared, he said, to withdraw its military forces and retire from Indochina if that was what the United States desired. Dulles replied that he would consider the idea but that he was personally convinced that Washington would prefer the French to remain.[55]

During the next few days the two governments attempted to reconcile what Faure called a "fundamental disagreement" over strategy in Vietnam. Faure agreed to support Diem on condition that his government was broadened and cease its anti-French propaganda and to withdraw French military forces according to the previously arranged schedule. Dulles replied that the United States would counsel Diem to broaden his government but pointed out that Diem was not the kind of leader who would accept dictation. That, indeed, was one of his strengths.[56]

On May 12, the three governments agreed on a set of principles that covered over their disagreements on Vietnam. They agreed to continue their support for the Diem regime if it broadened its base of support and attempted to solve the dispute with the sects by peaceful means. But Diem took matters into his own hands, extending his government's control over sect areas and bringing the Revolutionary Committee under control.[57]

Betting on a Long Shot

During the meeting between John Foster Dulles, Harold Macmillan, and Edgar Faure in May, Dulles commented in a moment of frustration that Vietnam was not worth a split between the United States and France. If a choice had to be made, he said, the United States was willing to pull out of Vietnam. Although the Secretary later remarked to the NSC that he had merely made a dramatic gesture to counter a French threat to pull out their military forces, it was undoubtedly an accurate statement of Washington's long-term priorities. Yet, as events were to show, it did not represent the administration's thinking at the time. Although the tripartite meeting in Paris had led to a fragile agreement to continue cooperating in an effort to help the Diem experiment succeed, the gap between the United States and France over the Vietnam issue was growing. Under de Gaulle it would become virtually complete.[58]

One of the reasons for French dislike of Diem undoubtedly was his own anti-French political views, and there is little doubt that they conspired against him. Yet there was also probably a genuine feeling in Paris that Diem could not succeed, a view that was shared in good measure by the British. Even as the United States extended its own commitment to Diem, administration officials were well aware that they were taking a large gamble. In one moment of candor Eisenhower told General Collins that Diem just changed the odds of success in Vietnam from 10 percent to 50 percent. Even Mike Mansfield, one of Diem's staunchest supporters, conceded that he was a long shot.[59]

The Eisenhower administration, then, went into the Diem experiment with its eyes wide open. Why was Washington prepared to stick with Diem when London and Paris were not? One factor appears to be that the administration had a different view of the situation than did its European allies. The British and the French were undoubtedly concerned for the future of the Western presence in Southeast Asia, but they were prepared, if necessary, to write off Vietnam as a lost cause and concentrate their efforts on protecting the remainder of the region from the revolutionary virus. The British felt they could hold Malaya, whatever happened in Indochina. Eisenhower administration officials were convinced that if Indochina fell to the communists, the psychological and political impact on the other states in Southeast Asia could be catastrophic.

Washington's perspective of the needs of the situation in South Vietnam also differed from that of its European allies. London and Paris saw Diem as an unmitigated disaster and not a realistic alternative to Ho Chi Minh. Most U.S. officials, as well as key members of Congress, were prepared to concede Diem's multiple failings, but—with the significant exception of General Collins—were convinced that his stubborn anticolonialism and single-mindedness were virtues as well as defects and were perhaps, as Dulles remarked in Paris, the only qualities that could save the country from communism. Certainly Washington, in a view that was probably shared by most Americans, harbored little hope for anyone placed in power by the French.

In the end, then, the administration entered the commitment with the realization that the gamble might not succeed but that it was worth trying. To General Collins's forebodings that it could lead to disaster, U.S. officials (who in any event suspected that Collins's fears were exaggerated) consoled themselves that at the least it would buy time to build up strength elsewhere in the region. This attitude was displayed in a Defense Department study completed in mid-April which called for a delaying action in South Vietnam to develop a favorable situation in neighboring areas, specifically in Thailand and Cambodia. With its eyes wide open, the administration had taken a major step into the quagmire of Vietnam.[60]

The Issue of National Elections

The agreement with the French to continue to support the Diem regime staved off the most immediate threat to the survival of the noncommunist section of Vietnam. But to Eisenhower administration officials, a second and potentially more serious challenge loomed in the summer of 1956—the national elections called for by the Political Declaration drawn up at the Geneva Conference. The problem was not simply that the elections might be held but that, according to most seasoned observers, the communists were almost certain to win them. Even Dwight D. Eisenhower, in his memoirs, admitted that if elections were held in 1956, Ho Chi Minh would receive 80 percent of the vote.[61]

During the Vietnam War, critics of U.S. involvement often cited Eisenhower's comment as proof of Ho Chi Minh's popularity among the Vietnamese people, a fact that U.S. policymakers at the time made no effort to conceal. But the issue was somewhat more complicated than a simple case of popular appeal. Administration officials were not only concerned about Ho's personal popularity and the absence of personal charisma and political organization among his noncommunist rivals but also at the likelihood that in the North, the DRV would manipulate the elections to its advantage, as had been the case in Eastern Europe following the end of World War II. The U.S. delegation at Geneva had vainly proposed that elections in Vietnam should be supervised by the United Nations to guarantee their fairness and reiterated that position in the statement issued at the close of the conference.

During the months following the peace agreement, U.S. officials periodically fretted about the issue and what to do about it. Some, like Ambassador
Donald Heath, simply proposed that the provisions for national elections be
ignored because they were not binding on either the United States or the
government of free Vietnam. One CIA report, predicting the likelihood of a
Vietminh victory, proposed using violations of the Geneva Accords by the DRV
as a pretext to circumvent them. A similar position was suggested when the
issue was raised by Secretary Dulles at a meeting at the State Department on
October 8, 1954.[62]

For the most part, French officials felt that the elections should be held.
The official position in Paris was that a failure to hold elections would violate
the spirit of Geneva, but Ambassador Dillon reported that in actuality the
French were probably afraid that if the elections did not take place, the DRV
would have a pretext to renew the war. Yet there is some evidence that French
officials were also concerned at the probable results of an election and tried to
head it off for that reason. One official admitted that the decision had been a
mistake and the results could be a disaster. In talks with U.S. officials in November, Prime Minister Mendès-France had alluded to the possibility of holding
elections only at the local level, in the hope of avoiding a landslide victory for
the Vietminh. In a cable to Ambassador Dillon following the meeting, Dulles
said that the administration had decided to reserve its position on elections
until the security situation in Indochina clarified.[63]

The issue came up again at an NSC meeting held on January 27, 1955, to
hear General Collins's report on the situation in South Vietnam. At that time
Secretary Dulles noted that it would be unrealistic to expect the communists to
agree to cancel the elections, but he added that there were other techniques,
"many of which are familiar to the Soviets," for preventing them from taking
place. Shortly after the meeting, studies were initiated in Washington and at the
U.S. Embassy in Saigon on possible means of averting or influencing the elections. On a trip to Southeast Asia in early March, Dulles raised the issue with
Foreign Minister Tran Van Do in Saigon. At that time the Diem regime apparently had no firm policy on elections. Dulles urged Diem to accept the principle
of holding elections and then insisting on procedures that would guarantee that
they would be carried out fairly. He felt that the DRV was unlikely to agree to
hold honest elections, and this would put the onus of refusal on Hanoi.[64]

In early April, Washington approached Saigon with a preliminary proposal
based on a suggestion for all-German elections that had been put forward by
Anthony Eden but was rejected by the communists. It began with the fundamental principle that no discussions on future national elections could take
place unless agreement had first been reached with the DRV on a series of
specific safeguards to guarantee the fairness and representative nature of the
elections. The administration believed that such an approach would put the

South Vietnamese government on a firm legal footing with regard to the Geneva Accords but would probably be unacceptable to the Hanoi regime because
of the strict compliance required to hold genuinely free elections.[65]

During the next few weeks, U.S. officials attempted to work out a joint
position on the issue which could be supported not only by the British and the
French but also by the Saigon government. On May 17, a draft NSC paper called
for a policy that would urge Saigon to proceed with consultations in July 1955 as
called for by the accords, while insisting on adequate guarantees that genuinely
free elections would take place in accordance with the stipulations contained in
the agreement. This position, the paper noted, was generally consistent with
free world policies regarding the divided countries of Korea and Germany and
would facilitate the administration's effort to obtain British and French support
for this course of action. If such a policy led to a renewal of hostilities in
Vietnam, the paper concluded, the United States should be prepared to resist
any communist attack on the South, if necessary with U.S. armed forces.[66]

When consulted, the British and the French, as well as the Canadians,
appeared amenable to the strategy. But Diem refused, despite a U.S. warning
that in so doing he would be exposing his government to severe international
criticism and providing the moral high ground to the DRV. Diem explained
that his government would not consider consultations with Hanoi until the
projected national assembly, scheduled to meet in August, had an opportunity
to consider the issue. Diem's reaction was discussed at a meeting of high-level
officials in the State Department in early June. Secretary Dulles explained that
U.S. policy was to suggest to Diem that he do everything possible to frustrate
the holding of elections by insisting on conditions the communists could not
accept. Then, if the communists decided to invade the South, the administration would promise in advance to intervene on his side. But he conceded that if
Diem refused to conform to the provisions of the Geneva settlement, the
United States would be in an awkward position. The DRV might react to such
an eventuality by invading the South. Would the United States, he asked rhetorically, be justified in considering such an act as a violation of the Geneva
Accords and invoke the Manila Pact?

The meeting reached no decision on the question of whether Saigon was
bound to adhere to the Geneva Accords, but there was a consensus that the
intent of the accords had been to settle the conflict through national elections
and that if Diem refused to hold consultations, he would face great difficulties
with the British and the French. The National Security Council discussed the
issue the following day and decided to postpone a decision until the attitude of
other concerned governments had become clear.[67]

During the next few weeks, U.S. officials tried to get Diem to soften his
opposition to any consultations with Hanoi. On July 15, the State Department
instructed the U.S. Embassy in Saigon to warn Diem that if he ignored the

Geneva formula without agreeing to a satisfactory substitute, his government would be in a "highly vulnerable position" because of communist pressures and a lack of sympathy from many Western and Asian leaders. But Diem remained adamant. In a speech given on the sixteenth he declared that his government was not bound to the Geneva Accords and would not agree to hold unification elections so long as the regime in the North did not renounce terrorism and place national interests above those of international communism. Diem had softened his text slightly to appease U.S., British, and French concerns, but the speech was followed by popular demonstrations (probably officially sponsored) against the ICC representatives in Saigon, an action that was hardly likely to endear South Vietnam to the people of India and Canada.[68]

Reaction abroad to Diem's speech was generally negative. In Geneva, where a summit meeting of Western leaders was taking place, French prime minister Faure complained to Eisenhower that Diem should give the impression he was willing to hold elections even if he did not intend to carry through with them and appealed to the president to persuade him at least to hold talks with leaders in Hanoi, who had already sent their own proposal to Saigon to schedule talks on future elections. At Geneva, the three Western leaders agreed on a formal statement advising Diem to reply to Hanoi's proposal. In its own message to Saigon containing the statement, the administration assured Diem that the United States was not attempting to force his government into automatically accepting any proposal made by the communists but that it was also important not to provide them with a pretext to revert to subversion in the South or raise the election issue at the diplomatic level under unfavorable conditions.[69]

In Great Power meetings at Geneva, U.S. tactics succeeded. The British and the French did not insist that formal consultations on elections be held between the two Vietnamese states on July 20 but simply called for some gesture from Saigon that would imply its willingness to take part at some future date in genuinely free elections. Surprisingly, the Soviet delegation did not press the issue and was apparently willing to accept a gesture. But Diem would not cooperate. In a radio broadcast on August 9 he made no response to the letter but simply reiterated that his government was not bound by the Geneva Accords and that conditions for free elections did not exist in the North.[70]

Dulles did not press the issue. At a press conference on August 30 he remarked that the United States had no objection to free elections but agreed with Diem that conditions were not ripe at the moment. But U.S. officials were not entirely comfortable with Diem's adamant refusal to hold talks with the DRV. When DRV prime minister Pham Van Dong complained of the delay in a letter to the British, the United States advised Diem to address a note to London acknowledging the letter from "authorities in Hanoi" and reaffirming support for elections under conditions that would guarantee a free expression of the national will and stating that he was actively studying additional steps to broaden his government to enable it to speak authoritatively for the Vietnamese people. The British and the French in general supported the U.S. approach, but British Foreign Secretary Harold Macmillan expressed concern at Diem's continuing refusal to hold talks with Hanoi and said it could cause India to withdraw from the ICC.[71]

Diem finally relented to U.S. pressure, and on October 7 he addressed a letter to the British reiterating his government's position on consultations. But Saigon's stalling tactics aroused impatience among Hanoi's allies, and in late October Chinese foreign minister Zhou Enlai appealed to the two Geneva co-chairmen to press Saigon to agree to consultations on the issue. In mid-November, Macmillan met with Soviet foreign minister Molotov, who insisted that something must be done to persuade Saigon to comply with the provisions of the accords but agreed for the moment to send a letter to all participants at the conference informing them of the impasse and asking what should be done.[72]

That initiative had little effect. In January 1956, China proposed that a new conference on Indochina be convened at Geneva, but the idea was opposed by both Washington and London. In talks with the British, Dulles argued that no decision on consultations should be held until elections for a national assembly took place in March. He agreed to raise the issue with Diem and try to persuade him to adopt a position that could be construed as conforming to the accords but stressed that he would not push Saigon into rigged elections. To derail the Chinese proposal, the British suggested a meeting of the Geneva co-chairmen in April. The Soviets approved that suggestion, and the idea of an international conference was abandoned. India said it would be satisfied with a statement that national elections would be discussed by July 1957.[73]

During the later phases of the Vietnam War, when U.S. combat troops had become actively involved in the fighting, the decision by the Eisenhower administration to support Diem's refusal to hold consultations on elections came under intense and often hostile scrutiny. Critics of the U.S. role in the war argued that by backing Diem in his refusal to hold talks with DRV representatives, the United States had taken a crucial step in breaking the Geneva Accords and undermining the legality of U.S. support for the government of South Vietnam (referred to in U.S. official documents as the GVN). Supporters of U.S. policy countered that neither Diem nor the United States was bound by the accords and thus they were fully justified in refusing talks with the North.[74]

It has always been difficult to formulate an impartial assessment of this issue because of the legal, political, and moral complexities involved. In the first place, the Geneva Accords were vague on the procedures for holding the elections and ambiguous on the commitment by the two Vietnams to hold them. Neither the South Vietnamese nor the United States had formally assented to the accords and had specifically referred to the problem of obtaining conditions for holding truly free elections. To deal with this dilemma, France (as surrogate for the Associated State of Vietnam until formal independence was granted) had committed South Vietnam in its name, but the latter had refused to be held to an agreement signed by a colonial power without its consent.

Second, there was a valid moral issue involved. The experience of Eastern Europe after World War II raised serious questions about the possibility of holding a free election in the North and provided a justification for insisting on adequate safeguards to obtain a fair representation of the national will. There are, however, equally valid reasons to doubt whether the Diem regime would permit an open expression of views in the South. The primary difference, as Eisenhower administration officials were well aware, was that the DRV was likely to be better organized in mobilizing the population in the areas under its control.

Some observers have claimed that the provisions for national elections in the Geneva Conference were simply a cosmetic means of obtaining the consent of the two Vietnams to the treaty and that no one really expected the elections to take place. Leaving aside the question of Hanoi's attitude on the issue, which will be discussed below, documentary evidence clearly shows that most of the governments represented at Geneva, including the British and the French, took the election provisions seriously and expected them to be held. Even U.S. officials in private discussions admitted that if elections did not take place, it would contravene the spirit of the Geneva Accords.

For all of the above reasons, then, the administration was in a quandary as to how to deal with the issue, obviously hoping that the elections would not take place but anxious as well to avoid the charge of having sabotaged them. The position that was eventually worked out with the British and the French, to agree to the holding of consultations but only on the basis of stringent conditions that would not have been acceptable to the DRV, was probably the best that could be achieved under the circumstances. Unfortunately, Diem refused to cooperate and the Eisenhower administration, against its better political instincts and fearful above all of the collapse of the anticommunist government in the South, decided to support him. It was a decision that would haunt future administrations, who were exposed to considerable criticism on legal grounds, not only from adversaries but also from allies.

The Diem Experiment

One of the ways the Eisenhower administration hoped to win broad international support for the new state in South Vietnam was by demonstrating that it represented the will of the Vietnamese people. Belief in the importance of democratic institutions had been a key element in the arsenal of the free world against the forces of international communism since the beginning of the Cold

War in the late 1940's, and both the Truman and the Eisenhower administrations had hoped that a Vietnamese government freely elected by the Vietnamese people would form a natural bulwark against the further expansion of communism in Southeast Asia.

From the start, however, the issue of democracy was a double-edged sword when Washington attempted to apply it to Vietnam. All knowledgeable observers were convinced that the Vietminh would be victorious in any all-Vietnamese elections. Then, after Geneva, it soon became clear that in a fractionalized society like South Vietnam, only a strong leader with some authoritarian instincts could hope to bring about the cohesion necessary to enable it to defeat a well-organized insurgency movement. Secretary Dulles had expressed this view in talks with French Prime Minister Edgar Faure in the spring of 1955 when he remarked that Asian governments, citing the example of Syngman Rhee in South Korea, always had strong leaders. It has often been said that U.S. government officials preferred authoritarian leaders to facilitate the containment of communism in Asia and justified the emergence of such leaders to buttress its policies in Asia. This is a misleading statement because most would undoubtedly have agreed that a stable democratic system was preferable to an authoritarian one, however stable it appeared on the surface. In fact, however, doubt about the relevance of Western-style democracy in newly emergent Asian societies was shared by many Asian specialists in the academic world, as well as by many Asian intellectuals. This attitude was enhanced during the late 1950's when in many newly independent countries in Asia, democratic institutions proved to be fragile. This led to a growing conviction among many social scientists in the West that Asian societies might require a transitional period or might even not be suited to Western-style democratic institutions.[75]

Such sentiments, of course, made it easier for U.S. officials to rationalize the emergence of such authoritarian leaders as Ngo Dinh Diem in South Vietnam. Although Diem was admittedly stubborn as well as authoritarian, one of his strengths, in the eyes of some U.S. officials, was that he was an uncompromising nationalist who would brook no interference in his determination to forge an independent nation.

The inherent contradiction between the U.S. desire for a strong leader and the maintenance of democratic principles created severe problems for the Eisenhower administration in its policy toward South Vietnam. During the winter of 1954–55, General Collins periodically discussed the nature of the future Vietnamese political system with Prime Minister Diem. Collins was under instructions not to interfere with Saigon's efforts to undertake political reform, but in conversations with Diem he tried to persuade him that he must learn to tolerate a political opposition. Diem was noncommittal, remarking on one occasion that he was considering a proposal to form a provisional national assembly that could provide the framework for a representative government until elections could be held for a constituent assembly. He said that he was not willing to tolerate political parties and had no intention of forming one himself.[76]

Diem had no lack of adversaries, of course, but they did not take the form of organized political parties. After having triumphed over the religious sects, he turned his attention to the problem of Chief of State Bao Dai. He had informed General Collins early in the year that he was inclined to reject a constitutional monarchy and get rid of Bao Dai, whose pro-French suscep-tibilities made him particularly unattractive to a nationalist like Diem. In Sep-tember he remarked to new U.S. ambassador Frederick Reinhardt, who had replaced Collins in April, that he might deal with the issue by means of a popular referendum asking voters to choose between himself and Bao Dai as chief of state. The government would then produce a draft constitution creating a strong presidential system of government.

Reinhardt argued against Diem's plan, pointing out that it would raise questions of the legitimacy of his claim to govern and suggesting that a better approach would be to create an elected assembly to consider such political changes. But Diem countered that such a body would be too cumbersome and would lead in the end to a weak parliamentary system on the French model. In a cable to Washington, Reinhardt recommended that the administration make it clear that U.S. support of Diem was conditional on his making progress on the election of a national assembly.[77]

But not all in Washington agreed. In a letter to Reinhardt, Kenneth T. Young, director of the Office of Philippine and Southeast Asian Affairs and a foreign service officer with considerable experience in the area, argued that the United States should not expect Asian countries to follow strictly the Western model and must be permitted "to find their own balance between the values of sufficient authority and effectiveness of executive leadership on the one hand and adequate responsible expression of the popular will on the other." Young himself declared that South Vietnam needed "a strong, centralized form of government with suitable outlets for voicing local and public opinion, includ-ing a 'responsible' opposition."[78]

In the end, Secretary Dulles split the difference. He agreed with Reinhardt that it was essential that the Vietnamese government broaden its base through the adoption of political reforms, but he shared Young's concern over the potential fallout of a national popular assembly which, unless the government possessed an effective political organization commanding a majority in the assembly, could harass the government and add to its already enormous bur-dens. Like Young, John Foster Dulles concluded that strong and stable executive leadership should have priority and that representative and constitutional pro-cedures "should be developed to the extent that they do not weaken central authority." It was under that assumption that the administration decided to support Diem's decision to establish a strong pro-government party, known as the Can Lao (Personalist Labor) Party.[79]

Reinhardt did not give up. In a cable to the State Department in mid-October, he admitted the danger of an unruly assembly but said that a greater threat existed if the government did not attempt to broaden its popular base. Regarding the danger of a fractionalized and obstreperous opposition in the national assembly, he said that Diem could be counted on to guarantee that there would be a comfortable pro-government majority.[80]

On October 25, 1955, with no forewarning to the United States, the government carried out a national referendum between Bao Dai and Ngo Dinh Diem. According to official figures, the latter received a landslide 98.2 percent of the total vote. An embassy report on the referendum, noting the one-sided election campaign for Diem and the absence of freedom for the opposition to organize (Bao Dai remained in France and did not contest the vote), called it a "travesty on democratic procedures" and no true measure of Diem's popularity in South Vietnam. One favorable sign was the large turnout—97.8 percent of all eligible voters—since Hanoi and some sect leaders had called for a boycott. There were reports, however, that the government may have packed the ballot boxes. The referendum represented the coup de grace to Franco-Vietnamese relations. The French, already smarting from negotiations that would lead to the complete withdrawal of French forces in April 1956, were angry at Diem's public humiliation of Bao Dai.[81]

Diem's autocratic political style (the CIA reported that he was "almost pathologically sensitive to criticism and potential opposition") was repeated the following March in elections for a national assembly. The result of the elections gave pro-government forces a solid majority. The National Revolutionary Movement (NRM—a pro-government united front)—received 47 seats, while Independents, most of them hand-picked by the government, were elected to 39. The following year, with U.S. assistance, a constitution was drafted and promulgated, and Ngo Dinh Diem was formally elected president of the new Republic of Vietnam (RVN).[82]

A second area of concern to U.S. officials was land reform. Under French colonial rule, much of the land in the South, notably in the Mekong River Delta, was in the hands of absentee landlords. There was a general recognition that land reform was necessary, but the Associated State under Bao Dai had done little to address the problem.

After the Geneva Conference, U.S. officials began to devote more attention to the issue. During the fall of 1954 Ambassador Donald Heath periodically urged on Washington the need for land reform, which he viewed as essential to combat communist influence in the South. But he admitted that Diem probably would not pursue it vigorously. It was one of the French criticisms against Diem that as a representative of mandarin interests he could not be relied upon to create a good program. During his visit to Washington in December, Prime Minister Mendès-France appealed to Dulles to push Diem on starting a land reform program. The U.S. mission in Saigon initiated a study of the land situation in November, and General Collins included the issue in the program that he drew up with General Ely a few weeks later. But there were obstacles to a serious effort to rectify the inequity in land distribution in the South. Not only was Diem's support unlikely, but the new government lacked a solid administrative base in rural areas, particularly in sect areas, which resisted government interference.[83]

In January 1955, Diem issued a land reform ordinance restricting landlords to 25 percent of the profit from the annual harvest, but it had little practical effect. In June the administration instructed Wolf I. Ladejinsky, a land reform specialist employed by the United States Operations Mission (USOM) in Saigon, to talk with Diem about the importance of a program to ease the problem of landlessness in rural areas of the South, citing the experience of other Asian societies such as Taiwan, the Philippines, and India. Diem did agree to appoint a minister of agricultural reform, but Ladejinsky was disappointed at the absence of urgency with which Diem and his key advisers approached the issue. In July 1956, the Saigon government finally promulgated a program to the U.S. Embassy calling for the distribution of excess land to tenants and asking for a loan or grant from the United States to help pay the costs. U.S. sources were critical of the vagueness of the program and fearful that it could lead to disillusionment among the peasants but eventually agreed to pay part of the costs.[84]

The bulk of the U.S. economic aid program was tied to the importation of consumer goods through the Commercial Import Program (CIP). Diem complained and wanted more direct aid in capital goods, but Ambassador Elbridge Durbrow, another career foreign service officer who replaced Frederick Reinhardt in March 1957, explained that the CIP program was needed to generate counterpart funds for local military expenses. After Diem persisted, the administration agreed to help promote foreign industrial investment but found that it was difficult to attract venture funds to South Vietnam because of the risk involved and a variety of government restrictions. Diem was anxious to promote government involvement and sought U.S. aid for joint state-private enterprises, but the administration was reluctant to get involved in government-owned firms. Eventually Washington responded to requests for advice from state-owned enterprises.[85]

The primary area of growing U.S. responsibility in South Vietnam was in the training and equipping of the Saigon government's armed forces and local self-defense militia. The main problem was the Geneva limitation on the size of the U.S. training mission, which had gradually replaced the French in the months following the Geneva Accords. The administration had promised Anthony Eden that it would not increase the size of the mission beyond the limit of

342 members which existed at the time of the signing of the accords. In December 1955 the Joint Chiefs requested an increase in the size of the mission, citing the departure of French personnel, but the State Department rejected the request, fearing political repercussions.

By early 1956 the attitude in the State Department began to change, and Secretary Dulles agreed to a proposal to send personnel on a temporary basis to recover U.S. equipment. In April, the United States established the Temporary Equipment Recovery Mission (TERM) and placed it under the MAAG mission. But the establishment of TERM created problems with U.S. allies as well as with the ICC, which questioned its legality and felt it would be provocative to the DRV. Nevertheless, the program was implemented in June. To avoid problems, the size of the mission was limited to 350 military personnel and civilians.[86]

Beyond the training mission, the United States provided limited support for the South Vietnamese armed forces. The administration had originally planned to reduce the size of these forces from 170,000 to 100,000 but eventually acceded to Diem's request to set a ceiling at 150,000. In December 1955, Diem requested U.S. aid for the Self-Defense Militia and the embassy approved it as a stopgap until the Civil Guard (Garde Civile) took on its functions to maintain law and order.[87]

Countering the Threat from the North

NSC 5429/5, approved in December 1954, called for the use of U.S. armed forces if necessary, appropriate, and feasible in the event of an overt communist attack on the area covered by the Manila Pact. There was a general assumption, however, that the primary threat in Southeast Asia was in the form of subversion, in which case primary reliance was to be placed on French forces and the FAVN. The administration took the threat of subversion seriously, however, and Point 9 of NSC 5429/5 said that

if requested by a legitimate local government which requires assistance to defeat local communist subversion or rebellion not constituting armed attack, the U.S. should view such a situation so gravely that, in addition to giving all possible covert and overt support within the Executive Branch authority, the President should at once consider requesting Congressional authority to take appropriate action, which might if necessary and feasible include the use of U.S. military forces either locally or against the external source of such subversion or rebellion (including Communist China if determined to be the source).[88]

During the spring of 1955, as the Diem regime fought to establish its authority over the religious sects, U.S. sources worried that the Vietminh possessed the capability to take over the South even without an overt attack, and a study undertaken by the Defense Department predicted that if remaining French military forces departed, it would be "extremely difficult if not impossible" to defend the South without the use of U.S. combat forces. After Diem refused to hold consultations with the DRV, the NSC called on the Defense Department for studies on how to handle a possible Vietminh attack on the South. The Joint Chiefs responded in September, warning that for the near future, unassisted South Vietnamese armed forces would be capable of "only limited resistance against determined overt aggression by Vietminh forces." In such a situation, the first U.S. operations would be immediate naval and air action to support the FAVN combined with an attack on the Vietminh. As soon as possible, mobile U.S. forces should be made available for joint operations with the FAVN. Such actions, the JCS warned, would be only minimal to protect the South from a communist conquest. To destroy Vietminh forces and occupy the North would require considerably more time and would depend on the energy and solidarity of the South Vietnamese as well as on possible restrictions on U.S. military operations. Without the use of nuclear weapons, the Joint Chiefs warned, such an operation would require "greater U.S. forces than the U.S. would be justified in providing from the overall point of view." The most effective deterrent, they believed, would be to station U.S. forces in the South, but this was prohibited before an act of aggression occurred by the terms of the Geneva Accords, so the next best step would be mobile ground forces in Southeast Asia. The JCS felt, however, that the major threat to South Vietnam was now subversion and thus concluded that additional mobile forces should not be deployed in Southeast Asia, but South Vietnamese forces, as well as those of Thailand and Cambodia, should be strengthened.[89]

In May 1956, the Joint Chiefs presented a plan for the defense of South Vietnam in case of an overt attack from the North. The plan called for South Vietnamese operations in a delaying action around Da Nang until assistance from allied forces arrived. It recommended that most of the fighting be done by Vietnamese and other Asian forces. But some worried that because the DRV had a two-to-one superiority of ground forces, U.S. air and naval support would have to be supplemented by at least two divisions of ground troops, to be used in an amphibious attack north of the demilitarized zone (DMZ).[90]

To some, the JCS position that nuclear weapons were needed for local war situations seemed too rigid. In January 1955, the NSC had passed Directive 5501 on basic national security policy. The directive said that in case of local war, the United States should be prepared to use highly mobile forces suitably equipped for local war as well as possessing atomic capabilities but not be dependent on the use of nuclear weapons for effective action. In revising the directive a few months later, the NSC Planning Board felt that U.S. forces should be sufficiently flexible so that a decision to intervene would not automatically mean a decision to employ nuclear weapons, and it called on the Defense Department to make a special presentation of such U.S. capabilities, using Vietnam as a test case. In particular, the board wished to know whether forces used in such operations would possess the capability for conventional combat without the use of nuclear weapons and what principles would govern any planned use of the latter in a local war situation.[91]

Admiral Radford presented his report on local war at an NSC meeting held on June 7. The report focused on the defense of South Vietnam but added that operations could be extended to the North if the circumstances were appropriate. The report confirmed that the United States could intervene in South Vietnam without serious disruption of its force levels elsewhere, whether or not nuclear weapons were used, so long as China did not intervene except to provide aid and advisers, and that other allied nations provided at least token forces. Radford said that in such a situation, nuclear weapons would probably not be needed against targets in North Vietnam, which could be destroyed by conventional capabilities, but he said that atomic weapons might be useful against concentrated Vietminh troops in the South. There was presently no indication, he concluded, that Hanoi intended to attack the South directly.

After Radford concluded his presentation, Secretary Dulles remarked that partial support for such an operation could be expected from Asian members of the Southeast Asia Treaty Organization (SEATO) but not from the British and the French. He then called on Walter Robertson to express the department's concern at the possible employment of nuclear weapons. Robertson warned that they would have the "very gravest impact" on Asian public opinion and he hoped that the United States would agree to use them only in the most crucial situation. The ensuing discussion was inconclusive, with Radford indicating his firm disagreement with Robertson's comments and the president remarking that it might be possible to send Nike missiles with nuclear warheads to Southeast Asia. The meeting concluded with a brief discussion of the president's authority to intervene against aggression on short notice without resort to congressional authorization. Dulles strongly recommended consultation, and Eisenhower agreed. The meeting noted the JCS report and agreed to encourage the South Vietnamese to heighten their planning for defense against possible external aggression and discreetly to manifest U.S. willingness to assist in such defense through the Manila pact, although the president rejected any formal action.[92]

On September 5, 1956, President Eisenhower approved NSC 5612/1, "U.S. Policy in Mainland Southeast Asia," which extended NSC 5429 and established policy for the area for the immediate future. On the whole, it was an optimistic document. Although it described the threat to the area from international communism as serious, it viewed the challenge as primarily covert and psychological, in the sense that the fall of one nation could lead to accommodation by the remainder. The administration saw the solution primarily in terms of the Manila Pact. If communist aggression should take place, the United States would invoke the Manila pact or the United Nations Charter so it could take appropriate military action. For the moment, U.S. forces were to serve mainly as a deterrent while the main emphasis would be on regional cooperation and the buildup of local forces to maintain regional independence, as well as on constitutional government and economic development.[93]

Hanoi Watches and Waits

For U.S. policymakers, one of the most crucial problems in attempting to stabilize the situation in South Vietnam was to estimate the intentions of the DRV. Would Hanoi decide to resume the war or accept, however reluctantly, the verdict of Geneva and seek a political solution? What was the attitude of China and the Soviet Union? Would their apparent willingness to sacrifice the interests of the Vietnamese revolution on the altar of peaceful coexistence continue, or would they shift to a policy of supporting the Vietminh when their changing interests appeared to require it?

On the whole, U.S. intelligence analysts believed that, at least for the time being, the threat to South Vietnam was primarily through political fragmentation or subversion. Between 1954 and 1957, CIA reports consistently predicted that Hanoi would not attack the South but would rely on subversive efforts to destabilize the fragile Saigon regime in hopes of an internal collapse or political takeover. There was a flurry of anxiety during the spring and summer of 1955 that Hanoi might turn to a military solution as a result of Diem's refusal to hold consultations on national elections, but that concern subsided with the passage of time, and by 1956 it had become the conventional wisdom in Washington that the DRV would refrain, at least for the time being, from an overt attack on the South, although many felt that it might initiate guerrilla war if the Diem government appeared to be stabilized.[94]

From the perspective of a generation later, that prognosis appears to have been reasonably accurate. Following the Geneva Conference, communist leaders in the North decided to accept the procedures called for by the Geneva Accords and await the results of the scheduled national elections throughout the country. That decision may have been unpopular among the more militant members of the party, particularly in the South, where the interests of Vietnamese reunification had been so clearly sacrificed to the needs of the North and of the Great Powers. There were, however, persuasive reasons for the DRV to accept the cease-fire. For one, both Moscow and Beijing had undoubtedly made it clear that they would not provide massive aid in the event of a resumption of the war. China had been a major supplier of military assistance to the Vietminh in the months leading up to Geneva, but Beijing was still hoping to improve relations with the West and apparently advised Vietnamese leaders to maintain a low profile.[95]

But there was an additional reason for accepting the results of Geneva, at least for the time being, and that was fear of increased U.S. military involvement. Whether leaders in Hanoi were aware of U.S. contingency plans for the use of armed forces in the event of an overt attack on South Vietnam from the North is unknown. Certainly they were aware of negotiations over SEATO and the possibility of the establishment of U.S. military bases or training missions in Laos and Cambodia. Ho Chi Minh must have cited these dangers to bring militant elements to accept the verdict of Geneva. In his Political Report given to the VWP Central Committee a few days before the signing of the treaty, Ho warned his more impetuous colleagues of the danger of U.S. intervention and argued persuasively for a period of peace which would provide time for the party to build up the regroupment zone in the North as a base from which to advance toward reunification of the entire country. The new policy, he said, would be to seek reunification through nationwide elections, but he also called for the strengthening of the Vietminh armed forces into a mighty people's army (to be known as the People's Army of Vietnam, or PAVN) "capable of meeting the requirements of the new situation."[96]

With the conclusion of the Geneva Accords, then, the party settled in for a period of peace and domestic reconstruction. A Politburo resolution issued in early September, "The New Situation, the New Mission, and the New Policy of the Party," called for a shift from war to peace, from the struggle for unification to building a new society. The resolution called for efforts in the South to use legal and illegal activities to consolidate peace and implement the Geneva Accords. This policy was confirmed at the Seventh Plenum of the VWP Central Committee in March 1955, which called for a policy of building up the North while waging a political struggle in the South and engaging in diplomatic work to win sympathy and support from the progressive peoples of the world.[97]

In adopting a diplomatic strategy, party leaders placed considerable emphasis on France. In his Political Report to the Central Committee in July, President Ho Chi Minh had noted that under the new government of Prime Minister Pierre Mendès-France, French policy toward the DRV had "noticeably changed," and he called for a more conciliatory policy toward France. This new approach was clearly demonstrated in the immediate post-Geneva period. The DRV welcomed the arrival of Jean Sainteny as delegate general of France in North Vietnam and stated its willingness to maintain cultural contacts with the French. In December Sainteny negotiated a "status agreement" at a subdiplomatic level with the DRV.

The warming of Franco-Vietminh relations concerned U.S. officials in Washington, who feared that the French might abandon their efforts to preserve an anticommunist government in the South. French sources, however, explained that Paris was attempting to encourage "Titoism" in Hanoi in the belief that Ho Chi Minh was more a nationalist than a communist. In March, Prime Minister Edgar Faure promised U.S. officials that France would not play

a "double game" in Vietnam and would not establish formal diplomatic relations with the DRV.

By contrast, the DRV adopted a policy of firm hostility to the United States,
which Ho Chi Minh had described in his July 1954 speech as the "main enemy"
of world peace. This attitude was reflected in more concrete ways. The administration had allowed its consulate in Hanoi to remain in operation even after
the return of the DRV to the city in October 1954. But after the DRV placed
severe restrictions on its operations and personnel, the consulate was officially
closed in December.[98]

A crucial component of the party's new strategy in the South rested on its
ability to retain a residual level of several thousand loyal Vietminh political
operatives below the DMZ to maintain the structure of the movement and
press for national elections. Some operated in the open, breaking up into
political committees at the local level to promote peace and elections. Others
operated covertly, burying weapons and maintaining the Vietminh organizational network to prepare for the possibility of a breakdown of the Geneva
process and a return to revolutionary war.[99]

Did party leaders in Hanoi actually expect national elections to take place?
Vietminh sources have sometimes been quoted to the effect that they had conceded that they would not. Yet there is ample evidence that they had adopted a
strategy that was based on the assumption that they would take place, and the
DRV may have hoped that pressure from the Geneva co-chairmen and other
nations, such as India, China, Canada, and France, would eventually compel
the Saigon regime and its U.S. ally to accept, however reluctantly, the necessity
of holding elections. Even in the West, many observers, including some officials
in the United States, appeared to believe that elections in some form would take
place, and it is difficult to believe that Hanoi would not have heard such reports.
A trip by President Ho Chi Minh and party general secretary Truong Chinh to
Moscow and Beijing in early summer must have been undertaken to ascertain
the views of Hanoi's major allies on the issue.[100]

Yet Ho and his colleagues were clearly prepared for the possibility that the
Geneva procedures would break down, and the refusal of the Diem regime to
hold consultations in the summer of 1955, however disappointing, did not lead
to a change in policy in Hanoi. At a plenary meeting of the Central Committee
held in August after Ho's return to the DRV, the party confirmed the existing
two-pronged policy of consolidating its power in the North while advancing
step-by-step toward reunification with the South. The primary decision taken
at the conference was the formation of a new national united front (called the
Fatherland Front) to rally the people of the entire country toward reunification
by peaceful means.[101]

During the next few months, party operatives in the South carried out a
moderate policy emphasizing political struggle combined with selective violent

activities and an effort to link up Vietminh military units with dissident elements of the religious sects. In the meantime, Diem attempted to root out Vietminh bases in rural areas while arresting members of the Vietminh-sponsored Saigon-Cholon Peace Committee, established at Hanoi's order to press for national elections. Party operations in the South were headed by Politburo member Le Duan, a veteran communist from Quang Tri Province, Central Vietnam, who had served as the senior Vietminh representative in the area since the early 1950's. Le Duan soon discovered that the failure to hold elections as called for by the Geneva Accords aroused considerable anxiety among supporters of the revolution in the South. Some became discouraged and dropped out of the movement, while others called for a more activist policy to counter Saigon's aggressive tactics. Similar feelings erupted among southern supporters of the Vietminh who had settled in the North following the signing of the Geneva Accords.[102]

In June, Ho Chi Minh sent an open letter to the "southern comrades" in which he defended the existing policy of seeking national reunification by peaceful means. Such appeals from southerners to come to the rescue of beleaguered comrades in the South, however, came at an awkward time for party leaders in Hanoi. Under the new leadership of Soviet Communist Party chief Nikita Khrushchev, the Soviet Union had just promulgated a new foreign policy emphasizing peaceful coexistence with the West and a peaceful road to socialism. In March, the VWP newspaper *Nhan Dan* had voiced its approval of the new policy line formulated in Moscow, but there were obviously some doubters. In a speech to the Central Committee in late April, General Secretary Truong Chinh (recently returned from attending the Communist Party of the Soviet Union's Twentieth Congress in January) conceded that "there are some people who do not yet believe in the correctness of this political program and in the policy of peaceful reunification of the country, holding that these are illusory and reformist." Such doubts existed even among senior officials in the party. While approving the existing policy of peaceful struggle and peaceful coexistence, the April plenum alluded to the possibility of a resumption of armed struggle if conditions required it. In a speech at the plenum, Ho Chi Minh pointed out that although in certain countries the road to socialism could be peaceful, in cases where the machinery of state, the armed forces, and the police were in the hands of the exploiting class, the oppressed peoples must prepare for armed struggle. President Ho was now apparently on the side of the doubters.[103]

Two months following the April plenum, the Politburo adopted a resolution entitled "The situation and missions of the revolution in the South" in an attempt to clarify party policy. According to the resolution, the basic form of struggle in the South was still political, but armed struggle for the purpose of self-defense was permissible under certain circumstances. The document stressed the importance of creating base areas and setting up a broad national front against the Diem regime and its U.S. protector. References in the press, however, suggested that opinion remained divided.[104]

In the South, Le Duan took the slight opening in Hanoi and attempted to expand it. In a short pamphlet written in October and presented at a Central Committee plenum two months later, he argued for a strategy that, though nonviolent on the surface, would call for a more vigorous use of self-defense forces to support the political struggle against the Saigon regime. The pamphlet, *The Path to Revolution in the South*, was approved by the Central Committee and became basic policy for the next two years. Le Duan's plan was to achieve victory by means of a general uprising to seize political power supported by low-level paramilitary activities. With authorization from the central authorities, during the next several months the revolutionary leadership in the South undertook to form small battalion-sized units to undertake low-level military activities while engaging in selective acts of terrorism to intimidate supporters of the Diem regime. At the same time, Hanoi launched a program to modernize its armed forces in preparation for a possible resumption of armed struggle in the South. Guaranteeing national security and building the armed forces was labeled by the Central Committee as "one of the main tasks of the whole party and people." Still, party leaders refrained from approving a return to the strategy of revolutionary war in the South.[105]

In August 1957 Ho Chi Minh went to Moscow, presumably to seek support for a more active policy in the South. On his return he announced that he had achieved "unity of views" with the new leadership in Moscow. Then he took a second trip to the USSR in November with Le Duan, now serving as acting general secretary of the party, to attend the conference of communist parties held in Moscow. It was a time of rising tension in the relationship between Moscow and Beijing, a rivalry that was based not only on China's disagreement with Khrushchev over destalinization but also on differences over the possibility of a policy of peaceful coexistence with the West. At the conference, however, the two communist powers apparently agreed to deemphasize their ideological differences and may have reached an accommodation to discourage a resumption of conflict in Indochina. The final declaration issued at the conference stressed the importance of peaceful coexistence. But Ho was able to insert a phrase in the declaration maintaining the possibility of a nonpeaceful road to socialism.[106]

The Diem Miracle

Hanoi's cautious half-step toward a more activist policy in the South received little attention in Washington. A National Intelligence Estimate issued by the CIA in May 1957 predicted that the DRV would probably continue its policy of "peaceful competition" with the Diem regime for the allegiance of the Vietnamese people but warned that it would continue its efforts to exploit dissatisfaction among various groups in the South.[107]

But in Saigon, President Ngo Dinh Diem was concerned about the security situation in Laos and Cambodia and the rising size and strength of the PAVN. During a state visit to Washington in May he requested an increase in the authorized size of the South Vietnamese armed forces (now formally known as the Army of the Republic of Vietnam, or ARVN). In a meeting at the White House on the ninth, he told President Eisenhower that the DRV now had 400,000 troops as compared with only 150,000 in the ARVN, a figure that had reflected the presence in the South of the French Expeditionary Corps. Now that French troops had been withdrawn, he needed an increase to 170,000 in addition to a shift from light to heavy divisions to cope with a possible invasion from the North. To handle internal security requirements, he hoped to build up the Civil Guard and local self-defense forces.

For Eisenhower, the problem was at least partly a budgetary one. He reminded Diem that he was protected by the "umbrella clause" in the Manila Pact. But Diem had some reservations about existing SEATO strategy, which relied on the introduction of external armed forces and the possible use of nuclear weapons in case of communist aggression in Southeast Asia. Only Thailand and the Philippines, he said, could provide immediate help in the form of troops. Moreover, he questioned the value of atomic weapons in Vietnam, where visibility was poor and there were few targets appropriate for an atomic attack. Eisenhower was not particularly impressed and pointed out that U.S. aid was not limitless, but he promised to do what he could.[108]

Diem's proposals for an increase in the size and strength of the South Vietnamese armed forces did have some support in the Pentagon, as well as from MAAG chief Lieutenant General Samuel T. Williams in Saigon. Williams felt that ARVN needed to be strengthened in both size and effectiveness, and he supported Diem's request for a heightened force limit of 170,000 troops. He also pointed out that all French military personnel had been withdrawn by early 1957 and requested an increase in the number of U.S. advisers by incorporating the TERM program into the existing MAAG operation.

But many civilian officials in Saigon and Washington were dubious about Diem's request. Some felt that his proposal for a strengthened Civil Guard was a subterfuge to build up a larger army and obtain increased military aid from the United States. Specialists connected with the Michigan State University advisory group viewed the Civil Guard as a civilian police force rather than a branch of the South Vietnamese army. They also had serious reservations about the self-defense forces, which were plagued by poor morale and heavily infiltrated by the communists. Some, too, felt that in emphasizing the military aspects of the problem, Diem and U.S. military advisers such as General Williams were ignoring the root causes of the unrest in the South, which was related to the growing alienation of much of the population from the Saigon regime. Ambassador Elbridge Durbrow reflected this view in a report submitted just before President Diem's visit to Washington in May. His report was generally positive. The economic situation was "remarkable," the military situation was "improving," and security had been achieved "in large measure." But he warned that the regime was courting trouble because of Diem's distrustful nature and the growing alienation of key groups within the population, including the sects, the overseas Chinese, and some Catholics.[109]

Durbrow's concern over the general political situation did not abate during the remainder of the year, and in a report submitted in December he warned that the Diem "miracle" (as his performance had been described by some observers in the United States during his state visit in May) was showing significant signs of losing momentum. Durbrow's primary criticism was directed at the president's autocratic style of leadership. Like many previous U.S. officials, Durbrow described him as distrustful, authoritarian, limited in vision, and lacking a broad political base of support within the country. He also emphasized the regime's concentration on issues of national security while ignoring the economic and social needs of the mass of the population. Its attempt to suppress the opposition by terror and intimidation often played into communist hands by alienating key groups within the country. Durbrow recommended that the United States apply pressure on Diem to take steps for the good of his own regime.[110]

To many members of the U.S. mission in Saigon, another source of Diem's remoteness was his reliance on his family and the Can Lao party. According to U.S. Embassy reports, the Can Lao Personalist Labor Party first emerged in the early 1950's among Vietnamese émigrés living in France, many of them admirers of the Personalist philosophy of the Catholic philosopher Emmanuel Mounier. The party was formed by Diem's younger brother Ngo Dinh Nhu in 1954 and quickly turned into a clandestine organization promoting the interests of the Diem regime. In the late 1950's it was estimated to contain between 16,000 and 20,000 members, most of them professionals and government officials. The party was organized along Leninist lines and had regional branches throughout the RVN.

Defenders of the Can Lao pointed out that it performed social and philanthropic services and provided a firm base of support for the regime, but many Vietnamese claimed that it was a root cause of much of the official corruption that was becoming endemic in Vietnamese society because members used their official connections to gain special favors from the government. Durbrow sought an opportunity to discuss the issue with Ngo Dinh Nhu, who was not only secretary general of the party but also a personal counselor to the president, pointing out that critical press reports of the party in the United States could antagonize Congress and reduce the level of U.S. aid to the RVN, but Nhu denied reports of financial wrongdoing by members of the party and said that they had been spread by the communists.[111]

Such criticism of Diem's performance was not universally shared by U.S. official representatives in the RVN. General Samuel T. Williams took issue with Durbrow's views about Diem and his assessment of the essential nature of the problem in South Vietnam. To Williams, the problem was military, and bickering between the U.S. mission and the Saigon government over the latter's shortcomings only distracted from the task at hand. Personal antipathy between Williams and the ambassador exacerbated the problem.[112]

Yet even critics of Ngo Dinh Diem were faced with the disagreeable fact that there were still no viable alternative candidates for leadership of the country. Even Ambassador Durbrow agreed that the opposition was lacking in leadership and in links with the rural population. Saigon intellectuals were viewed as lightweights, and their vocal unhappiness with the regime, though worrisome, was not viewed as politically significant. The most visible opposition figure, at least to U.S. observers, was Dr. Phan Quang Dan, a leading member of the Caravelle Group that issued a proclamation in 1959 demanding political and economic reforms and a broadening of the base of the Saigon government. Many Western journalists were impressed by Dr. Dan, but embassy sources dismissed him as inexperienced and saw few threats to Diem's authority from within the ranks of the military.

Another apparent reason for U.S. official ambivalence about Ngo Dinh Diem was the tendency of many U.S. observers at the time to see his autocratic style of government as natural for a society such as Vietnam. The failure of democratic institutions to take root in many Southeast Asian countries after the restoration of independence following World War II (two conspicuous examples were Burma and Indonesia) was disillusioning to many Western scholars and government officials, and it became the conventional wisdom among many observers that Asian societies were not yet suited for a pluralistic form of government. Ambassador Durbrow himself, although a vocal critic of Diem's style of leadership, conceded that Western political institutions might not be appropriate in Vietnam, at least for the time being. In a lengthy report on the overall situation in December 1959, he commented favorably on the "forced draft" approach that Diem had adopted and suggested that his philosophy of Personalism might be a better alternative to communist ideology than those that had been adopted in other societies in the region. Durbrow concluded that although Diem's government was not crafted on the American model, the United States should support him as long as he was benevolent and looked out for the interests of the population.[113]

Durbrow's warning that the United States should not assume that Western liberal democratic institutions and values were automatically applicable in Vietnam struck a responsive chord in Washington, where State Department officials had been attempting to formulate a coherent response to the rash of military takeovers throughout Asia. This problem was discussed by the NSC in June 1959 and prompted a circular airgram to U.S. missions in Asia and Africa, many of which were faced with the same issue. Later that month, in a draft revision to NSC 5429/5 entitled "Current Policy in the Far East," State Department officials made the same point: "To the extent possible as consistent with our continuing aim of encouraging democratic growth, especially respect for basic human rights, encourage strong responsible executive-type governments which are best suited to the current requirements of various countries taking into account their traditions, circumstances, and capabilities."[114]

Not all agreed with the new tendency to accept the trend toward authoritarian governments in Asia and turn it to the advantage of U.S. security needs. Interestingly, one word of caution came from the Pentagon. In a memo dated July 14, 1959, the Joint Chiefs warned of the potential difficulties involved in supporting authoritarian dictatorships, citing the examples of Syngman Rhee in Korea and Chiang Kai-shek in Taiwan. In the future, they suggested, "U.S. policy should avoid such personal commitments [to an individual ruler] and should be aimed toward the development of governmental institutions in the countries of the Far East that can survive changing chief executives with little or no disruption."[115]

Although reports from the U.S. Embassy in Saigon were somewhat ambivalent about alternatives, they did single out with considerable accuracy the increasing problems that the Diem regime was beginning to encounter in dealing with its critics in the intellectual community. Embassy officials were conspicuously less successful in evaluating the rising level of discontent in the countryside. The administration had urged the Saigon regime to undertake measures to reduce the unequal distribution of land that had been left over from the colonial period. Wolf Ladejinsky, the USOM official who later served as Diem's personal adviser for land reform affairs, had assisted Ngo Dinh Diem in producing the land reform law, passed by the National Assembly in 1957. After that, however, the embassy had not closely monitored the implementation of the program and had limited itself to the pious hope that it would enlist the allegiance of the rural population, despite prior warnings that Diem was not seriously committed to the issue.

It was not that the regime was blind to the danger of handing over the countryside to the forces of the revolution. Diem himself was concerned about the threat to his government in rural areas and had invested considerable energy in attempting to deal with the issue. But Diem had a curious blind spot about the relationship between rural poverty and insurgency, and his approach focused on eliminating support for the Vietminh rather than on the challenge of winning peasant "hearts and minds" by an effective program of agricultural development and land distribution. From the beginning, the land reform law was much less stringent than had been desired by U.S. specialists, and it was flouted with impunity by wealthy landlords, many of whom had close ties with the Saigon regime. As a result, the percentage of poor farmers who received land from the program was relatively insignificant. Although Washington had little concern for the problem, the Hanoi government was highly conscious of the relevance of land hunger to revolution and made a major effort to win support in the villages by promising to distribute land to the poor. By the late 1950's discontent with the regime in rural areas was increasing steadily.

Diem's response was characteristic. Viewing the problem in military rather than economic and social terms, he attempted to herd the rural population in threatened areas into so-called agrovilles, large community development centers that combined defense, economic, and administrative functions. In theory, the purpose of the new centers was to isolate the rural population from the guerrillas in the countryside and prevent the latter from obtaining recruits and provisions necessary for their survival and further growth. But the autocratic techniques used by the government to settle the peasants in the agrovilles led to widespread anger in rural areas and soon brought the program to a virtual halt. By 1959, such developments began to arouse the concern of the U.S. mission, and particularly of Wolf Ladejinsky.[116]

The Path to Revolution in the South

The growing discontent in the villages played into the hands of the revolutionary leadership in the South and spurred it to greater efforts to gear up for a major attempt to bring down the Diem regime. During 1958 some southern leaders had intensified their efforts to win approval from the central authorities in Hanoi for an acceleration of the armed struggle in the South, and some cadres began to undertake military operations on their own initiative. By the middle of 1958, local revolutionary authorities in Tay Ninh province, in the center of the rubber plantation region adjacent to the Cambodian border, began to integrate their local military forces into combined units to defend themselves against government sweep operations. In August, guerrilla units attacked and briefly occupied a district capital in the province. Further to the north, party operatives in the Central Highlands, armed with a copy of Le Duan's pamphlet *The Path to Revolution in the South,* began to organize minority tribal peoples to build a liberated base area in the Tra Bong district, in the mountainous western part of Quang Ngai province.

These events pointed out the need for party leaders in the DRV to make a decision. The Politburo was now under new leadership. After presenting his report on conditions in South Vietnam to the central authorities in December 1956, Le Duan had been named acting general secretary of the VWP. Party ideologist Truong Chinh had occupied the post since 1941 but had just been dismissed as a result of errors committed by the Hanoi regime in carrying out land reform in the North. President Ho Chi Minh was named titular general secretary, but Le Duan was assigned responsibility to carry out the day-to-day duties of the post. From then on, he would serve as a powerful advocate of an aggressive strategy to achieve national reunification with the South.

In late 1958, responding to the increasingly tense situation in South Vietnam, Le Duan left secretly for an inspection trip to evaluate the situation. Shortly after his return at the end of the year, a plenary session of the Central Committee was convened to discuss the situation and future actions. At the end of the meeting, the Central Committee approved a new policy which called for a return to revolutionary war to liberate the South. The new policy, however, still reflected the ambivalence that had characterized attitudes in Hanoi since the Geneva Conference. Though approving a return to the tactics of revolutionary war, the final communique, which was not issued until May, declared that the "political strength of the masses" would still be the main form of struggle, although it would now be supplemented by low-level military activities carried on by local guerrilla forces and village self-defense units of the type that had been used during the August Revolution. Two secret units—called Groups 559 and 759 from the date of their formation (May and July 1959)—were created to enhance the ability of the DRV to infiltrate additional cadres and supplies into the South by land through Laos and by sea. Most such cadres were former Vietminh supporters from the South who had emigrated to the North after the Geneva Conference and received training in revolutionary operations at camps set up near Hanoi. An additional unit was created to assist the Pathet Lao to escalate their own revolutionary activities against the royal government in Laos.[117]

In Hanoi, that meeting, known formally as the Fifteenth Plenum of the VWP, is sometimes described as an "extremely important milestone" in the struggle for national independence and reunification. But although it is generally considered Hanoi's opening shot in the Second Indochina War, it is still surrounded by ambiguity and confusion. What caused the decision to be made at that particular time? Why the delay of several months before the new policy was confirmed? What did the new strategy actually call for, and why?

Western observers have often assumed that communist leaders decided to escalate the struggle when they realized that Diem's errors had created a revolutionary situation in the South, opening an opportunity to overthrow the Saigon regime. Historical accounts written in Hanoi have confirmed that the rising discontent in the South was one factor in their decision, but they add that another reason was the intensified suppression of the revolutionary forces (now labeled Viet Cong, or "Vietnamese Communists" by the Saigon regime) by Diem's security apparatus during the late 1950's. According to DRV sources, as a result of Saigon's repressive efforts, by the end of the decade the party infra-structure in South Vietnam had been reduced to about 5,000 members. The revolution, in Hanoi's eyes, had to go either forward or backward. Repression had virtually destroyed the organizational base left in place in the South after the Geneva Conference. To survive, it was essential to strike back.

Some foreign observers have alleged that the decision was made as the result of pressure from revolutionary cadres in the South. There is probably at least some truth in this. During 1957 and 1958, a number of southern cadres went to Hanoi to argue their case and to request an escalation of military struggle. But it would be misleading to assume that the new policy was neces-sarily forced on a reluctant party leadership. Ho Chi Minh had argued for years that a policy of revolutionary violence might be required in South Vietnam, and Le Duan, now acting general secretary, took the same view. If there was a debate at the Fifteenth Plenum, it was probably more about timing and the proper mix of political and military tactics than about whether to adopt the new approach.

Even after the basic decision was reached, there was considerable debate over the relative importance of political and military forms of struggle. There had been much criticism within the party over the militarization of the conflict against the French, and many may have felt that a primarily political struggle was the best approach to adopt. Limited support from Moscow and Beijing, as well as anxiety over the possibility of a direct U.S. role in the conflict, may have persuaded some to hesitate before the abyss of a new war. Finally, some may have placed a higher priority on completing socialist transformation in the North. Whatever the reasons, the decision was probably controversial as well as momentous, which may help to explain the delay in announcing the results of the debate.[118]

Does it matter when and why Hanoi decided to return to a more revolu-tionary approach to reunify North and South? It does, because of the legal and moral implications involved. Who started the Vietnam War? Was it a civil war or an invasion from the North? These questions aroused considerable debate throughout the world in later years, when the war had become a controversial issue in the United States. Many Americans found it difficult to accept their government's claim that the war was an invasion initiated by the North. Critics of U.S. involvement point to the discontent with the Diem regime in the South and assert that, at the most, communist leaders in North Vietnam gave their support to an internal struggle within the South to overthrow a hated ruler. Those who supported U.S. policy do not necessarily absolve Ngo Dinh Diem of some responsibility for the situation, but they assert that without active sup-port from the North, the southern insurgency movement could have been handled by the security forces of the Saigon regime.

It is unlikely that any consensus on this issue will be reached until the passions aroused by the Vietnam War have died. On the basis of present evidence it is hard to reject the conclusion that the most persuasive answer is a combination of the two. Without external support from the North, it is doubtful that dissident forces inside South Vietnam would have possessed the strength or the self-discipline to overthrow the Diem regime so long as he received firm support from the United States. The importance of leadership provided by the North is now conceded even in Hanoi, and the argument earlier advanced by some Western critics of the war that the movement was essentially indigenous can no longer be considered as valid. Yet there is no doubt that the movement had deep roots in the South, without which no amount of effort by the DRV could have pushed the situation in the RVN to the point of revolution. Had the United States not intervened on the side of the South, the issue would undoubtedly have been decided in a matter of months rather than years.

Some would say, of course, that the issue of northern support for the insurgency in the South is irrelevant because the Geneva Accords, even while dividing Vietnam into two de facto states, affirmed that legally it was a single nation. When Ngo Dinh Diem, with the acquiescence of Washington, refused to hold consultations on national elections, Hanoi was absolved from responsibility to abide by the provisions of the agreement. That, at any rate, was the position taken by the United States in reaction to violations of the accords by the North. Were there moral or political factors justifying the decision by the RVN and the United States to ignore such legal provisions in the interest of a higher moral law? I shall return to these issues at the end of the book.[119]

During the next several months, bolstered by the steadily increasing level of personnel and matériel moving down the system of trails being constructed from the North to the South, the insurgent forces in South Vietnam waged a number of so-called spontaneous uprisings in various parts of the RVN. One took place in Tra Bong district in the Central Highlands, enabling local forces to build a liberalized zone in the area populated by over 1,000 people. Similar outbreaks occurred elsewhere, notably in the heart of the Mekong Delta, where a popular insurrection supported by local guerrilla units temporarily took over control of several villages in Kien Hoa province. The party leadership in the South remained cautious, however, instructing local echelons to concentrate on organizational work and political agitation until the proper time for a major advance in the revolution was at hand.[120]

The Origins of Counterinsurgency

Hanoi's decision to adopt a strategy of "revolutionary war" in 1959, once it became known in Washington, confirmed the assumptions of U.S. intelligence analysts since the end of the Geneva Conference, who had predicted subversion rather than overt armed attack as the DRV's most likely form of response to the failure to realize peaceful reunification with the South. Saigon and Washington agreed on the need to develop the capacity to counter such activities but disagreed on the way to cope with them. Diem preferred to build up the Civil Guard and the local Self-Defense Forces to bear the brunt of the counterguerrilla effort, preserving his regular armed forces in preparation for a possible invasion from the North. According to some observers, Diem also viewed the Civil Guard as a loyal force composed primarily of Catholics from North Vietnam that he could use against the army, the loyalty of whose high command structure he had reason to doubt. He was determined to place the Civil Guard under the Ministry of Defense to avoid the existence of two separate armed forces and to facilitate the shipment of military equipment to such forces through U.S. foreign aid.

Many officials in Washington were skeptical of Diem's plan for several reasons. They doubted the value of such forces in dealing with internal subversion and suspected that Diem's motive was simply to obtain support to increase the size of his armed forces. They also recommended that the Civil Guard be placed under the Ministry of Interior in conformity with the belief that it was essentially an internal police force. An additional problem with Diem's proposal, from Washington's point of view, was that it lacked the funding to train and equip the Civil Guard at its present level of over 50,000 men and felt that any such funds could be better used to improve the economy of the country. Eventually a compromise was reached whereby the administration agreed to train and equip the Civil Guard at a force level of 32,000 while Diem acquiesced in Washington's demand that training be provided by public safety specialists within the U.S. Operations Mission. But Diem, with the support of MAAG and some officials in the Defense Department in Washington, remained reluctant to abandon his plan to place the Civil Guard under the Ministry of Defense.[121]

Beyond the question of military organization lay the broader issue of strategy. U.S. intelligence analysts predicted that at least at the outset, Hanoi would adopt guerrilla tactics, whereas others such as MAAG chief General Samuel T. Williams and perhaps Ngo Dinh Diem himself foresaw the greater likelihood of a conventional war such as the one in Korea. Williams had supported Diem in his proposal to strengthen the Civil Guard and place it under the Ministry of Defense, but he thought the primary threat to the RVN would be an attack from the North. When in 1958 the ARVN General Staff wanted to create commando or ranger units to carry out counterguerrilla operations, Williams opposed the proposal as "hasty" and "ill-considered" on the grounds that it would deplete the strength of Saigon's conventional forces. General Williams was not blind to the need for counterguerrilla operations, but he was convinced that it would be better achieved by reorganized and better equipped Civil Guard units.[122]

To some civilian and military officials in Washington, the poor record of the South Vietnamese armed forces in coping with guerrilla operations suggested the need to create small, lightly armed units operating at the village level. One of the first to advocate this strategy was Colonel Edward G. Lansdale, now deputy special assistant for special operations in the office of the secretary of defense. When in the spring of 1959 President Diem asked for U.S. advice and assistance in developing counterinsurgency operations, Lansdale commented that the United States had little experience in this area and suggested that U.S. Army Special Warfare teams be assigned to MAAG as advisers, with instructions to study counterguerrilla tactics with ARVN combat units before giving advice.[123]

Lansdale's complaint that the U.S. Army had little experience in counterguerrilla warfare undoubtedly reflected the general preference in the Pentagon for large-unit warfare based on superior technology that had characterized U.S. strategic thinking during the twentieth century. But the alarming rise of guerrilla activities in South Vietnam during 1959 and early 1960 provoked rising concern in U.S. military circles, and in February 1960 Special Forces personnel were assigned to MAAG in Saigon to train ARVN commando units. A few weeks later, the Defense Department instructed MAAG to encourage ARVN to develop antiguerrilla capabilities within its regular force structure, reversing General Williams's advice the previous year. That same month, the Joint Chiefs initiated efforts to produce a counterinsurgency program for South Vietnam.

But differences soon arose between civilian and military officials over how to implement the plan and the conditions to impose on the Saigon regime for its implementation. In his year-end report written in December 1959, Ambassador Durbrow described the problem as primarily political and characterized the South Vietnamese leadership as more concerned with security than economic development. As the level of rebel activity increased during the early months of 1960, Durbrow conceded that the security problem was serious, but he continued to see the solution in political terms. Diem's government continued to lack a "sense of mission" and treated the population with suspicion and coercion rather than compassion and understanding. Citing a captured Viet Cong document that said that 70 percent of the population in rural areas was either embittered by or indifferent to the Saigon government, he warned that it was "highly unlikely that any solution can be found to the internal situation in South Viet-Nam if the RVN does not enjoy the support of the rural population." Durbrow was also concerned that the RVN was engaged in a bitter border dispute with Cambodia and encouraging rebel activities against the neutralist government of Norodom Sihanouk there, heightening the latter's sensitivities to threats from the pro-U.S. governments in Thailand and South Vietnam. In a cable to the State Department on May 3 he complained that Diem was not listening to U.S. advice and recommended that he be authorized to threaten a cutback in military assistance unless Diem would "come to his senses."[124]

Durbrow's cable of May 3 had been sent with the apparent concurrence of General Williams, but in a private letter to Edward Lansdale in Washington, Williams insisted emphatically that he had not concurred and in fact disagreed with the effort to pressure Diem. The message also caused a stir in Washington. In the State Department a cable was drafted by Vietnam Desk Officer Chalmers B. Wood approving Durbrow's request to threaten an aid cutoff to bring Diem to reason. But the draft drew an immediate response from the Defense Department, where officials questioned the value of such a negative approach and suggested instead that the United States attempt to work constructively with Diem to find a solution to the problem. This issue had just been considered in an Operations Plan for Vietnam approved by the interagency Operations Coordinating Board, which had recommended that the United States should be careful in giving advice to Diem so as "not to disturb a situation favorable to the free world."[125]

Apparently because of the lack of concurrence from Defense, the draft cable was not sent. The issue was raised briefly at a meeting of the NSC held on May 9, but apparently there was no discussion of whether to apply pressure on Diem to persuade him to be more receptive to U.S. advice. President Eisenhower simply noted that everything possible should be done to prevent a further deterioration of the situation because the United States "had rescued this country from a fate worse than death and it would be bad to lose it at this stage." That evening, a separate cable was dispatched to Saigon rejecting Durbrow's request to threaten sanctions on the grounds that the administration would have to follow through if Diem refused to cooperate, "thus weakening our over-all security posture in Asia." He was authorized to warn Diem that if U.S. aid was misused serious consideration would be given to backing up words with action.[126]

The dispute between the Departments of State and Defense was finally papered over at a meeting of the Operations Coordinating Board on May 25. The board's report recommended continuing support of the Saigon regime on the grounds that it was "independent, anti-Communist, and generally responsive to the needs of the people" while at the same time continuing to press Diem to broaden the popular base of his government and improve relations with Cambodia. There were few signs from Saigon that such an approach would succeed. In a conversation with Ambassador Durbrow and Wolf Ladejinsky, Diem rejected their plea for a more conciliatory attitude toward opposition elements in the RVN and refused to give up any territory to Cambodia despite pressure from the United States.[127]

With the dispute over how to deal with Diem at least temporarily resolved, the administration settled in to make the policy work. In mid-July, the NSC approved a new policy paper titled "U.S. Policy on Mainland Southeast Asia." The strategy for Vietnam was essentially unchanged, but the paper did note that if a particular country ceased to show a will to resist the communists, the United States should consider terminating its aid program.[128]

During the summer of 1960, the administration began following a two-pronged strategy on Vietnam: to pressure the RVN to develop a national course of action and to draw up a counterinsurgency program to deal with the threat from the communists. The effort evoked a new sense of urgency. A Special NIE issued in mid-August reported a rising level of insurgency activity in the South and warned that criticism of the Diem regime from civilian and military officials was growing at an alarming rate. If not reversed, it warned, such criticism "will almost certainly cause the collapse of Diem's regime."[129]

The report inspired the Joint Chiefs to instruct MAAG to send a representative to a meeting in Washington to discuss the situation. In preparation for the meeting, which was held in early September, the new MAAG chief, Lieutenant General Lionel C. McGarr, produced a paper which called for the temporary transfer of the Civil Guard to the RVN Defense Ministry, shifting the training program for the guard from USOM to MAAG, and an increase in the size of ARVN to 170,000. Ambassador Durbrow had found General McGarr easier to deal with than his predecessor, but he was angry at what he considered McGarr's precipitate action in producing the report. In his comments on the paper he supported the proposal to shift training responsibilities for the Civil Guard to MAAG, but he opposed its transfer to the Defense Ministry, which would encourage Diem to want it equally equipped with ARVN. Nor was he convinced of the need to increase the latter to 170,000 because the threat of aggression from the North was remote and it would add to Diem's proclivity to rely on force. It was better not to pamper Diem, he advised, just when he was starting to move in the right direction.[130]

Two weeks later, the Defense Department in Washington approved a draft plan for counterinsurgency operations in Vietnam. After approval by the State Department, it was sent to the U.S. Mission in Saigon in mid-October for comments. The plan had its origins in a CINCPAC staff study that had been drawn up in April and focused on the need to encourage the RVN to adopt a national emergency program to integrate all civilian and military resources under central control for the conduct of counterinsurgency operations. In the words of one military historian, it tended to emphasize the military and administrative aspects of the problem. In Saigon, General McGarr was enthusiastic. Ambassador Durbrow was not entirely opposed to it but felt that the key to success lay in the willingness of the regime to adopt political and military reforms. He recommended that a possible force increase of 20,000 be used as a club to press Diem to act in the political realm first.[131]

The Eleventh Hour

Ambassador Durbrow's stubborn insistence on the need to tie military aid to political reforms was a clear indication that although the issue had been finessed in Washington, it was still a matter of debate within the U.S. mission in Saigon. After his abortive request to apply sanctions in May, he was briefly optimistic that the situation was improving when Diem agreed to abandon the agroville program. But during the summer conditions continued to deteriorate and in September, with the support of Wolf Ladejinsky and RVN vice-president Nguyen Ngoc Tho, Durbrow recommended to Washington that he be authorized to approach Diem on getting rid of his brother Nhu and seek to broaden his political support. If he refused, Durbrow suggested that the United States seek an alternative leader.

In Washington, the reaction remained skeptical. Colonel Edward Lansdale, whom Diem had unsuccessfully requested be stationed with MAAG in Saigon, remarked that he had serious doubts that Durbrow could deal effectively with Diem in light of the accumulated mutual distrust between the two. On October 7, the State Department cabled Durbrow its approval of his proposal for a talk with Diem but cautioned him to be discreet in removing Nhu from power. It also agreed to consider the ambassador's suggestion for a letter from President Eisenhower expressing U.S. willingness to consider supporting the RVN.[132]

Durbrow saw Diem on October 14 and informed him that Washington had approved the transfer of the Civil Guard to the Ministry of Defense and that training responsibilities would be shifted from USOM to MAAG. But the president was unresponsive to Durbrow's appeal to consider replacing Ngo Dinh Nhu. Nor did such moves have any impact on the domestic situation in South Vietnam. In a brief visit to Saigon in mid-October, Assistant Secretary for Far Eastern Affairs J. Graham Parsons described the situation as at "the eleventh hour."

As if to emphasize Parsons's point, a military coup broke out on November 10 in Saigon. Paratroopers under the command of battalion commander Colonel Vuong Van Dong surrounded the presidential palace and demanded that Diem resign. The event took U.S. officials by surprise, and the first reaction in Washington was cautious. The administration expressed its "deep concern" at the turn of events and advised Ambassador Durbrow to seek a rapid stabilization of the political situation to prevent the communists from taking advantage of it for their own purposes. It hoped that Diem and his family would be treated with "all due respect."[133]

The coup leaders formed a Military Revolutionary Committee and began to negotiate with Diem about a new government. The latter contacted the U.S. Embassy through an intermediary and asked for U.S. Marines, but Durbrow refused. With Washington's approval, Durbrow tried to arrange a compromise that would lead to the restoration of a stable government with Diem in an "active role." On the twelfth Diem agreed to form a new government, but that afternoon loyalist troops moved in and Diem was able to restore his authority.[134]

On November 14 Durbrow met with President Diem and expressed his gratification that he had survived the coup. But the incident had further poisoned relations between the U.S. Embassy and the Saigon regime. Durbrow's role in the coup aroused the suspicion and anger of Diem and other members of his entourage, and on the seventeenth the president complained to General McGarr that MAAG was the only U.S. agency that gave him its full support and confidence. Around Saigon there were widespread rumors—possibly floated by the government—that the U.S. Embassy had supported the coup.[135]

In Washington, the State Department formally denied reports that the administration had in any way encouraged the coup. Durbrow later commented to State Department historians that he had been disturbed by the coup and given his full support to President Diem. But other members of the embassy staff declared that Durbrow had adopted a relatively neutralist attitude toward the coup, a posture they defended on the grounds that it was uncertain which side was going to win and both were anticommunist.[136]

The coup also exacerbated existing differences between civilian and military officials in Washington. The State Department approved Durbrow's approach, but several members of the Defense Department were highly critical of the ambassador and declared that his hostility to Diem made him a liability. Lansdale openly campaigned to have Durbrow removed from office.[137]

The friction hampered agreement on future policy as well. General McGarr recommended that the RVN request for a 20,000 increase in the size of the ARVN be approved, but Durbrow argued for a delay until Diem promised to move on political reforms. If he did not take effective action, the ambassador predicted, the United States might be compelled in the not distant future to undertake the difficult task of identifying and supporting an alternative leadership.[138] In Washington, State Department officials sided with Durbrow, although Assistant Secretary Parsons felt that the dispute was somewhat academic because the war on the communists and political reform must be pushed at the same time. In the meantime, the request for troops was delayed until final approval of the counterinsurgency program.[139]

Ambassador Durbrow met with Diem on December 23 and explained the reason for the delay, but the latter contemptuously remarked that there was no point in political reform if the troop increase was not approved. During the last two weeks of the year, Durbrow and General McGarr continued to argue over priorities until December 31, when Parsons advised the embassy to let the issue of reforms drop for the time being.[140]

Conclusions

There have been two popular theories as to how and why the United States became involved in Vietnam. One, frequently labeled the "quagmire thesis," holds that successive U.S. presidents gradually became entangled in the war by infinitesimal stages, each convinced that a limited commitment would lead eventually to victory. The other, popularly known as the "stalemate thesis," asserts that U.S. involvement in Vietnam was not, in the words of one well-known Vietnam observer, an "inadvertent descent into unknown quicksand," but a series of deliberate acts by presidents who saw the quagmire for what it was but could not bring themselves to accept a defeat during their term in office. Fearing defeat but generally pessimistic on long-term prospects, each did only what was minimally necessary to achieve a stalemate in Vietnam, to prevent a defeat rather than to secure a victory.[141]

Neither hypothesis, at least in its pure form, is applicable to the Eisenhower administration, although the second is closer to the mark. Certainly the administration did not slip into its commitment to the Diem regime by inadvertence. At the start, Washington knew the prospects were bleak. Yet it pressed on and occasionally even found some modest grounds for optimism. In a Christmas Eve cable to General Collins, Secretary Dulles found a few bright spots amid the prevailing gloom, including the recently concluded Manila pact, evidence of Franco-American cooperation, and what Dulles regarded as the "fundamentally anti-Communist" orientation of the Vietnamese people. At worst, he concluded, the investment in Vietnam was justified, if only to buy time to build up strength elsewhere in the area.[142]

The Eisenhower administration thus went into its commitment with its eyes open. And after Diem's suppression of the sects in April 1955, it had reason to hope that the gamble had paid off. Although Diem obviously caused exasperation and resentment among Vietnamese and foreigners alike with his imperious ways, he had managed to bring some order to a situation that, to many observers, had seemed virtually unmanageable after the Geneva Conference came to a close. Perhaps, many came to believe, a tough, no-nonsense leader was best for the Vietnamese people at this stage of their development. This sense of complacency about the situation in the South was graphically demonstrated by President Eisenhower, when he commented at a meeting of the NSC in May 1960 that "heretofore we have been proud of Diem and had thought he was doing a good job."[143]

But the rapid rise of urban discontent and the growth of the insurgency movement in the countryside at the end of the decade underlined the fragility of the much-advertised "miracle of South Vietnam." A few years later, when emotions engendered by the Vietnam War had reduced complex realities to simplicities and slogans, hawks and doves argued over whether the conflict was an internal civil rebellion against the Saigon regime or an invasion from the North. At the time, however, few knowledgeable observers doubted that there were two parts to the problem—the resentment in the South caused by Diem's own behavior and the heightened efforts by the communist leadership in the North to use the opportunity to promote national reunification under Hanoi's rule.

It was one thing to understand the nature of the problem, however, and another to know how to solve it. From the start, there were differences over priorities. MAAG officers in Saigon and officials at the Defense Department in Washington were inclined to believe that the crux of the problem was national security. If the insurgent forces could be defeated, Diem's weaknesses, though serious, would be manageable. But many civilian officials at the State Department and in the U.S. Embassy in Saigon felt that the underlying problem was Diem himself. If that was the case, there was no point in seeking military solutions until and unless Diem could be brought to accept U.S. advice to undertake political and social reforms.

Faced with contrasting hypotheses, the administration reacted with ambivalence. It was not blind to the political and socioeconomic aspects of the problem, and it recognized correctly that the immediate threat to South Vietnam was from internal subversion, although directed from Hanoi. Yet, in general, Washington appeared to view the problem as primarily military in nature. The Manila pact strongly emphasized the military threat at the expense of the need for political and economic reforms, and the bulk of U.S. aid to the RVN, as to other countries in the region, was military.

The fixation with international communism as a military threat was, of course, part of the zeitgeist of the 1950's. But it was exacerbated in the case of Vietnam by the difficulties of dealing with Ngo Dinh Diem. The problem was that Diem's very strengths as a nationalist leader made him impervious to advice from the United States. Whatever his imperfections, Diem's defenders could make a persuasive case that it would have been unrealistic to expect the Saigon regime to build a pluralistic society based on functioning democratic institutions at a time when independence had been newly restored and an organized revolutionary movement still existed within the country. Democratic governments formed on the Western model were established throughout the region at the dawn of independence after World War II, and virtually none remained intact at the end of the decade of the 1950's. Few if any faced opposition as experienced and formidable as Ngo Dinh Diem faced in South Vietnam. As a number of Western observers pointed out at the time, it was surely unreasonable to expect such fledgling governments faced with intimidating problems of economic backwardness, political inexperience, and ethnic and cultural diversity to have mastered techniques of political pluralism that had required generations if not centuries to perfect in Western society. Under the circumstances, as many U.S. observers rationalized at the time, an authoritarian form of government in South Vietnam was virtually inevitable, at least for the time being.

Then, too, the contempt often given to President Diem's allegedly naive philosophy of Personalism is somewhat out of place given the history of the past two decades. Although Diem's attempt to create a state ideology out of a synthesis of Confucianism and Catholic modernism was often naive and self-serving, it represented a shrewd if imperfect attempt to blend traditional and modern ideas in a society going through the painful process of social transformation, an approach that is being applied with varying degrees of success throughout the region today. In retrospect, idealistic American bureaucrats and academics hoping to force-feed the South Vietnamese people with a diet of American democratic capitalism were surely guilty of ignoring the lessons of historical and cultural reality.

But it is a long way from this to the assertion that Diem represented a realistic answer to the multiple problems of post-Geneva South Vietnam. Unlike most political leaders in the region, who came to power on the shoulders of nationwide anticolonialist movements with roots in both urban and rural areas, Diem had no political party and no mass popular base. To the contrary, he was a member of a religious minority that because of its talent and special privileges for centuries had aroused the suspicion and resentment of much of the local population. Diem had demonstrated his sectarian views on religion and his contempt for the population of the South during the Geneva Conference. Equally important, he lacked the charismatic appeal of a Sukarno, a Nehru, an U Nu, or a Ho Chi Minh to symbolize in his person the aspirations and ideals of his people.

Diem's economic credentials were equally suspect. As the French had pointed out, his instincts placed him on the side of the landlord class, and he had little grasp of the needs of poor farmers, who made up the bulk of the population in South Vietnam. If French warnings were not enough, Diem demonstrated his inability to compete with the rice-roots appeal of the Vietminh when he passed a land reform program that totally failed to deal with the fundamental land problem in the South.

Eisenhower administration officials were aware of these shortcomings from the start. But they responded to Diem's critics with the unanswerable rejoinder that there was no one else. That, of course, was the root of the problem and one that the administration never directly faced. What would the United States do if the Diem experiment failed? A partial answer emerged at the time of the attempted coup in November 1960, when the administration's confidence in him had reached its nadir. Washington would turn to whatever noncommunist leadership arose to fill the vacuum. If that antidote failed, as a last resort

Washington appeared willing to accept the loss of the remainder of Vietnam to the communists, while refocusing the efforts of the free world on stabilizing the remainder of the region. An outright invasion from the North, however, would probably have triggered U.S. military response.

South Vietnam was still far from that apocalyptic possibility during the Eisenhower administration's final months in office in the fall of 1960. The primary focus of Washington's attention at that time was on Laos, where communist gains in the civil war alarmed top officials and prompted the president, at the last meeting of the National Security Council under his administration, to remark that, if necessary, the United States would fight in Laos. Ironically, if we can rely on Eisenhower's recollection several years later, top administration officials did not foresee the coming crisis in South Vietnam.[144]

President Eisenhower has been praised for his prudence in keeping the United States out of the quagmire of Indochina. This praise is somewhat misplaced. Although he deserves credit for his prudence in refraining from direct involvement at the end of the Franco-Vietminh conflict, President Eisenhower bequeathed to his successor a Southeast Asia policy in a state of disarray. The administration's gamble that it could build a new nation with an untried and suspect leader was now about to exact its price. In the meantime, Washington was poised to intervene directly in the civil war in Laos. With American prestige now deeply committed to a region in turmoil, the next president would find that his options were perilously limited.

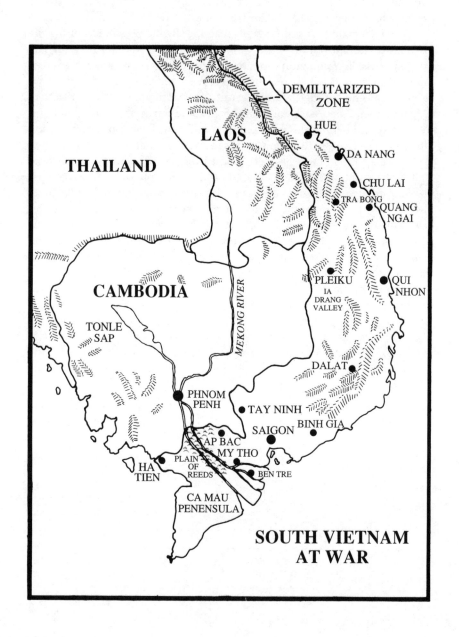

DEMILITARIZED
ZONE

LAOS

THAILAND

HUE

DA NANG

CHU LAI

TRA BONG

QUANG
NGAI

CAMBODIA

PLEIKU

QUI
NHON

IA
DRANG
VALLEY

TONLE
SAP

MEKONG RIVER

DALAT

PHNOM
PENH

TAY NINH

SAIGON

BINH GIA

AP BAC

MY THO

HA
TIEN

PLAIN
OF
REEDS

BEN TRE

CA MAU
PENENSULA

**SOUTH VIETNAM
AT WAR**

Chapter 8

Kennedy and Counterinsurgency

In briefings with President-elect John F. Kennedy, outgoing chief executive Dwight D. Eisenhower had said little about Vietnam but had stressed the crisis in Laos, where a rightist coup against Prime Minister Souvanna Phouma had provoked the Pathet Lao into attacking government forces in various areas of the country. But it was not long before the Kennedy team was hit with the seriousness of the situation in South Vietnam. On January 4, sixteen days before the inauguration of the new president, the U.S. Embassy in Saigon completed its counterinsurgency plan and sent it to Washington.

The report was somber, emphasizing the rise in effectiveness of insurgency operations and the growing weakness of the Saigon regime. It concluded that if Diem did not take "immediate and extraordinary action" to stimulate his government to reduce the insurgency and regain popular support, the Viet Cong could overthrow the RVN in the months to come. The authors recognized that the menace came from both internal and external sources but predicted that the greatest immediate threat was posed by the steady expansion of guerrilla forces inside the country, supported by the infiltration of regular forces and cadres from the North. It took no clear position on the issue of Ngo Dinh Diem, saying merely that he offered the best hope for defeating the Viet Cong if the necessary corrective measures were undertaken. It called for approving the RVN request for an increase in the size of ARVN from 150,000 to 170,000 and providing MAAG training for the 30,000-man Civil Guard.[1]

At approximately the same time, Brigadier General Edward G. Lansdale returned from his short visit to South Vietnam to evaluate the situation and report back to Washington. Lansdale painted an equally dismal picture of the situation, acknowledging, among other things, that the RVN had achieved better material than spiritual progress and had lost will, but he stressed that Diem was the only potential leader with executive ability and determination and warned that if Diem were overthrown he would be succeeded by squabbling, selfish, and mediocre people. Lansdale was scathing in his references to the defeatist attitude at the U.S. Embassy in Saigon and said that a vigorous new leadership was needed in South Vietnam, which he described as a "combat area of the Cold War" needing emergency treatment.[2]

The counterinsurgency plan was discussed at a meeting of key foreign policy advisers at the White House on January 28. Besides President Kennedy, other key officials in attendance were Vice-President Lyndon B. Johnson, Secretary of State Dean Rusk, Defense Secretary Robert S. McNamara, chairman of the JCS Lyman Lemnitzer, and General Lansdale, who presented a briefing on his trip to Saigon. The new president was no stranger to Vietnam. He had been actively interested in the area since the early 1950's, when, as a young congressman, he had briefly visited the area and then criticized French policies in Indochina and North Africa. He was also reported to be an admirer of General Lansdale, allegedly through reading the book *The Ugly American*, a fictional account of Lansdale's recent career fighting communist insurgency movements in South Vietnam and the Philippines.

The new Kennedy team had a mixed record in Asian affairs and foreign policy issues. The new secretary of state, Dean Rusk, was a Rhodes Scholar from the state of Georgia who had spent the war years in the China theater and served as assistant secretary for Far Eastern Affairs under President Truman. Other key members of the team, including Under Secretary of State Chester Bowles, Ambassador to the United Nations Adlai Stevenson, National Security Advisor McGeorge Bundy, and Defense Secretary Robert S. McNamara, had little experience in Asia and represented an unknown quantity.

In their approach to the Cold War they were equally diverse. The majority undoubtedly shared the deep suspicion of Moscow's intentions that had characterized their predecessors in the Eisenhower administration. Dean Rusk had established a reputation as a tough advocate of containment policies during his stint as assistant secretary for Far Eastern affairs in the early 1950's. But others, such as Chester Bowles and Adlai Stevenson, were identified with a more conciliatory approach in foreign affairs. Unlike the initial years of Dwight D. Eisenhower, there would be no broad consensus within the Kennedy administration on a program to "roll back the Iron Curtain."[3]

The somewhat ambivalent image toward the Cold War presented by the new administration was no accident. It undoubtedly reflected the relatively nonideological and pragmatic character of the new chief executive himself. Kennedy had displayed the complex nature of his foreign policy philosophy during the presidential campaign, when he had criticized the Eisenhower administration for allowing the alleged "missile gap" to take place, while simultaneously suggesting the withdrawal of Chiang Kai-shek's forces from the off-shore islands of Quemoy and Matsu. That contrapuntal emphasis on toughness and conciliation also appeared in his inaugural address, when he had combined a firm adherence to the doctrine of containment with a rhetorical challenge to Moscow to join with Washington in a new era of peaceful ideological competition between the capitalist and socialist camps. In effect, Kennedy was attempting to return the doctrine of containment to the more political and ideological orientation that its author, George F. Kennan, had recommended more than a decade before. The new Kennedy White House was undoubtedly influenced by the precarious nature of the world situation. When Kennedy took office, relations with Moscow were as tense as they had been for many years. In addition to the festering problems in Vietnam and Laos, a Great Power confrontation loomed over Berlin, and unstable conditions in Africa and the Caribbean created the possibility of escalating competition in those regions. Khrushchev had added to the tension when, in a speech in early January, he had bluntly declared that the Soviet Union would provide firm support to wars of national liberation around the globe.

The festering problems in Africa, Asia, and the Caribbean undoubtedly served to focus the attention of the new administration on the question of Soviet influence in the Third World. For Kennedy and a few of his foreign policy advisers, the importance of Asia, Africa, and Latin America was already axiomatic. The new president in particular had become convinced that those regions of the world would increasingly become the focus of East-West competition during his presidency, and he took seriously Khrushchev's threat to take advantage of unstable conditions in developing nations to promote the interests of Soviet foreign policy.

It was at least partly for that reason that the new administration was determined to formulate a grand strategy to replace the doctrine that had been adopted by its predecessor early in the previous decade. The doctrine of massive retaliation, as even its progenitors admitted, was relatively unsuitable for application to low-level conflicts in the Third World, where U.S. national interests did not necessarily justify the risk of nuclear confrontation with the USSR. The new administration wanted to formulate a new concept that would permit the United States to strengthen friendly forces against internal or external adversaries without the threat of escalation into a nuclear confrontation between the Great Powers. The result was the new doctrine of "flexible response."

The new strategy called for a measured response to any threat posed by a revolutionary disturbance in the Third World that would be sufficient to eliminate or reduce the threat but not risk an escalation of the conflict into a global crisis between the nuclear superpowers. In such conditions, the United States could avoid becoming paralyzed into inaction by the fear that U.S. involvement in the suppression of such insurgencies could trigger a confrontation with Moscow. The new doctrine was soon to be tested in Southeast Asia.

The meeting at the White House on January 28 had originally been scheduled to deal with the situation in Cuba, but Vietnam was added to the agenda at the president's request after he had been informed of the serious situation there during his first days in office. At first, Kennedy appeared skeptical of the counterinsurgency plan and its implications. He questioned the need for additional ARVN forces to suppress less than 10,000 guerrillas and asked rhetorically whether the problem was not more political and moral than military. But when it was explained that ARVN forces were needed both to suppress the guerrillas and to prepare for a possible conventional attack from the North, he raised no further objection, and two days after the meeting the White House approved the counterinsurgency plan and authorized the requested increase in the size of ARVN with additional funds to improve the quality of the Civil Guard. Kennedy, noting that Vietnam was one of the "four crisis areas" that faced the White House (in addition to Laos, Cuba, and the Congo), also approved a suggestion by Secretary Rusk to set up an interagency task force to make recommendations to the Country Team in Saigon.[4]

Significantly, there was little discussion during the meeting of Diem's qualifications for building a viable noncommunist society in South Vietnam. During the meeting General Lansdale repeated his criticism of the "defeatist" attitude of civilian officials at the U.S. Embassy in Saigon. Secretary Rusk attempted to defend Ambassador Durbrow but agreed that it might be time for a change. The president suggested that a letter of support from him to President Diem might help to improve relations between the two countries. At first, Kennedy appeared receptive to appointing Lansdale to replace Ambassador Durbrow, but resistance to the idea in the Pentagon and the State Department was widespread, and eventually a courtly career foreign service officer from Virginia, Frederick Nolting, was picked for the post.[5]

In Saigon, Ambassador Durbrow was receptive to Washington's suggestion for a message of general support for Diem, but he was opposed to a formal presidential letter, which would give Diem the impression that the United States had no choice and would back him against his rivals. He also expressed his skepticism that Lansdale's idea of a two-party opposition would work in South Vietnam. Possible alternatives to Diem lacked sophistication and had no realistic program. In the meantime, any effort to encourage a responsible opposition would be viewed as a threat by President Diem and encourage his opponents to plan anouther coup. The best road, Durbrow emphasized, was to induce Diem to introduce political reforms that would plant the seeds of democracy.[6]

Diem moved quickly to meet possible objections from the new administration in Washington. On February 6, he announced reforms to decentralize government authority and build new democratic institutions at the local level.

He also responded positively to the draft U.S. counterinsurgency program, which was presented to him on the thirteenth. But Diem resisted key parts of the plan. While the United States wanted to clear areas systematically, using small units to scour the jungles beyond the pacified area (called by some the "net and spear" approach) and then call in reserves when contact was made, Diem had a more ambitious vision and wanted to move more rapidly. These differences were magnified when Diem continued to resist delegating authority outside his family and delayed implementing the political reforms he had promised in February.

In March, Durbrow recommended that the administration withhold financial aid for the ARVN force increase unless Diem began to implement the counterinsurgency plan. But as before, he encountered opposition in Washington, where Lansdale and Walt W. Rostow, the new deputy special assistant for national security affairs under McGeorge Bundy, argued that Durbrow was not the man to pressure Diem because of the personality clash. Leave the arm-twisting, they advised, to someone with fresh capital. In the end, the issue was sidestepped as the administration sent a letter to Diem with no promise of specific support. Decisions on that score would be delayed pending a visit by Vice-President Lyndon B. Johnson to South Vietnam.[7]

The Crisis in Laos

One reason why the new Kennedy team did not focus quickly on the situation in Vietnam was that it was preoccupied with problems elsewhere—with the Soviet threat to cut Western access to Berlin, with the projected invasion of Cuba, and with the crisis in Laos, where the conflict between the government and the Pathet Lao continued. During his final months in office, Eisenhower had considered sending troops to Laos, which he had described to Kennedy as "the cork in the bottle," but the latter was reluctant to intervene. In Kennedy's view, and that of many of his advisers, the landlocked and heavily forested character of Laos, along with the lack of a firm anticommunist base in society, made the area difficult to defend. How could the administration defend a decision to fight in Laos and not in nearby Cuba? A task force on Laos created in February under Assistant Secretary Parsons agreed and recommended neutrality. Eventually Kennedy decided to seek a negotiated solution to the conflict in Laos, while attempting to stiffen the anticommunist regime in South Vietnam.[8]

The problem for Kennedy was how to stabilize the Royal Lao government sufficiently to make a compromise solution a realistic possibility. The JCS predicted that it might require 60,000 U.S. troops plus a call-up of the reserves. Moreover, there was no guarantee that China and the USSR would agree to a negotiated settlement. Would a cease-fire simply free the communists to attack Thailand and South Vietnam? After some consideration, Dean Rusk wanted to invite the neutralist former prime minister Souvanna Phouma back from Paris, where he had been serving in exile as ambassador under the rightist government in Vientiane.

In March, Secretary Rusk approached Soviet foreign minister Andrei Gromyko on convening a new Geneva Conference to seek an end to the conflict in Laos. In the meantime, the United States warned China at the Warsaw talks that it would intervene in strength unless an enforceable cease-fire was achieved. But on March 9 the Pathet Lao launched a spring offensive, and when the situation became critical the administration decided on a limited show of force with possible SEATO action, while placing Special Forces units in Okinawa on alert and sending the Seventh Fleet to the Gulf of Thailand. But Kennedy was acutely conscious that congressional and public opinion was opposed to military involvement in Laos, and in a nationwide television address on March 23 he appealed for a "truly neutral Laos." At first, both the Soviet Union and China rejected a cease-fire before negotiations, but eventually Moscow relented and agreed that a conference could begin after the conclusion of a cease-fire. On April 24, Great Britain and the USSR, the two co-chairs of the Geneva Conference, announced that a cease-fire would take place on May 3. The Geneva Conference on Laos was to begin two weeks later.[9]

While the administration grappled with the crisis in Laos, the new Vietnam Task Force struggled to come up with a concrete program of action to supplement the counterinsurgency plan in Vietnam. The committee was headed by Deputy Secretary of Defense Roswell L. Gilpatric, and key members included Walt W. Rostow, deputy special assistant for national security affairs, and Deputy Under Secretary of State U. Alexis Johnson. Lieutenant General Lionel G. McGarr, MAAG chief in Saigon, attended the first meeting and wasted no time in challenging advocates of a political approach. The main problem in South Vietnam, he said, was military. The psychological and economic aspects could be handled later. To hammer home his point he cited statistics that incidents inspired by insurgent forces had increased dramatically in 1960 in an attempt to secure liberated areas in the countryside. Only 42 percent of the country, McGarr said, was under the firm control of RVN.

McGarr recommended an increase in the size of MAAG and asked for 20,000 additional ARVN troops to cope with the rising level of Viet Cong activity. But he warned that additional forces would be required to secure the border with Cambodia and Laos. Even then, a fully effective military seal would be difficult to establish because of the jungles and swamps. McGarr expressed misgivings about the upcoming negotiations on Laos, pointing out that if the communists controlled southern Laos they could outflank the South Vietnamese, but Gilpatric responded that we "must assume that we cannot do too much about the Cambodian and Lao problems."[10]

A few days later the task force met again to consider a draft report written by Lansdale with the collaboration of other officials in the Departments of State and Defense. It painted a grim picture of the situation in South Vietnam, which it portrayed as the target of a communist "master plan" to take over all of Southeast Asia. It accepted General McGarr's contention that the immediate problem was internal security and called for a series of measures to improve the military situation, including an increase in the size of MAAG and U.S. financial support for all 68,000 members of the Civil Guard. Pointing out that there was neither time nor justification for "starting from scratch," the authors called for implementation of the counterinsurgency program and a series of mutually supporting military, political, social, and psychological measures to solve the problem. The key was psychological, to assure Diem of wholehearted U.S. support and to indicate to friends and foes alike that, "come what may, the United States intends to *win* this battle."[11]

The task force report was discussed at a meeting of the NSC on Thursday, April 27. The available minutes of that meeting are sketchy, but comments by several participants give a general picture of the course of discussion. The overall reaction to the report was favorable, but some felt that it was short on specifics and should be revised and reshaped before being presented to President Diem. There was also a continued conviction in some quarters that political reform should take priority over military operations. Special Counsel to the President Theodore C. Sorensen pointed out the importance of political reforms to potential success. "There is no clearer example of a country," he commented in a memo to the president on the following day, "that cannot be saved unless it saves itself." Robert W. Komer, then a member of the NSC staff, agreed on the need to get Diem to act and suggested a token commitment of U.S. troops as evidence of U.S. determination to help him. The debate over priorities would obviously be influenced by the composition of the new task force and the role of the ambassador. On April 29 Ambassador Nolting and Ambassador-designate to Thailand Kenneth T. Young appealed to Gilpatric to assign the major role to the State Department, with substantial authority to the ambassador. Gilpatric felt that State Department representatives had watered down the importance of the counterinsurgency program and linked it too tightly with political reform, but he agreed that the task force should be housed in the Department of State.[12]

On April 26, the Pathet Lao launched a major offensive to seize land before a projected cease-fire could be established. That evening the Joint Chiefs alerted CINCPAC of possible air strikes on North Vietnam and southern China. The following day, Kennedy consulted with congressional leaders, who advised against putting U.S. troops in Laos. The issue was also raised at a meeting of the NSC that same day. According to accounts of the meeting, the JCS must have been badly divided on possible courses of action and displayed a marked reluctance to become militarily engaged in the area without a presidential guarantee of a substantial commitment of forces, including the possible use of nuclear weapons against China and North Vietnam. The meeting reportedly undermined Kennedy's already fragile confidence in the advice he was receiving from the Pentagon (Walt Rostow later commented that it was "the worst White House meeting he attended in the entire Kennedy administration"). Occurring in conjunction with the Bay of Pigs disaster, it may have confirmed Kennedy in his decision not to send troops to Laos.[13]

In any event, no decision was taken at the meeting on possible actions in Laos, and the president asked the Joint Chiefs to present their views individually and in writing. But it was increasingly evident that Kennedy would seek a negotiated settlement there. The next day, an annex was added to the Vietnam Task Force report. The annex pointed out that a settlement in Laos would complicate the defense of the RVN, so to counter the impact of such a settlement, it advocated increasing the size of ARVN by two divisions. It also called for the formation of two additional U.S. training commands of 1,600 men each, with the assigned mission of raising the overall combat effectiveness of the South Vietnamese armed forces. These additional forces could help to compensate for the anticipated consolidation of communist control over eastern Laos. Finally, the annex proposed the formation of an additional Special Forces Group of 400 men to train and assist the ARVN armed forces in countering increased guerrilla activity anticipated as the result of a settlement in Laos. This represented a total of 3,600 U.S. military personnel beyond the currently authorized increase and a clear transgression of the provisions of the Geneva Accords.[14]

The NSC met to discuss these proposals at 10 A.M. on April 29. There is no available record of the meeting, but the president did not act on the task force request. He did approve an increase in MAAG to help train 20,000 additional South Vietnamese troops, and he authorized U.S. support for the entire Civil Guard of 68,000. But he took no action on sending troops to Laos. On the previous evening, in an apparent reference to the situation in Laos, he had said at a Democratic Party dinner in Chicago that the United States would meet its obligations but could only defend the freedom of those determined to be free.

At the close of the meeting, the NSC referred the draft report back to the task force for revision. Clearly, however, the troop issue was still open for further debate. That same day, high-level civilian and military officials held a meeting at the State Department on the situation in Laos and the advisability of introducing American troops to stem the communist advance near the administrative capital of Vientiane. Attorney General Robert F. Kennedy represented the president at the meeting.

According to the published record, the discussion was wide-ranging and frequently rambling. Chief of Naval Operations Admiral Arleigh Burke recommended sending troops to Vientiane, saying that if Laos were to be lost, the

United States would have to put troops into Thailand and South Vietnam. It would be easier to hold now than later, he said, to make it clear that the United States was not going to be driven out of Southeast Asia.

Army Chief of Staff General George Decker supported Burke, arguing that the United States could not win a conventional war in Southeast Asia. If action were taken, he said, the intent should be to win, introducing troops into Thailand and South Vietnam, bombing Hanoi and China and, if necessary, even using nuclear weapons. But many of the civilian participants were skeptical. McNamara remarked that it would be easy for the Pathet Lao and the Chinese Communists to prevent a successful U.S. landing at Vientiane, and others worried about the possibility of Chinese intervention. The meeting ended with an inconclusive discussion of where to draw the line in Southeast Asia. Robert Kennedy was one of the doubters, pointing out that the administration would look silly if it put troops into Laos and then backed down.[15]

During the next few days the situation continued to deteriorate, as the Pathet Lao stalled on accepting a cease-fire, and on May 1 a preliminary order was issued for possible military intervention in Laos. But the alert was canceled later the same day when the news broke that agreement on a cease-fire had been reached. Still, there was little optimism in Washington over the situation, and most officials felt that the chance of "salvaging anything out of the cease-fire and coalition government was slim indeed."[16]

Focus on Vietnam

By early May, then, there was a growing sense that the United States would not move troops into Laos but would attempt to draw the line in Thailand and South Vietnam. That certainly appears to have been the president's view. According to Richard Nixon, who discussed the issue with Kennedy at the time, the latter told him, "I just don't think we ought to get involved in Laos, particularly where we might find ourselves fighting millions of Chinese troops in the jungles." The decision was based partly on the political and geographical differences between the three countries but also on the domestic situation in the United States, where there was congressional support for action in South Vietnam and Thailand but not for Laos. Still, Kennedy worried about the political impact of a defeat in Laos, remarking to historian Arthur Schlesinger, Jr., that, unlike Eisenhower, he could not afford a defeat in Indochina.[17]

With the road to a negotiated settlement for Laos now open, attention in Washington turned back to the task force report on Vietnam. On May 1, Roswell Gilpatric submitted a new draft to the president. There had been two drafts, one written in the State Department and the other by the task force, with input from the Department of Defense. The former accepted the need to place military over political considerations for the time being, but it emphasized that military operations must be supplemented by a strong political and economic program. For the moment it advocated sticking with the present government, despite its acknowledged weaknesses. There was no alternative, it said, without running an "unacceptable degree of risk."[18]

The State Department draft report also placed heavy importance on psychological factors in controlling the spread of communism in Southeast Asia. In the event of the loss or division of Laos, it was doubtful that South Vietnam and other nations in the region would be able to resist communist pressures unless they were confident of U.S. determination to stem further communist expansion in the area. It therefore recommended measures to boost Saigon's confidence, including an increase in ARVN to 200,000, an increase in the size of MAAG to 3,200, and a bilateral treaty between the United States and the RVN, with an option to introduce U.S. troops into South Vietnam.[19]

The draft report written by the task force put less emphasis on the need for political reform, and it recommended that the task force be housed in the Department of Defense rather than the Department of State, with Roswell Gilpatric remaining as director and Edward Lansdale as his deputy. On May 4 the task force met to discuss the two drafts but was unable to reach a consensus on the key issues. The bulk of discussion was apparently devoted to the implications of introducing troops into South Vietnam and what their purpose would be once they were stationed there. Walt Rostow proposed that their mission be fourfold: (1) to serve as a trip-wire in case of a communist attack from beyond the border, (2) to train ARVN, (3) to release South Vietnamese forces for counterinsurgency activities, and (4) to meet an anticipated communist offensive.[20]

The final report, which generally followed the State Department version, was submitted to the president on May 8. Three days later, Kennedy approved NSAM-52, which announced a number of measures based on the task force report. The directive confirmed the military decisions taken on April 29, ordered a study of the proposal to increase the size of ARVN to 200,000, and directed additional study of the recommended size and composition of a U.S. military force if one were to be sent to South Vietnam. The president directed Ambassador Nolting to discuss a treaty with Diem, but without making any firm commitment, and ordered that the task force for Vietnam be housed in the Department of State, with foreign service officer Sterling Cottrell as director.[21]

The first round of discussions on Southeast Asia within the Kennedy administration had thus resulted in an increased military commitment to the Diem regime in the context of a decision to seek a negotiated settlement in Laos. The new administration had adopted a compromise policy that implied an increase in U.S. involvement in South Vietnam while avoiding a firm commitment to the Saigon regime and rejecting proposals from the Joint Chiefs to introduce U.S. troops into Laos and consider attacks on North Vietnam and possibly even China.

The decision had some important implications. In deciding to focus efforts on containing communist expansion in Thailand and Vietnam rather than in Laos, the administration was forced to accept on faith the assumption that after a negotiated settlement, infiltration into South Vietnam through Laos could be kept within manageable limits, either by Soviet pressure on Hanoi or by the threat of U.S. retaliation. Yet clearly, even at the time, administration officials were not optimistic that a settlement in Laos would substantially reduce infiltration. In discussions about military options during the spring of 1961 many participants anticipated the possibility that, in the event of an agreement over Laos, infiltration would continue and perhaps even increase. To many military officers in the Pentagon, who had been soured by the earlier experience with limited war (involving the introduction of U.S. combat troops but not the use of nuclear weapons) in Korea, the decision not to fight in Laos sent the wrong message to Hanoi and Beijing and set the stage for a more difficult task later. But to Kennedy and some of his civilian advisers, Laos was the wrong place to fight. The stage was set for a running debate over strategy that would continue well beyond the end of the administration.

One problem with the decision to negotiate in Laos was that in the context of the time, it made it more difficult for the new president to avoid taking a stand in South Vietnam. Comments that Kennedy made to colleagues at the time show clearly that, in his view, U.S. credibility had been badly shaken by the failure of the Bay of Pigs invasion and Khrushchev's blustering during the summit meeting in early June. If that credibility were to be restored, in Southeast Asia as in Moscow, the United States had to make a stand elsewhere. As Kennedy said to administration figures at the time, "Vietnam looks like the place."[22]

What is noteworthy about the decisions of May 1961 is that there was relatively little debate about the ability of Ngo Dinh Diem to serve as the centerpiece of the U.S. effort in Southeast Asia. The Kennedy team was not blind to the man's weaknesses. The president in particular had been skeptical of Diem's potential since the mid-1950's, when, on a visit to Saigon as a young congressman, he had been briefed by Edmund Gullion, who had pointed out that Diem's northern background and his Catholic religious beliefs, in addition to his Gallic manners, made him a liability as a nationalist leader. Nevertheless, most administration officials appeared to accept General Lansdale's judgment that he could be induced to reform once he had full confidence in the determination of the United States to provide him with support against the communist threat. There was also little discussion among principal administration figures of alternatives, with the exception of a brief memo from Walt W. Rostow to the president noting the possibility that Diem might be overthrown. Then, he said, it would be necessary to "move fast with the army types who may then emerge."[23]

Nor was there much consideration over whether South Vietnam was the place to stand and fight. In reading over the documentary evidence on the debates that took place at the time, one is struck by the imprecision of views expressed by senior administration figures in terms of U.S. objectives in the region and how to achieve them. Lacking in experience in Southeast Asia, and sometimes in defining national security issues, most of Kennedy's top advisers floundered over how to approach the problem. Could Southeast Asia be saved, and if so how and where? What were Hanoi's intentions? Would the war be a guerrilla war or an invasion? Should the United States send troops or not? If so, what would be their mission? In this debate, there was little of the caution that had characterized discussions on the issue during the Eisenhower presidency. Too many of the "best and the brightest" were essentially at sea when it came to formulating a strategy to stem the advance of communism in Southeast Asia. In the spring of 1961 Washington was entering a tunnel with no idea of a possible exit.

Perhaps the one administration figure who was most conscious of the dangers inherent in the situation was the president himself. Unlike many of his principal advisers, Kennedy was aware that the key question in South Vietnam was not simply whether Ngo Dinh Diem could serve as the centerpiece of the U.S. effort on the country but whether the Vietnamese people themselves wanted a noncommunist independent future or preferred unification under Ho Chi Minh and Hanoi. According to Roger Hilsman, eventually to serve as assistant secretary of state for Far Eastern affairs, Kennedy told him on numerous occasions that nothing should be done that would make it difficult for the United States to get out of South Vietnam. Yet in the end, he was forced to take the opening steps into the tunnel. Many writers on the period have noted that in so doing Kennedy had been boxed in by his own rhetoric and by the narrow margin of his electoral victory in the presidential election the previous year. This is undoubtedly a valid statement, but in fairness to Kennedy, the new president was faced with a crisis atmosphere not of his own making, and his options were severely limited. In the context of the time, with a belligerent Khrushchev testing Washington's resolve in Berlin and around the world, he could be accused of doing too little, or of not doing it well, but few Americans would have accused him of doing too much.[24]

Getting on Diem's Wavelength

It was left to Vice-President Lyndon Johnson to carry the new administration's message to South Vietnam. President Kennedy had written Diem a noncommittal letter on April 26 to congratulate him on his reinauguration as president of the RVN. Now Johnson, who had asked Kennedy for permission to make a state trip to Asia, would carry with him a much more concrete message from Washington that the United States was ready, as the new letter stated, "to join with you in an intensified endeavor to win the struggle against Communism and to further the social and economic advancement of Viet-Nam." Johnson arrived in Saigon on May 11. The following day he met with Diem and presented him with the president's letter. Diem's initial reaction was cautiously positive. The Kennedy administration's proposal for an increase in ARVN and full U.S. support for the Civil Guard was obviously welcome. In fact, Diem remarked pointedly, he had proposed such moves years ago. He was willing to increase the size of MAAG and to embark on an urgent program of social and economic reforms so long as they were "appropriate to Vietnam." But at a meeting with Johnson that evening, Diem was cautious about the introduction of U.S. combat troops into South Vietnam and said that he wanted U.S. or SEATO troops only in case of overt aggression. Nor did he desire a treaty with the United States.[25]

After leaving Saigon on May 13, Johnson went to Bangkok, where he attempted to reassure Thai leaders that the U.S. decision to accept negotiations on Laos did not mean that the administration was preparing to abandon Southeast Asia. On May 23 he returned to Washington. In a memo to the president reporting the results of his trip, he said that the opening of negotiations on Laos had created a sense of doubt and concern about U.S. intentions in Southeast Asia and weakened the ability of many Asian leaders to maintain a strongly pro-U.S. orientation. His visit had bought the administration some time, he said, but now it must follow through. SEATO, he said, is "not now and probably never will be the answer" because the French and British were unwilling to support decisive action. Asian countries were still sensitive about colonialism and would not want U.S. troops except for training purposes, but he warned that the United States should not neglect the probability that an open attack would bring calls for U.S. troops. But the greatest danger, he said, was not communism, but hunger, poverty, disease, and ignorance. That must be the point of attack. In a formal report he was more somber. "Danger flags are flying," he said, and if this effort fails, "our direct military involvement may be required to hold the situation."[26]

During the summer of 1961 the administration attempted to implement the counterinsurgency plan. From the start, Diem wanted more. In a formal letter to Kennedy in June, he asked for additional support for his armed forces, a request that was supported by General McGarr. There was also some welcome optimism from the embassy, when Ambassador Nolting, who had arrived at his post in early May, registered his approval of Diem's ability. The situation had definitely improved, he said, and we could "back him to the hilt on moral grounds." In Washington, the troop request, combined with continuing tension in Laos, provoked several administration officials to suggest the need for a new look at the overall situation in the region, and Walt Rostow, now emerging as the White House expert on the problem, suggested that General Maxwell Taylor, Kennedy's personal military adviser, go to Vietnam.[27]

Rostow, in fact, was a prime mover in the effort to end what he called the "reactive character" of U.S. activities in the area and to create a coherent program to stop the advance of communism in Southeast Asia. A professor of economics on leave from the Massachusetts Institute of Technology, Rostow had some experience in Asia (he had recently written a well-received book on Chinese economy) and specifically in the field of promoting economic development in Third World societies. Early in 1961 he had given a speech at the Special Warfare School at Fort Bragg in which he described communism as "the scavenger of the modernization process" and recommended the use of U.S. foreign aid to hasten less-developed nations threatened with communism through the difficult transitional period to advanced economic development.

With a temperament naturally inclined to seek rational solutions to practical problems, Rostow must have been disturbed by the lack of precision that characterized the debate over possible courses of action in Southeast Asia during the first months of the Kennedy administration. During the last part of July, the seemingly indefatigable Rostow attempted to stimulate discussion on strategy in Southeast Asia throughout the Washington bureaucracy. On the twenty-seventh he joined with General Maxwell Taylor, President Kennedy's special military representative, in submitting a memo to the president that tried to present alternative strategies in preparation for a meeting at the White House the following day.

The focus of the July 27 paper was to devise an integrated strategy to stem the advance of communism throughout the entire region. The authors said that the United States had three alternatives: (1) to disengage from the area as gracefully as possible, (2) to find a convenient political pretext to attack the source of aggression in Hanoi, or (3) to "build as much indigenous military, political and economic strength as we can in the area, in order to contain the thrust from Hanoi while preparing to intervene with U.S. military force if Communist China comes in or the situation otherwise gets out of hand." Both Rostow and Taylor were strongly inclined toward an active U.S. effort to stem the advance of communism in Southeast Asia and assumed that it was the policy of the administration to follow the third approach, but that some consideration of alternatives would be useful to assist in defining the appropriate course of action to adopt. The key issues to be determined, they pointed out, were (1) what settlement in Laos would be minimally acceptable to the United States, (2) should increased pressure on Hanoi be applied to expose its role in both Laos and South Vietnam, and (3) how should the administration respond to the request from Saigon for increased military assistance?[28]

The following day, John Steeves, chairman of a State Department Task Force on Southeast Asia, presented his committee's preliminary report on the region to the president. The report noted that there was a consensus on the following: (1) that it was essential to U.S. policy interests to ensure the security of Southeast Asia against further communist advancement, whether by political takeover or by covert or overt military means, (2) that the administration should decide now to resist such encroachment, by appropriate military means if necessary, and with or without unanimous SEATO support, (3) that a coordinated package involving the entire Southeast Asian peninsula was required, and (4) that North Vietnam be recognized as the immediate threat. The report concluded that any effective strategy should include an effective ICC, a noncommunist or divided Laos, a strengthened Thailand, a means of pressuring Hanoi (including the option of direct retaliation), and a new SEATO plan.

At 11 A.M. on July 28, Steeves discussed the committee report (and presumably the Rostow-Taylor memo) with the president and other top officials at the White House. The initial focus of the meeting was on Laos. Deputy Under Secretary of State U. Alexis Johnson, who had been a member of the Vietnam Task Force earlier in the year, reported that the administration was prepared to accept a negotiated settlement calling for a coalition government including the Pathet Lao, provided that the settlement provided for a stable government and a strong control mechanism. The problem was, he said, that the communists were not yet ready to accept a neutral Laos so a new element was needed to change their calculations. The administration was considering a plan to hold southern Laos with combined U.S. and allied forces, but if the North Vietnamese intervened in force, the United States might have to threaten air and naval operations in the area of Hanoi and Haiphong.

But President Kennedy was still skeptical of the military option, pointing out that in the past the United States had been too optimistic about Laos and that many military leaders were reluctant to become directly involved in combat in the area. Under Secretary Johnson replied that it would be helpful for future planning if it was at least clear that the United States was prepared to intervene if the situation required it, but Kennedy avoided a flat statement and simply reiterated that he was "at present very reluctant to make a decision to go into Laos" when he still had little confidence in the military practicability of the proposal before him. Let's press forward with negotiations, he said. Nothing would be worse than an unsuccessful intervention in this area. The remainder of the meeting was devoted to Vietnam. Kennedy agreed to examine the proposals put forward by the Southeast Asia Working Group and concurred that it would be useful for General Maxwell Taylor to undertake a fact-finding trip to the area. Rostow, who had impressed the president with his energy, would accompany him. In the meantime, the administration would look into Saigon's aid request.[29]

In early August President Kennedy sent a second letter to Diem. The issue of linking U.S. aid to Vietnamese reforms had been fought out once again in Washington, with officials in the Departments of State and Defense arguing for the need to create an atmosphere of trust with the Diem regime, while officials from ICA and the Bureau of the Budget, skeptical of Saigon because of past performance, wanted to impose stringent conditions on U.S. aid to guarantee results. The letter represented a compromise but leaned toward the former view, expressing a willingness to approve an increase in ARVN forces to 200,000 but adding that any expansion beyond that would require further study.[30]

The issue had probably already been decided. The administration's intention to extend further military and economic assistance to the RVN was set forth in NSAM-65, issued on August 11. In that memo, it was noted that for the present, national security considerations must be given top priority, but that military actions were useless unless political, social, and economic reforms were effectively carried through. It instructed Ambassador Nolting to continue efforts to persuade Diem to move in that direction. The White House had taken another step in extending the U.S. commitment to the Saigon regime.[31]

Plugging the Leak in the Dike

One of the primary concerns of administration officials during the summer of 1961 was the effect that the growing strength of the communists in Laos could have on the situation in Vietnam, especially on infiltration into the South. A National Intelligence Estimate published in mid-August had alerted readers to the problem. The U.S. Embassy in Saigon chipped in with its own evaluation, predicting a continuation of infiltration through Laos and increased military activity in the South in coming months. To administration officials, now conditioned to the idea that Hanoi and Beijing had a "master plan" based on the Maoist three-stage concept of people's war, such evidence indicated that communist strategy was building up to a major attack in the South, possibly in the coming year.[32]

In August, the administration sent William J. Jorden, a former reporter for the *New York Times* and now a member of the State Department's Policy Planning Council, to Saigon to gather documentation on the infiltration by communist forces into the RVN. Jorden spent several weeks in Southeast Asia and submitted his report on his return to the United States in late September. Jorden emphasized that the communist effort was not primarily "a movement of large organized units across the GVN border" but relied on local recruitment for the bulk of its following. But he added that the infiltration of personnel and matériel was on the increase and took place both by sea and by land. Jorden's report confirmed what many other U.S. officials believed and feared. Although the precise level of North Vietnamese assistance to the Viet Cong forces in the South could not be accurately estimated, it was becoming a significant factor in the equation and could only be made worse by the situation in Laos. Walt W. Rostow suggested that an investigating commission go to Southeast Asia to study the situation and lay the basis for a possible U.N. resolution condemning the DRV. An additional option that the administration began to pursue was to play on Moscow's presumed willingness to cooperate in the effort to achieve a settlement in Laos. On September 13, W. Averell Harriman, the veteran Democratic Party politician who was serving as the administration's ambassador at large, cabled from Geneva that the Soviet representative to the peace talks, George Pushkin, had promised him that Moscow "could and would control North Viet-Nam" and that Hanoi would abide by the terms of a treaty. Washington was interested, but not all were so sanguine. From Saigon, Nolting reported his skepticism. Even with a "strong ICC," a neutral Laos, he predicted, could not control infiltration from North into South Vietnam.[33]

Concern over the rising level of infiltration and of overall Viet Cong activity was not limited to U.S. officials. In Saigon, Diem was anxious over the situation and on September 30, two weeks after Viet Cong forces overran a provincial capital less than 30 miles from Saigon, he presented visiting CINC-PAC commander Admiral Harry Felt with a request for a bilateral defense treaty with the United States. Ambassador Nolting was surprised at the request and simply remarked that it would have to be studied. The State Department replied cautiously that the request would be reviewed "promptly and sympathetically" but pointed out that Article 19 of the Geneva Accords (restricting the authority of the states of Indochina to establish military alliances) must be taken into consideration.[34]

Debate in Hanoi

Anxiety in Washington and Saigon that Hanoi had a "master plan" to conquer the South was not entirely justified. When the Kennedy administration came into office in January 1961, communist leaders in North Vietnam were engaged in their own debate over the strategy to follow in the South. They too were divided over the proper mix of political and military struggle that would be required to secure victory.

The decision to return to the policy of revolutionary war that had been approved by the VWP Central Committee in May 1959 was not specific on what strategy to adopt. The resolution had simply noted that some combination of political and military struggle would be required. Debate over the proper approach had been submerged by an uneasy compromise that emphasized the need for a primary reliance on political activities to build up the mass base of the movement while gradually strengthening military forces for an ultimate confrontation with the Saigon regime.

During the next two years, tensions over strategy and tactics continued within the party. Some impatient cadres in the South were critical of what they felt was an overemphasis on political struggle and appealed for greater stress on military operations and a return in some form to the Maoist strategy of people's war that had been applied in somewhat modified form during the war against the French. Others adopted a contrasting view, arguing that military operations simply intensified the Saigon regime's efforts to repress the movement. They were in favor of continuing the stress on political activities that had been adopted after the Geneva Conference.

The debate had apparently not been resolved by the autumn of 1960 because the party's Third National Congress, held in September, did not make any significant decisions affecting existing strategy but simply noted that the period of stability in the South was at an end and disintegration was under way. To take advantage of this new stage of the revolution, the congress placed military and political struggle on an equal footing in the South, while heightening the level of support from the North. Party leaders clearly did not anticipate that a major commitment of resources from the North would be required because the same congress approved the DRV's first Five-Year Plan calling for rapid socialist industrialization.

In any event, the intensification of the effort in the South necessitated a new front organization to enlist the support of the mass of the population in South Vietnam in a common struggle against the Diem regime. The objectives of the new front were designed to appeal to all anti-Diem forces in the South and emphasized national independence and social justice rather than social revolution. In deference to regional sentiment in the South and to avoid any identification with the North, the new organization was called the National Front for the Liberation of South Vietnam, or NLF. Like its predecessors, in actuality the new front, formally founded in December 1960, was under the firm guidance of the party leadership in Hanoi.[35]

A factor of crucial importance was the level of support that Hanoi would receive from its major allies. Neither Moscow nor Beijing was anxious to see the situation in Indochina escalate into a major confrontation with the United States, and both must have expressed that view to Hanoi in the years immediately following the Geneva Accords in 1954. Still, the heightening of the Sino-Soviet dispute placed both under pressure to demonstrate their support for Vietnam and other wars of national liberation. The resolution issued at the close of the Conference of Communist and Workers' Parties held in Moscow in November 1960 reaffirmed the statement at the 1957 conference on nonpeaceful transition to socialism, and Ho Chi Minh played a conciliatory role in seeking to reduce the bitterness of the emerging Sino-Soviet dispute.

The VWP Third Congress of September 1960 had made a general commitment to the liberation of the South but had been vague on specifics. Published speeches given at the meeting sent conflicting signals. Politburo member Truong Chinh, now becoming identified with a cautious line on South Vietnam, warned unnamed comrades from the South not to be "too impatient," and Defense Minister Vo Nguyen Giap remarked that "a number of our comrades" did not fully understand that while Hanoi's policy was to preserve peace, it was necessary to be prepared "to cope with any maneuver of the enemy." Le Duan, who had been formally elected to the post of first secretary (replacing the title of general secretary, in imitation of a similar change in Moscow), had merely remarked that the task would be long and arduous, "not simple but complex, combining many forms of struggle."[36]

But the rapid evolution of the situation in South Vietnam clearly created a need to formulate a more specific approach, and four months later the Politburo met in Hanoi, in the words of an official history of the war, to "concretize" the results of the Third Party Congress. The resolution issued at the end of the meeting was decidedly optimistic, noting that the period of stability of the Saigon regime was at an end and a period of continuous crisis was about to begin. Based on that analysis, the Politburo called for an intensification of the military effort in the South aimed at final victory through a combined general offensive and uprising, with intensified military attacks in rural areas (divided for military purposes into two regions, the Central Highlands and the Mekong River Delta) coordinated with a mass popular insurrection in the major cities. A few weeks later, the scattered forces of the revolution in the South were unified into a new People's Liberation Armed Forces, or PLAF. Like the Vietminh armed forces that had been used in the war against the French, the PLAF would function at three levels—local self-defense units operating at the village level, guerrilla units under regional command, and conventional forces directed from the southern headquarters. To provide centralized direction for the effort, a new Central Office for South Vietnam (Trung uong cuc Mien Nam, also known as COSVN), directly subordinate to the Central Committee in Hanoi, was created in September.[37]

But the Politburo in Hanoi cautioned leading cadres in the South (many of whom were members of the VWP Central Committee or other central organs of the party) that the time for such an offensive and uprising had not yet arrived. In letters written to COSVN chairman Nguyen Van Linh following the January Politburo meeting, the VWP party leader Le Duan described the recent decisions and added his own appraisal of the overall situation. The revolution was progressing well, he said, but it was still in the "first stage" of development because enemy military strength was substantially intact and many ARVN soldiers were still ambivalent about the revolution. Criticizing some southern leaders for their recent tendency to feel that the general uprising could be launched without extensive preparation (such as the formation of liberated base areas and the adoption of a strategy of protracted war), Le Duan warned Linh not to be impetuous. A greater emphasis on military struggle might provoke an enemy reaction and make the party's political activities in the southern provinces more difficult to carry out. He cited the examples of the Bolshevik uprising and the August Revolution to point out that revolution could not succeed unless the enemy's armed forces had been militarily defeated or undermined by internal subversion.[38]

Why did party authorities in Hanoi opt for an approach that was more reminiscent of that used during the August Revolution than that applied during the war against the French? First, they had to take account of the fact that neither of their chief allies appeared willing to bankroll a major military effort to overthrow the Diem regime. More important, a resumption of hostilities could provoke a countermove on the part of the United States, including the possibility of U.S. military intervention in the war. For the time being, Le Duan and his colleagues undoubtedly hoped that the Diem regime was sufficiently vulnerable to be toppled without the open use of force.

The Taylor Mission

Although concern over the problem of Hanoi's involvement was rising in Washington, informed U.S. observers were conscious that infiltration was only one aspect of Saigon's problem. Inside South Vietnam, Diem's difficulties continued despite the more conciliatory attitude taken by the new administration in Washington. Discontent with the regime was on the increase among key elements in South Vietnamese society. A State Department intelligence report issued at the end of September stated that although coup rumors had subsided, the situation was still potentially explosive.

Such evidence led the Kennedy team for the first time to question the Diem regime. In October, Under Secretary of State Chester Bowles, who had broken ranks during the spring to suggest the possibility of a negotiated settlement in Vietnam, wrote a memo to Secretary Dean Rusk pointing out that a military response to the problem in Southeast Asia would involve U.S. prestige in a remote area under adverse circumstances. Bowles recommended a political approach, proposing that the concept of a neutral and independent Laos now being discussed at Geneva be broadened to include all Southeast Asia and guaranteed by all states involved in the area, including China and the Soviet Union. Bowles conceded that the communists might manipulate such a situation to their own advantage, but he said that the United States would then have a free hand to seek stronger action with international support.[39]

In a note to Harvard historian Arthur Schlesinger, Jr., then serving as special assistant at the White House, Bowles admitted that the reaction to his memo within the State Department had been "relatively negative." But he was not entirely alone in his doubts. A few days later, Averell Harriman, then with the U.S. delegation at the Laos peace talks in Geneva, cabled from Switzerland his concern that Diem was the problem and warning that the United States was sitting on a "powder keg" that might go off at any moment. Some foreign service officers in the U.S. Embassy in Saigon, such as Counselor for Political

Affairs Joseph Mendenhall, felt the same way, but Ambassador Nolting, while conceding Diem's limitations, felt that Washington should stick with him.[40]

In the meantime, others continued to anguish over the problem of infiltration. The Joint Chiefs had assessed a proposal by Walt Rostow to station SEATO forces in South Vietnam to stem infiltration from the North and rejected it as not feasible. Such troops, the JCS reasoned, would have to be deployed over several hundred miles of border and could be attacked by the enemy piecemeal or bypassed. At best, they would reduce but not eliminate infiltration. Moreover, the proposal would compound U.S. logistical problems by placing troops at the most vulnerable defense points if the DRV or China should decide to intervene. An alternative plan, to man only the seventeenth parallel, was also considered unsound because it was rarely used and would concede the bulk of northern and central Laos to the communists. The JCS concluded that what was needed was not a dispersal of allied forces along the border but a concentrated effort (represented by SEATO Plan 5, a proposal drawn up in May to hold key population centers in the Laotian lowlands with SEATO forces, or a variant thereof) to save all or most of Laos, thus securing the South Vietnamese frontier and freeing ARVN for operations against insurgent forces in the RVN.[41]

But at the State Department, some officials were still thinking of the SEATO option in connection with South Vietnam. At a meeting held at the White House on October 11, U. Alexis Johnson presented a plan for the possible introduction of SEATO forces in South Vietnam in combination with the stationing of U.N. observers to report on infiltration. Kennedy made no commitment but decided to follow through on the plan to send General Maxwell Taylor to Saigon to look into the feasibility of various plans to deal with the situation in the RVN. According to one of Taylor's biographers, the president told General Taylor that he hoped to avoid committing U.S. combat troops in South Vietnam.[42]

The Taylor team, which included Walt W. Rostow, Sterling Cottrell of the State Department, and Edward Lansdale, among others, arrived in Saigon on October 15 and immediately met a sense of urgency. General McGarr was concerned at the increased level of Viet Cong activity in the South, and Diem was worried about the situation in Laos, arguing to his guests that a treaty was needed now to reassure the Vietnamese people. He also wanted a contingency agreement by Washington to introduce U.S. armed forces when and if they were required. The Taylor group also discovered disquieting evidence of continuing political dissension in Saigon and the provinces. In a meeting with General Duong Van "Big" Minh, the popular southern-born military commander complained of declining ARVN morale, government favoritism toward Catholics, and problems in selecting province chiefs.[43]

The Taylor mission left Vietnam for Bangkok on the evening of October 25. Before his departure, General Taylor cabled his preliminary conclusions to

Washington. On November 1, he filed a formal report from the Philippines. South Vietnam, he reported, was suffering from a double crisis of confidence: in U.S. determination to stay in the area and in Diem's own tactics and administrative abilities. In the meantime, the communists had been very successful in taking advantage of the situation and were well on the way to victory through a strategy of subversion, bypassing the stage of conventional war.

Taylor recommended vigorous action by the United States to counter the adverse trends. To infuse the Saigon regime with a sense of purpose and reassure the Vietnamese people of the constancy of U.S. support, he recommended that a limited number of U.S. troops be introduced into Vietnam. The ostensible purpose would be to assist the RVN in recovering from disastrous floods that had struck Central Vietnam, but the real reason would be to provide a boost to Vietnamese morale and free ARVN for offensive operations against the Viet Cong. Then, to achieve a better management of Saigon's nation-building effort, Washington should provide U.S. administrators for direct insertion into the government machinery while increasing the size of MAAG and other forms of assistance. In sum, the United States would become a "limited partner" in the war.

The overall effect of Taylor's recommendations, of course, would be to involve the United States much more directly in the conflict and in the fate of the Saigon regime. Taylor emphasized that he was well aware of the risks involved in committing U.S. prestige and the possible unlimited growth of the commitment. But he argued that this was the most effective way to convince the Vietnamese of U.S. purpose and "an essential action if we are to reverse the present downward trend of events."[44]

Back in Washington, officials were already beginning to react to the cables that the Taylor mission had dispatched from Southeast Asia. The renewed indications of instability in Saigon had nagged at the minds of key policymakers and provoked a quiet consideration of alternatives to the Diem regime. On October 20, the State Department sent a secret memo to Nolting for his use in case of the possible overthrow of Ngo Dinh Diem. It stated that U.S. policy was to support Diem for as long as he was "effectively in control over the GVN." In the meantime, no action should be taken to encourage his opponents. In case of a coup attempt, the embassy should give full support to Diem until the chief of mission decided it was time for a change. Then the United States should be prepared to shift support quickly to any noncommunist individual or group that appeared most capable of establishing effective control over the government. The nature of support, noted the memo, should be strong enough to achieve rapid results but not so blatant as to make the person or group appear to be a U.S. puppet. In the meantime, the embassy was instructed to keep a list of Vietnamese who might be acceptable as alternative leaders.[45]

At the same time, the ground was already being prepared for the possible introduction of U.S. troops into South Vietnam. On October 25, the day General Taylor had cabled his preliminary recommendations from Bangkok, U. Alexis Johnson directed the Vietnam Task Force to study possible political and diplomatic preparations for sending troops. Several key figures in the administration, including Chester Bowles, George Ball (soon to replace Bowles as under secretary of state), and Secretary Rusk, however, had serious reservations about sending troops.

The president also received advice from Capitol Hill. Senator Mike Mansfield, long a key congressional supporter of President Diem, wrote a memo to Kennedy advising him to approach the introduction of troops into the RVN with the greatest caution. If U.S. troops were to be used, he said, they would be there without significant allied support and would be engaged against third-string communists but with the risk of direct involvement by China. That would involve the United States in an open-ended commitment at serious logistical disadvantages while weakening U.S. commitments elsewhere. Mansfield conceded that Vietnam was very important to U.S. security but pointed out that U.S. power could not be a substitute for political and economic reforms inside South Vietnam. He favored a substantial increase in U.S. military and economic aid to Vietnam but recommended leaving the physical burden to the South Vietnamese.[46]

There is no record of Kennedy's reaction to Mansfield's memo, but it is clear that the president was receiving advice on the crisis from a wide variety of sources inside and outside the government. One of the more vocal was Ambassador to India John Kenneth Galbraith, who was in Washington for the visit of Prime Minister Jawaharlal Nehru to the United States. On November 3 he submitted a "Plan for South Vietnam." Like Senator Mansfield, Galbraith was profoundly skeptical of the potential benefits of increased U.S. involvement. In fact, he went further. Mansfield still appeared to hope for the revival of a strong noncommunist regime in Saigon, whereas Galbraith despaired of the prospects for the survival of a "limping American satellite" and said the United States should seek to create an independent and politically neutral state in the South.

There were good reasons, Galbraith argued, to opt for a neutralist solution at that time—the Geneva Conference on Laos was reaching a climax, the Sino-Soviet dispute was acute, and reports of Maxwell Taylor's proposals had probably improved the administration's bargaining position. Key elements in his proposal were a U.N. resolution on the independence of the RVN, the dispatch of observer groups to report on infiltration; prompt agreement at Geneva on the neutralization of Laos with the understanding that it was not to be used as a corridor; an approach to the Soviets on mutual efforts to end the fighting in Southeast Asia; and discussions with Nehru on how to convince Ho Chi Minh that the U.S. objective was an independent South Vietnam not necessarily allied with the United States.[47]

Maxwell Taylor arrived in Washington on November 3 and immediately presented his formal report to the White House in a brief meeting with the president. The report was accompanied by reports from members of the mission as well as a paper from William Jorden of the Policy Planning Council. On balance, the report presented a depressing picture of the situation in Vietnam. Even Edward Lansdale, among those in attendance at the meeting, noted that Vietnam was "dangerously far down the road to a Communist takeover" and in a more critical state than during his last visit. As before, however, there was disagreement over the root of the problem. To Lansdale and others, the key was the security situation; to some State Department officials such as Sterling Cottrell and Jorden, the primary problem was Diem. Cottrell warned that because there was no guarantee the Saigon regime could succeed, it would be a mistake for the United States to commit itself irrevocably to the defeat of communism in South Vietnam. Yet a little later he recommended that if the United States was unable to reverse the trend, it should move to the Rostow plan of applying punitive measures on the DRV. Jorden was equally ambiguous. He felt that to give unquestioned support to Diem was to "court disaster," but a U.S. posture of neutrality would invite an explosion that would benefit the communists. Jorden recommended a compromise approach that would seek reforms acceptable to both Diem and his critics. If that failed, he proposed that Washington should find alternative leadership, although he admitted that engineering a coup involved risks and was not something the United States did well.[48]

President Kennedy said little about the report at the meeting except to make clear that he was instinctively opposed to introducing U.S. forces. He ordered that distribution of the Taylor report be restricted to key advisers, whom he directed to study the proposal for a meeting on November 7, after the departure of Prime Minister Nehru. Over the weekend, top officials had wrestled with the problem, with a primary focus on the troops issue. Defense Secretary McNamara wrote a memo to the president favoring Taylor's proposal on the grounds that the fall of South Vietnam would have serious strategic implications and that the chance of preventing that was small without the presence of U.S. forces. McNamara's views were seconded by the Joint Chiefs, who emphasized that the 8,000-man increment recommended by Taylor was too limited to solve the problem and should be seen as preparation for a larger force later. They also recommended warning Hanoi that the United States would take action against North Vietnam unless it stopped supporting the insurgency in the South.[49]

Secretary McNamara's memo, drafted by Assistant Secretary of Defense William P. Bundy, was apparently then shared with Dean Rusk with the intention of formulating a joint position to be communicated to the president. Rusk shared McNamara's concern over the impact of a communist victory in South Vietnam, but he was reluctant to make a major commitment of American prestige to what he labeled a losing horse. In a cable from Japan, where he was participating in trade talks, Rusk warned against any commitment without a guarantee of Diem's compliance with planned reforms. He was also concerned about the possibility of Chinese or Soviet intervention and the possible impact on negotiations on Laos. He agreed that a fully satisfactory settlement was unlikely but did not rule out the possibility of a settlement that would permit the return of Souvanna Phouma as prime minister of a neutralist coalition government. He did see the value of using the Taylor proposals to convey U.S. determination to Moscow and Beijing, so he approved the first seven points of the Taylor proposal and recommended that action on U.S. combat troops be deferred.[50]

While key administration officials responded to the Taylor report, the president was occupied with the visit of Prime Minister Jawaharlal Nehru of India. In a lunch with Nehru, Kennedy and Ambassador Galbraith probed Nehru's views on the issue and sought his support for a joint effort. Nehru's reply was disappointing; he simply expressed his disapproval of the dispatch of U.S. troops without offering suggestions of his own to deal with the problem.

The scheduled meeting at the White House on November 7 did not take place. One reason offered by State Department historians was the president's heavy schedule in connection with Nehru's visit to Washington. But there are also indications that Rusk may have told Kennedy that he and McNamara had not yet been able to formulate a joint position on the key issue because of Rusk's concern that a precipitate action could upset the possibility of a settlement on Laos. On the eighth, McNamara redrafted his memo of November 5 after consultation with the Joint Chiefs, who declared that 8,000 U.S. troops would be useful as an opening gambit only if accompanied by a clear indication that the United States was committed to prevent the fall of South Vietnam to the communists. He recommended such a commitment and, if Kennedy agreed, approval of the Taylor plan as a first step.

In the meantime, a revised version of the joint memo was being drafted in the State Department. The new draft conceded the unlikelihood that the fall of South Vietnam could be prevented without the introduction of a substantial number of U.S. armed forces but concluded that nevertheless it would be "desirable" if it could be saved without such a commitment so as to reduce the risk of a resumption of hostilities in Laos and open intervention by the major communist powers. To forestall that eventuality, the paper said that the only hope was a prompt revamping of the administrative and command structure of the RVN and "sharply increased" U.S. military and economic aid. A Lao-type settlement, it said, would be highly dangerous in South Vietnam. The author was not opposed to the introduction of U.S. troops *after* a successful settlement in Laos, however, and noted that such a decision could serve to stabilize the position in Indochina by demonstrating that a settlement in Laos was as far as

Washington was prepared to see communist influence develop. If troops were introduced, they should be placed near the DMZ to relieve South Vietnamese armed forces for offensive operations elsewhere, and other SEATO nations should contribute troops.

The State Department draft ran into immediate criticism in the Defense Department for its vagueness on timing, for its fear of upsetting an unsatisfactory settlement in Laos, for its suggestion to place U.S. troops in an area little used by the enemy, and for its statement of firm commitment without any military muscle. But the State Department wanted to postpone the decision. On November 9, Rusk, McNamara, and several of their aides met in the State Department to hammer out a compromise. Some of the disagreement was based on semantics, but Rusk remained reluctant to commit U.S. troops until the RVN had made a clear commitment, and Harriman wanted to proceed with the conference first.[51]

On November 11, a new joint memo drafted by U. Alexis Johnson and William Bundy was presented to the president for a meeting that day. It opened with the dire prediction that the loss of South Vietnam would have a catastrophic effect on U.S. national security and the near certainty that the remainder of Southeast Asia would move to a complete accommodation with communism if not formal incorporation within the communist bloc. It would destroy SEATO and undermine U.S. commitments elsewhere and would stimulate bitter controversy in the United States. The authors therefore felt that the administration had no choice but to commit itself to preventing the fall of South Vietnam to communism. They recognized that one aspect of the problem was the inept and divided government in South Vietnam and asserted that the United States must insist that the RVN "take the measures necessary to win the war against the guerrillas." But at the same time they believed that it would not be possible for the Saigon regime to win the internal struggle so long as infiltration continued unchecked and insurgent forces enjoyed a safe sanctuary beyond the frontier. "We should be prepared," it concluded, "to introduce United States combat forces if that should be necessary for success" and if necessary strike at the source of aggression in the North.[52]

The report distinguished between two categories of U.S. forces: small units to be used in direct support of an ARVN military effort and larger units with direct military missions. The first category should be introduced as soon as possible. The second, whose presence would pose the risk of a hostile reaction by Moscow and Beijing and possibly by the population of South Vietnam itself, should be given consideration but might not be needed.

The meeting with the president took place at noon in the White House. In the meantime, Kennedy had been discussing the issue with others such as George Ball and John McCloy, who were reluctant to commit troops in South Vietnam. He had scoffed at Ball's warning that the United States could end up like the French, with 300,000 troops bogged down in the jungles of Southeast Asia.[53]

Unfortunately, the documentary record of what took place at the meeting with his key advisers is sketchy. What is clear is that the president, citing congressional opposition and the danger of war with China, remained reluctant to make a decision to commit U.S. troops to the conflict in Vietnam except as a last resort. He was also opposed to a blanket statement of commitment and deferred action on the first recommendation—a commitment to prevent the fall of South Vietnam and recognition that U.S. forces might eventually be needed. But he did tentatively approve recommendations to undertake planning for the possible future introduction of U.S. forces as well as to increase military assistance and advisory personnel to the South Vietnamese armed forces. He also directed the preparation of a White Paper to publicize Hanoi's transgression of the Geneva Accords by infiltrating men and matériel into the South.[54]

The meeting at the White House on November 11 did not end the debate over Vietnam policy. On the same day, Averell Harriman drew up his own ideas on the subject in a memo to the president. Harriman argued that before U.S. troops were brought in, Washington should approach the Soviet Union about supplementing a settlement on Laos with a guarantee that Laotian territory would not be used as a staging area against South Vietnam. But Rostow opposed negotiations before the U.S. position in the region had been strengthened. To remedy the confusion, Maxwell Taylor asked for a second meeting of the National Security Council to resolve the issue.[55]

That meeting, held on the fifteenth, was attended by all cabinet officials except Vice-President Johnson, who was in Detroit and unable to return in time. Secretary Rusk opened the discussion by explaining the rationale for the memo presented on the eleventh, but from the outset Kennedy balked, expressing opposition to becoming involved on two sides of the world at once (presumably a reference to Berlin) and questioning the wisdom of a direct role in a conflict the origins of which, in his view, were ambiguous. Korea, he noted, was a clear case of aggression, and U.S. policy there had broad support from other members of the United Nations. The conflict in Vietnam was more obscure, and a U.S. decision to intervene might win little support from its major allies (both the British and the French had been consulted and expressed reservations about the introduction of U.S. troops into South Vietnam). He could make a good case against intervention in a country 10,000 miles away. Millions had already been spent against a guerrilla army of less than 20,000 men without any success.

Rusk conceded that U.S. allies opposed intervention, but he argued that a policy of firmness in South Vietnam similar to that which the administration had displayed in Berlin might achieve U.S. interests without resort to combat.

But Kennedy countered that the situation in South Vietnam was not as clear-cut as in Berlin, to which McNamara replied that the presence of U.S. troops would clarify the issue because they could be used against the Viet Cong as well as directly against the North. But Kennedy was still not convinced and responded that it was not clear how U.S. forces could be used against guerrillas, from whom they would be vulnerable to attack.

The president was also concerned about the attitude of Congress and U.S. public opinion and at the fact that the proposed actions would contravene the Geneva Accords. He expressed the view that the administration must act in such a way as to place responsibility for breaking the accords on Hanoi. In the end, he deferred a decision on the troops issue and directed that the next two or three weeks be used to complete studies on the proposed program. The final program, as approved as NSAM-111 on November 22, incorporated the bulk of the Taylor proposals but with no reference to preventing the fall of South Vietnam to communism.[56]

In the six months since the approval of the Vietnam Task Force report in May, the environment for making decisions on the Vietnam conflict had changed. On the one hand, the apocalyptic atmosphere that had accompanied the Berlin crisis, the Bay of Pigs, and the chaotic situation in Laos had eased. Although negotiations were still under way in Laos, it looked as though a settlement, however unsatisfactory, was beginning to take shape.

On the other hand, the overall situation in Vietnam, if anything, was worse than it had been in the spring. Rates of infiltration were up, as was the estimated size of the enemy forces. General McGarr reported from Saigon that the annual infiltration rate had increased to 17,000 as compared with 7,500 the previous year. Moreover, the weakness of the Diem regime was clearer. Whereas in the spring there was at least some hope that the situation could be managed, now it was clearer than ever that Diem was a key part of the problem.[57]

These events undermined the fragile confidence in Washington that Diem could do the job on his own and led to a break in the rough consensus that had characterized decision making in the spring. Most of Kennedy's key advisers were agreed on the need to increase U.S. involvement while sticking with Diem, at least for the time being. But dissident voices now began to be heard, as high officials in the State Department such as George Ball and Averell Harriman began to question the advisability of escalating the U.S. commitment. In a private letter to Kennedy on November 20, Galbraith applauded Kennedy's decision not to send troops and said there could be no solution without a change in government in Saigon. It was necessary to play the game for a while, he conceded, but in the end the United States must withdraw its support from Diem. Nothing succeeds, he remarked, like successors.[58]

In the end, Kennedy compromised. He followed the lead of his chief advisers and adopted a course leading to further involvement, but he rejected the recommendation contained in the Taylor report calling for the introduction of U.S. troops into the South. He also refused to make a firm commitment to save South Vietnam from communism. Kennedy's behavior during the November debate contained the seeds of a seemingly unending controversy among his advisers and other observers regarding his ultimate intentions in South Vietnam. Some, like Theodore Sorensen and historian Arthur Schlesinger, Jr., have interpreted his actions as a clear sign that he was unwilling to commit U.S. power to save South Vietnam from communism. Others, such as Walt W. Rostow, argue that Kennedy's commitment was firm and unalterable.

It is not easy from the perspective of 30 years to make a firm judgment on Kennedy's intentions on Vietnam in the fall of 1961. The factors that had impelled him to enhance the U.S. role in the spring still pertained: the narrow base of his domestic support, the need to reassure allies and convince adversaries of the constancy of U.S. foreign policy objectives. As he remarked to John McCloy, he had few options. But it is also clear from the record that Kennedy was more skeptical than most of his key advisers of the advisability of a major U.S. role in the Vietnam conflict. Not only did he reject the proposal to introduce U.S. troops into South Vietnam, but he questioned the political, moral, and legal purpose for their being there. In so doing he anticipated a number of the problems that would face policymakers in later years. In the end, he went only half as far as his advisers wished him to, and then with extreme reluctance. As he remarked to James Reston, he would not have made the decision to increase the U.S. commitment in South Vietnam had he not been struck by the relevance to Berlin. Even so, he was determined to pursue other courses of action and wrote Khrushchev with a proposal to remove the area from Great Power rivalry. And in a tacit indication of his concern at the monochromatic character of advice he was receiving from key advisers, he appointed Averell Harriman, one of the administration's freethinkers, to replace Walter McConaughy as assistant secretary of state for Far Eastern affairs.[59]

Limited Partnership

Even optimists within the administration were agreed that a key to the success of the new program was to achieve the wholehearted cooperation of the Saigon regime. Diem had always resisted pressure to undertake reforms in the political and social arenas. Would he accede now that Washington wanted a much greater role in the decison-making process?

In Saigon, Ambassador Nolting met with Diem on November 17, two days after the meeting in Washington that had led to the approval of the new program. Nolting had been informed about the decisions in a cable that pointed out that the new program called for a "much closer relationship than the present one of acting in an advisory capacity only." The United States, it said,

"would expect to share in the decision-making process in the political, economic, and military fields as they affected the security situation," and U.S.
aid would be dependent upon Diem's willingness to enact needed reforms to
broaden the base of his government. Nolting explained the administration's
reasons for deciding not to send combat troops to South Vietnam and informed him that its willingness to go ahead with the joint efforts depended on
Saigon reforms "of real substance and meaning" in the administrative, social,
and political realms. Nolting reported that Diem seemed to take the news better
than expected and had promised to help, while emphasizing that the RVN "did
not want to be a protectorate." A few days later, however, Nolting reported a
conversation with one of Diem's key advisers, who had told him that Diem was
disappointed in U.S. proposals and feared that the administration was preparing to back out of Vietnam as it was already doing in Laos.[60]

History would show that Diem's fear of a U.S. withdrawal was somewhat
premature, but his concern that it was about to tamper with the fabric of
Vietnamese life society was well founded. On November 22, Joseph Mendenhall, no admirer of Diem's, at Nolting's request, drew up a set of proposals to
improve the administration and broaden the base of support for the Diem
regime. Mendenhall included suggestions that had originated during the Eisenhower administration, to set up a "cabinet of all the talents" with participation
by opposition political parties, to liberalize censorship to win the support
of intellectuals, to remove Madame Nhu from the public eye, and to initiate
new economic programs and set up provincial councils to win support in the
countryside.

To Diem many of these suggestions were anathema. In discussions with
Ambassador Nolting he took the offensive, complaining that U.S. interference
was giving the label of nationalism to the communists and that the proposal to
create a broader political front was inappropriate. The immediate problem, he
said, was to provide security. Communist terrorism was undermining popular
support for his government because of fear. In private he was critical of the idea
of a cabinet of talents, claiming that the intellectuals were no good. To signal his
displeasure, the official press began to denounce U.S. interference in Vietnamese affairs.[61]

After less than a year in office, the Kennedy administration had collided
headlong with the same dilemma that had tormented its predecessor. Official
sources in Washington tried to dampen talk about pressuring Diem by instructing U.S. representatives in Saigon not to criticize the regime in public, but
rumors of a coup could not be contained. They came primarily from military
sources, where General Duong Van Minh was openly critical of his president.
Washington was aware of these rumors and explored them gingerly, but for
the time being nothing happened. From Saigon, Nolting urged patience, arguing that in time Diem would go along with U.S. suggestions. On December 5,

he informed him that the United States was ready to move ahead with the program.[62]

The issue of military assistance was explored at a meeting of senior civilian and military officials in Honolulu. Secretary McNamara set the tone with an attitude of energy and determination, announcing that the military could have practically anything it wanted short of combat troops. The goal, he told his listeners, was to win, and if something was needed, the military should ask for it. McNamara reportedly had little faith in gimmicks such as defoliants or exclusively air or naval operations but was convinced that victory would come "on the ground" inside Vietnam.[63]

To handle the task, the administration decided to create a new Military Assistance Command in South Vietnam. Not surprisingly, the idea did not receive universal approbation. Ambassador Nolting complained that it would inevitably result in overemphasizing the military aspects of the problem and encourage Diem to take the same view. Nolting had some support in the State Department, but his complaints were rejected by the White House, and in January a new Military Assistance Command, Vietnam (MACV), was created with General Paul Harkins as commander.[64]

With the U.S. commitment to provide increased military assistance to the RVN in place, the Defense Department looked into the specific concept of operations to move beyond the generalities of the counterinsurgency program. In September 1961, MAAG had produced a report called "Geographically Phased National Level Operation Plan for Counter-insurgency." It called for a three-phase operation. In the preparatory phase, priority target areas would be established, plans drawn up, and training programs gotten under way. A military phase would follow, devoted to clearing the targeted area with regular forces and then handing over the security task to the Civil Guard. Finally, there would be a security phase, when the Self-Defense Corps would assume the responsibility for civil order, and control would pass to civilian hands to move forward with economic reform programs.

For implementation, MAAG planners adopted the "oil spot technique" that had first been introduced many years earlier by the French. During the initial year, priority would be assigned to six provinces around Saigon and the area of Kontum in the Central Highlands. Later, attention would shift southward to the Mekong Delta and more remote areas in the Highlands and into the provinces north and east of Saigon. The plan would commence with an ARVN sweep into War Zone D to reduce the immediate danger to the capital area and increase Saigon's self-confidence.[65]

During his visit to Saigon in October, Maxwell Taylor had mentioned this plan to President Diem, who had been evasive, indicating only that he had a plan of his own. That plan was apparently based on the concept of operations presented to him by British adviser Robert G. K. Thompson. Well-known for his success in suppressing the communist insurrection in Malaya, Thompson had been invited to Saigon in September to head an advisory mission to the RVN. Although U.S. officials knew relatively little about the situation in Malaya and some argued that it was not relevant to Vietnam, others felt it was useful for Diem to consult him. Thompson was undoubtedly aware of the danger that inadequate consultation with U.S. officials could undermine his effectiveness so he stopped in Washington en route to Saigon and met with Maxwell Taylor and the Joint Chiefs.

In November, Thompson presented his plan to President Diem. It was similar to the U.S. version in its gradualist approach, but it differed in geographical focus and emphasis. Thompson placed his initial attention on the Mekong Delta and based his program on a concept that had been effective in Malaya—the so-called strategic hamlets. The goal was to win the people, not just kill terrorists, and to make primary use of the Civil Guard and the Self-Defense Corps rather than ARVN. The self-defense forces were the key to Thompson's plan because they would show the people how to defend themselves. Regular units would be used primarily for mobile operations to keep the Viet Cong off balance.[66]

Not surprisingly, the plan encountered criticism in U.S. military circles. Some of it might have been motivated simply by pique that Thompson had not consulted with U.S. officials as much as the British had promised, but there were clearly differences in substance. Ambassador Nolting reported that he agreed with much of Thompson's paper and called it an admirable conceptual statement for counterinsurgency operations. But he predicted that it could arouse difficulties by allowing Diem the opportunity to bypass his chain of command and retain control of operations in his own hands. General McGarr was harsher in his judgment, contending that its static security approach ignored the need for sizable conventional military forces and would take too long to implement.[67]

In Washington, however, Thompson's ideas received more sympathetic attention in quarters where the more conventional military approach was not popular. Significantly, even Maxwell Taylor was interested. In January 1962 Taylor recommended that the president give serious consideration to a similar plan entitled "A strategic concept for South Vietnam," which had been developed within the Washington bureaucracy. The author of the plan was Roger Hilsman, head of the Bureau of Intelligence and Research (INR) in the Department of State and a leading advocate of a primarily political counterinsurgency approach within the Kennedy administration. Hilsman had become familiar with the techniques of guerrilla war while serving with U.S. forces in Burma during World War II.

Hilsman's plan was based on three assumptions: that the problem in South Vietnam was more political than military, that a counterinsurgency program must provide the population with protection from the guerrillas, and that counterinsurgency forces must use the same tactics as the guerrillas. Like Thompson, Hilsman wanted a program based on strategic hamlets, beginning with highly populated areas like the Mekong Delta and along the central coast. And he agreed with Thompson that ARVN should be employed primarily to keep the Viet Cong off balance in areas already under Viet Cong control. It would be similar to the MAAG plan in that it would be a three-phase process from secure regions to insecure areas along the borders.

Hilsman presented his plan to the president on his return from a visit to Saigon in late January. Kennedy had instructed Hilsman and NSC staff member Michael Forrestal to make a trip to South Vietnam and submit a report presenting their ideas on their return. Kennedy was apparently impressed with Hilsman's ideas and instructed him to prepare a formal report while briefing other agencies of the government on its benefits. A few days later Hilsman discussed his paper with the Joint Chiefs, who were less impressed. They disliked the command arrangements and the downgrading of conventional tactics and did not recommend implementation of the proposal. But the general concept already had won approval in the White House, and eventually the administration agreed to support a modified version of the Thompson plan.[68]

Support at the highest level enabled Thompson to bypass disagreements with U.S. military representatives in Saigon. He agreed to compromise on the problem of command arrangements and also to delay giving priority to the police because they were not yet ready to handle security responsibilities. Diem gave his approval of the plan on March 19.

By early 1962, then, the Kennedy administration had formulated a strategy to defeat the communist insurgency in South Vietnam. For the moment, the debate between advocates of a political or military approach had been resolved in favor of the former. At the heart of the new program was the building of strategic hamlets to provide security for the population against the Viet Cong and create the basis for extending government control to the entire population. The U.S. role would be in the form of a "limited partnership" to supply materials and advice through growing adviser corps at all levels. But Hilsman and Thompson were not to have the last word. Diem and the Pentagon applied the program in their own fashion, while Hanoi watched and drew its own conclusions.[69]

Counterinsurgency in Action

From the start, Washington and Saigon differed over the implementation of the program. U.S. officials wanted to begin with a relatively secure area and move gradually into less secure regions, whereas Diem preferred to begin in Binh Duong province, an insecure area near Zone D, where, according to one estimate, only 10 of 46 villages were secure. Diem opposed a sweep into Zone D itself, which in his view would simply close the string on an empty bag, undermine morale, and achieve nothing. Washington gave in, and Operation Sunrise was Diem's operation from the start. It began on March 22, 1962, with Diem's brother Ngo Dinh Nhu in charge. He called for a threefold effort at social revolution—against divisive forces, the low standard of living, and communism.

The ultimate test of the new program, of course, lay in its ability to reduce the communist threat in the South. If some policymakers in Washington were correct, it would (to use Mao Zedong's famous metaphor) dry up the "sea" in which the guerrilla "fish" swam and eventually bring the insurgency to an end.

President Kennedy had attempted to resolve the tensions between advocates of a political or a military approach in Vietnam by a compromise program that in the end satisfied neither. In its stress on the importance of nation-building and strategic hamlets, the initial program reflected the views of those who maintained that the primary problem was political in nature. But Kennedy shied away from applying overt pressure on Diem in the hope that he could be brought to realize the necessity of basic changes in his administration and style of leadership. At the same time, he attempted to pacify the Pentagon by setting up a military command in Vietnam to provide a clear focus for the military effort.

As a result, the compromise achieved little. The bureaucratic tensions were softened, at least at the senior level. Ambassador Frederick Nolting, despite his evident discomfort with arrangements that undermined his leading role in the Country Team, attempted to cooperate with the new MACV commander, General Paul Harkins, and by all reports their personal relationship was excellent. But for policy, the arrangement was less successful because U.S. military officers in Saigon carried out their operations with little deference to the overall strategical objectives of the program.

One example of this tendency was the issue of using defoliants. President Kennedy had approved a limited program to use defoliants to destroy some mangrove swamps in unpopulated areas in the Mekong Delta. In early 1962, Diem requested that they be used in a crop destruction program to be carried out in areas invested by the Viet Cong. The Pentagon approved the program, and after some consideration, Ambassador Nolting gave his approval, subject to reevaluation and if undertaken on a case-by-case basis. But some civilian members of the Vietnam Task Force, supported by key senior officials in the administration such as Averell Harriman and United States Information Agency Director Edward R. Murrow, were concerned that the program might alienate the civilian population, while raising the specter of chemical warfare and damaging the reputation of the United States in world opinion. Kennedy himself was reluctant to undertake it, but when the Saigon regime became more insistent he relented and authorized it under strict conditions.[70]

The Kennedy administration attempted to monitor the success of the new program by setting up links between the U.S. mission and local South Vietnamese officials implementing the program in the field. But from the start, Diem resisted U.S. interference. He refused permission for U.S. provincial survey teams to evaluate the political situation in villages and limited their authority to reporting on military operations and intelligence. He also rejected a request by the United States Operations Mission to authorize it to bypass ministries in Saigon (which were notorious for their incompetence and inefficiency) to deal directly with the provinces.

In the eyes of many U.S. observers, the strategic hamlets were the key to the success of the program. During the spring of 1962, the Saigon regime undertook an ambitious program to build them throughout the country. The objective was to have 6,000 hamlets in operation by December 1962 and to complete the program by the end of the following year. By July there were already 2,400 in place. Many U.S. observers worried that the program would be too superficial and alienate the rural population.

Soon there were signs that such concerns were justified and that the regime was committing the same errors it had committed with the agrovilles in the late 1950's. Compulsory resettlement, lack of construction materials, and the government's refusal to pay the farmers for their labor caused widespread resentment. The U.S. mission approached Diem with a suggestion to provide various incentives to win the approval of the local population, but he demurred, pointing out that the peasants had plenty of time on their hands and needed no pay. To deal with the shortage of materials, the United States planned to provide a "hamlet kit" of useful materials for construction and defense, but unfortunately the kits would not be ready until the end of 1963. In the meantime, Robert K. G. Thompson worried that ARVN was assigned all the security tasks, leaving little responsibility to the people.

Despite these blemishes, Washington officials were cautiously optimistic that the strategic hamlet program was on the right path. On a visit to Saigon in May, Robert S. McNamara reported "restrained optimism" about the program and felt that victory was "clearly obtainable." The strategic hamlets continued to proliferate, reaching over 3,000 units by September.[71]

Although the administration still instructed U.S. officials in South Vietnam to refrain from criticizing Diem's behavior, nonofficial observers were under no such restrictions. Articles critical of the Saigon regime by members of the Michigan State advisory team led to the cancellation of its program in public administration in February. Even Wesley Fishel, a professor of political science from Michigan State and one of Diem's closest foreign friends and supporters, wrote that he was increasingly pessimistic because of the "most profound and distressing deterioration there." The escalation of the U.S. military effort was a salutary development, he said, but it was only enough to "warm the fingers and toes."[72]

Diem also encountered increasing criticism from the foreign press, which had begun to complain about the regime's propensity to censor critical articles. In early 1962, the government ordered the expulsion of journalist Homer Bigart of the *New York Times* and *Newsweek* reporter François Sully. Ambassador Nolting shared some of Diem's frustration with the increasingly critical tone of the journalistic community in Saigon, but he was concerned that Diem's harsh response could lead to an increasingly negative attitude within the press corps and undermine support for the program in Congress. Nolting was able to persuade Diem to rescind the expulsion order, but the problem continued, and the regime banned *Newsweek* in September. An NBC correspondent was expelled the following month.[73]

Diem's problems with the press caused anguish in Washington, which was receiving concerned cables on the subject from John Mecklin, director of USIA operations in Saigon. The administration attempted to persuade the regime to adopt a more tolerant attitude and asked the *New York Times* to transfer its reporter David Halberstam, one of Saigon's harshest critics, but both requests were rejected.

The Saigon press corps, however, was equally critical of the U.S. Embassy for not permitting journalists to accompany U.S. military personnel on combat operations such as Operation Farmgate, a program involving a squadron of T-28s, a training plane capable of carrying out limited combat operations. The plane had two pilots, a South Vietnamese and an American. The latter was technically assigned as a flight instructor but sometimes flew the plane in support of ARVN combat operations. Washington attempted to deal with the issue by allowing Nolting the discretion to permit journalists to participate in selected operations. But that did not resolve the essential issue of covert U.S. participation in combat operations, a role the White House vigorously denied. The administration conceded that the U.S. role had increased but called press reports of a U.S. combat role "factually wrong" and "lacking in perspective." Like Diem in dealing with the press, the administration bungled its attempt to handle the issue and eventually aroused concern in Congress.[74]

The new counterinsurgency program did indeed cause problems for Hanoi and its followers in the South. The decisions taken in Washington in November 1961, combined with the creation of MACV in January, confused commanders of the insurgency in the South and were convincing evidence to Hanoi that, despite its own efforts, the United States was prepared to escalate its role in the conflict. A COSVN conference held in October 1961 had analyzed the situation in the light of existing instructions from Hanoi and posed the possibility that an escalation by Washington could force the revolutionary movement to abandon its emphasis on a general uprising and force it into a total war similar to that which had taken place during the conflict against the French.

But at a meeting in Hanoi the following February, the Politburo concluded that although U.S. escalation complicated the task of completing national reunification, it did not essentially shift the balance of forces in South Vietnam. The enemy, it insisted, remained confused and divided, and the United States still hoped to avoid a major escalation of the war. In the meantime, the position of the revolution in the South had become stronger with the establishment of COSVN, the PLAF, and a broad united front against the Diem regime. In the months after its founding, revolutionary leaders in the South fleshed out the new NLF with a series of mass organizations based on gender, age, occupation, ethnic background, or religious belief. Of particular importance was the Farmers' Liberation Association, which attempted to win support from the rural population by promising to carry out a program to redistribute land from wealthy landowners to the poor. To win the support of women, a Women's Liberation Association was established on the promise of achieving sexual equality in a society that still practiced traditional Confucian norms of male superiority. In succeeding years, women played an active role in the movement, not only in the NLF but also in the armed forces, where some served in guerrilla units or in the village self-defense militia. To knit the movement closely to the central authorities in Hanoi, a branch of the VWP, formally known as the People's Revolutionary Party (PRP), was established in 1962 to provide an organizational framework for party members working in the South.

Based on the success already attained in the effort to build rice-roots support for the movement throughout the southern provinces, the Politburo in its February resolution reiterated the importance of balancing political and military struggle, maintaining the initiative, and strengthening revolutionary base areas. The primary immediate task was to destroy the strategic hamlets, using a combination of political and military techniques. The resolution cautioned against adventurism or excessive optimism and called for tactics of protracted war and self-reliance.[75]

Toward Peace in Laos

While Hanoi was attempting to cope with rapidly changing circumstances in South Vietnam, Washington was focusing its attention once more on Laos, where there was serious concern that the weak government and armed forces of rightist prime minister Phoumi Nousavan might collapse. In January, the Pathet Lao had besieged the northern mountain city of Nam Tha, not far from the border with Burma and China. The administration debated intervention, but sentiment in Congress appeared strongly hostile to direct U.S. military involvement, and some influential figures such as Senator Richard Russell of Georgia advised the president to get out of Laos. To assuage nervousness in Bangkok over a possible U.S. departure from Southeast Asia, the administration signed the so-called Thanat-Rusk Communique, a bilateral guarantee that the United States would meet its SEATO obligations in Thailand, even in the absence of support from other signatories of the pact. It also sent a division of U.S. troops to Thailand, a force too small to intervene in Laos but sufficient to signal to the enemy the dangers involved in violating the cease-fire.[76]

In May, as negotiations on a coalition government at Geneva continued without result, Pathet Lao forces tightened their grip on the perimeter of Nam Tha, and Laotian government troops fled in panic. Fearful that the fall of Laos could leave both Thailand and South Vietnam undefended, the administration once again turned to the threat of intervention, sending a signal that if communist pressure intensified, the United States would occupy lower Laos. Assistant Secretary Harriman and Roger Hilsman prepared a memo recommending a series of military moves to establish Washington's credibility and bring about a compromise at Geneva, including the dispatch of the Seventh Fleet to the Gulf of Thailand and the transfer of a U.S. battle group in Thailand to the Laotian border.

Kennedy approved the first recommendation but delayed on the second until senior Pentagon officials could be consulted. In a series of NSC meetings in mid-May, the president, with the consent of McNamara and the Joint Chiefs, approved the troop movement as a signal to Hanoi. But the disagreement between advocates of a political or a military solution now resurfaced. The former recommended a strategy calling for occupation of the lowland areas east of the Mekong, but not beyond the cease-fire line, to avoid provoking an escalation of the conflict. The latter called for the seizure of the entire Laotian panhandle to cut off infiltration, combined with possible ground and air attacks on North Vietnam.

No immediate decision was taken on these contingency plans, and in the end they were not needed because Pathet Lao forces failed to advance following their victory at Nam Tha, and Khrushchev agreed to the creation of a neutral Laos and assured Washington that Hanoi would comply with treaty provisions that prohibited the use of Laotian territory for infiltration into South Vietnam. Even U.S. advocates of an agreement were not optimistic that Hanoi would comply fully with its provisions, but they voiced the hope that the treaty would compel the North Vietnamese to be more circumspect in shipping men and matériel into the South. The final agreement, calling for a tripartite government of rightists, centrists, and revolutionaries under Prime Minister Souvanna Phouma and a division of the country into two separate zones administered by the Lao government and the Pathet Lao, was signed on July 23.[77]

Reassessment in Hanoi

On April 20, 1962, while negotiations on Laos were still under way, a high North Vietnamese official suggested that a new Geneva Conference be called to discuss the conflict in South Vietnam. Hanoi's initiative was based on the assumption that the "Laotian model" of a negotiated end to the conflict could be applied in South Vietnam. In a message to southern leaders in July, VWP first secretary Le Duan explained the thinking of the party Politburo on the subject. Le Duan conceded that the U.S. objective in Laos was different than it was in South Vietnam. Because Laos had a direct border with China, the Kennedy administration would be less likely to intervene directly there than in South Vietnam, where the only direct adversary was the DRV. But party leaders were also convinced that Washington was reluctant to intervene directly in the conflict in the South and believed that if not forced to the wall, the United States might be willing to accept a negotiated settlement, even if it were a defeat in disguise.

For that reason, as well as to preserve world peace (Le Duan's code phrase referring to warnings from Moscow and Beijing not to let the Indochina conflict get out of hand), Hanoi had instructed the Pathet Lao to refrain from taking advantage of their victory at Nam Tha to push for total victory in Laos. "How far we win, and how far they lose," he said, "is very important." The victory achieved by Laotian revolutionary forces at Geneva was a direct consequence of this strategy. Greater military efforts might have forced the United States into direct military intervention in the conflict. Full victory in Laos could be secured after the final triumph of communist forces in South Vietnam.[78]

With that purpose in mind, Hanoi called on southern leaders to place heightened emphasis on the importance of political struggle in preparation for possible negotiations. The united front in the South was to be broadened to include groups reluctant to join the NLF but willing to join in the struggle against the Diem regime. Individuals owing a secret allegiance to the party were to maintain their neutral status in public so that they could be called upon to serve as an "under the blanket" group of pro-NLF neutral forces in a possible coalition government formed as the result of a peace settlement. Such groups could then cooperate with the NLF faction in completing the unification process.[79]

Hanoi's idea of a negotiated settlement, then, called for the creation of a coalition government patterned after the tripartite model in Laos and the withdrawal of U.S. forces from the South. It was a solution that would avoid an abject humiliation of the United States but at the same time would represent a serious long-term strategic defeat for U.S. containment policy. It was predicated on the possibility that Washington was more concerned about the psychological impact of a defeat in South Vietnam than about the concrete impact such an eventuality would have on U.S. security interests in Asia.

In the meantime, party strategists set out to find ways to counter the enemy's strategic hamlet program, which had caused some confusion among political cadres and commanding officers of the PLAF. One captured document, apparently written for the benefit of local operatives in the South, listed

"eight lessons" on how to destroy the strategic hamlets and bring the population under the authority of the NLF. The preferable means was to destroy the
hamlets by frontal assault. If that was not successful, they should be infiltrated
and overthrown from within by a combination of military pressure, political
manipulation, the selective use of terror, and psychological techniques. Local
echelons were instructed not to become impatient and to return to the attack
even after the hamlets were rebuilt until the government presence in the area
had finally been eliminated.

Washington Rejects Negotiations

The idea of a negotiated settlement was indeed still under discussion in
Washington. Chester Bowles, the author of an abortive proposal the previous
year, raised the issue again in a memo to the president of April 4. Bowles
suggested that if the situation in Vietnam approached the point of stalemate,
the United States should move toward a negotiated settlement involving the
neutralization of Southeast Asia, the dissolution of SEATO, and a bilateral
guarantee of the independence of Thailand. On the same day, Ambassador
Galbraith wrote his own appeal to the president. Warning that the situation was
beginning to resemble the Franco-Vietminh conflict, he appealed to Kennedy
to keep the door open for a diplomatic solution.[80]

Kennedy showed the Galbraith memo to Harriman, who said he agreed on
some points but not others. Like Galbraith, he wanted to keep U.S. military
involvement to a minimum but did not think a peace conference or neutralization was advisable at this time. He agreed with Galbraith that Diem was a
"losing horse," but he saw no alternative. He concluded that a decision should
be delayed until Washington had a better idea of the situation in South Vietnam. Kennedy agreed but added that he wanted "to seize any favorable moment
to reduce our involvement" and authorized Galbraith to approach the government of India as a possible contact with the DRV. For the moment, he instructed Harriman to discuss the memo with McNamara. The latter rejected
Galbraith's implied parallel with the situation before the Geneva Conference
and said that a withdrawal would be "tantamount to abandoning South Vietnam to the Communists." This view was backed up by the Joint Chiefs, who
answered McNamara's request for comments by arguing that any reversal of
U.S. policy "could have disastrous effects, not only upon our relationship with
South Vietnam, but with the rest of our Asian and other allies as well."[81]

Kennedy's trial balloon on a negotiated settlement in South Vietnam thus
ran into heavy criticism within the administration, and at a meeting of the National Security Council on May 1 the Galbraith proposal was formally dropped
after both Roger Hilsman and Averell Harriman publicly opposed the idea. The
proposal to apply the Laotian model to South Vietnam continued to arouse

some interest in the White House, however, and caused considerable nervousness in Saigon. In a letter to Diem on July 9, President Kennedy tried to reassure him that Washington was well aware that the situation in South Vietnam was quite different from that in Laos. But Diem's concerns were not entirely without foundation, for Kennedy had instructed Harriman to broach the idea of a peace conference on South Vietnam with North Vietnamese representatives at Geneva. On July 22, at the invitation of a Burmese official, Averell Harriman had an informal discussion with DRV foreign minister Ung Van Khiem. According to the published record of the meeting, however, both sides limited themselves to a repetition of their standard positions, and the meeting ended without result.[82]

For the remainder of Kennedy's life, White House interest in a peace conference, fragile in any case, virtually evaporated. What had happened to scuttle the fragile hopes for a negotiated settlement? Undoubtedly one factor was the accumulating evidence that Hanoi was ignoring the provisions of the Geneva Accords that called for the withdrawal of Vietnamese forces from Laos. The settlement was supposed to provide for the withdrawal of foreign forces and the prohibition of any use of Laotian territory for infiltration into the RVN. But it soon became clear that a significant number of Vietnamese troops had remained in Laos after the accords (William Bundy quoted intelligence estimates to the effect that 6,000 of the 10,000 Vietnamese troops stayed in Laos after the signing of the agreement) and that, despite assurances to the contrary by Soviet officials at the Geneva Conference, infiltration was continuing at a significant, if not increased, level. In late November, Walt W. Rostow proposed that the issue be raised with Soviet Politburo member Anastas Mikoyan during the latter's visit to the United States, but the idea was rejected by the president.[83]

Hanoi's failure to abide by the Geneva Accords was no surprise to most officials in Washington, although it was undoubtedly evidence that the DRV could not be trusted to comply with agreements on other matters. Harriman was pessimistic that Hanoi would conform to the agreement and at best would behave in a more circumspect manner to avoid international criticism. But Harriman also wanted the administration to be scrupulous in its own observance of the terms of the agreement so that in any transgression, the onus would be on the other side. Kennedy agreed, and the administration took no action to bring attention to the issue. In the view of Walt W. Rostow, the failure to act decisively on the matter of infiltration was "the greatest single error in American policy in the 1960s."[84]

An additional reason why the Kennedy administration did not pursue the negotiating track in South Vietnam was that in the summer of 1962, for the first time in months, Washington was guardedly optimistic about the situation in Vietnam. Although some were skeptical, the first statistical evaluations of the new strategic hamlets were hopeful. Saigon sources reported that Viet Cong attacks were temporarily on the decline, creating a mood of cautious optimism that the program had turned the corner. This fragmentary evidence of improving conditions provided President Kennedy with a new opening to reduce the U.S. presence in South Vietnam. After the affair of the Galbraith memo in April, Kennedy began to urge Robert McNamara to draw up preliminary plans to begin the phased withdrawal of U.S. forces from the RVN. With continuing indications of success emanating from Saigon, the plan was made operational on July 23 during a visit by Secretary McNamara to the RVN. Withdrawal would begin at the end of 1963 from a peak of 12,000 and would decline to less than 2,000 in fiscal year 1968 (or sooner, if the possibility arose), when remaining personnel would consist of just headquarters and MAAG elements.[85]

Recent evidence suggests that the picture of progress might have been deliberately fabricated by U.S. military sources in Saigon and that evidence to the contrary began to filter back to Washington during the summer months. Whatever the truth of that charge, during the next few months there was a spurious sense of optimism throughout much of the Washington bureaucracy that the counterinsurgency program was working. In a meeting in Honolulu in July, McNamara reported "tremendous progress" in bringing the insurgency to an end and called for a gradual shift of responsibility to ARVN forces. General Paul Harkins proposed a major offensive by ARVN troops to take advantage of the disarray in the enemy camp, and Ambassador Nolting signaled his approval. A paper drafted by the State Department in October claimed that the Viet Cong were no longer winning the war and that there was a new sense of confidence in the South that the RVN would win. Buoyed by this false sense of progress, the White House inaugurated plans for a gradual disengagement of U.S. forces from South Vietnam.[86]

But that sense of optimism was not universal. In a memorandum written to Deputy Assistant Secretary of State for Far Eastern Affairs Edward E. Rice in August, Joseph Mendenhall warned that the overall trend in the South remained in favor of the communists and that the key problem was the continued alienation of the population by Diem and his brother Ngo Dinh Nhu. The U.S. consul in Hué reported that in Central Vietnam, the strategic hamlets were a facade and the regime had not yet won the allegiance of the local rural population. Averell Harriman was critical of the excessive optimism coming out of the U.S. mission in Saigon, and press reports by Western journalists in South Vietnam continued their relentless criticism of the regime and the failure of the U.S. mission there to grasp the reality of the situation.[87]

In November, at the request of the president, Senator Mike Mansfield led a senatorial group on a brief trip to Southeast Asia to evaluate the situation and report back to the White House. On his return, Mansfield discussed his conclusions in a personal conversation with Kennedy at Palm Beach in mid-December. In his report, he warned that although there was still a chance that the administration's counterinsurgency program would succeed, the target date for success—one or two years—was too optimistic. Moreover, Mansfield expressed serious reservations over the capacity of the current leadership in Saigon to carry out the task successfully. President Diem remained "a dedicated, sincere, hardworking, incorruptible and patriotic leader," but he was growing older and power was passing to his brother Ngo Dinh Nhu, who was talented but ambitious and fascinated with the manipulation of power. If present remedies did not work, he warned, there would be great temptation in Washington to make a massive U.S. military commitment, which he "most emphatically" did not recommend. "It is their country, their future which is most at stake," he emphasized, "not ours." Mansfield concluded by questioning whether it would not be preferable for the United States to reduce its commitments to the area while relying on a "vigorous diplomacy" to protect its interests and prevent a catastrophic unheaval in the region.[88]

Mansfield's gloomy estimate of the situation in South Vietnam (which was eventually released to the press and caused a stir in both Washington and Saigon) was evidently a considerable shock to the president. According to one confidant, he initially reacted with anger but ultimately found himself agreeing with Mansfield's estimate. It may have been as a way to assess Mansfield's conclusions that Kennedy asked Roger Hilsman and NSC staffer Michael Forrestal to undertake a short visit to Saigon at the end of the year to report on the situation. On their return in early January, they concluded that although there were signs of improvement in South Vietnam, the enemy was also stronger, and progress was slower than had been anticipated. They were particularly critical of the lack of coordination between political and military objectives in the war. In a secret annex meant only for the president, they recommended the replacement of Ambassador Nolting and suggested that contacts with opposition elements in South Vietnam be increased in case of a change of government in Saigon.[89]

As the year 1962 came to an end, then, there was considerable ambivalence in Washington over the situation in South Vietnam and a sense of growing frustration among senior officials that with all the information being provided, much of it in the form of statistics, a clear picture of what was taking place there was as elusive as ever.

A Perilous Situation

In his report to the president in December, Mike Mansfield had warned that although Hanoi was temporarily off balance, it would be unwise to assume that an enemy so determined and resourceful would not be able to devise new ways to cope with the challenge of the moment. Mansfield's view was prescient. Party leaders in Hanoi and the leadership in the South were indeed encountering problems in dealing with the strategic hamlets and the new mobility of

ARVN (the latter a consequence of the introduction of U.S. helicopters). In December, the Politburo met to consider ways to deal with the new situation. It concluded that the conflict in South Vietnam had become a full-fledged war and that the armed struggle must therefore be strengthened. While efforts to take advantage of the movement's political superiority must be maintained, a heightened emphasis was placed on the need to build up the PLAF to battalion level to destroy the strategic hamlets and strengthen liberated base areas in the Central Highlands and the Mekong Delta.[90]

The Politburo's call for a more aggressive attitude had quick results. After months of reacting to Saigon's initiatives, the VC struck back. In early January, at a village called Ap Bac near the Mekong Delta city of My Tho, the PLAF imposed a severe defeat on ARVN units supported by helicopters. Three American advisers were killed in the skirmish. Communist sources claimed nineteen U.S. dead and eight helicopters downed. According to a historical account in Hanoi, the battle showed the coming of age of the new revolutionary armed forces and had "important historical significance" in defeating the helicopter strategy of the enemy and shattering the confidence of ARVN.[91]

Later, VWP first secretary Le Duan would comment on the battle that the enemy now realized it would be difficult to achieve a military victory in South Vietnam. There is no doubt that it shook the confidence of some U.S. observers in Saigon (John Paul Vann, a prominent U.S. military adviser, labeled South Vietnamese soldiers "cowards" in the press), and coverage of the incident by foreign reporters was highly critical of ARVN's performance. But Le Duan was undoubtedly overstating the case (presumably he received his impressions from media sources in the United States), for senior U.S. officials remained relatively optimistic about the overall situation. Ambassador Nolting insisted that the war was going better than news reports suggested, and a team of military officers led by Army Chief of Staff General Earle C. Wheeler returned from a brief trip to Vietnam in late January with the optimistic conclusion that in the absence of increased pressure from the communists, "we are winning slowly on the present thrust." General Wheeler noted the need for an improvement in South Vietnamese combat capabilities and warned that Ho Chi Minh must be brought to account "for helping to keep the insurgency in South Vietnam alive," but he insisted that unless Hanoi was prepared to escalate the conflict, "the ingredients for eventual success" had already been assembled. To deter Hanoi, he proposed covert operations against North Vietnam or even reprisal air strikes against specific targets in the DRV.[92]

Washington's confidence about the situation in South Vietnam was dependent, of course, not only on the assumption of improved performance by ARVN forces but also on the continued stability of the Diem regime. Diem had critics in Washington, and some administration figures were increasingly convinced that the war could not be won as long as he was in charge in Saigon. On their return from South Vietnam in early January, Roger Hilsman and Michael Forrestal had reported that alienation against Ngo Dinh Diem and his family was on the increase, even among senior officials of the Saigon regime, and Chester Bowles returned to the attack with a memo to the president in early March. Bowles stated that he was deeply alarmed about the situation and suggested that the United States should make clear its openness to "alternative leadership" should Diem prove resistant to Washington's pleas to reform.

Press coverage by foreign reporters in Saigon was also growing increasingly hostile, and relations between South Vietnamese officials and foreign journalists covering the war had become chronically antagonistic. When asked by Washington if something could not be done to alleviate the problem, Ambassador Nolting replied that although part of the responsibility lay with the RVN, which was inordinately sensitive to criticism, the crux of the problem was that many U.S. journalists in South Vietnam were young and inexperienced and thus found it difficult to present a balanced view of the situation. He recommended a greater effort by the administration to present the facts about the war to editors of major newspapers in the United States.

There is some evidence that under the persuasion of such longtime associates as Senator Mike Mansfield, Kennedy was having new doubts about the increasingly perilous situation in Saigon. Sometime in early 1963 he called Mansfield into his office and told him that he now agreed on the need for a complete military withdrawal from South Vietnam beginning in early 1965, after the presidential election. Later he told Mansfield that he had changed his mind and that he wanted to begin withdrawing troops beginning early in 1964.

Was Kennedy now determined to pull out of South Vietnam even under conditions that might lead to a communist victory? The evidence is not clear, but Kennedy's aide Kenneth O'Donnell apparently thought so. After Mansfield's departure, the president told him: "In 1965, I'll become one of the most unpopular Presidents in history. I'll be damned everywhere as a Communist appeaser. But I don't care. If I tried to pull out completely now from Vietnam, we would have another Joe McCarthy scare on our hands, but I can do it after I'm reelected. So we had better make damned sure that I *am* reelected."[93]

While Kennedy wrestled with his private doubts about the war, other members of the administration began to give serious consideration to finding a replacement for Ngo Dinh Diem. The problem was that there were few signs that a viable "alternative leadership" existed. In a brief visit to the White House in early April, British counterinsurgency expert Robert G. K. Thompson asserted that the quality of the opposition was "poor." He predicted that if Diem were to be overthrown, the war could be lost in six months. On balance, most senior officials were inclined to stick with Diem, at least as long as progress was being achieved in the war against the Viet Cong. There was a general consensus that hostility to the regime still existed and there remained the ever-present danger of a coup, but some felt that the discontent was manageable as long as the administration kept its attention on the main threat from the communists.

On April 17, a National Intelligence Estimate reported that although there were some trouble spots in the war, the overall situation was improving. Under the surface, however, relations between the United States and the RVN were reaching a crisis point. Administration efforts to induce the Saigon regime to reform, combined with the growing U.S. presence in the RVN, provoked strong resistance from Diem and his immediate entourage. In early April he bluntly rejected a U.S. request for greater participation in implementing the counter-insurgency program, and there were open reports that Ngo Dinh Nhu planned to demand a reduction in the number of U.S. personnel in the RVN. Public Affairs Director John Mecklin advised Washington that U.S. criticism of the regime had created a "perilous situation" because Diem was bound to react, one way or another. An open break between the two governments could create a paradoxical situation, he noted. It would certainly damage the administration's policies in U.S. public opinion, but it might also induce the Saigon regime to "go along with us at the pressure points." Either way, Mecklin felt that it was essential to turn the struggle decisively against the communists before deterioration set in.[94]

The Buddhist Crisis

The spark that reignited the lingering doubts within the administration about the capacity of Ngo Dinh Diem to lead his country to victory over the Viet Cong was the Buddhist crisis that erupted in early May. The first incident took place on May 8, when Buddhist groups in Hué protested a government order prohibiting the displaying of Buddhist flags on a religious holy day. Buddhist leaders were especially upset because local authorities had taken no action when Catholic groups had displayed religious banners during a celebration of their own earlier in the year. To make matters worse, the Buddhist protests were suppressed by police with the loss of several lives. The responsibility for the bloodshed has never been explained. Buddhist sources blamed the government, but Diem refused to accept responsibility and claimed that the Viet Cong had provoked the incident. Some sources claimed that Americans were involved. Whatever the case, the incident renewed suspicion among Buddhist groups at the regime's alleged favoritism to Catholics and led to angry speeches and demonstrations at pagodas in and around Saigon and other South Vietnamese cities.

In Washington, the administration reviewed its contingency plans for the possible emergence of a new government in Saigon and a plan prepared for the director of the Vietnam Working Group in the State Department concluded that "the U.S. role should, if possible, be limited to indicating discreetly, but clearly the conditions under which the U.S. would recognize and support a new government." Should further steps be required, the paper recommended that the ambassador be authorized to act on his own judgment to prevent a "dangerous interregnum." In the meantime, it instructed Nolting to remonstrate with Diem about the regime's treatment of the Buddhist issue. Nolting spoke with Diem on the eighteenth and urged him to take action to reduce Buddhist irritation and calm the crisis. A few days later, Nolting left for an extended family vacation in the Mediterranean.[95]

After Nolting's departure, the tension escalated, as Buddhists held protest meetings in pagodas and some began to conspire actively for Diem's overthrow. President Diem attempted to defuse the anger by meeting with moderate elements among the Buddhist leadership, but actions and statements by Ngo Dinh Nhu and his wife raised anger to an even higher pitch. On June 11, the world was shocked when an elderly monk, Thich Quang Duc, set himself afire and burned to death on a street in downtown Saigon. Madame Nhu inflamed the situation further when she joked that she would be prepared to furnish the gasoline for "bonze barbecues." With American public opinion increasingly hostile, Washington instructed U.S. chargé William Trueheart (at his own suggestion) to warn Diem that if the South Vietnamese government did not act to defuse the crisis, the administration would publicly dissociate itself from the regime's actions.[96]

Diem agreed to open negotiations with the Buddhists. Talks began on the fourteenth and resulted in a compromise agreement permitting the Buddhists to fly their flag at religious ceremonies. Diem continued to reject responsibility for the May 8 incident but promised that guilty officials would be punished. But his actions were too little and too late. Buddhist leaders were by now determined to force a confrontation with the regime and found Western reporters, many of them now impassioned opponents of the regime, all too ready to cooperate in publicizing their grievances. According to one scholar, CIA agents were openly consorting with Buddhist activists at the Xa Loi pagoda in downtown Saigon.[97]

In Washington, the administration appeared paralyzed by indecision. An intelligence estimate prepared in INR in late June predicted that the protests would continue and that, if so, a successful coup was likely. It was generally agreed that Diem could not be pressured into following U.S. advice, and, in fact, pressure from Washington only seemed to make the Ngos even more stubborn. Relations with Saigon were now at an all-time low. Ngo Dinh Nhu openly sneered at the United States, warning that Americans should be sent home and hinting that the regime was in touch with representatives from the North regarding a separate peace. It was still official U.S. policy to seek to avoid a coup. Nevertheless, some State Department officials, such as George Ball, Averell Harriman, and Roger Hilsman, argued that the administration should speak out publicly against Nhu's actions, whatever the risk.

Frederick Nolting, just back in Washington from his trip to Europe, disagreed with that approach, but he was about to be replaced as ambassador by Henry Cabot Lodge. Lodge's appointment was announced on June 27, and it was widely speculated that he had been selected to defuse partisan criticism of the administration's Vietnam policy and to serve as a strong voice to carry Washington's message to Vietnam. The appointment of the new ambassador aroused the suspicions of Ngo Dinh Diem, who had worked effectively with Nolting. "They can send ten Lodges," he said, "but I will not permit myself or my country to be humiliated, not if they train their artillery on this palace."[98]

Green Light to Saigon

The possibility of a coup was discussed at a meeting in the White House on July 4. In a briefing for the president, Roger Hilsman noted that there was an "activist element" among the Buddhists that provided some justification for Diem's fear that they wished to bring about the overthrow of his government. Hilsman noted Nolting's view that a coup would lead inevitably to civil war and added that, in his view, such an eventuality was possible but not inevitable. It was an encouraging sign, he said, that the war against the Viet Cong in the countryside had been going well despite the growing instability and protest in the major cities.[99]

On July 9, Nolting returned to Saigon to await his replacement, who was due to arrive in mid-August. Nolting immediately attempted to repair the damage that he felt had been caused by his deputy William Trueheart's blunt efforts to threaten Diem with U.S. retaliation, and he advised Washington not to reiterate its threat to dissociate itself from the Saigon regime. But anti-Diem elements in the State Department were skeptical of Nolting's optimism and argued successfully for a continuation of the policy of "watchful waiting." Their views were supported by a Special NIE issued on July 10, which concluded that the chances of a coup were "better than even" if Diem failed to carry out his promises to conciliate the opposition. The authors hedged on the consequences of a coup but predicted that with continued U.S. support, a noncommunist successor government could provide "reasonably effective leadership" for the war effort.[100]

Nolting held his ground and cabled that he was more sanguine about the situation than were those in Washington. But despite his efforts, the tensions between the regime and the Buddhists were too high to defuse and incidents continued. The regime vacillated between conciliation and desperate efforts to suppress the movement by force or intimidation. On August 12, Nolting met with Diem and elicited a promise that the government would not, as rumored, launch a new crackdown on the Buddhists. Diem was worried that the shift in ambassadors would mean a change of policy in Washington, but Nolting reassured him that he had heard on "highest authority" that no change was contemplated. Three days later, after a final plea to President Diem to take action to reduce tensions, Nolting left for the United States.[101]

Buddhist leaders such as Tri Quang did not moderate the volume of their own demands and called openly for revolt against the Diem regime. On August 21, at the request of South Vietnamese military commanders, the regime declared martial law. At virtually the same moment, perhaps taking advantage of the absence of an ambassador at the U.S. Embassy, Nhu ordered a raid on the pagodas, allegedly killing several bonzes and forcing several others to return to their own provinces. Nhu had for long been viewed as the eminence grise of the Saigon regime, and his provocative and even contemptuous flouting of U.S. sensitivities angered officials in Washington. When senior ARVN officers approached a U.S. Embassy officer with an appeal that the United States make it clear that it would withdraw support from the Saigon regime unless Diem agreed to remove his brother from a position of responsibility, the response from Washington was immediate. In a telegram dispatched on the twenty-fourth, Ambassador Lodge (who had arrived two days earlier) was authorized to inform the generals that the United States could no longer tolerate the presence of Nhu in a position of power. Diem "must be given a chance" to get rid of his brother, otherwise the United States was prepared to accept the obvious implication that it could no longer support Diem. Lodge was instructed to examine alternative leadership and to make plans "as to how we might bring about Diem's replacement if this should become necessary."[102]

The famous "green light" August 24 telegram had been drafted by Roger Hilsman, with assistance from George Ball, Michael Forrestal, and Averell Harriman, and was cleared by telephone by the president and other senior administration officials, many of whom were out of town for the summer weekend. In the absence of Rusk and CIA director John McCone, their deputies Roswell Gilpatric and Richard Helms signed the cable, as did JCS chief Maxwell Taylor.

The following day, Ambassador Lodge cabled from Saigon his opposition to approaching Diem with further demands for reform, an action that in his view would simply provide Nhu with the time to arrest the plotters. Instead he proposed that he be authorized to approach the generals directly, without informing Diem, and that it be left up to them whether to retain Diem. Lodge stated that he would take no action on his instructions until he had received an answer.[103]

It was in those conditions that the president opened a meeting of his senior advisers at the White House on Monday. By then, Rusk and McNamara had apparently developed misgivings about the cable because of the informal man-

ner of its transmission and its blunt ultimatum to Diem. Maxwell Taylor, for
one, now criticized the cable for its vagueness and its failure to provide Diem
with an opportunity to change his ways. The discussion was inconclusive, and
Kennedy closed the meeting with instructions that further meetings would have
to be held to discuss the matter.[104]

During the next few days, senior officials attended several meetings with
the president at the White House, and although no one in attendance openly
rejected the contents of the cable, many were reluctant to give approval to the
removal of Diem until it was clear that he would not agree to get rid of his
brother and that the prospects for a successful coup were strong. In the end, it
was agreed to delay a decision pending the receipt of additional information
from Ambassador Lodge on coup plans and the likelihood of success. A second
cable was sent to Lodge providing him with authority to suspend aid to the
RVN if he felt it was advisable.

You Can't Hurry the East

In Saigon, Lodge was dubious that Diem and Nhu could be separated
(Diem, he said, "wishes he had more Nhus, not less") and wanted to push
ahead with plans for the coup, but on August 31 the generals backed off, perhaps
out of uncertainty over support from ARVN sources as well as from Washington. General Harkins reported that there was an "organization de confusion" among the plotters and remarked that "you can't hurry the east." Lodge
was disgusted (dealing with the generals, he complained, was like "pushing a
piece of spaghetti"), but the delay provided Washington with a respite to evaluate the situation. On the same day, the NSC met under the chairmanship of
Vice-President Lyndon Johnson to evaluate the situation. The disagreement
that had characterized meetings the previous few days had not been bridged,
and the debate was often acrimonious. Paul Kattenburg, a foreign service officer who had just returned from a brief trip to Saigon, reported that opposition
to Diem was increasing within the armed forces and the bureaucracy, but
former ambassador Nolting repeated his contention that support for the regime was stronger in rural areas. Kattenburg cited a warning by Henry Cabot
Lodge that the United States might be forced out of South Vietnam within six
months. If that was the case, he suggested, it would be better to withdraw
honorably. But Kattenburg's suggestion elicited no support from senior officials. Two things must be decided, declared Secretary Rusk. First, he said, we
must agree that "we will not withdraw until the war is won, and we will not run
a coup." Lyndon Johnson agreed that there was no alternative to Diem and that
it would be a disaster to pull out.[105]

The ambivalence among administration officials over the situation in South

Vietnam was reflected in the mind of President Kennedy himself. In comments in the course of several meetings with senior officials during the final days of August, Kennedy appeared reluctant to give final approval for the coup and welcomed the opportunity to delay while attempting to obtain more information on the situation from the U.S. Embassy in Saigon. But the president was less concerned with the wisdom of replacing Diem than with the possibility that the effort would fail. It would be better to back off, he felt, than to be involved in an operation that did not succeed.

For the moment, then, the administration delayed a decision while seeking further information on the prospects of success and making a last effort to detach Diem from his brother. In a television interview with CBS newsman Walter Cronkite on September 2, Kennedy rejected a prepared script and bluntly criticized the Diem regime for being out of touch with the people. When asked if the GVN still had time to regain popular support, Kennedy replied that it could, "with changes in policy and perhaps with personnel." It was their war, he said, to win or to lose. But he qualified that remark by adding that he did not agree with those who recommended a U.S. withdrawal. That, he concluded, "would be a great mistake."[106]

During the next few days, while plans for a coup were on hold, administration policy shifted from the conspiratorial to the diplomatic track. Ngo Dinh Nhu offered to resign and retire to Dalat, but Washington was skeptical of his sincerity and detected a stalling tactic. At a meeting of the NSC on September 6, Robert Kennedy again attempted to return to first principles. If the RVN could not resist a communist takeover, he said, the United States should get out. If the war could be won, but not with Diem, then Washington should provide Lodge with sanctions to deal with the generals. Characteristically, no one had an answer to such questions, and the meeting ended with an agreement to send a new mission, composed of General Victor Krulak and foreign service officer Joseph Mendenhall, to "get the facts."[107]

Krulak and Mendenhall left for Saigon the same day and presented their report to the NSC on their return four days later. But their conclusions did not clarify the situation. To the contrary, they sharpened the debate within the administration. Krulak had spent the bulk of his time in the countryside, where he was informed by U.S. military sources that the war against the Viet Cong was still going fairly well. Mendenhall (a critic of the Diem regime since the late 1950's) remained in Saigon, where he learned from U.S. and Vietnamese contacts that discontent with the Diem regime had not subsided. The report changed few minds among those in attendance at the meeting, and no decisions were reached. A follow-up meeting at the State Department the same day revealed a widening gap between those (including Robert McNamara, Maxwell Taylor, and Victor Krulak) who felt that Diem should be retained and those

(such as Averell Harriman, Roger Hilsman, and Agency for International Development official Rufus Phillips) who felt that the war would not be won
unless Diem was replaced.[108]

One option for the administration in dealing with the Diem regime was to
use the threat of the suspension of economic or military aid as leverage to
pressure Saigon into reforming its ways. Up until mid-September, Washington
had taken no action on the matter and had provided Ambassador Lodge with
discretionary authority to threaten an aid cutoff if he saw fit. On the eleventh,
Lodge entered the debate with a lengthy and sometimes eloquent cable emphasizing the inevitability that the instability in Saigon would eventually undermine the war effort in the countryside. It was time, he said, to suspend the aid
program so as to bring about "a drastic change in government."[109]

Lodge's recommendation was too precipitate for cautious minds in Washington, who were not yet convinced that Diem could not be persuaded to
remove his brother from office. There was also some concern that an aid cutoff
would damage the war effort. In a meeting held to discuss Lodge's proposal on
the evening of the eleventh, Dean Rusk recalled the U.S. decision to terminate
its support for Chiang Kai-shek, a decision that resulted in a communist takeover of mainland China. For the moment, no decision was taken on the matter
(in frustration, NSC staffer Michael Forrestal complained that U.S. policy was
in a "position of stall" and suggested to McGeorge Bundy that the paralysis
could be resolved only by a presidential decision). To provoke a decision, Roger
Hilsman drafted two cables to Saigon, the first authorizing Lodge to threaten
an aid cutoff to coerce Diem into reducing Nhu's authority (the pressure and
persuasion track) and the other to attempt to achieve a reconciliation with
Diem (the reconciliation track) and salvage whatever could be saved from the
wreckage of the dispute.

On the seventeenth, senior administration officials met at the White House
and decided to inform Ambassador Lodge that for the time being, no action to
remove the present government was envisioned. Lodge was authorized to press
Diem to reduce his brother's authority and to suspend U.S. aid programs if
necessary to emphasize U.S. displeasure. Washington noted Lodge's reluctance
to talk further with Diem unless he had more to say but said that such discussions "may conceivably be a means of exerting some persuasive effect even in
his present state of mind." Lodge, who still favored a coup, was quick to cable a
testy response. All this had been tried before without success, complained
Lodge, and suspension of aid would only harm the economy.[110]

The decision represented a qualified victory for those such as Roger Hilsman and Averell Harriman who wanted a "get tough" policy with Diem, but the
president had decided to send General Maxwell Taylor and Robert McNamara
on yet another inspection trip to Saigon, a decision that exasperated both
Harriman (who felt that Taylor and McNamara opposed his views) and Lodge

(who argued that the decision would be seen in Saigon as a sign that Washington had decided to "forgive and forget"). Kennedy's motives are not clear, but it seems plausible that, as had been the case so many times previously, an inspection trip was a means to avoid an immediate decision in the hope that conditions would eventually make such a decision unnecessary.[111]

Taylor and McNamara arrived in Saigon on September 23 and remained for several days. Not surprisingly, they received an ambiguous picture of the situation in their briefings with U.S. and Vietnamese officials. That ambiguity was fully reflected in the report they presented to the president on October 2, in which they concluded that the war was still going well, although the political situation was perilous and threatened further progress. But the trip had exerted an impact, for McNamara had now been brought around to the view that Diem had to change or go. Although there was no immediate sign of new military plans for a coup, dissatisfaction among the urban elite was deeply disturbing, and political tension was high in the cities. Pressure from Washington would only harden attitudes in Saigon, but without such pressure, the regime would simply go on as before. The report recommended that no action be taken for the moment to replace Diem but to "seek urgently to identify and build contacts with an alternative leadership if and when it appears." Prospects that a successor regime would represent an improvement were only about 50-50. In the meantime, aid through the Commercial Import Program should be withheld from the RVN without formal announcement, and purely "correct" relations should be maintained with the Diem regime. The report did conclude that the fight against the Viet Cong had made some progress and recommended that preparations should be initiated to begin removing U.S. military personnel in 1964, with an initial withdrawal of 1,000 U.S. troops by the end of the present calendar year.[112]

After meeting with McNamara, Taylor, and other senior officials on October 2 and 5, Kennedy approved the McNamara-Taylor report as NSAM-263, and Lodge was informed by cable that although no active encouragement should be given to a coup, an urgent covert effort to identify alternative leadership should be undertaken in preparation for possible future action. Lodge replied the same day that clandestine U.S. sources had been in touch with General Duong Van Minh, who sought to clarify the U.S. attitude in the event of a change of government in Saigon. During succeeding days Lodge pressed Washington to reassure the generals that the United States would continue to aid a new government "which gives promise of gaining support of the people and winning the war against the Communists." In his effort to persuade the administration to act, Lodge was undoubtedly aided by indications in late October that the military balance had begun to shift perceptibly toward the communists. There were also persistent reports that with encouragement from the French ambassador the regime was flirting with Hanoi. According to an INR report issued on

October 22, the level of Viet Cong attacks had accelerated in recent weeks, while morale and efficiency within ARVN and the RVN was on the decline.[113]

But Washington was still nervous at the possibility that the coup could abort and pressed Lodge for details on the generals' plans. In a message to Lodge on the twenty-fifth, McGeorge Bundy stressed the administration's concerns. "We are particularly concerned," he said, "about hazard that an unsuccessful coup, however carefully we avoid direct engagement, will be laid at our door by public opinion almost everywhere." Washington had no desire to thwart a coup, he concluded, but would like "to have option of judging and warning on any plan with poor prospects of success."[114]

But the generals, concerned at the risk of disclosure, were unwilling to share their plans with the Americans. On October 28, General Tran Van Don, one of the coup leaders, informed Ambassador Lodge that a coup was imminent but would give no date and said that it would be a purely Vietnamese operation. Lodge cabled the news to Washington and said that, short of informing Diem and Nhu, the United States could not influence the course of events. But administration officials were still paralyzed by anxiety and pressed the embassy for more information from the coup group on the prospects for success because a miscalculation "could result in jeopardizing U.S. position in Southeast Asia." Lodge replied that although he agreed that a miscalculation could harm U.S. interests in Southeast Asia, there were equally tremendous risks in doing nothing. "If we were convinced that the coup was going to fail," he remarked, "we would, of course, do everything we could to stop it."[115]

Washington was not totally reassured, and in a hectic meeting on the twenty-ninth, several administration officials voiced their reluctance to approve the go-ahead without further assurances that the coup would succeed. In a cable dispatched the following evening, McGeorge Bundy instructed Lodge that if he became convinced that a coup could not succeed, he should endeavor to persuade the generals to wait until the chances were better. "But once a coup under responsible leadership had begun," the message concluded, "it is in the interest of the U.S. government that it should succeed."[116]

On November 1, Lodge, accompanied by General Harkins and visiting CINCPAC commander Admiral Harry Felt, visited President Diem at the Presidential Palace. Harkins vehemently opposed a coup. "We have backed Diem for eight long hard years," he told Maxwell Taylor in Washington, and it seemed incongruous to "kick him around, and get rid of him." Admiral Felt was aware of the coup plans but not of the details. Diem appeared unsuspecting that the visitors were aware of his impending fate, remarking to Lodge that he knew there would be a coup but not who was organizing it. He was conciliatory in his private talk with Lodge, whom he asked to inform President Kennedy that he hoped to carry out the reforms suggested by the United States in his own time. But he indicated a continuing reluctance to replace Nhu, who had just announced the release of Buddhist demonstrators from jail.[117]

The coup began on the afternoon of November 1, when rebel units seized government and military installations and demanded the resignation of the Diem regime. The president and his brother tried to enlist support from senior military officers in the capital area, but when it became clear that no support would be forthcoming, Diem called Ambassador Lodge to ask for U.S. support to suppress the coup. Lodge, however, said that he could not act without authorization from Washington and offered to grant the president and his family asylum at the U.S. Embassy. Diem demurred and escaped with his brother from the Presidential Palace via a secret passageway to a Catholic church in the Chinese suburb of Cholon. There they were picked up by military officers loyal to the plotters and murdered en route back to Saigon.

The assassination of Diem and Nhu was a shock to President Kennedy, but the success of the coup was greeted with relief in the White House, and on November 7, the United States issued a press release announcing its recognition of the new provisional government, now controlled by a handful of military commanders led by General Duong Van Minh. Two weeks later, Lodge met with senior U.S. officials in Honolulu to report on the situation and record his ideas on future U.S. actions to promote stability in Saigon and a continuation against insurgent forces in the countryside.

In a meeting on November 20, Lodge gave an essentially optimistic assessment of the prospects in South Vietnam. The generals, he said, "appeared to be united and determined to step up the war effort." They were aware of the importance of psychological and socioeconomic factors as key components of success and were agreed on the need to end coercion in connection with the strategic hamlet program and the practice of arbitrary arrests and disregard of habeas corpus. Lodge cautioned his listeners, however, that Washington should not pressure the new government to move too rapidly toward democratic practices on the Western model. Vietnam, he said, was not ready for government by election. General Harkins reported that Viet Cong incidents had risen markedly after the coup but had now subsided. After the close of the conference, Ambassador Lodge and the remainder of the party returned to the United States to report to the president. McGeorge Bundy prepared a draft memorandum embodying the results of the meeting for presidential consideration. Shortly after their arrival in Washington, John Kennedy was assassinated in Dallas.[118]

Conclusions

Few periods of the U.S. involvement in the Vietnam War are as marked by controversy as that of the Kennedy presidency. The adoption of the counterinsurgency program in the fall of 1961, which led to a substantial increase in U.S. involvement in the war, the 1962 settlement at Geneva, which led to the creation of a tripartite government under the leadership of the neutralist Souvanna Phouma in Laos, the decision to replace Ngo Dinh Diem, and the question of what President Kennedy would have done about Vietnam had he lived, all have inspired debate over the legacy of the Kennedy administration on the later course of the Vietnam War. To some, Kennedy bears a heavy responsibility for his role in leading his country into the quagmire of Vietnam. To others, his assassination destroyed the last chance to avoid a descent into the tragedy of Vietnam.

With regard to the first issue, it is not entirely fair to fault the Kennedy administration for its decision in 1961 to extend the U.S. commitment in South Vietnam. When John Kennedy came into office he faced a crisis in Laos and a major challenge to U.S. national security in Berlin. A few days before the inauguration, Soviet party leader Nikita Khrushchev had uttered a belligerent speech threatening Soviet support for national liberation struggles throughout the Third World. In Vietnam, the revolutionary movement had begun to revive from the period of relative quiescence and once again was threatening the stability of the already fragile Saigon regime. The new administration, beset by problems elsewhere in the world, did not have much time to consider its policies in Southeast Asia at leisure.

It has been charged that the new president contributed to his own dilemma by intervening in Cuba and adopting a foreign policy based on the Cold War vision of a world divided by hostile ideologies. It is no doubt true that Kennedy was transfixed by the perceived threat from international communism, and the rhetorical eloquence of his inauguration speech created a self-imposed challenge that he was unable to master. But in his fear of communism, Kennedy was a product of his age. Cold War sentiment remained a powerful force in the America of the early 1960's. Failure to react to the challenge of revolution in Southeast Asia would have provoked the charge from Republicans of Kennedy's "softness on communism" and a widespread public view that the new president lacked the capacity to lead the nation in dangerous times. His narrow victory in the presidential election the previous year made that a risk the new president could not take.

In fact, however, in 1961 Kennedy was less infected by the Cold War mentality than most of his contemporaries in Washington. More than the majority of his foreign policy advisers, Kennedy saw the risks inherent in intervention on the side of the fragile Saigon regime. Tragically, the events in Berlin, Cuba— admittedly of his own making—and Laos dangerously narrowed his options and made disengagement from South Vietnam virtually impossible. As it was, Kennedy sensed the indigenous character of the events taking place in Vietnam and generally took the side of those of his advisers who wished to adopt a political rather than a military approach to the war.

Paradoxically, whereas John F. Kennedy is charged by some with adopting a Cold War strategy in South Vietnam, he is faulted by others for failing to move decisively to meet a similar communist challenge in Laos. Recent critics have charged that the primary failure of the Kennedy strategy was not in Vietnam but in Laos, where Kennedy accepted a compromise settlement in an effort to end the conflict there and limit infiltration through the Laotian panhandle into South Vietnam. Administration officials hoped that the Soviet Union would live up to its verbal assurances and pressure the DRV to limit the infiltration of cadres, troops, and matériel into the South. According to Norman B. Hannah, a former foreign service officer who served as deputy director of the Office of Southeast Asian Affairs in the State Department and at CINCPAC headquarters during the Vietnam War, this "tacit agreement" with Moscow that North Vietnam would not use Laotian territory to attack the South was a "massive failure" in logic and gave the Hanoi regime a decided advantage in pursuing its aims in South Vietnam. If Southeast Asia was important to U.S. national security, and Hannah believes that it was, the Kennedy administration should have been willing to make the effort to use U.S. and SEATO forces to prevent a communist victory in Laos, rather than accepting a disguised defeat at the conference table.[119]

The later course of the Vietnam War, when it became clear that the massive infiltration of North Vietnamese troops had become a crucial factor in the struggle for the South, does lend some credence to Hannah's criticism. Kennedy administration officials, including Averell Harriman, were aware that the settlement at Geneva would not end infiltration through Laos, but they hoped that Hanoi would be more discreet in making use of the area for the shipment of men and supplies to the South. That judgment was severely mistaken, at least after the escalation of the war in 1965. Whether the hope in Washington that the Geneva Accords would limit infiltration was a massive failure in logic, as Hannah contends, it was undoubtedly a major miscalculation.[120]

But there are two serious problems with Hannah's assumptions. First, there is persuasive evidence that a military approach in Laos would not have received wide support either in Congress or in the country at large, where few viewed Laos as crucial to U.S. security interests in Asia. Even hardheaded stalwarts of the Cold War view such as Senator Richard Russell had serious reservations about a confrontation with communism in Laos, where existing political forces gave little promise to sustain a massive American effort.

Second, Hannah seriously underestimates the problems that the United States would have encountered in deciding to embark on a massive military effort in Laos and North Vietnam. A protracted conflict with the Pathet Lao and Vietnamese forces (and a strategy of protracted war is undoubtedly what Hanoi would have adopted under the circumstances) would have presented major logistical problems and sorely strained public support for the administration's strategy of containment in Southeast Asia. There was of course the additional risk that a U.S. move into Laos would have triggered war with China, whose willingness to go to war with India over the boundary with Tibet suggests that Chinese leaders were not averse to the use of force to protect their vital interests. All in all, it is difficult not to accept the administration's judgment that Laos was not the place to take a major stand against the threat of international communism and that Kennedy's decision to negotiate on Laos, in the face of a massive policy split among his advisers, was the prudent one. As Harriman himself commented, the Geneva Accords was "a good bad deal."[121]

Having decided not to follow the military option in Laos, however, Kennedy found himself even more burdened by the albatross of the Diem regime. That burden was a legacy of the Eisenhower administration, of course, but Kennedy handled the issue no better than had his predecessor. The decision to acquiesce in a military coup to overthrow the Diem regime is usually identified with the Buddhist crisis in the spring of 1963, and strictly speaking that is true, but the option of removing Diem if he no longer served the purposes of U.S. containment policy was implicit in the minds of some Kennedy administration officials from the beginning.

Was it a mistake to replace Diem? Kennedy's defenders argue that by the fall of 1963, Diem was unable to govern, but critics retort that whatever his faults he was the only political figure with the ability and the determination to resist a communist takeover in South Vietnam. The latter judgment appeared to be confirmed after Diem's assassination, when a series of unstable governments engaged in a game of "musical chairs" in Saigon until the rise of Nguyen Cao Ky and Nguyen Van Thieu in the late spring of 1965. Should Washington have simply swallowed its discomfort and followed the policy of "sink or swim with Ngo Dinh Diem," as many senior officials, including Vice-President Lyndon Johnson, advised?[122]

The contention by Kennedy's critics that Ngo Dinh Diem was the only political figure capable of resisting a communist takeover in South Vietnam may have been valid in the late 1950's, but it was no longer the case in 1963. Whether or not the military figures that followed the overthrow of the Ngo Dinh Diem regime were capable of leading their people on an anticommunist crusade, Diem himself was no longer capable of doing so in the final months of his regime. Ambassador Nolting's comment that Diem continued to have support in rural areas is beside the point. The pattern of violent change in modern times shows that the fate of revolutions is usually decided not in the countryside but in the cities and within the ranks of the armed forces. When Diem lost support within the urban middle class and among the senior ranks of the army, his fate was sealed, short of a massive effort by the United States to keep him in power. The decline in security conditions in rural areas in late October was a clear sign that the urban crisis had begun to affect the countryside. The chaos of the immediate post-Diem period is not an indication that the overthrow of

Diem was an error but a sign of the state to which Diem's own action had brought South Vietnamese society. Whether or not the Kennedy administration was justified in conspiring for his overthrow, Diem's career as the dominant political figure in South Vietnam was clearly coming to an end.

Even if Diem had been able to survive the efforts of his opponents to defeat him, it seems clear that the Kennedy administration would have encountered major problems in retaining support for its policies in Congress and among the U.S. public. Restiveness over the behavior of the Diem regime had created a volatile mood among the American people and could have become a major factor in the presidential election in 1964. Moreover, it is likely that as the crisis continued, the DRV would have intensified its efforts to destabilize the Saigon regime and placed more pressure on it.

What would have happened if Kennedy had lived? Kennedy confidants are irrevocably split over the issue. Dean Rusk insists that never in his conversations on the subject of Vietnam with President Kennedy did the latter ever suggest the possibility of withdrawal. William P. Bundy points out that not even during the Buddhist crisis in the spring of 1963 (which, in the words of Leslie H. Gelb and Richard K. Betts, created a "perfect pretext" for disengagement) did Kennedy suggest withdrawal or a negotiated settlement. But other sources maintain that the president had made it clear from the outset that he had no intention of committing U.S. combat troops to South Vietnam and point to his decision to remove U.S. military advisers on a gradual basis as an indication that, come what may, President Kennedy was determined to extricate the United States from the quagmire of Vietnam. Filmmaker Oliver Stone, in his controversial movie *JFK*, even argues that Kennedy's determination to withdraw from South Vietnam contributed to his assassination.[123]

It is impossible to know for sure what Kennedy would have done had he lived, and speculation on the issue is ultimately fruitless. But a few observations may be in order. Kennedy's actions and comments about Vietnam throughout his presidency suggest the agonized ambivalence that he experienced in grappling with the problem. Unlike many of his advisers, who saw no alternative to the defense of South Vietnam, Kennedy was clearly tortured by doubts about the wisdom of involvement there, while at the same time fearful of the high price of withdrawal. His Hamlet-like indecision on the issue was reflected in the policies his administration adopted from the outset and maintained until his death.

It does not seem unlikely that the president had made a private decision in the spring of 1963 to begin the withdrawal of U.S. forces on a gradual basis, whatever the effect on the course of the war. The Buddhist crisis must have confirmed many of his doubts about the survivability of the RVN and the wisdom of a U.S. commitment there. That he did not confide his doubts to some of his senior advisers such as Dean Rusk can be explained as a consequence of past experience, when his trial balloons on a reduced U.S. role had been treated with scant respect by key members of his cabinet and administration.

But the course of his behavior during the later stages of the Saigon political crisis during the summer and fall does not support the view that he was determined to extricate the United States from the quagmire of South Vietnam, regardless of the consequences. Had he truly intended to withdraw, as some contend, there was no better pretext than the situation that Ngo Dinh Diem had created by his treatment of the Buddhists. The political costs of a withdrawal under those conditions would have been significant but manageable. Yet Kennedy ultimately decided to acquiesce in the replacement of Diem with a new leadership that was clearly committed to continuing the war effort. Would he have supported such a risky move if he had intended to cut the ground out from under that new government by withdrawing U.S. advisers early the following year? The most plausible conclusion is that Kennedy briefly hoped that new leadership in Saigon could revitalize the war effort, thus creating conditions for a gradual withdrawal of U.S. forces under more favorable circumstances.

In the end, Kennedy could neither go in with force nor disengage with honor. That was his tragedy and the mark of his administration. Theodore Sorensen speculates that Kennedy "was simply going to weather it out, a nasty, untidy mess to which there was no other acceptable solution." Whatever the case, Kennedy's indecision in Vietnam did not help the situation and probably made it worse. Journalist James Reston, recalling that Kennedy had told him that he had to show determination in Vietnam to make up for the disastrous impression created by the failed Bay of Pigs invasion, felt that the consequent decision to send additional advisers to South Vietnam was "a critical mistake" that started the slide into the Vietnam War. The judgment on Kennedy's Vietnam policy, then, must be mixed. President Eisenhower had left him with few options to work with, and Kennedy deserves credit, at the least, for resisting a greater debacle in Laos. But like Eisenhower, Kennedy bequeathed a legacy in Vietnam that was virtually bankrupt. It would be the new president, Lyndon Baines Johnson, who would be called to pay the price for the miscalculations of his predecessors.[124]

Chapter 9

Into the Quagmire

Henry Cabot Lodge returned to Washington only a few days after Lyndon Johnson assumed the presidency following the death of John Kennedy. As vice-president, Johnson had had relatively little direct involvement in the Vietnam War since his visit there in 1961, when he had carried the new administration's initial message to Saigon. But he had attended high-level meetings that dealt with the issue and was generally known as a staunch supporter of the Diem regime.

President Johnson met with Lodge on November 24. According to a memorandum written by CIA director John McCone, Lodge reported that the situation in Saigon since the coup was improved, leaving the new president with the impression that the United States was, in McCone's phrase, "on the road to victory." McCone noted that the CIA's view of the competence and projected public support for the new government was less optimistic. Johnson then expressed his opinion about past U.S. policy in South Vietnam. He wanted less emphasis placed on the need for social reforms, saying it was not necessary to reform every Asian into a U.S. image. He also emphasized that the bickering within the U.S. mission in Saigon must stop. Anyone who did not conform to policy, he said, "should be removed." In a conversation with his aide Bill Moyers immediately following the meeting, Johnson expressed his concern at the effect a U.S. defeat in Vietnam would have on attitudes in Moscow and Beijing and voiced his determination to back the South Vietnamese. When asked by Moyers what he had said to his advisers at the meeting, Johnson answered: "I'm not going to let Vietnam go the way of China. I told them to go back and tell those generals in Saigon that Lyndon Johnson intends to stand by our word, but by

God, I want them to get off their butts and get out in those jungles and whip hell out of some communists."[1]

After the meeting with Lodge, the president announced to the press that existing U.S. policies in South Vietnam would continue. On November 26 he approved NSAM-273, which essentially affirmed the decisions adopted in Honolulu while making a few changes in the wording of the draft that McGeorge Bundy had originally prepared for John Kennedy. Those changes were relatively minor but had the effect of strengthening the U.S. role in assisting the South Vietnamese war effort. The new directive confirmed U.S. support for the new government, maintaining aid levels as they had been under the previous regime. There was otherwise no change in strategy. The basic objective was to assist the Saigon government to help itself, while reaffirming the previously stated intention of removing 1,000 U.S. troops by the end of 1963 and bringing the insurgency movement to an end by the close of 1965.

The new administration, then, made no immediate changes in Vietnam policy, despite the tumultuous events that had taken place in recent weeks. But there were clear signs of a possible change in emphasis. The new president suffered none of the doubts of his predecessor about the war and whether it could be pressed to a satisfactory conclusion. Whether he was aware of Kennedy's private concerns about Vietnam policy is uncertain. According to one source, Johnson had made a private vow that Kennedy had been correct on Vietnam and that he himself must see it through. It was also necessary to provide support to the new government in Saigon. Whatever the new president's previous convictions that there was no realistic alternative to Diem, he, like most other administration officials, desperately wanted the new government to succeed, and Lodge's early optimism gave them that hope.[2]

Under the surface impression of unity and continuity, however, many of the old dilemmas remained. What was needed first—political stability or military success? As had been the case since the mid-1950's, there were strong differences on that question. Curiously, the new chief executive appeared to focus on the latter, whereas military opinion now weighed in on the side of the former. From Saigon, for example, came a MACV assessment that political reform was necessary before military victories could be expected. But a special CIA report prepared at the request of Defense Secretary McNamara said the opposite. Military victories in the field were desperately needed, it noted, to raise morale in Saigon. The report's conclusions were gloomy, estimating that the new government had at best an even chance to withstand the forces of revolution over the next few months.[3]

As it turned out, the question was somewhat academic, for in the weeks that followed the fall of the Diem regime, progress on either count was hard to come by. From the start, the new government in Saigon was plagued with factionalism because General Duong Van Minh proved to be a weak leader.

Secretary McNamara visited Saigon in the middle of December, and his report on the visit reflected a sense of urgency over the continued political instability in Saigon and the strategic hamlet program, which was virtually dead in the water. Most disquieting were the rumors that senior officials in Saigon were sympathetic to French president Charles de Gaulle's recent proposal for the neutralization of all of Southeast Asia. McNamara found the situation "very disturbing" and predicted that unless current trends were reversed, South Vietnam could fall under a communist government within two or three months.[4]

Our Boy in Saigon

On January 30, 1964, the government of Duong Van Minh was overthrown by Major General Nguyen Khanh, a younger member of the coup group and commander of ARVN's IV Corps in the Mekong Delta. Nguyen Khanh explained to Ambassador Lodge that he had launched the operation to prevent "neutralists" from taking power, but some U.S. officials were convinced that such concerns were merely a cloak to hide Khanh's political ambition. In his book on the period, George McT. Kahin contends that the coup had full backing from the United States, but the evidence is hardly conclusive. Still, it seems clear that Lodge and other senior U.S. officials in Saigon were aware of Khanh's intentions and at a minimum gave him assurances of U.S. backing in the event his bid for power was successful. Once the changeover had been completed, Lodge expressed his satisfaction that there finally was an able leader in Saigon who listened to U.S. advice. The evidence to date, he said, was "that he is able, that he has got a lot of drive, and that he is not tolerating any delay." We need a "tough and ruthless commander," he concluded. Perhaps Khanh would be it.[5]

But evidence soon began to accumulate that Lodge's optimism was misplaced. Although the political situation now appeared somewhat more stable, the military situation did not improve, leading to a flurry of new suggestions in Washington for a change in strategy. From the Joint Chiefs came a proposal to increase the U.S. military presence in Vietnam, placing U.S. advisers at all levels in the RVN, to remove restrictions on cross-border operations into Cambodia, and to adopt additional punitive measures against the source of aggression in Hanoi. From outside the administration came increasing calls for a negotiated settlement followed by a U.S. withdrawal. French president Charles de Gaulle called for a peace conference to neutralize the entire area. Among well-known Americans who echoed de Gaulle's views were Senator Mike Mansfield and columnist Walter Lippmann. On February 1, President Johnson announced at a press conference that in principle the administration had no objection to the neutralization of all of Vietnam but that there was no current indication that the Viet Cong were prepared to leave their neighbors in peace. For the time being, he said, the best way to achieve peace was "to stop the invasion of South

Viet-Nam by some of its neighbors and supporters." In early March there were renewed rumors of a coup in Saigon, prompting President Johnson to remark that we must make it clear that General Khanh is "our boy" in Saigon.[6]

Following a now familiar pattern, the White House reacted to the confused situation by sending Maxwell Taylor and Robert S. McNamara on a fact-finding visit to the RVN to evaluate the situation and make policy recommendations. Arriving on March 8, they talked with Nguyen Khanh, who promised to establish a national service act to mobilize the population for the struggle and to increase efforts to pacify the provinces around Saigon. The strength of the South Vietnamese armed forces was to be increased from 226,000 to 251,000, that of the Civil Guard from 90,000 to 119,636, and the Self-Defense Forces were scheduled to increase from 257,000 to 422,000.[7]

McNamara's report to the president was discussed by the National Security Council on March 17. The secretary was candid about the deteriorating situation in the RVN: 40 percent of the country was now under Viet Cong control or influence, and 22 of the country's 43 provinces were controlled to a significant degree by revolutionary forces. Desertion, apathy, and draft-dodging were commonplace. But McNamara was not yet ready to recommend withdrawal. If South Vietnam were to go communist, he warned, almost all of Southeast Asia would also fall under communist domination or under the domination of forces not now explicitly communist but likely to become so. Even the Philippines would be shaky, and the threat to India, Australia, and New Zealand would be greatly increased.

McNamara presented three possible courses of action: neutrality through negotiations, military operations against North Vietnam, and the adoption of measures to improve the situation in South Vietnam. The first, he said, was incompatible with U.S. objectives as set forth in NSAM-273, and the time was not propitious to explore the second scenario. That left the third option, to strengthen the RVN and its armed forces. McNamara rejected the idea of introducing U.S. combat troops or taking over operational command, pointing out that it would be psychologically damaging to Vietnamese morale. Moreover, intervention by the United States on a large scale, combined with U.S. or RVN actions against the North, would disturb key allies and other nations.[8]

The Joint Chiefs were not happy with the latest McNamara-Taylor report and in particular its rejection of tougher measures against the North. In a memo to the secretary dated March 14, they argued that the policies recommended in the report were militarily inadequate. Action against the DRV was needed to discourage Hanoi from giving further support to revolutionary forces in the South as well as to raise morale in Saigon. The JCS recommended that the United States establish military bases in the South for the purpose of undertaking offensive operations against North Vietnam and along the Laotian and Cambodian borders.[9]

But President Johnson agreed with McNamara that overt military operations against the DRV would be premature and that the immediate task was to "strengthen the southern base." He approved McNamara's report as NSAM-288 on March 17 and authorized preparations for possible retaliatory actions against the North on a contingency basis. In the meantime, he wanted to develop "the strongest possible military and political base for possible later action." Johnson also attempted to squelch the growing interest in a negotiated settlement. He talked personally with Senator Mansfield and Walter Lippmann and instructed Ambassador Bohlen in Paris to discuss the matter with President de Gaulle.[10]

As had been the case with his predecessor, President Johnson's first major decisions on Vietnam followed a middle ground, satisfying neither hawks nor doves. He had refused the recommendations of military advisers but left the door open for escalation in the future.

Hanoi's Response

There is not much hard evidence on Hanoi's reaction to the overthrow of the Diem regime. It has been suggested that Vietnamese leaders were astonished that the United States would overthrow its own ally. That may be true, but internal documents indicate that party leaders had speculated since as early as 1960 that Washington might eventually decide to replace Diem with a more obedient puppet. In a letter to Nguyen Van Linh in 1962, Le Duan had predicted that Washington might bring about new leadership in Saigon and then seek to negotiate a U.S. withdrawal. Whatever the case, Hanoi leaders undoubtedly took heart from the coup and viewed it as a confirmation of their own strategy of focusing their attack on the weak political base of the Saigon regime. Whoever succeeded him, party leaders were convinced, would be nothing more than a puppet of the Americans and an easier mark for the revolutionary forces in the South.[11]

Although Ho Chi Minh and his colleagues undoubtedly had a full measure of ideological contempt for their new adversaries in Saigon, they may have been uncertain of their intentions with regard to prosecuting the war effort. In the immediate aftermath of the coup, the NLF sent signals hinting at a possible negotiated settlement and reduced the level of attacks in the South. When those signals were rebuffed, Viet Cong attacks intensified.[12]

In December, the Ninth Plenum of the VWP was convened to discuss the new situation. It was by now apparent that Hanoi's hope that the overthrow of Diem would provide a pretext for a U.S. withdrawal from the South was overly optimistic. In fact, the early signs were that the U.S. role in the war was on the increase. This apparent Americanization of the war brought into question the DRV strategy of placing equal emphasis on political and military struggle and strengthened the argument of those who felt that Hanoi should adopt a more aggressive policy in the South.

Party strategists had concluded that the United States could react to height-

ened pressure from the North in two possible ways—by maintaining the existing strategy of special war or by moving to a higher level of involvement,
including the introduction of U.S. combat troops. Although there was apparently a vigorous debate on the issue at the conference, it was the dominant view
that Washington would be most likely to escalate if it became convinced that the
revolutionary forces would be unable to resist a growing U.S. presence. Such a
development would be unacceptable to Hanoi because it would make it significantly more difficult to maintain the momentum of the revolution.

The plenum therefore approved a decision to strengthen the PLAF as
rapidly as possible in order to realize a basic change in the balance of forces and
achieve victory in a short time. In that process, the role of armed struggle would
become "direct and decisive" because the most urgent immediate task was to
destroy ARVN in preparation for a general offensive and uprising.

How could the North, the solid "rear base" of the revolution, best help its
comrades in the South? There have been persistent but unconfirmed reports
that some leading party members may have called for the direct intervention of
the PAVN in the struggle in the South. In the end, however, the introduction of
large numbers of North Vietnamese main force units was rejected, probably
out of concern that such actions could trigger an escalation of the U.S. role in
the conflict. The plenum did call for increased aid from the North to deal with
the heightened U.S. military effort but indicated that the roles of the two zones
would continue to be different, thus implying that the PAVN would play, at
most, a limited combat role in the South.[13]

An additional reason why party leaders may have decided not to escalate
the direct role of the DRV in the struggle in the South was that it would strain
relations with its two major allies, the Soviet Union and China. Hanoi was
prepared to ignore advice from Moscow and Beijing where its own vital interests were at issue, but it could not afford to take lightly the risk of a total
estrangement from either because of their role as major suppliers of military
assistance to the DRV. To avert such an eventuality, Hanoi sent out a circular
letter to fraternal parties explaining the decision and promising that even if the
United States should intervene directly in the South, the DRV would restrain
Washington from escalating the struggle and extending the war to North Vietnam.

The decisions reached at the December plenum exacerbated existing policy
differences over strategy in the South and also caused increasing strains with
the Soviet Union. Le Duan publicly criticized unnamed party comrades who
had been influenced by "modern revisionism" (a clear reference to the Khrushchev policy of peaceful coexistence with the West) and praised Moscow's rival
China for "having satisfactorily carried out most satisfactorily the instructions
of the great Lenin."[14]

During the first three months of 1964, U.S. intelligence sources reported significant gains for the insurgent forces. Viet Cong units were beginning to organize in batallions and even regiments and were now armed with heavy equipment from China and the Eastern European countries. According to some estimates, 40 percent of the territory of the RVN was now under VC control or influence. In the meantime, infiltration from the North was continuing, but at a lower rate than in 1962. One reason for the declining rate of infiltration may have been that Hanoi's supply of southerners sent north after the Geneva Accords had begun to dry up. An increasing number of infiltrators were North Vietnamese draftees. According to a study of the problem by MACV in August, there were as yet no indications of the movement of regular units of the PAVN into South Vietnam.[15]

Focus on the North

While Hanoi was trying to find a way to win in the South without substantially increasing the role of the North, Washington was discussing various ways of persuading Hanoi to desist from its growing involvement in the conflict in South Vietnam. The first consideration of direct action against the DRV had come in May 1963, when the Joint Chiefs asked CINCPAC to prepare a plan for covert operations by the RVN against the North. The plan was approved by the JCS on September 9 as OPLAN 34-A and was seriously discussed at the Honolulu conference in November. It was given final approval by the White House early the following year. Advocates of the plan hoped that it would increase the cost of the war to the North and convince Ho Chi Minh to give up his goal to unify the country. But some U.S. officials doubted that it would have a significant effect on attitudes in Hanoi and contended that only air attacks and other "punitive or attritional" operations would be likely to achieve the goal of convincing Hanoi to cease support for the Viet Cong.

Phase I of OPLAN 34-A began on February 1, 1964. On February 20, the president directed a speedup of contingency plans for pressuring North Vietnam to produce "maximum credible deterrent effect" on Hanoi. To study the issue, an interagency study group was formed under Robert H. Johnson, a member of the State Department's Policy Planning Council, and William H. Sullivan. At first, the committee members were skeptical of the efficacy of bombing and singled out additional possible actions, including the stationing of U.S. forces in Thailand, a blockade of Haiphong harbor, and authorizing hot pursuit in strikes into Laos and Cambodia as well as air strikes on North Vietnam. The group warned that China and the Soviet Union might intervene militarily but argued that the United States should be prepared to follow through against China if necessary. The positive benefits would be to demonstrate simultaneously U.S. resolve and restraint, reduce the capabilities of the Viet Cong, and improve the situation in the South for what it described as "virtually inevitable" negotiations. But it doubted that Hanoi would stop or reduce Viet Cong operations unless the United States escalated its role in South Vietnam and improved the situation there.[16]

At first President Johnson made no decision on the issue. Secretary McNamara recommended against retaliatory action "at this time" because such operations would be "extremely delicate" and hard to justify. There was also a possibility of counterescalation by Hanoi as well as the unlikelihood of achieving the stated objectives. But he did recommend planning for retaliatory action on a "tit-for-tat" basis. State Department officials doubted the value of "tit-for-tat" operations, arguing that it would be difficult under such circumstances to present a picture of escalating pressures, and they envisaged McNamara's proposals only as a contingency plan for possible future actions.

At the pivotal meeting of the National Security Council on March 17, President Johnson approved Secretary McNamara's recommendations. The Joint Chiefs responded to the directive by instructing CINCPAC to prepare a program of border control and graduated overt military pressure by South Vietnamese and U.S. forces against Hanoi. In response, CINCPAC drew up a three-phase plan called OPLAN 37-64, involving operations against infiltration routes into the South as well as against targets in the North. Phase I would concentrate on air and ground strikes in South Vietnam and along the borders with Laos and Cambodia. Phase II would involve "tit-for-tat" amphibious and air raids against targets in the DRV. The final phase would entail intensive operations against the North. Most of the air strikes would be undertaken by the RVN armed forces, with some assistance from U.S. aircraft.[17]

There was less agreement on proposals from some quarters for punitive raids on Laos. There was general agreement that information on the nature and magnitude of DRV aid to the southern insurgency through Laos was lacking and that efforts to control the traffic by diplomatic means had failed. The Joint Chiefs, who wanted an integrated approach to the security of Southeast Asia, with the role of the DRV as the key, felt that raids on Laos were justified and that existing "self-imposed restrictions" were uncalled for. Many State Department officials agreed with the Pentagon that Laos and Vietnam were part of the same problem but feared that attacks on Laos would make it more difficult for Prime Minister Souvanna Phouma to protect Laotian sovereignty and the fragile "tacit agreement" at Geneva. For the time being President Johnson agreed with the State Department and reserved judgment on measures against infiltration trails running through Laos.[18]

During the next few weeks, administration officials dealing with the Vietnam conflict shifted their primary focus from the South to the North. A general consensus still existed that the war could not be won until the situation in South Vietnam had stabilized, but some sought the key to that stability in Hanoi, not in Saigon. At a meeting of senior U.S. officials in Saigon in mid-

April, the primary focus of attention was on how to convey to party leaders in Hanoi the message that the United States was prepared to apply increasingly large military pressure on the DRV to compel it to reduce or eliminate its role in supporting the insurgency in South Vietnam. Ambassador Lodge suggested that the administration's message be taken to Hanoi by the new Canadian representative on the ICC, diplomat J. Blair Seaborn. He further proposed that Washington offer positive incentives to Hanoi by using a "carrot and stick" approach to make the offer more attractive.

The White House approved the initiative, and when Ottawa agreed, Seaborn met with DRV prime minister Pham Van Dong on June 17 to discuss the issue. But Hanoi was unmoved. Pham Van Dong received the Canadian diplomat affably and indicated his understanding of the seriousness of Washington's intentions but declared that DRV support for the struggle of liberation in the South was unshakable.[19]

Why did the administration gradually shift its focus from Saigon to Hanoi as the best means of reversing the deteriorating situation in South Vietnam? There was little evidence that the DRV had decided to increase its involvement in the South. One reason, perhaps, was that the situation in South Vietnam had changed. Although Diem and his family—often considered a contributory factor in the domestic unrest in the country—had been removed from the scene, the means of stabilizing the political situation and reducing the threat of the Viet Cong seemed as elusive as ever. Although Washington was not interested in Nguyen Khanh's quixotic proposal for a "march to the North," it did seem persuaded that one means of raising morale in Saigon and buying time for strengthening the South Vietnamese government and armed forces was to reduce if not remove the pressure from the North.

Another possible factor was the changed situation in Washington. In the months that followed the assassination of John F. Kennedy, the influence of those who were skeptical of the military option was on the decline. Roger Hilsman and Robert F. Kennedy had left the administration, and others such as Averell Harriman did not have the ear of the new president, who, though still unwilling to follow the advice of his more militant advisers, was clearly more receptive to the military option than had been his predecessor. Although many of the key advisers of the Kennedy team, such as Dean Rusk, Robert S. McNamara, and McGeorge Bundy, remained at their posts, many of the other voices that had encouraged John F. Kennedy in his skepticism about Vietnam had been stilled.

The ground had thus been prepared for a possible extension of the war into North Vietnam. While bureaucrats awaited a final decision on the matter from the White House, attention turned to the equally important problem of reinvigorating the war effort in South Vietnam, where political factionalism, religious tensions between Catholics and Buddhists, and a "business as usual attitude" all combined to undermine progress in the war against the Viet Cong. Clashes between Buddhist and Catholic groups erupted periodically on the streets of Saigon, and the endemic factionalism that had long characterized South Vietnamese politics reached new heights. On May 14, Ambassador Lodge reported that "Big" Minh was planning a new coup to overthrow the government of General Khanh. The latter, he insisted, was definitely the best alternative.

On May 21, Secretary Rusk cabled Ambassador Lodge in Saigon to request his ideas on how to shake the RVN leaders "by the scruff of the neck" to end their bickering and concentrate on the defeat of the Viet Cong. It would be ironic, he remarked, if the United States struck the North only to lose the South. A few days later, in a meeting at the State Department, a proposal by Joseph Mendenhall to infuse the pacification program with a new vigor by introducing additional U.S. personnel in key provinces near Saigon and along the central coast was discussed. Similar talks were under way to develop a plan to introduce U.S. officials at various levels of RVN administration. The basic objective of the plan was to stiffen the war effort in Saigon by placing a "tall American" at every point of stress and strain.[20]

In the meantime, a new Pathet Lao offensive broke out in Laos. The Pathet Lao representatives had voluntarily withdrawn from Prime Minister Souvanna Phouma's tripartite government in April 1963, nominally because of the rising danger of assassinations. In succeeding months, Souvanna Phouma accused the Pathet Lao of cooperating with North Vietnamese forces in attacking his own government units. He continued his efforts to reconstitute the tripartite arrangements created at Geneva, however, and in April 1964 he was briefly arrested by right-wing forces in the capital of Vientiane, leading him to reconstitute his government as a coalition of neutralist and rightist elements. The enemy offensive added a sense of urgency to the situation in Washington. On May 24, the National Security Council met without the president and discussed the possibility of applying force against North Vietnam to bring about new negotiations or the removal of Pathet Lao units from Laos. The following day, McGeorge Bundy drafted a memo to the president recommending the use of "selected and carefully graduated military force against North Vietnam" unless a prior warning to that effect produced sufficient improvement in the region to make such action unnecessary.[21]

The president's senior advisers convened at Honolulu on June 1 to discuss all aspects of the conflict in Vietnam. The primary focus of the meeting was to discuss whether to recommend an extension of the war to the North. Ambassador Lodge advocated action against the DRV as a means of boosting morale and fostering a "feeling of unity" in South Vietnam. A representative of the Joint Chiefs remarked testily that the United States "should not waste critical time" on a series of "messages" but should take "positive, prompt, and mean-

ingful military action" to indicate its determination to bring North Vietnamese
support for the insurgency to an end. Such meaningful military action should
consist of attacks on military targets in North Vietnam to destroy the "will and
capabilities" of the DRV to support the insurgencies in South Vietnam and
Laos. But Defense Secretary Robert S. McNamara did not agree, arguing that
operations against the North should not be taken until preparations for countering possible North Vietnamese or Chinese retaliatory action (involving the
possible introduction of U.S. combat troops) had been completed. Dean Rusk
agreed, on the grounds that U.S. public opinion was badly divided on the
administration's policies in Southeast Asia (according to the *Pentagon Papers*, a
recent Gallup poll had shown that only 37 percent of those surveyed were
convinced U.S. national security interests were involved in Southeast Asia) and
should be prepared for a possible escalation of the war. Rusk favored seeking
congressional authorization for future U.S. military actions in the area. In the
end, the conferees agreed to recommend postponing a decision to expand the
war into North Vietnam.[22]

The conference also debated how far to increase the U.S. role in the policymaking process in Saigon. Whereas the meeting at the State Department in late
May had called for focusing U.S. efforts on key provinces in South Vietnam, a
Vietnam Coordinating Committee under William H. Sullivan recommended a
de facto U.S. takeover of the RVN machinery. Both Ambassador Lodge and
General William Westmoreland, who had just replaced General Paul Harkins as
commander of MACV, were opposed to the approach, however, and it was
dropped in favor of an alternative proposal to increase the U.S. advisory role in
key provinces of the RVN.

The results of the deliberations at Honolulu were reported to President
Johnson on June 3. The president had just had an extended conversation with
journalist Walter Lippmann and Under Secretary of State George Ball on the
situation in Southeast Asia. Both had warned him against precipitate action in
conditions when the country was not united on the issue and the United States
could be portrayed as a warmonger in world public opinion. According to Ball,
the president had appeared receptive to their arguments.

There is no documentary record of the June 3 meeting, but later events
indicate that President Johnson accepted the conclusions reached at the conference and decided to delay any further action to initiate the process of seeking
a congressional resolution while continuing to study targets for possible air
attacks in the DRV. From Saigon came a message from Henry Cabot Lodge
appealing to the president to avoid the dilemma of "either doing nothing or
doing something imprudent." Arguing against the dispatch of U.S. combat
troops to Southeast Asia, he called for the limited use of naval and air power for
carefully selected objectives. Pitting the manpower of a nation of 190 million
against that of a nation of 900 million, he said, would put us on "the short end

of the stick." Better, he pointed out, to use U.S. superior military power to put us "on the long end of the stick." A few days later, the CIA's Board of National Estimates predicted that

> with the possible exception of Cambodia, it is likely that no nation in the area would quickly succumb to communism as a result of the fall of Laos and South Vietnam. Furthermore, a continuation of the spread of communism in the area would not be inexorable, and any spread which did occur would take time—time in which the total situation might change in any of a number of ways unfavorable to the communist cause.

The estimate did conceded that the loss of Laos and South Vietnam would be "profoundly damaging" to U.S. prestige and credibility in the Far East and would enhance the prestige of China at the expense of the allegedly more moderate USSR.[23]

Toward the Tonkin Gulf

The overall results of the policy debate in May and early June, then, had been relatively modest in terms of concrete actions. During the next few weeks, the only major decision on Vietnam announced by the White House was a modest increase in the number of U.S. military advisers in the RVN. It has been speculated that election year politics were involved, but an analysis of the documents suggests that administration officials were aware that major decisions were pending and hoped to solidify support in Congress and among the wider public for an expanded U.S. role in the war. William P. Bundy recalls that senior officials were convinced that although the military situation in Laos and South Vietnam was serious, it was not desperate enough to warrant hasty action at a time when domestic issues needed attention and the country was still reeling from the assassination of John Kennedy the previous autumn. In the meantime, Congress was restive and the nation was seriously divided on U.S. Southeast Asia policy. Senior officials realized that the administration would have to make a strong case to justify an increase in the U.S. role in the Vietnam War.[24]

Lyndon Johnson, of course, had his own problems. It was a presidential election year, and criticism of his policies in Vietnam were coming from both the left and the right. As always, congressional and public opinion demanded vigorous efforts to stem the advance of communism while at the same time expressing reluctance to become directly involved in a military conflict in an area of questionable importance to the security of the United States. If Johnson took no action, he was vulnerable to attacks from the future Republican presidential nominee of being "soft on communism." If he escalated, he lost one of his most promising themes in the upcoming presidential campaign—that he was more likely to be able to keep the country out of war than his saber-rattling opponent.

By early summer, then, the administration was poised on the brink of another escalation of the Vietnam conflict but not yet ready to jump into the abyss. On June 22 the White House issued NSAM-308 calling for an intensive effort "to bring to the American people a complete and accurate picture of the United States involvement in Southeast Asia, and to show why this involvement is essential." Senior administration officials had debated the advisability of seeking a congressional resolution that would give the White House increased latitude in Southeast Asia but advised against it for the time being, on the grounds that the risks would outweigh the advantages until such time as a firm decision on drastic action had been reached.[25]

On June 23, President Johnson announced the resignation of Henry Cabot Lodge as ambassador to South Vietnam and the appointment of General Maxwell Taylor as his replacement. During the first few weeks after Taylor's arrival in Saigon in early July, the situation in the RVN did not change significantly. Chronic factionalism and religious strife continued to undermine political stability and reduce the effectiveness of the regime, but General Khanh appeared to be generally in control of the situation and anxious to cooperate with the new U.S. envoy. Insurgent activities throughout the country were up slightly from earlier in the year, but there was no indication of a major campaign in the offing nor, although draftees of North Vietnamese origin were beginning to appear with increasing frequency in PLAF units, any clear indication that main force troops of the PAVN had begun to appear in the South. There was some consideration of launching air attacks on enemy infiltration routes through the Laotian panhandle, but Ambassador Leonard Unger in Vientiane successfully argued against the idea on the grounds that such raids would have only marginal effects in South Vietnam and would greatly complicate the political situation in Laos.

On August 2, North Vietnamese patrol boats attacked the U.S. destroyer *Maddox* while the vessel was on patrol in the Tonkin Gulf off the central coast of North Vietnam. Concluding that the attack had been launched at the initiative of local North Vietnamese authorities, the White House took no action except to order the dispatch of a protest note to Hanoi and the continuation of the patrols. If attacked, the ships were authorized to destroy the attacking forces but not to penetrate into hostile waters or airspace. Two days later, a second attack on the *Maddox* and a second destroyer, the *C. Turner Joy*, allegedly occurred. In reprisal for the second attack, the administration ordered retaliatory air strikes to be launched on North Vietnamese patrol boat bases and other targets on the central coast of the DRV and requested a resolution from Congress authorizing the president to take necessary action to protect U.S. interests in the region.

The so-called Tonkin Gulf incident would later become one of the controversial episodes in a controversial war. Critics would dispute the administration's claim that the attacks had been unprovoked, and doubts were raised as to whether the second incident had actually occurred. This is not the place for an extended discussion of the evidence relating to the Tonkin Gulf incident. But a few comments about the incident and its overall relationship to the administration's policy in Vietnam are in order.

First, there appears to be no doubt that the first incident occurred. As described by a history of the war published in Hanoi, "On 2 August 1964 one of our torpedo squadrons chased the destroyer *Maddox* from our coastal waters, which is regarded as our first victory over the U.S. navy." The evidence for the second attack is less conclusive. After its initial report of the attack, the *Maddox* later the same day cabled that because of "freak weather effects" and "over-eager" sonarmen, a review of the action made many of the reported contacts "appear doubtful." Senior officials gathered at the Pentagon, however, examined the evidence, concluded that the attack had indeed taken place, and decided to use the incident to launch an immediate retaliation and present the draft resolution to Congress.

Second, the administration was being less than truthful in claiming that the attack had been totally unprovoked. The North Vietnamese attack on August 2 was probably precipitated by the conjunction of two military operations—the DESOTO patrols undertaken by U.S. naval units to obtain intelligence on DRV radar installations along the central coast, and Operation OPLAN 34-A, the guerrilla raids into North Vietnam launched by South Vietnamese military units which had been approved earlier in the year. Senior administration officials were aware that OPLAN 34-A operations were under way in the general vicinity of the DESOTO patrols of August 2, but, according to William P. Bundy, they did not believe that such operations could "reasonably constitute a provocation" because the distances between the two were considerable. That may be so, but a cable from the State Department to the embassy in Saigon dated August 3 noted: "We believe that present OPLAN 34A activities are beginning to rattle Hanoi, and *Maddox* incident is directly related to their effort to resist these activities. We have no intention yielding to pressure." Whatever the case, it is probable that North Vietnamese military commanders thought that the two were related, and the administration was aware that that indeed was the case.[26]

Did the administration deliberately schedule the operations as a means of provoking the DRV into retaliatory action, as some have charged, thus providing a pretext to seek a congressional resolution? Although final evidence on this point is lacking, it seems doubtful that the entire incident had been staged for the purpose of justifying a U.S. retaliation. But once the incident had taken place, the White House was quick to use it to its own advantage and seek approval from Congress for broader authority to conduct operations to protect U.S. security interests in Southeast Asia.

In later years, when the Vietnam War had become increasingly unpopular among the American public, many congressmen would claim that they had been duped into approving the resolution, which was introduced on August 5 and passed in both houses with a near-unanimous vote two days later. In fact, key congressmen were aware of most of the facts involved, although not of the ambiguity of the evidence relating to the second attack. Rank-and-file members were not privy to the details of the incident, but a general attitude prevailed that the circumstances of the Tonkin Gulf incident were less important than the fact that the president wanted congressional authorization to take action to protect the American flag in hostile waters. Few were willing to oppose him in that request.[27]

Hanoi Raises the Ante

In his insightful account of the war, political scientist William S. Turley remarks about the Tonkin Gulf incident that Hanoi "probably had grown impatient waiting for the United States to make the first move." That observation is undoubtedly true of the more militant elements in the party and military leadership, although it hardly squares with the overall objective of North Vietnamese strategy, which was to avoid provoking the United States into a direct intervention in the war.[28]

Hanoi's strategy during the spring and summer of 1964 had been relatively cautious, given the fragile situation in South Vietnam. While continuing to infiltrate personnel and supplies down the Ho Chi Minh Trail, Hanoi still hesitated to send units of the PAVN to take part in combat operations in the South. Viet Cong operations in rural areas were up somewhat from early in the year, and there were an increasing number of attacks on RVN and U.S. installations and personnel, leading to suggestions in Washington that U.S. dependents be removed. But Hanoi still held back from major assaults and appeared willing to increase the pressure gradually in preparation for a possible general offensive and uprising in the near future. Similar actions were taken to restrain the Pathet Lao in Laos.

Under these circumstances, it seems unlikely that Hanoi would have wished to provoke the United States into a possible escalation of the war. At this stage of the conflict, insurgent forces in the South still generally refrained from direct attacks on U.S. advisers and installations. Polish diplomat Mieczyslaw Maneli reports that North Vietnamese leaders constantly asked him and other Eastern Europeans resident in Hanoi how they should behave toward the Americans to avoid a direct confrontation. On the other hand, Hanoi was clearly willing to bear the costs of escalation. Party leaders were bitingly critical of Moscow's failure to provide them with firm support, and elements within North Vietnamese society suspected of sympathy with Khrushchev's policy of "revisionism" were systematically removed from the party and the government.

The strong U.S. response to the Tonkin Gulf incident was a clear signal that the Johnson administration was not on the verge of withdrawing from South Vietnam. To Hanoi, events in Saigon were promising and suggested that the RVN was beginning to come apart. Restiveness was growing within the armed forces, and wide sectors of the population, including affluent members of the urban bourgeoisie, now opposed the Khanh clique.

For central authorities in Hanoi, then, the U.S. reprisal raids might have been a disappointment but not a deterrent. In meetings of senior party officials after the incident, the central authorities decided to expand insurgent military operations in the South in the hope of achieving a "decisive victory" within one or two years. The liberated base area in the Central Highlands was to be strengthened, the remaining strategic hamlets in the Mekong Delta were to be destroyed, and the military strength of the PLAF, especially its main force units, was to be increased to wage "annihilating battles" against the enemy's armed forces. In the meantime, propaganda and agitational work in the cities was to be accelerated in preparation for a general uprising when the appropriate opportunity arose.

There is no clear indication when the decision to send North Vietnamese regular forces to the South was reached, but it is probable that preparations for such a move began at this time. According to U.S. intelligence sources, the first units of the PAVN departed from their camps in September and October and arrived in the South at the end of the year. Although party strategists were undoubtedly aware that Washington would register these moves, they apparently hoped that the news would stimulate dissent and hasten a U.S. withdrawal. A resolution issued by the Politburo in late December portrayed the United States as bitterly divided on the war and increasingly isolated from its chief allies on the issue.[29]

Assessing the Options: The Logic of Escalation

It has been said that the Tonkin Gulf incident represented a psychological "crossing of the threshold" and made further U.S. escalation in Vietnam not only easier but almost inevitable. Whether or not that is the case, the Johnson administration did not make immediate use of the congressional resolution as a rationale for vastly stepped-up attacks on the DRV. After the retaliatory moves taken immediately following the Tonkin Gulf incident had been completed, U.S. actions were relatively restrained. After a third "incident" in the Tonkin Gulf in mid-September, DESOTO patrols and OPLAN 34-A operations were temporarily suspended to guarantee that Hanoi would bear the onus of any further escalation of the conflict. The evidence for the attack had been unconvincing, and it was later concluded that it had not taken place.[30]

Yet many administration officials were concerned that the limited character of the U.S. response might signal to Hanoi that the United States would not continue to take vigorous action to pursue its interests in Southeast Asia. As one of the authors of the *Pentagon Papers* noted, a consensus had begun to develop that additional and continuous pressure had to be imposed on Hanoi lest the lesson of the days of Tonkin be forgotten. In the State Department, Assistant Secretary William Bundy wrote a memo entitled "Next courses of action in Southeast Asia" in which he called for a three-phase process involving steadily increasing pressure and culminating in action against military-related targets in the DRV after the beginning of the new year to persuade Hanoi to remove its forces from South Vietnam and Laos. CINCPAC agreed, pointing out that the U.S. reprisal raids had "created a momentum" that must not be lost. The Joint Chiefs chimed in with their views, urging actions to "sustain the U.S. advantage [recently] gained" and warning that a failure to maintain military pressure could signal a "lack of resolve." Other appeals for additional moves came from Walt W. Rostow and from John T. McNaughton, assistant secretary for international security affairs in the Department of Defense. If South Vietnam collapsed despite major U.S. efforts, McNaughton concluded, the United States should abandon the Saigon regime, leaving the image of "a patient who died despite the extraordinary efforts of a good doctor."[31]

One reason for the rising concern in Washington was the growing conviction that the situation in Saigon was becoming intractable. When the administration had first begun to consider actions against the North, one of the primary justifications for such a move had been that it would raise morale in the South and help to stabilize the Saigon regime. At that time there was some hope that Nguyen Khanh could provide the leadership necessary to mobilize public support behind his government and energize the counterinsurgency program. By late summer it became clear that this hope was illusory, and many Washington officials were convinced that the regime was too fragile to support a bombing campaign against the North.

One of the problems was that U.S. officials, influenced by the euphoric comments of Ambassador Lodge in Saigon, had placed excessive faith in General Khanh. From the start, he faced opposition from older military figures around General Duong Van Minh, in addition to rising pressure from civilians and religious groups for a greater role in the government. The squabbling continued into the summer and seriously hindered the pacification program. A few days after the Tonkin Gulf incident, Nguyen Khanh set up a new charter to strengthen his position and remove his rivals from the Military Revolutionary Council. But his attempts at governmental reorganization merely served to galvanize the opposition into action. During the next few days, large student demonstrations broke out, and Buddhist activists formed a movement called the Salvation of Buddhism in Danger, demanding the abolition of Khanh's charter and the holding of new elections in the fall. Nguyen Khanh attempted to dampen the protests by promising to revise the constitution and reduce censorship, but the demonstrations continued and on August 25 he suddenly resigned. When no one stepped forward to fill the vacuum, a triumvirate leadership of Tran Thien Khiem, Duong Van Minh, and Nguyen Khanh was formed amid anarchy in the streets.[32]

For most of the president's senior advisers, the question of the hour was not whether to escalate but how far and how fast to proceed. The question was discussed at a strategy meeting held without the president on September 7. Maxwell Taylor returned from Saigon to provide his assessment of the situation in South Vietnam, where the government of Nguyen Khanh was hanging by a thread. Other participants were secretaries Rusk and McNamara, the new JCS chairman Earle "Bus" Wheeler, and CIA director John McCone. Taylor had sent a cable on the situation before his departure from Saigon in which he described the limitations of the South Vietnamese government and its leader. Noting that the administration was faced with the choice of passively watching the emergence of political conditions that would force the United States to withdraw in failure or assuming greater responsibility for the outcome, he called for a more active U.S. role in the conflict while hoping for fortuitous developments on the international scene.[33]

At the meeting, General Wheeler presented a proposal on behalf of the JCS for a series of "deliberately provocative actions" by the United States to provoke the DRV, followed by a systematic U.S. bombing campaign of ascending severity to destroy the will and capabilities of the DRV to support the insurgencies in South Vietnam and Laos. But a majority at the meeting rejected the proposal. Maxwell Taylor, for one, felt that the RVN was too weak for the United States to assume a deliberate risk of escalation. But it was agreed to keep open the possibility of bombing in the future, "depending on GVN progress and Communist reaction in the meantime." An agreement was also reached to recommend a series of actions—including the resumption of U.S. patrols in the Tonkin Gulf as well as OPLAN 34-A operations, talks with the Laotian government on limited RVN operations in Laos, and preparations for retaliation on a tit-for-tat basis to any provocative action against U.S. units by the Viet Cong or the DRV—to strengthen RVN morale and "show the Communists we still mean business." The results of the meeting were summed up in a memo drafted by William Bundy.[34]

The president met with his senior foreign policy advisers to discuss their recommendations on the ninth. The latter presented their conclusions that drastic action against the North should not be adopted until the South had been strengthened, at which Johnson exploded at the behavior of a "group of men" in Saigon who lacked a sense of responsibility for the public interest and regularly estimated matters in terms of their own personal gains and losses. Dean Rusk, noting that the Sino-Soviet split was deepening, suggested that the administration adopt the recommendations of September 7 and "play for the breaks." The president attempted to press his advisers for ways to strengthen the RVN, but with little success. Maxwell Taylor suggested that U.S. advisers be integrated into the GVN administrative apparatus, but John McCone worried that such actions could provoke anti-American feeling in Saigon. When Johnson asked what could be done if Nguyen Khanh fell from power, General Taylor replied that so long as the army was solid, the real power of the RVN would be secure. The army would be reliable, he predicted, if it had confidence in U.S. support. On one issue, the group was of one mind. When Johnson asked rhetorically if anyone doubted whether the effort was justified, all agreed that it was. If we lost South Vietnam, said General Wheeler, we would lose Southeast Asia, and all countries in the area would look to China as the rising power in the area. The reason for waiting, the president concluded, was thus simply that "with a weak and wobbly situation it would be unwise to attack until we could stabilize our base." On the following day, the president approved the group's recommendations as NSAM-314.[35]

The September policy debate, then, produced little in concrete actions to turn the tide in South Vietnam. No major departure from existing policy would be adopted until the situation cleared in Saigon. But though an author of the *Pentagon Papers* perhaps overstates the case when he comments that a general consensus had developed among senior officials that "some form of additional and continuous pressure should be exerted against North Vietnam," there was a general feeling that more was needed, and further decisions loomed on the horizon. For the moment, all hinged on the fragile situation in Saigon.[36]

On September 13, three days after Lyndon Johnson approved NSAM-314, a second coup restored Nguyen Khanh to sole power. To placate his political opponents, Khanh agreed to rule behind a facade of civilian rule with the appointment of a High National Council of Elders and a new constitution with the elderly Cao Dai dignitary Pham Khac Suu as chief of state and the Saigon politician Tran Van Huong as prime minister.[37]

The instability in Saigon did not have immediate consequences on the war in the countryside, where Ambassador Taylor reported that the number of Viet Cong attacks on military installations was down, but he warned that there was evidence that the rate of infiltration had increased markedly and an increasing number were regular troops of the PAVN. Taylor concluded that the administration must be prepared to adopt "new and drastic methods to reduce and eventually end such infiltration if we are ever to succeed in South Vietnam."[38]

Such comments were music to the Joint Chiefs, who responded by calling for stronger measures to cut off infiltration routes by seizing control of border areas and applying direct military pressure against the North. But recent events in Saigon had confirmed the growing doubts of one senior administration official over the correctness of U.S. policy in Vietnam and prompted him into action. In recent meetings of the president's foreign policy advisers, George Ball had registered his disagreement with the policy of military escalation. In early October, shortly after the appearance of a new Special National Intelligence Estimate that had portrayed an "almost leaderless" Saigon regime in a state of rapid deterioration, he marshaled his arguments in a lengthy memorandum and sent it to Dean Rusk, Robert McNamara, and McGeorge Bundy for comments.

The memo was a wide-ranging critique of U.S. policy and assumptions in Southeast Asia. No one, he said, could demonstrate that action against North Vietnam would create political cohesion in Saigon or persuade Hanoi to stop helping the Viet Cong. To the contrary, bombing the DRV could trigger a "major invasion of South Vietnam by North Vietnamese forces" that would force the United States to introduce its own combat troops. Under the circumstances, it would be difficult to control the risks and prevent further escalation. Once on the tiger's back, he warned (quoting a Chinese proverb), it would be hard to dismount. Ball attempted to anticipate objections from those who contended, in his words, that Washington had to "stop the extension of Communist power into South Vietnam if our policies were to have any credence." Our allies, he said, were convinced that the United States was "engaged in a fruitless struggle in South Vietnam" and feared that in our single-minded determination to save the country from communism we would lose interest in their problems. "What we might gain by establishing the steadfastness of our commitments," he warned, "we could lose by an erosion of confidence in our judgment," a result that could eventuate if we pursued a course that many regarded as "neither prudent nor necessary." How, then, to proceed? Ball pointed out that the United States originally committed itself to assist South Vietnam only "so long as the Vietnamese people wish us to help" and so long as they maintained a decent standard of performance. Washington could now demand that the Saigon regime and people demonstrate such unity and purpose. Such a demand might serve to rally the RVN to decisive action. More likely, it would lead to a collapse of will and negotiations with the Viet Cong. That, he concluded, would be a good thing.[39]

Ball's reasoning fell on deaf ears. McNamara in particular appeared shocked that his colleague would, in Ball's phraseology, "challenge the verities" and implied that he had been imprudent in putting his views on paper. Ball considered bringing the document to the president's attention but decided to delay doing so until after the presidential election, when he could hope to win Johnson's full attention. That opportunity would not arise until the following February.

November Policy Review

On November 1, 1964, Viet Cong units launched a mortar attack on a U.S. air base at Bien Hoa, about twenty miles north of Saigon, killing four U.S.

servicemen and destroying several aircraft. NSAM-314 had said that the United States "should be prepared to respond as appropriate" to any attack on U.S. units in South Vietnam, and both Maxwell Taylor and the Joint Chiefs recommended immediate retaliatory air strikes against the North, but at a meeting at the White House that same day, Johnson decided not to retaliate, and a press release issued after the meeting was noncommittal. Administration officials explained that if the United States decided to retaliate in the future, it must be for a broader reason than the strike at Bien Hoa.[40]

The attack at Bien Hoa, however, did result in the creation of an NSC Working Group to study alternatives and then report to a Principals Group of NSC members who would in turn propose future courses of action to the president. The working group was chaired by William Bundy and included Michael Forrestal and Robert Johnson of the State Department, John McNaughton from the Department of Defense, as well as representatives from the CIA and the Joint Chiefs.

According to its instruction, the working group was supposed to examine alternatives, but according to one of the authors of the *Pentagon Papers*, there was a general agreement among the members that there was no realistic alternative to escalation. They therefore began with the shared assumption that U.S. prestige was heavily committed to the maintenance of a noncommunist government in South Vietnam and "only less heavily" to a neutralized Laos. They perceived three objectives: (1) the general principle of helping a country defend itself against communist subversion and attack, (2) the specific consequences of communist control of South Vietnam and Laos for the security of the remainder of Southeast Asia (although the effects in Thailand would be mainly in terms of morale), and (3) the importance of South Vietnam as a "test case" of the U.S. capacity to defeat a war of national liberation. A defeat in South Vietnam, the group concluded, would be a "major blow" to U.S. containment policy worldwide.

The primary disagreement within the working group was over the effect that the application of military pressure would have on the DRV. Bundy favored it as a means of demonstrating toughness, McNaughton because there were no prospects for stability in Saigon. But representatives from the intelligence agencies were pessimistic and argued that even a damaged DRV could support the war at a low level and would hope for international pressure to force a U.S. withdrawal. The JCS representative was not as pessimistic and reiterated the Joint Chiefs' proposal to destroy enemy capabilities. Something less than total destruction, he said, might be all that was required.

In the end, the working group avoided any agreed recommendation on the issue. In predicting Hanoi's reaction to U.S. escalation, it simply said that the decision would be influenced by the U.S. posture and the extent and nature of the U.S. escalation, as well as how Washington communicated its intentions. The final report asserted that U.S. attacks could cripple Hanoi's primitive industrial and transportation network and reduce its capability to wage guerrilla war but concluded that it would not create unmanageable control problems and predicted that the DRV "would probably be willing to suffer some damage to the country in the course of a test of wills with the U.S. over the course of events in South Vietnam." It further predicted that Moscow and Beijing would provide assistance but that Moscow, under new leadership since the overthrow of Nikita Khrushchev in October, did not wish to run a major risk of war. One interesting aspect of the working group's deliberations was its debate over the possibility of failure. An early draft by William Bundy had declared that even if the United States made a major military commitment with the possible use of nuclear weapons, it was possible that South Vietnam, because of its "bad colonial heritage" and the enduring strength of the communist government in the North, "might still come apart." The United States, noted Bundy, had never thought that it could "defend a government or a people that had ceased to care strongly about defending themselves, or that were unable to maintain the fundamentals of government." The impression around the world, he noted, was that these elements were lacking in South Vietnam. Even then, however, Bundy was not ready to give up. In that case, he said, the U.S. objectives would be to hold the situation together as long as possible to buy time to strengthen other areas of Asia, to adopt sufficient forceful measures so that even in the worst case the United States would emerge with its standing as the principal helper against communist expansion as little impaired as possible, and to make clear to the world and to Asia that if South Vietnam were to fail, it was owing to "special factors" that "do not apply to other nations that we are committed to defend."[41]

Reaction to Bundy's memo was mixed. Forrestal and Sullivan suggested that more attention needed to be devoted to how China fit into the equation, while the JCS representative countered that Bundy's paper understated the gravity of the loss of South Vietnam and overstated the potential risks of U.S. action to prevent that loss. If South Vietnam were lost, said Vice-Admiral L. M. Mustin, there would be no point for the United States to attempt to strengthen other countries in the region. It would be, he said, "thoroughly non-productive" to attempt it. He also took issue with Bundy's justification for a possible defeat. The U.S. standing as the principal helper against communist expansion would suffer abject humiliation and Bundy's rationale would be a slight paraphrase of Aesop's fox and grapes story, transparent to any intelligent outside observer. The fall of South Vietnam, he concluded, would be near disastrous or worse. Cambodia, Thailand, and possibly Burma and Malaysia would almost automatically fall to communist domination. Mitigating circumstances would not alter the situation, and the results would be grave regardless of the foreseeable variants. To the Joint Chiefs, South Vietnam was as important as Berlin from a symbolic point of view and more important from a military perspective.[42]

The final report followed the Bundy draft in assessing the consequences of a communist victory. The effect on NATO, it predicted, would not be severe so long as the United States did not remove its military forces from Western Europe and become isolationist. In Asia, the effect would "depend heavily on the circumstances in which South Vietnam was lost and on whether the loss did in fact greatly weaken or lead to the early loss of other areas in Southeast Asia." The fall of Saigon could have serious repercussions in India and Iran, but the possible consequences in Southeast Asia itself were highly differentiated and by no means automatic. The domino theory was viewed as "over-simplified" and applied only if China entered Southeast Asia militarily or if U.S. forces were withdrawn in the event of a military defeat. But it conceded that Laos would be hard to hold and that Cambodia would bend sharply to the communist side. Thailand would come under pressure, and Indonesia would be encouraged to increase pressure on Malaysia (where President Sukarno was promoting the policy of "konfrontasi" to unite all Malay peoples under Indonesian rule). The final report concluded that there were

enough "ifs" in the above analysis so that it cannot be concluded that the loss of South Vietnam would soon have the totally crippling effect in Southeast Asia and Asia generally that the loss of Berlin would have in Europe; but it could be that bad, driving us to the progressive loss of other areas or to taking a stand at some point [so that] there would almost certainly be a major conflict and perhaps the great risk of nuclear war.

As before, Admiral Mustin disagreed with many of these conclusions and presented a minority report, which was included as an appendix to the final working group report. Mustin reiterated the conclusion of the JCS that the domino theory was "the most realistic estimate for Cambodia and Thailand, probably Burma, possibly Malaysia."[43]

The working group did not recommend specific policies, but it did list possible courses for future action, ranging from continuing the present strategy (Option A), a rapid and sustained increase in military pressure on the North (Option B), and a more gradual approach, combined with the possible introduction of U.S. ground troops, to bring about negotiations (Option C). The working group did not select its own recommendation on the various options and, according to William Bundy, probably could not have reached a consensus on the issue.

The working group report was scheduled to be discussed at a meeting of high-level officials in late November. The meeting, attended by Dean Rusk, Robert McNamara, John McCone, General Earle Wheeler, George Ball, and the two Bundys, convened on the twenty-fourth and opened with a discussion of the central question of whether the RVN could survive even if aid to the insurgency forces from the North could be curtailed. A consensus was reached that the security situation in South Vietnam "could be handled in time if the government could maintain itself" but that, even in that event, the struggle would be a long one. All but George Ball concurred that the loss of South Vietnam would be more serious than stated in the working group report and closer to the JCS assessment. Dean Rusk argued that the confidence of other nations in the United States would be affected by the loss of South Vietnam despite their possible indifference to the struggle in Southeast Asia. He did not accept the rationale that Washington would get international credit merely for trying. The harder we tried and failed, he said, the worse the situation would be.

Having disposed of the issue of objectives, the committee then engaged in a lengthy discussion of options. It was generally agreed that the present policy was a failure and should be discarded. A proposal by George Ball to seek a new Geneva Conference was rejected as nothing but a smoke screen for a communist takeover. There was some sympathy for the view that withdrawal would be less damaging than an unsuccessful escalation and that a unified Vietnam might prove to be an obstacle to future Chinese expansion in Southeast Asia. But in general, such an option was considered too risky in its potential consequences.

As before, administration officials had come to an agreement on the logic of escalation but could not concur on how far or how fast to proceed. Option B—heavy pressure on the North—was rejected as risking war with China, despite continued support for such a policy from the Joint Chiefs and General Wheeler's argument that the chances of war with Beijing were not significant. There was a brief discussion of the possible use of nuclear weapons. Secretary McNamara said that he could not imagine a case in which they would be considered, but McGeorge Bundy noted that there might be pressure to use them from political or military circles. General Wheeler said they would not normally be used for interdiction purposes but perhaps might become necessary in extremis to save a military force threatened with destruction. No decision was taken on Rostow's proposal to introduce U.S. ground troops, but several participants expressed the view that they might serve a useful purpose. McNamara, though expressing a preference for massive air deployment, said they could provide a general security force, in which General Wheeler concurred. Rusk saw their value in demonstrating U.S. resolve, while CIA director John McCone remarked that they might serve to stabilize the situation, as in Lebanon. The meeting adjourned without making any recommendation, pending the return of Ambassador Taylor from Saigon.[44]

On November 27 the principals met again with Maxwell Taylor in attendance. His assessment of the situation in Saigon was bleak on all counts. The government was unstable, pacification operations were at a standstill, and the rate of infiltration was on the rise. On the key question of priorities, Taylor straddled the issue. Without a better government, he warned, nothing would work. Yet even an effective government in Saigon could not succeed until the DRV was forced to cease supporting the Viet Cong. He agreed that operations against the North might serve as a means of improving RVN morale but warned that even reprisal attacks might not hold the present government upright. Like the others, Taylor was ambivalent on options, but on balance he preferred a policy that combined Option A (existing strategy) with the beginning stages of Option C, gradually escalated military pressure on the North. But he warned that even reprisal attacks might not preserve the present government.[45]

The meeting ended inconclusively, exuding an overall air of pessimism. There was a recognition that nothing might help, and when Taylor was asked whether the United States could carry on if the regime collapsed or asked us out, he replied that such an eventuality would be hard to visualize, and all agreed it should be avoided. Taylor warned that an ultimatum to "perform or else" would be a gamble but that a simple statement that the United States could not help in the absence of a stable government might help. The principals met twice more in the following days and approved a draft NSAM that incorporated Taylor's suggestion of a combination of Options A and C. The transition to a second phase of "graduated military pressures directed systematically against the DRV" would take place if the situation in the RVN improved and Hanoi refused to yield on acceptable terms, or "if the GVN can only be kept going through stronger action." Unlike the original Option C designed by the working group, it was not combined with a flexible policy on negotiations to bring Hanoi to the conference table.[46]

On December 1, the principals presented their draft NSAM to the president. It called for the temporary continuation of the present policy supplemented by selected new operations such as armed reconnaissance of infiltration routes in Laos and an accelerated counterinsurgency program. If results were not shortly forthcoming, the focus would shift to graduated military pressure directed specifically against the DRV. Targets would begin with infiltration routes and move gradually northward. The ultimate goal would be to bring Hanoi to the negotiating table under circumstances favorable to the United States. No formal decision was reached or published at the close of the meeting, but based on available evidence and an account of the meeting at the Johnson Library, the president approved only the first stage of the principals' report, reserving judgment on later actions until further measures had been taken to improve the situation in South Vietnam.

What would happen if political conditions in Saigon continued to deteriorate? Here the evidence is ambiguous. According to notes of the meeting taken by John McNaughton, Johnson remarked that there was "no point hitting North if South not together." But he quotes the president as adding that he wanted to give Taylor "one last chance" before the "Day of Reckoning." If the response was "more of the same," he said, "then I'll be talking to you General [Wheeler]." The November policy review had thus not resulted in major decisions for new actions to reverse the drift in South Vietnam. Once again, the president had rejected the option of unleashing military pressure against the DRV, ostensibly on the ground that the crux of the problem remained in Saigon. "Hesitate to sock neighbor," McNaughton's notes quote the president, "if fever 104." Yet an expansion of war into the North now appeared virtually inevitable because it could be done whether or not the situation in South Vietnam improved. "If need be," he had remarked at the meeting of December 1, "create a new Diem, so when tell Wheeler to slap we can take slap back."[47]

Agony of Indecision

Ambassador Taylor met with the president on December 3 to finalize plans for his return to Saigon. In the message that he was to present to the South Vietnamese, Taylor was to emphasize that although action against the North could reduce the threat to the RVN, the administration was not prepared to escalate the conflict until there was a government in Saigon "capable of handling the serious problems involved in such an expansion and of exploiting the favorable effects which may be anticipated from an end of support and direction by North Vietnam." Minimal criteria for such a decision included a government able to speak for and to its people, capable of maintaining law and order in populated areas of the country, and able to make plans for the efficient conduct of operations against the Viet Cong.[48]

During the next several weeks, there was little change in the situation. In Saigon, bickering among the various political and military factions continued despite Ambassador Taylor's appeal for unity and culminated in the dismissal of the government of Tran Van Huong by Nguyen Khanh and the latter's sole takeover of power. Taylor, who had liked Huong, lost his patience, lecturing some of the younger military leaders on the need for national unity and suggesting that Nguyen Khanh himself resign and leave the country. Student riots, sponsored by the Buddhists, echoed through the streets of the city and on television screens in the United States. On Christmas Eve, a bomb exploded at the Brink's Hotel in downtown Saigon, killing 2 Americans and wounding nearly 40 more. The embassy, supported by the Joint Chiefs, called for immediate reprisals against the DRV, but the request was turned down on the grounds that there was no clear evidence of Viet Cong involvement. A cable from the Department of State to the U.S. Embassy in Saigon also pointed out that a reprisal launched on Christmas Day could create a strong reaction in U.S. public opinion that the administration was trying to shoot its way out of an internal political crisis.[49]

The sense of unease about the war in South Vietnam had now reached to include key members of Congress, including Senators Mike Mansfield, William Fulbright, and Frank Church of Idaho. A survey of senatorial opinion on the war at the time indicated that nearly half of those who responded suggested a negotiated settlement as soon as Saigon's bargaining position had improved. Ten favored immediate negotiations, eight proposed military action against the DRV, and three called for an immediate withdrawal of U.S. forces and military aid. Eleven called for a continuation of existing policy.[50]

President Johnson appeared to be in an agony of indecision. Increased involvement in "that bitch of a war on the other side of the world" would distract attention and resources from domestic Great Society programs. But withdrawal would expose him and his administration to the charge (feared by all Democrats since the fall of China in 1949) of cowardice and appeasement of the communists. He had little faith in the efficacy of large-scale bombing and instinctively preferred to concentrate on defeating the insurgent forces with the aid of U.S. combat troops on the ground in South Vietnam but had equally little confidence in the political leadership in Saigon. Whichever way he moved, he was bound to be crucified.[51]

The continued drift in Saigon inspired new thoughts about solutions in Washington. In early January, William Bundy wrote a memo to Secretary Rusk evaluating the situation and courses of action open to the administration. There were, he said, only two real alternatives. The first was to let the situation drift, which would lead eventually to a government in Saigon dominated by the NLF. This could lead to the creation of a united Vietnam with some degree of independence from China, thus producing a pause in communist pressure on Southeast Asia. But Laos would become untenable and Cambodia, as well as Thailand, would be forced to accommodate to the new situation in one way or another. Although American public opinion would probably not be "too sharply critical," it would still represent a humiliating defeat for the United States.[52]

The alternative was to take stronger action. This option, Bundy admitted, presented "grave difficulties" because it would commit the United States to a weak ally in Saigon and inspire harsh criticism from friends and allies such as India and Japan. Most important, there would be no guarantees that Saigon could be stiffened or that Hanoi could be induced to call off its support for the insurgents in the South. Yet, on balance, Bundy preferred the latter because, as he put it, it presented at least the "faint hope of really improving the Vietnamese situation and, above all, would put us in a much stronger position to hold the next line of defense—namely Thailand." Even if the situation in South Vietnam deteriorated to the point of communist takeover, he said, "we would have appeared to Asians to have done a lot more about it."[53]

In the Pentagon, John McNaughton was experiencing similar thoughts. In a memo to McNamara drafted a few weeks later, he warned against the temptation to use the deterioration in Saigon as an excuse to "dump" South Vietnam. The U.S. objective, he said, was not to "help friend" but to contain China. If Saigon fell, the conflict would simply shift to Malaysia or Thailand (in the margin, McNamara commented, "These will go fast") and continue with side effects of accommodation elsewhere in Asia. Negotiations offered no solution, although they might serve to confuse the "psychological impact of loss." For the moment, there was no alternative but to keep "plugging away" while waiting for the next "reprisal opportunity" and beginning to educate the American public that the confrontation in Southeast Asia might last for years.[54]

Incident at Pleiku

That next "reprisal opportunity" was not long in coming. The U.S. Embassy in Saigon had received reports that U.S. citizens and installations might become the target of terrorist attacks similar to the incidents at the Brink's Hotel and the Bien Hoa Air Base. Admiral U. S. Grant Sharp in Honolulu had suggested the removal of U.S. dependents from South Vietnam, but that had been delayed because of its possible psychological effect on the Vietnamese. On February 7, Saigon time, the Viet Cong attacked a U.S. Special Forces Camp at Pleiku in the Central Highlands, killing several American servicemen and wounding many others.

Hanoi, of course, had been watching with interest as Washington agonized over a solution to the problem in Vietnam. After the Tonkin Gulf incident in August 1964, the Politburo had set in motion an accelerated effort to bring about a decisive victory through combined political and military struggle within a period of one or two years. In preparation for that scenario, it appointed a senior military commander, General Nguyen Chi Thanh, to take charge of all operations in the South. Born in a rural village near the imperial capital of Hué in 1914, he had become active in party activities during the 1930's and spent much of World War II in jail. After the war he directed Vietminh activities in the central provinces and was named to head the political directorate of the Vietminh armed forces in 1951. The same year, he became a founding member of the VWP Politburo. In succeeding years he became a convinced advocate of Maoist methods in the DRV and was promoted to the highest military rank—a rank shared only with General Vo Nguyen Giap—in 1959.[55]

During the early 1960's General Thanh became directly involved in overseeing military operations in the South, and shortly after the Tonkin Gulf incident he visited the area to evaluate the situation and present his recommendations to the party leadership. Nguyen Chi Thanh was a man of action rather than a theorist, and it is likely that he was instrumental in bringing about the decision to introduce North Vietnamese troops into the war and seek a victory by military means, despite concerns among some of his colleagues that Hanoi lacked the firepower to deal with the challenge of a growing U.S. role in the war. General Thanh adopted the Maoist view that revolutionary spirit could overcome the technological superiority of the enemy. His plan was to consolidate a liberated base area in the strategic Central Highlands and advance from there into the lowlands to engage in battles to destroy a significant proportion of the enemy's armed forces. Such victories would serve as a springboard for a general offensive and uprising to bring about the fall of the Saigon regime.[56]

Events in the world arena now came to Hanoi's aid. After Soviet leader Nikita Khrushchev was overthrown in late October, the new Soviet party leadership under Alexei Kosygin and Leonid Brezhnev was quick to demonstrate more sympathy for Vietnamese appeals for support. When Prime Minister Pham Van Dong visited Moscow to take part in celebrations of the Bolshevik Revolution in early November, the Soviet Union agreed to increase its assistance to the DRV and reportedly also agreed to support a general offensive in the South if the United States refused to negotiate. In return, Hanoi promised to "harmonize" its own interests with those of the "international proletariat."

In December, Viet Cong units attacked a Catholic village at Binh Gia, east of Saigon, and inflicted heavy casualties on South Vietnamese armed forces. Hanoi sources labeled the battle a major victory, which signaled the revolutionary movement's increased ability to meet the challenge of the enemy's tactics of mobile warfare. But it also demonstrated the continuing inability of the PLAF to follow up on its battlefield successes. A captured document providing a year-end assessment of the situation remarked that insurgent forces did not yet possess sufficient military strength to impose a decisive defeat on the enemy.[57]

The party tried to keep up with the rapidly evolving situation without provoking the United States into direct action. At a meeting of the Politburo in early January 1965, Hanoi called for accelerated efforts to destroy the South Vietnamese armed forces and prepare conditions for a general uprising in the major cities. In a letter reporting the results of the meeting to Nguyen Chi Thanh, now the COSVN chief in the South, Le Duan raised the fundamental question: could the PLAF defeat ARVN before it had a chance to revive (as had taken place in Laos) or the United States decided to intervene? If so, Washington would have no choice but to negotiate a compromise settlement and withdraw.

Le Duan answered his own question in the affirmative. He admitted that the balance of forces was not as favorable to the revolution as it had been just before the Geneva Conference in 1954, but he asserted that the guerrilla movement was stronger now and the overall political situation was more advantageous. If several ARVN divisions could be disabled and other units could be lured out of the cities through guerrilla attacks in rural areas, then urban uprisings in major cities like Saigon, Da Nang, and Hué would have a good chance of success. Then politics would become a key factor. A coalition of neutralist forces, secretly guided by the party, could form a government in Saigon and demand a U.S. withdrawal. Le Duan admitted that there was no

guarantee of success, but he quoted Lenin: "Let's act and then see." Even if they
did not succeed, he said, they could always retire and try again.[58]

"Aggression from the North"

An emergency meeting of the NSC, supplemented by the attendance of
Senator Mike Mansfield and Speaker of the House of Representatives John
McCormack, convened in the White House as soon as the news of the attack at
Pleiku reached Washington. The meeting resulted in a quick decision to launch
air strikes on DRV staging areas in the North Vietnamese panhandle. Accord-
ing to the partial record of discussion at the meeting, all in attendance agreed
that the administration must retaliate. Even Mansfield commented that the
Pleiku incident had "opened many eyes." Early on the morning of February 7,
Washington time, U.S. carrier-based planes in the Tonkin Gulf struck at Dong
Hoi and other sites in the DRV. The following day, the president instructed
McNamara to draw up a program of sustained reprisals, and the White House
announced that dependents would be evacuated from the RVN.[59]

Hanoi reacted, but not in the way Washington had hoped. On February 10,
Viet Cong units attacked a U.S. Army billet at Qui Nhon, on the central coast of
the RVN, killing 21 Americans. Washington retaliated with another air strike
near Dong Hoi. The White House attempted to downplay the importance of
the strikes so as not to provoke China and the Soviet Union. Senior officials
were particularly sensitive to the fact that Soviet Premier Alexei Kosygin was
then on a state visit to Hanoi. But it was clear that changes were in the wind.
The air strikes were no longer labeled as reprisals but as a response to aggression
and, as the author of the *Pentagon Papers* has remarked, "were designed to
signal changes in the ground rules in the conflict in the South." The Pleiku
incident resulted in a decisive shift in the administration's focus of emphasis
from the South to the North. The key to the solution of the war, from Washington's perspective, was now in Hanoi rather than Saigon. It would remain
there until the final departure of U.S. troops in 1973.[60]

A team of administration officials led by McGeorge Bundy was in Saigon at
the time of the Pleiku incident. With Ambassador Taylor's concurrence, they
immediately cabled to Washington their recommendation for prompt retaliation against the DRV. En route home Bundy drafted a memo in which he
proposed a policy of sustained reprisals, including air and naval actions (but
something less than the Phase II of the program drafted in December), against
North Vietnam. In a short but hard-hitting report he conceded that the prospects in South Vietnam were "grim." Without new U.S. action, he warned,
defeat appeared inevitable, if not within weeks or months, then certainly within
a year or so. But Bundy expressed disagreement with the existing assumption
that the United States could not take further action without the promise of a

more stable government in Saigon. Although Nguyen Khanh had weaknesses, he was still the best man available for present purposes. To launch a new policy of reprisals against the North, he insisted, the government "need be no stronger than it is today." Key problems, he argued, were Saigon's lack of confidence in the clarity and firmness of the U.S. commitment and the widespread belief that Washington possessed neither the will nor the patience to stay the course in Vietnam. Retaliatory measures against the DRV would not only instill that confidence but also give Washington more leverage in Saigon. Bundy admitted that such actions would not necessarily turn the tide (he placed the odds of success at 25 to 75 percent), but the value seemed to him to exceed the cost. "It will damp down the charge that we did not do all we could have done," he said, and set a high price for future guerrilla wars. Negotiations would mean "surrender on the installment plan."[61]

In Saigon, Ambassador Taylor generally concurred with Bundy's analysis, but he felt that the main goal was to weaken Hanoi's will and only secondarily to boost GVN morale and destroy Hanoi's ability to support the insurgency. To achieve that purpose, he recommended a policy of graduated reprisals combined with a demand that the DRV return to the terms of the Geneva Accords of 1954 and 1962. In return, the United States would promise not to resort to the use of force to upset the accords with regard to the DRV. The military still wanted stronger measures. CINCPAC called for "steady, relentless movements" to convince Hanoi and Beijing of the prohibitive cost of supporting the Viet Cong.

A meeting of the National Security Council was held on February 10, shortly after the Viet Cong attack at Qui Nhon and the return of the Bundy mission from Saigon. There was apparently a consensus at the meeting that additional air strikes should be launched against the DRV, although Vice-President Hubert Humphrey wanted to delay action until Kosygin had departed for Moscow. The primary item of debate was how far north to stage the strikes. Within 24 hours of the Viet Cong attack, U.S. and South Vietnamese aircraft struck again in two areas in the panhandle region. The press release announcing the raids was careful to avoid the term "retaliation" and stressed that they were a response to "continued aggression" from Hanoi. On February 28, the administration released a new White Paper entitled *Aggression from the North* in which it attempted to document the growing DRV role in supporting the insurgency movement in the South.[62]

The Pleiku incident opened the floodgates. On February 13 President Johnson approved a new policy calling for "a program of measured and limited air action jointly with the GVN against selected targets in the DRV south of the 19th parallel until further notice." The first strikes were scheduled for February 26, but bad weather forced a postponement until March 2. At first the attacks were sporadic, but after both Taylor and Westmoreland called for an increased tempo, in mid-March the president agreed to increase and regularize the bombing campaign, leaving the timing to field commanders. The primary emphasis was on interdiction of infiltration into the South. But the White House made it clear that it was "important not to kill the hostage." The stated objective of the attacks was not to destroy the enemy's capabilities but to break his will by denying him victory. When asked for the rationale for the decision, President Johnson replied that it was to avoid an instant and total Chinese response.[63]

The Fork in the Y

In his memo written immediately following the attack on Pleiku, McGeorge Bundy had not mentioned the use of troops, but the question had been in the air. In November, the NSC working group had considered the establishment of an allied force near the DMZ as part of a Phase II concept to provide a blocking force against a possible North Vietnamese invasion until reinforcements arrived, and the issue had been turned over to the JCS for possible implementation. But the Joint Chiefs were not at that time enthusiastic over the introduction of U.S. combat troops into South Vietnam, preferring to rely on air power to limit Hanoi's capabilities to bolster the insurgency in the RVN. Neither Dean Rusk nor Robert McNamara favored the use of U.S. troops, and the idea was apparently dropped at that time, although it remained in the air as part of a possible Phase II concept.[64]

But the Pleiku incident and the change in U.S. bombing strategy that followed led to a reevaluation of the concept. In their response to Secretary McNamara's February 8 request for recommendations on how to react to the Pleiku attack, JCS chairman Earle Wheeler and Air Force Chief of Staff General John B. McConnell proposed the dispatch of three U.S. combat divisions to Southeast Asia. Two weeks later, in a cable sent through the U.S. Embassy, General Westmoreland expressed concern at reports that there were 6,000 Viet Cong in the region of the U.S. air base at Da Nang and submitted a request for U.S. troops to guard the base. In forwarding Westmoreland's request to Washington, Taylor expressed his strong reservations about the concept. In his view, it would encourage the South Vietnamese government to "unload other ground force tasks upon us" and turn the conflict over to white-faced soldiers that could not be assimilated by the population. We could not hope to win such a war, he warned, any more than the French had. Taylor was also skeptical that the two battalions requested by General Westmoreland would provide adequate security and suggested a reduction to one battalion. But CINCPAC supported Westmoreland's request and pointed out that the deployment of two U.S. Marine battalions at Da Nang would free ARVN for more offensive operations. President Johnson approved Westmoreland's request on February 26, and Taylor was asked to seek approval from the RVN. This was no easy matter, for although Nguyen Khanh had expressed a willingness in December, the new civilian government under Phan Huy Quat had serious reservations about introducing U.S. troops and wanted them as inconspicuous as possible. The final decision was announced to the press on March 6 and described as a "limited mission" to relieve ARVN forces and strengthen the general security of the Da Nang air base complex.[65]

Why, after so much hesitation and soul-searching over the advisability of increasing the U.S. role in the conflict, did Johnson now move so quickly? What was there about the situation in February 1965 that changed earlier perspectives? Participants in the decisions offer several possibilities. One factor, as one of the authors of the *Pentagon Papers* noted, was that the situation in South Vietnam was alarming. During the early weeks of 1965 the Nguyen Khanh regime deteriorated rapidly, and a new government under Phan Huy Quat, formed on February 16, looked no better. Pacification was at a standstill, and apathy was rampant in Saigon. Intelligence sources reported a marked increase in infiltration from the North and insurgent activity and a rapid deterioration of the situation in the Central Highlands provinces, especially in Binh Dinh, which was now virtually lost to the Viet Cong. Many feared that the VC would cut Highway 9 and divide the country in two. To some observers, their attacks at Binh Gia signaled the end of the second phase and beginning of the third phase of Hanoi's strategy of people's war. It was these concerns that incited Ambassador Taylor to propose retaliatory actions for their "pulmotor" effect on Saigon.

Another factor that influenced minds in Washington was the growing evidence of Hanoi's role in the war. Administration officials had conclusive evidence in the form of intercepts that at least two PAVN regiments had arrived in the South the previous December, but on CIA advice such evidence had not been included in the White Paper issued in late February. Were intelligence sources correct in asserting that Hanoi had begun to infiltrate substantial numbers of main force units down the Ho Chi Minh Trail from the North? That is a highly controversial question for which there are as yet no definitive answers. What does seem clear is that until late 1964, party leaders had refrained from sending large numbers of North Vietnamese regular forces to the South to avoid providing Washington with a pretext for widening the war. During the late fall and winter of 1964–65 it is likely that the infiltration of PAVN units increased as DRV strategists attempted to bring about a rapid collapse of the Saigon regime before Maxwell Taylor's "pulmotor" had time to take effect.

According to Hanoi sources, however, party leaders were not yet prepared to make a basic change in their own approach. In a letter written to COSVN chief Nguyen Chi Thanh sometime in February, Le Duan reported that the Politburo had decided that there was no reason to change the existing strategy calling for a protracted struggle to culminate in a general offensive and uprising. Could the armed forces of the Saigon regime be defeated without a change in strategy (presumably meaning the large-scale influx of regular forces from the North) before the United States could decide to escalate its own role in the war? Le Duan answered his own rhetorical question in the affirmative. It would all depend, he said, on the cleverness of revolutionary forces and the reaction of the United States. The United States, like all Great Powers, was reluctant to get bogged down in an inconclusive conflict. If the insurgent forces could defeat Saigon's armed forces before the United States had time to interfere, then it might decide to draw back because it would lose less prestige by withdrawing from a limited commitment than one on a larger scale.

What, then, were the Politboro's instructions to Nguyen Chi Thanh and his colleagues? The key to victory, it said, was to strengthen all elements of the revolutionary armed forces to place maximum pressure on the Saigon regime and its own armed forces. Guerrilla troops were to tie down ARVN units by launching attacks throughout the country. Simultaneously, main force units must be strengthened and concentrated to open up new offensive campaigns (such as at Binh Gia the previous December) to force the enemy to disperse his forces and draw them away from the cities. If such actions were to take place, the urban movement would be able to intensify its own efforts to prepare for a general uprising in Saigon and other major cities of the GVN to be launched at a time of accelerated military attacks in the countryside. If the two operations could be effectively coordinated, victory could be achieved before the end of the year, leading to the creation of a neutralist government in Saigon under NLF control. Le Duan conceded that victory was not certain, but even so, the movement in rural areas was so strong that success was only a matter of time.[66]

Washington's decision to launch sustained air attacks on the DRV and introduce U.S. combat troops into the RVN in February and March undoubtedly brought Hanoi's strategy of avoiding the direct involvement of the North into question. But it apparently did not lead to an immediate change in approach. At its Eleventh Plenum in late March, the party Central Committee issued a resolution conceding that the United States was in the process of taking a more direct part in the war. But it argued that U.S. policymakers were badly divided over strategy and that the current objective of the Johnson administration might be to widen the war in order to negotiate from strength and thus limit the scope of the U.S. defeat. The resolution predicted, however, that the United States would encounter major problems if it attempted to escalate the war because of the weakened state of the Saigon regime and the growing strength of the revolutionary forces. Other factors favoring the insurgency were the declining morale of the enemy and an increasingly favorable world situation. To party leaders, then, the U.S. decision to escalate had not changed the basic situation, and there was still a chance to defeat the enemy in the stage of special war. Under those circumstances, the roles of South and North remained different, with the latter still serving as the rear base of the struggle, supporting the liberation movement in the South while continuing to engage in domestic construction. Hanoi was not yet ready to throw its entire strength into the war effort.[67]

Administration officials were probably also affected by the evolving world situation. Although the new government in Moscow, like its predecessor, appeared unwilling to run the risk of a wider war in Southeast Asia, the Kosygin visit had shown that Soviet leaders were prepared to increase their assistance to the DRV in the war in the South. In the meantime, China had not reacted to the fall of Khrushchev by moving closer to Moscow. To the contrary, Beijing appeared increasingly belligerent, and the Chinese official press predicted that Thailand would be the next apple in Southeast Asia to fall from the tree of imperialism. Such statements, combined with Sukarno's continued policy of "konfrontasi" with Malaysia, made moderate leaders in Southeast Asia edgy and persuaded policymakers in Washington that only strong action by the United States could halt the deterioration of the situation in the region. As a joint memorandum written by McGeorge Bundy and Secretary McNamara had expressed it in late January, the administration was now at "the fork in the Y," from which it must either advance or retreat.[68]

The Debate over Troops

What was the administration's purpose in introducing combat troops? The press statement announcing the decision to send the first units had implied that it was a temporary measure, and Maxwell Taylor had similarly informed the government of Phan Huy Quat (which was not consulted on the decision, according to a Vietnamese source) that their deployment was purely defensive and temporary in nature. But that was certainly not the view of many senior U.S. military officers concerned with the problem of Vietnam. Although at the beginning of the year General Wheeler had described the purpose of such troops as providing base security, by early March Pentagon sources probably viewed them as the opening wedge for the introduction of large numbers to play an active role in the Vietnam War.[69]

This was certainly the view of General Westmoreland in Saigon, who was concerned at the prospects for a Viet Cong summer offensive and convinced that ARVN could not handle it. On March 17, he asked Ambassador Taylor to agree to a proposal to deploy an additional battalion of U.S. Marines to protect the airstrip at Phu Bai, north of Da Nang. This, he explained, would relieve ARVN from sedentary duties and strengthen the situation in the northern provinces as well as ending talk of a U.S. withdrawal.

But the ambassador still opposed deploying troops. In a cable to Washington the following day, Taylor presented his arguments. "The introduction of a U.S. division," he said, "obviously increases U.S. involvement in the counter-insurgency, exposes greater forces and invites greater losses." It would raise sensitive questions of command with the Saigon regime and could encourage it to adopt an attitude of "let the United States do it." It would increase U.S. vulnerability to communist propaganda and Third Country criticism as it appeared to assume the old French role of alien colonizer and conqueror. Finally, he concluded, "there is considerable doubt that the number of GVN forces which our action would relieve would have any great significance in reducing the power gap." So he opposed the introduction of a U.S. division into South Vietnam "unless there are clear and tangible advantages outweighing the numerous disadvantages."[70]

On March 19 CINCPAC forwarded Westmoreland's proposal to the Joint Chiefs, who gave their approval on March 25. Westmoreland had an ally in Washington in General Harold Johnson, army chief of staff, who had just returned from a visit to Saigon in early March. Johnson reported that the situation was so perilous that only U.S. forces could save it. His recommendation to Secretary McNamara on March 14 called for more U.S. ground troops to deter Hanoi, defeat the Viet Cong, and create a stable RVN. One division would provide security, while four other divisions of U.S. and SEATO troops would be posted on the DMZ to stop infiltration. The Joint Chiefs backed him up three days later.

At the end of March, Maxwell Taylor returned briefly to Washington to present his own point of view. Taylor was not unalterably opposed to the use of U.S. troops, but he wanted to clarify their mission. He was concerned that an American takeover of the war would lead to growing antiforeign sentiment in South Vietnam and wanted to impose strict limits on U.S. combat activities, placing them in territorial enclaves from which they might launch carefully selected offensive operations and thereby test both their effectiveness and the impact of their use on the attitudes of the Saigon government and the local population.[71]

Curiously, there was little debate within the administration over the advisability of introducing U.S. combat units, a decision that had been avoided by two previous presidents as a turning point marking an American takeover of the war. Significantly, support for the idea came from civilian officials involved in war planning, including McGeorge Bundy, the president's adviser for national security affairs, and John McNaughton in the Department of Defense. In a memo to the president dated March 21, the former had posed the following question: "In terms of U.S. politics which is better: to 'lose' now or to 'lose' after committing 100,000 men? Tentative answer: the latter." A similar conclusion was drawn by John McNaughton. Above all, he said in his own memo to McNamara on the twenty-fourth, it was necessary for the United States to have been a "good doctor," to have "kept promises, been tough, taken risks, gotten bloodied, and hurt the enemy very badly." What inspired these men, both of whom had serious reservations about the likelihood of victory in South Vietnam, to support an escalation of the U.S. military role in the war without any guarantee of success? In both cases, the decisive factor was the effect of a humiliating defeat on U.S. prestige. In Bundy's view, the "cardinal" U.S. goal in Vietnam was "Not to be a Paper Tiger. Not to have it thought that when we commit ourselves we really mean no major risk. This means, essentially, a willingness to fight China if necessary." McNaughton agreed. The primary U.S. objective in Vietnam was to avoid a humiliating defeat and preserve the U.S. reputation as a guarantor of the security of its allies.[72]

After discussions with his advisers, President Johnson approved NSAM-328 in early April. The new directive approved the deployment of two new marine battalions at Phu Bai and Da Nang, in Central Vietnam, and a substantial increase in the size of U.S. logistical support forces. Key U.S. allies, such as South Korea, Australia, and New Zealand, would be encouraged to contribute combat units to the common effort in South Vietnam. Johnson also approved a change of mission for U.S. Marines beyond providing base security "to permit their more active use under conditions to be established and approved by the Secretary of Defense in consultation with the Secretary of State." Finally, NSAM-328 called for a continuation of Rolling Thunder, as the bombing operations against the DRV were labeled, at a slowly ascending level, depending on Viet Cong activity in the South.[73]

In the decisions incorporated in NSAM-328, Lyndon Johnson had followed a by now classic pattern in presidential decision making on Vietnam. He had approved a deepening of the U.S. commitment to South Vietnam but had granted less military muscle than his more ardent military advisers had requested. In so doing, he carefully instructed subordinates that the decisions should be implemented with a minimum of publicity and should be "understood as being gradual and wholly consistent with existing policy."[74]

Did President Johnson and his key advisers realize how momentous was the step they were taking with the introduction of U.S. combat forces into the Vietnam War, or were they persuaded that the actions taken in NSAM-328 would lead in the near future to a satisfactory resolution of the conflict? I will return to this question at the end of this chapter, but a few comments are in order here. According to the memoirs of presidential adviser Clark Clifford, responsibility for the decision rests partly with the president's military advisers, who did not warn the White House that "the bombing of the North would inevitably lead to requests for ground troops." By this reading of the situation, President Johnson and his civilian advisers had been unaware of the likelihood that U.S. troops would be needed to stave off the collapse of South Vietnam and were duped into accepting their deployment by duplicitous minds in the Pentagon. This appears to be a serious misreading of the actual situation. There is no clear evidence that the Joint Chiefs were convinced that the use of U.S. combat forces was the best way to reverse the drift toward defeat in South Vietnam and appeared to prefer the massive application of U.S. air power. According to journalist David Halberstam, the president himself had publicly lectured Army Chief of Staff Harold Johnson before the latter's fact-finding trip to Saigon in early March:

Bomb, bomb, bomb. That's all you know. Well, I want to know why there's nothing else. You generals have all been educated at the taxpayer's expense, and you're not giving me any ideas and any solutions for this damn little piss-ant country. Now, I don't need ten generals to come in here ten times and tell me to bomb. I want some solutions. I want some answers.[75]

It is true that initially many civilian officials were reluctant to recommend the massive deployment of U.S. combat forces in South Vietnam and hoped that their use would be limited to base security duties. Such was apparently the case with Secretary of State Dean Rusk. But once the decision had been made, some seemed not only to accept it but even to rationalize its potential benefits. As for Lyndon Johnson himself, he seemed well aware of the implications of what he was doing. Although he had initially approved less than the Joint Chiefs had requested, in the next few days he would prove willing to approve far more than almost any of his advisers had anticipated. When bombing and feelers for peace talks failed to solve the problem, Lyndon Johnson was indeed, as he had threatened at the beginning of the war, going to "turn it over to the generals."

If Lyndon Johnson was well aware that his decisions in early April could lead to a vastly expanded U.S. involvement in the Vietnam War, why was he so concerned to disguise their implications when addressing the American public? The evidence shows that Lyndon Johnson was clearly aware that his actions could lead to escalation and wanted to prepare the ground. On April 3, Rusk told Taylor that the president felt that he must not force the pace too fast, or the Congress and public opinion, which had been held in line up to now, would no longer support the administration's actions in Vietnam.

Saving Face for Washington

While statesmen and generals debated the issue of troops in Hanoi and Washington, there was a flurry of activity on the diplomatic scene. During the first weeks of 1965, some consideration was given in Washington to seeking a negotiated settlement of the war. During the month of January, administration officials assessed various plans for achieving a cease-fire, and the French probed for a reaction from Hanoi through contacts with Chinese and DRV diplomatic representatives in Paris. Mai Van Bo, Hanoi's commercial representative to France, appeared to express some interest in a French proposal to draw up guarantees for a neutral and totally independent South Vietnam and a strong ICC but was evasive on whether Hanoi would bring to an end its political and military activities in the South. Senior U.S. officials such as Dean Rusk were convinced that Hanoi was not prepared to accept true neutrality for South Vietnam and did not pursue the issue. Those conclusions appeared to be confirmed in early March, when Mai Van Bo reported to the French that, in light of the U.S. attacks on the DRV, negotiations were no longer a matter for consideration in Hanoi. Similar efforts to sound out Hanoi by Canadian ICC representative Seaborn had no greater success. The latter reported that, in his view, DRV leaders were convinced that the United States had launched air strikes only to improve its bargaining position for a peace conference to end a war that it now recognized as lost. Under the circumstances, he said, Hanoi hoped to avoid the experience of 1954 and pursue the full victory "which it sees in sight."[76]

Not all in Washington were skeptical of embarking on the road to negotiations. George Ball had acquiesced in the decision to launch air strikes after the Pleiku incident, but he had drafted a memorandum pointing out the dangers of war with China if the United States moved its air attacks northward into the Red River Delta. The president read the paper without comment. A few days later, Ball presented his October 1964 memorandum recommending a negotiated settlement of the war to Johnson, who read it with interest and ordered a meeting of senior officials to discuss Ball's ideas. But the meeting was inconclusive and, in Ball's words, "made no converts," even the president, who made critical remarks of his own. Yet, according to William Bundy, Ball's efforts had not been entirely fruitless because the latter's warning about Chinese involvement may have been a factor in persuading Johnson to limit the extent of the air campaign against the DRV.[77]

Still, the president was not dead set against peace talks. One of the factors involved in the decision to escalate the U.S. military role in the Vietnam conflict was the belief on the part of some administration officials that a strengthened U.S. position in South Vietnam, combined with sustained air strikes against the DRV, might induce North Vietnamese leaders to settle the conflict on Washington's terms. During the late fall and winter of 1964–65, the Johnson administration had sent signals to Hanoi. There had been no response until after the Pleiku incident and the announcement of the launching of the U.S. bombing campaign of the North, when DRV sources had indicated tersely that Hanoi was not interested in negotiations. Party leaders were well aware of Washington's tactics and were determined not to enter negotiations until overall conditions were favorable.

For a brief period, Washington apparently lost interest, assuming that Hanoi was not prepared to compromise. But by late March and April, administration officials began once again to allude to the possibility of a peaceful settlement of the conflict. Undoubtedly they were partly motivated by the need to undercut public criticism of the administration's tough stance on negotiations. But there is evidence that some officials felt that a position on negotiations needed to be developed in preparation for inevitable peace talks in the future. On April 7, one day after granting approval of NSAM-328, President Johnson gave a highly publicized speech at the Johns Hopkins University in which he offered to engage in "unconditional discussions" on a settlement of the war and offered financial inducements in the form of U.S. economic assistance to develop the basin of the Mekong River.[78]

Johnson's speech had its desired effect in the United States, where it was praised in the press for its statesmanlike quality. But it had little effect in Hanoi. The following day, the DRV announced its own terms for a settlement of the conflict in South Vietnam. Three of the so-called Four Points—calling for U.S. withdrawal and recognition of the basic national rights of the Vietnamese people, return to the provisions of the 1954 Geneva Accords, and the peaceful reunification of the two zones of Vietnam, to be achieved by the Vietnamese people themselves without any foreign interference—were acceptable to Washington, at least in principle. But Point Three, stating that "[the] internal affairs of South Vietnam must be settled by the South Vietnamese people themselves in accordance with the program of the South Vietnam National Front for Liberation, without any foreign interference," was totally unacceptable.[79]

Hanoi's terms, in any case, were vague. Were they to be read as preconditions for negotiation or as the basis for discussion during peace talks? Administration officials doubted that Hanoi was serious but were sufficiently interested to ask Blair Seaborn to find out. In early May, to indicate its willingness to explore the possibility of peace talks, Washington announced a short bombing pause to encourage Hanoi to respond. But the DRV made no response to Washington's gesture and, according to Seaborn, continued to be uninterested in negotiations. Seaborn's estimate was accurate, for Hanoi was playing for time in the hope that its bargaining position would improve in the future. In a letter written to General Nguyen Chi Thanh after the announcement of the Four Points, Le Duan indicated that the moment was not appropriate for negotiations. "Only when the insurrection [in South Vietnam] is successful," he pointed out, "will the problem of establishing a 'neutral central administration' be posed again." As for Hanoi's Four Points, they were "intended to pave the way for a U.S. withdrawal with a lesser loss of face."[80]

Killing with Kindness

One interested party who had not been satisfied with the president's decision on troops was General William Westmoreland. On April 11 he asked for additional U.S. units to secure vital installations in the Bien Hoa–Vung Tau area. Johnson was sympathetic to the proposal, but Maxwell Taylor was not. He had already informed Prime Minister Phan Huy Quat about the decision to increase U.S. troop strength, and although the latter had agreed to the decision, he had doubts about the value of U.S. troops and felt that Saigon needed political support more than military assistance. Now Taylor complained that it was his understanding from talks in Washington that it had been decided to experiment with the marines before taking further action.

But Johnson had already decided, and on the fifteenth Taylor received a cable stating that "highest authority believes the situation in South Vietnam has been deteriorating and that, in addition to actions against the North, something new must be added in the South to achieve victory." Calling for "a strong experiment in the encadrement of U.S. troops with the Vietnamese," the president approved the request for the deployment of an additional brigade to the Bien Hoa–Vung Tau area to take part in combat operations as well as to provide base security. Taylor responded with an acerbic message to McGeorge Bundy complaining that the latest decision "shows far greater willingness to get into the ground war than I had discovered in Washington during my recent trip." "There is such a thing," he said pointedly, "as killing with kindness." Taylor's deputy U. Alexis Johnson agreed, cabling his own view that the Vietnamese people were a volatile and hypersensitive people.[81]

The issue was referred to a hastily convened meeting of high-level officials with Taylor in Honolulu on April 20. The participants were able to reach a consensus on some issues, including an agreement on the assumption that the DRV would not be willing to accept a peace settlement for at least six months and that the path to negotiations would come more from a Viet Cong defeat in the South than from the infliction of pain in the North. Such conclusions had several implications. With regard to the Rolling Thunder program, it was important to maintain the bombing at the present level, with a primary emphasis on attempting to reduce infiltration. On the issue of ground troops, the conference reached a compromise, calling for a modified version of Taylor's enclave approach, involving the active defense of key coastal areas. The participants may have been influenced in these decisions by an appeal from Ambassador Taylor, who warned that it was important not to "kill the hostage" by attempting more than Saigon could handle. On his return to Saigon, Taylor obtained Pham Huy Quat's concurrence with the decisions, although the latter was not entirely persuaded that the situation in the RVN was sufficiently perilous to merit a massive U.S. takeover of the war.[82]

One thing had been settled by the decisions of early April. With the addition of troops, the focus of most administration officials returned to the situation in South Vietnam. Only John McCone, retiring director of the CIA, and of course the Joint Chiefs, felt that the growing U.S. military presence had to be supplemented by heavy and sustained attacks on vital areas of the DRV. Most civilian officials, skeptical of the potential effects of bombing and fearful of war with China, viewed the bombing campaign primarily as a means of reducing infiltration from the North.

The growing U.S. military presence markedly reduced the likelihood of a collapse of South Vietnam. But the chronic instability of the Saigon regime continued. In early June Prime Minister Phan Huy Quat was forced to resign and was replaced by a military junta under the leadership of Air Vice Marshal Nguyen Cao Ky. Ky and his close ally, Army General Nguyen Van Thieu, had earlier been members of the "Young Turk" faction in Nguyen Khanh's government. In the meantime, the Viet Cong continued to take advantage of the disarray in Saigon. Insurgent activities increased during the spring, and U.S. intelligence sources estimated that infiltration was on the increase.

General Westmoreland was quick to react. He had not attended the meetings in Washington in April and had reportedly been disappointed at the slow force buildup, which was provisionally limited to a ceiling of 95,000 men. Westmoreland also criticized the enclave approach as too negative. On June 7 he requested large-scale reinforcements, following up four days later with a request to undertake offensive operations throughout South Vietnam. CINCPAC supported his request and sent it to Washington.

The request arrived in Washington at a delicate time. A State Department press officer had just divulged that U.S. troops would engage in combat operations in South Vietnam, resulting in a sudden rise of public anxiety over the course of the war. From the embassy in Saigon, Ambassador Taylor and his deputy U. Alexis Johnson undercut Westmoreland's proposal by arguing that more U.S. troops would only make the GVN nervous. Civilian officials in Washington, moreover, had reached a temporary consensus on holding the line at the presently established level. In a letter to President Johnson in mid-May, his close confidant Clark Clifford had advised him to keep the level of U.S. ground forces to a minimum, warning that the war would become "a quagmire" without any realistic hope of ultimate victory. Even President Johnson appeared to have some doubts about whether the increase in U.S. troop strength would not result in a reduced South Vietnamese effort. At a meeting of the NSC on the eleventh, Johnson concluded that the United States must delay and deter the Viet Cong and their North Vietnamese allies as much as possible, without going all out. If Westmoreland's request were granted, he said, "it means that we get in deeper and it is harder to get out." We must determine, he concluded, "which course gives us the maximum protection at the least cost."[83]

But the upward pressure continued. Responding to an increase in Viet Cong activity and the fall of the government of Phan Huy Quat, the White House announced on the sixteenth that U.S. force levels in the RVN would be increased to 70,000 men. Viewing this as the last chance to hold the line against the further Americanization of the war, on June 18 George Ball sent a memo to the president in which he appealed for a "trial period" of three months to evaluate the situation before committing an "endless flow of forces to bog down in the jungles and rice paddies of South Vietnam." The more involved the United States became, he pointed out, the harder it would be to get out. Lyndon Johnson did not often agree with George Ball on the subject of Vietnam, but he always read his memos carefully. After a stormy meeting with his foreign policy advisers on June 23, during which Robert McNamara appealed for more troops, Johnson instructed both McNamara and Ball to produce memos justifying their respective positions. Ball's paper, dated June 28, repeated arguments that he had unsuccessfully presented previously. The United States, he said, should demand that the Saigon regime fulfill the conditions on its performance that had been set forth by President Eisenhower a decade earlier. If the request were refused, or if the government were to collapse, the United States should withdraw. "Any prudent military commander," he pointed out, "carefully selects the terrain on which to stand and fight, and no great captain has ever been blamed for a successful tactical withdrawal."[84]

McNamara's own memo, revised from an earlier draft written on June 26, was sent to the president on July 1 and contained a recommendation to increase the size of the foreign military presence in the RVN by an additional 44 battalions (34 from the United States and 10 from other countries) and included other possible actions such as the mining of North Vietnamese harbors. McNamara admitted that this substantial investment would not begin to pay off until the tide in the war had turned (certainly not in less than several months and perhaps not for a year or more), and he conceded the possibility that a massive foreign presence could provoke anti-American sentiment in South Vietnam and lead to the rejection of the government that supported that presence. But he predicted that the program would be acceptable to the American people because it was "a combined military-political program designed and likely to bring about a favorable solution to the Vietnam problem."[85]

Both the Ball and the McNamara memos were circulated for comment within the administration, where they were exposed to searching and frequently scathing criticism. McGeorge Bundy wrote a note to McNamara on June 30 expressing his concern that the open-ended nature of his proposal put the nation on "a slippery slope toward total U.S. responsibility and corresponding fecklessness on the Vietnamese side." William Bundy was uncomfortable with the stark choice represented by the two proposals between extreme positions and drafted a memo of his own containing the recommendation that U.S. force levels be maintained at the present limit of 85,000. Bundy contended that a large-scale increase in the U.S. presence would simply compound the consequences of a possible defeat, while withdrawal under circumstances described by George Ball would have catastrophic effects at a time when, on the surface, the war did not appear to be going badly. Moreover, he said, the American public would not be able to understand the sudden reversal of the administration's position. Bundy was not excessively optimistic about the prospects for success at the present level of U.S. military commitment but felt that there was a "fair chance" that within four to six months a stalemate could result, leading to a possible political settlement.[86]

President Johnson met with his key advisers on July 2 to discuss the papers. In the meantime, Dean Rusk had written a brief memo presenting his own ideas. The memo essentially supported McNamara's recommendation to send additional troops on the grounds that the United States must prevent a defeat in South Vietnam, even at the risk of general war. Discussion at the meeting apparently did not take the form of a review of the options contained in the papers themselves but only on practical actions to be adopted in the near future. Johnson did not make a formal decision on troops at the close of the meeting, but according to other sources he may have already decided in favor of McNamara's recommendation. On July 7, he sent McNamara (accompanied by General Wheeler and Henry Cabot Lodge, who was replacing Maxwell Taylor for another tour as ambassador to the RVN) on another fact-finding mission to Saigon. On the eighth he met with a panel of senior advisers, including Dean Acheson, Omar Bradley, Arthur A. Larson, Paul Hoffman, and John McCloy, to solicit their views. With the exception of Larson and Hoffman, who suggested that the issue be presented to the United Nations, the remaining "wise men" urged the president to stand firm and add as many ground troops as were required. A few days earlier, former president Eisenhower had similarly advised Johnson to go "all out."[87]

The view that Lyndon Johnson had already decided to accept McNamara's recommendations is strengthened by comments that he made at a press conference on the thirteenth. "Increased aggression from the North," he warned, "may require an increased American response on the ground in South Viet-Nam. . . . It is quite possible that new and serious decisions will be necessary in the near future. Any substantial increase in the present level of our efforts . . . will require steps to insure that our reserves of men and equipment of the United States remain entirely adequate for any and all emergencies." Four days later he authorized a cable to McNamara, who was still in Saigon, instructing him to prepare a proposal for a 34-battalion increase in the size of the U.S. military presence in South Vietnam.[88]

On his return to Washington on July 21, McNamara presented a memorandum summarizing his conclusions from the trip to Saigon. The defense secretary proposed an increase in U.S. force levels by 34 battalions to 175,000 men by October, with a further escalation of 100,000 in 1966. At General Westmoreland's request, McNamara proposed that the role of U.S. forces be changed from a purely defensive posture into an active role to seize the initiative and take the battle to the enemy. He also recommended an increase in the number of air sorties over North Vietnam (while still avoiding striking population and industrial targets not directly related to war production) and a willingness to mine the DRV harbors in case the Viet Cong or the DRV should commit "a particularly damaging or horrendous act" in South Vietnam. McNamara admitted that it was not clear how such substantial numbers of U.S. troops could eventually be disengaged from Vietnam, but he concluded that the strategy he had presented "stands a good chance of achieving an acceptable outcome within a reasonable time in Vietnam."[89]

The president met with his key advisers in the White House on July 21. Unlike the earlier meeting on July 2, Johnson encouraged a thorough rehash of the issues and listened carefully as George Ball restated his opposition to the escalation of the war, which he described as a "perilous voyage." The president pressed General Wheeler to explain how U.S. troops could force the enemy to fight the war on American terms. McGeorge Bundy agreed that victory would not come easily, but he argued that it would be disastrous to withdraw. There would be ample time to get out, he concluded, after a good try had been made.

At the end of the discussion all but George Ball expressed support for McNamara's proposals and, in an atmosphere redolent of memories of Munich (Henry Cabot Lodge had raised the issue at the meeting), Lyndon Johnson summed up. Withdrawal would be a disaster. A massive escalation in the bombing campaign over the DRV would not necessarily achieve U.S. objectives and could widen the war. Standing pat (in Johnson's phrase, "hunkering up") was only slow defeat. In evident agony over the cost of his decision to his Great Society program, Johnson appeared to recognize that only McNamara's plan offered a hope for success.

Discussions continued during the next few days. At a quiet meeting held at Camp David of Johnson, Robert McNamara, and Clark Clifford on the twenty-fifth, the latter for the first time voiced to the president his own doubts about the war. Hold to the present course for a while, he advised, and then seek an honorable way out. Johnson listened but was not persuaded. That night a State Department cable circulated to key U.S. embassies around the world declared that "while final decisions have not been made here, I can tell you that it now appears certain that it will be necessary to increase United States armed forces in South Vietnam by a number which may equal or exceed the 80,000 already there." Ironically, it may have been Lyndon Johnson's dream of the Great Society that impelled him into South Vietnam. He would not allow his domestic programs, now before Congress, to be scuttled on the reefs of an acrimonious debate about who lost the war.[90]

On July 27, the president held a meeting to explain the decision to key congressmen. Most supported the decision, but there were dissenters. Senator Mike Mansfield registered his disagreement with the president's course of action, saying the United States had pledged only to assist South Vietnam in its own defense. The present government in Saigon lacked both competence and legitimacy, and the United States owed it "no pledge of any kind." As for the war, even a total victory would be costly and could lose the support of the American people. The best hope, he concluded, was for a quick stalemate and negotiations. The following day, at a press conference held in the White House, President Johnson announced that 50,000 more U.S. troops would be sent to South Vietnam, and more would be dispatched later. Explaining his decision, Johnson referred to the lessons of history that the United States must be the guardian at the gate. Citing the Munich conference in 1938, he declared that success only feeds the appetite of aggressor nations. The United States is in Vietnam, he said, to fulfill the solemn pledges of three presidents to defend this small nation. We cannot dishonor our word or abandon our commitment.[91]

Coping with Limited War

The decisions reached in mid-July fully committed the United States, for the first time since the end of the Korean conflict, to a major land war in Asia. Maxwell Taylor's enclave strategy had been abandoned, and U.S. combat troops would become fully engaged in the fighting in Vietnam. As George Ball had been warning since early in the decade, American soldiers would be fighting and dying in the jungles and rice paddies of South Vietnam.

Yet, even in committing U.S. lives and prestige to a major land war in Southeast Asia, Lyndon Johnson ignored the advice of Henry Cabot Lodge and the wishes of the Joint Chiefs and rejected proposals to take the war directly to the North. One reason was to minimize the risk that Congress would reject the Great Society program, then under consideration on Capitol Hill. The nation, Johnson insisted, could have both "guns and butter." But the White House also adopted the gradualist approach to avoid the danger of a larger conflict and the possibility of whipping up war fever in the United States. "In Vietnam," Dean Rusk remarked many years later, "we wanted to do it calmly and in cold blood." The essence of the strategy of flexible response was to enable the United States to deal with local conflicts in areas of limited importance to its national security without running the risk of a nuclear confrontation with the major communist powers.[92]

Concern over Chinese intervention had guided U.S. policy in Indochina since the Truman era, and some Johnson administration officials had been seriously concerned at the possibility of a violent Chinese reaction to heavy U.S. attacks on the DRV. Since February of 1965, the White House had been attempting to signal to Beijing that its purposes in Vietnam were purely defensive. China's response had been ambiguous. Mao Zedong had remarked to the American journalist Edgar Snow that China would not take a direct part in the

Vietnam conflict unless it were attacked by U.S. forces, but an article in *People's Daily* in late March had warned that China regarded the struggle of the Vietnamese people as its own struggle and would send all necessary material assistance to help repel aggression. When the U.S. side raised that issue at the bilateral talks in Warsaw in late April, the Chinese representative Wang Bingnan cited a statement by Zhou Enlai that China was ready to send the necessary aid, including manpower, "whenever the South Vietnamese people want them."[93]

Wang Bingnan reiterated these views during a meeting with U.S. ambassador John Cabot in Warsaw in late June. Responding to Cabot's charge that the DRV and China were committing aggression against South Vietnam, he declared that the U.S. bombing of North Vietnam had rendered the DMZ irrelevant. The Chinese people, he said, had the right to assist the poeple of South Vietnam in striking back "on whatever scale is necessary" until U.S. forces were thoroughly defeated.[94]

In their own calculations about the future course of the war, North Vietnamese party leaders had undoubtedly counted on the deterrent effect on the United States of possible Chinese intervention. Le Duan had said as much in his letter to Nguyen Chi Thanh in May, and Beijing had encouraged such beliefs by signing an agreement with the DRV in April which called on China to provide support forces and some combat personnel to their fraternal allies. At the same time, however, China reportedly signaled Washington that it would not supply combat troops to North Vietnam so long as the United States and its ally in Saigon did not cross the seventeenth parallel.[95]

Hanoi undoubtedly watched the gradual buildup of U.S. military forces during the spring of 1965 with considerable misgivings. Party leaders may have realized that their chances for bringing about the collapse of the Saigon regime before the United States had time to respond had substantially diminished. In a letter written to colleagues in the South early in 1966, Politburo member Le Duc Tho conceded that the situation in the South had evolved more rapidly than Hanoi had anticipated. "Things," he pointed out, "do not always develop in strict accordance with our subjective judgments and intentions."[96]

Still, if Hanoi sources are to be believed, they were not despondent. In his letter to Nguyen Chi Thanh, Le Duan attempted to put the situation into perspective. The introduction of U.S. combat troops had undoubtedly changed the situation, he conceded. The North no longer had the capacity to inflict "mortal blows" on enemy forces, and they would undoubtedly cause damage to revolutionary base areas and reduce the level of infiltration from the North. But he insisted that the basic situation had not radically changed. The enemy was internally divided, hesitant over strategy, and desperately seeking a negotiated settlement to avoid a humiliating defeat.

There was no need, Le Duan concluded, to change the party's basic strategy in the South. The chronic weakness of the Saigon regime remained the fundamental reality of the war, and if ARVN forces could be routed quickly, the addition of 100,000 U.S. troops could not prevent the collapse of Washington's puppet. Southern leaders should therefore continue to prepare for the general offensive and uprising. If the U.S. buildup continued and temporarily stabilized the situation in the South, he said, his side would switch to the strategy of protracted war, a strategy they knew well, and the United States would lack the patience to pursue. "We will fight," he concluded, "whatever way the U.S. wants." Even if the North was invaded, they were prepared and would win.[97]

By the end of the summer, Hanoi could no longer be in any doubt about the extent of Washington's commitment. The size of the U.S. troop presence was about to surpass 100,000, and many units were moving into strategic positions in the Central Highlands, as well as along the coast of Central Vietnam. Units of the First Cavalry Division were deployed at An Khe, on Route 19, to keep the highway to the coast open and prevent an anticipated enemy attack on the provincial capital of Pleiku.

The first contacts between PLAF and U.S. combat troops had been mildly encouraging to party strategists in Hanoi. In August, U.S. forces launched a search-and-destroy mission into the Batangan peninsula, a few miles south of the U.S. Marine Base at Chu Lai. The peninsula was an area traditionally sympathetic to the revolution and was infested with combat villages (well-armed villages and hamlets under NLF control). Local Viet Cong units fought back fiercely, and although they absorbed heavy casualties they inflicted heavy damage. Party histories cite the battle of Van Tuong (named for a hamlet located near the center of the fighting) as evidence that local PLAF forces could hold their own in a pitched battle against U.S. troops. Perhaps more important, the U.S. military command did not achieve its primary purpose in the operation. After U.S. troops left the area, it reverted to Viet Cong control.[98]

Hanoi's hopes for firm Chinese support, however, were being dashed by events in Beijing. In July, China reportedly rejected a North Vietnamese request for pilots, arguing that it would not deter U.S. air strikes on the North. During the summer months a bitter debate took place among Chinese leaders over whether to cooperate with Moscow in providing aid to Hanoi. While some held that fraternal solidarity claimed precedence over China's dispute with the USSR, others, led by Mao Zedong and Defense Minister Lin Biao, rejected any idea of united action with Moscow in the Vietnam War. By September, Mao's faction had won the debate, a victory symbolized by the publication of Lin Biao's famous article "Long live the victory of people's war" in September. Although some Western observers viewed the article as a declaration of war against the West, North Vietnamese leaders correctly interpreted it as a subtle hint to them to follow the path of self-reliance and adopt a policy of protracted war in the South. In a speech the following May, Le Duan issued a sharp rejoinder to Beijing, pointing out that "it is not fortuitous that in the history of our country, each time we arose to oppose foreign aggression, we took the offensive and not the defensive. . . . Taking the offensive is a strategy, while taking the defensive is only a stratagem."[99]

In September 1965, the Politburo met to evaluate its options and map future courses of action. Party leaders admitted that with the steady increase in U.S. military strength in South Vietnam, the conflict had become a limited war. That did not mean that the concept of the general offensive and uprising was now invalid, but it did indicate that the struggle, as Le Duan described it in a letter to Nguyen Chi Thanh, would be "fiercer and longer." It would become a protracted war, and the resources of the entire nation must be mobilized against the enemy in the South.[100]

In his letter to General Thanh, which was not written until November, Le Duan repeated the views that he had expressed in his letter the previous May. Washington's decision to escalate the war complicated the situation but did not change the fundamental strategic perspective. The unstable political situation in Saigon was still the enemy's Achilles' heel. If ARVN could be demoralized and routed, it was still possible to win through a general offensive and uprising. But with American forces now serving as a shield, revolutionary units must occasionally confront American units to maintain the initiative and weaken the enemy position.

Le Duan was careful to explain that southern commanders must be cautious and selective in confronting the Americans. They should be attacked only where they were relatively weak and vulnerable. In general, it was advisable to concentrate attacks on the weaker and more demoralized ARVN forces. But when U.S. troops prevented the revolutionary movement from consolidating its hold on the crucial Central Highlands, they must be confronted and defeated. The key, Le Duan pointed out, was to stick to the tradition of always maintaining the initiative and adopting an offensive posture.

If revolutionary commanders in the South were astute in interpreting these instructions, Le Duan concluded, it would still be possible, even with the addition of half a million U.S. troops, to win "a decisive victory in a relatively short period of time." A decisive victory, he carefully explained, is not the same as a total victory, in which the enemy forces are entirely vanquished. But a decisive victory along the lines of the battle of Dien Bien Phu in 1954 could lead to the collapse of the Saigon regime and the withdrawal of American forces. Le Duan dismissed the possibility that the United States would invade North Vietnam. If so, he predicted, it would encounter the united strength of the entire socialist camp.

In October, PAVN units confronted U.S. troops for the first time in the Battle of Ia Drang Valley. The battle began with a North Vietnamese attack on an ARVN post at Pleime, a few miles south of the mountain city of Pleiku in the Central Highlands. The attacking units then withdrew to Chu Pong Mountain, a longtime insurgent stronghold close to the Cambodian border, where they engaged pursuing American troops of the First Cavalry Division. North Vietnamese casualties were heavy, but they inflicted heavy losses on U.S. forces and led General Vo Nguyen Giap to remark that the Battle of Ia Drang had demonstrated the ability of the PAVN to deal with the Americans.[101]

In December, a plenary session of the VWP Central Committee approved the Politburo's directives. The goal was to mobilize the force of the entire nation (a code phrase for the decision to commit large numbers of North Vietnamese troops into the South) and force the United States to get bogged down and accept defeat at the level of limited war. The resolution issued at the close of the conference stressed the virtue of self-reliance (a tacit reference to Lin Biao's advice in September) but also expressed the hope that sympathy and support would be forthcoming from progressive peoples and governments around the world. Hanoi had accepted Washington's challenge. The stage was now set for the most violent period of the Vietnam War.[102]

Conclusions

It has been said that Lyndon Johnson's decision to escalate the U.S. role in South Vietnam was inevitable, a logical outgrowth of policies that had been adopted since the Viet Cong attack on the Special Forces camp at Pleiku in February. In his unpublished memoirs, William Bundy denies this and asserts that the decisions of mid-July were both new and avoidable and that there were other alternatives that could have been adopted. The circumstances appear to support the latter assertion. During the three weeks before the fateful meeting of July 21, the administration geared up for a major review of Vietnam policy, and key administration officials adopted a variety of positions on the issue which were given a lengthy hearing by the president before the final decision on the twenty-fifth.

On the other hand, the record also suggests that Lyndon Johnson had begun to conclude as early as the beginning of the year that if other methods failed, he would have to turn the war over to his generals. If such is the case, in his mind the decisions of July were a natural if not an inevitable outgrowth of his initial decision to introduce U.S. combat forces in the early spring. However reluctantly and painfully, Johnson found himself entangled in a web compacted of fears of falling dominoes, the actions of previous presidents, and the symbols of Munich. The advice of the vast majority of his advisers and a generation of foreign policy gurus helped to strengthen that web. In the written record of those agonizing last days of strategy debate, the shape of the final decision is implicit. It was clearly not just "Lyndon Johnson's War."

Some observers have contended that Lyndon Johnson duped the public by campaigning on a peace plank in the presidential election of 1964 although he was already privately convinced that only American military power could bring victory in Vietnam. Did Johnson deliberately delay the bombing of the North and the introduction of U.S. combat troops to guarantee reelection and avoid a public outcry against the Americanization of the war? We cannot, of course, gain access to the president's private thoughts. But his comments to his advisers cited here suggest that at least until late February or March of 1965, Johnson held out some hope that actions short of the introduction of U.S. forces could bring about a satisfactory solution to the conflict. Only when it became clear that conditions in the South were continuing to deteriorate during the early months of 1965 did he recognize that a greater effort was needed. As he had warned early in the year, once convinced that lesser actions would not do the trick, he would now "turn it over to his generals." Having decided to introduce American troops, however, he deliberately downplayed the impact on U.S. public opinion to avoid unnecessary damage to his domestic programs, a decision that would later arouse harsh criticism from those who wanted an all-out approach to the war.

Why did Johnson feel that he had to meet the challenge with the introduction of U.S. combat troops? After all, both Eisenhower and Kennedy had backed away from a similar decision at key stages in their own administrations. The easy answer is that the situation in South Vietnam was more perilous in 1965 than it had been in either 1954 or 1961. According to many knowledgeable observers, a failure to act would lead in short order to the collapse of the regime. Yet that is not an entirely persuasive answer because it is not clear that either of his predecessors would have committed U.S. troops even in extremis. Kennedy had emphasized that it was "their war," and during the Indochina crisis in 1954 John Foster Dulles (presumably speaking for Eisenhower) had rejected the unilateral introduction of U.S. combat troops into Indochina on the grounds that U.S. national security was not directly threatened there.

By contrast, Johnson consistently acted as if U.S. national security was directly engaged in South Vietnam. In this, of course, he was not alone. Although George Ball and some Asian specialists in the State Department were skeptical of the relevance of the domino theory in contemporary Southeast Asia, most high-level administration officials appeared convinced that a communist victory in South Vietnam would lead to a dangerous unraveling of the balance of power in Asia and of U.S. influence in the remainder of the world. Laos and Cambodia would fall in short order, and the resistance of other nations in the region to communism would be severely weakened. According to William Bundy, administration officials were well aware of the national character of the Hanoi regime but were convinced that other countries in the region could not stand up to the psychological effect of a communist victory and would be increasingly vulnerable to the pressures emanating from an aggressive government in mainland China. In portraying the conflict in South Vietnam as a direct challenge to the interests of the free world, Lyndon Johnson was reflect-ing the views of the majority of his advisers, as well as some of the leading figures in the foreign policy establishment since the end of World War II.[103]

In the end, however, the decision was the president's to make, and there is ample evidence that Lyndon Johnson suffered few if any of the doubts that had inhibited previous presidents in committing U.S. power and prestige to the survival of a noncommunist Vietnam. Not only in public statements such as the press conference on July 28 but also in private discussions with his advisers, Johnson constantly stressed the importance of American credibility in honor-ing the U.S. commitment in Vietnam. During the critical meeting of July 21, even while probing General Wheeler sharply on the risks of engaging in a land war in Asia, he plaintively responded to George Ball's recommendation to withdraw: "Wouldn't we lose all credibility by breaking the word of three Presidents?"[104]

In his own mind, then, Lyndon Johnson was not breaking with tradition but was firmly embarked on a course that was based on the inherited wisdom of three administrations. To Johnson, this was the logical course to follow and one that avoided the humiliation of defeat and the risk of general war. The Ameri-can people did not wish the United States to "pack up and leave," but they also opposed a decision to blow the enemy out of the water. In the view from the White House, the administration was clearly following the moderate course in Vietnam.

One factor that apparently did not weigh heavily in the decision was public opinion. John Kennedy, at least in the early months of his term in office, had few options because of the perilous world situation and the need to demon-strate his toughness in foreign policy to Moscow and to the American people, but Lyndon Johnson was under no such pressure. To the contrary, public opinion surveys taken in 1965 showed that doubts about the war had reached a critical level among the American public, and (as some of his advisers admit-ted) withdrawal would not have posed a critical problem to his administration, although Johnson feared that it would unleash a storm of criticism from the right, as had happened in the early 1950's. In fact, comments by senior advisers as early as the summer of 1964 suggest a belief that the importance of Vietnam had yet to be demonstrated to the American people and their representatives in Congress.[105]

Did Lyndon Johnson and his advisers believe that the decisions reached in mid-July would bring victory? Although the evidence is not conclusive, it seems reasonably clear that, with the exception of Defense Secretary McNamara (who still appeared to hold an optimistic view of future prospects in the war), most civilian officials approached the decision with a strong sense of concern, if not foreboding. Dean Rusk apparently did not wish to contemplate the possibility of failure, but sub-cabinet-level advisers such as John McNaughton and William Bundy had already begun to contemplate the possibility the previous fall, while contending that defeat after a major effort was preferable to unilateral withdrawal.[106] Johnson himself, at the NSC meeting on July 27, remarked that although the troop increase might bring an improvement in the situation, at a minimum it would enable the RVN to get through the critical monsoon season and hold on until January. In July 1965, there was no visible "light at the end of the tunnel."

Chapter 10

The Limits of Containment

At the end of April 1975, almost exactly ten years after the first U.S. Marines waded ashore on the beaches of Central Vietnam, North Vietnamese troops entered the Presidential Palace and brought an end to the Saigon regime. By that time, the Vietnam War had become the most unpopular conflict in American history and the national consensus over the doctrine of containment, the cornerstone of U.S. foreign policy since the end of World War II, had been shattered. During the next two decades, the aftershocks of the war reverberated throughout American society, from the growing structural problems in the economy to the difficulties encountered by Vietnam veterans and what President Jimmy Carter described as a persistent "malaise" in the American psyche. Policymakers, journalists, and scholars interested in foreign affairs speculated over the effect that the end of the war would have on U.S. foreign policy and the strategy of containment, and every new foreign policy challenge aroused public cries of "no more Vietnams."

For many Americans, the war raised fundamental questions about the national purpose. What were we trying to achieve in Vietnam? Was the war, as President Ronald Reagan would phrase it, a "noble cause"? Or was it, as others said, a shameful and misguided aberration, best forgotten and never repeated? Or, finally, were leftist commentators closer to the mark in describing it as the inevitable consequence of a capitalist America turned imperialist and policeman of the world?[1]

Questions have also been raised about the strategy applied in Vietnam. Some critics have maintained that by introducing combat troops the United

States excessively militarized the conflict and unduly minimized the "other war" to "win the hearts and minds" of the Vietnamese people. Others have argued that the war was lost not because the United States overemphasized the importance of military force but, to the contrary, because it did not effectively use its military advantage to press the war to a successful conclusion. Still others have asserted that the argument between the political and military approaches was a sterile one because, short of the total destruction of the North, the war was essentially unwinnable because of the superiority of the revolutionary movement to the chronically weak regime in Saigon.

Out of such controversy has come the lingering debate over the so-called lessons of Vietnam. During the immediate postwar years, the phrase usually had the connotation of avoiding similar entanglements in foreign disputes in the future—the polar opposite, in that respect, of the "lessons of Munich" of a generation before. It was often applied to U.S. military involvement in Central America and specifically to the civil struggle in El Salvador. More recently, however, it has been used by those who contend that the problem in Vietnam was not that the United States became involved but that it did not make better use of its tremendous superiority in firepower to impose its will on the enemy. President George Bush popularized that view during the Gulf War, when he promised that the United States would not fight "another Vietnam" but would carry the war to the finish.[2]

What has been most characteristic about such debates has been that almost all the participants focused on the search for simple answers to the problems and complexities of Vietnam. Most have been waged with a combination of moral fervor and the intellectual certainty that there were clear-cut differences in Vietnam between black and white, good and evil, and winning and losing. Few indeed have waded into the morass of Vietnam with the conviction, as expressed once by McGeorge Bundy, that "gray is the color of the complex truth."

For the diplomatic historian faced with the challenge of reaching an understanding of the meaning of Vietnam, however, a more nuanced view is essential, at least as a prerequisite to analysis if not as a set of conclusions. For in investigating the record of the long U.S. involvement in Indochina, any but the most hardened and single-minded observer must concede that U.S. policymakers were often faced with excruciating choices and painful moral dilemmas in meeting the challenges of Vietnam. Whether they made the right choices or drew the proper conclusions is, of course, a matter of opinion. A bitter and tragic experience, filled with missteps, misjudgments, and mistakes, it certainly was. A simple matter it most certainly was not.

With that as prologue, let us explore some of the issues and controversies that have been raised by the war on the basis of the available record.

The Objective

Critics have often charged that U.S. objectives in the Vietnam War were not clear. That criticism was most often voiced during the height of the war in the late 1960's, when it sometimes appeared uncertain whether the U.S. goal was to win the war, to keep from losing it, or simply to prevent the enemy from winning by military force alone. At first glance, such criticism appears mis-placed because in the broadest sense it appears obvious that the U.S. objective was quite clear—to prevent a communist takeover of Indochina. What was actually at issue was the strategy that was applied to achieve that objective.

Yet the critics are correct in maintaining that often there was a lack of clarity about U.S. goals in Indochina, and that ambiguity contributed in major ways to the failure to adopt an effective and proper strategy to deal with the problem. It is also evident that the ambivalence over objectives was rooted in the theory of containment and in how it was applied on the mainland of Southeast Asia. From the outset, U.S. policymakers were divided about the implications of the concept and about how and whether it should be applied to Southeast Asia. Was mainland Southeast Asia defensible or not? Was it vital to the security of the United States? The failure to reach clear answers to these questions continued to plague the formulation of policy throughout the Viet-nam War and certainly contributed to the strategical failures that led to the final conquest of Saigon in 1975.

The United States first decided to become involved in the Indochina conflict in the late 1940's, when the Truman administration gradually and somewhat reluctantly began to provide aid to the French struggle against the Vietminh. The immediate decision was clearly linked to the rising fear of communism in the United States, a fear that had been exacerbated by the communist conquest of China in 1949. Yet, as we have seen, the assumptions behind the policy of containment in Asia predated the formulation of the Cold War concept of containment and were rooted in the U.S. experience with Japan in World War II and in the "One World" philosophy of Franklin D. Roosevelt. The growing concern over the expansionist tendencies of the Soviet Union and Communist China simply added a coherent source of threat to that vision. In its origins, at least, U.S. involvement in Indochina was not an aberration but a natural out-growth of evolving U.S. interests in the area.[3]

How realistic was Washington's fear of falling dominoes? Today, when the USSR has disappeared from the maps of the world and the socialist camp is in a state of almost complete disarray, it is difficult to conjure up the sense of vulnerability that was felt by many Americans in the immediate post–World War II era, when memories of the Axis alliance were fresh and the fear of communism was fueled by daily evidence of the consolidation of Soviet power in Eastern Europe. Such fears, whether or not they were justified, were felt not only in Washington but in London, in Paris, and in other European and Asian capitals as well. The communist conquest of China, followed by public statements of support for world revolution in Beijing and the entry of Chinese volunteers into the Korean War, brought a new sense of heightened danger to the noncommunist nations of Asia, at a time when newly independent states were badly in need of time to strengthen fragile political institutions and build a sense of national self-confidence. It is hard to question the logic of the Truman administration's decision to intervene in the region. The U.S. experience during World War II, buttressed by the postwar fervor to build a world safe for democracy, made it virtually inevitable that Washington would take action to defend the nation's interests in Southeast Asia.

Whether the Truman administration adopted the proper response to the challenge, however, is a legitimate matter for debate. The failure to test Ho Chi Minh's sincerity, though understandable in light of U.S. global priorities at the time, doomed Washington to an alternative (the abortive "Bao Dai experiment") that knowledgeable observers agreed had little chance to succeed. In retrospect, the administration might have been better advised to take a chance on Ho Chi Minh while strengthening other nations in the area. That it did not adopt that strategy can be ascribed not only to the growing intensity of Cold War fears in Washington but also to anxiety over undermining relations with the French.

In any event, what was crucial about President Truman's decision to intervene in the Franco-Vietminh conflict was its highly qualified character. That decision was based not on the intrinsic importance of Indochina (or even mainland Southeast Asia) to U.S. national security but on the impact that a communist conquest of the Red River Valley could have on the region as a whole (usually defined at the time as the arc of Asia from Japan to the Suez Canal). In that sense, the importance of Indochina was not absolute but derivative. That view was fully reflected in official statements at the time that if Indochina could not be saved, an effort there was necessary to buy time for strengthening other nations in the region. Implicit in those projections (although never spelled out) was the assumption that the United States would not become directly involved in the conflict. For the time being, U.S. objectives and strategy in Indochina were roughly in synchronization.

Despite the anticommunist rhetoric of the Republican presidential campaign of 1952, the Eisenhower administration initially accepted the limitations inherent in its predecessor's qualified commitment to resist a communist takeover of Vietnam. Although Eisenhower apparently gave serious consideration to the introduction of U.S. combat forces before and during the Geneva Conference, he eventually rejected the idea, and Dulles later rationalized the decision by remarking that U.S. national interests were not directly at stake in

Indochina. That judgment was given legal sanction in the SEATO treaty, which placed the United States under only limited obligations to take action in the event of an armed attack against a nation signatory to the treaty.

Yet the Eisenhower administration soon adopted other measures that indicated that it was prepared to take considerable risks to protect its limited investment in Southeast Asia. After the signing of the Geneva Accords it committed the weight of U.S. prestige to the precarious Diem regime despite the president's own admission that it had at best an even chance to survive. The commitment was not legally binding, but it was politically and morally open-ended. Later the administration drew up contingency plans for the introduction of U.S. forces into the RVN in the event of an invasion from the North. In the final months of his administration, Eisenhower may have been on the verge of sending troops to stop the advance of Pathet Lao forces in Laos, and one can only speculate what he would have done had he been faced with the imminent collapse of the Diem regime in Saigon. For what it is worth, he gave firm encouragement to Lyndon Johnson's decision to dispatch U.S. combat troops to South Vietnam in 1965.

Was Eisenhower's decision to extend the degree of U.S. commitment to the survival of a noncommunist regime in Vietnam justified? That, of course, is a matter of judgment, but conditions had changed considerably since President Truman had taken the first hesitant steps into Indochina at the beginning of the decade. In the years since U.S. recognition of the Bao Dai government in 1950, the nations of the region had achieved a greater degree of stability, and the internal threat of a communist takeover had begun to recede in Burma, Malaya, and Indonesia. By the same token, in the mid-1950's both China and the Soviet Union had adopted a more moderate stance in global affairs, and both had signaled their preference for a peaceful solution to the conflict in Indochina and an improvement in their relations with the United States. Finally, America's closest allies were no longer urging that it take strong action to resist communist expansion in Southeast Asia. To the contrary, both Paris and London appeared willing to accept the implications of the judgment at Geneva. For all of Eisenhower's insistence on the need for joint action in Indochina, if a new war broke out in the area it was clear that the United States would act virtually alone.

When the Kennedy administration came into office in January 1961, it thus inherited not only a growing crisis in Indochina but also a growing U.S. commitment to the area. On various occasions, Kennedy had voiced his reluctance to become directly involved, but the tense international situation at the time of his inauguration reduced his room for maneuver, and the actions of his administration often added to the impression that the U.S. commitment to Vietnam, if not to Laos, was virtually absolute. Whatever the views of Kennedy himself, most of his key advisers apparently thought so, if not because of the threat of falling dominoes (McNamara and the Joint Chiefs), then because of the need for Washington to honor its word (Dean Rusk). Although there has been considerable speculation over Kennedy's ultimate intentions, the fact is that the U.S. presence in South Vietnam had increased substantially during his steward-ship in the White House, and withdrawal was becoming increasingly difficult. Although Kennedy clearly recognized the nature of his dilemma in Indochina, he had not resolved it at the time of his death, and the legacy he left to his successor was more perilous than the one he had inherited at the time of his inauguration.

Lyndon Johnson did not share Kennedy's reluctance to commit U.S. power and prestige to the survival of the Saigon regime, and under his administration, the U.S. commitment appeared to be virtually limitless. Yet his insistence on adopting a strategy that avoided unnecessary provocation to China and his reluctance to subordinate his Great Society program to "that bitch of a war" in Vietnam made it clear (not least to his adversary in Hanoi) that he was not prepared to go all-out in Indochina. Like Kennedy, Johnson anguished over the dilemma, but he failed to resolve the growing contradiction between ends and means in the Vietnam War, and that failure destroyed his presidency. It re-mained to Richard Nixon to resolve the dilemma by reaching beyond Hanoi to come to terms with the real source of U.S. anxieties, the communist govern-ment in China. That maneuver succeeded in creating conditions for the United States to leave Vietnam with its prestige reasonably intact, but it also demon-strated Nixon's tacit acceptance of the assumption that Vietnam was expend-able, an assumption that became a reality with the fall of Saigon in the spring of 1975.

To the casual observer, the fall of Saigon marked the final debacle of U.S. policy in Indochina. In the United States as in the world at large, the Vietnam War is usually portrayed as an American failure. Yet the events that have trans-pired in the years that followed showed that, on the whole, the United States had actually achieved its larger purpose in Southeast Asia. A glance at the region today suggests that from the standpoint of U.S. national interests, the situation is more favorable than could have been anticipated two decades ear-lier. Not only is much of mainland Southeast Asia reasonably stable and pros-perous, but the nations of the region have begun to band together for their own security, and Vietnam itself now serves as a potential bulwark against future Chinese expansion into the area. It has been said (among others, by the staunchly anticommunist leader Lee Kuan-yew in Singapore) that U.S. actions in Vietnam were instrumental in helping to bring about that situation.

Lee Kuan-yew has a point. In its ultimate purpose—to buy time for the remainder of the region to stabilize—the United States did achieve its objective by (in John McNaughton's phrase) "getting bloodied" in Vietnam. The funda-mental issue, then, is not whether the United States successfully applied the theory of containment to Southeast Asia (clearly, in the larger sense, it did), but whether the bloody war in Vietnam, which had so many other regrettable consequences for the formulation and implementation of U.S. foreign policy, was necessary to achieve that purpose.

Unfortunately, that question is exceedingly difficult to answer because of its highly speculative nature and the numerous factors involved. To contain communist expansion in the region as a whole without intervening militarily in Vietnam, it would have been necessary to limit the U.S. commitment to South Vietnam while accepting the likelihood, if not the certainty, that all of Vietnam (and perhaps Laos and Cambodia as well) might eventually fall under communist rule. Such a policy could only have been adopted at a time when the United States was not yet morally and politically committed to the survival of a noncommunist Vietnam, when there was relative stability in Great Power relations and within the region as a whole, and when it had become reasonably clear that a noncommunist solution in Vietnam was improbable without a substantial commitment from the United States.

Such a time existed only once in the long history of the Indochinese conflict: in the years immediately following the Geneva Conference. Had the Eisenhower administration indicated its willingness to accept the implications of the Geneva Conference by favoring national elections and limiting its commitment to the Saigon government, while at the same time taking steps to strengthen the SEATO alliance and negotiating with China on an overall reduction of the tensions in the area, the United States might have managed, if necessary, to execute a strategic retreat in Vietnam without abandoning its ultimate interests in the region. At a minimum, the United States would have ended up fighting under conditions more favorable than those that existed in Vietnam.

There is no way to know, of course, whether such a strategy would have succeeded. Political conditions in the area were still relatively fragile, and the impact of a communist victory in Vietnam could have sent shock waves of uncertainty throughout the region (and certainly in the remaining states of Indochina) and triggered an attitude of uncertainty on the part of U.S. allies in other parts of the globe. But the administration could have countered such dangers by taking strong action elsewhere in the region with the firm support of its chief European allies. Most important, it would have spared the country the need to fight a war that it was unlikely to win in order to preserve a government in a country whose legal status was murky at best and whose destiny was not vital to the security of the United States. Many observers abroad had already discounted the Saigon experiment as doomed to failure, and its loss would have done relatively little harm to U.S. national security interests in Asia. Such a policy would have placed the United States in full compliance with an international agreement reached by most of the major nations of the globe while at the same time providing the South Vietnamese with a fighting chance to secure their own destiny. There were risks, of course, but they were certainly no greater than the actual cost of an eventual war that divided the country, undermined the national economy, and badly damaged the confidence of the American people in their own government.

Given the anticommunist anxieties that gripped the American people during the mid-1950's, such a policy would undoubtedly have encountered criticism from broad segments of the population. But President Eisenhower, whose anticommunist credentials were unquestioned (except perhaps for the extreme right wing of his party) was in a better position to take such action than was a chief executive from the Democratic Party. And Eisenhower had demonstrated by his restrained actions in Eastern Europe and the Middle East that he could act prudently in the face of such sentiment when U.S. national interests required it. It is one of the many tragedies of the Vietnam War that he was unable to do so in Southeast Asia.

The Strategy

Not all would agree that the choice in Vietnam was simply between losing now or losing later. To many, there was an alternative possibility, that the United States could have won the war in Vietnam by pursuing a different strategy. Debate among policymakers over the proper approach to apply in Vietnam dated back to the late 1950's and early 1960's and was centered primarily on a disagreement between advocates of a military or a political approach. Could the application of military force through the use of superior technology overcome the techniques of revolutionary war based on the tactics of guerrilla warfare and political agitation and propaganda, or must the latter be opposed by a strategy of counterinsurgency that focused on a program of social and political reforms to "win the hearts and minds" of the people?

During the Kennedy administration, the United States adopted a strategy that relied on elements of both strategies but with a slight bias (matching the president's own views) toward the political approach. Under Lyndon Johnson, with the Saigon regime in steady decline, the advocates of a more military approach gained the clear advantage, although pacification and political reform were by no means abandoned. Still, many proponents of the use of military force were exasperated at President Johnson's refusal to take maximum advantage of U.S. material and technological superiority by invading North Vietnam or Laos and engaging in intensified bombing of the DRV.

That debate was rejoined after the fall of Saigon. To some critics who spoke out in the immediate postwar years, the cardinal error committed by U.S. policymakers had been to assume that an insurgency movement with substantial popular support (such as had been represented by the revolutionary movement in South Vietnam) could be defeated by superior military technology alone. Such critics argued that the United States could have achieved its objectives in Vietnam had it carried through on a nation-building program designed to strengthen the Saigon regime and undermine popular support for the guerrillas. A prominent advocate of this point of view was the AID official Robert Komer, who argues in his book *Bureaucracy at War: U.S. Performance in the Vietnam Conflict* that the failure to strengthen the foundations of the Saigon regime undermined and ultimately doomed the military effort to failure. A similar view had been expressed by former CIA director William Colby, who has contended in *Lost Victory: A Firsthand Account of America's Sixteen-Year Involvement in Vietnam* that had the successful pacification operations of the late 1960's been implemented earlier, the Viet Cong might not have gained the momentum needed to encourage Hanoi to engage its regular forces and the American people might have shown the patience to tolerate an extended period of low-level U.S. counterinsurgency operations.

Both Komer and Colby make a good case for the importance of political and socioeconomic reforms in the Vietnam War, and they demonstrate that too often pacification operations and political reforms were subordinated to military factors by U.S. policymakers. Unfortunately, neither writer provides a convincing prescription for victory in the face of Saigon's chronic weakness and Hanoi's determination to pursue the struggle at whatever cost. Both Komer and Colby focus on the success of the pacification program in the late 1960's, when the Saigon government was relatively stable and operating behind the shield of a massive U.S. military presence. But, as Komer concedes, the most crucial time for carrying out a successful program would have been before the escalation of the war on both sides after 1964. That is precisely the period when the Saigon regime was either too stubborn (under Diem) or too incompetent (under his successors) to implement such a policy effectively. The underlying fact is that without substantial external support, noncommunist nationalists were never a match for their communist rivals, and no amount of American effort was likely to change that. The failure to win the hearts and minds of the Vietnamese people lay not in Washington but in Saigon.

This is not to say that a greater emphasis on nation building in the late 1950's and early 1960's would not have been worth the effort. Had the Diem regime been more sensitive to the sources of dissatisfaction in South Vietnam, it might have responded to the challenge and deprived the guerrilla fish access to the sea. But it is clear that there was little that the United States could do to influence the behavior of Ngo Dinh Diem, and indeed it was correctly believed that one of his few strengths was his refusal to serve as an American puppet. By the time a new leadership was installed in South Vietnam the situation was so perilous that only a substantial U.S. military presence could prevent a communist victory. When Hanoi responded by escalating its own role in the struggle, the opportunity to achieve success by a primarily political effort had already passed.

On the other side of the political spectrum, some critics have asserted that the United States failed to achieve its goals in Vietnam not because it over-emphasized the importance of military force but, to the contrary, because it did not effectively use its military advantage to press the war to a successful conclusion. In this view, the United States should have made better use of its tremendous superiority in firepower to impose its will on the enemy.

The best-known advocate of such an approach is Harry G. Summers, Jr., whose book *On Strategy* aroused a firestorm of controversy when it was published by Presidio Press in 1982. Summers, a U.S. military officer with service in Vietnam and later a lecturer at the Army War College in Carlisle, Pennsylvania, does not argue that superior firepower alone could necessarily defeat a revolutionary war. Rather, he contends that in South Vietnam the DRV waged a conventional war disguised as a revolutionary war. Until 1963, he concedes, Hanoi had adopted a low-level strategy based primarily on guerrilla warfare, and up to that time the U.S. policy of counterinsurgency was the correct approach. But after the fall of Ngo Dinh Diem in November, Hanoi shifted increasingly to a conventional strategy involving the introduction of regular units of the PAVN. The guerrilla tactics carried out by local Viet Cong forces were essentially a ruse to disguise the fact that the brunt of the conflict would be borne by regular units of the North Vietnamese army. It was not fate, he said, but four PAVN divisions that won the battle for Saigon in April 1975.

It is the main theme of Summers's book that the United States did not respond correctly to the shift in Hanoi's strategy in the mid-1960's but continued to fight the phantom of guerrilla war. In so doing, U.S. policymakers ignored the famous dictum of the German military strategist Karl von Clausewitz to "know your enemy" and focused their efforts on nation building and counterguerrilla tactics in the South rather than concentrating on the source of the problem by destroying the ability of the North to wage the war.

What strategy should the United States have adopted in the face of Hanoi's escalation of the conflict? Once again, Summers found his answer in Clausewitz. The purpose of military force is to achieve a political end. The United States should have clearly determined that its national objective was to achieve a victory in Vietnam. Then it should have mobilized the support of the American people through a declaration of war and applied sufficient force to compel Hanoi to sue for peace. Instead, President Johnson, fearful of Chinese intervention and reluctant to jeopardize his Great Society program by massive escalation of U.S. involvement in Southeast Asia, attempted to wage the war through a strategy of gradual escalation and without a clear statement of U.S. national objectives, thus confusing the American public and undermining public support for the war.

Summers concedes that the Johnson administration had some justification for being wary of a wider war, but he argues that the likelihood of direct Chinese intervention in Vietnam was small. In any event, the United States did not need a total victory in Vietnam but could have achieved its objectives through a limited incursion into North Vietnam or even a tactical offensive against PAVN units in the South.

Summers's critique was soon followed by others. In his *25-Year War: America's Military Role in Vietnam*, published in 1984, General Bruce Palmer, Jr., another U.S. Army officer with experience in Vietnam, criticized the policy of gradual escalation and contended that U.S. combat forces should have been used to seal off infiltration routes into South Vietnam while naval units imposed a blockade of North Vietnam to face its leaders with an ever-present threat of invasion. Then, behind the shield provided by American military power, the most important task of the war—the strengthening of the South Vietnamese armed forces—could be carried out under favorable circumstances. A similar argument was advanced by Norman B. Hannah, a retired foreign service officer with experience in Laos. The ultimate cause of the U.S. failure in Vietnam, he argued in *The Key to Failure: Laos and the Vietnam War*, could be traced to the 1962 Geneva Accords on Laos, which provided Hanoi with carte blanche to use Laotian territory as an infiltration route for North Vietnamese troops destined to fight in the South. Like Palmer, Hannah argued that U.S. forces should have cut such routes to force a settlement.

These are three serious critiques of U.S. strategy in Vietnam. They point very effectively to the underlying political and military weakness of the gradualist approach applied by the Johnson administration. It did not wear down the enemy, nor did it display American resolve. To the contrary, as Bruce Palmer has argued, it provided the Hanoi regime with the time to build its own defenses while simultaneously eroding support for the war in the United States. In moving cautiously, as Dean Rusk admitted in an interview after his departure from office, the Johnson administration may have underestimated the resourcefulness of the enemy and overestimated the patience of the American public.[4]

These points are well taken. Although the quality of U.S. intelligence reporting on the strength and tenacity of the communist movement and its leaders since the late 1940's had been quite high, many U.S. policymakers, particularly during the Kennedy and Johnson years, exhibited an overly optimistic expectation that the mere demonstration of U.S. "resolve" would force Hanoi to discard or at least adjust downward its schedule for victory in the South. Such expectations not only showed a blindness to the determination of Ho Chi Minh and his colleagues but also a surprising insensitivity to the legendary impatience of the American people. Not only had previous U.S. statesmen from George C. Marshall to Dwight Eisenhower recognized the inadvisability of a long and inconclusive war, even North Vietnamese leaders, drawing on the example of the Chinese Civil War and the Korean conflict, recognized that a gradualist approach was a recipe for American failure.

But to point out some of the reasons for the failure of U.S. strategy is a far cry from providing a feasible alternative. Although the authors cited above would not necessarily agree on the most effective solution to the Vietnam problem, they all share the conviction that the war was winnable and that the solution lay in the proper application of U.S. military power. How persuasive are these views? To make an assessment, we must take a closer look at some of the assumptions held by the advocates of a military solution and expose them to critical scrutiny.

It is one of the Summers's key contentions that the Vietnam War was not a revolutionary war but a conventional war in revolutionary guise. It thus demanded a conventional military approach rather than the counterinsurgency, nation-building approach that, in Summers's view, was actually applied. His contention is based essentially on that fact that during the later stages of the Vietnam War, regular units of the PAVN played an increasingly heavy role in the fighting in the South. The final "Ho Chi Minh Campaign," which ended with the seizure of Saigon at the end of April 1975, was a classical conventional assault carried out by North Vietnamese troops.

Few knowledgeable observers today would disagree with Summers that after 1965, Hanoi's strategy relied increasingly on regular units of the North Vietnamese army as the basis of its fighting forces in the South. And, as Hanoi now delights in pointing out, infiltration rates into the South through the Laotian panhandle were probably heavier than U.S. estimates at the time and were a major factor in the final campaign that drove the Saigon regime to its knees. Given these realities, a counterinsurgency approach such as had been recommended by some Kennedy administration officials in the early 1960's would have had little chance of success.

But to argue from the fact that Hanoi's strategy was essentially conventional and that a purely military response on the part of the United States would have successfully countered it is to misunderstand the concept of revolutionary war and the impact it has had on Vietnamese society. Revolutionary war was never simply a guerrilla strategy; it was a sophisticated combination of political and military techniques designed to take advantage of the strengths of the revolutionary movement and the weaknesses of the enemy and to seek victory by whatever means were most appropriate to the problem at hand. As such, it relied on both guerrilla and conventional military tactics, as well as on various forms of political and paramilitary struggle to undermine the position of the enemy and build support for the revolutionary movement. During the early stages of the Vietnam War, as Summers concedes, Hanoi relied primarily on low-level forms of struggle, and with considerable success. There is ample evidence that revolutionary forces would have taken over control of the South in 1965 had it not been for the introduction of U.S. combat troops.

The character of Hanoi's strategy did begin to change after the fall of the Diem regime, and by the end of 1965 regular units of the PAVN were already beginning to play a dominant role in the fighting. But even then Hanoi did not rely strictly on conventional techniques but on a highly sophisticated approach consisting of a mixture of lightning attacks by regular and guerrilla forces in areas of Hanoi's own choosing to demoralize the enemy and keep the war on the front page of U.S. newspapers. Guerrilla tactics and political struggle were thus not just a ruse, as Summers suggests, but were an integral part of the revolutionary strategy adopted by party leaders in Hanoi. If Summers is justified in claiming that defenders of a political approach ignored the key role of the North Vietnamese troops in affecting the course of the war, then he can be equally accused of ignoring the importance of political and paramilitary factors in determining the outcome.

To advocates of a more aggressive military approach to the war in Vietnam like Harry Summers, the political and social conditions in South Vietnam were somewhat irrelevant. If the Saigon regime was weak and overall conditions were unstable, then that weakness was a direct product of the presence of large numbers of North Vietnamese troops in the South. It thus follows naturally that if the proper strategy had been adopted to seal off the South from contact with the North, or to destroy the war-making capacity of the North, then the insurgency movement in South Vietnam would have withered on the vine.

It would be fatuous to deny that the United States could have won the war by an all-out assault that, in the words of one prominent military figure, would have bombed the North Vietnamese "back into the Stone Age." By and large, however, critics of U.S. strategy stopped short of advocating an all-out approach and recommended actions that fell short of the total destruction of North Vietnam: more aggressive operations by U.S. combat units in the South to eliminate North Vietnamese units and cut infiltration routes through the DMZ and the Laotian panhandle and heavier pressure on the DRV by means of sustained and destructive bombing raids on industrial and military targets throughout North Vietnam. Some argued for a blockade by the Seventh Fleet or a limited invasion of the North Vietnamese panhandle by U.S. combat troops.

The recommendation that U.S. combat forces should have assumed a more aggressive stance in the South is puzzling, for it was General Westmoreland's strategy to launch aggressive "search-and-destroy" operations throughout the country to engage the enemy's main forces to end the threat from the North. Although that approach did have some success in improving security near urban areas and imposing heavy casualties on enemy forces, by and large enemy main force units avoided contact with U.S. combat troops and frustrated U.S. efforts to engage them in conventional battles. Advocates of a more aggressive approach in the South have not persuasively indicated how they could have induced Hanoi to agree to engage in a purely conventional war if it did not choose to do so.

Virtually all advocates of the more aggressive approach contend that U.S. forces should have launched a major effort to seal off infiltration routes into the South by occupying the area south of the DMZ and into the Laotian panhandle. On the surface, this appeared to be an attractive alternative to the gradualist approach because a good case can be made that the failure to stop infiltration into the South was a key to the eventual outcome of the Vietnam War. But here too there are hidden problems. It would have been an enormous undertaking, requiring the establishment of a string of firebases and a system of electronic surveillance through a dense jungle terrain fully three times as wide as the defensive line established south of the DMZ in Central Vietnam. Ironically, it would have placed U.S. forces in a defensive posture and exposed them to attacks by the enemy at the latter's own choosing. This was undoubtedly one of the key reasons why the proposal to build such a barrier won only limited support from war planners in the Pentagon during the Johnson administration.[5]

Even if infiltration routes in the area of the DMZ could have been cut, however, there is no guarantee that men and supplies could not have been shipped into South Vietnam by other routes, by sea along the vast and indefensible coastline, or through the port of Sihanoukville, in Cambodia. In all likelihood, a U.S. effort to seal off the Ho Chi Minh Trail would not have led to an end of the conflict but to the spread of the war into Cambodia and Thailand and a reactivation of Pathet Lao operations in Laos.

Such a strategy would thus not only have been costly but also offered little possibility of a quick solution to the war, as Summers, for one, appears to assume. Even if such a strategy held the possibility of long-term success, Hanoi could hope to resume its activities once U.S. troops had been withdrawn. Would the American people have had the patience for such a drawn-out and inconclusive struggle? The answer is self-evident.

To advocates of a military approach, one solution to such problems would have been to engage in heavy air and naval attacks on the North as a means of compelling the Hanoi regime to reduce or eliminate its support for the revolutionary movement in the South. For the most part, critics assume that heavier bombing of key targets in the DRV combined with the presence of U.S. naval forces in the Tonkin Gulf to blockade the northern provinces and threaten the possibility of an invasion would have forced the regime to maintain adequate military forces in the North and thus reduce its capacity to intervene in South Vietnam.

The primary reason why the Johnson administration did not adopt such a strategy was undoubtedly the concern of Washington officials over the likelihood of Chinese intervention. For the most part, critics dismiss this possibility. Summers himself contends that the likelihood of Chinese intervention was small and that Beijing bluffed the United States into thinking that it might intervene in the war, thus paralyzing U.S. strategy.[6]

It is undoubtedly true that China was anxious to avoid direct involvement in the Vietnam War and signaled that fact to the United States at key instances. But it is too facile to declare flatly that China had no intention of engaging actively in Vietnam. Several studies have shown that Vietnam policy aroused vigorous debate within the party leadership in Beijing in 1965, and it is not unlikely that a more aggressive U.S. stance that threatened the survival of the Hanoi regime would have provoked China, as had happened during the Korean War, to intervene directly in the struggle. It might also have tipped the delicate balance of forces within the CCP leadership in favor of those who advocated detente with Moscow to wage a common struggle against U.S. imperialism in Asia.

If the above is true, then a policy of all-out military power would have been costly, uncertain in its prospects, divisive in its domestic repercussions, and risky by possibly widening the conflict. Such a course could be justified only if a strong case could be made that Vietnam was vital to the security of the United States. But did the ends justify such means? It has been argued above that the importance of Vietnam was always derivative rather than absolute, a fact that was tacitly if not explicitly conceded by every president from Truman to Nixon. To return to Clausewitz, if the purpose of military force is to achieve a political end, the United States should have determined that the objective of the strategy of containment in Southeast Asia was not necessarily to win in Vietnam but to act in such a way as to provide the noncommunist Vietnamese with an opportunity to fight for their own survival while at the same time seeking to guarantee that the remainder of the region did not fall into the communist orbit.

Under such circumstances, the standard rules of war do not apply. To many Americans, it is axiomatic that if a war is worth being fought, or a challenge is undertaken, it must be fought to the end. But under the doctrine of containment, the goal was not necessarily to prevent the loss of any particular country to communism but to protect key regions around the world from falling under the influence of Moscow (or later Beijing). Such a concept allows for tactical retreats from untenable positions much as a military commander will withdraw his forces from an exposed position to make a stronger stand elsewhere. It was the fundamental error of containment strategy as practiced during much of the 1950's and 1960's that every country and every area, no matter how exposed and vulnerable, had to be defended from the menace of international communism.

The rationale for the U.S. commitment to Vietnam, of course, was not that

Vietnam was intrinsically important to U.S. national security but that the psychological impact of a communist victory there could lead the leaders of Third World nations to lose confidence in the U.S. ability or willingness to protect them from internal or external attack and thus to decide to accommodate themselves to communist power. The leaders of Thailand no doubt informed U.S. officials of that danger on frequent occasions, and Dean Rusk has stated that although the neutral nations in Southeast Asia did not publicly support U.S. policy in the 1960's, they "would have been dismayed" if the United States had withdrawn from Vietnam. That may be so, but a prudent policy making it clear that a U.S. commitment would be undertaken only when the nation concerned showed the willingness and the ability to resist communist pressures with modest external assistance would undoubtedly have provided adequate reassurance to such leaders. It is safe to say that Vietnam rarely or never met either of those two qualifications.[7]

Not only did the United States commit its prestige to a nation whose chances of survival were dubious under the best of circumstances, but the Kennedy and Johnson administrations transformed Vietnam into the very symbol of U.S. resolve to resist the expansion of international communism. Had Vietnam been crucial to U.S. national security, or had the insurgency movement there been directly sponsored by Moscow or Beijing as a test of that resolve, Washington may have been justified in girding its forces to meet the challenge. But Soviet and Chinese behavior at the Geneva Conference in 1954 had made it clear that neither viewed a communist victory throughout Indochina as a high priority, and in fact they consider it an annoying distraction from other foreign policy objectives. That China provided more direct assistance and encouragement to the DRV during the early 1960's can be explained at least in part by the Dulles policy of forcing Beijing into a posture of angry isolation.

What can explain this gross inflation of the U.S. national interest by otherwise intelligent and rational men? In part, it was a consequence of the hasty actions and inflated rhetoric that gradually transformed a country of purely derivative importance to the free world into the symbol of U.S. determination to resist the expansion of communism in Asia. Yet these measures in turn were caused by the increasing paranoia brought about by the tensions aroused by the Cold War, a paranoia that caused U.S. officials to see a Chinese plot or the master hand of the Kremlin behind every decision taken in Hanoi.

Exaggeration of the national interest and excessive fear of an adversary, of course, is not a phenomenon limited to the era of the Cold War. It was displayed by major European powers during the height of the imperialist hysteria in China at the end of the nineteenth century and in the Balkans after the assassination of Archduke Franz Ferdinand of Austria-Hungary in the summer of 1914. It was a factor in the decision by the Japanese government to expand its influence into China and Southeast Asia by military means before World

War II. In such times, political leaders are prone to toss aside their rational calculations about national interest and intervene in areas that have little intrinsic importance to their national security out of fear that rivals may gain an advantage there. In some instances, such as the threat posed by Hitler's Germany in the 1930's, the fear is justified. In most cases, the danger is overstated and the threat is self-fulfilling.

Was there no way, then, for the United States to win in Vietnam short of the virtually total destruction of the DRV? That would seem to be the implication of a study by historian Gabriel Kolko. Kolko, in *Anatomy of a War: Vietnam, the United States, and the Modern Historical Experience,* argues that the political failure of the noncommunist nationalist movement in Vietnam can be traced back to the historical weakness of the Vietnamese bourgeoisie under repressive French colonial rule. The basic pattern of modern Vietnamese history, he asserts, was "the non-Communists' endemic inability to relate to the dynamics of their own times." This left the door open for the Vietnamese communist movement under the leadership of Ho Chi Minh and gave him a momentum the United States was never able to overcome.

This is not the place for a lengthy analysis of the factors that underlay the unique strength of the communist movement in Vietnam. I am inclined to assign more importance to cultural and historical factors during the precolonial era than to the impact of French colonial rule. Yet there is no doubt that, for whatever reason, there were deep-seated historical reasons for the communist triumph in Vietnam, and it is perhaps more accurate to describe the war as a victory for Hanoi than as a defeat for Washington. It is probably too much to say that these obstacles posed an insuperable challenge to a U.S. version of nation building (after all, societies do evolve), but they undoubtedly called for a degree of ingenuity, persistence, and sensitivity to local historical and cultural factors that have all too often been in short supply in U.S. foreign policy.

The Lessons of Vietnam

What conclusions can be drawn from the above analysis? What lessons can be drawn from the experience? Debate over the so-called lessons of Vietnam began shortly after the fall of Saigon and has continued to this day. Countless books and articles have been written on the subject by officials, journalists, scholars, and other political pundits. Many of these efforts have been useful, although predictably the lessons drawn have usually been strongly influenced by the political bias of the individual observer. In general, the recommendations have gravitated toward two poles of thought: the "never again" school and the "go all-out" approach.

Some critics have argued that the entire project was a mistake and shows how traditional U.S. foreign policy was distorted by the anxieties and fears of the Cold War. A good example of this school of thought is George McT. Kahin, whose study *Intervention: How America Became Involved in Vietnam* is relentlessly critical of the decision by several U.S. presidents to intervene in the conflict in Vietnam. Kahin describes Truman's decision to assist the French in Indochina as "the first in a continuing series of steps to apply external power in the effort to control the threat of nationalism and create an artificial, externally sustained state that lacked any substantial indigenous foundation."[8]

In my judgment, this characterization of Truman's Indochina policy is somewhat harsh. It misconstrues the motives of Truman and his key advisers and the means they used to carry out their policy. The case has been presented in this book that the original commitment to Indochina was rooted in the traditional American belief in the universality of democratic ideals, the importance of open markets, and the need to create a world safe for political and cultural self-determination. The Truman policy was sometimes shortsighted and unimaginative, and it no doubt ascribed altruistic motives to actions that were actually taken for purely national interest, but the strategy he adopted in Indochina was reasonably prudent and was based on a reasonable concern for the future of the free world alliance and the course of events in Southeast Asia. Most Washington officials were undoubtedly ignorant of the popular roots of the Vietnamese communist movement and assumed (based on recent experience in Eastern Europe) that communism and indigenous nationalism were inherently incompatible. Such officials believed that with the departure of the French, a vigorous new brand of noncommunist Vietnamese nationalism would begin to thrive. In the internationalist mood of the time, it is not surprising that the administration would opt to use U.S. power and influence to assist in the emergence of societies based on the democratic capitalist model. In many other cases around the world, and elsewhere in Asia itself, that assumption eventually paid dividends.

If such is the case, it was not the original commitment that was at the root of the problem but the later failure to learn from bitter experience that raised Vietnam from a matter of only derivative importance into the symbol of U.S. determination to resist communist expansion throughout the world. Here Kahin has a point. By the late 1950's it was readily apparent to many informed observers that noncommunist nationalist forces in South Vietnam lacked the coherence and the will to compete effectively with Ho Chi Minh's disciplined and dedicated followers. The Eisenhower administration and its successors were well aware of that weakness, yet they deliberately committed U.S. prestige, and eventually thousands of American lives, to the survival of a failed experiment.

Was this course of events inevitable? It has been argued that the United States entered the war in Vietnam not by accident but by design. According to author Patrick Hatcher, the problem arose when U.S. policymakers began to ignore George Kennan's advice to adopt a prudent posture in competing with the Soviet Union around the world and decided to take maximum risks in opposing communist expansion wherever it appeared.[9]

Hatcher assigns the bulk of the blame for that transition from minimalism to maximalism (to use his phraseology) to the Kennedy and Johnson administrations. Eisenhower, he notes, was better at "losing small," at trying to win but minimizing risks, whereas Kennedy and Johnson did not know how to lose small. This is not entirely fair, at least in the case of Indochina. It was Kennedy, after all, who defused the crisis that Eisenhower had created in Laos by taking the issue to the negotiating table. It has been argued here that in Vietnam Eisenhower had a hand in creating the problem by committing U.S. prestige to a losing proposition. It was John F. Kennedy (and Lyndon Johnson after him) who paid the price for Eisenhower's miscalculation.[10]

Still, Hatcher's central argument is well taken. The essential error committed by U.S. policymakers in Southeast Asia was not the decision to include the region under the umbrella of the U.S. strategy of containment—history has validated that effort as successful—but the assumption that the survival of noncommunist Vietnam was essential to that success. Events since the fall of Saigon make it clear that a more prudent policy would in all likelihood have achieved the overall purposes of containment without the tragic expenditure of lives and resources that were invested in the abortive effort to preserve Vietnam as the keystone in the arch of containment in Asia.

Hatcher and others have contended that the process was unavoidable, an ineluctable consequence of the Cold War zeitgeist that reigned in the United States in the 1950's and 1960's. This is not the place for an extended discussion of the dynamic forces driving postwar U.S. foreign policy, but it is certainly true that the Cold War mentality in the United States took on a momentum of its own, ultimately distorting the prudent calculations of early containment theorists. Perhaps that was an inevitable consequence of the growing U.S. fear of communism, but even at the height of the Cold War, U.S. presidents were capable of adopting cautious positions in the face of strong pressures for escalation. Eisenhower wisely ignored hawkish elements in his administration by refusing to intervene in Indochina in 1954 and in the Hungarian Revolution two years later. A decade later, Lyndon Johnson resisted pressures from maximalists to intensify the war against the DRV on the reasonable grounds that such action would risk a world nuclear confrontation.

In general, then, it was always within the power of the White House to reverse the seemingly inexorable trend toward intervention in Vietnam. But by the late 1950's, Vietnam had taken on such symbolic importance as the keystone of the arch of defense in Southeast Asia that few U.S. policymakers could bring themselves to argue for a reversal of the process. In that sense, Washington reaped what it had sown. Had President Eisenhower adopted a more prudent attitude toward the Diem regime, had John F. Kennedy possessed the strength of will to act on his own doubts about the survivability of that regime in the early 1960's, Lyndon Johnson would not have felt compelled to intervene with U.S. troops, and the effects of failure in Vietnam could have been kept within tolerable limits.

Proponents of the "never again" school, then, are mistaken in citing the Vietnam War as proof that all efforts to help friendly Third World governments to defeat internal insurgency movements are inadvisable because they lead inevitably to direct intervention or outright failure. In many cases, U.S. efforts to provide such assistance have succeeded. But they are certainly correct in warning of the dangers that such actions can all too easily escalate unless the costs of the operations are carefully calibrated and great care is exercised in reconciling the means and the ends. No such effort was ever undertaken in Vietnam.

A second "lesson" that has often been drawn from the Vietnam War is that U.S. military forces should not be committed abroad unless the United States is prepared to go for final victory. It was this lesson that was cited by President George Bush when he stated at a press conference on the day opening the Gulf War: "I've told the American people before that this will not be another Vietnam," he declared. "Our troops will have the best possible support in the entire world, and they will not be asked to fight with one hand behind their back."[11]

Few would deny that the United States should use to the degree necessary its enormous power when it must act to protect a vital interest. But it has been argued here that although Vietnam was an important link in the chain of containment in Asia, it was never defined as an area of vital importance to the security of the United States and that U.S. participation in the Vietnam conflict was not only tragic but also, in terms of U.S. national interests, essentially unnecessary. That fact was tacitly conceded in the U.S. reaction to the fall of Saigon in 1975. If that is the case, the crucial point of the argument is not whether the United States should have gone all out in Vietnam, but how far should it have gone in assisting the South Vietnamese to carry on the struggle themselves. Truman, Eisenhower, and Kennedy, all of whom had legitimate doubts about how far to go in seeking a noncommunist solution in Vietnam, yet believed that it was in the national interest to provide military assistance to the Saigon regime short of the commitment of U.S. combat troops to enable it to resist a communist takeover. Was that belief wrong? Did the provision of military assistance and training programs to the Vietnamese armed forces in the 1950's inevitably put the United States on a "slippery slope" to direct involvement in the 1960's? Where does one draw the line between limited assistance and actual intervention? Is it possible or desirable in some cases to provide military assistance to an ally or a client without making a formal commitment or going all out?

As policymakers who dealt with the Vietnam issue were well aware, these are not easy questions to answer. Yet some general comments may be useful. In implementing its policy of containment, the United States was justified in providing military assistance to countries whose survival was in the national interest yet were not crucial to U.S. national security. To do less in the case of South Vietnam would have virtually doomed the RVN to defeat because the DRV was receiving military assistance from its own allies. But the granting of military assistance does not, and should not, imply that additional forms of support, including U.S. combat troops, are likely to follow. Direct U.S. military intervention should have been made available only in cases of crucial importance to the United States. Certainly they should not have been provided to any ally unless the prospects for victory at a reasonable cost were relatively good.[12]

Neither of these factors ever pertained in Vietnam. Yet under Presidents Eisenhower and Kennedy, this line was never clearly drawn. Both gave active consideration to the introduction of U.S. combat troops even in the face of evidence of the uncertain prospects for success and doubts about the crucial importance of the area to U.S. national security. A clearer definition of U.S. objectives, as had gradually emerged during the 1961 crisis in Laos, would have permitted policymakers to reduce if not eliminate the danger that Vietnam would take on enormous symbolic importance in the global balance of forces and place the country on the slippery slope to direct involvement. The failure to set those limits doomed the United States to fighting a war that it was not willing to use all its resources to win.

It might be argued that the establishment of such well-defined limits incites the enemy to intensify his own efforts. But the lack of limits also encouraged the leaders of U.S. client states to believe that they could always rely on the immense power of their patron, thus relieving them of the responsibility to secure their own destiny. If applied in Vietnam, such limits would have forced Saigon to face the challenge of nation building that it alone could bring to successful realization. Failure to do so would only have demonstrated that the conditions for successful containment did not exist.

It was proper, then, to provide military aid to the Diem regime, so long as the latter appeared to be willing to make reasonably effective use of it (a serious question in Diem's case). But it was an error to tie the survival of that regime to U.S. prestige and international credibility, thus reducing the room for maneuver of future chief executives when the situation in Saigon declined to the point of crisis.

Was U.S. intervention in Vietnam a noble cause? This problem is too complex and loaded with political and moral connotations to be subject to rational analysis. The judgment expressed here is that the original motives for attempting to contain the spread of communism in Southeast Asia were commendable and on the whole justified but that the decision to intervene in the conflict in Vietnam was marred by ignorance, shortsightedness, a degree of national hubris, and a lamentable tendency on the part of some U.S. policymakers to identify U.S. national interests with the forces of Truth and Goodness in the world. Although countless Americans who took part in the experiment were undoubtedly motivated by high moral principles, it was not, on the whole, a noble effort.

Are there any lessons in the Vietnam experience applicable to postwar foreign policy? Some undoubtedly think so. The interpretation of the "lessons of Vietnam" has become a veritable growth industry and has spawned books and academic conferences as well as sterile debates in the political arena. The "never again" school argued strenuously against U.S. military assistance to El Salvador on the grounds that it would lead inexorably to direct intervention. The "all-out" school, with the encouragement of George Bush, raised its banner during the war in the Persian Gulf. It has been argued here that there are indeed some useful lessons for policymakers faced with crises in foreign affairs. It is crucially necessary to understand the enemy as well as to understand one's own strengths and weaknesses. It is vital to define U.S. interests precisely and adopt an appropriate strategy to deal successfully with those interests. It is especially important for a Great Power not to exaggerate national security needs or lose a sense of proportion in world affairs. Such a perspective would have enabled U.S. policymakers to view the conflict in Vietnam for what it was—a civil war with some implications for regional stability—but not, at least after the mid-1950's, with the potential for shaking the global balance of power. It is increasingly clear today that Vietnam, however it is governed, serves as a useful counterbalance to Chinese ambitions in the area.

But it should be apparent that one of the primary lessons of the Vietnam War is that "lessons" from previous wars should be drawn with extreme care. Everyone knows the dictum that generals always refight the last war, and badly. That same caution can be applied in the conduct of foreign affairs. It was the "lessons of Munich" which provided the guiding principle for U.S. involvement in Vietnam. Those lessons had some relevance to the global situation after the end of World War II, but they were highly misleading when applied to the situation in Indochina, where Ho Chi Minh (whatever his communist predilections) was no Adolf Hitler. The image of Munich, according to which the enemy had to be stopped at the gate before he was fighting on the doorstep, was a powerful stimulus to American policymakers faced with the conflict in Southeast Asia. A better example might have been Mukden, where in 1931 the United States protested against the Japanese takeover of Manchuria but took no military action. Although some have decried the failure of the United States to act more decisively in response to that example of "international outlawry," it was a prudent response in view of the isolationist sentiments of the American people and the pacifist attitudes in the world community at that time. When Japan finally attacked Pearl Harbor in December 1941, the American people, and much of the world at large, were prepared to back President Roosevelt in a massive effort to defeat the Axis.

The course of events since the end of the Vietnam War suggests that the "lessons of Vietnam" are indeed limited. Much was made of the so-called Vietnam syndrome, according to which the American people would be unwilling to support the application of U.S. military power in Third World crises because of the fear of "many Vietnams." The Vietnam syndrome had a short shelf-life. The "never again" school argued against the provision of U.S. military assistance to the government in El Salvador, but the Reagan administration ignored the protests and the operation was, by current estimate, a modest success. A few years later, George Bush led U.S. combat troops into Panama with the praise of a large majority of Americans. Whether or not the move was justified, it did not lead the United States into another quagmire in Central America.

The arguments of the "all-out" school are equally subject to doubt. Although George Bush relentlessly reminded the American people that the Gulf War would not be "another Vietnam," he placed clear limits on the use of American power by rejecting a ground attack on Baghdad and leaving the Saddam Hussein regime intact. Whether or not such a strategy was appropriate, it was a clear sign that George Bush, for all his jingoist rhetoric, recognized the need for the prudent application of U.S. military power in the conduct of foreign affairs.

In any event, there is reasonable doubt that nations are able to learn abiding lessons from past experience. The American people, many of whom are too young to remember any "lessons" from Vietnam, quickly forgot the problems that were encountered by the lack of clear goals in Vietnam and cheered the decisions of their leaders in Panama and the Persian Gulf, where the objectives were no less imprecise. The unfortunate fact, for nations as for individuals, is that each generation must learn from its own experience. If that is the case, the nation could all too willingly march blindly into another Vietnam in the future.[13]

Fortunately, the decline and fall of the Cold War makes such a development unlikely, at least for the foreseeable future. The dissolution of the Soviet Union and the collapse of the socialist camp demonstrated the overall success of the strategy of containment, while suggesting that George Kennan's prescription for a prudent and minimalist approach to the dangers of Soviet expansionism while hoping for a change of attitude in Moscow was essentially correct. Whether or not Vietnam was an aberration from or a symptom of the traditional principles of U.S. foreign policy, it can be said of the containment strategy in Vietnam that, although the United States may have lost the battle, it won the war.

Reference Matter

Notes

The following abbreviations are used in the notes:

CCP	Chinese Communist Party
CINCPAC	Commander in Chief, Pacific
COSVN	Central Office for South Vietnam
Cuoc Khang Chien	*Cuoc Khang Chien Than Thanh cua Nhan Dan Viet Nam*
DDRS	*Declassified Documents Reference System*
DOS	Department of State
DSB	*Department of State Bulletin*
ECA	Economic Cooperation Administration
EDC	European Defense Community
FE	Office of Far Eastern Affairs
FRUS	*Foreign Relations of the United States*
History of JCS	U.S. Department of Defense, *History of the Joint Chiefs of Staff*
ICC	International Control Commission
ICP	Indochinese Communist Party
INR	Bureau of Intelligence and Research
MAAG	Military Assistance Advisory Group
MACV	Military Assistance Command, Vietnam
NIE	National Intelligence Estimate
NSC	National Security Council
OSS	Office of Strategic Services
PSA	Office of Philippine and Southeast Asian Affairs
RG 59	U.S. Department of State: Central Files (Indochina), National Archives

SD   Secretary of Defense
SEAC   Southeast Asia Command
SEATO   Southeast Asia Treaty Organization
SS   Secretary of State
USVN   *United States–Vietnam Relations, 1945–1967*
VDRN   *Vietnam Documents and Research Notes*

Chapter 1

1. For a study of this issue, see Friend, *Between Two Empires.*
2. For an analysis, see Gordon, *Toward Disengagement in Asia.*
3. Ibid., chap. 3.
4. Hess, *United States' Emergence,* pp. 34–35.
5. Quoted in *USVN,* book 7, pt. V.B.1, p. 30.
6. *DSB,* Apr. 18, 1942, p. 33, quoted in Drachman, *United States Diplomacy Toward Vietnam,* p. 35. Roosevelt's letter to Marshal Pétain is in *FRUS,* 1941, pp. 205–6. For Hull's comment, see DOS Release no. 374, in *DSB,* Aug. 2, 1941, p. 87, quoted in Drachman, p. 135.
7. For FDR's conversation with Stalin at Tehran, see Hess, *United States' Emergence,* pp. 80–81.
8. Ibid., pp. 61–67.
9. De Gaulle, *War Memoirs,* p. 187.
10. *Direction de la documentation, notes, documentaires et études,* no. 548 (Feb. 15, 1947), quoted in Cameron, ed., *Viet-Nam Crisis,* pp. 11–12; translation by Cameron. The request for membership in the Pacific War Council was transmitted to Washington by the U.S. Embassy in Chungking. See office memo from Landon, dated March 2, 1945, in RG 59, 851 G.00/3-245.
11. Hess, *United States' Emergence,* pp. 80–81.
12. Ibid., p. 382, n. 16.
13. Memo from Under Secretary of State Stettinius to President Roosevelt, Nov. 2, 1944, in *FRUS,* 1944, 3: 778–79; Memorandum from President Roosevelt to Secretary of State Stettinius, Jan. 1, in *FRUS,* 1945, 7: 293.
14. Drachman, *United States Diplomacy Toward Vietnam,* p. 67; Patti, *Why Vietnam,* pp. 121–22.
15. Memo by Roosevelt to Stettinius, October 16, 1944, in *FRUS,* 1944, 3: 777.
16. Cook, *Constitutionalist Party,* chap. 1.
17. For Ho Chi Minh's own account of his conversion to Leninism, see Gettleman, ed., *Vietnam,* pp. 30–32.
18. There have been a number of accounts of the conditions surrounding the creation of the ICP. For a recent version based on original documentation, see Huynh, *Vietnamese Communism.*
19. One prominent exception to this general rule was the radical Cochinchinese intellectual Nguyen An Ninh. Although descended from a scholar-gentry family in the Mekong Delta and educated in Paris, Ninh was sensitive to the plight of the poor and in the mid-1920's attempted to organize resistance to the French at the village level. Arrested by the French, he later cooperated with the ICP although he never joined the party. He died in prison in 1939.

20. See my *Rise of Nationalism* for details.

21. For an account of the revolt by a historian in Hanoi, see Tran, *Les Soviets du Nghe Tinh.*

22. Duiker, *Rise of Nationalism*, pp. 275–76.

23. Patti, *Why Vietnam*, pp. 46–48. Patti's book is an essential source for information on U.S. intelligence operations in South China and Indochina during World War II. The so-called Anti-Invasion Association mentioned by Patti is presumably the International Anti-Aggression League mentioned by Vietnamese defector Hoang Van Hoan in his memoirs, *A Drop in the Ocean.* See p. 195.

24. Ho Chi Minh had visited the United States while serving aboard a French steamship before World War I and had reportedly established contact with radical black groups in Harlem. For his attitude toward the United States during this period, see Patti, *Why Vietnam*, passim.

25. Hess, *United States' Emergence*, pp. 85–86. For a memorandum reporting the views of the U.S. naval attaché in Chungking on Chinese activities with Vietnamese groups in South China, see RG 59, 851 G.00/2-545. Cordell Hull forwarded a memo representing the views of Asianists to the White House in September 1944. See Hess, p. 108.

26. I am grateful to Chalmers Roberts for his comment on that point. Letter from Chalmers Roberts, Mar. 23, 1992.

27. Hess, *United States' Emergence*, pp. 103–4. On Hull's views, see his memo quoted on p. 107.

28. Quoted in Drachman, *United States Diplomacy Toward Vietnam*, p. 53. For Roosevelt's comments at Yalta, see *FRUS*, 1945, pp. 770, 994. Also see Memo by Leo Pasvolsky, Apr. 13, 1945, ibid., p. 288.

29. See Conversation between the president and Charles Taussig, Mar. 15, 1945, in *FRUS*, 1945, p. 124. This was confirmed by Quentin Roosevelt, who cited the president to the effect that if the French promised to assume the role of tutor in Indochina, the United States would not oppose it so long as independence was assured (Patti, *Why Vietnam*, p. 121). For an indication that some State Department officials assumed that FDR had approved the Yalta formula, see the Memo by WE/EUR to the President, "American Policy with Respect to Indochina," in RG 59, 851 G.00/5-945. For a useful analysis of the debate over self-government and independence in discussions about trusteeships, see Gibbons, *U.S. Government and the Vietnam War*, 1: 15.

30. Hess, *United States' Emergence*, pp. 147–49. The Blakeslee memorandum, "U.S. Policy with regard to the Future of Indochina," is in RG 59, 851 G.00/4-545. It is excerpted in Porter, ed., *Vietnam: A History in Documents*, pp. 12–16.

31. "Suggested Reexamination of American Policy with respect to Indochina," in RG 59, 851 G.00/4-245.

32. FE's suggested revisions are in RG 59, 851 G.00/4-2145. Also see Porter, ed., *Vietnam: A History in Documents*, pp. 17–18. The opinions of the European Division apparently had the support of the president. See the comments by Hull in his *Memoirs*, 2: 1599.

33. Patti, *Why Vietnam*, p. 117. See the telegram from Joseph Grew to Ambassador Caffery, May 6, 1945, in *FRUS*, 1945, 6: 307. The remark by Bidault is quoted in Drachman, *United States Diplomacy Toward Vietnam*, p. 56.

34. *FRUS*, 1945, 6: 307–8, has excerpts.

35. Gibbons, *U.S. Government and the Vietnam War*, p. 21.

36. Quoted in Patti, *Why Vietnam*, p. 128.

37. The thesis regarding the position that Roosevelt would have adopted on Indochina had he lived is similar to the larger question as to whether the Cold War would have taken place if Truman had not become president. The presently available evidence indicates that Roosevelt was increasingly distrustful of Stalin in the days before his death, which suggests that Soviet-American relations would have suffered even if he had lived. For a provocative but unproven hypothesis regarding Roosevelt's final intentions regarding Indochina, see Tonnesson, *Vietnamese Revolution*, esp. chaps. 4–7.

38. See the department's telegram to the U.S. Embassy in Paris dated March 22, 1945, in RG 59, 851 G.oo/3-2245, instructing the embassy to inform Georges Bidault that this did not represent a commitment to provide U.S. military assistance. At first Wedemeyer resisted these instructions, but Halifax persisted and said that operations would not prejudice the future settlement in the area. Wedemeyer relented. See Drachman, *United States Diplomacy Toward Vietnam*, p. 72.

39. This problem is discussed in Patti, *Why Vietnam*, chaps. 11–14.

40. Ibid., p. 120.

41. According to Drachman, *United States Diplomacy Toward Vietnam*, p. 88, Sabattier was concerned about U.S. restrictions. For Sabattier's views, see Sabattier, *Le Destin de l'Indochine*, pp. 455–62.

42. This incident is cited in several contemporary accounts. See Patti, *Why Vietnam*, pp. 58–60.

43. Iriye, *Cold War*, chap. 2.

Chapter 2

1. Not surprisingly, there has been some disagreement over the circumstances of Bao Dai's abdication. Tran Huy Lieu, the chief of the Vietminh delegation to Hué, asserts that it was voluntary. Bao Dai contends he was pressured. The question has important implications, of course, regarding the legality of the new Provisional Republic of Vietnam. For these two views, see Tran Huy Lieu, "Tuoc an kiem cua Hoang de Bao Dai," in *Nghien Cuu Lich Su* (Historical research), no. 18 (Sept. 1960), pp. 46–51. Bao Dai's account is in *Dragon d'Annam*, pp. 118–23.

2. Party historians now concede that the dissolution of the ICP was a tactical ploy. See *Lich Su Dang Cong San Viet Nam*, 1: 475, and Hoang Van Hoan, *Drop in the Ocean*, p. 224.

3. Letter from Chalmers Roberts, Mar. 23, 1992. It has sometimes been assumed that Gracey was acting on his own, but SEAC records indicate that he was carrying out orders from Mountbatten's headquarters in Ceylon. According to one source, SEAC headquarters felt that the "eventual reoccupation of French Indochina is a matter for the French." The U.S. Embassy in Paris reported on October 12, 1945, that the British government considered the French civil administration the sole authority south of the sixteenth parallel. See Spector, *Advice and Support*, p. 64. For a sympathetic portrayal of Douglas Gracey, see Dunn, *First Vietnam War*.

4. Memorandum of Conversation (Dunn), Aug. 29, 1945, in *FRUS*, 1945, 7: 540–42.

5. *History of JCS*, p. 74. Evidence of pro-Vietminh attitudes among U.S. officers stationed in Indochina can be found in Patti, *Why Vietnam*, passim. For a report

reflecting the views of OSS representatives in Hanoi on the new government, see Donovan to Ballantine, Sept. 5, 1945, in RG 59, 851 G.00/9-545.

6. Memo from FE (Vincent) to Under Secretary Acheson, Sept. 28, 1945, in RG 59, 851 G.00/9-2845. Vincent's conversation with Sir George Sansom of the British Embassy is in ibid., 851 G.00/9-2445.

7. Memo, Bonbright to Matthews (EUR), Oct. 2, 1945, in RG 59, 851 G.00/10-245.

8. *Pentagon Papers*, 1: 16.

9. *USVN*, book 1, pt. 1, pp. 73–74. According to Hoang Van Hoan, at a conference of Vietminh representatives held just before the end of World War II, Ho Chi Minh had predicted that Vietnam might not receive total independence until five years after the war. In the meantime, the Vietnamese might have to accept partial independence within the confines of a French Union. See Hoang Van Hoan, *Drop in the Ocean*, p. 215.

10. Hess, *United States' Emergence*, p. 180, n. 44, citing RG 59, 851 G.00/10-2245. Also see the testimony of Abbot Low Moffat and Frank White, May 11, 1972, U.S. Senate Foreign Relations Committee, "United States and Vietnam," pp. 187–88, 201–2.

11. Hess, *United States' Emergence*, p. 183, citing testimony of Frank White, U.S. Senate Foreign Relations Committee, "United States and Vietnam."

12. *USVN*, book 8, pt. B.2, pp. 53–55. Patti and Nordlinger were more impressed with Vietminh military capabilities than Gallagher and predicted that they could use guerrilla warfare effectively against the French. See Hess, *United States' Emergence*, p. 183, n. 58, citing memoranda of conversation, Dec. 5, 1945, RG 59, 851 G.00/12-545.

13. Ho's letter of January 18, 1946, is located in U.S. Senate Foreign Relations Committee, "United States and Vietnam," pp. 10–11. For the Landon cables, see *FRUS*, 1946, 8: 26–27.

14. Caffery to SS, Feb. 6, 1946, in *USVN*, book 8, p. 59.

15. Byrnes to French Ambassador Henri Bonnet, Apr. 12, 1946, ibid., pt. B.2, pp. 64–65.

16. For a useful summary of the talks, see Hammer, *Struggle for Indochina*, pp. 159–63.

17. Reed to Byrnes, Apr. 27, 1946, in *FRUS*, 1946, 8: 37–38.

18. O'Sullivan to the Secretary, June 5, 1946, ibid., pp. 43–45.

19. Paris 3801, Aug. 2, 1946, in RG 59, 851 G.00/8-246.

20. Memorandum, Moffat to Vincent, Aug. 9, 1946, in *FRUS*, 1946, 8: 52–54.

21. Caffery to Byrnes, Sept. 11, 1946, ibid. In a letter to the secretary on the sixteenth, Caffery said that Ho had behaved "with dignity" and in a tactful way during the negotiations. See RG 59, 851 G.00/9-1646.

22. Caffery to Byrnes, Sept. 12, 1946, in *USVN*, book 1, pt. 1.C, pp. 102–4.

23. DOS 241 to Reed in Saigon, Aug. 9, 1946, in RG 59, 851 G.00/8-946. Assistant SS to Saigon, Sept. 9 and 10, 1946, and Caffery to SS, Nov. 11, 1946, in *FRUS*, 1946, 8: 57, 63. For rumors of Vietminh contacts with the CCP, see Oct. 19, 1946, p. 62.

24. Saigon 349 to the Secretary, Aug. 29, 1946, in RG 59, 851 G.00/8-2946.

25. There have been numerous charges and countercharges as to who was to blame for the clashes between the Vietminh and the opposition. For a series of cables from the U.S. consulate in Hanoi, see Hanoi cables 63, 68, and 69, from July 1 to July 26, 1946, ibid.

26. Paris 5858 to the Secretary, Nov. 29, 1946, ibid.

27. Assistant SS to Saigon (Moffat), Dec. 5, 1946, in *FRUS*, 1946, 8: 67–68.

28. For Moffat's report, see U.S. Senate Foreign Relations Committee, "United States and Vietnam," Appendix 2, pp. 41–42.

29. See Hess, *United States' Emergence*, chap. 8, for an overview.

30. DOS Circular Airgram, Dec. 17, 1946, in RG 59, 851 G.oo/12-1746.

31. "Cong viec khan cap bay gio" (Urgent tasks for today), in *Van Kien Dang* (1945–54), vol. 1 (1945–46), pp. 101–3.

32. Hanoi 147 to Secretary, Dec. 18, 1946, in RG 59, 851 G.oo/12-1846. On December 20, O'Sullivan cabled that the attack had clearly been premeditated, but from Saigon Reed reported rumors that an attempted coup may have forced Ho into desperate action. For a provocative analysis of the beginning of the Franco-Vietminh War, see Tonnesson, *1946.*

33. Memorandum of Conversation, "Possible Viet-Minh representative en route to Washington," in RG 59, 851 G.oo/10-3145.

34. Patti, *Why Vietnam*, p. 392.

35. For a view of the importance of Europe in administration calculations, see Clark Clifford Oral History, p. 10.

Chapter 3

1. For a brief discussion of the conditions surounding the enunciation of the containment doctrine, see Gaddis, *Strategies of Containment*, pp. 28–30.

2. For d'Argenlieu's comments, see Saigon to SS, Dec. 24, 1946, in *FRUS*, 1946, 8: 78–79.

3. Byrnes to Caffery, Dec. 24, 1946, ibid., pp. 77–78.

4. Assistant SS to U.S. Embassy in London, Dec. 27, 1946, ibid., pp. 79–80. Ronald Spector points out that Truman administration officials were concerned that U.S. pressure to bring the fighting in Indochina to an end might drive the French to reject U.S. plans to forge an anti-Soviet alliance in Europe. See Spector, *Advice and Support*, p. 83.

5. Moffat (Singapore) to SS, Jan. 7, 1947, in *FRUS*, 1947, 6: 54–55.

6. Minister in Siam (Stanton) to SS, Jan. 7, 1947, ibid., pp. 56–58. Ambassador Stanton received a lecture for his pains. See ibid.

7. Vincent memo to Under Secretary of State, Jan. 8, 1947, ibid., pp. 58–59. One reason for the French rejection may have been suspicion of U.S. objectives. An article by Marius Moutet in the French journal *Le Populaire* had recently criticized the United States for practicing "economic imperialism" in Asia.

8. SS to Caffery, Feb. 3, 1947, ibid., pp. 77–78.

9. *History of JCS*, p. 132.

10. Cited in Hammer, *Struggle for Indochina*, p. 197. Caffery's discussion with Bidault is reported in DOS to Reed in Saigon, Feb. 7, 1947, in RG 59, 851 G.oo/2-747.

11. Assistant SS to Caffery, Mar. 24, 1947, in *FRUS*, 1947, 6: 81. Marius Moutet described Ho's offer as a "small step forward" because it omitted his previous demand for a return to the military status quo ante. See Caffery to DOS, Mar. 3, 1947, in RG 59, 851 G.oo/3-347. But the initiative was derailed by a debate within the French government over whether the letter was fraudulent. The French political situation is described in Hammer, *Struggle for Indochina*, pp. 199–200.

12. Paris to SS, Apr. 11, 1947; Saigon to SS, Feb. 7, 1947, in RG 59, 851 G.oo/2-747.

13. Hanoi to SS, May 7, 1947, in *FRUS*, 1947, 6: 95. A DRV official quietly approached the U.S. ambassador in Bangkok, and the department had responded with cautious

approval, but little came of it. See Bangkok to SS, Apr. 17, 1947; SS to Bangkok, Apr. 25, 1947; Bangkok to SS, Apr. 24, 1947; SS to Hanoi, May 2, 1947; SS to Hanoi, May 9, 1947. These cables are available in RG 59, 851 G.oo.

14. Hammer, *Struggle for Indochina*, p. 207. A translated report on the Ho-Mus meeting was provided in Hanoi to SS, June 20, 1947, in RG 59, 851 G.oo/6-2047.

15. Bao Dai, *Dragon d'Annam*, p. 182. Bollaert's comment is quoted in Hammer, *Struggle for Indochina*, p. 209.

16. Bao Dai, *Dragon d'Annam*, pp. 173–77.

17. Marshall to Caffery, May 13, 1947, in *FRUS*, 1947, 6: 95–97.

18. Reed to Acheson, June 14, 1947, in ibid., pp. 64–66.

19. Marshall to Reed in Saigon, July 17, 1947, ibid., pp. 117–18.

20. Reed to SS, July 14, 1947, ibid., pp. 121–26.

21. Spector, *Advice and Support*, pp. 84–85.

22. Bao Dai, *Dragon d'Annam*, p. 182. Bollaert's speech is reported in Reed to DOS, Sept. 11, 1947, in RG 59, 851 G.oo/9-1147. The speech was a shock to Bao Dai, who had convened a conference of noncommunist nationalists in Hong Kong in September to reformulate a common declaration for negotiations with the French. From Hanoi, O'Sullivan reported that the French were split on Indochina policy. Bollaert, supported by Marius Moutet, wanted to deal with Ho Chi Minh, but Ramadier did not. Bollaert was recalled to Paris for consultations. See O'Sullivan to DOS, Aug. 1, 1947, in RG 59, 851 G.oo/8-147.

23. SS to Caffery, Sept. 11, 1947, in *FRUS*, 1947, 6: 135–36.

24. Bao Dai, *Dragon d'Annam*, pp. 182, 188–91.

25. One of the notable quotes was the following: "I believe that it must be the policy of the United States to support free peoples who are resisting attempted subjugation by armed minorities or by outside pressure" (Graebner, ed., *Cold War Diplomacy*, pp. 186–89).

26. Blum, *Drawing the Line*, p. 108. But some feel that this concept of globalism made the distinction meaningless. See Hixson, *Kennan*, p. 222.

27. Gaddis, *Strategies of Containment*, p. 57.

28. Quoted in Nogee and Donaldson, *Soviet Foreign Policy*, pp. 84–85.

29. Understandably, it seemed to some like the shift to the left by Stalin in 1928 all over again. See Shulman, *Stalin's Foreign Policy Reappraised*, p. 16.

30. Ibid., p. 90, and Tanigawa Yoshihiko, "The Cominform and Southeast Asia," in Iriye, ed., *Origins of the Cold War*, p. 364.

31. For a description of the dispute, see Yoshihiko, "Cominform," in Iriye, ed., *Origins of the Cold War*, pp. 362–77. Also see Allan W. Cameron, "The Soviet Union and Vietnam: The Origins of Involvement," in Duncan, ed., *Soviet Policy*, pp. 114–15.

32. McLane, *Soviet Strategies*, p. 360, says the conference "quickened the tempo" of revolution in Southeast Asia.

33. See Yoshihiko, "Cominform," in Iriye, ed., *Origins of the Cold War*, pp. 369–71.

34. Ibid., pp. 371–72. For a discussion of the U.S. reaction to the Calcutta Conference, see Blum, *Drawing the Line*, p. 110.

35. Norman A. Graebner, "Containment in Asia: The Road to Vietnam," in Osborn et al., eds., *Democracy, Strategy, and Vietnam*, p. 17.

36. Spector, *Advice and Support*, p. 92; Blum, *Drawing the Line*, pp. 119–20, citing

memo Landon to Penfield, Feb. 17, 1948, Folder and box unknown, Lot 54 D190, RG 59, and "Southeast Asia Conference—Communist Activities in Southeast Asia," June 21–26, 1948, Southeast Asia Conference Folder, Lot 54D, 190, ibid.

37. *History of JCS*, p. 134.

38. SS to Caffery, July 3, 14, 1948, in *FRUS*, 1948, 6: 29 and 33. According to George McT. Kahin, the Truman administration was well aware that much U.S. aid to France was ultimately used in Indochina. But he appears to believe that it was a deliberate policy, which is not supported by evidence at my disposal. See his *Intervention*, p. 8.

39. SS to Caffery, Aug. 30, 1948, in *FRUS*, 1948, 6: 30. Saigon to SS, Aug. 20, 1948, ibid., p. 39.

40. Memo, Reed to Butterworth, Aug. 13, 1948, cited in Blum, *Drawing the Line*, p. 108.

41. *USVN*, book 8, pp. 144–48.

42. Ibid.

43. Bao Dai, *Dragon d'Annam*, pp. 211–14.

44. Lockhart, *Nation in Arms*, pp. 186–93; *CKC*, 1: 239.

45. "Nghi quyet hoi nghi Truong uong mo rang ngay 15–17 1–1948," (Resolution of the Enlarged Central Committee on January 15–17, 1948), in *Van Kien Dang*, 1945–54, vol. 2, no. 1, pp. 166–98. The resolution mentioned the possibility of civil war between progressive and reactionary forces in France and predicted that the United States would intervene in Indochina if that were to take place. See pp. 168–69.

46. Saigon to DOS, Nov. 5, 1948, in *FRUS*, 1948, 6: 54–55.

47. Bao Dai, *Dragon d'Annam*, pp. 214–20. For the accords, see Appendix IV.

48. Acheson to American Embassy (Paris), Feb. 25, 1949, in *FRUS*, 1949, vol. 7, pt. 1, pp. 8–9.

49. Caffery to SS, Mar. 16, 1949, in *FRUS*, 1948, 6: 12–14.

50. Reed to Butterworth, Apr. 14, 1949, in RG 59, 851 G.oo/4-1449, cited in Hess, *United States' Emergence*, p. 323. Also see Reed to Butterworth, memo, May 16, 1949, blind memo, attached to memo, Reed to Butterworth, May 16, 1949, Lot 54D, 190 RG 59, in Blum, *Drawing the Line*, p. 122.

51. Blum, *Drawing the Line*, p. 122.

52. SS to Gibson, May 20, 1949, in *FRUS*, 1949, vol. 7, pt. 1, pp. 29–30.

53. SS to Abbott, May 2, 1949, ibid., pp. 21–22.

54. SS to Abbott, May 4, 1949, ibid., pp. 23–25; Abbott to Acheson, May 6, 1949, ibid., p. 22.

55. SS to Abbott, May 20, 1949, ibid., p. 29.

56. Memorandum of Conversation by Charlton Ogburn, May 17, 1949, ibid., pp. 27–28.

57. Meeting of the NSC, Apr. 2, 1949, in NSC "Meetings of 1949" Folder, Truman Library.

58. PPS-51 is in *FRUS*, 1949, vol. 7, pt. 2, pp. 1128–33. For a discussion, see Blum, *Drawing the Line*, pp. 104–5.

59. Blum, *Drawing the Line*, pp. 120–23. Also see Rotter, *Path to Vietnam*, p. 76. The memos by Charles Reed are in RG 59, 851 G.oo/4-1449 and 851 G.oo/5-1749.

60. The memo is in *FRUS*, 1949, vol. 7, pt. 2, pp. 1135–37. For a brief discussion of the context, see Bullock, *Bevin*, p. 673.

61. Memorandum of Conversation by Douglas MacArthur II, May 24, 1949, in *FRUS*, 1949, vol. 7, pt. 1, pp. 30–32.

62. Bruce to SS, May 30, June 2, 1949, ibid., pp. 34–35, 36.

63. Draft message of June 6, 1949, ibid., pp. 39–45; Bruce's reply, June 13, 1949, ibid., pp. 45–46.

64. U.S. Ambassador in London to SS, June 15, 1949; Assistant SS to Bruce, June 16, 1949; U.S. Ambassador in New Delhi to SS, June 17, 1949, ibid., pp. 55–56, 75, and 57–58.

65. The statement was printed in the *DSB*, July 18, 1949, p. 75. Ogburn's memo to Reed is discussed in Blum, *Drawing the Line*, p. 118.

66. Jessup, *Birth of Nations*, chap. 5.

67. Memorandum of Conversation, Sept. 17, 1949, in *FRUS*, 1949, vol. 7, pt. 1, pp. 83–89.

68. Blum, *Drawing the Line*, pp. 109–10.

69. For Davies's memo, see *FRUS*, 1949, vol. 7, pt. 2, pp. 1147–51. Also see Blum, *Drawing the Line*, pp. 90–91, and Jessup, *Birth*, pp. 24–25.

70. Blum, *Drawing the Line*, p. 91.

71. Ibid., p. 92; Jessup, *Birth*, p. 29.

72. Memorandum by Secretary of Defense Louis Johnson to Executive Secretary of the NSC, June 10, 1949, in *USVN*, book 8, p. 226.

73. Jessup, *Birth*, p. 169; Blum, *Drawing the Line*, pp. 154–57.

74. Blum, *Drawing the Line*, p. 163.

75. NSC 48/1 was approved on December 23, 1949. A copy is in *USVN*, book 8, pp. 225–65. It was slightly amended as NSC 48/2 on December 29. For the changes, see ibid., pp. 265–72. The State Department draft is in *FRUS*, 1949, vol. 7, pt. 2, pp. 1209–14. Also see Blum, *Drawing the Line*, pp. 165–77, and Rotter, *Path to Vietnam*, pp. 120–24.

76. Blum, *Drawing the Line*, p. 147. Also see "Review of the World Situation," Oct. 19, 1949, President's Secretary's Files, "NSC Meeting No. 47" Folder, Truman Library.

77. See the Revers report in Bao Dai, *Dragon d'Annam*, p. 245.

78. The Fosdick memo to Jessup, Nov. 4, 1949, is in Porter, ed., *Vietnam: Definitive Documentation*, document 143, pp. 214–15.

79. The Yost memo is discussed in Jessup, *Birth*, pp. 166–69. Jessup commented that it represented departmental thinking at that time.

80. Blum, *Drawing the Line*, p. 148.

81. Ibid., p. 151.

82. The exchange of messages is in *FRUS*, 1949, vol. 7, pt. 2, pp. 105–10.

Chapter 4

1. The classic statement of Vietminh strategy during their war against the French is Truong Chinh's *Resistance Will Win*. For a discussion and references, see my *Communist Road*, pp. 128–31.

2. The assumption that Soviet support for the Vietminh movement was limited in the years immediately following the end of World War II has been generally accepted among Vietnam observers, although firm evidence is lacking. For one oft-quoted reference, see Isaacs, *No Peace for Asia*, p. 173. The most useful source on Soviet policy toward Indochina after World War II remains McLane's *Soviet Strategies*. For an account that focuses primarily on more recent events, see Pike, *Vietnam and the Soviet Union*. Both Moscow and Hanoi remain reticent about the nature of Soviet support for the Vietminh after

World War II, although sources on both sides concede privately that it was minimal. I am grateful to Kurihara Hirohide for his insights on this issue.

3. It has sometimes been asserted that Vietminh military strategy was an imitation of the Maoist concept of people's war. Actually, it was primarily the product of local inspiration, although there are similarities, and Vietminh leaders were not averse to making use of Maoist ideas when they appeared appropriate to conditions in Vietnam (interview with Professor Le Mau Han, University of Hanoi, Dec. 13, 1990). For a discussion, see my *Communist Road*, esp. chaps. 4–6. For a brief account of early party-to-party relations, see my *China and Vietnam*. The most detailed account is Chen's *Vietnam and China*. An account by a Chinese researcher which adds little to existing knowledge on the subject is Ying Yu, *Zhongguo Renmin*.

4. Chen, *Vietnam and China*, p. 228. There are numerous intelligence reports relating to increasing Sino-Vietnamese contacts in the State Department files. See, for example, Saigon's cable 1577, Mar. 9, 1951, in RG 59, 751 G.00/3-951.

5. *FRUS*, 1949, vol. 7, pt. 1, pp. 140–41. Reports have just surfaced of a secret trip by Ho Chi Minh to China during this period. See Le Phat, "Ghi nho ve mot chuyen di voi bac" (Recollections of a journey with uncle) in the journal *Lao Dong* (Labor), Spring 1990.

6. For a brief reference and discussion, see Gurtov, *First Vietnam Crisis*, pp. 7–8. Also see Chen, *Vietnam and China*, pp. 14–20.

7. Ying Yu, *Zhongguo Renmin*, p. 56, says only that he visited China early in 1950 and asked for assistance. A cable from the U.S. mission in Hong Kong noted the curious fact that Chinese recognition was announced while both Mao Zedong and Zhou Enlai were in Moscow for negotiations over a Sino-Soviet aid pact. See U.S. Consul (Hong Kong) to DOS, Feb. 8, 1950, in RG 59, 751 G.00/2-850.

8. See Taylor, *China and Southeast Asia*, p. 5.

9. Chen, *Vietnam and China*, pp. 230–37; Georges Boudarel, "L'Ideocratie importée au Vietnam avec le maoisme," in Boudarel et al., *La Bureaucratie*.

10. Bao Dai, *Dragon d'Annam*, p. 269; Abbott to SS, Nov. 22, 1949, in *FRUS*, 1949, vol. 7, pt. 1, pp. 98–99.

11. Schuman told Acheson that India's attitude may have been affected by problems with the French over the latter's control over Pondichery, but Nehru remarked to Acheson that Bao Dai lacked character, ability, and reputation and was receiving no help from the French. When Acheson asked him about alternatives, Nehru felt that Ho was the only choice, although he conceded that Ho was a genuine communist. Nehru argued that the experience of Eastern Europe was unlikely to be repeated in Southeast Asia because the communist parties there had begun as nationalist organizations, not puppets of Moscow. Memo of Conversation, Dean Acheson with Jawaharlal Nehru, Oct. 12, 1949, in Memorandum of Conversation File (Oct.–Nov. 1949), Acheson Papers. For comments on the reluctance of other Asian nations to recognize the new Associated State of Vietnam, see Memorandum of Conversation with the Foreign Minister of Burma, Aug. 25, 1949, in *FRUS*, 1949, vol. 7, pt. 2, 691–93, and Memorandum of Conversation with Carlos Romulo, Mar. 10, 1950, in Acheson Papers.

12. Memo from Lacy to Assistant SS (Rusk), Sept. 5, 1950, in *FRUS*, 1950, vol. 6, pp. 140–41. From Bangkok, Ambassador Stanton attempted to explain the Thai attitude, pointing out that they were more concerned about colonialism than about the danger of

communism. Threats from Washington to withhold support, he warned, would have little influence on their thinking (ibid., 6: 697).

13. Memorandum of Dean Acheson to President Truman, Feb. 2, 1950, ibid., pp. 716–17.

14. The Thai argued that Bao Dai was simply a French creation and that U.S. military aid would not provide the "missing component." See *USVN*, book 8, pp. 280–81, and Bangkok to DOS, Mar. 3, 1950, in RG 59, 751 G.00/3-350. The U.S. statement of recognition is in the *DSB*, Feb. 20, 1950, pp. 291–92.

15. Memorandum of Conversation by SS, Feb. 16, 1950, in *FRUS*, 1950, 6: 730–33.

16. For a discussion, see Bullock, *Bevin*, pp. 744–45.

17. Quoted in Blum, *Drawing the Line*, p. 183; *DSB*, Jan. 23, 1950, pp. 111–18.

18. Jessup, *Birth*, p. 189; Memorandum of Conversation by Philip Jessup, Feb. 6, 1950, in *FRUS*, 1950, 6: 11–18; Rotter, *Path to Vietnam*, pp. 186–90.

19. Problem Paper by Working Group in DOS, Feb. 1, 1950, in *FRUS*, 1950, 6: 711–15. The recommendations by the JCS are in *History of JCS*, citing (TS) JCS 1721/43, Jan. 16, 1950, CCS 452 China (4-3-45), sec. 7, pt. 7. For a rebuttal by Charlton Ogburn, see his memo to Butterworth, Mar. 21, 1950, in RG 59, 751 G.00/3-2150. The Vietminh, he said, had withstood 150,000 French troops for four years and would not wilt before the psychological impact of U.S. assistance.

20. Country Report by Bureau of Far Eastern Affairs for Director of Mutual Defense Assistance Program (Bruce), n.d., in *FRUS*, 1950, 6: 735–38. The report was issued on February 16.

21. Dean Acheson to Bruce, Mar. 29, 1950, ibid., pp. 771–72.

22. For a copy of NSC 64, see ibid., pp. 744–47.

23. The JCS views on NSC 64 are contained in their memorandum to the Secretary of Defense, Apr. 10, 1950, in *USVN*, book 8, pp. 308–13.

24. Chargé in Saigon (Gullion) to SS, Mar. 18, 1950, in *FRUS*, 1950, 6: 762–63.

25. *History of JCS*, p. 160, citing (TS) JCS 1992/11, Mar. 29, 1950.

26. Chargé in France (Bonbright) to SS, May 11, 1950, in *FRUS*, 1950, 6: 813–15. The U.S. mission in Saigon reported that the French conspired to overthrow Nguyen Phan Long out of distrust of his pro-U.S. attitudes. See Saigon to DOS, Apr. 15, 1950, in RG 59, 751 G.00/4-1550. For references to the Nguyen Phan Long regime, see Bao Dai, *Dragon d'Annam*, p. 278; Shaplen, *Lost Revolution*, p. 67; and Jessup, *Birth*, p. 173. The French told Jessup that Nguyen Phan Long was intelligent but knew nothing of politics or administration.

27. The final communique is in *FRUS*, 1950, 6: 1085–86.

28. For the report of the Griffin mission, see ibid., pp. 762–63. Also see SEA File: General (1950–52), in Melby Papers. For a discussion, see Rotter, *Path to Vietnam*, pp. 190–96.

29. Shaplen, *Lost Revolution*, p. 67; Gibbons, *U.S. Government and the Vietnam War*, 1: 70.

30. For comments on the situation by the U.S. mission in Saigon, see *FRUS*, 1950, 6: 794–95.

31. Rusk's testimony before Congress is in Porter, ed., *Vietnam: Definitive Documentation*, document 178.

32. Gaddis, *Strategies of Containment*, chap. 4. For a comment evaluating the pos-

sibility that public criticism provoked Acheson into a more aggressive attitude, see Isaacson and Thomas, *Wise Men*, p. 494.

33. Gibbons, *U.S. Government and the Vietnam War*, 1: 64–67. Charlton Ogburn complained that Edmund Gullion had been in Indochina too short a time to make categorical assertions about the importance of U.S. aid in turning the tide against the Vietminh.

34. Memoranda of Conversation (May–June 1950), Acheson Papers. For a reference to panic in Western Europe, see Meeting of June 27, 1950, in White House Office with Senators and Congressmen, in Subject File (Japan-Korea, July 19, 1950), Box 71, Elsey Papers. Also see Memorandum of Conversation, Dean Acheson with Ambassador Morgenstierne of Norway, June 30, 1950, in Memoranda of Conversation (1950), Acheson Papers.

35. *History of JCS*, pp. 170–71, citing MDAP Status Report for October 1950, Oct. 31, 1950; *USVN*, book 8, p. 338; Memorandum from SS to the President, July 3, 1950, in *FRUS*, 1950, 6: 835–36.

36. Melby drafted the China White Paper that attempted to justify U.S. policy in China during the civil war.

37. For the Melby report and other papers connected with the mission, see Box 9, Southeast Asia File, Melby Papers. Also see *FRUS*, 1950, 6: 164–73. For Melby's private pessimism about the possibility of Franco-Vietnamese cooperation, see his undated telegram to Rusk and Lacy, in Melby Chron. File 1950 (Nov.–Dec.), Melby Papers.

38. The mission had just been raised from legation to embassy status at U.S. insistence.

39. Telegram, Heath to DOS, Aug. 9, 1950, in *FRUS*, 1950, 6: 849–51; Telegram, Heath to DOS, Aug. 23, 1950, ibid., pp. 864–67. The embassy in Paris chipped in, saying that an effort to persuade the French to grant national independence to the Associated States would be a waste of time (Bruce to DOS, Aug. 17, 1950, ibid., pp. 859–60).

40. Memo, "United States Policy Toward Indochina in the Light of Recent Developments," Aug. 16, 1950, ibid., pp. 857–58. Dean Acheson doubted the likelihood of a Chinese invasion because of historical antipathy between the Chinese and Vietnamese peoples. He assumed that the existing policy of limited aid would continue. But Acheson was concerned that the French might seek a separate arrangement with Beijing and told Bruce to warn them that China would not honor any agreement and would also try to undermine unity among the Western allies (For Bruce from Secretary, n.d., in RG 59, 751 G.00/7-1550).

41. Kennan, *Memoirs*, 2: 59, cited in Jessup, *Birth*, p. 194. Kennan assumed that the entire country of Vietnam would eventually come under some form of Vietminh authority. Ogburn's memo is in *FRUS*, 1950, 6: 862–64. He complained that Europeanists like Woodruff Wallner derided Asianists for their preoccupation with "little brown feet."

42. Cable, Acheson to Heath, Sept. 1, 1950, in *FRUS*, 1950, 6: 868–70.

43. *History of JCS*, p. 190, citing (TS) JCS 1924/26, Aug. 14, 1950, CCS 092 USSR (3-27-45), sec. 48, and (TS) NSC 73/4, Aug. 25, 1950, same file, sec. 49.

44. *History of JCS*, p. 191, citing Memo, Bradley to Louis Johnson, Indochina, Sept. 7, 1950, in CCS 092 Asia (6-25-48), excerpted in *USVN*, book 8, pp. 358–59. In a memo to the secretary, Dean Rusk said that he assumed the United States would intervene in Indochina only if China invaded, if U.S. commitments elsewhere permitted it, and if

such intervention was under the auspices of the United Nations (Memo, Rusk to Secretary, Sept. 12, 1950, in RG 59, 751 G.00/9-1250).

45. Webb to Heath, Sept. 16, 1950, in *FRUS*, 1950, 6: 880–81, presents a summary of the conversation.

46. *History of JCS*, p. 193, citing (TS) Memo by CSA, "Possible Future Action in Indochina," Oct. 18, 1950, in (TS) CCS 092 Asia (6-25-48), sec. 7. Any such commitment, he said, was to be on condition that it did not endanger the U.S. strategic position in the event of a global war, offered a "reasonable chance of success," and was undertaken in concert with other members of the United Nations ("Draft Statement on U.S. Policy on Indochina for USC Consideration," Oct. 11, 1950, in *FRUS*, 1950, 6: 888–90. Also see *USVN*, book 8, pp. 349–54).

47. *USVN*, book 8, p. 391. The U.S. Embassy in Saigon reported French intelligence sources on the level of Chinese assistance to and cooperation with the Vietminh. See Heath to DOS, Sept. 11, 1950, in RG 59, 751 G.00/9-1150. General Erskine, a member of the Melby mission, reported in midsummer that the Vietminh had about 45 battalions, compared to 100 in the French Expeditionary Force. He said that French defenses in the border area were poor, and in the event of a Vietminh attack they would be "practically annihilated." See Box 10, Melby Papers.

48. Bao Dai, *Dragon d'Annam*, p. 262. Carpentier complained that de Lattre was "impulsive" and that they could not work together. See Heath to DOS, Dec. 14, 1950, in RG 59, 751 G.00/12-1450.

49. *History of JCS*, pp. 179–87. Some French personnel, however, were unhappy about de Lattre's domineering presence and requested transfers. See Saigon 1056, Joint Weeka 50, Dec. 12, 1950, in RG 59, 751 G.00/12-1250.

50. Heath to SS, Oct. 15, 1950, in *FRUS*, 1950, 6: 894–96; Heath to DOS, Oct. 14, 1950, in RG 59, 751 G.00/10-1450. Later Heath made an assessment of the battlefield situation in the aftermath of the Vietminh border offensive. See Heath to SS, Nov. 4, 1950, in *USVN*, book 8, pp. 405–8.

51. SS to Heath, Oct. 30, 1950, in *FRUS*, 1950, 6: 913. The telegram to Bao Dai is in ibid., pp. 894–96. In a comment to Phillipe Devillers, Bao Dai responded that critics did not understand the need to adopt an imperial style in dealing with the people. See Devillers, *Histoire du Vietnam*, p. 458.

52. The press conference is reported in *FRUS*, 1950, 6: 938. Acheson's comment on "primary responsibility" is in Acheson to Bruce, Nov. 1, 1950, ibid., pp. 920–21. Letourneau's statement is reported in Bruce to SS, Nov. 24, 1950, ibid., pp. 936–37.

53. The Joint Strategic Survey Committee report is subenclosure B, in *FRUS*, 1950, 6: 886–88.

54. Memorandum for the Secretary of Defense, "Possible Future Action in Indochina," Nov. 28, 1950, in *USVN*, book 8, pp. 400–404. Also, see *FRUS*, 1950, 6: 945–48. The draft report is dated October 11, 1950, and is in RG 59, 751 G.00/10-1150.

55. William Lacy of PSA replied to Ohly. See RG 59, 751 G.00/1-1751. Spector, *Advice and Support*, pp. 129–31, citing Memo, Ohly for SS, Nov. 20, 1950, and Memo, Merchant for Rusk, Jan. 17, 1951. For Ohly's memo, see *FRUS*, 1950, 6: 925–30. Dean Acheson later commented that "having put our hand at the plow, we could not look back." See Gelb and Betts, *Irony of Vietnam*, p. 45, citing Acheson, *Present at the Creation*, p. 674.

56. The NIE is in *FRUS*, 1950, 6: 958–63. General de Lattre was skeptical that the

Chinese would intervene, at least for the present. See U.S. Consul (Hong Kong) to DOS, Jan. 10, 1951, in RG 59, 751 G.00/1-1051. The U.S. military attaché in Saigon agreed.

57. Heath's view of Bao Dai is recorded in Heath to SS, Jan. 20, 1951, in *FRUS*, 1951, vol. 6, pt. 1, pp. 350–52. Ngo Dinh Diem had already begun to consult with Department of State officials on the situation, usually at his own request. See Memorandum of Conversation, Ngo Dinh Diem with Gibson and Hoey of PSA, Jan. 15, 1951, in RG 59, 751 G.00/1-1551.

58. For a reference, see my *Communist Road*, p. 355, no. 33. Also see the captured document enclosed in Heath to DOS, Aug. 21, 1950, in RG 59, 751 G.00/7-2150.

59. The most dramatic account of the battle is Fall, *Street Without Joy*. U.S. sources claimed that the French could not have succeeded without U.S. aid, but de Lattre won plaudits for his decisiveness. See Spector, *Advice and Support*, p. 137, and *History of JCS*, p. 199.

60. See the Vietminh training document sent by the U.S. Consulate in Hanoi to DOS, July 12, 1950, in RG 59, 751 G.-001/7-1250. Also see Brown and Zasloff, *Apprentice Revolutionaries*, pp. 46–48.

61. United States Department of State, *Working Paper on North Viet-Nam's Role in the War in South Viet-Nam* (Washington, D.C., 1968), Appendix 1, vol. 6, pt. 1, p. 2-2.

62. For a discussion, see my *Vietnam Since the Fall of Saigon*, p. 132, and Duiker, *Communist Road*, p. 140.

63. Heath to SS, Feb. 24, 1950, in *FRUS*, 1951, vol. 6, pt. 1, p. 384. According to U.S. sources, even Bao Dai never liked Huu because he was too pro-French. See Heath to DOS, Feb. 7, 1951, in RG 59, 751 G.00/2-751. Also see Bao Dai, *Dragon d'Annam*, pp. 271–73.

64. Memorandum by the JCS to Secretary of Defense George C. Marshall, Jan. 10, 1951, in *FRUS*, 1951, vol. 6, pt. 1, pp. 347–48; SS to SD, Jan. 26, 1951, ibid., p. 365. The Truman-Pleven talks are summarized in Acheson to Heath, Jan. 30, 1951, ibid., pp. 368–69.

65. NIE, "Resistance of Thailand and Burma to Communist Pressure in the Event of a Communist Victory in Indochina in 1951," Mar. 20, 1951, ibid., pp. 27–31. Also see Rusk's memo to Matthews, Jan. 31, 1951, ibid., pp. 16–26.

66. Heath to SS, Mar. 23, 1951, ibid., pp. 409–10.

67. The study is in *USVN*, book 8, pp. 438–45.

68. The letter is in *FRUS*, 1951, vol. 6, pt. 1, p. 137. For Acheson's letter to Marshall, see *FRUS*, 1950, 6: 1363. The JCS reply is in *FRUS*, 1951, vol. 6, pt. 1, pp. 132–33.

69. U.S. Political Adviser to Supreme Commander, Allied Forces in the Pacific, to SS, Feb. 2, 1951, in *FRUS*, 1951, vol. 6, pt. 1, p. 144.

70. Struble's report said that the British were pessimistic about Burma, which they described as a "weak spot," and the French were critical of the Thai, whose foreign policy "blows and bends with the wind." One reason for concern over Thailand was the report that the Thai Communist Party had just established a new united front to overthrow the regime of Pibul Songgkram. For documents on the Singapore conference, see *FRUS*, 1951, vol. 6, pt. 1, pp. 64–71.

71. Heath to SS, June 29, 1951, ibid., pp. 432–39. Ambassador Bruce in Paris of course agreed with Heath. The French had primary responsibility, he pointed out, and the Vietnamese should "never be permitted to forget the essential irreplaceable contribution

the French are making toward their independence and the fate they would meet if the French were to withdraw" (Bruce to SS, July 9, 1951, ibid., pp. 442–43).

72. Chief of Special Economic and Technical Mission at Saigon (Blum) to ECA, July 12, 1951, ibid., pp. 450–52.

73. Memo, Livingston Merchant to Assistant SS, July 27, 1951, ibid., pp. 462–64.

74. Spector, *Advice and Support*, p. 153, citing Brigadier General Francis Brink, "A Study of the Vietnamese Army," Mar. 21, 1951, updated May 7, 1951.

75. Records of a Meeting at the Pentagon Building, Sept. 20, 1951, in *FRUS*, 1951, vol. 6, pt. 1, pp. 517–21. Also see *History of JCS*, pp. 217–20. De Lattre's claim that the Vietminh could be eliminated within two years without Chinese intervention was not universally shared in Indochina. In talks with Gullion, Admiral de Bourgoing, French naval commissioner of Indochina, said that the war could not be won in the absence of a general settlement elsewhere in Asia because there was no reason why Chinese aid to the Vietminh would not increase. This, Gullion said, was a typical view by French officers and foreign military attachés in Indochina. The British felt that France would need fifteen to twenty years. See Gullion to SS, Oct. 4, 1951, in *FRUS*, 1951, vol. 6, pt. 1, pp. 530–31.

76. *History of JCS*, p. 219, citing (TS) Memo, JCS to SD, "Combat Operations in Indochina," Nov. 19, 1951, CCS Asia (6-25-48), sec. 19.

77. Minutes of a Meeting at the Department of State with de Lattre de Tassigny, Sept. 17, 1951, in *FRUS*, 1951, vol. 6, pt. 1, pp. 506–16.

78. To ECA from Goodyear, Nov. 30, 1951, ibid., pp. 548–50.

79. Heath to SS, Dec. 9, 1951, ibid., pp. 558–59.

80. The British aide-mémoire is discussed in Assistant SS to SS (Rome), Nov. 21, 1951, ibid., pp. 115–16. The JCS response to Secretary of Defense Lovett is contained in *History of JCS*, p. 221, citing (TS) Memo, JCS to SD, "Combat Operations in Indochina," Nov. 19, 1951, CCS Asia (6-25-48), sec. 19.

81. Ambassador of United Kingdom to SS, Dec. 17, 1951, in *FRUS*, 1951, vol. 6, pt. 1, pp. 123–24. The French agreed in an aide-mémoire presented to the U.S. Embassy on December 28. See Bruce to DOS, in RG 59, 751 G.00/12-2951.

82. "Substance of Discussions of State-JCS Meeting at the Pentagon Building," Dec. 21, 1951, in *FRUS*, 1951, vol. 6, pt. 1, pp. 569–70.

83. Ambassador in France to SS, Dec. 26, 1951, ibid., pp. 573–78. The Pleven note in English translation is ibid., pp. 571–72.

84. *History of JCS*, p. 240, citing U.S. intelligence report by Joint Intelligence Committee (S) JIC 529/10, Jan. 9, 1952, CCS 092 Asia (6-25-48) BP p. 3, JCS Records; Lovett to SS, Jan. 2, 1952, in RG 59, 751 G.5/3-252.

85. The conference is reported in *History of JCS*, pp. 240–41, and in *USVN*, book 8, pp. 465–67.

86. *USVN*, book 8, p. 467.

87. Spector, *Advice and Support*, p. 152, citing Memo, Admiral Davis, Feb. 5, 1952, subject: Report of the Five Power Ad Hoc Committee on Southeast Asia, CCS 092 Asia (6-25-48), sec. 24, JCS Records. The use of the atom bomb was not mentioned. The JCS statement is in *DSB*, Feb. 11, 1952, cited in *History of JCS*, p. 243.

88. For the draft position paper prepared in the State Department, see *FRUS*, 1951, vol. 6, pt. 2, pp. 261–62.

89. For the JCS response, see Memorandum by the JCS to SD (Lovett), Jan. 28, 1952, ibid., pp. 263–64.

90. NSC-124 is in *FRUS*, 1952–54, vol. 12, pt. 1, pp. 119–23. Excerpts are in *USVN*, book 8, pp. 468–76. Much of the NSC study was based on a memo by William S. B. Lacy of the Office of Philippine and Southeast Asian Affairs in answer to a French request for additional assistance. But the State Department memorandum had assumed no direct Chinese intervention so had not mentioned the issue. For a reference, see Allison, *Ambassador*, p. 188.

91. Memorandum for the Secretary of Defense, "United States Objectives and Courses of Action with respect to Communist Aggression in Southeast Asia," Mar. 4, 1952, in *USVN*, book 8, pp. 486–92.

92. Ibid., p. 489.

93. NIE, Mar. 3, 1952, in *FRUS*, 1951, vol. 13, pt. 1, pp. 53–61. But Heath and Brink thought it was too pessimistic. See Heath to SS , Apr. 5, 1952, in *FRUS*, 1951, vol. 6, pt. 1, p. 99.

94. Editorial Note in *FRUS*, 1952, vol. 13, pt. 1, pp. 61–62.

95. Draft—Indochina Section of NSC Paper, ibid., pp. 82–89. It was cleared at a meeting at the State Department on April 1.

96. Memorandum by the JCS to SD (Lovett), ibid., pp. 113–17.

97. Memo by Assistant SS for Far Eastern Affairs (Allison) to SS, May 7, 1952, ibid., pp. 124–29; Allison, *Ambassador*, pp. 190–91.

98. The JCS in particular stressed the need to pressure the French at every opportunity. See the carton "NSC Meeting No. 120," Truman Library. NSC 124/2 is in *FRUS*, 1952–54, vol. 12, pt. 1, pp. 123–24, and in *USVN*, book 8, pp. 520–34. Also see President's Security Files: NSC Minutes 1952–53, meetings of May 3 and June 25, 1952, Truman Papers.

99. United States Minutes of Tripartite Foreign Ministers Meeting with France and the United Kingdom at the Quai d'Orsay, May 28, 1952, in *FRUS*, 1952, vol. 13, pt. 1, pp. 157–66. In June Acheson discussed the situation with British ambassador Sir Oliver Franks and remarked that it would be futile to put ground troops in Indochina because the United States didn't have them, and "we can't have another Korea." The only hope was to change China's mind.

100. For a brief reference to the formation of a communist organization in Cambodia, see my *Communist Road*, pp. 142–43.

101. *History of JCS*, p. 233. On rumors of negotiations, see *FRUS*, 1952–54, vol. 13, pt. 1, pp. 66–67.

102. Heath to SS, May 12, 1952, in *FRUS*, 1952–54, vol. 13, pt. 1, pp. 134–35.

103. For minutes of the meetings with Letourneau, see SS to Legation in Saigon, June 20, 1952, ibid., pp. 204–8. The communique is in *DSB*, June 30, 1952, p. 1010. The United States told Letourneau the United States would probably provide France with an additional $150 million in aid. In his memoirs, Anthony Eden said Acheson complained to him that the French refused to provide information on the situation in Indochina and was surprised to hear that Washington had agreed to provide more assistance to Paris. John Allison cited an unnamed colleague that Letourneau used "waffling" English to be imprecise on political issues but "precise French" when referring to U.S. aid (*Ambassador*, p. 193).

104. *History of JCS*, pp. 255–59; Radford, *Pearl Harbor to Vietnam*, pp. 354–55. On the London meeting, see *FRUS*, 1952–54, vol. 13, pt. 1, pp. 212–13.

105. For an evaluation of Vietminh morale, see U.S. Consul at Hanoi (Sturm) to SS, Sept. 19, 1952, in *FRUS*, 1952–54, vol. 13, pt. 1, p. 252. The NIE is in ibid., pp. 243–49. For Bao Dai's comments on Nguyen Van Tam, see Bao Dai, *Dragon d'Annam*, p. 298. For Heath's views, see *FRUS*, 1952–54, vol. 13, pt. 1, pp. 188, 224–25.

106. Ministerial Council of the North Atlantic Council Meeting, in *FRUS*, 1952–54, vol. 13, pt. 1, pp. 318–21; SS to French Embassy, Jan. 16, 1953, ibid., pp. 351–52; Acheson, *Present at the Creation*, pp. 676–77.

107. Shaplen, *Lost Revolution*, pp. 78–79.

108. Memo to Rusk, Jan. 15, 1951, in *FRUS*, 1951, vol. 6, pt. 1, pp. 6–9.

109. President's Security File, Minutes of the NSC (1952–53), meeting of Apr. 9, 1952, Truman Papers.

Chapter 5

1. Anderson, *Trapped by Success*, pp. 20–21; Gaddis, *Strategies of Containment*, pp. 147–48. Dulles admitted that the doctrine of massive retaliation was an imperfect means of dealing with political threats.

2. For the full text, see *Public Papers of the Presidents, 1953*, pp. 12–34.

3. Heath to SS, Feb. 4, 1953, in *FRUS*, 1952–54, vol. 13, pt. 1, pp. 378–81. For Truman's comment to Eisenhower, see Truman, *Memoirs*, 2: 519.

4. For a report on Secretary Dulles's meeting with the French, see *FRUS*, 1952–54, vol. 13, pt. 1, pp. 377–78. Also see the position paper prepared by Philip W. Bonsal, ibid., pp. 363–66.

5. Memo by OIC/VLC Affairs (Hoey) to Assistant SS Allison, Mar. 16, 1953, ibid., pp. 413–14.

6. *USVN*, book 9, pp. 11–14.

7. For documentary sources on the talks, see *FRUS*, 1952–54, vol. 13, pt. 1, pp. 429–35, 450–53. For State Department reaction to the plan, see ibid., pp. 458–64. The communique is in ibid., pp. 436–37. Dulles's comment at the NSC meeting is reported in Anderson, *Trapped by Success*, p. 17.

8. Memo by the JCS to SD (Wilson), Apr. 21, 1953, in *FRUS*, 1952–54, vol. 13, pt. 1, pp. 493–95. There is a discussion in Spector, *Advice and Support*, pp. 70–71.

9. Substance of Discussions of State-JCS Meeting at the Pentagon Building, Apr. 23, 1953, in *FRUS*, 1952–54, vol. 13, pt. 1, pp. 496–503. For the JCS memo to Secretary Wilson on the French plan, see ibid., pp. 493–95, or *USVN*, book 9, pp. 24–26.

10. U.S. Minutes of U.S.-French Conversation, 1st Session at Quai d'Orsay, Apr. 22, 1953, in *FRUS*, 1952–54, vol. 13, pt. 1, pp. 483–85. For an indication of French reluctance about the relevance of Korea, see Bao Dai, *Dragon d'Annam*, p. 307.

11. Dillon to SS, May 23, 1953, in *FRUS*, 1952–54, vol. 13, pt. 1, pp. 579–80.

12. Memorandum of Discussion at 141st Meeting of the NSC, Apr. 28, 1953, ibid., pp. 516–19.

13. There is no verbatim record of Sihanouk's talks with the president and vice-president, but for a general appraisal of his views, see Memo by Donald Heath to Assistant SS, Apr. 20, 1953, ibid., pp. 475–77.

14. SS to Embassy in France, May 6, 1953, ibid., pp. 550–51. On Guillaume and Valluy, see ibid., pp. 561–62.

15. *History of JCS*, p. 291, citing (TS) Memo, Secy JCS to JSPC, "Possible Courses of Action in Indochina," Jan. 23, 1953, CCS 092 Asia (6-25-48), sec. 37.

16. *History of JCS*, p. 259; Radford, *Pearl Harbor to Vietnam*, p. 355.

17. *FRUS*, 1952–54, vol. 2, pt. 1, pp. 305–8.

18. Memorandum of Discussion at the 143d Meeting of the NSC, May 6, 1953, in *FRUS*, 1952–54, vol. 13, pt. 1, pp. 546–49.

19. *History of JCS*, pp. 293–95, citing (TS) JCS 1992/227, June 22, 1953. An extract is in *FRUS*, 1952–54, vol. 13, pt. 1, pp. 615–16.

20. For comments on Navarre, see Spector, *Advice and Support*, p. 173.

21. Report of U.S. Joint Mission to Indochina, Lieutenant General John O'Daniel Through CINCPAC to JCS, July 14, 1953, in *USVN*, book 9, pp. 69–104. See the comments in Spector, *Advice and Support*, p. 174. Robert McClintock, then counselor of embassy in Saigon, did not agree and says that Navarre was "intellectually indisposed" to listen to O'Daniel and the two never saw eye to eye. McClintock once observed that to expect Navarre and O'Daniel to work in unison was "about as optimistic as to harness a water buffalo and a gazelle to pull through a rice paddy." See McClintock, *Meaning of Limited War*, p. 170.

22. Bao Dai, *Dragon d'Annam*, p. 312. For comments on Joseph Laniel, see Cable, *Geneva Conference*, p. 14.

23. See the CIA Estimate in *USVN*, book 9, pp. 46–57.

24. Chargé in France (Achilles) to DOS, July 8, 1953, in *FRUS*, 1952–54, vol. 13, pt. 1, pp. 643–44.

25. Substance of Discussions of State-JCS Meeting at the Pentagon Building, July 10, 1953, ibid., pp. 648–52.

26. United States Minutes of the First United States–French Meeting at Residence of SS, July 12, 1953, ibid., pp. 656–67.

27. See the views of Assistant Secretary Walter Robertson, ibid., pp. 556–59.

28. Record of Actions by the NSC at Its 158th Meeting, Aug. 6, 1953, ibid., pp. 718–19; Substance of Discussions of State-JCS Staff Meeting at the Pentagon Building, Sept. 4, 1953, ibid., pp. 751–57. For the JCS conditions see ibid., pp. 744–46. There was some discussion of making U.S. assistance conditional on French approval of the European Defense Community. That suggestion was rejected, but the administration did indicate it would seek assurances from Laniel that Paris would push for it. See Memo, Douglas MacArthur II to Sec., Sept. 8, 1953, in RG 59, 751 G.00/9-853.

29. Ambassador in France (Dillon) to SS, July 22, 1953, in *FRUS*, 1952–54, vol. 13, pt. 1, p. 693. An article in *Life* magazine, dated August 3, criticized French policies in Indochina and claimed the war was "all but lost." Both the French government and Ambassador Heath responded testily, and the magazine's editors agreed to publish a rejoinder by Heath entitled "France Is Fighting the Good Fight" in September. For the dispute, see Saigon cables 391, 397, and 461, in RG 59, 751 G.00/9-353, 9-454, and 9-1653.

30. *History of JCS*, pp. 285–86. In an article in *Le Monde*, journalist Jacques Servan-Schreiber charged the French government with playing a "double jeu."

31. Heath to DOS, Aug. 1, 1953, in *FRUS*, 1952–54, vol. 13, pt. 1, pp. 710–11. Bao Dai's reaction is in *Dragon d'Annam*, p. 314.

32. Bao Dai, *Dragon d'Annam*, p. 315; Bui Diem, *Jaws of History*, pp. 78–80. For Heath's background comments, see *FRUS*, 1952–54, vol. 13, pt. 1, p. 836.

33. Ambassador in Saigon to DOS, Oct. 26, 1953, in *FRUS*, 1952–54, vol. 13, pt. 1, pp. 848–50.

34. *New York Times*, Oct. 28, 1953. A few weeks later, Laniel said that France would welcome a diplomatic settlement if an "honorable solution" could be found (ibid., Nov. 13, 1953).

35. Spector, *Advice and Support*, p. 179.

36. The secretary's speech of September 2 is in the *DSB*, Sept. 14, 1953, pp. 342–43.

37. SS to DOS, Oct. 17, 1953, in *FRUS*, 1952–54, vol. 13, pt. 1, pp. 830–32. Bonnet's report is in Memorandum of Conversation by Counselor (MacArthur), Oct. 9, 1953, ibid., pp. 823–24.

38. See *History of JCS*, pp. 180–81, and Spector, *Advice and Support*, pp. 329–31.

39. General Navarre thought he had to protect Laos for political reasons and insists that he was never told of a government directive to give up territory to protect French forces in Indochina. See the *New York Times*, Jan. 26, 1969. For Navarre's own account of why he decided to reoccupy Dien Bien Phu, see his *Agonie de l'Indochine*. For his comments at the time to Donald Heath, see *FRUS*, 1952–54, vol. 13, pt. 1, p. 881.

40. Vo Nguyen Giap, *People's War*, pp. 140–48; Hoang Van Thai, article in *Vietnam Courier*, Mar. 1984.

41. Joyaux, *La Chine*, pp. 68–71; Taylor, *China and Southeast Asia*, pp. 10–11. The French press was reporting that both Moscow and Beijing favored a settlement but that the Vietminh remained opposed. See Dillon to DOS, Sept. 15, 1953, in RG 59, 751 G.00/9-1553.

42. Cable, *Geneva Conference*, p. 35; Taylor, *China and Southeast Asia*, p. 11.

43. U.S. Ambassador in Moscow (Bohlen) to DOS, Sept. 3, 1953. Actually, Ho's speech was set in the context of the recent cease-fire in Korea and did not reject negotiations but said that they should take place only under favorable conditions. See Ho Chi Minh, *Toan Tap*, 6: 459. Nikita Khrushchev says that Zhou Enlai told him Ho Chi Minh was desperate for a settlement because of high casualties suffered by his forces. This seems doubtful. If so, Ho may have said it to obtain increased assistance from China. See Nikita Khrushchev, *Khrushchev Remembers*, p. 533. For a French explanation of Ho's willingness to negotiate, see *FRUS*, 1952–54, vol. 13, pt. 1, pp. 888–90. Also see Joyaux, *La Chine*, p. 68.

44. U.S. Embassy (Stockholm) to DOS, Nov. 29, 1953, in RG 59, 751 G.00/11-2953. In an accompanying editorial, the journal expressed skepticism about Ho's sincerity and said that his comments appeared "inspired by Moscow," but Quai d'Orsay sources admitted they were "brilliantly timed" to coincide with the demand for negotiations in Paris. A Vietnamese-language version of the interview is in Ho Chi Minh, *Toan Tap*, 6: 494–96. Also see Joyaux, *La Chine*, p. 91.

45. Chargé in Paris (Achilles) to DOS, Nov. 30, 1953, in *FRUS*, 1952–54, vol. 13, pt. 1, pp. 887–88.

46. SS to Assistant SS, Dec. 7, 1953, ibid., pp. 901–2; Memorandum by the Counselor (MacArthur), Dec. 4, 1953, ibid., pp. 897–98. For a reference to the testy relations between the heads of state, see Cable, *Geneva Conference*, pp. 36–37.

47. Special Estimate, "Probable Consequences of Certain Possible Developments in

Indochina before Mid-1954 in Non-Communist Asia," Nov. 16, 1953, in *FRUS*, 1952–54, vol. 13, pt. 1, pp. 865–74.

48. *History of JCS*, pp. 333–36, citing (TS) NSC 177, Dec. 30, 1953, Encl to (TS) JCS 1992/265, Jan. 4, CCS 092 Asia (6-25-48), sec. 53, in NSC Microfilm 0143. All this is in "An Account of the Events and Decisions leading to the loss of North Indochina" prepared by the Office of the Special Assistant to the JCS for National Security Affairs, Oct. 25, 1954.

49. NSC 162/2, Oct. 30, 1953, in *FRUS*, 1952–54, vol. 12, pt. 1, p. 584.

50. *History of JCS*, pp. 339–40. For the report by the Plans Division, see *USVN*, book 1, pt. 2, pp. 3–6. Also see Spector, *Advice and Support*, p. 195.

51. *History of JCS*, p. 339.

52. Ibid., p. 341; Radford, *Pearl Harbor to Vietnam*, pp. 381–82.

53. *History of JCS*, p. 342; "Account of the Events and Decisions," p. 35. For a view by Assistant Secretary of State Walter Robertson on the Special Annex, see *FRUS*, 1952–54, vol. 13, pt. 1, pp. 944–45.

54. Memorandum of Discussion at the 179th Meeting of the NSC, Jan. 8, 1954, in *FRUS*, 1952–54, vol. 13, pt. 1, pp. 947–54.

55. Memorandum of Discussion at the 180th Meeting of the NSC, Jan. 14, 1954, ibid., pp. 961–64. The full text is in *USVN*, book 9, pp. 217–38.

56. The JCS recommendations are in *FRUS*, 1952–54, vol. 13, pt. 1, pp. 968–71.

57. Memorandum by C. D. Jackson, Special Assistant to the President, Jan. 18, 1954, ibid., pp. 981–82.

58. *Public Papers of the Presidents, 1954*, pp. 245–55. For the deliberations of the special committee, see Memorandum of the Meeting of the President's Special Committee on Indochina, Jan. 29, 1954, in *FRUS*, 1952–54, vol. 13, pt. 1, pp. 1002–6.

59. The British agreed. See Cable, *Geneva Conference*, p. 43.

60. Memo for the Record by the Counselor (MacArthur), Jan. 27, 1954, in *FRUS*, 1952–54, vol. 13, pt. 1, pp. 998–1000; Cable, *Geneva Conference*, pp. 43–44.

61. Memorandum of Discussion at the 186th Meeting of the NSC, Feb. 26, 1954, in *FRUS*, 1952–54, vol. 13, pt. 1, pp. 1080–81. The Soviet Union had demanded a single conference dealing with both Korea and Indochina. The French wanted two meetings, one for each issue. As a compromise, the conference was convened to discuss Korea but with an indication that Indochina could also be discussed, at which time the United States, France, the United Kingdom, the USSR, and other interested states would be invited. For Dulles's "Report on Berlin" broadcast to the nation on February 24, see *DSB*, Mar. 8, 1954, pp. 343–47.

62. Report by the President's Special Committee on Indochina, Mar. 2, 1954, in *FRUS*, 1952–54, vol. 13, pt. 1, pp. 1109–16.

63. *USVN*, book 9, pp. 266–70.

64. The Erskine Working Group report, "Military Implications of the U.S. Position on Indochina in Geneva," Mar. 17, 1954, ibid., pp. 271–75. Also see Memo for SD, ibid., pp. 266–71, and *History of JCS*, pp. 365–66.

65. Memorandum of Discussion at the 187th Meeting of the NSC, Mar. 4, 1954, in *FRUS*, 1952–54, vol. 13, pt. 1, p. 1094.

66. Memorandum by SS to the President, Mar. 23, 1954, ibid., pp. 1141–42; Memorandum of Conversation, by William R. Tyler of the Office of Western European Affairs, Mar. 23, 1954, ibid., pp. 1142–44. According to Douglas Dillon, a U.S. Air Force general

had developed plans to use B-29s at Dien Bien Phu and had informed Navarre of the idea. Perhaps that was why, he said, the French were surprised that Washington eventually rejected the idea. See Dillon to Douglas MacArthur II, July 15, 1954, in RG 59, 751 G.00/7-1554. In any case, Ely was confused at the meaning of Dulles's comments and later asked for clarification. See Memo "Indochina," in RG 59, 751 G.00/3-2454.

67. Radford's discussions with General Ely were reported by the former in Memorandum by the Chairman of the JCS (Radford) to the President, Mar. 24, 1954, in *FRUS*, 1952–54, vol. 13, pt. 1, pp. 1158–59. For his memo on the talks to the Special Committee on Indochina, see *USVN*, book 9, pp. 277–85. Also see *History of JCS*, p. 373, and Radford, *Pearl Harbor to Vietnam*, pp. 393–94. Ely presented a memo to Radford asking whether U.S. aircraft could be used to alleviate the situation. See *FRUS*, 1952–54, vol. 13, pt. 1, p. 1160.

68. Radford, *Pearl Harbor to Vietnam*, pp. 393–94. In Radford's support is his apparent refusal of Ely's request to sign a minute stating that "there was complete agreement on the terms of General Ely's memorandum, dated 23 March, dealing with intervention by US aircraft in Indochina in case of an emergency, it being understood that this intervention could be either by Naval or Air Force units as the need arises, depending on the development of the situation." See *History of JCS*, pp. 373–373a. For Ely's account, see Ely, *Indochine*, p. 63. For Radford's account to the president, see note 67 above. Later Senator Lyndon B. Johnson asked Secretary Dulles how General Ely had gotten the wrong impression of U.S. intentions. Dulles denied that he was responsible and said he had no idea where Ely had gotten the idea. See *FRUS*, 1952–54, vol. 13, pt. 2, p. 1473. For an overview of the issue, see Herring and Immerman, "Eisenhower," p. 347. Herring thinks Admiral Radford was probably less circumspect than he allows (ibid., p. 348). Radford later remarked to a senior U.S. government official, however, that his real aim in urging intervention in Indochina was to find a pretext to strike at mainland China. See Chalmers Roberts's article "How Close to War in '54?", *Washington Post*, Oct. 24, 1971.

69. Memorandum of Telephone Conversation Between the Secretary of State and the Chairman of the Joint Chiefs of Staff (Radford), Mar. 24, 1954, in *FRUS*, 1952–54, vol. 13, pt. 1, p. 1151.

70. Memorandum of Discussion at the 190th Meeting of the NSC, Mar. 25, 1954, ibid., pp. 1163–68.

71. The full text is in *DSB*, Apr. 12, 1954, pp. 539–42. At a press conference on March 31 Eisenhower evaded questions on the implications of the speech. See Herring and Immerman, "Eisenhower," p. 351.

72. Boudarel, "Comment Giap"; Heath to DOS, Mar. 31, 1954, in *FRUS*, 1952–54, vol. 13, pt. 1, pp. 1190–91.

73. Memorandum of Discussion at the 191st Meeting of the NSC, Apr. 1, 1954, in *FRUS*, 1952–54, vol. 13, pt. 1, pp. 1200–1202. Also see p. 1204. For Radford's meeting with the other members of the JCS, see ibid., 1198–99. For General Ridgway's explanation of why he rejected Radford's proposal, see ibid., pp. 1220–21. The Special Annex was recirculated to the members of the Planning Board as a result of the meeting of the NSC on March 25, 1954. See ibid., pp. 1182–83. The full text is in ibid., pp. 1183–86.

74. Memorandum of Conversation with the President, Apr. 2, 1954, ibid., pp. 1210–11. The draft resolution is on pp. 1211–12.

75. For the comments of the JCS, see ibid., pp. 1220–23.

76. Memorandum of the File of the SS, Apr. 5, 1954, ibid., pp. 1224–25. Also see Herring and Immerman, "Eisenhower," p. 353; Adams, *Firsthand Report*, p. 122.

77. Anderson agrees with the latter conclusion, *Trapped by Success*, pp. 32–33. For the argument that he wanted to isolate the hawks, see Gelb and Betts, *Irony of Vietnam*, p. 57.

78. Ambassador in France (Dillon) to DOS, Apr. 6, 1954, in *FRUS*, 1952–54, vol. 13, pt. 1, pp. 1248–49.

79. Memorandum of Discussion at the 192d Meeting of the NSC, Apr. 6, 1954, ibid., pp. 1250–65. The Planning Board report is in *USVN*, book 9, pp. 298–331.

80. *USVN*, book 9, pp. 346–58, has Part II of the Special Committee report. Part I is in *FRUS*, 1952–54, vol. 13, pt. 1, pp. 1109–17. In his memoirs, Richard Nixon claims that Eisenhower "backed down considerably" at the meeting from the position he had taken earlier in the month. See *RN*, p. 151.

81. Meeting of the NSC, Apr. 6, 1954, in *FRUS*, 1952–54, vol. 13, pt. 1, pp. 1260–65.

82. For a summary, see DOS to Paris, Apr. 3, 1954, in *USVN*, book 9, pp. 293–94, for text. The letter is in *FRUS*, 1952–54, vol. 13, pt. 1, pp. 1238–41.

83. Cable, *Geneva Conference*, pp. 12–19.

84. Ibid., p. 57.

85. Ibid. The final communique is in *DSB*, Apr. 26, 1954, p. 622.

86. First Secretary of the Embassy in France (Godbey) to DOS, Apr. 21, 1954, in *FRUS*, 1952–54, vol. 13, pt. 1, pp. 1328–34; Memorandum of Conversation by SS, Apr. 14, 1954, ibid., pp. 1335–36.

87. SS to DOS, Apr. 22, 1954, ibid., pp. 1362–63. Cable, *Geneva Conference*, pp. 59–60, says the explanation of the Colombo Conference was only a pretext. Eden did not want to be boxed in. Cable admits that Dulles was probably correct in resenting Eden's duplicity.

88. Minutes of Tripartite Meeting of Foreign Ministers, Apr. 22, 1954, in *FRUS*, 1952–54, 16: 544–48. The "breaking point" quote is in *FRUS*, 1952–54, vol. 13, pt. 1, p. 1374. Geneva to Secretary, Apr. 25, 1954, in RG 59, 751 G.00/4-2554. Actually, CINCPAC had sent a U.S. representative to Saigon to consider giving air support and had moved a carrier task force to the South China Sea. But Radford admitted to Eden in Paris that even an immediate U.S. air strike might not save Dien Bien Phu although it could forestall a general collapse. See *History of JCS*, p. 388.

89. For references to the "misunderstanding" see *FRUS*, 1952–54, vol. 13, pt. 1, pp. 1927 and 1933; Prados, *Sky Would Fall*, pp. 152–54; Herring and Immerman, "Eisenhower," pp. 357–58. Bidault's charge that Dulles offered France U.S. atomic weapons is in his memoirs, *Resistance*, p. 196. Emphasis is in the text and it is not a direct quote. See *FRUS*, 1952–54, vol. 13, pt. 2, pp. 1446–48.

90. Memorandum of Conversation by the Assistant SS for European Affairs (Merchant), Apr. 26, 1954, in *FRUS*, 1952–54, vol. 13, pt. 1, pp. 1386–91. For an earlier conversation, see p. 1362. Radford did not help by suggesting the need for Royal Air Force units in Hong Kong and Malaya.

91. SS to DOS, Apr. 24, 1954, ibid., p. 1398.

92. Cable, *Geneva Conference*, pp. 62–64.

93. SS to DOS, Apr. 23, 1954, in *FRUS*, 1952–54, vol. 13, pt. 1, pp. 1374–75; Herring and Immerman, "Eisenhower," p. 360; Eisenhower, *Mandate for Change*, p. 354; Radford, *Pearl Harbor to Vietnam*, pp. 408–9; Cable, *Geneva Conference*, p. 63. Radford's com-

ments on his talks in London are in *FRUS*, 1952–54, vol. 13, pt. 2, pp. 1416–17. The meeting with Churchill is reported in ibid., pp. 1436–37. The Eden-Dulles talks are in *FRUS*, 1952–54, 16: 553–57, 576–77.

94. *FRUS*, 1952–54, vol. 13, pt. 1, p. 1266. Dillon was convinced that only a limited number of officials in the French government were aware of the request to the United States for military intervention. Dulles conceded that if Dien Bien Phu fell before the United States intervened, Paris could repudiate any agreement for united action, but he was prepared to take that risk. See ibid., pp. 1404–5.

95. Draft State Department Press Release, ibid., pp. 1346–48; *Public Papers of the Presidents, 1954*, pp. 381–89.

96. *FRUS*, 1952–54, 16: 604–5. For the full account of the press conference, see *Public Papers of the Presidents, 1954*, pp. 427–28.

97. NSC meeting of Apr. 29, 1954, in *FRUS*, 1952–54, vol. 13, pt. 2, pp. 1431–35. Nixon, *RN*, pp. 153–54; Prados, *Sky Would Fall*, pp. 167–68; Eisenhower, *Mandate for Change*, pp. 354–55.

98. Editorial Note in *FRUS*, 1952–54, 16: 698.

99. In his memoirs, Richard Nixon states that when, many years later, Eisenhower was asked whether he and Dulles were serious about sending troops to Vietnam, Ike had replied "all the way." In his later years, of course, Eisenhower was quite hawkish on Vietnam, but there seems no reason to doubt the veracity of his memory. See *RN*, p. 155.

Chapter 6

1. SS to U.S. Delegation, May 12, 1954, in *FRUS*, 1952–54, 16: 778–79.

2. SS to U.S. Delegation, May 13, 1954, ibid., pp. 787–89.

3. Memorandum of Discussion at the NSC Meeting, May 8, 1954, in *FRUS*, 1952–54, vol. 13, pt. 2, pp. 1505–6.

4. The Vietminh proposal was presented at the Second Plenary Session on May 10. See *FRUS*, 1952–54, 16: 753–55.

5. For U.S. comments on the Vietminh proposals, see ibid., pp. 770–72. Also see Randle, *Geneva 1954*, pp. 208–9.

6. Laniel promised Bao Dai the French would not accept partition. See *FRUS*, 1952–54, 16: 323.

7. Sixth Restricted Session on Indochina, May 25, 1954, in *FRUS*, 1952–54, 16: 922. Soviet sources had predicted that the Vietminh would not propose partition but would seek nationwide elections in all three Associated States. The communists would lose in Cambodia and Laos, said Popov, but would win 60 percent of the vote in Vietnam. See the interview of journalist Kingsbury Smith with Popov, editor of *Izvestiya*, in U.S. Delegation to DOS, May 4, 1954, in RG 59, 751 G.00/5-454. For the possible reasons why the Vietminh preferred partition, see Duiker, *Communist Road*, p. 164.

8. U.S. Delegation to DOS, May 27, 1954, in *FRUS*, 1952–54, 16: 952.

9. U.S. Delegation to DOS, June 2, 1954, ibid., pp. 1005–8.

10. U.S. Delegation to DOS, June 7, 1954, ibid., pp. 1054–56. For the views of officials in the Defense Department, see *USVN*, book 9, pp. 498–99.

11. U.S. Delegation to DOS, May 26, 1954, in *FRUS*, 1952–54, 16: 933; SS to U.S. Delegation, May 28, 1954, ibid., p. 966.

12. First Plenary Session on Indochina, May 8, 1954, ibid., pp. 734–36.

13. Seventh Plenary Session on Indochina, June 10, 1954, ibid., p. 1116. For the Zhou Enlai–Eden meeting, see U.S. Delegation to DOS, May 20, 1954, ibid., pp. 863–64.

14. Smith-Eden Meeting, June 9, 1954, ibid., pp. 1083–85. Cable, *Geneva Conference*, p. 93, says Eden cabled Churchill that if the communists refused to cooperate, the conference should be adjourned. Cable thinks the comment represented a failure of nerve on Eden's part. Eden told Walter Bedell Smith that three issues appeared irreconcilable: a separate treaty for Laos and Cambodia, the status and powers of the ICC, and the composition of the ICC. See U.S. Delegation to DOS, June 9, 1954, in RG 59, 751 G.00/6-954.

15. Dillon to SS, May 10, 1954, in *USVN*, book 9, pp. 446–48. *FRUS*, 1952–54, vol. 13, pt. 2, pp. 1522–25.

16. SS to Dillon, May 11, 1954, in *FRUS*, 1952–54, vol. 13, pt. 2, pp. 1534–36. For a record of the meeting at the White House, see ibid., pp. 1527–28.

17. SS to Dillon, May 15, 1954, ibid., pp. 1569–77. Later he told Dillon to remind Laniel that Paris should not assume that the same conditions would pertain *after* a settlement was reached. See ibid., p. 1576. Dillon was concerned about a French rejection of the European Defense Community and appealed for a favorable decision on the marines. See *USVN*, book 9, pp. 472–74.

18. The plan is in *USVN*, book 9, pp. 477–79. Also see Radford, *Pearl Harbor to Vietnam*, pp. 425–27.

19. Memorandum of Conversation with Cutler, June 1, 1954, in *FRUS*, 1952–54, vol. 13, pt. 2, pp. 1647–49. Also see *History of JCS*, pp. 417–20; Dillon to SS, May 29, 1954, in *FRUS*, 1952–54, vol. 13, pt. 2, p. 1635; Dulles's response, ibid., pp. 1659–60.

20. The speech is in *DSB*, June 28, 1954, pp. 971–73. For Valluy's request, see Memo for the Record, June 2, 1954, in RG 59, 751 G.00/6-254.

21. Dillon to SS, June 14, 1954, in *FRUS*, 1952–54, vol. 13, pt. 2, pp. 1687–89; SS to Dillon, June 14, 1954, ibid., pp. 1689–90. The Australian attitude is presented in "Clarification of Press Statement on Indochina," May 11, 1954, in RG 59, 751 G.00/5-1154.

22. See his talk with Ambassador Dillon in *FRUS*, 1952–54, vol. 13, pt. 2, p. 1725. Lacouture claims that Mendès-France accepted a one-month deadline because of the deteriorating situation in Indochina. General Valluy had estimated after the battle of Dien Bien Phu that the Vietminh battle corps could be ready for an attack on the Red River Delta within ten days. See *History of JCS*, p. 422; Lacouture, *Mendès-France*, p. 227.

23. For Zhou's proposal at the Thirteenth Restricted Session on June 14, see *FRUS*, 1952–54, 16: 1139–40. His meeting with Eden on the sixteenth is recorded in ibid., pp. 1170–71. Zhou confirmed his position in a meeting with Mendès-France on June 23. See "Entrevue Mendès-France–Zhou En-lai a Berne," in Mendès-France, *Oeuvres*, pp. 73–74.

24. Fifteenth Restricted Session on Indochina, June 18, 1954, in *FRUS*, 1952–54, 16: 1179–85.

25. "Entrevue," p. 73. Zhou Enlai told Nehru that Chinese communism was "not for export" and that Beijing would accept governments of the people's own choosing in Laos and Cambodia. See Aldrich to SS, July 2, 1954, in RG 59, 751 G.00/7-254.

26. The Vietminh were also worried about SEATO, although they found it expedient to blame China for the problem. See U.S. Delegation to DOS, June 23, 1954, in *FRUS*, 1952–54, 16: 1227 and 1232.

27. Lacouture, *Mendès-France*, p. 221; Smith-Chauvel meeting, June 16, 1954, in *FRUS*, 1952–54, 16: 1154–55.

28. SS to U.S. Delegation, June 17, 1954, in *FRUS*, 1952–54, 16: 1172. U. Alexis Johnson's meeting with Jean Chauvel is reported in ibid., pp. 1176–78.

29. Smith-Molotov meeting, June 18, 1954, ibid., p. 1191.

30. U.S. Delegation to DOS, June 26, 1954, ibid., p. 1253. Mendès-France told Chauvel he felt that the DRV was counting on the July 20 deadline to force Paris to make concessions. They were pressed, he conceded, but not enough to accept the thirteenth parallel. See "Lettre a Chauvel," in Mendès-France, *Oeuvres*, pp. 99–100.

31. Summary of five-power talks, July 5, 1954, in *FRUS*, 1952–54, 16: 1283–86. Eden had a great deal of respect for Bedell Smith and called him a "splendid friend throughout." Cable, *Geneva Conference*, p. 70, suspects that Smith was influenced by Eden.

32. Bonsal to Heath, July 14, 1954, in *FRUS*, 1952–54, 16: 1374; Heath's letter to Bonsal, ibid., pp. 1280–82.

33. Meeting, June 30, 1954, ibid., pp. 1766–68; *FRUS*, 1952–54, vol. 13, pt. 2, pp. 1754–55.

34. French aide-mémoire, June 26, 1954, in *FRUS*, 1952–54, vol. 13, pt. 2, pp. 1755–57. According to Cable, Churchill wanted the U.S.-U.K. meeting to do some "fence mending" (*Geneva Conference*, p. 100).

35. For the conditions, see *FRUS*, 1952–54, vol. 13, pt. 2, p. 1758.

36. See references in ibid., pp. 1763, 1789, and 1804. Diem complained to Robert McClintock about the French evacuation of the provinces south of the Red River Delta and said that if the French abandoned Hanoi, it would be "practically impossible" to set up a viable state in the center and the South (McClintock to DOS, July 4, 1954, in RG 59, 751 G.00/7-454).

37. Dillon to SS, July 4, 1954, in *FRUS*, 1952–54, vol. 13, pt. 2, pp. 1784–85. Also see pp. 1788, 1794, and 1795–97.

38. Ibid., p. 1798, citing Hagerty diary. The reason Eisenhower gave was that it would "give the Democrats a chance to say that we sat idly by and let Indochina be sold down the river to the Communists without raising a finger or turning a hair." Later he added that it would provide free propaganda to the communists and a pretext for the French to blame the United States for the debacle (*FRUS*, 1952–54, 16: 1334).

39. Eisenhower, *Mandate for Change*, cited in *FRUS*, 1952–54, vol. 13, pt. 2, p. 1807. Lacouture, *Mendès-France*, pp. 244–45.

40. Memorandum of Conversation by U.S. Delegation, July 13, 1954; Mendès-France, *Oeuvres*, pp. 117–21; Memorandum of Conversation, by U. Alexis Johnson, July 13, 1954, in *FRUS*, 1952–54, 16: 1348–55; Eisenhower, *Mandate for Change*, pp. 369–70. Zhou Enlai's role in the compromise is discussed in U.S. Delegation to DOS, July 14, 1954, in *FRUS*, 1952–54, 16: 1368–69.

41. Memorandum of Conversation, by U. Alexis Johnson, July 13, 1954, in *FRUS*, 1952–54, 16: 1353–54.

42. Ibid., pp. 1361–62. The communique is on pp. 1362–64. The French promised to seek to achieve an agreement that conformed to the seven points. The United States stated that it was prepared to respect the terms of the treaty if it conformed to the seven points but not if they differed.

43. NSC Meeting, in *FRUS*, 1952–54, vol. 13, pt. 2, pp. 1834–40.

44. SS to Under Secretary of State, July 16, 1954, in *FRUS*, 1952–54, 16: 1390–92. Dulles and the president discussed what action to take if the Vietminh rejected French proposals. Dulles felt that asking Congress for wartime powers was too drastic because it would frighten the public. It would be preferable to take the issue to the United Nations. See ibid., p. 1852, citing Hagerty diary.

45. U.S. Delegation to DOS, July 19, 1954, in *FRUS*, 1952–54, 16: 1466. Walter Bedell Smith's talks with Eden and Mendès-France are on pp. 1405–7.

46. Ibid., p. 1491.

47. ibid., p. 1500.

48. The press conference is excerpted in ibid., p. 1503.

49. The Dulles press conference is reprinted in *DSB*, Aug. 2, 1954, pp. 163–64. An excerpt is in *FRUS*, 1952–54, 16: 1550.

50. Kattenburg, *Vietnam Trauma*, p. 47.

51. Ambrose, *Eisenhower*, p. 170.

52. Cable, *Geneva Conference*, pp. 49–50.

53. Special NIE, June 15, 1954, in *FRUS*, 1952–54, vol. 13, pt. 2, p. 1708. Mayers, *Cracking the Monolith*, pp. 129–31.

54. Dillon to DOS, July 22, 1954, in RG 59, 751 G.00/7-2254. The French source was Secretary of State for War Chevallier.

55. Le Duan, *Thu Vao Nam*, letter of May 1965, p. 130.

Chapter 7

1. Press conference of Secretary of State John Foster Dulles, in *DSB*, Aug. 2, 1954, p. 163. Dulles said much the same thing at an NSC meeting on July 22, noting that "the remaining free areas of Indochina must be built up if the dike against Communism is to be held." See *FRUS*, 1952–54, vol. 13, pt. 2, p. 1870.

2. NIE, "Post-Geneva Outlook in Indochina," in *USVN*, book 10, pp. 691–98.

3. Bao Dai spent the winter months in Ban Me Thuot and then returned to France in April to be "au coeur du debat" (*Dragon d'Annam*, p. 321). Heath's comments are in Heath to Bonsal, July 4, 1954, in *FRUS*, 1952–54, 16: 1282. Not all U.S. officials wanted him to return to Vietnam. See McClintock's cable in *FRUS*, 1952–54, vol. 13, pt. 2, p. 1690.

4. Memorandum of Discussion at the 199th Meeting of the NSC, May 27, 1954, in *FRUS*, 1952–54, 16: 943. For Dulles's earlier comment, see SS to U.S. Delegation, May 22, 1954, ibid., p. 892.

5. Dulles to U.S. Delegation, June 5, 1954, ibid., p. 1044.

6. Bao Dai, *Dragon d'Annam*, pp. 325–28; *FRUS*, 1952–54, 16: 1289. For McClintock's comment that he was considered to be in the American pocket, see *FRUS*, 1952–54, 16: 1784. It is interesting that as early as 1950 Vietminh sources predicted that the United States would eventually replace Bao Dai with Ngo Dinh Diem. See O'Sullivan to SS, Oct. 6, 1950, in RG 59, 751 G.00/10-650.

7. Robert Scheer, "The Genesis of United States Support for Ngo Dinh Diem," in Gettleman, ed., *Vietnam*, pp. 235–53. On support for Diem, see Kattenburg, *Vietnam Trauma*, p. 53, n. 27.

8. McClintock to DOS, July 4, 1954, in *FRUS*, 1952–54, vol. 13, pt. 2, pp. 1782–84; Dillon's comment, ibid., pp. 1608–9. McClintock was counselor of the U.S. Embassy in Saigon.

9. Warner, *Last Confucian*, p. 92; *FRUS*, 1952–54, 16: 1136. Bao Dai told Heath that Diem was an "incapable," obstinate, and inordinately proud, with little support outside the Catholic community. See *FRUS*, 1952–54, vol. 13, pt. 2, p. 22.

10. Kattenburg, *Vietnam Trauma*, p. 53; Anderson, *Trapped by Success*, pp. 52–54. For the minutes of a meeting between Ngo Dinh Diem and high-ranking U.S. officials in May 1953, see *FRUS*, 1952–54, vol. 13, pt. 2, pp. 553–54. Dulles's comment is in *FRUS*, 1952–54, 16: 892. A Special NIE published in June pointed out that despite his honesty and zeal, he had "not yet demonstrated the necessary ability to deal with practical problems of politics and administration." Though conceding that he had the support of Catholics, the report said many influential groups, including the army, opposed him. See Special NIE, "Current Trends in South Vietnam," in *USVN*, book 10, p. 752.

11. Ambassador at Saigon to the DOS, July 7, 1954, in *FRUS*, 1952–54, vol. 13, pt. 2, p. 1789. Also see *FRUS*, 1952–54, 16: 1339–40.

12. Ambassador in France to DOS, Aug. 4, 1954, in *FRUS*, 1952–54, vol. 13, pt. 2, pp. 1920–21; Dulles's comments, ibid., pp. 1888–89. For Dulles's comments on the possibility of getting the French out of South Vietnam, see ibid., p. 1869.

13. Ambassador at Saigon to DOS, July 23, 1954, ibid., pp. 1872–73; Chief of the United States Military Assistance Advisory Group in Indochina (O'Daniel) to the Department of the Army, July 27, 1954, ibid., 1883–85.

14. SS to the Embassy in France, Aug. 18, 1954, ibid., pp. 1957–59. Dulles told Dillon he did not wish to give the impression that Diem was a U.S. protégé or that the administration was irrevocably committed to him. For the NSC meeting, see *FRUS*, 1952–54, 16: 724–33.

15. According to the memoirs of Pierre Mendès-France, this was not so. In a message to André Bettencourt, Mendès-France admitted that Washington may have gotten the impression that Paris would approve the EDC but says he warned Dulles in July that there was little support for it in the National Assembly. The French premier said he had made no promises. See "Le Malentendu Franco-Americaine," Sept. 16, 1954, in Mendès-France, *Oeuvres*, pp. 343–44.

16. Memorandum of Conversation by the Deputy Director of the Office of Western European Affairs (Tyler), Aug. 27, 1954, in *FRUS*, 1952–54, vol. 13, pt. 2, pp. 1991–93; Ambassador in Vietnam to DOS, Aug. 26, 1954, ibid., pp. 1985–87. Also see ibid., pp. 1988–90 and 1993–94.

17. Assistant SS to Dillon, Sept. 17, 1954, ibid., pp. 2034–35.

18. Sainteny reported that Ho was congenial and expressed a desire for a continued French economic and cultural presence in the DRV. He insisted that he was not a slave to hard-liners in the VWP. See U.S. Consul (Hanoi) to SS, Oct. 26, 1954, in RG 59, 751 G.00/10-2654. The communique is in *FRUS*, 1952–54, vol. 13, pt. 2, pp. 2097–98. For an account of the talks, see ibid., pp. 2083–84. London opposed U.S. aid to Cambodia as illegal. See ibid., p. 2079.

19. Assistant SS to Ambassador in Vietnam, Sept. 28, 1954, in *FRUS*, 1952–54, vol. 13, pt. 2, pp. 2085–86; Ambassador in Vietnam to DOS, Sept. 29, 1954, ibid., pp. 2092–93.

20. Ambassador in Vietnam to DOS, Oct. 22, 1954, ibid., pp. 2151–53.

21. The letter is in ibid., pp. 2166–67. For the NSC meeting of October 22, see ibid., pp. 2153–58.

22. Ambassador in Vietnam to DOS, Oct. 23, 1954, ibid., pp. 2163–64.

23. Buszynski, *SEATO*, pp. 18–19; *FRUS*, 1952–54, vol. 12, pt. 1, p. 651. The Thai did not want India included, which, in their view, would guarantee "united inaction." See *FRUS*, 1952–54, 16: 801–3.

24. Minutes of Meeting of the NSC, July 23, 1954, in *FRUS*, 1952–54, vol. 12, pt. 1, p. 653.

25. Minutes of a Meeting on Southeast Asia, July 24, 1954, ibid., pp. 665–71.

26. Memo for SD, Aug. 11, 1954, in *USVN*, book 10, pp. 709–13.

27. Ibid.

28. Memorandum by the Regional Planning Adviser in the Bureau of Far Eastern Affairs (Ogburn) to the Assistant SS for Far Eastern Affairs (Robertson), Aug. 11, 1954, in *FRUS*, 1952–54, vol. 12, pt. 1, p. 719.

29. Memorandum of Discussion at the 210th Meeting of the NSC, Aug. 12, 1954, in *FRUS*, 1952–54, vol. 12, pt. 1, pp. 724–33.

30. See SD (Wilson) to SS, Aug. 17, 1954, and Memoranda of Conversation with the President and Secretary of State, Aug. 17, 1954, ibid., pp. 739–40 and 735.

31. Minutes of the meeting of Aug. 18, 1954, ibid., pp. 744–47.

32. For discussions on membership, see ibid., pp. 648, 742, 802–3, and 835. Also see Kahin, *Intervention*, p. 72.

33. Memorandum of Conversation, Prepared in the DOS, Aug. 30, 1954, in *FRUS*, 1952–54, vol. 12, pt. 1, p. 820.

34. For French views, see Bonnet to SS, Oct. 26, 1954, in *FRUS*, 1952–54, vol. 13, pt. 2, pp. 2186–87. For U.S. views, see ibid., pp. 2198–99.

35. Memorandum of Discussion at the 219th Meeting of the NSC, Oct. 26, 1954, ibid., pp. 2183–85.

36. Eisenhower letter, ibid., pp. 2205–7. For Collins's private meeting with Dulles and Radford, see ibid., pp. 2198–99.

37. SS to Embassy in Saigon, Nov. 20, 1954, ibid., p. 2274. Dulles's comment about U.S. prestige is on p. 2271. Mendès-France says that he told Dulles that if the United States wanted France to recognize U.S. leadership in Asia, it was contradictory to drive the French out of Indochina. See "Entretiens Franco-Americains de Washington sur l'Indochine," Nov. 18–19, 1954, in *Oeuvres*, pp. 470–74.

38. NIE of Nov. 23, 1954, in *FRUS*, 1952–54, vol. 13, pt. 2, pp. 2286–1301.

39. For Mansfield's views, see Assistant SS to Embassy in France, Dec. 17, 1954, ibid., pp. 2393–94. Collins's report, ibid., p. 2379. For Heath's comments, see pp. 2391–92. Relations between Diem and Phan Huy Quat are discussed in Bui Diem, *Jaws of History*, pp. 86–88.

40. Alternatives under consideration were Phan Huy Quat, Bao Dai, Nguyen Van Tam, and Tran Van Huu. See Ambassador in France to DOS, Dec. 19, 1954, in *FRUS*, 1952–54, vol. 13, pt. 2, pp. 2400–2405. General Ely admits that some officials in Paris wanted to play a "double jeu" (i.e., play an evenhanded role with the North and the South). See Ely, *Indochine*, p. 235.

41. SS to Embassy in Vietnam, Dec. 24, 1954, in *FRUS*, 1952–54, vol. 13, pt. 2, pp. 2419–20.

42. Memorandum of Discussion at the 234th Meeting of the NSC, Jan. 27, 1955, in *FRUS*, 1955–57, 1: 62–70. For Collins's report, see ibid., pp. 54–57. The supplement is *USVN*, book 10, pp. 865–82.

43. Telegram from the Special Representative in Vietnam (Collins) to DOS, Mar. 31, 1955, in *FRUS*, 1955–57, 1: 168–71.

44. Telegram from SS to the Embassy in Vietnam, Apr. 1, 1955, ibid., pp. 179–80. For the secretary's telephone conversation with the president, see ibid., pp. 175–76.

45. DOS to Collins, Apr. 4, 1955, in RG 59, 751 G.00/4-455; Telegram from the Special Representative in Vietnam (Collins) to SS, Apr. 7, 1955, in *FRUS*, 1955–57, 1: 218–21; Collins, *Lightning Joe*, pp. 402–3. For a dissenting voice from the CIA, see *FRUS*, 1955–57, 1: 199–202.

46. The memo by Kenneth T. Young is in RG 59, 751 G.00/4-1155, with the draft telegram attached. Also see Anderson, *Trapped by Success*, p. 107. For the cables, see *FRUS*, 1955–57, 1: Apr. 11, 1955. In a phone conversation with his brother Allen, John Foster Dulles said that he was inclined to go along with Diem, but the president leaned toward Collins's view (ibid., p. 235).

47. DOS to Dillon, Apr. 18, 1955, in RG 59, 751 G.00/4-1855; Telegram from the Special Representative in Vietnam (Collins) to DOS, Apr. 19, 1955, in *FRUS*, 1955–57, 1: 268–70; ibid., pp. 250–51. For his recall, see DOS to Collins, Apr. 16, 1955, in RG 59, 751 G.00/4-1655; Collins, *Lightning Joe*, p. 404; Lansdale, *In the Midst of Wars*, pp. 250–51.

48. Collins, *Lightning Joe*, p. 405; Memorandum from Sebald to SS, Apr. 23, 1955, in *FRUS*, 1955–57, 1: 280–81; Memo for Secretary from Herbert Hoover, Jr., in RG 59, 751 G.00/4-2355.

49. SS to Embassy in France, Apr. 27, 1955, in *FRUS*, 1955–57, 1: 294–98.

50. Telegram from SS to the Embassy in France, Apr. 27, 1955, ibid., p. 301; ibid., pp. 305–6 and 337; Lansdale, *In the Midst of Wars*, p. 300.

51. Memorandum of Discussion at the 246th Meeting of the NSC, Apr. 28, 1955, in *FRUS*, 1955–57, 1: 307–12; DOS to Dillon, Apr. 28, 1955, ibid., pp. 312–13.

52. Collins, *Lightning Joe*, p. 406; Special NIE, May 2, 1955, in *FRUS*, 1955–57, 1: 347.

53. Special NIE, May 2, 1955, in *FRUS*, 1955–57, 1: 346–50; Telegram from SS to the Embassy in Vietnam, May 3, 1955, ibid., pp. 353–55.

54. Telegram from the Special Representative in Vietnam (Collins) to DOS, May 5, 1955, ibid., p. 368; Collins, *Lightning Joe*, p. 408.

55. Telegram from SS to DOS, May 8, 1955, in *FRUS*, 1955–57, 1: 372–78.

56. In a letter to President Eisenhower, Dulles said he had made a major effort to persuade the French to give their backing to Diem. Dulles pointed out that, like Syngman Rhee, Diem was distasteful, but that all Asian governments were run by strong leaders. Faure was skeptical but willing to give Diem a chance, and Dulles felt he had made a convert. See SS to DOS, May 12, 1955, ibid., pp. 399–400.

57. Telegram from SS to DOS, May 12, 1955, ibid., pp. 401–5.

58. See ibid., p. 415.

59. Collins, *Lightning Joe*, p. 411; Memorandum for the Record, by Senator Mike Mansfield, in *FRUS*, 1955–57, 1: 277.

60. *USVN*, book 10, pp. 925–26.

61. For other estimates, see NIE-63-5-54, "Post-Geneva Outlook in Indochina," Aug. 13, 1954, in RG 59, 751 G.00/8-1354; Minutes of a Meeting on Southeast Asia, July 24, 1954, in *FRUS*, 1952–54, vol. 12, pt. 1, p. 667. In that meeting, Dulles conceded that the communists would probably win the elections because they possessed a population

advantage of 13 million in the North to 9 million in the South and would "vote as a bloc." The NIE predicted that the communists "would almost certainly win."

62. "Post-Geneva Outlook"; Ambassador in Vietnam to DOS, Oct. 28, 1954, in *FRUS*, 1952–54, vol. 13, pt. 2, p. 2191; Meeting at the DOS, Oct. 8, 1954, ibid., p. 2123.

63. SS to Dillon, Oct. 25, 1954, in *FRUS*, 1952–54, vol. 13, pt. 2, p. 2182. The British government conceded that the Political Declaration had no legal basis. See the comments to the House of Commons in London to DOS, Mar. 23, 1955, in RG 59, 751 G.00/3-2355.

64. Memorandum of Conversation, Mar. 1, 1955, in *FRUS*, 1955–57, 1: 103–4.

65. SS to the Embassy in Vietnam, Apr. 5, 1955, in *FRUS*, 1955–57, 1: 208–9.

66. U.S. Policy on All-Vietnam Elections, ibid., pp. 410–12. This draft statement was initially prepared by the State Department and submitted to the NSC Planning Board, where it was revised. The JCS wanted to remove the stipulation that the United States might act alone, but the State Department opposed the proposal. See ibid., p. 438.

67. Memorandum of Conversation, June 8, 1955, ibid., pp. 439–41. The NSC meeting is reported in ibid., p. 433.

68. The text of the declaration is in Cameron, ed., *Viet-Nam Crisis*, 1: 383–84. The U.S. appeal to Diem is in Acting SS to Embassy in Vietnam, July 15, 1955, in *FRUS*, 1955–57, 1: 487–88.

69. SS to the Embassy in Vietnam, July 22, 1955, in *FRUS*, 1955–57, 1: 494–95.

70. The tripartite meeting is reported in a letter from Kenneth T. Young to Ambassador Reinhardt; see ibid., pp. 499–503.

71. SS to DOS, Sept. 27, 1955, ibid., p. 546. For a reference to Dulles's press conference, see ibid., p. 534.

72. The British letter is in Cameron, ed., *Viet-Nam Crisis*, 1: 414–15. For Macmillan's meeting with Molotov, see *FRUS*, 1955–57, 1: 579.

73. The Chinese proposal is reported in *FRUS*, 1955–57, 1: 628. According to Paul Kattenburg, the Soviets received at least a dozen notes from the DRV protesting the lack of consultations (*Vietnam Trauma*, p. 62).

74. Lewy, *America in Vietnam*, p. 8.

75. One alleged example of this tendency, according to Kenneth T. Young, was Rupert Emerson, the noted Southeast Asian specialist. See Emerson, *Representative Government*, pp. 16, 192. For Young's comment, see *FRUS*, 1955–57, 1: 552. Also see Frances Fitzgerald, *Fire in the Lake*, p. 121.

76. Special Representative in Vietnam (Collins) to DOS, Feb. 23, 1955, in *FRUS*, 1955–57, 1: 92.

77. Ambassador in Vietnam to DOS, Sept. 29, 1955, ibid., p. 547. Lansdale worked on him as well. See *In the Midst of Wars*, pp. 331–32.

78. Letter from Kenneth T. Young to Ambassador Reinhardt, Oct. 5, 1954, in *FRUS*, 1955–57, 1: 551–54.

79. SS to the Embassy in Vietnam, Oct. 6, 1955, ibid., p. 559.

80. Embassy in Vietnam to SS, Oct. 14, 1955, ibid., pp. 562–63.

81. Ambassador in Vietnam to DOS, Nov. 29, 1955, ibid., pp. 589–94.

82. For a U.S. report on the elections, see Chargé in Vietnam to DOS, Mar. 23, 1956, ibid., pp. 662–66. Also see Lansdale, *In the Midst of Wars*, p. 350.

83. Fall, *Vietnam Witness*, pp. 178–79.

84. Acting SS to the Embassy in Vietnam, Apr. 12, 1957, in *FRUS*, 1955–57, 1: 779; Anderson, *Trapped by Success*, pp. 152–54. Washington's concern over the issue was expressed in SS to Reinhardt, in *FRUS*, 1955–57, 1: 525–26. For a conversation between Ladejinsky and Diem on the issue, see ibid., pp. 455–58.

85. See the memo dated Sept. 27, 1956, in *FRUS*, 1955–57, 1: 742–43.

86. For overseas reactions to the creation of TERM, see ibid., pp. 646 and 657.

87. Reinhardt to DOS, Dec. 5, 1955, ibid., pp. 596–97.

88. Note by the Executive Secretary to the NSC, Dec. 22, 1954, in *USVN*, book 10, p. 845.

89. Memo for the Executive Secretary, NSC, Sept. 15, 1955, ibid., pp. 1001–15; Spector, *Advice and Support*, pp. 269–70. For a reply from the State Department's Policy Planning Staff, drafted by Charles Stelle, see *FRUS*, 1955–57, 1: 560–62. Stelle said that the best alternative would be a clear affirmation of U.S. intent to take vigorous action under the Manila Pact.

90. Telegram from CINCPAC to CNO, June 1, 1956, in *FRUS*, 1955–57, 1: 689–91; Memorandum of Conversation, May 28, 1956, ibid., pp. 685–86.

91. See the memo from Robert Bowie to the Planning Board, June 6, 1956, ibid., pp. 693–95. He was concerned at the JCS policy that without nuclear weapons the United States would be unable to take effective action in local wars and that the JCS would seek authorization to use such weapons without recourse to the political situation. He asked the secretary of state to obtain a clarification.

92. Radford's report, ibid., pp. 703–09; minutes of the NSC meeting of June 7, ibid., pp. 695–703. Also see Spector, *Advice and Support*, pp. 271–72.

93. *USVN*, book 10, pp. 1083–85. See the comments in Gelb and Betts, *Irony of Vietnam*, pp. 183–84.

94. The NIEs of July 27, October 26, and May 14, 1955, are in *FRUS*, 1955–57, 1: 498–99, 564, and 818–19; for an NIE dated July 17 on the same subject, see *USVN*, book 10, pp. 1066–82.

95. *Vietnam: The Anti-U.S. Resistance War for National Salvation, 1954–1975: Military Events*, p. 10. The original version, *Cuoc Khang Chien*, appeared in English translation in Joint Publications Research Service, 80,968, June 3, 1982. Smith, *International History*, 1: 31–32; Duiker, *Communist Road*, p. 172. For Ho's admission that the fighters in the South might be discouraged, see his speech in *Toan Tap*, 6: 585.

96. Ho Chi Minh, *Toan Tap*, 6: 588; Duiker, *Communist Road*, p. 172, n. 3.

97. *Cuoc Khang Chien*, pp. 5, 9–10. An excerpt from the September resolution is in *Lich Su Dang*, 3: 5–10.

98. Devillers and Lacouture say that the DRV cordoned the U.S. consulate in November when the United States claimed that accreditation was not necessary because a mission existed in Saigon. See Devillers and Lacouture, *Fin d'une guerre*, p. 389.

99. Gabriel Kolko says there were 15,000 Vietminh in the South in 1957, and 130,000 had gone to the North in 1955. Most observers accept a lower figure. Kolko, *Anatomy of a War*, pp. 98–99. CINCPAC estimated there were 10,000 Vietminh left in the South. See *FRUS*, 1955–57, 1: 511.

100. Beijing apparently advised Hanoi that the elections would not be held. See *Beijing Review*, Nov. 23, 1979. Smith asserts that Hanoi did not expect elections to take place (*International History*, 1: 30). Also see Thayer, *War by Other Means*, pp. 6–7.

101. *Cuoc Khang Chien*, p. 14. See details on p. 15. On the First Congress, see Smith, *International History*, 1: 64.

102. Post, *Revolution*, 2: 121–22; Duiker, *Communist Road*, p. 176.

103. Ho Chi Minh's letter is in *Toan Tap*, 7: 453–57. See *Cuoc Khang Chien*, p. 16; Truong Chinh's speech is cited in Smyser, *Independent Vietnamese*, p. 7.

104. *Cuoc Khang Chien*, p. 17; Duiker, *Communist Road*, p. 178, n. 17. On the leadership crisis, see Smyser, *Independent Vietnamese*, p. 21.

105. *Cuoc Khang Chien*, pp. 19–20. Vo Nguyen Giap, "Strengthening national defense and building up the people's armed forces," in *VDRN*, document 98, p. 45.

106. Smyser cites communist sources that the declaration was worked out by China and the Soviet Union. Whether or not that is the case, the reference to nonpeaceful transition is strikingly similar to Ho's speech at the April 1956 Plenum. See Smyser, *Independent Vietnamese*, pp. 17–21; Duiker, *Communist Road*, pp. 182–83.

107. The NIE of May 14, 1957, is in *FRUS*, 1955–57, 1: 818–19.

108. For Diem's visit with Eisenhower, see ibid., pp. 794–99.

109. Ambassador in Vietnam (Durbrow) to SS, Apr. 29, 1957, ibid., pp. 787–92. For a discussion of the civilian-military debate, see Spector, *Advice and Support*, pp. 320–25.

110. Ambassador in Vietnam to DOS, Dec. 5, 1957, in *FRUS*, 1955–57, 1: 869–84.

111. Chargé in Vietnam (Elting) to DOS, July 30, 1959, in *FRUS*, 1958–60, 1: 221–25.

112. Spector, *Advice and Support*, p. 277.

113. Ambassador in Vietnam to DOS, Dec. 7, 1959, in *FRUS*, 1958–60, 1: 256–71.

114. The draft revision of NSC 5429/5 is in *USVN*, book 10, pp. 1196–1210.

115. Ibid., p. 1217.

116. The embassy was not well informed but agreed that the GVN was using too much force and too little persuasion. See *FRUS*, 1958–60, 1: 189, 194.

117. *Cuoc Khang Chien*, pp. 29–33; Duiker, *Communist Road*, pp. 187–88.

118. Sources in Hanoi explain that the reason for the delay in announcing the decision was the need to confer with southern leaders and Hanoi's major allies (interview in Hanoi with Dang Xuan Ky, Dec. 5, 1990).

119. See the discussion in Kahin, *Intervention*, pp. 106–9; *Cuoc Khang Chien*, p. 30.

120. The instructions by the southern leadership are in Race Documents, number 1044, a collection of materials deposited by Jeffrey Race in the Center for Research Libraries, Chicago, Illinois. For the spontaneous uprisings, see Duiker, *Communist Road*, pp. 190–93.

121. Spector, *Advice and Support*, pp. 320–25; *USVN*, book 10, p. 1167; Memorandum of Conversation, Mar. 13, 1958, in *FRUS*, 1958–60, 1: 23–25.

122. Spector, *Advice and Support*, pp. 360–61.

123. Memorandum from Lansdale to O'Donnell, June 4, 1959, in *FRUS*, 1958–60, 1: 206.

124. Ambassador in Vietnam to DOS, May 3, 1960, in *FRUS*, 1958–60, 1: 433–37. On the ninth he discussed it with Diem, who was "not happy." See ibid., p. 325.

125. Board report, ibid., pp. 412–25; Williams's letter, ibid., pp. 442–45. The Defense Department reaction is in *USVN*, vol. 4, book 2, p. A5.

126. SS to Embassy in Vietnam, May 9, 1960, in *FRUS*, 1958–60, 1: 448–49; Memorandum of Discussion at the 444th Meeting of the NSC, May 9, 1960, ibid., pp. 446–48. One reason given was that the administration was facing difficulties with other Asian allies at the time and could not afford an additional problem.

127. Board report, ibid., pp. 498–500.

128. *USVN*, book 10, pp. 1281–98.

129. The Special NIE is in *FRUS*, 1958–60, 1: 536–41.

130. Ambassador in Vietnam to DOS, Sept. 5, 1960, ibid., pp. 556–60.

131. Durbrow's letter expressing this view is in ibid., pp. 621–31. J. Graham Parsons, the new assistant secretary for Far Eastern Affairs, essentially agreed. After a brief visit to Saigon in October he expressed his concern in a cable to Durbrow. See Ambassador in Thailand to Embassy in Vietnam, Oct. 21, 1960, ibid., pp. 611–13.

132. SS to Embassy in Vietnam, Oct. 7, 1960, pp. 591–94. There was no discussion of alternative leadership, according to Parsons. See interview with Parsons, *FRUS*, 1958–61, 1: 594. Durbrow's cable was drafted by Joseph Mendenhall, one of Diem's most persistent critics in the U.S. Embassy.

133. For an embassy account of the events, see Ambassador in Vietnam to DOS, Nov. 12, 1960, in ibid., pp. 641–43.

134. For a remark indicating Washington's approval of Durbrow's posture during the coup, see ibid., p. 640.

135. Diem's complaint to McGarr is in Memorandum from the Chief of MAAG to the Ambassador in Vietnam, Nov. 17, 1960, ibid., p. 677. Rumors of U.S. support of the coup are reported in ibid., p. 680. They were firmly denied by the administration.

136. For comments by members of the embassy staff on Durbrow's role during the coup, see Editorial Note, ibid., pp. 660–63. Also see Memo from Wood to Anderson, Dec. 2, 1960, ibid., pp. 705–7.

137. For Lansdale's suggestion that Durbrow be removed as ambassador on the grounds that he had totally lost credibility with President Diem, see Memorandum from Lansdale to Gates, Nov. 12, 1960, ibid., p. 653. Also see ibid., p. 682.

138. Letter from Ambassador in Vietnam to Assistant SS Parsons, Nov. 30, 1960, ibid., p. 694; letter from Chief of MAAG to CINCPAC, Nov. 21, 1960, ibid., pp. 695–703.

139. Letter from Acting Assistant Secretary Steeves to Ambassador in Vietnam, Dec. 20, 1960, ibid., pp. 737–38.

140. Acting SS to Embassy in Vietnam, Dec. 31, 1960, ibid., pp. 751–52.

141. Gelb and Betts, *Irony of Vietnam*, pp. 25–26.

142. DOS to Collins, Dec. 24, 1954, in *FRUS*, 1952–54, vol. 13, pt. 2, pp. 2419–20. According to William P. Bundy, the theme of "buying time" in Vietnam in order to save other countries within the region was also prevalent among working-level officials in Washington, at least until Diem was able to consolidate his power in May 1955 (letter to the author from William P. Bundy, Dec. 1992).

143. For Eisenhower's comment, see *FRUS*, 1958–60, 1: 447.

144. Rostow, *Diffusion of Power*, pp. 663–64. In an interview with NBC, the only problem that Eisenhower recalled in South Vietnam was Diem's nepotistic tendencies.

Chapter 8

1. Paper Prepared by the Country Team Staff Committee, Jan. 4, 1961, in *FRUS*, 1961, 1: 1–12. For Eisenhower's briefing of Kennedy on the situation in Laos, see Rusk, *As I Saw It*, p. 428. Eisenhower allegedly advised Kennedy to put U.S. troops in Laos, "with others if possible, alone if necessary." To Rusk, Eisenhower's advice contrasted sharply with his

own behavior in 1954. Recent scholarship raises some doubt about whether Ike had been as categorical in advising the introduction of U.S. troops into Laos as such recollections indicate, noting that he was often inclined to speculate on questions about which he had not yet made up his mind. For some analysis of the issue, see Greenstein and Immerman, "What Did Eisenhower Tell Kennedy?"

2. *USVN*, vol. 1, book 11, p. 2.

3. For information on the background of the new Kennedy team, see Halberstam, *The Best and the Brightest*, p. 159. Also see the manuscript of William P. Bundy, in Box 1, Carton 12, William P. Bundy Papers. In a speech in April 1954 Kennedy said that there was no solution in Indochina without true independence. See *FRUS*, 1952–54, vol. 13, pt. 1, p. 1266.

4. Two memorandums on the meeting are in *FRUS*, 1961–63, 1: 13–15 and 16–19. According to Walt W. Rostow, Kennedy talked to him shortly after the meeting and said, "This is the worst one we've got, isn't it? You know, Eisenhower never mentioned it. He talked at length about Laos, but never uttered the word Vietnam" (Rostow, *Diffusion of Power*, p. 265).

5. There were allegations that Kennedy offered the ambassadorial job to Lansdale after the meeting but that Rusk had argued against the idea on the grounds of Lansdale's "lone wolf" reputation. See Halberstam, *The Best and the Brightest*, pp. 30–31. Assistant Secretary Parsons briefed Rusk on Lansdale. See *FRUS*, 1961–63, 1: 19–20. Rusk makes no mention of the issue in his autobiography.

6. Embassy in Vietnam to DOS, Jan. 31, 1961, in *FRUS*, 1961–63, 1: 25–28. Lansdale wrote privately to Diem asking him not to jail opponents. See ibid., pp. 20–23.

7. *USVN*, pt. 4.B.1, book 2, pp. 9–11. For Rostow's view of Durbrow, see *FRUS*, 1961–63, 1: 72.

8. Kennedy was prepared for the idea of neutralization by a briefing paper drawn up for his talk with Eisenhower in January. Eisenhower advised against a coalition government because it had failed in China. See Gibbons, *U.S. Government and the Vietnam War*, 2: 8; Rusk, *As I Saw It*, p. 428; Schlesinger, *Thousand Days*, pp. 336–37. According to William P. Bundy, administration officials were convinced that Soviet interest in Laos was focused on limiting Chinese influence in the area. See Bundy manuscript, chap. 3, p. 15.

9. Dommen, *Conflict in Laos*, pp. 196–97; Rostow, *Diffusion of Power*, pp. 266–68.

10. The minutes of the first meeting are in *FRUS*, 1961–63, 1: 77–80. Kenneth T. Young's report on the meeting is in *DDRS*, 1975, p. 317c.

11. *USVN*, book 11, pt. 1, pp. 42–56, has the first draft. A later draft, with annex, is in *DDRS*, 1978, p. 147a.

12. Memorandum from the Ambassador-designate to Vietnam (Nolting) to SS, Apr. 29, 1961, in *FRUS*, 1961–63, 1: 87–88. Sorensen's and Komer's comments are in ibid., pp. 84–86. The discussions in the NSC meeting of April 28 are briefly reported in ibid., pp. 82–83.

13. The Rostow quote is in Schlesinger, *Thousand Days*, p. 337. Schlesinger says Kennedy told him that if it had not been for the crisis in Cuba, "we might be about to intervene in Laos" (ibid., p. 339). For Rostow's own later reference that it was an "extraordinarily disheveled meeting," see Rostow, *Diffusion of Power*, p. 269.

14. The annex is in *USVN*, book 11, pt. B.1, pp. 58–61. An earlier draft by Lansdale called for the commitment of U.S. troops instead of an increase in ARVN to demon-

strate the U.S. resolve to use force of arms if there was no Laos settlement. See *USVN*, book 2, pt. 4.B.2, p. 32.

15. Information on the meeting in the State Department is in *USVN*, book 11, pt. 1, pp. 62–66. Also see Gibbons, *U.S. Government and the Vietnam War*, 2: 27–28.

16. Gibbons, *U.S. Government and the Vietnam War*, 2: 32–33.

17. Schlesinger, *Thousand Days*, pp. 337–39.

18. The State Department draft is in *FRUS*, 1961–63, 1: 93–115. The quote is on p. 97.

19. Ibid., p. 108.

20. *USVN*, book 11, pp. 67–68. A brief report of the May 4 NSC meeting is in *FRUS*, 1961–63, 1: 125. Nolting said that there were no dissenters within the task force that Diem was the best bet to make a fresh start. But he admitted that Rusk was pessimistic. See Nolting, *Trust to Tragedy*, pp. 14–17.

21. For the task force report, see *USVN*, book 11, pp. 69–130. NSAM-52 is in *FRUS*, 1961–63, 1: 132–34.

22. Rusk, *As I Saw It*, p. 430; Schlesinger, *Thousand Days*, p. 339; Kahin, *Intervention*, p. 474, n. 16. Journalist James Reston recounts that after Kennedy's tempestuous meeting with Khrushchev in Vienna the former had told him privately that Khrushchev had pressured him on Berlin because he was convinced that anyone who had made such a mess of the Bay of Pigs fiasco "had no guts." It was now essential to demonstrate our firmness, Kennedy told Reston, and the place to do it was in Vietnam. The revelation astonished him. See Reston, *Deadline*, p. 291.

23. *USVN*, book 2, pt. 4.B.1, p. ii. Letter to the author from Roger Hilsman, May 21, 1992. For Rostow's comment, see *FRUS*, 1961–63, 1: 131.

24. Letter from Hilsman, May 21, 1992. For a more critical view, see Kahin, *Intervention*, p. 129.

25. Telegram from Embassy in Vietnam to DOS, May 13, 1961, in *FRUS*, 1961–63, 1: 136–38. Kennedy's letter is in *USVN*, book 11, pp. 132–35. The evening talk is in *DDRS*, 1981, p. 537. On May 15 Diem replied that he was gratified that Johnson had asked him for suggestions. We are "not accustomed to being asked for our views as to our needs." See *USVN*, book 11, pt. 1, pp. 155–56. A later letter is in ibid., pp. 167–73.

26. *USVN*, book 11, pt. 1, pp. 159–66. The formal report is in *FRUS*, 1961–63, 1: 152–57. For a report on the trip by Ambassador to Thailand Kenneth T. Young, see ibid., pp. 143–46. Johnson's "veep to the people" approach nettled some old-timers, he said, but it was effective. For a second undated report by the vice-president, see ibid., pp. 152–57.

27. Nolting's reaction is in the telegram from the Embassy in Vietnam to DOS, July 14, 1961, in *FRUS*, 1961–63, 1: 216–20. Nolting admitted that some embassy officials, notably political counselor Joseph Mendenhall, were pessimistic. See Nolting, *Trust to Tragedy*, pp. 25–27. British and French observers thought that Diem was hopeless and that the situation was getting worse. But British foreign secretary Lord Home thought there was no alternative. See *FRUS*, 1961–63, 1: 269. For Rostow's ideas on the problem, see ibid., pp. 256–57.

28. The paper is in *FRUS*, 1961–63, 1: 248–49.

29. Memorandum of a Discussion, July 28, 1961, ibid., pp. 252–56; task force report, ibid., pp. 250–51. See also Kinnard, *Certain Trumpet*, p. 95.

30. The letter is in *FRUS*, 1961–63, 1: 263–66. Nolting was instructed to press Diem on political reforms. See ibid., pp. 262–63.

31. NSAM-65, dated Aug. 11, 1961, is in *USVN*, book 11, pp. 241–44.

32. Ibid., pp. 245–46; *FRUS*, 1961–63, 1: 301–4.

33. Nolting's reaction is in *FRUS*, 1961–63, 1: 301–4; Jorden's report, Sept. 27, 1961, ibid., pp. 310–14. For Rostow's suggestions, see ibid., pp. 314–15.

34. For Nolting's telegram and the response from Washington, see ibid., p. 316.

35. See the speech by Ton Duc Thang in *Third National Congress*, 3: 24–26.

36. The documents of the congress are in *Third National Congress*. Vo Nguyen Giap's speech is in vol. 1, p. 54, Le Duan's, ibid., p. 62.

37. *Cuoc Khang Chien*, pp. 74–75. The COSVN had originally been set up during the Franco-Vietminh conflict but had been replaced by regional committees after the Geneva Accords.

38. Le Duan, *Thu Vao Nam*, letters of Feb. and Apr. 1961, pp. 31–50. An abbreviated English-language version of the book entitled *Letters to the South* was published by the Foreign Languages Publishing House in Hanoi in 1986.

39. Memorandum from the Under SS to SS, Oct. 5, 1961, in *FRUS*, 1961–63, 1: 322–25. The report by the Bureau of Intelligence and Research (INR) is in *USVN*, book 11, pp. 258–90.

40. Telegram from the Consulate General in Switzerland to DOS, Oct. 13, 1961, in *FRUS*, 1961–63, 1: 363–64; ibid., pp. 327, 369.

41. *USVN*, book 11, pp. 297–99. The JCS said that if Plan 5 was politically unacceptable, they would propose an interim course of action to provide for the defense of Vietnam but not of Thailand and Laos. See *FRUS*, 1961–63, 1: 330–32. For an NIE entitled "Probable Communist Reaction to Certain SEATO Undertakings in Vietnam," see *USVN*, book 11, pp. 313–21.

42. Kinnard, *Certain Trumpet*, p. 97; Memorandum for the Record by Deputy SD (Gilpatric), Oct. 11, 1961, in *FRUS*, 1961–63, 1: 343–44. The final instructions are in Taylor, *Swords and Plowshares*, p. 225. For State Department ideas, see *FRUS*, 1961–63, 1: 337–42.

43. For Minh's complaints, see *FRUS*, 1961–63, 1: 395–98; McGarr's comments, ibid., pp. 347–59; Mendenhall's estimate, ibid., pp. 416–17.

44. *USVN*, book 11, pp. 331–42; Taylor, *Swords and Plowshares*, pp. 242–44. Kahin, *Intervention*, p. 136, charges that Taylor appeared unaware of the character of the Diem regime.

45. The memo is in *FRUS*, 1961–63, 1: 408–11. An earlier one was apparently sent to Durbrow in April. See ibid., p. 407.

46. Memorandum from Senator Mansfield to the President, Nov. 2, 1961, in *FRUS*, 1961–63, 1: 467–70; Rusk, *As I Saw It*, p. 464.

47. Paper Prepared by the Ambassador to India (Galbraith), Nov. 3, 1961, in *FRUS*, 1961–63, 1: 474–76. For a related proposal, see Bowles, *Promises to Keep*, p. 409.

48. Taylor's report with appendixes is in *FRUS*, 1961–63, 1: 477–532.

49. Note by SD (McNamara), Nov. 6, 1961, ibid., pp. 543–44; Memo by McNamara, Nov. 5, 1961, ibid., pp. 538–40; Memorandum for the Record, Nov. 6, 1961, ibid., pp. 532–35. According to George Ball, after the meeting he told President Kennedy that he felt that to commit U.S. forces in Vietnam would be a "tragic error." See Ball, *Past Has Another Pattern*, pp. 366–67. The presidential order to limit distribution of the Taylor report caused a number of administration officials to tender their resignations on the

grounds that it made it impossible for them to carry out their duties (letter from Hilsman, May 21, 1992).

50. For the draft, see *FRUS*, 1961–63, 1: 550–52. Bundy manuscript, chap. 4, pp. 24–25. In his memoirs, Dean Rusk says that he did not oppose the introduction of U.S. troops into South Vietnam at that time but felt that careful study was needed before a decision (*As I Saw It*, p. 432).

51. The State Department draft is in *FRUS*, 1961–63, 1: 561–66. The Rusk-McNamara meeting is reported in ibid., pp. 572–73. Also see Bundy manuscript, chap. 4, p. 28.

52. *USVN*, book 11, pp. 359–67.

53. Ball, *Past Has Another Pattern*, p. 366; Gibbons, *U.S. Government and the Vietnam War*, 2: pp. 80–84.

54. The memorandum of conversation of the November 11 meeting is in *FRUS*, 1961–63, 1: 577–78. Also see Taylor, *Swords and Plowshares*, p. 248; Gelb and Betts, *Irony of Vietnam*, p. 77; and Gibbons, *U.S. Government and the Vietnam War*, 2: 89–90.

55. For the decision to convene a second meeting, see *FRUS*, 1961–63, 1: 588. Harriman's memo is on pp. 580–82.

56. Notes on NSC meeting, Nov. 15, 1961, in *FRUS*, 1961–63, 1: 607–10; NSAM-111, ibid., pp. 656–57.

57. For statistics on infiltration, see ibid., pp. 661–63. According to Rostow, about 70 percent were local recruits, 25 percent were South Vietnamese trained in the North, and 5 percent were northerners.

58. Galbraith's memo is in *USVN*, book 11, pp. 406–18. Rostow replied that Galbraith ignored the problem of infiltration. See *FRUS*, 1961–63, 1: 661–63.

59. Gelb and Betts, *Irony of Vietnam*, p. 77; Bundy manuscript, chap. 4, p. 34. Historian Arthur Schlesinger says Kennedy told him that once troops were introduced, it would be "like taking a drink. The effect wears off, and you have to take another" (*Thousand Days*, p. 547).

60. Nolting to DOS, Nov. 22, 1961, in *FRUS*, 1961–63, 1: 649–52.

61. Nolting's conversation with Diem is reported in ibid., pp. 666–68.

62. For contingency plans drawn up in Washington in case of a coup in Saigon, see ibid., pp. 683–87.

63. The Honolulu Conference is reported briefly in ibid., pp. 739–42.

64. Memorandum from SD (McNamara) to the Chairman of the JCS (Lemnitzer), Nov. 13, 1961, ibid., pp. 589–90; ibid., pp. 720–23. Nolting's views are in ibid., pp. 731–32. Also see ibid., 2: 36, 47, 70, 95, 111, 129, and 171. There was also some unhappiness in Washington at the appointment of General Harkins. McGeorge Bundy complained that he was too old. See ibid., 1: 766. We need the right man, he said, not just a convenient way of relieving General McGarr.

65. *USVN*, book 3, pt. 4.B.2. p. 8.

66. Thompson's plan is in *USVN*, book 11, pp. 345–58. The strategic hamlets differed from the "New Villages" in Malaya in that the former attempted to use existing hamlets but reconfigured them for defensive purposes. The New Villages consisted of Chinese nationals rounded up from the surrounding jungles or outside the towns who were placed in artificial communities where they began life anew (letter to author from Charles Cross, Mar. 31, 1992).

67. *USVN*, book 3, pp. 11–13.

68. Letter from Hilsman, May 21, 1992. Hilsman's plan is in *FRUS*, 1961–63, 2: 73–90. For his discussion of the report with the JCS, see ibid., pp. 113–16. Also see Hilsman, *To Move a Nation*, pp. 426, 438–39.

69. Hilsman cites a speech by General Earle C. Wheeler in November 1962 in which the latter insisted that the problem was essentially a military one. See Hilsman, *To Move a Nation*, p. 426. According to Hilsman, both his and Thompson's plans were bastardized by Ngo Dinh Nhu (letter from Hilsman, May 21, 1992).

70. For reservations on defoliants by Harriman and Murrow, see *FRUS*, 1961–63, 2: 163, 590, and 620–21. For Kennedy's skepticism, see pp. 367, 670. The issue came up periodically later in the Kennedy administration. See *FRUS*, 1961–63, vols. 3 and 4, passim.

71. Paper Prepared in the Department of Defense, n.d., in *FRUS*, 1961–63, 2: 387.

72. Ibid., p. 151.

73. For a reference, see ibid., pp. 279–80.

74. DOS to Nolting, Apr. 4, 1962, ibid., pp. 305–6, 323–24; Gibbons, *U.S. Government and the Vietnam War*, 2: 108.

75. *Cuoc Khang Chien*, p. 50; *Mot So Van Kien cua Dang ve Chong My, Cuu Nuoc*, 1: 136–58.

76. For a discussion, see Gibbons, *U.S. Government and the Vietnam War*, 2: 114; letter from Hilsman, May 21, 1992.

77. Hilsman, *To Move a Nation*, pp. 151–55.

78. Le Duan, *Thu Vao Nam*, letter of July 1962, pp. 51–69.

79. See *Duiker, Communist Road*, pp. 205–6.

80. Ambassador to India to the President, Apr. 4, 1962, in *FRUS*, 1961–63, 2: 297–300. He had talked to Kennedy about it on the first and the latter had encouraged him to put his ideas in writing. Gibbons, *U.S. Government and the Vietnam War*, 2: 119–20; Newman, *JFK and Vietnam*, p. 236.

81. Memorandum of Conversation between Kennedy and Harriman, Apr. 6, 1963, in *FRUS*, 1961–63, 2: 309; Memorandum from Williams to McNamara, Apr. 14, 1962, ibid., pp. 324–27.

82. Ibid., pp. 543–46. According to William H. Sullivan, one of Harriman's aides, "we hit a stone wall." See Gibbons, *U.S. Government and the Vietnam War*, 2: 121. According to Charles Cross, then a foreign service officer dealing in Laotian affairs, there was some casual interest among U.S. officials in the possibility of applying the Laotian model in South Vietnam if a noncommunist centrist of appropriate stature could be located. Such an individual, however, never appeared in Diem's Vietnam. In any case, Cross among others doubted that Hanoi would accept a coalition government in Saigon unless it could dominate it (letter from Cross, Mar. 31, 1992).

83. Rostow, *Diffusion of Power*, pp. 288–90; Hilsman, *To Move a Nation*, p. 153; Bundy manuscript, chap. 8, pp. 4–5. Charles Cross relates an anecdote from a meeting between Mikoyan and Harriman. Mikoyan raised the charge that Kuomintang troops operating in Burma were crossing over into northwestern Laos. Harriman denied the charge and then added, to Mikoyan's amusement, "Besides, Chiang Kai-shek doesn't do what we tell him to do any more than Mao Zedong does what you tell him to do" (letter from Cross, Mar. 31, 1992).

84. Rostow, *Diffusion of Power*, p. 290.

85. *USVN*, book 3, pt. 4.B.4, pp. 1–4; letter from Hilsman, May 21, 1992; Gibbons, *U.S. Government and the Vietnam War*, 2: 125; Newman, *JFK and Vietnam*, pp. 266–88.

86. Record of the Sixth Secretary of Defense Conference, July 23, 1962, in *FRUS*, 1961–63, 2: 548. MACV estimated that it would require one year to turn the responsibility over to ARVN, while Secretary McNamara remarked that a three-year estimate would be more realistic. An INR report echoed such optimistic comments in a report dated June 18, 1962, although it cautioned that much remained to be done. See *USVN*, book 12, pt. 4.B.4, pp. 469–80. On Harkins's plans for an offensive, see *FRUS*, 1961–63, 2: 788–90, and Hilsman, *To Move a Nation*, p. 464. Also see Bundy manuscript, chap. 8, pp. 18–19.

87. Letter from Harriman to Nolting, Oct. 12, 1962, in *FRUS*, 1961–63, 2: 693–96; Memorandum from Robert Johnson to Rostow, Oct. 16, 1962, ibid., pp. 703–7.

88. Report by Mansfield, Dec. 18, 1962, ibid., pp. 779–87.

89. Hilsman, *To Move a Nation*, pp. 463–65; Gibbons, *U.S. Government and the Vietnam War*, 2: 135.

90. *Cuoc Khang Chien*, p. 50.

91. Ibid., pp. 52–53.

92. Wheeler's trip is reported in *FRUS*, 1961–63, 3: 73–94. For comments on the battle by U.S. officials and the foreign press, see pp. 1–3. For Hilsman's view that Ap Bac was a "stunning defeat for the Government forces," see *To Move a Nation*, 447–49. The April NIE is in *USVN*, book 12, pt. 4.B.4, pp. 469–80.

93. O'Donnell, *Johnny, We Hardly Knew Ye*, p. 16; Charlton and Moncrieff, *Many Reasons Why*, p. 81; Newman, *JFK and Vietnam*, pp. 322–25.

94. Mecklin's comment is in *FRUS*, 1961–63, 3: 152–56. The NIE is in ibid., pp. 232–35.

95. Nolting, *Trust to Tragedy*, p. 104; *FRUS*, 1961–63, 3: 314. The contingency plan is in ibid., pp. 317–26. Nolting admits that local officials were partly at fault but says that the question of who instigated the riots is unclear (*Trust to Tragedy*, p. 106).

96. Trueheart to DOS, June 11, 1963, in *FRUS*, 1961–63, 3: 378–81.

97. On charges of CIA involvement, see Hammer, *Death in November*, p. 156.

98. Trueheart to DOS, June 25, 1963, in *FRUS*, 1961–63, 3: 414. There was discontent about Nolting's performance among some officials in Washington, who felt that stronger leadership was needed in Saigon. See the Hilsman-Forrestal report of January 1963, ibid., p. 61. Kennedy liked Nolting and felt that he had been generally effective as ambassador but recognized the need for a replacement. The INR report is in ibid., pp. 405–9.

99. The meeting of July 4 is in ibid., pp. 451–53, and *USVN*, book 12, pt. 2, pp. 526–28.

100. The NIE is in *USVN*, book 12, pt. 2, pp. 529–35, and *FRUS*, 1961–63, 3: 483–85. Nolting's response is in ibid., pp. 528–29. For charges that Nolting restricted critical commentary by his staff, see *FRUS*, 1961–63, 4: 382.

101. Nolting to DOS, Aug. 12, 1963, in *FRUS*, 1961–63, 3: 562–64.

102. DOS to Lodge, Aug. 24, 1963, ibid., pp. 628–29.

103. Ibid., pp. 634–35.

104. The meetings of August 26 and 27 are reported in ibid., pp. 638–41 and 661–65. Also see Rusk, *As I Saw It*, p. 437; Schlesinger, *Thousand Days*, p. 991; Hilsman, *To Move a Nation*, p. 498; Bundy manuscript, chap. 9, pp. 10–11. According to Roger Hilsman, at the Monday meeting, Kennedy polled everyone present and each agreed to accept the existing cable as amended by Ambassador Lodge (letter from Hilsman, May 21, 1992).

105. Memorandum of a Conversation, Aug. 31, 1963, in *FRUS*, 1961–63, 4: 69–74;

Pentagon Papers, 2: 741–43; Kattenburg, *Vietnam Trauma*, p. 120; Gibbons, *U.S. Government and the Vietnam War*, 2: 161.

106. The interview is in *FRUS*, 1961–63, 4: 93–95. In a draft version (ibid., p. 82), Kennedy said that the United States was willing to help "so long as it is wanted and can be effective." But it was "hard to see how we can continue this effort if the essential conditions for success were no longer present."

107. The September 6 meeting is reported in ibid., pp. 117–20.

108. Ibid., pp. 161–67, 169–71; Bundy manuscript, chap. 9, p. 15.

109. Lodge to DOS, Sept. 11, 1963, in *FRUS*, 1961–63, 4: 171–74.

110. There is no record available of this meeting. In attendance were Rusk, McCone, McNamara, Robert Kennedy, and Harriman. Lodge's response is in *FRUS*, 1961–63, 4: 258–59. For a discussion, see *USVN*, book 3, pt. 4.B.5, p. 29.

111. Ellen Hammer claims that Kennedy approved the trip as a means of convincing McNamara and other senior Pentagon officials that there was no alternative to a policy of stiff sanctions against the Diem regime. William P. Bundy denies the assertion and declares that the president had not made up his mind (letter from Bundy, Dec. 1992). Also see Hammer, *Death in November*, p. 212. In a personal message to Lodge, the president reassured the ambassador that any indication of comfort to Diem would be avoided. His purpose, he said, was to make s ɪre that the senior military advisers understood the situation on the spot. Whether such high-level visits achieved their purpose is another matter. As Charles Cross has pointed out, briefings for senior officials were carefully planned and the briefers followed the party line in selecting their statistics (letter from Cross, Mar. 31, 1992). For the president's letter to Lodge, see *FRUS*, 1961–63, 4: 256–57. Kennedy's instructions to Taylor and McNamara are on pp. 280–82. For Lodge's views, see p. 255.

112. *FRUS*, 1961–63, 4: 336–46; *Pentagon Papers*, 2: 751–66. McNamara recognized that the decision was a crucial one but still hoped that Diem could be saved. One factor that may have influenced his views was an interview with an unnamed scholar in Saigon. Report by McNamara, Sept. 26, 1963, in *FRUS*, 1961–63, 4: 293–95.

113. Lieutenant General Lucien Conein of the CIA had encountered General Tran Van Don at Tan Son Nhut airport on October 2, and the latter had requested a private meeting later that day, at which time he informed Conein that General Duong Van Minh wished to meet with him. The meeting with "Big" Minh took place on the fifth. Conein's account of the meeting at Tan Son Nhut is in *FRUS*, 1961–63, 4: 354–55. The report of the meeting between Minh and Conein on the fifth is in ibid., pp. 365–77. The cable to Lodge is on pp. 371–79. For a lengthy account of the alleged contacts between Hanoi and Saigon, see Maneli, *War of the Vanquished*, chap. 6. Although the reports may have been encouraged by the Saigon regime to arouse anxiety in Washington, William Bundy doubts that any U.S. officials took them seriously (letter from Bundy, Dec. 1992).

114. *FRUS*, 1961–63, 4: 437; *Pentagon Papers*, 2: 782.

115. Lodge to DOS, Oct. 28, 1963, in *FRUS*, 1961–63, 4: 449; Bundy to Lodge, Oct. 29, 1963, ibid., pp. 473–75; Lodge to DOS, Oct. 30, 1963, ibid., p. 488.

116. The cable to Saigon is in *FRUS*, 1961–63, 4: 500–502.

117. Ibid., p. 499; Hammer, *Death in November*, pp. 283–84.

118. Newman, *JFK and Vietnam*, pp. 438–39; Memorandum of Discussion at the Special Meeting on Vietnam, Nov. 20, 1963, in *FRUS*, 1961–63, 4: 608–24.

119. Hannah, *Key to Failure*, p. 91. According to Charles Cross, if there was indeed a "massive failure in logic," it was in the assumption that Hanoi's flagrant disregard of the Laos accords would engender world support for a strengthened U.S. presence in South Vietnam (letter from Cross, Mar. 31, 1992).

120. Hilsman, *To Move a Nation*, p. 459.

121. For a discussion of congressional and public attitudes toward Laos, see Gibbons, *U.S. Government and the Vietnam War*, 2: 29–30.

122. William Colby, then a senior CIA official in Saigon, cites NLF chairman Nguyen Huu Tho remarking that the overthrow of Diem was "a gift from Heaven for us." See Colby, *Lost Victory*, p. 158.

123. Rusk, *As I Saw It*, p. 441; Gelb and Betts, *Irony of Vietnam*, p. 93; Bundy manuscript, chap. 9, p. 15; Hilsman, *To Move a Nation*, pp. 536–37; letter from Hilsman, May 21, 1992.

124. Sorenson, *Kennedy*, p. 661; Reston, *Deadline*, pp. 291–94.

Chapter 9

1. According to a study by John Newman, other Johnson advisers were convinced that Lodge had given the new president a pessimistic assessment of the war. See Newman, *JFK and Vietnam*, pp. 442–43. In any case, Johnson lost no time in reminding his advisers of his views on the overthrow of Ngo Dinh Diem. See the minutes of his meeting with foreign policy advisers on December 1, 1964, in Meeting Notes File, Box 1, Johnson Papers.

2. Newman, *JFK and Vietnam*, pp. 444–46; see nn. 16 and 17 for citations. According to Newman, McGeorge Bundy told him that NSAM-273 had been strengthened because the new president "held stronger views on the war than Kennedy did." See Memorandum for the Record of a Meeting, Nov. 24, 1963, in *FRUS, 1961–63*, 4: 635–37. NSAM-273 is on pp. 637–40; *USVN*, book 3, pt. 4.C.1, p. 3. For Johnson's meeting with Henry Cabot Lodge, see Meeting Notes File, Box 1, Johnson Papers.

3. Harkins's report is in *USVN*, Book 3, pt. 4.C.1, p. 32. "No amount of military effort or capability," it said, "can compensate for poor politics. Therefore, although all the prospects of an improved military posture are good, the ultimate achievement of the established military goal depends primarily upon the quality of support achieved by the political leadership of Vietnam at all levels." The CIA report is cited in ibid., p. iii.

4. McNamara's report, Dec. 21, 1963, is cited in ibid., p. 19. Also see *FRUS, 1961–63*, 4: 732–35.

5. Lodge to DOS, in *FRUS, 1964–68*, 1: 53–55. Lodge was impressed with Khanh but said he did not know him well. See ibid., p. 39. A CIA report on the possibility of new leadership is in ibid., pp. 36–37. Kahin, *Intervention*, chap. 7. For the U.S. reaction to the coup, see *USVN*, book 3, pt 4.C.1, p. 30.

6. Excerpts from the press conference are in *FRUS, 1964–68*, 1: 56. Comments by the JCS are in *USVN*, book 3, pt. 4.C.1, pp. 37–40.

7. *USVN*, book 3, pt. 4.C.1, p. 43. For the military situation at the time, see the Special NIE dated February 12, 1964, in *FRUS, 1964–68*, 1: 71–72.

8. *USVN*, book 3, pt. 4.C.1, pp. 47–48. NSC Meetings File, Box 1, Johnson Papers, has an account of the meeting of March 17. William Bundy recalls that the administration

was impressed with Nguyen Khanh at that time and more optimistic about the overall situation in the RVN. See Bundy manuscript, chap. 12, p. 26.

9. *USVN*, book 3, pt. 4.C.1, pp. 54–55; *FRUS*, 1964–68, 1: 149–50.

10. *USVN*, book 3, pt. 4.C.1, pp. 56–59.

11. Sources in Hanoi today frequently voice respect for Diem because of his nationalist credentials while voicing scorn for his successors as puppets of the Americans and the French.

12. *Nhung Su Kien Lich Su Dang*, 3: 275–77.

13. The plenum resolution is reproduced in English translation in *VDRN*, document 96. The series was issued by the U.S. Information Service in Saigon.

14. Ibid., document 98, "The World Situation and Our International Mission."

15. The statistics are from an infiltration study reproduced in *FRUS*, 1964–68, 1: 871–72.

16. Thies, *When Governments Collide*, pp. 21–22; *USVN*, book 3, pt. 4.C.2, pp. 2, 8.

17. Halberstam, *The Best and the Brightest*, pp. 435–36. For skepticism in the State Department see Thies, *When Governments Collide*, pp. 28–29.

18. Hannah, *Key to Failure*, p. 121.

19. For a discussion, see Gibbons, *U.S. Government and the Vietnam War*, 2: 244–45. The Seaborn report is in the National Security File, Vietnam Country File, LBJ Library.

20. *USVN*, book 3, pt. 4.C.1, pp. 76–77; Gibbons, *U.S. Government and the Vietnam War*, 2: 252–54; Lodge to DOS, May 14, 1964, in *FRUS*, 1964–68, 1: 322.

21. The draft memo from McGeorge Bundy is in *FRUS*, 1964–68, 1: 374–75. Brown and Zasloff, *Apprentice Revolutionaries*, pp. 92–93.

22. *USVN*, book 3, pt. 4.C.2, pp. 29, 36–37. The minutes of the Honolulu meeting are in *FRUS*, 1964–68, 1: 412–34.

23. *USVN*, book 3, pt. 4.C.2, p. 36; *FRUS*, 1964–68, 1: 484–87; Lodge's letter to LBJ, ibid., pp. 459–61.

24. Bundy manuscript, chap. 13, pp. 28–31.

25. NSAM-308 is in *FRUS*, 1964–68, 1: 523.

26. Meeting of the National Security Council, Aug. 4, 1964, in *FRUS*, 1964–68, 1: 611–12; Letter from William P. Bundy, Dec. 1992.

27. Senator William Fulbright, who later became a critic of the administration's Vietnam policies, took the position that the resolution was necessary and that the president could be trusted to use his authority wisely. For congressional reaction, see Gibbons, *U.S. Government and the Vietnam War*, 2: 322, 326–42.

28. Turley, *Second Indochina War*, p. 61.

29. *Nhung Su Kien*, 3: 309–12.

30. The incident, and the White House reaction to it, are discussed in Gibbons, *U.S. Government and the Vietnam War*, 2: 355–57. Also see Memorandum by McGeorge Bundy, Sept. 20, 1964, in *FRUS*, 1964–68, 1: 778–81.

31. *USVN*, book 4, pt. 4.C.2(b), p. 20. The memo is in *Pentagon Papers*, 3: 524–29.

32. See the Memorandum on the Situation in South Vietnam, June 13, 1964, in *FRUS*, 1964–68, 1: 500–507; Taylor to DOS, Aug. 25, 1964, ibid., pp. 703–4; *USVN*, book 3, pt. 4.C.1, pp. 95–96.

33. Taylor to DOS, Sept. 6, 1964, in *FRUS*, 1964–68, 1: 733–36.

34. The Bundy memo is in Tab A, ibid., pp. 747–49. *Pentagon Papers*, 3: document 191,

pp. 561–62; Bundy manuscript, chap. 20, pp. 9–10. The September 7 meeting is reported in *USVN*, book 4, pt. 4.C.2(b), pp. 25–26. Also see *USVN*, book 3, pt. 4.C.1, p. 97.

35. *USVN*, book 4, pt. 4.C.2(b), pp. 34–35; *FRUS*, 1964–68, 1: 758–60.

36. *USVN*, book 4, pt. 4.C.2(b), p. 25; Rusk, *As I Saw It*, p. 447; Bundy manuscript, chap. 20, p. 11.

37. See the editorial note in *FRUS*, 1964–68, 1: 764.

38. Taylor's cable is in *Pentagon Papers*, 3: document 210, pp. 583–84.

39. Ball's memo is in the *Atlantic* 230 (July 1972): 35–48. The Special NIE, dated Oct. 1, 1964, is in *FRUS*, 1964–68, 1: 806–11.

40. For a DRV report on the attack on Bien Hoa, see *Nhung Su Kien*, 3: 315. The recommendation of the JCS is in *USVN*, book 4, pt. 4.C.2(b), p. 4.

41. *USVN*, book 4, pt. 4.C.2(c), pp. 13–14; *Pentagon Papers*, 3: 588–90.

42. For the comments by the JCS, see *Pentagon Papers*, 3: document 228, pp. 621–28. For comments by William Bundy and Michael Forrestal, see ibid., documents 218 and 219.

43. See the analysis in *USVN*, book 4, pt. 4.C.2(c), pp. 16–18. Also see NSF Country File: Vietnam, Box 45, Johnson Papers.

44. Meeting Notes File, Box 1, Meeting of Nov. 24, 1964; Box 45, Memo of Executive Committee Meeting, Nov. 24, 1964, Johnson Papers. *USVN*, book 4, pt. 4.C.2(c), pp. 31–37.

45. *Pentagon Papers*, 3: document 244, pp. 674–76.

46. Ibid., document 245.

47. NSF Meeting: Notes File, Box 1, Johnson Papers. Also see *Pentagon Papers*, 3: 249–51; *FRUS*, 1964–68, 1: 965–68. According to my notes from the LBJ Library, the correct phrase was "so when tell Wheeler to slap we can take slap back."

48. *USVN*, book 3, pt. 4.C.2, pp. 100–102.

49. *Pentagon Papers*, 3: 262. Hanoi took credit for the attack on the Brink's Hotel. See *Nhung Su Kien*, 3: 319. According to William P. Bundy, the real reason was that the president was in Texas for the Christmas holidays and did not want to make a decision in those circumstances (letter from Bundy, Dec. 1992).

50. Bundy manuscript, chap. 20, p. 16; *Pentagon Papers*, 3: 263. For Mansfield's letter to Johnson, see Gibbons, *U.S. Government and the Vietnam War*, 2: 377–79.

51. Taylor, *Swords and Plowshares*, p. 333; Kearns, *Johnson*, pp. 251–52; Halberstam, *The Best and the Brightest*, p. 507.

52. *Pentagon Papers*, 3: 684–85.

53. Ibid., p. 686.

54. Ibid., pp. 686–87.

55. Biographical information on Nguyen Chi Thanh is in Boudarel, *Cent fleurs*, pp. 98–99. For Le Duan's comment, see *Thu Vao Nam*, p. 141.

56. *Nhung Su Kien*, 3: 309–12.

57. Duiker, *Communist Road*, p. 232, n. 56, has citations.

58. *Thu Vao Nam*, letter to Xuan [Nguyen Chi Thanh], Feb. 1965.

59. Meeting Notes File, Box 1, Johnson Papers.

60. *Pentagon Papers*, 3: 304.

61. Ibid., pp. 309–15, has the memo.

62. Notes of the NSC meeting are in Meeting Notes File, Box 1, Johnson Papers.

George Ball says that Humphrey was excluded from foreign policy discussions for months because of his comments.

63. *USVN*, book 4, pt. 4.C.3, p. 94; Ball, *Past Has Another Pattern*, p. 391.

64. *USVN*, book 4, pt. 4.C.3, pp. 66–67.

65. *USVN*, book 4, pt. 4.C.4, pp. 6–7.

66. Letter to Anh Xuan, Feb. 1965, in *Thu Vao Nam*; Bundy manuscript, chap. 22, p. 36. According to Bundy, chap. 25, p. 3, Washington now knew that PAVN regiments began coming south after December 1964.

67. *Mot So*, pp. 211–27.

68. Bundy manuscript, chap. 21, pp. 13–14.

69. Bui Diem, *Jaws of History*, p. 130.

70. *USVN*, book 4, pt. 4.C.4, pp. 57–58.

71. Gibbons, *U.S. Government and the Vietnam War*, 3: 177, n. 24.

72. Ibid., p. 179, citing from the Bundy memo. For McNaughton's memo, see *Pentagon Papers*, 3: 694–702.

73. *Pentagon Papers*, 3: 702–3.

74. Berman, *Planning a Tragedy*, p. 57.

75. Clifford, *Counsel to the President*, pp. 406–7; Gelb and Betts, *Irony of Vietnam*, p. 121; Halberstam, *The Best and the Brightest*, p. 684; Bui Diem, *Jaws of History*, p. 138.

76. Herring, *Secret History*, pp. 39, 42.

77. Ball reports meeting with Lyndon Johnson in *Past Has Another Pattern*, pp. 391–93. For a comment, see Bundy manuscript, chap. 23, pp. 15–16.

78. See the discussion in the Bundy manuscript, chap. 23, pp. 25–29, and Gibbons, *U.S. Government and the Vietnam War*, 3: 217–18.

79. Porter, *A Peace Denied*, p. 28.

80. Le Duan, *Thu Vao Nam*, letter of May 1965; Herring, *Secret Diplomacy*, pp. 42–44; Bundy manuscript, chap. 24. *USVN*, book 4, pt. 4.C.3, p. 128.

81. *USVN*, book 4, pt. 4.C.5, p. 64. Also see *USVN*, book 3, pt. 4.C.1, p. 116.

82. *USVN*, book 4, pt. 4.C.3, p. 100; Bui Diem, *Jaws of History*, p. 139.

83. NSC Meetings File, vol. 3, Tab 34, June 11, 1965, Vietnam; NSC Country File, Box 75, Letter of May 17, 1965, Johnson Papers.

84. Ball, *Past Has Another Pattern*, pp. 393–96. For a brief account of the meeting, see VanDeMark, *Into the Quagmire*, pp. 166–67.

85. Quoted in Gibbons, *U.S. Government and the Vietnam War*, 3: 329–32.

86. Bundy manuscript, chap. 27, passim. Gibbons, *U.S. Government and the Vietnam War*, 3: 340–42. Ball wrote a second memo toning down the recommendations contained in the first one. For a slightly garbled version, see *Pentagon Papers*, 4: 615–19.

87. Ike's conversation with Johnson is reported in Gibbons, *U.S. Government and the Vietnam War*, 3: 343–44. See this source for a useful discussion of the meeting of July 2. Also see Bundy manuscript, chap. 27, pp. 13–14. He says the meeting with the senior advisers was so short that it made him uneasy. For Rusk's views, see *As I Saw It*, pp. 450–51.

88. Cooper, *Lost Crusade*, p. 338.

89. Excerpts of McNamara's report are in the *Pentagon Papers*, 4: 297–99, 619–22; NSC File, NSC History, Box 40, Tab 396, Johnson Papers.

90. LBJ Meeting Notes File, Box 1, meeting with congressional leaders, meetings of

July 21–27, 1965, Johnson Papers; *Pentagon Papers*, 4: . 299; Bundy manuscript, chap. 27, pp. 31–33; Ball, *Past Has Another Pattern*, pp. 399–403; VanDeMark, *Into the Quagmire*, pp. 184–207.

91. LBJ Meeting Notes File, Box 1, Meetings of July 21–27, 1965; Box 75, Presidential News Conference of July 28, 1965, "Why we are in Vietnam," Johnson Papers.

92. Dean Rusk, Oral History, July 28, 1969, Johnson Library.

93. NSF (Poland) Country File, Box 202, citing State Department Airgram from American Embassy in Warsaw, Apr. 26, 1965, Johnson Papers.

94. Ibid., State Department Airgram from American Embassy in Warsaw, July 5, 1965.

95. Duiker, *China and Vietnam*, p. 49.

96. Working Paper on North Viet-Nam's Role in the War in South Viet-Nam (Washington, D.C., 1968), appendix item 302.

97. Le Duan, *Thu Vao Nam*, p. 136.

98. For an account of the battle, see Turley, *Second Indochina War*, p. 76.

99. Quoted in Duiker, *China and Vietnam*, pp. 49–50.

100. *Cuoc Khang Chien*, pp. 83–84. Le Duan, *Thu Vao Nam*, letter of Nov. 1965, p. 135.

101. For two accounts of the Battle of Ia Drang Valley, see Herring, "The 1st Cavalry and the Ia Drang Valley," and Moore and Galloway, *We Were Soldiers Once.*

102. *Cuoc Khang Chien*, p. 85. For excerpts of the resolution, see *Mot So* 2: 1–34.

103. Bundy manuscript, chap. 28, pp. 1–18.

104. Ball, *Past Has Another Pattern*, p. 401; NSC Meetings File, Vol. 3, Tab 35, July 27, 1965, Johnson Papers.

105. For public opinion surveys taken at the time, see Gibbons, *U.S. Government and the Vietnam War*, 3: 351–53.

106. Dean Rusk was optimistic at the meeting of July 21 and did not predict heavy casualties unless China decided to enter the conflict. See Meeting Notes File, Box 1, Meeting of July 21, 1965, Johnson Papers.

Chapter 10

1. For a survey of the literature, see Podhoretz, *Why We Were in Vietnam*. Podhoretz felt that there were moral reasons for U.S. involvement in the war.

2. *New York Times*, Jan. 17, 1991.

3. See Norman A. Graebner, "Containment in Asia: The Road to Vietnam," in Osborn, et al., eds., *Democracy, Strategy, and Vietnam*, p. 13.

4. Dean Rusk Oral History, July 28, 1969, Johnson Library.

5. The debate over whether to construct a barrier against infiltration from the North is chronicled in *USVN*, Book 5, pt. 4.C.6, pp. 65–67.

6. According to a recent comment by Walt W. Rostow, Johnson's fear of Chinese intervention made him "too cautious" in Vietnam. See *New York Times*, Jan. 23, 1991, p. 8.

7. Dean Rusk Oral History, Jan. 2, 1970, Johnson Library.

8. Kahin, *Intervention*, p. 33.

9. Hatcher, *Suicide of an Elite*, p. 3.

10. Ibid., p. 286.

11. *New York Times*, Jan. 17, 1991.

12. It has been said that this approach limits the United States to the "fun wars." The point is not that the United States must only fight easy wars, but it must not fight difficult wars unless it knows what it is fighting for.

13. These comments are provoked in part by my experience in teaching college courses on the Vietnam War for the last two decades. When surveyed at key points in the course about their own views on the war, students in recent years almost invariably support the U.S. commitment to Vietnam down to the mid-1960's. After that time they begin to divide into the traditional dichotomy of hawks and doves. Most such students have no firm views on the war or its lessons and are simply curious about why it became such a major factor in modern American life. It is a sobering experience.

Bibliography

Primary Sources: United States, Great Britain, and France

PUBLISHED DOCUMENTS

CIA Research Reports, 1946–76 (Vietnam and Southeast Asia)
Department of State Bulletin
Joint Chiefs of Staff, Records for the Far East, 1946–1953
National Security Council, Documents, 1947–77
Pentagon Papers (Gravel Edition). Boston: Beacon Press, 1971.
Public Papers of the Presidents of the United States: Dwight D. Eisenhower, 1953, 1954.
    Washington, D.C.: U.S. Government Printing Office. 1960.
U.S. Department of State. *Foreign Relations of the United States, 1944–64.*
United States Senate, Committee on Foreign Relations. "The United States and Vietnam,
    1944–1947," Staff Study no. 2 (April 3, 1972).
United States–Vietnam Relations, 1945–1967 (Washington, D.C.: U.S. Government Print-
    ing Office, 1971).
U.S. Department of State. *Working Paper on North Viet-Nam's Role in South Viet-Nam.*
    Washington, D.C.: U.S. Government Printing Office, 1968.

UNPUBLISHED MATERIALS

Dean Acheson Papers, Truman Library
McGeorge Bundy Papers, Johnson Library
William P. Bundy Papers, Johnson Library
George M. Elsey Papers, Truman Library
James P. Hendrick Papers, Truman Library
Lyndon B. Johnson Papers, Johnson Library
John F. Melby Papers, Truman Library
Harry S. Truman Papers, Truman Library

U.S. Department of State: Central Files (Indochina), 1945–54, Record Group 59, National Archives

U.S. Department of State: Central Files (Indochina), 1954–59, Record Group 59, National Archives

ORAL HISTORIES

Ball, George, Johnson Library

Chang Fa-k'uei, Columbia University Oral History Project

Clifford, Clark, Truman Library

Rostow, Walt W., Johnson Library

Rusk, Dean, Johnson Library

MEMOIRS AND OFFICIAL HISTORIES

Acheson, Dean. *Present at the Creation: My Years in the State Department.* New York: Norton, 1974.

Adams, Sherman. *Firsthand Report: The Story of the Eisenhower Administration.* New York: Harper & Row, 1961.

Allison, John M. *Ambassador from the Prairie.* Boston: Houghton Mifflin, 1972.

Ball, George. *The Past Has Another Pattern: Memoirs.* New York: Norton, 1982.

Bao Dai. *Le Dragon d'Annam.* Paris: Plon, 1980.

Bidault, Georges. *Resistance: The Political Biography of Georges Bidault.* New York: Praeger, 1967.

Bowles, Chester. *Promises to Keep: My Years in Public Life, 1941–1969.* New York: Harper & Row, 1971.

Clifford, Clark M., with Richard Holbrooke. *Counsel to the President: A Memoir.* New York: Random House, 1991.

Colby, William, with James McCargar. *Lost Victory: A Firsthand Account of America's Sixteen-Year Involvement in Vietnam.* Chicago: Contemporary Books, 1989.

Collins, J. Lawton. *Lightning Joe: An Autobiography.* Baton Rouge: Louisiana State University Press, 1979.

de Gaulle, Charles. *The War Memoirs of Charles de Gaulle (1944–1946).* Vol. 3: *Salvation.* Translated by Richard Howard. New York: Simon & Schuster, 1960.

Eden, Anthony. *Full Circle: The Memoirs of Anthony Eden.* Boston: Houghton Mifflin, 1960.

Eisenhower, Dwight D. *Mandate for Change, 1953–1956.* Garden City, N.Y.: Doubleday, 1963.

Gettleman, Marvin, ed. *Vietnam: History, Documents, and Opinions on a Major World Crisis.* New York: Fawcett, 1965.

Hull, Cordell. *The Memoirs of Cordell Hull.* 2 vols. New York: Macmillan, 1949.

Johnson, U. Alexis. *The Right Hand of Power: The Memoirs of an American Diplomat.* Englewood Cliffs, N.J.: Prentice-Hall, 1984.

Khrushchev, Nikita. *Khrushchev Remembers.* New York: Bantam, 1971.

Lansdale, Edward G. *In the Midst of Wars.* New York: Harper & Row, 1972.

Mendès-France, Pierre. *Œuvres complètes.* Vol. 3. Paris: Gallimard, 1986.

Nixon, Richard M. *RN: The Memoirs of Richard Nixon.* New York: Grosset & Dunlap, 1978.

Nolting, Frederick. *From Trust to Tragedy: The Political Memoirs of Frederick Nolting, Kennedy's Ambassador to Diem's Vietnam.* New York: Praeger, 1989.

Radford, Arthur W. *From Pearl Harbor to Vietnam: The Memoirs of Admiral Arthur W. Radford.* Stanford: Hoover Institution Press, 1980.

Reston, James. *Deadline: A Memoir.* New York: Random House, 1991.

Rusk, Dean, as told to Richard Rusk. *As I Saw It.* New York: W. W. Norton, 1990.

Truman, Harry S. *Memoirs.* 2 vols. Garden City, N.Y.: Doubleday, 1955–56.

Westmoreland, General William C. *A Soldier Reports.* Garden City, N.Y.: Doubleday, 1976.

U.S. Department of Defense. *A History of the Joint Chiefs of Staff: The Joint Chiefs of Staff and the War in Vietnam.* Vol. 1. Wilmington, Del.: Michael Glazier, 1982.

Primary Sources: Vietnam

UNPUBLISHED MATERIALS

Catalog of Viet Cong Documents (Pike Documents, Series II), microfilm held at Cornell University Library, February 1969.

Communist Vietnamese Publications. Microfilm series edited by the Library of Congress, Washington, D.C.

Documents of the National Liberation Front for South Vietnam (Pike Documents, Series I), microfilm series held at the Center for International Studies, Chicago, Illinois, 1967.

PUBLISHED MATERIALS

Cuoc Khang Chien Chong My Cuu Nuoc 1954–1975: Nhung Su Kien Quan Su (The anti-U.S. war for national salvation, 1954: Military events). Hanoi: Nhan Dan, 1980.

Cuoc Khang Chien Than Thanh cua Nhan Dan Viet Nam (The sacred war of the Vietnamese people). 4 vols. Hanoi: Su That, 1960.

Ho Chi Minh. *Toan Tap* (Collected works). 10 vols. Hanoi, 1980–89.

———. *Selected Writings.* Hanoi: Foreign Languages Press, 1977.

Hoang Tung and Duc Vuong. *Dong Chi Truong Chinh* (Comrade Truong Chinh). Vol. 1. Hanoi: Su That, 1990.

Hoang Van Hoan. *A Drop in the Ocean: Hoang Van Hoan's Revolutionary Reminiscences.* Beijing: Foreign Languages Press, 1988.

Le Duan. *Thu Vao Nam* (Letters to the South). Hanoi: Su That, 1986.

Lich Su Dang Cong San Viet Nam (A history of the Vietnamese Communist Party). Vol. 1. Hanoi: Su That, 1984.

Lich Su Dang Cong San Viet Nam: Trich Van Kien Dang (A history of the Vietnamese Communist Party: Selected documents). 3 vols. Hanoi: Su That, 1979.

Lich Su Quan Doi Nhan Dan Viet Nam (A history of the People's Army of Vietnam). Vol. 1. Hanoi: Quan Doi Nhan Dan, 1974.

McGarvey, Patrick, ed. *Visions of Victory: Selected Vietnamese Communist Military Writings, 1964–1968.* Stanford: Hoover Institution Press, 1969.

Mot So Van Kien cua Dang ve Chong My, Cuu Nuoc (A collection of documents on the anti-U.S. national salvation struggle). 3 vols. Hanoi, 1985.

"Party Account of the Situation in the Nam Bo Region of South Vietnam from 1954–1960." Manuscript, n.d. Copy in author's possession.

Third National Congress of the Vietnam Workers' Party. 3 vols. Hanoi, 1960.

Van Kien Dang, 1930–1945 (Party documents, 1930–1945). 3 vols. Hanoi: Ban Nghien Cuu Lich Su Trung Uong Xuat Ban 1977–78.

Van Kien Dang, 1945–1954 (Party documents, 1945–1954). 4 vols. Hanoi: Ban Nghien Cuu Lich Su Trung Uong Xuat Ban, 1979–80.

Van Kien Dang ve Khang Chien Chong Thuc Dan Phap (Party documents on the struggle against the French colonialists). Vol. 2. Hanoi, 1988.

Van Kien Toan Quoc Dai Bieu Dai Hoi Lan Thu Hai cua Dang (Documents of the Second National Congress of the Party). Hanoi, 1951.

Vietnam Documents and Research Notes (Saigon: U.S. Mission in Vietnam, n.d.).

Secondary Sources: Books, Articles, and Monographs

Ambrose, Stephen E. *Eisenhower.* 2 vols. New York: Simon & Schuster, 1983–84.

Anderson, David L. *Trapped by Success: The Eisenhower Administration and Vietnam, 1953–1961.* New York: Columbia University Press, 1991.

Berman, Larry. *Lyndon Johnson's War.* New York: Norton, 1989.

———. *Planning a Tragedy.* New York: Norton, 1982.

Billings-Yun, Melanie. *Decision Against War: Eisenhower and Dien Bien Phu, 1954.* New York: Columbia University Press, 1988.

Blum, Robert M. *Drawing the Line: The Origins of the American Containment Policy in Asia.* New York: Norton, 1982.

Boudarel, Georges, et al. *La Bureaucratie au Vietnam.* Paris: L'Harmattan, 1983.

———. *Cent fleurs écloses dans la nuit du Vietnam.* Paris: Jacques Bertoin, 1991.

———. "Comment Giap a failli perdre la bataille de Dien Bien Phu." *Le Nouvel Observateur,* Apr. 8, 1983.

Brown, MacAlister, and Joseph J. Zasloff. *Apprentice Revolutionaries: The Communist Movement in Laos, 1930–1985.* Stanford: Hoover Institution Press, 1986.

Bui Diem, with David Chanoff. *In the Jaws of History.* Boston: Houghton Mifflin, 1987.

Bullock, Allen. *Ernest Bevin: Foreign Secretary, 1945–1951.* New York: Norton, 1983.

Buszynski, Leszek. *SEATO: The Failure of an Alliance Strategy.* Singapore: Singapore University Press, 1983.

Cable, James. *The Geneva Conference of 1954 in Indochina.* New York: St. Martin's Press, 1986.

Cameron, Allan W., ed. *Viet-Nam Crisis: A Documentary History.* Ithaca: Cornell University Press, 1971.

Charlton, Michael, and Anthony Moncrieff. *Many Reasons Why: The American Involvement in Vietnam.* New York: Hill & Wang, 1978.

Chen, King C. *Vietnam and China, 1938–1954.* Princeton: Princeton University Press, 1969.

Cook, Megan. *The Constitutionalist Party in Cochin China: The Years of Decline, 1930–1942.* Monash Papers on Southeast Asia, no. 6. Clayton, Australia, 1977.

Cooper, Chester L. *The Lost Crusade: America in Vietnam.* Greenwich: Fawcett, 1972.

Dacy, Douglas C. *Foreign Aid, War, and Economic Development: South Vietnam, 1955–1975.* Cambridge: Cambridge University Press, 1986.

Deibel, Terry L., and John Lewis Gaddis. *Containment: Concept and Policy.* Washington, D.C.: National Defense University Press, 1986.

Devillers, Phillipe. *Histoire du Vietnam, 1940–1952.* Paris: Editions du Seuil, 1952.

Devillers, Phillipe, and Jean Lacouture. *La Fin d'une guerre.* Paris: Editions du Seuil, 1960.

Dommen, Arthur J. *Conflict in Laos: The Politics of Neutralization.* New York: Praeger, 1967.

Drachman, Edward R. *United States Diplomacy Toward Vietnam, 1940–1945.* Cranbury, N.J.: Fairleigh Dickinson Press, 1970.

Duiker, William J. *China and Vietnam: The Roots of Conflict.* Berkeley: Institute of East Asian Studies, 1987.

——. *The Communist Road to Power in Vietnam.* Boulder: Westview Press, 1981.

——. *The Rise of Nationalism in Vietnam, 1900–1941.* Ithaca: Cornell University Press, 1976.

——. *Vietnam Since the Fall of Saigon.* Updated ed. Athens: Ohio University Press, 1989.

Duncan, W. Raymond, ed. *Soviet Policy in Developing Countries.* New York: Wiley, 1970.

Dunn, Peter. *The First Vietnam War.* New York: St. Martin's Press, 1985.

Ely, Paul. *L'Indochine dans la Tourmente.* Paris: Plon, 1954.

Emerson, Rupert. *Representative Government in Southeast Asia.* Cambridge, Mass.: Harvard University Press, 1955.

Fall, Bernard B. *Street Without Joy.* Harrisburg: Stackpole Press, 1961.

——. *Vietnam Witness, 1953–1966.* New York: Praeger, 1966.

——, ed. *Ho Chi Minh on Revolution: Selected Writings, 1920–1966.* New York: Signet, 1966.

Fitzgerald, Frances. *Fire in the Lake.* New York: Vintage, 1972.

Friend, Theodore. *Between Two Empires: The Ordeal of the Philippines, 1929–1946.* New Haven: Yale University Press, 1965.

Gaddis, John Lewis. *Strategies of Containment.* Oxford: Oxford University Press, 1982.

Gelb, Leslie H., and Richard K. Betts. *The Irony of Vietnam: The System Worked.* Washington, D.C.: Brookings Institution, 1979.

Gibbons, William Conrad. *The U.S. Government and the Vietnam War: Executive and Legislative Roles and Relationships.* Vols. 1–3. Princeton: Princeton University Press, 1986–89.

Goodman, Allan. *The Lost Peace.* Stanford: Hoover Institution Press, 1978.

Gordon, Bernard. *Toward Disengagement in Asia: A Strategy for American Foreign Policy.* Englewood Cliffs, N.J.: Prentice-Hall, 1969.

Graebner, Norman A., ed. *Cold War Diplomacy.* Rev. ed. New York: Van Nostrand, 1977.

Greenstein, Fred I., and Richard H. Immerman. "What Did Eisenhower Tell Kennedy About Indochina? The Politics of Misperception." *Journal of American History* 79 (Sept. 1992): 568–87.

Gurtov, Melvin. *The First Vietnam Crisis: Chinese Communist Strategy and United States Involvement, 1953–1954.* New York: Columbia University Press, 1967.

Halberstam, David. *The Best and the Brightest.* New York: Random House, 1972.

——. *The Making of a Quagmire.* New York: Random House, 1964.

Hammer, Ellen J. *A Death in November: America in Vietnam, 1963*. New York: Oxford University Press, 1987.

———. *The Struggle for Indochina, 1940–1955*. Stanford: Stanford University Press, 1954.

Hannah, Norman B. *The Key to Failure: Laos and the Vietnam War*. Lanham, Md.: Madison Books, 1987.

Harrison, James Pinckney. *The Endless War: Fifty Years of Struggle in Vietnam*. London: Free Press, 1982.

Hatcher, Patrick Lloyd. *The Suicide of an Elite: American Internationalists and Vietnam*. Stanford: Stanford University Press, 1990.

Herring, George C. *America's Longest War: The United States and Vietnam, 1950–1975*. New York: Knopf, 1986.

———. "The 1st Cavalry and the Ia Drang Valley, 18 October–24 November 1965." In Charles E. Heller and William A. Stofft, *America's First Battles, 1776–1965*. Lawrence: University Press of Kansas, 1986.

———, ed. *Secret History of the Vietnam War: The Negotiating Volumes of the Pentagon Papers*. Austin: University of Texas Press, 1983.

Herring, George C., and Richard H. Immerman. "Eisenhower, Dulles, and Dienbienphu: 'The Day We Didn't Go to War' Revisited." *Journal of American History* 71 (Sept. 1984): 343–63.

Hess, Gary R. *The United States' Emergence as a Southeast Asian Power, 1940–1950*. New York: Columbia University Press, 1987.

Hilsman, Roger. *To Move a Nation: The Politics of Foreign Policy in the Administration of John F. Kennedy*. Garden City, N.Y.: Doubleday, 1967.

Hixson, Walter. *George F. Kennan: Cold War Iconoclast*. New York: Columbia University Press, 1989.

Huynh Kim Khanh. *Vietnamese Communism, 1925–1945*. Ithaca: Cornell University Press, 1981.

Iriye, Akira. *The Cold War in Asia: A Historical Introduction*. Englewood Cliffs, N.J.: Prentice-Hall, 1974.

———, ed. *The Origins of the Cold War in Asia*. New York: Columbia University Press, 1977.

Isaacs, Harold. *No Peace for Asia*. New York: Macmillan, 1947.

Isaacson, Walter, and Evan Thomas. *The Wise Men: Six Friends and the World They Made*. New York: Simon & Schuster, 1986.

Jessup, Philip. *Birth of Nations*. New York: Columbia University Press, 1974.

Joyaux, François. *La Chine et le règlement du premier conflit de l'Indochine: Genève 1954*. Paris: Sorbonne, 1979.

Kahin, George McT. *Intervention: How America Became Involved in Vietnam*. Garden City, N.Y.: Anchor Press/Doubleday, 1987.

Kahin, George McT., and John Wilson Lewis. *The United States in Vietnam*. New York: Delta, 1967.

Kattenburg, Paul M. *The Vietnam Trauma in American Foreign Policy, 1945–1975*. New Brunswick: Transaction, 1980.

Kearns, Doris. *Lyndon Johnson and the American Dream*. New York: Signet, 1976.

Kinnard, Douglas. *The Certain Trumpet: Maxwell Taylor and the American Experience in Vietnam*. Washington, D.C.: Brassey's, 1991.

Kolko, Gabriel. *Anatomy of a War: Vietnam, the United States, and the Modern Historical Experience.* New York: Pantheon, 1985.

Komer, Robert. *Bureaucracy at War: U.S. Performance in the Vietnam Conflict.* Boulder: Westview Press, 1986.

Lacouture, Jean. *Pierre Mendès-France.* Translated by Georges Moloch. New York: Holmes and Meier, 1984.

Lewy, Guenter. *America in Vietnam.* Oxford: Oxford University Press, 1968.

Lockhart, Greg. *Nation in Arms: The Origins of the People's Army of Vietnam.* Wellington: Allen & Unwin, 1989.

Lomperis, Timothy. *The War Everyone Lost—and Won.* Baton Rouge: Louisiana State University Press, 1984.

Manelli, Mieczyslaw. *War of the Vanquished.* New York: Harper & Row, 1971.

Matthews, Lloyd, and Dale Brown. *Assessing the Vietnam War.* Washington, D.C.: Pergamon-Brassey's, 1987.

Mayers, David Allan. *Cracking the Monolith: U.S. Policy Against the Sino-Soviet Alliance, 1949–1955.* Baton Rouge: Louisiana State University Press, 1986.

McAlister, John T., and Paul Mus. *The Vietnamese and Their Revolution.* New York: Harper & Row, 1970.

McClintock, Robert. *The Meaning of Limited War.* Boston: Houghton Mifflin, 1967.

McLane, Charles B. *Soviet Strategies in Southeast Asia.* Princeton: Princeton University Press, 1966.

Montgomery, John D. *The Politics of Foreign Aid: American Experience in Southeast Asia.* New York: Praeger, 1967.

Moore, Lt. General Harold G., and Joseph L. Galloway. *We Were Soldiers Once . . . and Young.* New York: Random House, 1992.

Navarre, Henri. *Agonie de l'Indochine (1953–1954).* Paris: Plon, 1956.

Newman, John M. *JFK and Vietnam: Deception, Intrigue, and the Struggle for Power.* New York: Warner Books, 1992.

Nguyen Kien Giang. *Viet-nam Nam Dau tien sau Cach mang Thang Tam* (Vietnam in the years immediately following the August Revolution). Hanoi, 1961.

Nixon, Richard M. *No More Vietnams.* New York: Arbor House, 1985.

Nogee, Joseph L., and Robert A. Donaldson. *Soviet Foreign Policy Since World War II.* New York: Pergamon, 1984.

O'Donnell, Kenneth. *Johnny, We Hardly Knew Ye.* Boston: Little, Brown, 1976.

Osborne, George K., et al., eds. *Democracy, Strategy, and Vietnam: Implications for American Policymaking.* Lexington, Mass.: Lexington Books, 1987.

Palmer, General Bruce, Jr. *The 25-Year War: America's Military Role in Vietnam.* Lexington: University Press of Kentucky, 1984.

Parker, F. Charles IV. *Strategy for a Stalemate.* New York: Paragon, 1989.

Patti, Archimedes. *Why Vietnam: Prelude to America's Albatross.* Berkeley: University of California Press, 1980.

Pike, Douglas. *Viet Cong: The Organization and Techniques of the National Liberation Front of South Vietnam.* Cambridge, Mass.: MIT Press, 1966.

———. *Vietnam and the Soviet Union: Anatomy of an Alliance.* Boulder: Westview Press, 1987.

Podhoretz, Norman. *Why We Were in Vietnam.* New York: Simon & Schuster, 1982.

Porter, Gareth. *A Peace Denied: The United States, Vietnam, and the Paris Agreement.* Bloomington: Indiana University Press, 1975.

——, ed. *Vietnam: A History in Documents.* New York: New American Library, 1979.

——. *Vietnam: The Definitive Documentation of Human Decisions.* New York: Meridian, 1979.

Post, Ken. *Revolution, Socialism, and Nationalism in Viet Nam.* Aldershot: Dartmouth Publishing Co., 1989.

Prados, John. *The Sky Would Fall.* New York: Dial Press, 1983.

Race, Jeffrey. *War Comes to Long An: Revolutionary Conflict in a Vietnamese Province.* Berkeley: University of California Press, 1972.

Randle, Robert F. *Geneva 1954: The Settlement of the Indochina War.* Princeton: Princeton University Press, 1969.

Randolph, R. Sean. *The United States and Thailand: Alliance Dynamics, 1950–1985.* Berkeley: Institute of East Asia Studies, 1986.

Roberts, Chalmers. "The Day We Didn't Go to War." *Reporter,* Sept. 14, 1954.

Rostow, Walt W. *The Diffusion of Power: An Essay in Recent History.* New York: Macmillan, 1972.

Rotter, Andrew J. *The Path to Vietnam: Origins of the American Commitment to Southeast Asia.* Ithaca: Cornell University Press, 1989.

Rousset, Pierre. *Le Parti Communiste Vietnamien.* Paris: Maspero, 1975.

Sabbatier, Gabriel. *Le Destin de l'Indochine: Souvenirs et documents (1945–1951).* Paris: Plon, 1952.

Schandler, Herbert Y. *The Unmaking of a President: Lyndon Johnson and Vietnam.* Princeton: Princeton University Press, 1977.

Schlesinger, Arthur M., Jr. *A Thousand Days: John F. Kennedy in the White House.* Boston: Houghton Mifflin, 1965.

Scheer, Robert. *How the United States Got Involved in Vietnam.* Santa Barbara: Center for the Study of Democratic Institutions, 1965.

Scigliano, Robert. *South Vietnam: Nation Under Stress.* Boston: Houghton Mifflin, 1963.

Shaplen, Robert. *The Lost Revolution.* New York: Harper & Row, 1966.

Sheehan, Neil. *A Bright and Shining Lie: John Paul Vann and America in Vietnam.* New York: Random House, 1988.

Shulman, Marshall D. *Stalin's Foreign Policy Reappraised.* New York: Atheneum, 1965.

Smith, R. B. *An International History of the Vietnam War.* 2 vols. New York: St. Martin's Press, 1983–85.

Smyser, W. R. *The Independent Vietnamese: Vietnamese Communism Between Russia and China, 1956–1969.* Athens: Ohio University Papers in International Studies, 1980.

Sorensen, Theodore. *Kennedy.* New York: Harper & Row, 1965.

Spector, Ronald H. *Advice and Support: The Early Years.* Washington, D.C.: Center for Military History, 1983.

Summers, Harry G., Jr. *On Strategy.* Novato, Calif.: Presidio Press, 1982.

Taylor, Jay. *China and Southeast Asia: Peking's Relations with Revolutionary Movements.* 2d ed. New York: Praeger, 1976.

Taylor, Maxwell. *Swords and Plowshares.* New York: Norton, 1972.

Thayer, Carlyle A. *War By Other Means: National Liberation and Revolution in Viet-Nam, 1954–60.* London: Allen & Unwin, 1989.

Thies, Wallace J. *When Governments Collide: Coercion and Diplomacy in the Vietnam Conflict, 1964–1968*. Berkeley: University of California Press, 1980.

Tonnesson, Stein. *1946: Déclenchement de la guerre d'Indochine*. Paris: L'Harmattan, 1987.

———. *The Vietnamese Revolution of 1945: Roosevelt, Ho Chi Minh, and de Gaulle in a World at War*. London: Sage, 1991.

Tran Huy Lieu, *Les Soviets du Nghe Tinh*. Hanoi: Foreign Languages Press, 1960.

Tran Van Don. *Our Endless War: Inside Vietnam*. San Rafael, Calif.: Presidio Press, 1978.

Truong Chinh. *Primer for Revolt*. New York: Praeger, 1963.

Turley, William S. *The Second Indochina War: A Short Political and Military History, 1954–1975*. New York: Mentor, 1986.

Valentine, Douglas. *The Phoenix Program*. New York: Morrow, 1990.

VanDeMark, Brian. *Into the Quagmire*. Oxford: Oxford University Press, 1991.

Van Tien Dung. *Our Great Spring Victory*. New York: Monthly Review Press, 1977.

Vo Nguyen Giap. *Banner of People's War: The Party's Military Line*. New York: Praeger, 1970.

———. *Military Art of People's War*. New York: Monthly Review Press, 1970.

———. *People's War, People's Army*. New York: Bantam, 1962.

Wang Bingnan. *Zhong-Mei Huitan Jiu nian Huigu* (A retrospective view of nine years of Sino-U.S. negotiations). Beijing, 1985.

Warner, Denis. *The Last Confucian*. Baltimore: Penguin, 1963.

Ying Yu. *Zhongguo Renmin zhi you Hu Zhimin* (Ho Chi Minh: Friend of the Chinese people). Beijing: Commercial Press, 1987.

Yuen Foong Khong. *Analogies at War: Korea, Munich, Dien Bien Phu, and the Vietnam Decisions of 1965*. Princeton: Princeton University Press, 1992.

Index

In this index an "f" after a number indicates a separate reference on the next page, and an "ff" indicates separate references on the next two pages. A continuous discussion over two or more pages is indicated by a span of page numbers, e.g., "pp. 57–58." *Passim* is used for a cluster of references in close but not consecutive sequence.

morale in, 310, 312–17, 325–26, 342; post-Diem situation in, 311, 317, 325–28, 332–34, 350
Vietnam Syndrome, 384
Vietnamese National Army (VNA), 69, 72, 91, 99–106 *passim*, 115, 125–28, 134, 143, 169, 179; U.S. aid to, 95, 125–29 *passim*, 134, 139, 149–51, 156, 174, 195–200 *passim*, 205, 222
Vietnamese Nationalist Party (VNQDD), 17, 19, 44, 106
Vietnamese Workers' Party (VWP), 107–9, 145, 226, 235–36, 265–67, 313–14, 342
Vincent, John Carter, 37, 42, 54, 92
Vo Nguyen Giap, 44–45, 56, 89, 106, 145–46, 266–67, 336, 358
von Clausewitz, Karl, 371
Vuong, Colonel Van Dong, 242

Wang Bingnan, 355
War Zone D, 279, 281
Washington Conference (1922), 7
Webb, James, 75
Wedemeyer, Albert, 14, 29, 36, 62

Welles, Sumner, 10–11
Westmoreland, General William C., 319, 339–44 *passim*, 348–52, 374
Whampoa Academy, 88
Wheeler, General Earle C., 292, 326–27, 340, 343, 352–53, 360
White Man's Burden, 6
White Paper (1961), 275
Williams, General Samuel T., 230–32, 238–40
Wilson, Charles E., 132, 151, 155–63 *passim*, 201–4
Women, role of, 285
Wood, Chalmers B., 240

Yalta Conference (1945), 24–31 *passim*
Yalta system, 31–32, 188, 192
Yost, Charles, 81
Young, Kenneth T., 202, 208, 219, 255
Yugoslavia, 64

Zhdanov, Andrei, 63
Zhou Enlai, 146, 201, 216, 355; at Geneva Conference, 178–93 *passim*

Library of Congress Cataloging-in-Publication Data

Duiker, William J., 1932–
    U.S. containment policy and the conflict in Indochina / William J.
Duiker.
    p.   cm.
Includes bibliographical references and index.
ISBN 0-8047-2283-8 (acid-free paper)
1. Indochina—Politics and government—1945–   2. United States—
Foreign relations—Indochina. 3. Indochina—Foreign relations—
United States. 4. Vietnamese Conflict, 1961–1975—United States.
I. Title.
DS550.D8 1994
327.730597—dc20   93-41544   CIP